League Express

LEAGUE
Publications Ltd

RUGBY LEAGUE
2020-2021
Strange Days Indeed

League Publications Ltd

First published in Great Britain in 2020 by
League Publications Ltd, Wellington House, Briggate, Brighouse, West Yorkshire HD6 1DN

A CIP catalogue record for this book is available from the British Library
ISBN 978-1-901347-39-5

Designed and Typeset by League Publications Limited
Printed by H Charlesworth & Co Ltd, Wakefield

Contributing Editor
Tim Butcher

Statistics, production and design
Daniel Spencer

Contributors

Thomas Alderson	Martyn Sadler	
Robbie Andrews	Matthew Shaw	
Robson Andrews	Steve Slater	
Aaron Bower	Joe Smith	
Steve Brady	Tom Smith	
Phil Caplan	Andrew Steel	
Joshua Chapman	Doug Thomson	
Lewis Coleman	Callum Walker	
Alex Davis	Gareth Walker	
John Drake	Jordan Weir	
Matt Dyson	Nick White	
Dan Fowler	Ricky Wilby	
Ian Golden	Ian Wilson	
Ryan Gould	Peter Wilson	
Phil Hodgson		
Ash Hope		
Steven Hughes		
Mike Hyde		
Stephen Ibbetson		
Andrew Jackson		
Steve Kilmartin		
David Kuzio		
Callum Linford		
Lorraine Marsden		
Bryn May		
Keith McGhie		
Dave Parkinson		
Arindam Rej		
Huw Richards		
Ian Rigg		

Pictures
Dean Williams
Steve Gaunt
Magi Haroun
Simon Hall
Matthew Merrick
Bernard Platt
SWPix
Steve Jones/RLPix
Craig Milner
Richard Long
NRL Imagery
Mark Cosgrove
Terry Donnelly
Catalans Dragons
Paul Clayton
Craig Cresswell
David Greaves
Tom Pearson
Sean Gosling
Craig Hawkhead
Gareth Lyons
Alex Coleman
Dave Lofthouse
Steve Miller
Dave Murgatroyd
Prime Images
Bernard Rieu
Craig Thomas
Mal Walker
Neville Wright

Main cover picture
Dean Williams

CONTENTS

ACKNOWLEDGEMENTS

The *League Express Yearbook 2020-2021* is the 25th of League Publications Ltd's annual series of Rugby League Yearbooks, which began in the first year of Super League in 1996.

This historical record of the Rugby League year would not be possible without the hard work and dedication of all the contributors to *Rugby Leaguer & Rugby League Express*, *Rugby League World* magazine and the totalrl.com website.

We are able to include some wonderful action photography provided by, in particular Dean Williams, Steve Gaunt, Magi Haroun, Simon Hall, Matthew Merrick, Bernard Platt, SWPix, Steve Jones and NRL Imagery.

Thanks to the Rugby Football League for their help during the year and to the historians and statisticians at clubs who help us resolve any anomalies.

Acknowledgement also to the *Rothmans Yearbook 1999*, compiled by our late friend Ray Fletcher, the *British Rugby Records Book* from London Publications and to the club officials, and some supporters, who helped us verify records.

Thanks also to Opta Sportdata, who compile the Opta Index Analysis in our statistical section.

Special thanks to Matthew Shaw, Lorraine Marsden and Alex Davis, who respectively wrote the Championship & League 1, Women and NRL sections.

The comprehensive statistical review is once again awesome, compiled, under trying circumstances, by Daniel Spencer, who also designed the book.

TIM BUTCHER
Contributing Editor

INTRODUCTION

The 2020 season was like no other in the past. And it is unlikely to be replicated any time in the future. For starters, the first game was played on the 31st January and the last on 27th November.

At the start of the year, the Rugby League season just seemed to be carrying on as normal, with Super League having the added dimension of including Toronto Wolfpack as one of its member teams.

But behind the headlines there was something developing, even if it struggled to gain the attention of sports fans. On 23rd January 2020, the central government of China imposed a lockdown in the city of Wuhan and other conurbations in the province of Hubei in an effort to quarantine the centre of an outbreak of what was labelled coronavirus disease 2019 (Covid-19).

At the start of the Rugby League year the virus was an exotic and remote nightly news item. Western governments were slow to react to a phenomenon that within a few months would be affecting them very badly. The whole world was caught in a crisis that was declared a global pandemic by the World Health Organisation on March 3rd 2020. The virus caused an almost total lockdown of society in the spring and ebbed through the British summer but refused to go away before coming back with a bang towards the end of the year.

It had obvious repercussions for the game. The Rugby Football League suspended its competitions on 16th March and initially planned a restart on April 2nd. But it wasn't until August 2nd before fixtures could resume - with the lower leagues unable to play at all for the rest of the year - and all games were played in empty stadiums.

The impact on economies, with many people unable to work from home and most workplaces closed down, was huge, governments having to provide massive financial support for individuals and businesses. That proved a lifeline for Rugby League clubs, with the RFL also negotiating a loan of 16 million pounds from the government for which stricken clubs could apply. With income streams through attendances totally cut off, the continuation of Sky's distribution money also helped clubs to stay alive, although all players and employees were asked to take pay cuts.

The result of it all was the most bizarre season in the history of the game.

The Super League Grand Final was played on a Friday night, 28 days before Christmas, at the KCOM Stadium in Hull in front of empty stands.

The Challenge Cup Final was played in mid-October. It was staged at Wembley. But there were no fans present. The competition was sailing along nicely until the country went into its first lockdown. Before it could start up again, there had to be a re-draw as non-Super League clubs and Toronto who had battled their way through to the sixth round were unable to take any further part.

Magic Weekend, due to return to Newcastle in May, didn't happen.

The revived mandatory reserves competition hardly got going at all before it was abandoned. The Academy competition went the same way.

The Championship and League 1 couldn't find a viable way to re-start their

competitions without spectator income. A proposed end-of-year competition for the lower leagues couldn't attract enough clubs to get started.

And remember Storm Ciara, which hit the UK on the second Sunday in February?

Before that, with the Great Britain Lions still in the middle of their disappointing tour in the southern hemisphere, the global sport of Rugby League was given a major boost in profile when Toronto Wolfpack, gearing up for their first season of Super League after having won the 2019 Championship Grand Final, announced the signing of Sonny Bill Williams.

Williams agreed a multi-million dollar two-year deal with the Wolfpack in what many believed was a seismic moment for top-flight Rugby League in the northern hemisphere.

But within months, Toronto was forced to withdraw from the rest of the 2020 season before it resumed. And, early in November 2020, Super League's decision-making body, which was in real terms made up of the remaining eleven clubs, rejected an application from Toronto to re-join the top tier in 2021. It was a body blow to expansionists across the game.

The Wolfpack had had their record from the 2020 season expunged, with the RFL announcing there would be no promotion and relegation in 2020. Invitations were invited from Championship clubs to take the spare place in the following season's Super League.

It made little difference to the 2020 table, as Toronto had lost all six pre-lockdown league games. Even those hadn't gone to plan, with a home fixture against St Helens scheduled to be played at Allianz Park in London having to be switched to Warrington when Saracens rugby union club were punished for salary cap transgressions.

When the Canadian government shut off its borders in mid-March, the Wolfpack's fate looked sealed. The Rugby League season looked doomed.

But by the end of the year, the commitment of clubs and players had seen the season through to a satisfactory conclusion. Super League games started up again, for the TV audience at least, on August 2nd in front of empty stands. It was an over-demanding schedule for players, one positive of which was the premature appearance of some of the next generation of stars, that in the end proved too much, with strict Covid protocols causing a string of postponements and cancellations. Both Hull KR and Castleford Tigers were unable to complete their fixtures before the RFL took the sensible option of ending the regular season early ahead of an expanded play-off series.

As it evolved the season became 'make do and mend' with the Covid-enforced fixture re-arrangements making it just about impossible to keep track of which round was which. And with the Challenge Cup to fit in, the schedule meant some players having to play four games in nine days.

Nobody seemed to care that Salford would have finished seventh if they hadn't been deducted wins for a financial commitment they made in 2013 or that Warrington might have finished second, instead of third, if St Helens had travelled and lost to Catalans in the final week of the season. Or that the table would be decided on win percentages. A Hull derby played at St Helens might also turn out to be a unique event.

After 302 days, the season finally came to an end as the competition's two most consistent sides tore one another apart in a brutal Super League Grand Final.

St Helens' second consecutive title was won in the most dramatic way when future star Jack Welsby scored a try after the hooter sounded at the KCOM Stadium to seal an 8-4 win over League Leaders Wigan. No contest could have been tighter or harder fought.

Not even the Challenge Cup Final which Leeds Rhinos edged against Salford with a late Luke Gale field goal.

Not even the State of Origin series down under, played at the end of the year. The deciding game in Brisbane was Origin at its brilliant best with Queensland emerging 20-14 victors. The fact that a capacity crowd was allowed into the stadium - the largest crowd that had gathered for a sporting event in the world since the pandemic was declared in March - made it a truly special occasion.

Introduction

The game in Australia had been a shining light. The plan by the NRL to re-start the season down under on 28th May was thought barmy, although they did just that, and with great success, gradually introducing crowds at games. It was a beacon for League fans across the world.

The Rugby League season was a bright shining light in a year of gloom but sport was put into perspective by the stories around two huge Rugby League personalities. The biggest and most poignant was the news that former Leeds and Great Britain halfback Rob Burrow had been diagnosed with Motor Neurone Disease late in 2019, at the age of 37. Throughout the year, Burrow didn't shirk from facing the disease with the strength and fortitude he had shown through his glorious playing career.

That was mirrored by Hull KR and former St Helens prop Mose Masoe, who was carried off after an innocuous looking knock as he made a tackle in the Robins' friendly defeat at Wakefield. Tragically the Samoan's career was over with a serious spinal injury. He spent nearly three months in a hospital bed and was told he would be lucky to ever walk again. Eight months later he took his first steps unassisted.

TIM BUTCHER
Contributing Editor

The 25th League Express Yearbook contains the full story of the domestic year, the Australian season and match facts for all Super League, Challenge Cup games involving professional teams, Championship and League 1 games. Every player who has played in Super League is also listed along with those players to have made their debuts this year. We have also selected six individuals who we judge to have made the biggest impact on Rugby League in 2020, and scoring and attendance records for every club.

League Publications publishes the weekly newspaper Rugby Leaguer & Rugby League Express and the UK's most popular League website 'totalrl.com'.

1
PERSONALITIES OF 2020

James Graham
St Helens

Amidst the joy and celebration amongst the St Helens squad after the Super League Grand Final it might have been hard to pick out the single happiest person. But if you had to, the obvious choice would be James Graham.

For starters, Graham had been able to see out his career in perfect fashion, despite serious concerns over his chances of even playing in the final after suffering a head injury in the semi-final victory over Catalans Dragons a week earlier.

And what a way for Graham to bring a distinguished 17-year career to an end, with a second Super League title, his first since 2006, having previously been part of five Grand Final-losing Saints sides.

The 35-year-old had appeared in seven Super League Grand Finals with Saints and the chance to to add to his solitary Grand Final victory was one of the main motivations for returning from Australia to finish the season at his boyhood club.

Graham signed off as one of a handful of English players to have played in both Super League and NRL Grand Finals (he was on the losing side in two of those as well) in addition to winning three consecutive Challenge Cup Finals with Saints between 2006 and 2008, the year he was named Super League's Man of Steel.

He spent eight years in the NRL with Canterbury Bulldogs and St George Illawarra Dragons, playing 186 games, before returning mid-season to help Saints' quest to retain the Super League crown.

James Graham will go down as one of St Helens' and Super League's greatest players, after making his senior debut on 15th August 2003 as a 17-year old, in a 26-10 home win over Castleford.

Saints fans would have been forgiven for thinking they had seen the last of him when he decided to test himself in the NRL. The 2011 season was a tough one for Saints, when they played all their home matches at Widnes following the sale of Knowsley Road and before the completion of the new stadium, though they still made the Grand Final, going down to Leeds 32-16. That was Graham's last game before moving to the NRL.

Graham gained immediate respect in Australia with his fierce competitiveness and a ball-handling ability rarely found in props at the time.

He played 26 games in his debut NRL season and was part of the Bulldogs team which lost the Grand Final to Melbourne Storm. Two years later he featured in the Grand Final again for the Bulldogs, this time losing to South Sydney Rabbitohs.

Graham is the most-capped England player in Rugby League history with 44, while his total of 53 caps including nine for Great Britain makes him the second most-capped player in British Rugby League history, one behind Adrian Morley.

As well as being the Man of Steel winner in 2008, he was also twice named international prop of the year and won the Dally M award for front-rowers in his first season in 2012.

There was an early worrying moment in the Grand Final when the veteran prop was hit in the ribs off the ball by Thomas Leuluai and was laid out in pain. If anybody thought that was the last we'd see of James Graham, they were wrong. He went onto play a huge part in Saints' Grand Final win and seemed to take personal responsibility for pressuring every Wigan kick.

Total commitment. That summed up the playing career of James Graham.

Sean O'Loughlin
Wigan Warriors

If Rugby League fans of any club would have been allowed to attend the 2020 Grand Final they would surely have wanted to join in the guard of honour that St Helens' players made to applaud Sean O'Loughlin from the KCOM pitch.

The Wigan and England captain didn't go out on a high in his last game but his dignified reaction to the heart-breaking last-second defeat in the Grand Final was typical of one of the giants of the modern game.

When he announced at the start of November that he would be retiring at the end of the season, the Wigan club immediately announced he would be inducted into the club's Hall of Fame the following year.

He will become the 15th member, joining Andy Farrell, Shaun Edwards, Dean Bell, Ellery Hanley, Andy Gregory, Eric Ashton, Billy Boston, Brian McTigue, Ken Gee, Joe Egan, Jim Sullivan, Frano Botica, Colin Clarke and Martin Offiah.

O'Loughlin became the oldest player to compete in a Grand Final, having turned 38 three days before the game, taking over the record from Jamie Peacock, who played for Leeds against Wigan in 2015 at the age of 37 years, 300 days.

It seems like ancient history that way back in 2006, the 24-year-old O'Loughlin was made club captain by Ian Millward. He had some big boots to fill in his brother-in-law Andy Farrell, who had taken the union shilling the previous summer.

It proved a difficult transition for the club, a season that went from bad to worse and the loose forward received some stick from supporters for what they saw as his lack of leadership as the side languished in the relegation zone. Exit Millward, enter Brian Noble and Wigan made eighth spot in the table. It was onwards and upwards from there.

After joining Wigan's Academy from Wigan St Patricks, O'Loughlin made his first team debut for his hometown club, under coach Stuart Raper, with current coach Adrian Lam playing at halfback, on Friday 5th April 2002, coming off the bench in a 20-18 home defeat to Hull FC.

It had been long apparent that O'Loughlin, the son of former Wigan players Keiron and nephew of Kevin, was going to be a top player, having represented Great Britain Academy on the tour of Australia in 2001 and captaining the England A team against New Zealand A and on the tour of Fiji and Tonga the following year. He gained full international recognition in 2004 when he represented Great Britain in the Tri-Nations tournament.

By then he had played, at stand-off, in his first Grand Final in the side that lost to Bradford in the 2003 decider.

O'Loughlin quickly developed into a great player and a great leader who earned respect from teammates and opponents, despite his 2005 season being wiped out by a knee reconstruction.

The list of honours that he has led Wigan to is remarkable - one World Club Challenge, four Super League titles, two Challenge Cups and three League Leaders' Shields. A loose forward without peer, he made the Super League Dream Team a record seven times.

The 2020 Grand Final was only his eighth game of the season after a Covid and injury-disrupted year. But, revered by colleagues and opposition players alike, Sean O'Loughlin will live in the memory as one of the modern greats.

Paul McShane
Castleford Tigers

It was not the best of seasons for Castleford Tigers but at the end of 2020 they were celebrating when their versatile hooker Paul McShane was named the Steve Prescott Man of Steel as the best player in Super League XXV.

As for most things in life in 2020, the awards ceremony wasn't quite the same. The award was made without the glitzy occasion it has become known for. And the 3,2,1 point system that had been copied from League Express's Albert Goldthorpe Medal the previous year, had to be tweaked, with teams having played a different number of games. McShane was second on the table, based on points awarded but from a shortlist of the top five players, panel chairman Ellery Hanley was given the final decision. Wigan Warriors' Bevan French and Liam Farrell were also shortlisted for the award, along with Aidan Sezer of Huddersfield Giants and St Helens' Lachlan Coote.

McShane became the Tigers' fifth Man of Steel, after Adrian Vowles (1999), Rangi Chase (2011), Daryl Clark (2014) and Luke Gale (2017).

The Tigers were flying before the game was shut down in March, level at the top of the table with Wigan on five wins from seven. But they only won two games after the resumption in August and finished eighth. Hit by Covid issues the club couldn't get a side out for its last three fixtures.

But through some tough times, hooker-halfback McShane was consistently outstanding. He had developed into one the game's best schemers at the back of the play-the-ball and displayed great handling and kicking skills that create bags of tries close to the line. Add to that a total commitment in defence - he made 604 tackles in 2020 and in 2018 he was the league"s top tackler with 1160. And in his spare time he coaches amateur side Hunslet Club Parkside.

At the start of 2018 he signed a new five-year Tigers contract to the end of 2022. It would be hard to see McShane, who turned 31 in November wanting to play anywhere else in Super League.

It has been in no way plain sailing. As a star of the Leeds Rhinos Academy he looked on course for a long career at his hometown club, making his debut in the first game of the 2009 season as a 19-year-old, laying on a try for Lee Smith with his first touch after he came off the bench in a 28-6 defeat of Crusaders.

But despite playing 63 games for the Rhinos over five seasons - with loan spells at Hull FC and Widnes and finishing the 2013 season playing on dual registration with Hunslet - he submitted a transfer request after Leeds' signing of Paul Aiton from Wakefield. McShane soon moved in the opposite direction.

He excelled as Wakefield's first-choice hooker - he registered 27 appearances for Trinity in 2014 - but in late July 2015, after playing 24 times for Wakefield that season - McShane was involved in a swap deal between Trinity and Castleford that saw the Tigers hooker Scott Moore come to Belle Vue on-loan, with McShane signing a two-and-a-half year contract with the Tigers.

Joining Trinity's near neighbours Castleford injected fresh life into his career and the belief instilled in him by head coach Daryl Powell has seen McShane become a stand-out performer in Super League.

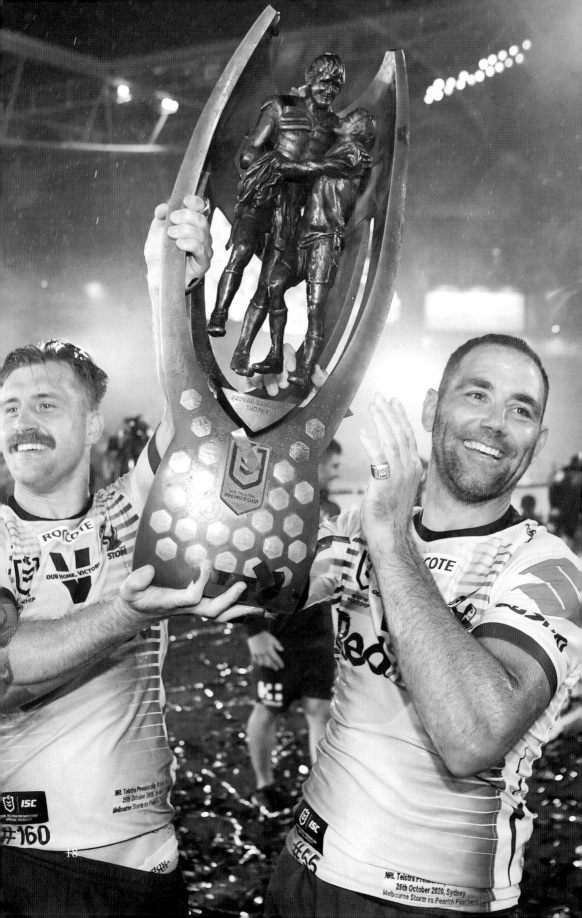

Cameron Smith
Melbourne Storm

'Everyone back home in Victoria. This one's for you, you beauty!'

If Cameron Smith really had decided to retire, he rounded off his stellar career in perfect fashion when he paid a post-Grand Final tribute to the people of the state where, not too long before, with Aussie Rules the undisputed football king, it would have been thought impossible to support a top Rugby League club.

Smith had just captained the Storm to a fourth (legitimate, they had two taken off them for salary cap transgressions) NRL Premiership, scoring 14 points, including a try in a 26–20 Grand Final victory over Minor Premiers Penrith Panthers. It was the eighth time he had led the Storm into the NRL decider.

The latest Premiership win was like no other. The year 2020 brought challenges to every sports team in the world but the Storm, along with New Zealand Warriors, had it tougher than most. When the NRL season was resumed on May 28th, the global coronavirus pandemic was almost under control in Australia. But a rise in cases of Covid-19 in Melbourne led to a tightening of restrictions and that meant that if the Storm were to participate in the 2020 competition, they would have to leave the state and set up a 'bubble' elsewhere. That they did, although they had no idea for how long their collective exile on the Sunshine Coast in Queensland would last. It lasted five months.

Many of the Storm players claimed the adversity had strengthened their camaraderie and that team spirit was apparent as they had to withstand a magnificent comeback by the Panthers in the Grand Final.

They might not have done it without the unparalleled leadership skills of Cameron Smith, who for composure and calmness had no peer.

At the end of the season Smith, who passed his 37th birthday in June, left everybody guessing about his future. Would he retire, go round one more time with the Storm. Play for another NRL club?

The debate about whether he was the greatest player in the game's history had already started however, with strong opinions given on both sides of the argument.

There is some serious competition for the accolade but Smith's achievements stand up to comparison. He won the Dally M Medal twice as the NRL's player of the year in 2006 and 2017, the Golden Boot in 2007 and 2017, as well as being named the NRL's Dally M Hooker of the Year for the ninth time at the end of the 2020 season.

He is also the highest all-time points scorer in NRL history, having surpassed Hazem El Masri's 2,418 points in 2019 and finished 2020 on a total of 2,786. And he made a record 430 appearances in the NRL after making his debut in 2002, all for the Storm.

Smith became regular captain of Melbourne in 2008 and by then he had established himself as a Queensland Origin player. In all he played in 15 series, 42 games in all, won 11 (his first in 2003 was already lost when he was drafted into the Maroons side for the third game) and was awarded the Wally Lewis Medal as player of the series four times. He lifted two World Cups for Australia in 2013 and 2017.

It's hard to imagine a Storm team without Cameron Smith.

Rob Burrow & Mose Masoe

Two stories of personal misfortune that ran through the Rugby League year of 2020 have provided inspiration for the many.

One of the most memorable occasions of the year came in January when Rugby League fans from far and wide gathered at a sold-out Headingley stadium to show their support for Leeds Rhinos' legendary scrum-half Rob Burrow. The month before Burrow, just over two years since his last game for the club, had been diagnosed with Motor Neurone Disease. A moving TV interview with the inimitable Burrow in December had stunned the world of Rugby League and a fund set up by the Rhinos Foundation in his support raised over £70,000 in the first 24 hours. By the end of 2020 that figure had risen to hundreds of thousand of pounds to help support Burrow and his young family and to help fund research into a disease that had no cure.

Jamie Jones-Buchanan's testimonial game game with Bradford Bulls on Sunday 12th January was made a joint fundraiser. The result was a sell-out crowd at Headingley and a highly emotional occasion. A whole host of former Rhinos greats, including Kevin Sinfield, Jamie Peacock and Danny McGuire, briefly came out of retirement to feature in the game, with Burrow entering the game five minutes from the end. 'The Pocket Rocket' who played 17 seasons at Leeds, had been a pivotal member of the Rhinos 'golden generation' and defied the odds so many times with his bravery, skill and speed that thrilled fans of every club.

Burrow and his wife of 20 years, Lindsey, the mother to his three young children, have shown towering strength of character and have worked hard at raising the profile of the cruel disease.

On the same day as the Headingley crowd paid tribute to Rob Burrow, Hull Kingston Rovers were playing a pre-season friendly at Wakefield. Like most pre-season warm-ups it wan't expected to present too many dramas.

But, early in the game, the Robins' giant prop Mose Masoe stayed down after making a tackle by his own posts and after lengthy treatment was carried from the field and rushed to hospital.

Tragically the Samoan's career was over with a serious spinal injury. He spent nearly three months in a hospital bed and was told he would be lucky to ever walk again. But, eight months later he took his first steps unassisted and, late in the year, League fans were heartened to see Masoe attending Hull KR matches, despite still needing the use of crutches. His cheery nature and a determination not to be wheelchair-bound was an inspiration to all.

British fans first got sight of Masoe playing in the 2013 Rugby League World Cup and the next season he was part of St Helens' Grand Final-winning side. After a return to the NRL was wiped out by a knee injury, he was back in British Rugby League with promotion-bound Hull KR.

The inspirational nature of Masoe's story is matched only by that of Rob Burrow.

2
THE 2020 SEASON

DECEMBER 2019
Wolfpack raise the stakes

While the Great Britain Lions were still in the middle of their disappointing tour in the southern hemisphere, the global sport of Rugby League was given a major boost in profile in November when Toronto Wolfpack, gearing up for their first season of Super League after having won the 2019 Championship Grand Final, announced the signing of Sonny Bill Williams.

Williams agreed a multi-million dollar two-year deal with the Wolfpack in what many believed was a seismic moment for top-flight Rugby League in the northern hemisphere.

Super League CEO Robert Elstone hailed the New Zealander's signing the biggest in the competition's history. It was to be the two-time rugby union world cup winner's third stint in League, the backrower having started his career with Canterbury Bulldogs in 2004.

Williams' switch back to Rugby League came just a week after he featured in the union world cup in Japan.

The Wolfpack had also signed Leeds Rhinos prop Brad Singleton, who was still under contract with the Rhinos, after a decade at Headingley during which time he won two Grand Final rings and a Challenge Cup medal.

Singleton was attracted by the prospect of teaming up again with Toronto coach Brian McDermott, who himself signed a new five-year contract with the club.

A raft of players who had helped the Wolfpack achieve their rapid promotion signed new contracts. Adam Sidlow, Andy Ackers, Liam Kay, Chase Stanley, Blake Wallace, Gary Wheeler and Gadwin Springer agreed two-year contracts, while Hakim Miloudi, Bodene Thompson and Josh McCrone were re-signed for the 2020 season.

There was, almost inevitably, some fall out in the off season as French Rugby League chiefs hit back at their former international captain Jason Baitieri, following his decision to walk out of their Australian tour.

The Catalans Dragons loose forward quit the national team following defeat in the World Cup Nines at the end of October, with two fixtures remaining for the full French side against the Junior Kangaroos and Western Rams, Baitieri blaming a 'lack of professionalism' from officials at the French Federation.

Several of Baitieri's teammates expressed their support for his stance. The Federation responded with a detailed statement, revealing player payments and slamming what they saw as a growing club versus country clash which was harming French development at international level.

Catalans Dragons were fined £27,500 after an RFL investigation into the events which followed their Super League win over Warrington Wolves in Perpignan on August 3rd. The Dragons' fine included a thousand pounds suspended from 2018 following a home Super 8s defeat to St Helens. Ten thousand pounds of the new fine was suspended until the end of the 2021 season. The club also had to bear two-thirds of the costs of the investigation.

The Wolves were fined £15,000, five thousand suspended until the end of the 2021

Sonny Bill Williams meets the media after signing for Toronto Wolfpack

season, and had to pay the remaining third of the costs. Both clubs acknowledged that the events at the end of a fiery game, which saw fighting between both sets of supporters, brought the game into disrepute.

On the field the Dragons were hoping for better things after their 2019 season fizzled out. Former halfback Josh Drinkwater returned to the club after a season at Hull KR, to partner marquee sining James Maloney.

Drinkwater first joined the Catalans following a serious injury to Luke Walsh early in the 2018 season but was released despite a successful stint (which included an historic Challenge Cup Final victory) owing to the club's long-term plan to bring in St Helens' halfback Matty Smith. But Smith's failure to settle into the Dragons side in 2019 saw him released from his contract.

Another Hull KR player, former Wigan backrower Joel Tomkins, joined his brother Sam at the Dragons, while Wigan winger Tom Davies also headed to Perpignan. But Catalans were left searching for another top-flight recruit following the sudden departure of Fiji international Brayden Wiliame. The 26-year-old centre, who had a year left on his current contract in Perpignan, was released on compassionate grounds for family reasons and joined the NRL's Dragons, St George Illawarra.

Clubs were still recruiting well into the off-season. Super League runners-up Salford were keen to fill the huge gap made by Man of Steel Jackson Hastings' departure to Wigan and signed former England stand-off Kevin Brown, whose 2019 season with Warrington was wiped out by an Achilles injury. The 35-year-old was joined at the AJ Bell Stadium by

Sebastine Ikahihifo. The Huddersfield forward, signed on a season-long loan, was a Dream Team member in 2017 but had struggled to replicate that form since, seemingly falling out of favour with Giants head coach Simon Woolford.

Ikahihifo's exit freed up a quota spot at the Giants and significant salary-cap space, which opened the door for the arrival of Aidan Sezer at the John Smith's Stadium. The halfback had played a major part in Canberra's march to the 2019 NRL Grand Final and was heavily predicted to lead the Giants to better things.

Castleford also had to do some halfback tweaking after losing Luke Gale to Leeds Rhinos. They signed 2018 Dream Team halfback Danny Richardson, whose opportunities at St Helens in 2019 had been limited.

Leeds also signed boom hooker Kruise Leeming as part of a swap deal with Huddersfield that saw Owen Trout go the other way. Another Leeds player, fullback Ashton Golding, as well as Kiwi prop James Gavet, were signed by the Giants.

Australian forward Matt Prior joined the Rhinos from the NRL's Cronulla Sharks, ending the club's long pursuit of the State of Origin representative. Prior's signing coincided with the departure of captain Trent Merrin, who left the club after just one season to return to the NRL with St George Illawarra Dragons. Loose forward Stevie Ward was named the Rhinos' new captain.

Gareth Ellis signed a new one-year deal with Hull FC, meaning he would be the oldest player in Super League in 2020, due to turn 39 years of age in May.

Across the River Hull, Hull KR coach Tony Smith was almost totally re-building his squad, with 20 players brought into Craven Park. Among them were five players from Bradford Bulls, who were the subject of controversy after the club, due to play their Championship home games at Dewsbury in 2020 because of the high cost of renting and maintaining Odsal, was bought by a consortium that included former RFL chief executive Nigel Wood. The current CEO of the Rugby League International Federation had headed the RFL when it bought Odsal Stadium in 2012. Calls for an independent inquiry into the latest developments at the troubled former Super League trailblazer were eventually rejected.

Wigan captain Sean O'Loughlin was set to play out the final season of his glittering career after signing a one-year contract extension with the club for what would be his nineteenth season at the DW Stadium. O'Loughlin, 36, who made his first-grade debut against Hull FC in April 2002, had led Wigan to four Super League titles, two Challenge Cups and a World Club Challenge title since being made captain in 2006.

One club making no signings at all in the close-season was St Helens. But the Super League champions did secure young star threequarter Jack Welsby on a new four-year contract.

St Helens and Salford dominated the 2019 League Express Readers' Poll awards. Six Saints players were named in the team of the year, reflecting their excellence in 2019. Lachlan Coote, Tommy Makinson, Regan Grace, Jonny Lomax, James Roby and Luke Thompson all made the team, with Roby being voted as both mature player and club captain of the year.

By far the biggest and most poignant story of the month was the news that former Leeds and Great Britain halfback Rob Burrow had been diagnosed with Motor Neurone Disease at the age of 37.

The Rhinos Foundation set up the Rob Burrow Fund following the announcement, with over £70,000 being raised in 24 hours. By the end of the year that figure had risen to hundreds of thousand of pounds to help support Burrow and his young family and to help fund research into a disease that had no cure.

Leeds announced that their game with Bradford Bulls on Sunday 12th January would be a joint fundraiser in line with Jamie Jones-Buchanan's testimonial game, with over 5,500 tickets sold in the first two days. The Bulls donated all their ticket sales from the game to the fund.

JANUARY
Front-page news

The New Year's Honours list once again provided thin pickings for Rugby League, with only two individuals recognised, with MBEs, for services to Rugby League. Lizzie Jones was honoured for services to Rugby League and to charity after founding the Danny Jones Defibrillator Fund following the loss of her husband, Danny, in May 2015. Over the last four years, the fund had raised almost £200,000 and purchased life-saving equipment, safeguarding the health of more than 40,000 Rugby League players and officials. Wales Rugby League president Mike Nicholas was also recognised for his work in the sport.

Rugby League did get royal recognition in the month of January on the back of the draw for the 2021 World Cup which was conducted in Buckingham Palace by the Duke of Sussex, the Patron of the Rugby Football League.

In itself that wouldn't have gained the competition much profile. But Prince Harry had been almost the sole focus of attention in the media since before Christmas after his announcement that he and his wife would be withdrawing from royal duties. On the Saturday after the draw took place, HM The Queen and Buckingham Palace announced at he would be changing his royal status to do just that.

The Thursday event was Prince Harry's first official engagement since the media storm blew up and the following day the story of the World Cup draw appeared on the front page of six national newspapers, as well as appearing in a multitude of television news programmes all over the world.

The following Monday, the Duke flew to Canada to begin a new life with is family.

The other huge event that gained national media attention was the Testimonial game for Rhinos stalwart Jamie Jones-Buchanan between Leeds Rhinos and Bradford Bulls, played on the Sunday before the World Cup draw. JJB had agreed to share the proceeds of the game with Rob Burrow, whose diagnosis with Motor Neurone Disease (MND) had shocked the world of Rugby League.

The result was a sell-out crowd at Headingley and a highly moving occasion. Former Leeds and Great Britain great Burrow struggled to contain his emotions immediately after the Rhinos beat Bradford 34-10 in a game that helped raise funds for him and his family following the recent announcement of his illness.

A whole host of former Rhinos greats, including Kevin Sinfield, Jamie Peacock and

CORAL CHALLENGE CUP - ROUND 1

Saturday 11th January 2020
Barrow Island 84 Rhondda Outlaws 6
British Army 26 Oulton Raiders 10
Distington 50 Bedford Tigers 10
Edinburgh Eagles 10 Ashton Bears 58
Featherstone Lions 12 West Bowling 24
Ince Rose Bridge 50 East Hull 10
Leigh Miners Rangers 28 Stanningley 26
Milford 47 Wigan St Judes 12
Pilkington Recs 18 West Hull 28
Rochdale Mayfield 32 London Chargers 12
Siddal 38 Saddleworth Rangers 0
Skirlaugh 8 Hunslet Club Parkside 6
Thornhill Trojans 22 Thatto Heath Crusaders 16
Underbank Rangers 22 Lock Lane 10
Upton 30 Jarrow Vikings 4
West Bank Bears 26 Royal Navy 24
Wigan St Patricks 30 Dewsbury Moor 14
York Acorn 36 Hammersmith Hills Hoists 14

Sunday 12th January 2020
Great Britain Police 66 Torfaen Tigers 0
Normanton Knights 30 Longhorns 24
RAF 10 Bentley 18
Sherwood Wolf Hunt 26 Wests Warriors 24

CORAL CHALLENGE CUP - ROUND 2

Saturday 25th January 2020
British Army 17 Skirlaugh 16
Great Britain Police 18 Rochdale Mayfield 19
Leigh Miners Rangers 26 Upton 6
Milford 12 Ince Rose Bridge 19
Siddal 62 Ashton Bears 4
Thornhill Trojans 58 Normanton Knights 14
Underbank Rangers 28 Distington 14
West Bank Bears 18 Bentley 20
Wigan St Patricks 10 West Hull 30
York Acorn 34 Barrow Island 14

Sunday 26th January 2020
Sherwood Wolf Hunt 6 West Bowling 38

Rob Burrow salutes the Headingley crowd, flanked by his former Leeds Rhinos teammates

Danny McGuire, briefly came out of retirement to feature in the game.

It was also a poignant occasion for Jones-Buchanan. 'For all the right reasons, it was the most memorable occasion of my career without a doubt. 2015 (when the Rhinos won the treble) was a symbol of what we were all about and why we were so successful. We had everything, but in particular we had team spirit.

'The way the Rugby League fraternity has come together for Rob is unbelievable. It was symbolic of what this club has been about for 20 years. It's the most powerful moment of my career.'

Toronto head coach Brian McDermott, who had signed a five-year contract with the club, pleaded for the Rugby Football League to grant the Wolfpack a salary-cap dispensation for the good of the sport's development in North America. McDermott suggested that Toronto were facing the same issues London had in paying players more to get them to sign at an expansion club, creating cap issues.

After signing Sonny Bill Williams on a multi-million dollar deal, Toronto made no secret of their desire to sign more of the biggest names in world rugby.

Clubs were informed of proposals to increase the Wolfpack's permissible salary cap spend by five per cent - London Broncos were allowed an extra ten per cent - equivalent to £105,000. The additional cap spend had been proposed to reflect the increased living costs in Toronto compared to the north of England. The proposal was met with a huge backlash by Super League clubs who considered the extra cap might increase their own chances of relegation.

Super League CEO Robert Elstone described the impasse on the eve of the new season as 'crazy'. Ultimately, proposals to give the Wolfpack an additional five per cent allowance on the £2.1m cap were vetoed by Super League clubs in the last week of January, voting by eight-to–one against approving the move. However the Wolfpack had a dispensation approved to allow them to sign two young players to their squad, thus extending their squad to 25 players.

With applications from clubs in New York and Ottawa to join League One still being assessed, Serbian club Red Star Belgrade and Spanish club Valencia Hurracanes announced they too would be making bids to enter the competition.

Meanwhile, with Super League XXV set to kick off at the end of January, some clubs were already struggling with injuries.

The worst was suffered by Hull prop Mose Masoe in the Robins' friendly win at Wakefield. Masoe was carried off after an innocuous looking knock as he made a tackle.

Tragically the Samoan's career was over with a serious spinal injury. He spent nearly three months in a hospital bed and was told he would be lucky to ever walk again. Eight months later he took his first, albeit tentative, steps unassisted.

Super League title sponsor Betfred announced that the £250 given to the Man of the Match in a live TV game to donate to a charity of his choice would be doubled, with that amount being split and going towards fundraising efforts for Masoe and Rob Burrow.

The Robins' injury toll didn't look good. Masoe's fellow co-captain Weller Hauraki was set for several months on the sideline with an ankle injury and Dean Hadley was facing three months out after a gruesome injury - dislocating his thumb through his skin - in the club's pre-season victory over Featherstone.

Wakefield Trinity had seen a string of injuries to their top payers scupper their season in 2019 and they were already on the back foot, with middle forwards a particular problem before the season kicked off. With David Fifita and Tinirau Arona not fully recovered from injuries suffered in 2019, George King was carried off with an ankle injury in the 30-4 Boxing Day defeat at Leeds. And Chris Green also picked up an ankle injury during Trinity's warm weather training camp in Alicante. Wakefield signed out-of-favour Wigan prop Romain Navarrete on a season-long loan but were trumped in attempts to sign Leilani Latu, the Gold Coast forward, who eventually joined Warrington Wolves.

New Castleford winger Sosaia Feki would also be missing the start of the season after suffering a calf tear in a 16-10 pre-season defeat by Toronto - missing Sonny Bill Williams - in Michael Shenton's Testimonial game.

And Catalans winger Lewis Tierney fractured an eye socket during a pre-season clash with Toulouse at Carcassonne. With Brayden Wiliame having left before Christmas the Dragons were still on the hunt for a top-class threequarter. At the end of the month they had found one in former Melbourne and Brisbane centre Israel Folau, who had spent the last eight years playing rugby union, after a two-year spell in Aussie Rules, but was at the time on the outer.

Folau's statements on Instagram about what he understood the Bible to say about same-sex marriage and homosexuality had brought him into conflict with the administrators of Rugby Australia. They terminated his contract, although Folau took the body to the Federal Circuit Court of Australia and an out-of-court settlement was reached.

The Catalans' decision to recruit Folau caused uproar in the UK, France and Australia, because of his outspoken comments. Wigan Warriors immediately announced that their home game against the Dragons on March 22nd would be promoted as a Pride Day in support of LGBT (lesbian, gay, bisexual, and transgender) groups. Players would be wearing rainbow socks and laces during the game and supporters were being encouraged to attend and make their feelings known at the game.

Conscious of Folau's legal challenge to the ARU, Rugby League's ruling authorities in the UK made clear their frustration at being unable to deny his registration.

FEBRUARY
Storm brewing

Round 1

Super League XXV kicked off on the last Thursday night of January with a humdinger of a contest between Wigan and Warrington at the DW Stadium, which the Warriors edged 16-10.

Both sides came out of the game with optimism, the Warriors because their defensive commitment saw them home, the Wolves because they went down to twelve men after the 23rd minute of a relentless clash. Warrington captain Chris Hill was the man given his marching orders after an incident that saw the Wolves fall behind when a penalty try was awarded for his high tackle on Sam Powell. Nobody could argue that Powell would have scored but for Hill's foul and he copped a three-match penalty notice the following Monday.

Instead of folding, the Wolves stood toe-to-toe with their local rivals and were still in the contest with the clock ticking down, despite going down to eleven men at one point when Mike Cooper was sin-binned.

Wigan had the game's matchwinner in fullback Bevan French, who scored a try and made another, Zak Hardaker playing in the centre. Warrington had their own star at the back in young debutant Matty Ashton, signed from Swinton, who was immersed in the action all game, showing a fearlessness that thrilled the Wolves fans. There were three other debutants in Jackson Hastings and George Burgess for Wigan and Warrington's former Wigan centre Anthony Gelling, who proved his usual handful.

Warrington started the game positively, showing a willingness to keep the ball alive as they built an early eight-point lead.

After Stefan Ratchford slotted an early penalty, Ben Murdoch-Masila roared onto a Blake Austin pass and bumped off George Burgess to score. Marquee signing Burgess was playing his first game since June after a suspension-hit 2019 and was withdrawn shortly after with a hip complaint that left him unable to return.

But his side was gaining a foothold in the game and responded when French picked a pass up off his bootlaces, dummied between props Hill and Cooper and danced over to cross under the crossbar.

Then came Hill's rash tackle, which led to a lengthy delay as Powell was stretchered off, and the penalty try that put the home side ahead for the first time. Ratchford closed the gap to two points at the break with another penalty and even then the controversy wasn't over, as Morgan Smithies was placed on report for an alleged eye gouge on Blake Austin. The 2019 Albert Goldthorpe Rookie of the Year faced no charge.

The third quarter settled into an attritional battle and was completely scoreless. But the game burst into life again when Cooper was shown a yellow card for obstructing French as he chased his own kick to the line.

The Wigan fullback then immediately turned provider for Liam Marshall with a peach of a long pass, though Hardaker's missed conversion kept the visitors' hopes alive.

Hardaker had a try ruled out by video for Ashton stepping into touch unnoticed

Hull KR debutant Shaun Kenny-Dowall on the charge against Wakefield

moments before and when Cooper returned the Warriors had to show great spirit to hold out.

The next night, home side St Helens looked like the same team that had won Super League in 2019, despite a new coach in Kristian Woolf, as they hammered their Grand Final opponents at Old Trafford, Salford Red Devils by 48-8.

It was a ruthless display that threw down the gauntlet to all their rivals, not just the Red Devils. And they did it without James Roby, Tommy Makinson and Morgan Knowles.

Alex Walmsley, Kevin Naiqama and Jack Welsby all bagged braces, while Jonny Lomax pulled the strings in a merciless performance.

Salford had lost eight players from the side that made a fairytale run to the Grand Final the previous October - most notably Steve Prescott Man of Steel Jackson Hastings to Wigan - and they looked set for another period of re-building.

Saints fullback Lachlan Coote limped from the field in the 46th minute with a medial collateral ligament injury to his knee that kept him out until round seven, the only blemish on a near-perfect season opener for the reigning champions. Youngster Jack Welsby moved back to fullback with aplomb and Saints' attacking machine never missed a beat.

Dan Sarginson (from Wigan), Kevin Brown (Warrington), Sebastine Ikahihifo (Huddersfield), Luke Yates (London), James Greenwood (Hull KR) and Rhys Williams (London) all made their Red Devils debuts, filling a massive void left by outgoing stars such as Hastings (to Wigan), Josh Jones (Hull FC), George Griffin, Derrell Olpherts (both Castleford) and Jake Bibby (Wigan).

On the same night, Hull KR also had a plethora of debutants but it worked in their favour as they were good value for their 30-12 home victory over Wakefield.

Greg Minikin, Shaun Kenny-Dowall, who captained Rovers in the injury absence of Weller Hauraki, Jamie Ellis, Ryan Brierley, Harvey Livett, Jordan Abdull, Matthew Storton, Will Maher and Elliot Minchella all made debuts. But it was a face from 2019, Ben Crooks, playing on the left wing, who made the headlines with four tries.

February

Joe Westerman scored a try for Wakefield on debut along with on-loan Wigan prop Romain Navarrete. But Wakefield, light on front-row options, were beaten convincingly and were hit with another injury blow as Danny Brough left the field on 54 minutes after a knee injury in the first half.

Pre-season predictions that Rovers would struggle looked far off the mark.

Huddersfield were also forecast to be among the strugglers but on the Saturday evening they were full value for their 32-12 win over the Catalans in Perpignan. Former Canberra Raiders scrum-half Aidan Sezer took control from start to finish with an imperial display - notching a try and six conversions - which brought the inevitable chants of 'Hail Sezer' from the small band of Giants supporters who had travelled to the south of France.

Sezer outshone his fellow Aussie debutants in the opposite ranks – James Maloney and Josh Drinkwater, Joel Tomkins also on debut – with some creative attacking moves, linking up seamlessly with stand-off Lee Gaskell and his tactical and goal-kicking display was near-perfect.

Huddersfield's pack, led by Adam O'Brien at hooker, put out the Dragons' fire, with the home team unable to cope with the rampaging Matty English, James Gavet - on debut also alongside former Dragon Kenny Edwards - and Joe Wardle. Winger Jermaine McGillvary looked back to his best with a double strike that was enough to decide the contest.

A double-header at Headingley on the Sunday was highly anticipated and drew a capacity crowd - the Wolfpack's first three home games were to be played on English soil because of the harsh Toronto winters.

The Canadian side was outplayed by Castleford Tigers, who emerged 28-10 winners after going behind to a well-worked fourth-minute try for Liam Kay. Jake Trueman was the stand-out player for Castleford, alongside debutant Danny Richardson as Peter Mata'utia's try shortly after half-time killed the game as a contest.

Derrell Olpherts and Tyla Hepi both made their Castleford bows but the media focus was on the Wolfpack debut of Sonny Bill Williams. Coach Brian McDermott had predicted it would take Williams two-thirds of the season to get back to his best and that looked a sound assessment.

The moment many neutrals had waited for arrived on 26 minutes when Williams came onto the field in place of Tom Olbison. But he knocked-on with his very first touch of the ball and at times looked awkward as he tried to re-adapt to League.

The second game was expected to be much tighter. But Hull FC made everyone sit up as they beat Leeds easily by 30-4.

The Airlie Birds' success was forged by a new-look pack - Tevita Satae, Manu Ma'u, Josh Jones and Jordan Johnstone (Danny Houghton was out injured) all showed up well - that completely out-muscled their Rhinos counterparts. They were aggressive, ran smart and offloaded at will. In the halves, Jake Connor, picked ahead of Albert Kelly, thrived off the space provided by his middles and Marc Sneyd provided the control to suffocate Leeds in to surrender.

Ratu Naulago scored two tries, as well as creating Hull's first for Carlos Tuimavave with a superb break and Andre Savelio scored a rampaging try and made another for Jamie Shaul. Naulago's second try on 56 minutes put Hull 24-0 ahead and it was all over for Leeds as neither new signing Luke Gale or Robert Lui could get a foothold in the game. Prop Matt Prior and back-rower Alex Mellor were other Rhinos debutants.

There were no major rule changes going into the new season but the shot clock, introduced for scrums and goal-line drop-outs in 2019, were both cut by five seconds – meaning 30 seconds for a scrum and 25 seconds for a drop-out. Clubs were also required to name a 21-man squad, rather than a 19-man one, for all games. Any player brought in for a match from outside the named 21 would cost his team an interchange.

Any strike to the head would entail an automatic sin-binning. And a change in the policing of play-the-balls was also announced, stressing the responsibility on the tackled

player to place the ball at his feet, not on an opposition player and 'to maintain balance and control and make a genuine attempt to make contact on the ball with the foot'.

There was no discernible improvement at the play-the-ball on the evidence of round one. But that didn't detract from an entertaining opening weekend.

Round 2

The Rugby League programme was badly affected by Storm Ciara which hit the UK on the second Sunday in February.

Both Super League fixtures that were scheduled for West Yorkshire on the Sunday afternoon – Huddersfield Giants v Leeds Rhinos and Wakefield Trinity v Catalans Dragons – were postponed because of a combination of heavy rain and strong winds. Attempts were made to have the Wakefield-Catalans game rearranged for the following Monday night but standing water on the Belle Vue pitch scuppered that plan.

It meant only four of the scheduled round-two games went ahead, with the first of them, on the Thursday night, providing a minor shock, Warrington beating St Helens by 19-nil at the Halliwell Jones Stadium.

The reigning Champions' ruthless opening-weekend dismantling of the last year's Grand Final opponents Salford had prompted talk of another campaign of total dominance, after which Saints finished an unprecedented 16 points ahead of the field.

But they were comprehensively beaten by a Warrington side fuelled by desire and taking a bold approach throughout, building on the promise they showed in the 12-man defeat at Wigan.

In mitigation, Saints, already without Lachlan Coote, Morgan Knowles, Tommy Makinson and James Roby, lost Alex Walmsley in the warm-up, before Mark Percival was withdrawn in the opening stages of the second half.

The Wolves were without key trio Gareth Widdop, yet to make his debut, Chris Hill and Jack Hughes but they took the game to their opponents from the off and, with long-term talismen Daryl Clark and Stefan Ratchford leading from the front, they overwhelmed their opponents for the majority of the clash.

Blake Austin was also influential in the middle of the field while young fullback Matty Ashton enhanced his rapidly growing reputation with another all-action effort from the back.

St Helens were behind from the 18th minute when Ratchford slotted a penalty before hooker Clark - having been held up over the line just moments earlier - plunged over from dummy-half. In between, Ashton had produced an electrifying break up the middle, only to be correctly penalised for passing off the floor after Jonny Lomax's outstanding cover tackle.

Ratchford was then involved twice in a move that also included Ben Currie cleverly knocking the ball back. It ended with Tom Lineham touching down out wide and Austin made the lead 13 at the break with a coolly taken field goal.

With centre Percival joining a crowded Saints treatment table in the opening stages of the second half, a comeback never looked likely and any flickering hopes were extinguished when Ratchford and Currie combined for a brilliant try saver on Kevin Naiqama out wide.

Austin, Ben Murdoch-Masila and Ashton then combined smoothly for Josh Charnley to finish and although Ratchford missed the conversion, his second penalty put a three-score gap between the teams.

Saints had not been nilled since losing at Wigan in August 2016, and they thought they had broken their duck when Lomax dived for the line in the closing stages. But the try was ruled out by video referee James Child.

Danny Houghton was back for Hull FC the following night and he celebrated his 350th club appearance with a 25-16 win in the derby at a packed KCOM Stadium.

Castleford's Paul McShane drives towards the Wigan line

It was a close contest that was decided in the minutes around the hour mark, with centre Josh Griffin and halfback Marc Sneyd doing the damage after Jamie Ellis's penalty that would have given Rovers an 18-12 lead bounced back off an upright.

Moments later, Griffin punched a hole down the left wing, outstripping virtually all with his break, before turning a high pass back inside for Sneyd to cling onto and crash over.

Then Sneyd's deep kick pinned the Robins' defence back in their own half, giving them minimal gains in a flustered set, before he turned supplier for Griffin with a tight bullet pass to send the centre sailing through a gap on the left edge. It put some daylight between the two sides and Sneyd's field goal two minutes from time finished the scoring.

Rovers' third try from Ben Crooks eleven minutes after the break, that Ellis goaled from the touchline for a 16-12 lead, was an absolute pearler, a glorious team move, sparked by an Ellis break on halfway and featuring ten last-gasp passes, including two from Shaun Kenny-Dowall, to take the ball from the right wing to the left corner.

On the same night, eight points from halfback Danny Richardson was enough to hand a severely depleted Castleford a hard-fought 16-12 home victory over a Wigan side that was never really allowed to get into gear.

It was impressive for the Tigers, considering the men they were without. Adam Milner, Tyla Hepi and George Griffin were all absent following head knocks, whilst Greg Eden was sidelined with a knee injury and Peter Mata'utia sat out the first of his two-game ban after being suspended for a late shot in Castleford's victory against the Wolfpack.

Down to the bare bones, head coach Daryl Powell did welcome back Oliver Holmes, whilst James Clare, Junior Moors and Lewis Peachey made their first appearances of 2020 and 17-year-old Sam Hall made his debut for the Tigers.

Harry Smith replaced the injured Sam Powell and Jake Shorrocks came into Wigan's matchday 17, taking George Burgess's place in Adrian Lam's only changes for Wigan, with Sean O'Loughlin making his 500th career appearance.

Paul McShane took control in an arm-wrestle of a game that the Tigers led by 12-6 at half-time, Liam Byrne crashing over after Derrell Olpherts and Cheyse Blair tries had given the home side a 10-6 lead. Richardson added a penalty just before the break.

The only scores of the second half were two more Richardson penalty goals that stretched Castleford's lead to ten on 62 minutes. That was until Wigan finally found space for Joe Burgess to race into the left corner in the last minute of the game.

On the Saturday afternoon, Salford had to dig deep to record a 24-16 home win over Toronto.

It was an even first half, with just two points separating the two at the break in a 40-minute period that didn't produce many try-scoring opportunities.

The Wolfpack, with Sonny Bill Williams looking more impressive on his first start, took the lead after 18 minutes when Gary Wheeler went over after only being on the field for a matter of seconds, while Salford - with young Aussie hooker Connor Jones on debut - led at the break after Kevin Brown followed up Tui Lolohea's kick by the side of the posts.

Two brilliant tries at the start of the second half through Lolohea and Rhys Williams - a cracking break from his own red zone from the restart and imperious rounding of fullback Wheeler - looked like knocking the stuffing out of Toronto. Instead it spurred them on.

With Salford leading by 12 points, it looked like they would cruise to victory. But Wheeler's second try and one for Brad Singleton saw the Wolfpack level the game heading into the last ten minutes.

Toronto probably deserved something with the way they hit back in the second half. But late tries from Dan Sarginson and Niall Evalds saw them crash to their second defeat of the season.

Round 3

Israel Folau touched down with his first touch of the ball in the seventh minute of Catalans Dragons' Saturday-evening 36-18 third round win over Castleford in Perpignan - in front of a large number of journalists, photographers and camera crews from France, the UK and Australia.

Folau played the full eighty minutes, ten years after his last game of Rugby League and nine months after his last game in Australian rugby union. The storm caused by his extreme religious views on homosexuality, expressed on social media, had divided opinion in the Rugby League world, with the Dragons receiving heavy criticism for offering Folau a career lifeline.

His teammate Sam Tomkins did him a favour by stealing some of the limelight with a virtuoso man-of-the-match performance. He tip-toed through the Tigers defence in his unique hop, skip and jump style for a hat-trick which sealed Catalans' first win of the season, a week after their game at Wakefield had been postponed due to the weather.

Tomkins opened the scoring just two minutes in, thanks to James Maloney's deft pass, to raise a cheer from the home supporters. However, the ground fell silent five minutes later when Josh Drinkwater hoisted a kick to the leaden skies. It fell into the hands of the leaping Folau and he touched down to audible gasps around the Gilbert Brutus.

Derrell Olpherts hit back for Castleford in the 14th minute, thanks to a brilliant in-goal collect and re-start by Danny Richardson, who raced up the middle to find his winger to complete a length-of-the pitch strike.

A Maloney penalty kept the scoreboard ticking, then Tomkins and Fouad Yaha worked hard to get Samisoni Langi over the line. But Castleford kept themselves in

contention with a try just before half-time as Cheyse Blair benefited from two penalties in the build-up to his touchdown in the right corner.

It took ten minutes of the second half before Tomkins scored his second, with a mazy run to the right. And when Olpherts was sin-binned for delaying a restart, Catalans went in for the kill.

Tomkins and Langi combined for Yaha to score in the 61st minute and, despite James Clare's response four minutes later, it was Tomkins who finished proceedings with his triple just before the final hooter, with Maloney adding his sixth conversion of the evening.

It was the Tigers' first defeat of the season and Hull FC had similar fortune after beginning the season with two wins against Leeds Rhinos and Hull Kingston Rovers. After their nilling to the Wolves, St Helens asserted their dominance on the Sunday afternoon with a 32-18 victory at KCOM Stadium, after trailing 6-2 at the break, courtesy of a converted solo Carlos Tuimavave try for the home side.

But, within 20 minutes of the restart, Matthew Costello, Luke Thompson, Louie McCarthy-Scarsbrook and James Bentley had gone over for Saints. Aaron Smith added a fifth try between replies from Tuimavave and Jamie Shaul.

So after only three rounds there remained only one hundred per cent record, after Huddersfield's Friday-night 12-10 win at Salford.

Aidan Sezer kicked a late penalty to make it two wins out of two for Huddersfield - their best start to a Super League season for six years.

After the Red Devils lost James Greenwood to concussion after 12 minutes, Adam O'Brien's sneaky scurry from dummy-half put them in front before Ken Sio responded for Salford on the end of a wide move involving Kevin Brown and Niall Evalds.

In a tight second half, Dan Sarginson's score put Salford ahead but teenager Louis Senior's try from a superb wide ball from Sezer levelled the match at 10-10.

The Red Devils nearly pinched it with six minutes to go, when a penalty saw them in field-goal territory. Tui Lolohea went for it but it went agonisingly wide. Replays showed that James Gavet had deflected it wide of the posts.

From that set came the major changing point. Joe Wardle shoved Brown off the ball and a penalty was awarded to Salford 30 metres from the Huddersfield line. But with consultation, the referee changed his decision and sin-binned Brown, who had led with his head into Jordan Turner's face.

From that, Evalds fumbled a loose ball, Lee Mossop was penalised for interference on his own line and Sezer kicked the easy penalty.

Salford's short kick-off attempt failed, but they got the ball back with 55 seconds to go. Pauli Pauli wrestled and swatted defenders away and offloaded to Kris Welham, who set Sio away. One on one with Darnell McIntosh, Sio grubbered past him. But McIntosh, only playing fullback because Ashton Golding was out long term with a pre-season hamstring injury, superbly turned and won the foot-race to ultimately win the Giants the game.

Brown apologised to Turner but insisted he did not mean to headbutt the Giants player. He was subsequently banned for two games.

Bevan French's strong start to the season continued on the Thursday as he scored twice and again won the man-of-the-match award as Wigan defeated Toronto 32-10.

The Wolfpack went into the game with just 18 fit players - a figure which was made worse when Jon Wilkin pulled out minutes before kick-off. Sonny Bill Williams was absent, back in New Zealand for the birth of his fourth child. Wilkin's late replacement, James Cunningham, lasted only seven minutes before limping off with a hamstring injury.

Toronto were well in the contest for the opening hour, before a late flurry of four tries took the game away from them.

Matty Russell's try put the Wolfpack ahead but Harry Smith and Bevan French went over six minutes apart as the hosts led at half-time. Toronto made a great start to the

Huddersfield's Darnell McIntosh wrapped up by Salford's Tyrone McCarthy and Dan Sarginson

second half with Bodene Thompson's try but a fantastic counter-attack by the Warriors saw Joe Burgess power over.

Burgess made up for some early mistakes as he raced away to put the Warriors back in front following a Josh McCrone kick into Wigan's in-goal. A quick tap on the twenty from French saw him offload to Jackson Hastings, who carried it on before sending the winger over from sixty metres out. Zak Hardaker converted to make it 16-10.

That was the turning point. Hastings ran across the field before finding French, who then stepped back inside and raced over for his second try. Hardaker's third conversion put the Warriors twelve in front.

Sean O'Loughlin thought he had sealed the win as he stepped inside with the line at his mercy but he was prevented from scoring with a flailing high arm from Hakim Miloudi, which saw the centre miss the rest of the game as he was sent to the sin bin for the second game in succession, while the Wigan captain left the field, obviously in some discomfort. The RFL Disciplinary later took no further action.

But Wigan took full advantage of the extra man with two tries in the final five minutes, both falling to Liam Farrell. The first saw him take an inside ball from Hastings to go over before making his second from nothing as he spied a gap and ended up under the posts.

Gareth O'Brien played his first game of the year, having previously been left out of Toronto's opening two fixtures.

Leeds got their first win, and in some style, on the Friday night as they beat Hull KR 52-10 at Headingley.

The Rhinos scored nine tries as Harry Newman, back at centre, tormented Rovers with his electrifying sidestep, picking up two tries and laying on a spectacular score for Ash Handley.

February

Leeds looked fresh following the postponement of their round-two game at Huddersfield and raced clear with Newman's two tries and a Cameron Smith score, Greg Minikin scoring just before the break for a 20-4 scoreline. The Rhinos pushed on after the break as Jack Walker, Ash Handley, Smith, Konrad Hurrell, James Donaldson and Richie Myler tries took them beyond 50 points. Rovers' only second-half score came through Jordan Abdull's converted try.

Warrington marquee signing Gareth Widdop made his Super League debut on the Sunday at Wakefield but could not help the Wolves avoid a surprise 18-8 defeat. With the wind swirling and the pitch heavy in parts, Trinity put in a highly improved display from their opening round defeat at Hull KR.

It was a disappointment for the Wolves, who had mastered St Helens a week before, as youngster Matty Ashton, a sensation in the opening two rounds, was dropped to make way for Widdop, as Stefan Ratchford reverted to fullback and Jake Mamo came in to the centre to replace Anthony Gelling. Gelling had been stood down by Warrington after being arrested by Cheshire Police on suspicion of wounding in a domestic incident.

There were no tries after an hour, with Wakefield leading 6-2 on penalties, but Ratchford broke the try-drought when he sped onto a Ben Currie offload from close range and converted for an 8-6 lead.

But Trinity showed great determination to re-take an ascendancy as Matty Ashurst crashed over in the 71st minute before Tom Johnstone sealed it when he scooped up a loose ball and raced away from halfway.

Round 4

Huddersfield Giants topped the table after a 22-4 Friday-night win over Hull KR at blustery Hull College Craven Park. The last time the Giants started a season this well, with three straight wins, in 2013, they ended it as league leaders for the first time in 81 years.

The Giants had the second worst defence in the competition in 2019, conceding 776 points at an average of 26 per game. After three games in 2002 they had conceded 26 at an average of just over eight.

The Robins, light on forwards, lost another unexpectedly before the game as George Lawler was forced to pull out with a stiff neck. He was replaced by the returning Mitch Garbutt, while Joe Keyes came in for his debut for the injured Jamie Ellis.

Huddersfield were the better side down the middle and Samoan prop Suaia Matagi was a big reason for that, deserving his bustling try on the hourmark that ended the contest.

The Giants put in a dominant display to lead 10-0 at the break thanks to tries from Louis Senior and Lee Gaskell. Prop James Gavet was stretchered off with a neck injury in the opening minutes of the second half but they extended their lead to 22-0 through Paul Clough and Matagi. Ben Crooks scored a consolation for Rovers in the final minutes.

Castleford and Wigan were level on points with the Giants after their wins over the weekend.

The Tigers took on Wakefield at the Jungle in the Friday TV game, with wet and windy conditions again affecting play, and emerged 32-15 winners after a dominant second half.

Trinity looked likely in the first forty minutes with scores from Joe Westerman, off a disguised flat ball from Jacob Miller, and a Tom Johnstone special in the left corner, although they only led 15-14 at the break as Castleford scored three tries of their own from Cheyse Blair, James Clare and Derrell Olpherts. Only a Miller field goal on the half-time hooter separated the sides.

Expectation of a nip-and-tuck second half were well wide of the mark as Clare's second try and two more to Oliver Holmes and Derrell Olpherts, while James Batchelor was in the sin bin for a professional foul, saw the Tigers stretch away.

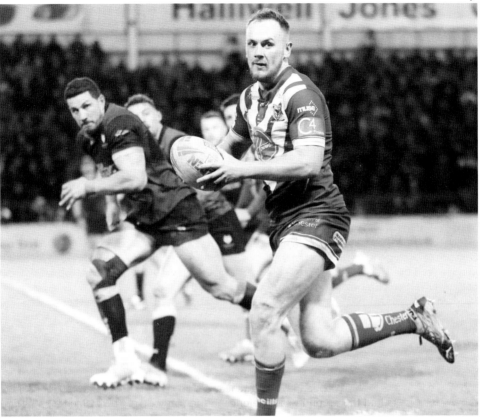

Warrington's Ben Currie makes a break against Toronto Wolfpack

In mitigation, Wakefield centre Joe Arundel had limped out of the game just before half-time and forward Jay Pitts filled in both at left centre and later on the right wing. Arundel's season was ended with an ACL, while Ryan Hampshire broke his jaw.

Wigan looked strong in their 26-12 Sunday-afternoon home win over Hull FC. Bevan French produced another eye-catching performance as they overran Hull in the second half.

The Aussie speedster was a handful all afternoon and he managed to score a try and had a hand in another as Wigan ran in four tries to two, while Hull crashed to a second consecutive Super League defeat.

The Warriors led 10-8 at the break following an entertaining half that ended with both teams having players in the sin bin, Josh Griffin and Liam Farrell taking a rest after a 39th minute melee. Hull came back from 8-0 down, French scoring a try in the third minute and Zak Hardaker kicking two goals. Adam Swift got Hull's try on 25 minutes after a Griffin interception and Marc Sneyd kicked two goals before a late penalty from Hardaker put Wigan back in front at the interval.

Tries from Dom Manfredi, back from a serious knee injury suffered the previous July, Jackson Hastings and Willie Isa saw Wigan take control after the break, Griffin scoring a fine consolation five minutes from time.

On the Friday night, Sonny Bill Williams was back for Toronto and former Catalans star Tony Gigot made his debut off the bench after joining the club on a month's trial. Gigot turned in an impressive spell at the back in the hour he was on the field but he couldn't prevent the Wolfpack falling to their fourth straight loss, this time by 32-22 at Warrington.

But Toronto were much improved, fighting back impressively to level up the match in the second half, after going three scores down early on. But two calmly taken Stefan Ratchford penalties and a late try from Ben Murdoch-Masila secured the points for the Wolves.

Toronto thought they'd snatched the game-clinching play with five minutes to go when Hakim Miloudi threw himself at the line but Josh Charnley did just enough to deny the Frenchman and Warrington survived.

Matty Ashton was back and his ability to split Toronto's line with raw pace as he rounded the cover defence to score in the 36th minute brought the crowd to its feet.

On the Saturday, former Man of Steel and new Rhinos halfback Luke Gale contributed ten points - including a vital try just before the break - as Leeds piled on four unanswered tries for a 22-8 victory, erasing Salford's early 8-0 edge to register back-to-back wins in their first away trip of 2020.

With Leeds staring down the barrel of an eight-point half-time deficit, despite having the wind at their backs - Niall Evalds had scorched in and Tui Lolohea muscled his way through Gale down the same right edge - Brad Dwyer unlocked the Red Devils' defence from dummy-half to set up Gale for the try that swung the momentum.

The turning point came on 50 minutes as Myler's and Gale's manic chase of a swirling Robert Lui bomb pinned Evalds in his in-goal. The decision attracted the fury of the home fans and Salford coach Ian Watson, who believed the fullback had been tackled in the air. And their mood didn't improve when Luke Briscoe acrobatically finished in the corner off the next set, poking Leeds' noses in front.

Mikolaj Oledzki went in shortly after, before a Gale penalty and Jack Walker's breakaway score sealed Leeds' victory.

World Club Challenge

Sydney Roosters retained the World Club Champions title with a 20-12 win over St Helens at a packed Totally Wicked Stadium on the Saturday night of round four.

Centre Joseph Manu scored twice as the National Rugby League premiers claimed a record fifth World Club Challenge title.

Saints, missing Mark Percival, Regan Grace and Lachlan Coote, made a lightning start as they charged downfield in the sixth minute to set up position. Theo Fages took the ball infield from the right and found Luke Thompson, who powered over from close range.

But the Roosters hit back to lead 8-6 at half-time as Daniel Tupou and Manu went over in opposite corners.

After the break, Saints dominated

BETFRED SUPER LEAGUE
Sunday 23rd February

	P	W	D	L	F	A	D	Pts
Huddersfield Giants	3	3	0	0	66	26	40	6
Wigan Warriors	4	3	0	1	86	48	38	6
Castleford Tigers	4	3	0	1	94	73	21	6
St Helens	3	2	0	1	80	45	35	4
Leeds Rhinos	3	2	0	1	78	48	30	4
Warrington Wolves	4	2	0	2	69	56	13	4
Hull FC	4	2	0	2	85	78	7	4
Catalans Dragons	2	1	0	1	48	50	-2	2
Wakefield Trinity	3	1	0	2	45	70	-25	2
Salford Red Devils	4	1	0	3	50	98	-48	2
Hull Kingston Rovers	4	1	0	3	60	111	-51	2
Toronto Wolfpack	4	0	0	4	58	116	-58	0

BETFRED WORLD CLUB CHALLENGE

Saturday 22nd February 2020

ST HELENS 12 SYDNEY ROOSTERS 20

SAINTS: 22 Jack Welsby; 2 Tommy Makinson; 3 Kevin Naiqama; 20 James Bentley; 21 Matthew Costello; 6 Jonny Lomax; 7 Theo Fages; 8 Alex Walmsley; 9 James Roby (C); 10 Luke Thompson; 11 Zeb Taia; 12 Dominique Peyroux; 14 Morgan Knowles. Subs (all used): 13 Louie McCarthy-Scarsbrook; 15 Matty Lees; 18 Joseph Paulo; 19 Aaron Smith.
Tries: Thompson (6), Walmsley (79); **Goals:** Makinson 2/2.
ROOSTERS: 1 James Tedesco; 2 Daniel Tupou; 3 Angus Crichton; 4 Joseph Manu; 5 Brett Morris; 6 Luke Keary; 7 Kyle Flanagan; 8 Jared Waerea-Hargreaves; 9 Jake Friend (C); 10 Sio Siua Taukeiaho; 11 Sitili Tupouniua; 12 Mitchell Aubusson; 13 Victor Radley. Subs (all used): 14 Sam Verrills; 15 Isaac Liu; 16 Nat Butcher; 17 Lindsay Collins.
Tries: Tupou (11), Manu (20, 61), Keary (68);
Goals: Flanagan 0/3, Taukeiaho 2/2.
Rugby Leaguer & League Express Men of the Match:
Saints: Alex Walmsley; *Roosters:* Luke Keary.
Penalty count: 11-6; **Half-time:** 6-8; **Referee:** Chris Kendall; **Attendance:** 16,108 *(at Totally Wicked Stadium).*

St Helens' Alex Walmsley meets Sydney Roosters' Isaac Liu and Nat Butcher head on

possession and position and spent what felt like the entire third quarter camped on the Roosters' line. Chances came, and chances went. There were near-misses and perhaps even one call that could have gone their way when Tommy Makinson appeared to have scored but was denied by the video referee.

But despite defending non-stop for 20 relentless minutes, the Roosters summoned some quality from within, forging a way downfield via a penalty and, with their first real attack of the half, crossing in the right-hand corner when Manu claimed his second.

That made it 12-6 and, while there was certainly still enough time for the Saints to reply, the psychological impact of that moment was huge. From there, the Roosters gradually restored control and finished the game off seven minutes later when the outstanding Luke Keary crossed from long range off Sio Siua Taukeiaho's great break. With Taukeiaho converting to make it 18-6 and then adding a penalty just a few minutes later, the Saints' chance had gone.

They did at least score a consolation in the dying seconds. Alex Walmsley was the try-scorer, showing real power close to the line to force his way over.

MARCH
Into the unknown

Round 5

Wigan leap-frogged Huddersfield to the top of the table after their Sunday afternoon contest at the John Smith's Stadium ended in a one-sided 42-10 romp.

The Giants went into the game with the competition's only one hundred per cent record and for 35 minutes of the game it looked like they would continue their winning run. They were deservedly 10-4 ahead with little over five minutes to go until half-time, when halfback Aidan Sezer was sin-binned for a high tackle on Thomas Leuluai.

By the time Sezer returned on the other side of the break, Wigan had scored four tries and 20 points to completely change the course of the match. The outstanding Liam Marshall scored two of them as part of a 14-minute hat-trick, to help secure a monster win.

Two tackles after Sezer was yellow-carded, Jackson Hastings and Bevan French combined to send Marshall over out wide. When Huddersfield were penalised again in the next set, Sam Powell burrowed his way over from dummy-half.

The Warriors would cross again before the break. Marshall was again the finisher and this time his try covered the length of the field, touching down with ten seconds left on the clock following his own kick over, allowing Zak Hardaker's conversion to make it 20-10.

Sezer was still off the field when Wigan struck again soon after the restart. Harry Smith, who was on for Leuluai as he took a concussion test, kicked a 40/20 to create the platform and Hardaker sent Dom Manfredi over in the right corner.

Even Sezer's return couldn't stem the tide. Smith this time took the defence on with ball in hand, allowing Chris Hankinson to put Marshall over for his hat-trick.

It was 32-unanswered points when prop Oliver Partington took what looked a regulation drive, burst straight through the middle and stepped Louis Senior to score under the posts. Marshall was denied a fourth by a forward pass call but George Burgess crashed over under the posts in the closing stages to complete the rout.

The Warriors also leapt over Castleford who had gone top the previous Thursday night with an eventually comfortable 28-8 win at Hull KR.

The Robins, already light in the middle, made three enforced changes to their pack with Matt Parcell and Harvey Livett ruled out through injury and Robbie Mulhern suspended for a match for dangerous challenge in the defeat at Huddersfield. They were replaced by Jez Litten, youngster Owen Harrison and debutant Matty Gee.

The Robins took the lead after earning a penalty. Joe Keyes' well-flighted kick to the corner was plucked out of the sky by Super League's leading scorer at the time, Ben Crooks, who beat Derrell Olpherts to the ball in the air to grab his seventh of the campaign. Ryan Brierley converted.

As the half wore on, Castleford exposed the Robins down the middle with three long-range breaks from Jordan Rankin, Michael Shenton and gamestar Paul McShane, the latter linking with Danny Richardson who sent Shenton into the corner. The Robins

Wigan's Liam Marshall dives past Huddersfield's Jordan Turner to score

ultimately still held a half-time lead, with Brierley converting a penalty goal from under the posts in the final action of the first 40 minutes.

But the Tigers, after coming back from the break early to warm up for the second week running, bossed the second half, scoring 22-unanswered points. Within two minutes Brierley had been sin-binned for colliding with Grant Millington as the two went for a kick in-goal. Richardson scored eight points during Brierley's absence. First, he brought the game level with a goal from the foul, before stepping inside Hull KR's scrambling defence for a try and converting. James Clare touched down acrobatically in the left corner and Mike McMeeken added a late try as Richardson finished with six goals out of six attempts.

The only cloud on the Tigers' horizon was a training injury setback for star off-season signing Sosaia Feki, the former Cronulla winger re-aggravating a calf injury that had already seen him miss the opening five rounds.

There was a blow-out the following night at Headingley where Leeds hammered Warrington 36-0. It seemed a long time since round two when the Wolves had looked destined to be the team to beat when they nilled St Helens.

Jack Walker's third try in as many games, two Rhyse Martin penalties and a Richie Myler score put the dominant hosts 14-0 up at the break. Brad Dwyer finished a scrappy third try for Leeds before Konrad Hurrell crashed over in the corner. Two tries in two minutes from Ava Seumanufagai and Ash Handley competed the victory.

Myler came on from the bench and played fullback for almost an hour after an injury to young fullback Walker. After the arrival at Headingley in the off season of halfback Luke Gale, Myler had dropped down the pecking order but had responded brilliantly to coach Richard Agar's plan to use him as a utility player.

Rhinos captain Stevie Ward was facing an uncertain future after being stood down 'indefinitely' because of problems recovering from a concussion injury he suffered in the opening week of the season against Hull FC. The Rhinos moved to secure England international forward Joe Greenwood on a two-month loan deal from Wigan. He was selected in the initial 21-man squad to face Warrington but did not make the 17-man team.

March

Saints coach Kristian Woolf was left hugely satisfied with the relentless pressure his side put on Toronto with their defence after the champions came out 32-0 winners over the Canadian side in Warrington on the Saturday. The Wolfpack's home game had been scheduled to be played at Saracens' Allianz Park in London but the union side had hit hard times after salary cap transgressions.

Coming off the back of an energy-sapping World Club Challenge defeat to Sydney Roosters, there would have been plenty of reasons for Saints to be below their best. But that wasn't the case as stand-off Jonny Lomax ran in his first two Super League tries of the season. James Bentley, Louie McCarthy-Scarsbrook and Aaron Smith crossed too before the Wolfpack were reduced to 12 men when Bodene Thompson was shown a red card for a shoulder charge on Matty Lees. Bodene got a zero-match penalty notice.

The Wolfpack certainly couldn't afford to lose many more players. The 36-year-old Jon Wilkin was playing through the pain, with Toronto's injury toll resulting in him delaying knee surgery and the Wolfpack added Wigan Warriors forwards Ben Kilner and Jack Wells to their roster, both on a one-month loan. Prop Brad Singleton ruptured the lateral medial ligament in his knee and was expected to miss four months.

On the Sunday, Catalans came away from the KCOM Stadium with a 34-29 win. The Airlie Birds looked to be on their way to a comfortable victory at one stage, leading 28-10 after 60 minutes and seemingly in complete control.

However, a remarkable collapse from Hull, with Sam Tomkins inspiring the comeback, led to James Maloney eventually scoring in the dying seconds to secure a brilliant win.

The same afternoon, injury-hit Wakefield Trinity collected their second win of the season, emerging 22-12 winners at Salford.

Props Kelepi Tanginoa and Romain Navarrete steamrolled the Salford pack, with Tanginoa marking his 26th birthday with a try and the three Albert Goldthorpe Medal points in a powerhouse display.

Tireless winger Bill Tupou, who scored a spectacular second-half try, cartwheeling over the right corner post, and makeshift halves pairing Max Jowitt and Jacob Miller also impressed in a gutsy four-tries-to-three triumph. Ken Sio finished with two good tries for the Red Devils as Wakefield made only one error in the second half.

Round 6

Rugby League was about to be hit by the global crisis caused by the spread of a new coronavirus that had first hit parts of China at the very end of 2019 and had seen its first fatality in the United Kingdom early in the month.

League Express had revealed that the Rugby Football League had sent a detailed document to clubs with advice on the Covid-19 virus, which included confirmation they had consulted with Sky Sports about playing games behind closed doors should the virus spread in the UK.

A number of other sports across the world had dramatically altered their schedules and this year's Olympic Games was destined to be cancelled. The RFL was hopeful that their competitions could carry on.

Wigan went two points clear at the top of the table after a 30-16 Sunday-afternoon home win over beleaguered Hull KR.

Nobody fancied injury-shot Hull KR's chances but they pushed Wigan all the way, with the game never really over until Liam Marshall's final try on 63 minutes. Five tries in total, Jackson Hastings ran in two, a number of which involved the outstanding Bevan French, were enough to move the hosts back to the top of the table after a bruising battle.

French's pace and footwork leading up to Hastings' second on 36 minutes was superb. Zak Hardaker converted that to give Wigan an 18-12 half-time lead - Liam Farrell, who was in the form of his life, had got the other Wigan try. Winger Ethan Ryan had raced

over for a try on his Super League debut as Rovers took a 6-0 lead and then Greg Minikin had levelled at 12-all.

Eight minutes after the break, Ryan Brierley's try, which he couldn't convert, made it 18-16. Eight minutes after that try, back-to-back penalties sprung the hosts into a position to strike, which they duly did when Tommy Leuluai's flat pass sent Sam Powell over. Then, seven minutes after that, they closed the game out once and for all.

Already leading by eight after Zak Hardaker had maintained his perfect record from the tee, the Warriors secured victory when Marshall squeezed over in the corner following an assist from the outstanding Farrell.

The Robins' injury crisis deepened as they suffered injuries to Robbie Mulhern, Will Maher, Joe Keyes and Matthew Storton, which left them with just one fit interchange for most of the final half-hour.

Later in the week, Ben Flower accepted a two-match penalty notice for a dangerous tackle on Storton and his front-row partner Oliver Partington was given a four-match ban for a similar challenge on Mulhern. Both Wigan players were found guilty of attacking opponents' legs while they were being held upright in a tackle.

Castleford had lost their chance to stay level with Wigan on the Friday night as they were pipped at Warrington, Blake Austin's field goal a minute from time giving the Wolves a 9-8 victory.

The win was a huge relief for Wolves' coach Steve Price who, after just five games, was under pressure after a woeful drubbing at the hands of Leeds Rhinos a week earlier.

Winger Tom Lineham dived over on 22 minutes to give Warrington a narrow two-point half-time lead after Danny Richardson's goal. A Stefan Ratchford penalty goal five minutes after the break extended the lead to 6-2 before Castleford were awarded a penalty try for Keanan Brand's high tackle as Calum Turner was about to score in the corner after taking a superb pass from Michael Shenton.

Richardson converted from in front of the sticks but, seven minutes later, Ratchford levelled with another penalty goal from under the Castleford sticks to set up a field-goal frenzy.

Austin went first, with arguably the best positioned of the incoming parade of attempts, but he kicked his wide of the posts from a central position. Castleford now had seven tackles from the 20-metre tap. It provided Richardson an opportunity, but he also went wide.

Next up was Gareth Widdop. But, from distance, he was short and slightly wayward.

The fourth halfback, Jake Trueman, tried next, perhaps unwisely. From distance, he kicked wide and the decision seemed to annoy his partner Richardson, who wanted to play for field position instead.

But Castleford got the next opportunity anyway after a Warrington knock-on and when Paul McShane scampered to make 15 quick metres, a Castleford one-pointer seemed certain.

The issue was that McShane's dart meant that Castleford couldn't put blockers in the way of Warrington, so when Richardson got the ball, he was closed down, forced to re-balance under pressure and miss. Joe Philbin's effort to make it to Richardson was perhaps as much a match-winning moment as the one to come.

Austin stepped up, with about 65 seconds remaining, to finally land a one-pointer and secure Warrington the points.

Leeds and Huddersfield moved into joint second with Castleford with Friday-night wins.

The Rhinos made short work of Toronto at home, winning 66-12. The Wolfpack could not contain the growing momentum of the Rhinos, epitomised by their halfback partnership.

That was best seen in the second try in only the seventh minute. Luke Gale, on his

Salford's Gil Dudson gets to grips with Catalans Dragons' Sam Tomkins

300th career appearance, started the move and Robert Lui sent Rhyse Martin into a hole. He picked up Gale again on the inside, who slowed to wait for support before his sweet reverse flick for the linking Richie Myler allowed him to evade the cover.

Toronto also had little answer to the power of Mikolaj Oledzki or the drive of Cameron Smith off the bench up the middle, where the battle was won. Harry Newman further enhanced a reputation that had seen the 20-year old drafted into a full England gathering.

Konrad Hurrell was menacing, finishing with the final try as the hooter went when he ripped up the centre to the posts.

The Giants meanwhile, won a memorable game at St Helens by 12-10. Saints dominated Huddersfield in every aspect of the game except the one that matters most - the scoreboard. They failed to convert a mountain of pressure into points in the opening hour to leave the door ajar for Huddersfield, who struck with 15 minutes remaining through a long-range Jake Wardle try, coolly converted by star halfback Aidan Sezer.

On paper, a pre-game mismatch was compounded by the absence of Huddersfield's regular props Matty English and Suaia Matagi (suspended), which was hardly what they needed up against Alex Walmsley and Luke Thompson. Darnell McIntosh returned at fullback, though and Tom Holmes and Oliver Wilson got their first games of the season off the bench.

Then the Giants lost Lee Gaskell (hamstring) and Ukuma Ta'ai (knee) in the first half. But their defence scrambled superbly to hand the reigning Super League champions their first home defeat since 2018.

On the same night there was another one-point game as Marc Sneyd's 81st-minute, 35-metre field goal gave Hull FC a 27-26 win at Wakefield.

Sneyd had kicked the first-ever golden point winner in February 2019 and he was again on hand to give Hull FC a hard-fought victory over a stoic Wakefield side that would never go away, even after the Airlie Birds took a 20-6 half-time lead.

Mahe Fonua, Jamie Shaul and Kieran Buchanan scored tries in 13 first-half minutes as Hull led 20-6 at the break.

But Jay Pitts and Ryan Atkins touched down to give Wakefield hope and Tom Johnstone went over twice in the corner late on - both spectacular one-handed finishes. Max Jowitt couldn't convert either of the tries from the touchline, hitting the post with the first attempt, which took the game to golden point and Sneyd's winning touch.

Salford gave a battling performance at Catalans but lost out 30-14, mainly thanks to a controlled performance from James Maloney.

The Dragons led 18-0 at half-time with tries to Michael McIlorum and a brace from Matt Whitley and looked to be coasting. But Salford hit back early in the second half with a dazzling solo run from fullback Niall Evalds, who stepped around Sam Tomkins to score on the right, with Tui Lolohea adding the extras. Ken Sio gave the visitors hope with a clever touchdown on the right corner flag before being bundled into touch.

A Maloney penalty made the score 20-10 with 20 minutes to go before Salford took advantage of a fumble from Tomkins for Sio to add his second on the right. Lolohea failed to convert and Lewis Tierney struck the killer blow for Catalans with a dazzling midfield dash resulting in a try for his fellow winger Fouad Yaha.

Tierney got his own try following good work from Israel Folau and Maloney's conversion rounded things off.

Round 7

The third week in March proved to be the most dramatic of times for Rugby League. While most sports put fixtures on hold because of the coronavirus pandemic, after consultation with the government, the Rugby Football League decided to carry on with matches, with all the ties in the fifth round of the Challenge Cup and all the remaining Super League matches in England being played.

But Catalans Dragons' President Bernard Guasch said his club was facing a 'real disaster' after it became Super League's first victim of the virus outbreak.

Leeds Rhinos were due to travel to Perpignan for the Saturday round seven clash against the Dragons but they decided not to fly out on the Friday when an un-named squad member reported symptoms of the virus, although he later tested negative.

The game had been scheduled to be played behind closed doors anyway because of a decision by the French government to ban all crowds of over a thousand. The following Tuesday the whole of France went into total lockdown, with severe restrictions on people's movements, in an effort to slow down the spread of the virus.

On the Thursday night, Lee Radford became the first Super League coach to lose his job after Hull FC crashed to a 38-4 defeat at home to Warrington.

News of Radford's sacking came in unique fashion as club owner Adam Pearson made the announcement on Sky Sports, barely 12 minutes after the final whistle. That immediately generated criticism from Rugby League supporters on social media.

Pearson later revealed he had already told Radford that he would be leaving the club before he broke the news on TV.

'I went to see Lee straight after the end of the game and we had ten or 15 minutes talking,' said Pearson. 'I don't think he was surprised (by the decision). I told him: 'I think that's it. And he said 'yes, I agree.' He always said to me he'd know when it was time to go. He had a really good innings and we should always remember what he has done for this club; his legacy is winning at Wembley and winning back-to-back Challenge Cups, which

Warrington's Blake Austin is closed down by Hull FC's Masi Matongo and Marc Sneyd

no one has ever done with Hull.

'But aspects of that performance were unacceptable and he knows that. Sky needed an interview so I said I'd handle Sky for him and he said 'great'. That's when I went out to do it. That is as clear as day.'

In the days after, several Hull players apologised and took responsibility for Radford's seven-year reign coming to an end.

Both sides went into the contest with their coaches under pressure and desperate to build some confidence after several frustrating weeks of poor form.

But it was the Wire who came out as the deserved victors after showing grit and determination in the first half before cutting loose with some crisp attacking rugby in the second, to get their first away win in the league since last July.

The contest was a real arm wrestle up until half-time, with only an individual piece of brilliance from Blake Austin and a try from Tom Lineham from a Hull mistake the difference.

However, the second half was a different story as the hosts capitulated, with Warrington running riot, adding five more well-taken tries - Austin and Gareth Widdop ended with two tries apiece - to subject the Airlie Birds to an embarrassing defeat.

The game also saw Anthony Gelling make a try-scoring return to the side after having been suspended following his arrest earlier in the season.

The following night, leaders Wigan's running streak came to an end with an 18-14 defeat at Salford.

Wigan looked in control for long periods, leading 14-2 through Jackson Hastings and Sam Powell tries and three Chris Hankinson goals in the first half, with just over 20 minutes remaining.

But then Niall Evalds injected himself into the contest with two quick-fire tries from nothing, his second that levelled the scores a length-of-the-field run after scooping up Powell's attacking grubber, before Kevin Brown put the home side in front for the first time as the clock ticked down.

Even then there was time for table-topping Wigan to mount one final attack after Harry Smith forced a goal-line drop-out.

But Dan Sarginson, who was outstanding against his former club, produced a crucial spot-tackle on the dangerous Bevan French to give Ian Watson's side just their second win from seven.

On the Sunday, Castleford put in a superb performance at home to beat St Helens by 28-14.

Two of Saints' three tries came in the final seven minutes. By then, the game was long over as a contest, with Castleford forging a deserved 22-4 lead that they never really looked likely to relinquish at any stage.

St Helens were architects of their own downfall to some extent, with a poor completion rate and, perhaps more importantly, ill-discipline, with two players sin-binned during the course of the game - Matty Lees and Louie McCarthy-Scarsbrook both seeing yellow.

With the outstanding Paul McShane pulling the strings from hooker and Danny Richardson and Jake Trueman again looking exciting in the halves, the Tigers were very much worthy winners as they moved level with Wigan at the top.

Leading 14-4 at half-time through a try from Peter Mata'utia and a double to Derrell Olpherts, his second a miraculous finish in the right corner, the Tigers were able to build after the break with two more tries, through Cheyse Blair and Trueman, to secure an ultimately comfortable victory.

BETFRED SUPER LEAGUE								
Sunday 15th March								
	P	W	D	L	F	A	D	Pts
Wigan Warriors	7	5	0	2	172	92	80	10
Castleford Tigers	7	5	0	2	158	104	54	10
Leeds Rhinos	5	4	0	1	180	60	120	8
Warrington Wolves	7	4	0	3	116	104	12	8
Huddersfield Giants	5	4	0	1	88	78	10	8
St Helens	6	3	0	3	136	85	51	6
Catalans Dragons	4	3	0	1	112	93	19	6
Hull FC	7	3	0	4	145	176	-31	6
Wakefield Trinity	5	2	0	3	93	109	-16	4
Salford Red Devils	7	2	0	5	94	164	-70	4
Hull Kingston Rovers	6	1	0	5	84	169	-85	2
Toronto Wolfpack	6	0	0	6	70	214	-144	0

Challenge Cup Round 5

The four lowest-placed Super League sides from 2019 entered the Challenge Cup at the fifth-round stage, with three progressing.

Surprisingly, win-less Toronto were one of them, winning a Wednesday night all-Super League clash at Huddersfield, by 18-0.

To nil a hitherto in-form Giants on their, albeit soaked, home turf was unexpected but to do it just six days after shipping in 11 tries at Headingley was astonishing. Coach Brian McDermott was quick to point out that the dreadful wet and windy weather at the John Smith's Stadium played its part, once the visitors had rocketed to a 12-0 lead in even time through two Ricky Leutele tries. It was 16-0 at half-time thanks to two Gareth O'Brien penalties and one more penalty goal from the fullback was the only score of the second half.

The Canadian side had Chase Stanley making his first appearance of the season after visa difficulties, while Joe Mellor and Darcy Lussick were back from injury, albeit the latter was among three replacements not used, or needed, by McDermott in a rare

Wakefield's Jay Pitts attempts to break free against Bradford

departure from the norm.

Wakefield coach Chris Chester admitted that winning and the return to action of David Fifita and Danny Brough were the only real positives to come out of the Friday-night Cup derby against Bradford.

Trinity were 17-14 victors after trailing 14-7 to the Championship battlers, led by former Wakefield coach John Kear, who were the better side for the first 60 minutes. Reece Lyne's 70th minute try proved the winner as Wakefield scraped home.

It was just at tight at Hull College Craven Park on the Sunday as Nick Rawsthorne's last-gasp try brought joy to the faces of Hull Kingston Rovers fans for the first time in a month and a half as they survived a real scare against Leigh, finally winning 22-19.

Rovers did not make it easy for themselves despite the excellent work of the relatively untested teenager Mikey Lewis in the halves – and they would have been left to rue their missed chances had Josh Woods' 70th-minute field goal been the final say.

Instead, John Duffy's Centurions saw their own unbeaten streak sacrificed in a game marked by sporadically scrappy ill-discipline, with Adam Higson sin-binned on two separate occasions for professional fouls, the second with seven minutes to go as Leigh led 19-18.

* On Monday 16th March, the Rugby Football League and Super League Europe announced a suspension of fixtures in the Betfred Super League, initially until April 3rd. Championship, League 1 and the community game followed suit the next day.

MARCH - JULY
An uncertain world

Not just Rugby League was thrown into chaos, confusion and uncertainty by the deadly virus that became known as Covid-19. The whole world was caught in a crisis, that was declared a global pandemic by the World Health Organisation on March 3rd 2020, that ebbed through the British summer but refused to go away.

Catalans' experience had illustrated on 16th March what was soon to come in the United Kingdom when a total lockdown was announced by French President Emmanuel Macron. Cafes and bars and all non-essential locations were closed. Public gatherings were not allowed and individuals were only allowed out of their house on essential business - and they had to carry a government form to prove it. A month after, the French government banned all sporting fixtures until September.

When the Rugby Football League suspended its competitions on 16th March, it initially planned a restart on April 2nd.

That proved wildly optimistic In a televised announcement on 23rd March, UK Prime Minister Boris Johnson said: 'From this evening I must give the British people a very simple instruction - you must stay at home.'

The instruction included the 'very limited purposes' for which people were allowed to leave their homes, such as shopping for necessities, one form of exercise a day or travelling to work if they could not work from home. It also banned gatherings of more than two people from different households in public. Non-essential shops were told to close and social events including weddings were stopped.

Toronto Wolfpack faced an even bigger dilemma. The Canadian government shut off its borders in mid-March, meaning that even if Super League fixtures could resume, there was little chance of the outpost club being able to play any home fixtures.

There was no definitive figure but by the end of October it was estimated the virus had killed over a million people worldwide, with the risk of death or long-lasting effects greater in old people and the socially disadvantaged. In the UK alone, over fifty thousand deaths were recorded by the beginning of November.

The virus was highly contagious through airborne transmission and touch. Facemasks became an everyday sight, with a concerted campaign to increase hand-washing.

The impact on economies, with many people unable to work from home and most workplaces closed down, was huge, governments having to provide massive financial support for individuals and businesses.

This proved a lifeline for Rugby League clubs, with the RFL also negotiating a loan of 16 million pounds from the government for which stricken clubs could apply. With income streams through attendances totally cut off, the continuation of Sky's distribution money also helped clubs to stay alive, although all players and employees were asked to take pay cuts. As to re-commencing the playing season, the best-case scenario was staging games behind closed doors to fulfil TV contracts.

A plan by the NRL to re-start the season down under on 28th May was thought barmy, although they did just that, and with great success, gradually introducing crowds at games.

The RFL laid plans to restart Super League from 2nd June onwards, the cases of Covid infection having dropped off dramatically by then. But it was another two months before the competition could resume, with all games being played at one venue per round, behind closed doors, to control the spread of the virus.

A significant cancellation was the Ashes Test series due to be played at the the end of the season. Magic Weekend, due to return to Newcastle at the end of May, was cancelled. The Academy and Reserves competitions were cancelled Championship and League 1 were cancelled, a huge blow to clubs who had invested heavily in winning promotion. An end-of-year competition for lower league clubs fizzled out when only five clubs entered.

On Monday 20th July, Toronto Wolfpack withdrew from the rest of the 2020 season

A statement from the club read: 'This decision has not been taken lightly, and in consideration of a range of factors specific to the club as the only transatlantic team in the league.

'The Covid pandemic has presented unexpected and overwhelming financial challenges to the Wolfpack organisation. Greatly reduced ticket, sponsorship, merchandise and game day revenue streams have resulted from the loss of all 11 of the team's home Super League games in Toronto. The Wolfpack would be left covering significant additional costs simply to complete a season of games in the UK including Covid testing, stadium rentals, medical costs and player pay increases to align with the rest of the league.

'The club fully intend to field a team in the 2021 season, and will be working with SLE and the RFL to understand this process moving into the next season.

'The Wolfpack would also like to thank our loyal fans for their ongoing support during a hugely challenging time.'

The statement came amid rumours that players had not been receiving their salaries on time and unlike British clubs the Wolfpack were unable to tap into the UK government's nation-wide 'furlough scheme', which saw playing and non-playing staff receive eighty per cent of their salaries while unable to work.

Toronto didn't receive any monies from Super League's central distribution to help keep them going. And all the Wolfpack's overseas players' six-month UK visas - which would have covered them in a normal season - had run out.

Their players were told to find other clubs for the rest of the year and some - Liam Kay to Wakefield, Andy Ackers to Salford - had already made permanent moves.

Toronto had also signed Kallum Watkins on a three-year contract after his decision to leave Gold Coast Titans and lined up Ryan Hall (Sydney Roosters), Leeds' Stevie Ward and Richie Myler as well as Wigan prop Ben Flower.

On the following Thursday, the Wolfpack had their record from the 2020 season expunged, with the RFL announcing there would be no promotion and relegation that year.

That made little difference to the table, as Toronto had lost all six pre-lockdown games.

On 16th July, Super League released a fixture schedule that would entail a total of 22 regular-season rounds instead of 29, starting on 2nd August. Dates and venues in the back end of the campaign were to be reviewed as the season progressed, in line with government advice and the requirements of host broadcaster Sky Sports.

Toronto's opponents would have a bye, although Featherstone Rovers proposed, fruitlessly, they would take Toronto's Super League place.

Warrington's Halliwell Jones Stadium, Leeds' Emerald Headingley Stadium and St Helens' Totally Wicked Stadium hosted all games in August.

There was a hope that limited crowds would return before the end of the season, which was to end with the Grand Final on November 28th after a four-team straight knockout play-off instead of the five-team system. But that hope was quashed when

the virus threatened a second wave in mid-September and some of the government's lockdown regulations were re-introduced.

On 17th October, Manchester United's Champions League draw gave then two home games astride the weekend of November 28th and the Grand Final could not be played at Old Trafford. Instead of postponing the final for a week, it was decided to stage it at Hull's KCOM Stadium on Friday 27th November.

Clubs returned to training for a mini-pre-season, with Huddersfield Giants the first back on 11th July. Strict testing of players, staff and officials took place on an ongoing basis.

There were to be two significant changes that teams had to prepare for – the 'six-again' rule was brought into Super League and matches were to be played without scrums, the game being restarted with a play-the-ball.

The 'six again' rule allowed the referee to restart the tackle count instead of awarding penalties for infringements around the ruck, with a hooter sounding to signify the decision. The rule had already been employed in the NRL since its restart on 28th May and had led to a speeding up of the game, thus not allowing defences to re-group after deliberately conceding a penalty by messing around at the play-the-ball.

It certainly speeded up the game, with players quickly adapting to the new rules.

On the restart Sunday, which was a catch-up weekend involving four clubs, the ball was in play for roughly 13 minutes longer in each of the games than in 2020 pre-lockdown, or those in the 2019 season, 66 minutes compared to 53.

St Helens' fixture against the Dragons was the second shortest game in Super League history, lasting 84 minutes and 30 seconds (the shortest was Hull KR v Wigan Warriors in 2019 - 83 minutes and 24 seconds). The average game time in 2019 (and pre-lockdown) had been 90 minutes and 43 seconds. And that was six minutes shorter than the 2018 average, a change largely attributable to the introduction of shot clock for scrums and dropouts.

After the first few rounds, the tackles per game stat was at its highest level of all time, with the average being 798 post-lockdown compared to 723 pre-lockdown.

The quick play-the-ball average was up from 31 to 89 a game. There were 81 quick play-the-balls in Castleford Tigers' match against St Helens compared to 47 when they met just before lockdown.

Wigan Warriors' match with Leeds Rhinos had 102 quick play-the-balls which, in the absence of scrums, was generating a relentless pace to the game.

In the end, even a 22-game regular season proved to be unfeasible after the postponement of scheduled fixtures due to positive Covid tests at many clubs. And when fixtures went ahead, there were very few that weren't affected by player withdrawals, putting a great strain on clubs, players and staff.

On 9th September, Super League announced that the table would now be determined by points percentage, due to the possibility that not all clubs would be able to play the same number of matches. The switch, which applied immediately, saw Catalans Dragons move from fourth in the table to top.

To qualify for the play-offs, a team had to play a minimum of 15 games, unless they would end the regular season in the top four on competition points anyway. However, at the time, the RFL said that rule could be reviewed if four or more clubs failed to complete the required number of matches.

A club could postpone a game if seven or more players were unavailable for 'Covid-related reasons' including test and trace - but clubs could choose to go ahead with fixtures if they wished.

As the post-lockdown season progressed it became obvious that the revised schedule was overly optimistic. The four-team play-offs over two weeks eventually became a six-team play-off over three weeks as the regular season was cut short because of so many postponements and cancellations.

March - July

The plan to stage the Challenge Cup Final on July 18th, as opposed to the last weekend in August, also foundered, the 2020 showpiece postponed in May.

On July 17th the RFL announced the final would be played on Saturday October 17th. The Cup had reached the last-16 stage following the completion of the eight fifth round ties on the last weekend before the suspension of the season in March.

But continuation of that proved impossible. With Toronto already withdrawn, it became obvious that the four Championship clubs, Sheffield Eagles, Featherstone Rovers, Widnes Vikings and York City Knights, along with Newcastle Thunder from League 1, couldn't take part. The competition had to be reshaped, the ten Super League clubs remaining included in a re-draw for the sixth round and the quarter-finals.

Two sixth round ties were to be played at the John Smith's Stadium in Huddersfield on Saturday August 22nd. The remaining six clubs received a bye to the quarter-finals.

Catalans President Bernard Guasch was furious that his club faced an additional away game when they were drawn to play Wakefield Trinity at Huddersfield in the sixth round. Under pressure to finance air travel to and from the UK for a re-drawn Super League fixture list, Guasch was angry that his club now faced another expensive trip.

Still, there was some sense of relief when the Super League resumed on Sunday 2nd August, even if games were played in front of cardboard fans and with simulated crowd noise.

AUGUST
Back in business

Round 4

St Helens kicked off the revived season on the first Sunday of August with a crushing 34-6 victory over Catalans Dragons behind closed doors at Headingley.

The game was played with cardboard cutout 'fans in the stand' and with artificial crowd noise, which added an atmosphere to Sky Sports' TV broadcast.

The star for St Helens was fullback Lachlan Coote, who scored two tries and kicked five goals in a performance that delighted Saints coach Kristian Woolf, who was particularly happy with the return of Great Britain and England international James Graham. Graham had re-joined the reigning champions until the end of the season.

Prior to the game, the players from both sides 'took the knee' in support of the Black Lives Matter movement, although Catalans centre Israel Folau was the only player not to join in the players' action.

Before the lockdown, St Helens had made a slow start to the season, when they won only three of their first six league games, including the game against Toronto, which had now been removed from the league table. And during the lockdown, they had seen the departure of boom prop forward Luke Thompson to the NRL with Canterbury Bulldogs. But the defending Champions looked more than comfortable with the new rules that instantly speeded everything up.

From the kick-off, eleven breathless minutes of play went without pause at an electric pace as both sides looked to avoid falling foul of the 'six-again' rule.

The first rest resulted in the first points when James Maloney was penalised for a tackle off the ball and Coote stepped up to kick a penalty goal.

Four minutes later, Saints crossed for the first post-lockdown try. A shift to the left saw the ball find Zeb Taia, who superbly palmed the ball on his inside to Coote, who pushed through a hole and stretched out for a wonderful set-piece try.

It was 28-0 on the hour mark by the time Maloney got a consolation for the Dragons. But Saints had the last word when Alex Walmsley swatted away the giant Julian Bousquet, putting him to the deck before storming to the line.

In mitigation the Dragons were missing Sam Tomkins, serving the final match of a two-game ban for tripping in the home win over Salford. And Michael McIlorum failed a head-injury assessment after leaving the field on 17 minutes. Tomkins' absence saw young Frenchman Arthur Mourgue given a chance to impress at fullback. But the prospect of flying to the UK every weekend throughout October looked like badly affecting the Dragons' chances for 2020.

Round 2

The double header concluded with an astonishing 27-26 win by Leeds over Huddersfield.

The Giants had totally dominated the Rhinos for over an hour and they led 26-6 after 63 minutes when Louis Senior went over for his second try. But three Rhinos tries

Catalans trio Arthur Mourgue, Michael McIlorum and Julian Bousquet attempt to halt St Helens' Theo Fages

in four minutes, another two minutes from time and a Luke Gale golden-point field goal resulted in the most astonishing of comebacks.

The build-up revolved around two debutants. Ashton Golding and Kruise Leeming swapped clubs in the off-season but their respective careers in different colours couldn't take off pre-lockdown due to injuries.

Golding played a great game in the Claret and Gold, with some key defensive moments, including a miracle tackle on Richie Myler early on that prevented the Leeds fullback from grounding the ball.

After Aidan Sezer's conversion of Louis Senior's second try the result looked done and dusted. Gale scored what appeared to be nothing but a consolation as he dived in.

But Huddersfield collapsed and Leeds sparked into life. Jordan Turner and Aaron Murphy both went off injured. Huddersfield changed things around but it didn't work. The next set, Harry Newman was sent scorching down the left edge. A play later, Luke Briscoe somehow scored in the corner.

When Alex Mellor crossed against his former side - a try given much to the annoyance of Huddersfield who felt he was held up - it definitely wasn't over.

And the Giants couldn't hold as Konrad Hurrell crashed over in typical fashion. Rhyse Martin converted and suddenly, it was all square.

In golden point, Huddersfield had the first chance, with Lee Gaskell, who ended the game with a broken thumb, slicing a field-goal attempt wide. Crucially it went dead. Leeds had a seven-tackle set. It was enough for Gale to produce his party piece.

Round 8

In the build up to the first full post-lockdown round, with all games again staged at Headingley, the RFL revealed that from a total of 2,019 tests on players, staff and officials in the previous four weeks, none had tested positive for Covid-19.

Catalans Dragons came back to Headingley six days after their humbling by St Helens and looked to be heading to another heavy defeat, this time to Castleford, when they trailed 14-0 in as many minutes after two Michael Shenton tries and three goals from Danny Richardson.

The Dragons were mis-firing but when Peter Mata'utia was sent to the sin bin on 31 minutes for a dangerous tackle on Samisoni Langi - he copped a two-match ban - with the Tigers still ten points to the good after a Tom Davies try, they clicked into gear, allowing centre Israel Folau's class to lead them to a stunning 40-14 victory.

Folau had put Davies in, Alrix Da Costa burrowed over after Mata'utia's departure and Folau's try gave Catalans the lead at half-time.

It was a superb try and gave a reminder of Folau's brilliance as he sped around Shenton from his own half, then produced a monstrous fend on the covering Greg Eden.

Benjamin Garcia's try five minutes after the turnaround began a one-sided half, Derrell Olpherts offloading in his own in-goal to no-one and Garcia touching down. Folau continued to shine with assists for Joel Tomkins and another Davies try before Jason Baitieri's try finished proceedings.

It was Castleford's first experience of the 'set restart' rule and Tigers coach Daryl Powell reckoned his side would get better once they get used to the style of the new game.

Warrington Wolves seemed to have little difficulty in adapting to the new rules as they eventually got on top of Hull KR, Daryl Clark starring in a 40-10 win.

The Robins played with innovation from the first whistle, as a short kick-off from Jamie Ellis caught Anthony Gelling unaware and they got the ball back.

From there, a shift to the left edge saw Ryan Brierley find an unorthodox run from Matty Gee to create an overlap, and he put Super League's leading try-scorer Ben Crooks to the line for a simple try within 60 seconds of the start.

Brierley couldn't convert from the touchline but it was an early warning shot from the Robins, who showed no fear in zinging the ball all over the place throughout the game.

It appeared to fluster Warrington, who were sloppy early on. Gelling's poor start worsened when he was sin-binned for a tip tackle on Gee on 12 minutes, a two-match ban ensued the following week, and from the penalty, Weller Hauraki almost doubled the lead but dropped the ball attempting to score.

That scare seemed to finally spark the Wolves into life. Daryl Clark began to cause issues for the Robins, which resulted in Shaun Kenny-Dowall being sent from the field for ten minutes after a professional foul.

From that set, Clark almost burrowed over but lost the ball under pressure from Hauraki, while three minutes later Stefan Ratchford's looping ball looking for Tom Lineham sailed out of play.

Eventually, the Wolves got on the board on 23 minutes through a Gareth Widdop/ Ben Currie combination that sent Lineham into the corner. Ratchford converted from out wide for a two-point lead and from then on, with Brierley and Adam Quinlan standing out in more adventurous Rovers play, the Warrington middles took control.

Warrington were one of the clubs in the transfer market during the lockdown and they had caused a stir in May when they announced that Australian superstar Greg Inglis was to come out of retirement to play for them in 2021.

On the Sunday, Hull FC were taken to the cleaners by Salford, halfbacks Tui Lolohea and Chris Atkin starring in a 54-18 Red Devils win, their short kicking game into the in-

Salford's Dan Sarginson is put under pressure by Hull FC's Albert Kelly

goal working like clockwork.

Ken Sio, Rhys Williams and Lolohea all finished with try-doubles for Salford, who learned in the lockdown that star fullback Niall Evalds would be leaving them to join Castleford at the end of the season.

It was a disappointing first game in charge for Hull's interim coach Andy Last and a far cry from round one in February when Hull were 30-4 winners at Leeds. After that, inconsistent form and only two more victories in the following six games, led to Lee Radford's dismissal in the immediate aftermath of the Airlie Birds' last match before lockdown, a 38-4 home defeat by Warrington.

Long-time club servant Last, who had been Radford's assistant, stepped up, only to have to wait 150 days to take charge in a game.

After Salford hit the front on 21 minutes, when Lolohea claimed his first try, Hull had just one spell in the second half, during which Jamie Shaul's four-pointer and Marc Sneyd's two cut the lead to 28-18, when they looked capable of mounting a genuine comeback attempt.

But industrious Australian forward Luke Yates' 59th-minute try swung the match back towards Ian Watson's side, who scored four more to complete a comprehensive triumph.

The needless 62nd-minute sin binning of Hull winger Ratu Naulago for kicking the ball away to delay a Salford restart was another frustration.

Wigan went clear at the top of the table after they were left clinging on for a 23-22 win over Wakefield, as Trinity cut a 16-point losing margin with 14 minutes remaining.

The Warriors probably deserved the two points as young halfback Harry Smith claimed the headlines with what proved the match-winning field goal three minutes from time. But nobody had expected it to be so close after watching Adrian Lam's side move into a comfortable 22-6 lead after an hour, which they thoroughly merited.

Wakefield's comeback was started on 66 minutes with an unbelievable one-handed finish in the left corner by Tom Johnstone, who was carrying an elbow injury that would keep him out for six weeks.

Chris Chester handed debuts to lockdown signings Tony Gigot and Liam Kay, with the former starting at fullback and Kay, making his second debut for Trinity, going in on the wing and scoring two late tries.

Sean O'Loughlin withdrew on the eve of the game for the Warriors, meaning Ethan Havard started, with the now established triumvirate of Bevan French, Jackson Hastings and Thomas Leuluai in the spine. Zak Hardaker stood out in the right centre.

Tony Clubb was still out with a neck problem, while centre Oliver Gildart continued his recovery from a dislocated shoulder sustained on Great Britain's tour of New Zealand the previous autumn.

After the game, Chester said his players wanted more knowledge about the 'Black Lives Matter' movement before deciding to take the knee prior to Super League matches. Trinity's players remained standing together, a policy that continued, while Wigan's players took part in the symbolic act that showed support for the movement.

The weekend closed with St Helens reaffirming the form of the previous week, beating the Rhinos 48-0, the first time Leeds had been nilled at Headingley since March 17th 1992.

The tormentor-in-chief was Alex Walmsley. The England prop completely out-played his opponents and set the tone early by clattering Australian prop Matt Prior in a bruising collision. Crucially, Walmsley got a quick play-the-ball away and Leeds were left retreating as Jonny Lomax galloped forward. Off another quick play-the-ball, James Graham was able to clatter over for his first try since his Saints return. Lachlan Coote converted his first of eight goals in a perfect night with the boot.

On the back of Saints' pack power, winger Regan Grace scored what many people hailed the most thrilling hat-trick ever.

Grace's first, just before the hooter, meant the contest was over at the break at 24-0. Coote gave Grace a licence to run, and run he did. His lightning acceleration saw him scorch through a gap in Leeds' defence, his footwork saw him evade Ash Handley and his balance saw him dodge Luke Gale and race under the posts.

Grace's second, a leap to touch down under pressure, was followed by another spectacular length-of-the-field effort to complete his treble.

Round 9

The global pandemic had not gone away and Rugby League demonstrated it was in a 'make-do' situation when an outbreak of the virus ran rife through Hull FC. A total of 12 people, including nine players and three members of the club's backroom staff, tested positive for the virus by the end of the week leading up to round nine.

Initially, six players, five of who played in the previous week's game with Salford, and two members of the coaching staff, tested positive. Hull FC owner Adam Pearson said he believed the virus had been transmitted after a player went to hospital with his new-born child. They were unable to fulfil their fixture against Castleford the following Sunday.

Hull's opponents the previous Sunday, Salford, were also unable to play Catalans on the Saturday. Eleven of their players have been forced to self-isolate for fourteen days as a result of the RFL's track and trace system, although the Red Devils reported a second round of full negative results after undergoing additional testing.

It meant a re-hashing of the fixtures, with Wakefield playing Catalans in what was a round-two fixture postponed by storm Ciara, instead of St Helens, who now played Castleford in a brought-forward round-16 game.

All the games were staged at an empty Totally Wicked Stadium in St Helens, with Huddersfield Giants losing by a late field goal for the second game running.

Luke Gale was the man for Leeds in Huddersfield's previous fixture and in this game Blake Austin held his nerve in the 75th minute to send Warrington into third place with a 19-18 win.

It was tough on the Giants, who were down to the bare bones by the hour mark, having lost four players with injury or concussion, including key halfback Aidan Sezer with a hamstring injury.

Wigan's Jackson Hastings and Sam Powell congratulate Liam Farrell on scoring against Leeds

It was all square at the break at 8-8 after a try each from Ukuma Ta'ai and Ben Currie and two goals each from Stefan Ratchford and Sezer. Gareth Widdop scored just a minute into the second half but a wonderful Sezer pass gave Jermaine McGillvary acres of space to finish in the corner to get the Giants right back in it. The former Canberra halfback couldn't convert, however, as the Giants still trailed by two points.

Things began to get desperate for the Giants and a gamble chip-kick by Tom Holmes on 57 minutes failed to come off, with Austin sweeping up. The number six refused to die with the ball and instead shipped it out wide, which laid the groundwork for a brilliant score. First Widdop sent Toby King away before the centre fed Tom Lineham, who had enough pace to outstrip the Giants' defence. Ratchford, surprisingly, missed the conversion, meaning Huddersfield remained just six points behind.

They were down to just 13 men a minute later as captain Sezer limped off, leaving the direction to 24-year-old Holmes and Sezer's replacement, 22-year-old Oliver Russell.

It was the latter that somehow restored parity with only seven minutes of the game remaining. A last-tackle play appeared to be going awry until the ball fell to Leroy Cudjoe. The experienced centre by-passed four Warrington defenders before offloading to Russell, who dived low to ground the ball.

The youngster showed a cool head to convert and make it 18-18. But Austin stepped up with five minutes to go, slotting over the one-pointer from 40 metres out.

Huddersfield tried desperately to claw their way back but a dropped ball by Russell as he shaped to find a field goal himself, ended any realistic hope.

On the Sunday, current league leaders Wigan dominated Leeds in a 28-10 victory, on-form stalwart Liam Farrell scoring his 100th try for the Warriors.

The Rhinos, who had second rower Bodene Thompson on debut after he was signed on loan from Toronto, showed a marked improvement on their 48-0 rout by St Helens, which had prompted coach Richard Agar to accuse them of lacking effort. They were still in contention until Jake Bibby touched down for Wigan's fourth try six minutes from the end.

By then Luke Gale was off the field, sin-binned for a dangerous lift on Jackson Hastings and Bevan French followed up a kick by Hastings for his second try to seal it.

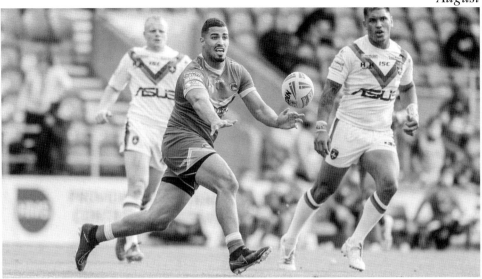

Catalans' Fouad Yaha gets a pass away against Wakefield

Round 2

In a game which had been postponed in February by high winds and rain, Catalans Dragons took Wakefield, who were technically the home side, to the cleaners, Matt Whitley and Tom Davies scoring hat-tricks in a 58-0 romp in St Helens.

It had been five months since Sam Tomkins last took to a Rugby League field. The former Wigan star had incurred a two-match suspension for tripping before lockdown. And his return made a massive difference to the Dragons' attack, despite Israel Folau not travelling after the birth of his child earlier in the week

Tomkins put Samisoni Langi through a hole after only two minutes and it was one-way traffic after that, with Wakefield losing winger Lee Kershaw, Tony Gigot and Kelepi Tanginoa to injury in the first half.

The Dragons had been given a special exemption to travel to the UK to continue their campaign despite new quarantine restrictions on travel from France, reportedly spending 50,000 euros on travel each matchday.

The following Monday Sam Tomkins took a one-match penalty notice for a trip on Ryan Hampshire, while Sam Moa got two matches for a high tackle on former teammate Romain Navarrete in the last minute of the game. Trinity centre Reece Lyne also got two games for a crusher on Benjamin Jullien.

Round 16

St Helens emerged with a 10-0 Sunday win over Castleford on their home ground after a titanic struggle, only one try scored, a decisive one in the end, scored by Theo Fages three minutes from time.

The Tigers, with Gareth O'Brien making his second loan debut after signing from Toronto, completed 20 of their 22 sets in the first half and, with the game level at 0-0, it was anyone's for the taking in the second half.

But in the early minutes of the second period, Saints began to assert their authority. The catalyst for the momentum to swing in their favour was a yellow card for Grant Millington after a shoulder charge and, from that, Lachlan Coote broke the deadlock with a penalty.

Seven minutes later, Coote was on hand to kick his second penalty after the Tigers

St Helens' James Graham gets to grips with Castleford's Gareth O'Brien

were penalised at the ruck - it took Castleford 68 minutes to earn their first and only penalty from the whistle of James Child.

Michael Shenton came close but was denied after an intervention from the video referee and, with three minutes left, the reigning champions flexed their muscles definitively. Alex Walmsley set Coote free downfield and Fages was on hand to capitalise, racing away past a scrambling Tigers defence to touch down left of the posts. Coote potted the simplest of conversions to make it 10-0.

Saints' winger Tommy Makinson was to miss the next five matches after pleading guilty to grabbing Castleford prop forward Liam Watts' testicles in the thirteenth minute of the game.

Challenge Cup Round 6

The revised Challenge Cup schedule, enforced by the inability of Championship clubs to compete, ran into further trouble, with Hull FC's tie with Castleford postponed and rearranged for Sunday, September 13th.

Which left one game for the BBC cameras, with Wakefield putting in an improved performance against Catalans, going down 36-24, a week on from a humiliating 58-0 reverse.

The Dragons were missing suspended Sam Tomkins, as well as Samisoni Langi, who scored two tries the previous week, and Julian Bousquet, although on the plus side Israel Folau was back in their side. After his brilliance against Castleford two weeks before, Folau was relatively quiet.

Stars of the show were halfback Josh Drinkwater and the Dragons' Papua New Guinean centre David Mead. In wet conditions, Drinkwater had the ball on a string virtually throughout the game, giving a kicking masterclass. He gave the final assist for five of the Dragons' six tries. All the Dragons' three first-half tries came from Drinkwater kicks, while Mead finished with a hat-trick.

Injury-hit Trinity had Giants winger Innes Senior on loan for his debut and late Tinirau Arona and Jacob Miller tries made the scoreline respectable.

The following week, the Dragons were left reeling by four positive Covid-19 test results, leaving the club in strict 14-day isolation quarantine and forcing the postponement of two fixtures.

Round 18

Castleford were due a bye weekend at the end of August, courtesy of Toronto's withdrawal but after the positive Covid-19 results at Catalans they agreed to play Wigan in a brought forward game.

In wet conditions at Warrington, the Warriors battled back from being 12 points down for a third straight win, by 30-22, to consolidate their position at the top of the Super League table.

Castleford looked like they might add to February's 16-12 victory over the Warriors at the Mend-a-Hose Jungle when they repelled early Wigan advances and scored two converted tries in five minutes midway through the opening half to lead 12-0.

Wigan lost in-form winger Liam Marshall to a long-term knee injury but fortune swung back in their favour as the game wore on, with Liam Farrell grabbing two of five tries that eventually overcame the battling Tigers.

The Warriors welcomed back Thomas Leuluai in the halves for his 300th Super League appearance after overcoming an ankle injury that kept him out of the 28-10 victory over Leeds two weeks earlier.

Morgan Smithies was sin-binned just after the break for a crusher tackle on James Clare that saw the Tigers winger stretchered off. The 19-year-old Smithies was banned for four games for that and for another two matches for a head butt.

Round 10

Leeds got back on the winning trail with a 50-12 hammering of Salford.

Richie Myler, playing fullback in the injury absence of Jack Walker, was in scintillating form, scoring three tries and having a hand in everything Leeds did well, along with stand-off Robert Lui. Winger Ash Handley also finished with a hat-trick.

There were mitigating factors for the Red Devils, having had just two full training sessions going into the game. Almost half of Ian Watson's squad and the coach himself had spent much of the previous two weeks self-isolating, following the spate of positive Covid-19 tests at their last opponents Hull FC, their only game since the season restart.

From the off Leeds looked faster and more energetic as opposed to the lacklustre Salford. And the Red Devils weren't helped just four minutes in when winger Ken Sio limped off after trying to kick infield. Kris Welham moved to the wing, with prop Ryan Lannon in the centre.

The next day, Sunday, James Roby guided St Helens to a fourth straight post-lockdown win, by 32-18, from the unfamiliar position of scrum-half but not before a spirited effort from Hull Kingston Rovers.

Roby switched from hooker when Theo Fages limped off with a hyper-extended knee on the half-hour mark in another game where Super League's injury toll continued to rise.

Rovers' fullback Adam Quinlan suffered a broken and dislocated wrist in the second half to add to some horrendous luck in 2020 but his side had plenty of cause for optimism otherwise.

The Robins looked like succumbing to a heavy defeat when they trailed 12-0 after less than 16 minutes but were level by half-time and also stirred again when they fell 18 points behind in the second half. But they never looked likely winners against a Saints team that, while not at its best, still had enough to keep the pressure on Wigan at the top, with further excellent performances from fullback Lachlan Coote and backrower James Bentley.

Unlike Salford, Hull FC's Covid-19 hiatus seemed to have done them good as they beat Huddersfield Giants, missing halves Lee Gaskell and Aidan Sezer, by 31-12.

The game - Andy Last's first victory as Hull coach - was in effect decided by half-

Hull FC's Jack Brown races clear of Huddersfield's Jordan Turner

time, courtesy of five first-half tries, some of them absolutely superb.

Last had promised he would make changes in the wake of the heavy defeat to Salford and he was as good as his word, dropping the likes of Danny Houghton and Mahe Fonua to the bench.

Jordan Johnstone excelled in Houghton's place, while Albert Kelly was at his brilliant best. Without several big names, the youthful fervour provided by the likes of Johnstone and props Jack Brown and Joe Cator played a big role.

BETFRED SUPER LEAGUE
Sunday 30th August

	P	W	D	L	F	A	D	Pts
Wigan Warriors	9	7	0	2	221	136	85	14
St Helens	9	6	0	3	228	109	119	12
Warrington Wolves	9	6	0	3	179	110	69	12
Catalans Dragons	7	5	0	2	216	141	75	10
Leeds Rhinos	8	5	0	3	201	162	39	10
Castleford Tigers	9	4	0	5	166	174	-8	8
Huddersfield Giants	8	4	0	4	144	155	-11	8
Hull FC	9	4	0	5	194	242	-48	8
Salford Red Devils	8	2	0	6	136	216	-80	4
Wakefield Trinity	8	2	0	6	115	226	-111	4
Hull Kingston Rovers	8	1	0	7	112	241	-129	2

Huddersfield might have been the better of the two sides after the break but the game had been decided by then. Fonua's try on 33 minutes to make it 28-0 had already put the game beyond the Giants.

In the final game, Warrington beat down-at-heel Wakefield 36-0.

Trinity looked out for the count from the off. The outbreak of Covid-19 at Catalans forced two of Wakefield's players - Alex Walker and Jay Pitts - into isolation, while Liam Kay was forced to do the same as a result of a potential contact of a family member. That, coupled with injury after injury, as well as the bizarre refusal of David Fifita to wear a GPS tracker - considered a key component of the 'track and trace' system to control the spread of the virus - had left Wakefield threadbare.

Warrington looked clinical as Blake Austin, after a quiet few games, was back to his brilliant best as he recorded a hat-trick. Ben Murdoch-Masila began a two-match suspension for a high tackle on Matty English in their win over Huddersfield and was replaced by Samy Kibula, the Congo-born prop debuting for the Wolves.

SEPTEMBER
Living with Covid

Round 11

Wakefield Trinity's game with Leeds was postponed after two of their players, one of whom played in the defeat to Warrington, tested positive for the virus.

Warrington's playing and coaching staff returned a full set of negative test results, although six Wolves players had to self-isolate for 14 days following test and trace analysis of their meeting with Wakefield.

Castleford's Jesse Sene-Lefao was stood down for coming into contact with a person who tested positive for Covid-19, despite him being named in their initial 21-man squad for the Tigers' game against Salford.

That week players were warned by the RFL they would be fined £250 if they celebrated scoring tries by hugging or jumping on a try-scorer.

The RFL had already tried to clamp down on players' behaviour off the field, which saw some receive retrospective bans. Jackson Hastings of Wigan, James Gavet of the Giants and Warrington's Riley Dean were all banned for 14 days for behaviour that included the use of public gyms, public pools and a failure to wear a facemask.

It was typical of the chaos that ran through Rugby League's attempt to play through the continuing global problem.

So on the first Thursday night of September, there were only two games staged at Headingley instead of three.

The first provided a major blowout as bottom side Hull KR hammered top side Wigan by 34-18, four days after they had pushed St Helens close.

Stand-off Jordan Abdull was the kingpin for Rovers on his recall, setting up tries with clever offloads and kicks in much the same way as he had for London Broncos the year before.

Wigan took a 6-0 lead when Sam Powell burrowed over. But Rovers grew in confidence, and suddenly they were 16-6 ahead after scoring three tries in seven minutes. The first came from Elliot Minchella, when he supported a superb Jez Litten break. The second came from Greg Minikin on the left after some smart Rovers' handling. The third came from Minchella again, who took advantage of an astonishing flipped back pass by Abdull out of his left hand.

As the second half started, everyone waited for Wigan to assert themselves. But it was the Robins who scored two quick tries in five minutes to extend their lead to 20 points.

Dean Hadley scored the first from an Abdull kick, while Minikin scored his hat-trick from a superb pass by Kane Linnett. There was no way back for Wigan,

In the second game, Salford looked to have regained their mojo when they led Castleford 18-0 after 11 minutes.

But with halfback Danny Richardson and prop Liam Watts causing mayhem around the ruck, the Tigers fought back to lead 24-18 before a Luke Yates try made it 24-all at the break. And after another nip-and-tuck 40 minutes, the Tigers edged it 37-30, Grant Millington's 72nd minute try sealing the win.

Warrington's Jake Mamo crosses to score against Hull FC

On the Friday, St Helens were slick and powerful in their 54-6 thrashing of Huddersfield.

Prior to the game, Giants coach Simon Woolford explained that he would have only 16 fit men for the game, with Reiss Butterworth and Owen Trout making debuts off the bench.

Trout got Huddersfield's only try before four tries in 12 second-half minutes by St Helens blew the young Giants away. Lachlan Coote and Regan Grace both finished with try doubles.

Warrington's 37-12 win over Hull FC was particularly impressive, given the disruption the Wolves faced leading into the game.

Six Warrington forwards were forced into self-isolation before the match. Chris Hill, Joe Philbin, Jack Hughes, Jason Clark, Matt Davis and Samy Kibula were all stood down. Ben Murdoch-Masila was suspended and Sitaleki Akauola remained unavailable. Gareth Widdop, one of Warrington's marquee halfbacks, was also out after testing positive for the virus.

But they still had more than enough to power past a Hull FC side who themselves were without a string of key men, Marc Sneyd, Scott Taylor, Josh Jones, Ratu Naulago, Andre Savelio, Masi Matongo, Joe Cator, Chris Satae and Gareth Ellis all missing.

The game was evenly balanced before Blake Austin's field goal late in the first half. Hull never hit their straps after that as prop Mike Cooper put in a huge performance in the middle. Prop Leilani Latu scored a try on his belated debut.

Round 12

On Wednesday 9th September, the Rugby
Football League announced that the Super
League table in 2020 would be determined
by points percentage instead of league
points, following several postponements
because of positive Covid-19 test results.
There was already a distinct possibility that
not all clubs would be able to play the same
number of matches.

The switch, which was applied
immediately, saw Catalans Dragons
move from fourth in the table to top. The
Dragons, who had a win percentage of
71.43 per cent from their seven games,
leapt above previous leaders St Helens,
Warrington Wolves and Wigan Warriors,
who all sat on 14 points from their ten
matches. The three were now on 70 per
cent, followed by Leeds Rhinos in fifth on
62.5 per cent and Castleford in sixth on 50
per cent.

At this stage, the top four clubs at
the end of the regular season would still
qualify for the play-offs. To do that, a team
had to play a minimum of 15 games, unless
they would end the regular season in the top four on competition points anyway.

The RFL said that rule could be reviewed if four or more clubs failed to complete
the required number of matches.

Clubs could postpone a game if seven or more players were unavailable for 'Covid-
related reasons, including test and trace but they could choose to go ahead with fixtures
if they wished.

A tweak was also made to the salary cap to help clubs with player rotations
amongst an increasingly crowded schedule.

Clubs could field any registered players - including loan recalls - provided the
player had a cap value of £30,000 or less. Additionally, if any player was unable to return
after a positive Covid-19 test, their salary cap would be removed from a club's total,
enabling the club to sign a replacement.

All the round 12 games went ahead, with Thursday and Friday night games staged
at St Helens and, on the Saturday, Catalans staging their first home game since the
lockdown, the French government allowing crowds, capped at 5,000, to attend sporting
fixtures.

On the Thursday night, two weakened teams met and Hull FC edged Wakefield 26-23
after a compelling game.

Wakefield had youngsters halfback Connor Bailey and backrower Yusuf Aydin on
debut and had Ben Jones-Bishop back for his first game of the season after overcoming a
serious lung illness.

Hull coach Andy Last rested a host of players, with the Challenge Cup tie with
Castleford to play the following Sunday.

After leading by only 14-13 at half-time, Hull went 26-13 in front with tries from
Andre Savelio and Jordan Lane, before two tries from Kelepi Tanginoa made for a tense
final five minutes, with Hull's young fullback Connor Wynne in the sin bin.

BETFRED SUPER LEAGUE
Sunday 6th September

	P	W	D	L	F	A	D	Pts
St Helens	10	7	0	3	282	115	167	14
Warrington Wolves	10	7	0	3	216	122	94	14
Wigan Warriors	10	7	0	3	239	170	69	14
Catalans Dragons	7	5	0	2	216	141	75	10
Leeds Rhinos	8	5	0	3	201	162	39	10
Castleford Tigers	10	5	0	5	203	204	-1	10
Huddersfield Giants	9	4	0	5	150	209	-59	8
Hull FC	10	4	0	6	206	279	-73	8
Salford Red Devils	9	2	0	7	166	253	-87	4
Wakefield Trinity	8	2	0	6	115	226	-111	4
Hull Kingston Rovers	9	2	0	7	146	259	-113	4

BETFRED SUPER LEAGUE
Wednesday 9th September

	P	W	D	L	F	A	D	Win %
Catalans Dragons	7	5	0	2	216	141	75	71.43
St Helens	10	7	0	3	282	115	167	70.00
Warrington Wolves	10	7	0	3	216	122	94	70.00
Wigan Warriors	10	7	0	3	239	170	69	70.00
Leeds Rhinos	8	5	0	3	201	162	39	62.50
Castleford Tigers	10	5	0	5	203	204	-1	50.00
Huddersfield Giants	9	4	0	5	150	209	-59	44.44
Hull FC	10	4	0	6	206	279	-73	40.00
Wakefield Trinity	8	2	0	6	115	226	-111	25.00
Salford Red Devils	9	2	0	7	166	253	-87	22.22
Hull Kingston Rovers	9	2	0	7	146	259	-113	22.22

September

Hull's Cup opponents Castleford had their game with Warrington pinched from under their noses, the Wolves continuing their 100 per cent post-lockdown record with a 12-10 win.

With less than two minutes remaining and the Tigers holding a four-point lead, having dominated the majority of an absorbing encounter, substitute Declan Patton released Ben Currie on a charge down the left edge.

Roaring up alongside him in the blink of an eye was fullback Matty Ashton, who raced to the line, despite the desperate ankle tap effort from a chasing Peter Mata'utia.

Warrington coach Steve Price handed a debut to young forward Eribe Doro on the bench and, with Daryl Clark absent due to the imminent birth of his child, Danny Walker started at hooker, while Stefan Ratchford switched from loose forward to scrum-half.

Castleford thought they had opened the scoring early on, only for Danny Richardson to have a try debatably ruled out for a double movement. But, soon after, he helped create the first try as his kick bounced off an upright and Gareth O'Brien was the quickest to react.

It stayed at 6-0 until just before half-time, despite the Tigers having ample opportunities to add to their score, when Josh Charnley plucked a Blake Austin kick out of the air to set up Anthony Gelling.

The Wolves then started the second half the brighter, only to prove wasteful themselves. And when Jake Mamo was sin-binned for a professional foul, Castleford re-established their lead through a disputed Darrell Olpherts effort out wide.

Warrington might have thought it was not their night when the video referee also ruled against them for a possible penalty try to Austin but they stuck to their guns and came up with Ashton's thrilling late winner.

The following night, Hull KR gave St Helens a run for their money for the second time in three weeks, only beaten 21-20 by a Theo Fages field goal in golden-point time.

Regan Grace's try put Saints 8-6 up at half-time after Dean Hadley's opener. Both sides then traded tries, with Jack Welsby and Alex Walmsley going over for Saints and Shaun Kenny-Dowall and Ethan Ryan scoring for Rovers.

A high hit from Kevin Naiqama on Kane Linnett allowed Will Dagger to tee up a kick from out wide to level the scores in the final minute of normal time. It also meant Kristian Woolf's side returned to the field a man short with Naiqama in the sin bin.

Hull KR received the extra-time kick-off and they ran the ball on the last play. On this occasion, it backfired, as the ball went out of play.

That gave Lachlan Coote a chance to win the game with a field goal but he scraped it wide, providing the Robins with a seven-tackle set. But Jordan Abdull was caught with the ball on the last just inside the Saints half and, spearheaded by Walmsley, Saints charged upfield for Fages to kick the golden point.

Leeds overcame a Covid-19 scare as seven of their players were temporarily stood down for their game against Huddersfield.

A family member of a player had displayed symptoms, so the club stood him down as well as the players highlighted by the track and trace system. Had the tests come back negative in time, those players would have been available for selection. But the results didn't come back until Saturday morning. They were all given the all clear but it was too late.

The uncertainty didn't prevent the Rhinos winning 13-12 - the second time they had beaten the Giants by a single point since lockdown.

For the second time in a matter of weeks, a field goal from Luke Gale separated the two sides. This time there was no stunning 13-minute comeback. But the Rhinos did have to overcome a poor first-half performance that left them ten points adrift.

The Giants were able to welcome back captain Aidan Sezer in the halves, Darnell McIntosh on the wing, Ashton Golding at fullback and Michael Lawrence in the middle. New signing, former Origin backrower Chris McQueen, who had arrived on a three-month trial, made his debut.

Catalans' Benjamin Garcia in action against Wigan, in the first game to be played in front of fans since the restart

But they lost Adam O'Brien early on. The form Huddersfield hooker was stretchered from the field and spent the weekend in Whiston hospital. He was cleared of a long-term neck injury but was out for the season.

Konrad Hurrell and Tom Briscoe tries put the Rhinos 12-10 up before the hour mark, though Oliver Russell's third penalty goal levelled it up before Gale's one-pointer five minutes from time.

That weekend, the Giants confirmed that head coach Simon Woolford would be leaving his job at the end of the season. Woolford had been heavily linked with a return to the NRL as assistant coach at high-flying Penrith Panthers.

One Catalans player was currently self-isolating but their Saturday home game against Wigan went ahead in front of a crowd of 5,000.

The sweltering heat didn't affect Wigan as they bounced back from their shock defeat to Hull KR with a commanding 28-12 win, with only two late Dragons tries saving their blushes.

Adrian Lam's young pack put Catalans Dragons on the back foot throughout with Sam Powell thriving out of dummy half. Winger Joe Burgess scored a try-double.

The result meant Catalans lost their four-day long spot at the top of the table, sinking to fifth, with St Helens top again on points difference from Warrington and Wigan.

Hull FC's Jamie Shaul leaves Castleford's Oliver Holmes grounded

Challenge Cup Round 6

On the Sunday, Hull FC centre Carlos Tuimavave celebrated a new four-year contract at the KCOM Stadium with a two-try performance that saw his team head into the Challenge Cup quarter-finals the following weekend after a 29-16 victory over Castleford Tigers.

Tuimavave's tries came in the first half of a tightly contested encounter, with his second coming on the stroke of half-time when he intercepted a ball in his own half to gallop to the tryline and extend Hull's lead to 18-6, although they lost star fullback Jamie Shaul to a head knock and he didn't play after the break.

Three minutes into the second half came a crucial blow for Castleford. An innocuous kick was defused by Hull. Instead of labouring their way back to the 20-metre line, Bureta Faraimo instead freed Ratu Naulago. The Fijian raced away unchallenged to the posts and, suddenly, in the blink of an eye, Hull led by 18.

Castleford fought back. Within two minutes of Naulago's try, Peter Mata'utia's pass sent Oliver Holmes over. And ten minutes after Holmes' try, Mata'utia turned from provider to chief benefactor when he capitalised on a great wraparound play including Paul McShane and Liam Watts to narrow the gap to eight.

But two penalties from Jake Connor in the final quarter ensured Hull's progression before Connor finished it off with a late field goal.

Tigers winger Sosaia Feki finally made his debut but lasted just 24 minutes before picking up a knee injury. Hamstring and calf injuries had seen him miss the entire campaign since his high-profile move from the NRL's Cronulla Sharks.

The match was originally scheduled for 22nd August but called off after six Hull players tested positive for Covid-19 and both sides were clearly exhausted at the end of a punishing schedule.

Wakefield's Tony Gigot and Josh Wood combine to halt Huddersfield's Darnell McIntosh

Round 7

Huddersfield Giants had started the search for a new head coach after Simon Woolford unexpectedly departed the club just over a week after the club confirmed he would leave at the end of the season.

Assistant Luke Robinson took charge in a caretaker capacity and the Giants picked up their first win post-lockdown with a 29-6 success over struggling Wakefield Trinity in a hastily re-arranged game played at Huddersfield's John Smith's Stadium, despite it being a home fixture for Trinity, on a Thursday afternoon with a 3pm kick-off. The round-7 game hadn't been played in March because of both clubs' entry into the Challenge Cup at the fifth-round stage.

Huddersfield were forced into changes after three players were identified by the RFL's track and trace system as a result of a positive test at Leeds. But they won the game at a canter, with Aidan Sezer calling the shots and Chris McQueen impressing.

Converted tries from McQueen and Suaia Matagi and Jordan Turner's field goal put the Giants 13-0 ahead at the break.

Further scores from James Gavet, Sezer and Jake Wardle wrapped up the win before Kelepi Tanginoa got Trinity on the scoreboard with 11 minutes to play.

Challenge Cup Quarter Finals

Salford and Leeds were the first two teams to go through to the Cup semi-finals on the Friday night in St Helens, after two contrasting games.

The Red Devils' 22-18 golden-point win over Catalans was the result of a fine comeback against a Dragons side that totally dominated the first quarter, after which they

led 12-0 through Fouad Yaha and James Maloney tries.

Josh Drinkwater, Michael McIlorum and Sam Moa were all back for the Dragons and they looked in total control, with Salford's star turn, fullback Niall Evalds, out with a calf injury suffered in their last match, the defeat by Castleford.

Dan Sarginson switched to the fullback role and Kallum Watkins made an eagerly anticipated debut with his hometown club after signing a three-year deal.

Salford hadn't been in the game at all by the 25-minute mark but that changed quickly. Jason Baitieri's concession of a penalty swung the momentum. Off the back of it, Krisnan Inu got the ball in space on the left, bumped away from Israel Folau and offloaded brilliantly to Sarginson as the Red Devils got themselves on the board. After assisting the try, Inu converted from the touchline.

Moments later, déjà vu struck when Kevin Brown passed long to Inu. This time, he bumped away from Lewis Tierney, spun and put the ball down himself, though he couldn't convert to level the scores at the break.

With Pauli Pauli in the sin bin for a high tackle on James Maloney, Matt Whitley's converted try made it 18-10 but James Greenwood reached out a long arm six minutes later for Inu to convert.

With time ticking away, Sam Kasiano saw yellow for repeated team offences and Inu took the ball back to kick the two points to level the game.

Still Salford came at the Dragons but now with a man advantage. Inu had two goes at a one-pointer, both missing to the right, sending the game to golden point.

On the second set, Salford raided the short side and found the Dragons wanting for numbers, allowing Sarginson to saunter into the left corner and run behind the posts to seal a memorable win.

Hull KR came into their quarter-final after two confidence-boosting performances against Wigan and St Helens in the previous two weeks. But they found Leeds too hot to handle, going down 48-18 to a well-organised and highly professional Rhinos display.

The Rhinos were forced to make several changes from the squad that gained a narrow one-point victory a week earlier against the Giants.

Alex Sutcliffe and Brad Dwyer were both out with suspensions, while Bodene Thompson and Brett Ferres, who had made his second Rhinos' debut a week ago, were both out of the squad.

The Robins were without the suspended Jordan Abdull - the stand-off was banned for two games after admitting grabbing the testicles of James Bentley in the defeat to St Helens - with coach Tony Smith recalling Jamie Ellis into the halfbacks to partner Mikey Lewis.

The Rhinos took control early on and never relinquished their grip on the game, leading 30-0 at half-time. And although the Robins drew the second half, with each side scoring 18 points, they were always too far behind to be playing for anything other than pride.

Leeds backrower Rhyse Martin scored 20 points with a try and eight goals and played a prominent role throughout as Kruise Leeming's try for the Rhinos (his first for the club) just before half-time gave Leeds a 30-0 lead and ensured there would be no way back for the Robins.

On the Saturday at Salford there were also two contrasting games.

Warrington managed to hold off St Helens by 20-18 in a high-quality thriller.

Both sides went into the quarter-final with confidence high, the Wolves on a seven-game winning run and Saints a six-match victorious streak. And both sides played well.

Warrington welcomed back Chris Hill, Joe Philbin and Jack Hughes following their isolation in line with Covid-19 protocols but Gareth Widdop remained out. Tom Lineham also began an eight-match ban for a 'squirrel grip' (grabbing the testicles) on Alex Foster in his side's narrow win over Castleford.

Mark Percival returned for St Helens and he was in the thick of the action early

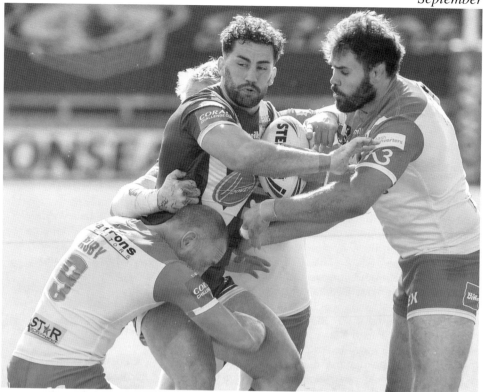

Warrington's Toby King tackled by St Helens' James Roby, Alex Walmsley and James Graham

on before limping off with a recurrence of a hamstring injury on 23 minutes, with Saints leading 8-0.

In the last 11 minutes of the first half that looked crucial as Anthony Gelling, Josh Charnley and Matty Ashton tries, two of which Stefan Ratchford goaled, made it 16-8 to Warrington at the break.

Saints fought back in style, two desperate tackles denying Lachlan Coote and Regan Grace before Grace finally grounded and Coote's exceptional touchline conversion reduced the deficit to 16-14.

Josh Charnley's try in the right corner, the final pass coming off Gelling's head, was cancelled out by Kevin Naiqama with a one-handed put down in the 70th minute. With neither converted, Warrington led 20-18 and that's how it remained.

Wigan were dominant against outgunned Hull FC in their 36-4 win, the Warriors running in seven tries in an almost faultless 80 minutes

Marc Sneyd, a two-time Lance Todd Trophy winner, made an earlier than anticipated return from a knee injury sustained in August as Hull found themselves without a number of players that featured when they beat Castleford to set up the tie six days earlier.

Albert Kelly and Ratu Naulago both sustained hamstring strains in the second half of that sixth-round clash, while Jamie Shaul was not deemed fit to play after he failed a head injury assessment. Wigan captain Sean O'Loughlin made his first appearance since the restart.

Liam Farrell and Bevan French both scored two tries as Joe Burgess's long-range effort after the half-time hooter took the game out of Hull's reach at 26-0. Second-half tries through Farrell and Oliver Gildart finished it off before Mahe Fonua scored a consolation for Hull.

September
Round 13

With St Helens on a bye, in a round played on Thursday and Friday at Warrington's Halliwell Jones Stadium, Warrington and Wigan took the chance to move above them to the top of the table.

The Wolves emerged 30-16 winners over Catalans, who had to overcome some adversity to make the game. The Dragons' private-charter jet had to be diverted from Perpignan to Toulouse because of high winds, leaving players and staff on a 130-mile road-race across southern France to catch the flight. They landed at Liverpool airport with just 90 minutes to kick-off and were able to have only a brief warm-up session.

Coach Steve McNamara also had to deal with the last-minute withdrawal of second row Benjamin Jullien, who made a U-turn on the road to Toulouse when his wife went into labour and gave birth to a baby daughter.

The disruption didn't stop the Dragons making the first game on the Friday night a great contest and McNamara was proud of his troops, although he still believed they could have taken something from the game.

It was a ninth win in a row for the Wolves. Anthony Gelling scored after a fine Blake Austin run on the back of a Mike Cooper offload but Tom Davies and Samisoni Langi crossed, both thanks to fine passes from Sam Tomkins, as Catalans fought back.

Matty Ashton levelled before the break, chasing Gareth Widdop's clever kick on the run, while Matt Davis sent them ahead after the restart two plays after an outstanding goal-line drop-out return by Joe Philbin.

Austin and Fouad Yaha exchanged well-worked tries before hooker Danny Walker wrapped up victory for the Wire late on with a short-range try.

Following the match, Catalans flew back to Toulouse to collect their vehicles and drive back to Perpignan, arriving around 4.00am on Saturday morning.

Wigan beat Wakefield, according to coach Chris Chester down to their last 17 men, by 28-16.

Trinity raced into a 12-0 lead through tries from the returning Jacob Miller and Tinirau Arona. But Wigan replied before the break through Jackson Hastings - after a one-two with the impressive Liam Farrell - and Bevan French, supporting Joe Burgess on the inside.

The second half was a tight affair, with Trinity hammering the Warriors line without scoring before Sam Powell went over from close range.

After Bill Tupou had a try ruled out by the video referee, Oliver Gildart and the fleet-footed French sealed it for Wigan, while Tom Johnstone's late reply for Wakefield marked his return.

Leeds' centre prodigy Harry Newman suffered a double leg fracture in the Rhinos' 41-16 win over Hull KR. Newman sustained the injury 30 minutes in and was taken to hospital after being carried off on a stretcher.

By that point the Rhinos were 18-0 up, through converted tries from Rhyse Martin, Ash Handley and James Donaldson and scored seven tries in all, including two for Handley, as they beat Rovers for the second time in six days.

The Robins made a string of changes, with Greg Minikin, Jordan Abdull, Matt Parcell, Dean Hadley, Mikey Lewis and Kane Linnett all out of the side.

Coming in was homegrown product Will Tate at fullback, who showed glimpses of promise to mark his debut, Nick Rawsthorne for his first Super League start and halfback Joe Keyes, who was given a rare chance to impress. Ryan Brierley, Will Maher, Kyle Trout, Jimmy Keinhorst and Owen Harrison were also brought into the side. They managed scores through Keinhorst, Brierley and Shaun Kenny-Dowall.

Kevin Brown produced a vintage halfback performance as Salford came from behind to almost certainly end Hull FC's play-off hopes with a 28-22 win.

The Black and Whites twice led in the first half and spent ten minutes playing

Leeds' Richie Myler holds off Hull KR's Ryan Brierley to score

against twelve men, with the otherwise impressive Dan Sarginson in the sin bin.

But Brown - looking increasingly comfortable alongside Tui Lolohea at halfback - created two tries and provided a constant threat with the ball as the Red Devils replicated their Challenge Cup form in the league. Krisnan Inu scored two well-taken tries and Rhys Williams one, while Kallum Watkins was showing signs that his mid-season capture was shrewd business.

Hull's Challenge Cup exit to Wigan formed the view they had little more to play for than pride after a seventh league defeat. Fullback Jamie Shaul scored his 100th Hull FC try in a double and Jordan Lane enhanced his growing reputation with a fine try.

Huddersfield and Castleford fought out a hugely entertaining game which the Giants edged 31-19, with the result in doubt until Jermaine McGillvary's hat-trick try in the last minute.

There were some great individual performances on both sides, great teamwork, and superb tries. The star of the show was Giants centre Jake Wardle, who gave a performance that combined speed with anticipation, scoring a try that demonstrated both those qualities as well as some stunning footwork. And Aidan Sezer orchestrated the comeback with a 15-point haul.

Tigers coach Daryl Powell recalled Gareth O'Brien, Jesse Sene-Lefao, Nathan Massey and Greg Eden into his matchday squad, as well as youngster Jack Sanderson, who was making his debut as the Tigers' 1,000th player.

Castleford edged the first half as O'Brien's penalty and field goal sent them in 13-12 ahead after the Giants bounced back from 10-0 down to lead 12-10.

Sanderson's debut try and an O'Brien goal built on the lead. However, McGillvary's converted try just after the hour put the Giants a point behind and Sezer's field goal on 68 minutes levelled at 19-all.

And it was the Giants who forged ahead, as a brilliant dash down the left by Wardle saw him pass to Sezer for another superb try, with Sezer converting.

The Giants' captain then missed a field-goal attempt and the Tigers replied with good work by Mike McMeeken in shrugging off tackles and keeping the ball alive. But the attack came to nought when Calum Turner knocked the ball on in a challenge by Sam Wood.

And the result was finally decided after another great run down the wing by Wardle. The young centre took the tackle, resisting the urge to keep the ball alive. From the play-the-ball Jordan Turner kicked to the right corner and McGillvary caught it to touch down despite a determined attempt at a tackle by Jesse Sene-Lefao. Sezer's touchline conversion was the icing on the cake for the Giants.

September

Round 14

By the end of September, when under normal circumstances the Rugby League season would be hurtling to its climax, the chance of any further action in the lower leagues this year had gone and the Super League fixture list was becoming more hectic as the re-jigged total of 22 rounds had to be fitted in somehow.

Add to that, the Challenge Cup semi-finals were programmed in for the first weekend of October, meaning four teams had to cram two games into four days.

The result was that round 14 provided the opportunity for up and coming players to show their wares, including a number of players with famous fathers making their Super League debuts. They included Umyla Hanley, the son of Ellery, for Wigan, Catalans' coach Steve McNamara's son Ben for Hull, Jarrod O'Connor, son of Sky commentator Terry, for Leeds and James Harrison, the son of Karl, also for Leeds.

On Tuesday at Salford's AJ Bell Stadium, the Red Devils beat Warrington 20-18 in a dress rehearsal for one of the Cup semi-finals.

A young Wolves side, with an average age of just over 21-years-old, trailed Salford Red Devils for only the final 80 seconds of their game. Wolves coach Steve Price handed Super League debuts to Nathan Roebuck and Connor Wrench in the backs, while Kyle Shelford made his first club appearance from the bench late on. Cole Oakley was also named in the 17 but wasn't used. Josh Thewlis and Riley Dean were each handed just their third Super League appearance, with Ellis Longstaff getting the second game of his career.

Salford had their own debutants on show too, with Widnes loanees Olly Ashall-Bott and Tom Gilmore starting, alongside Luis Roberts. They also welcomed captain Lee Mossop back from a calf injury and Ryan Lannon from a broken hand.

Tries from Roebuck, Thewlis and Dean opened up an 18-point lead just before the break as the Wolves youngsters took charge.

But Salford clawed their way back and when, on 71 minutes, Gilmore was on the end of an Andy Ackers break and Kristian Inu added the conversion it was all square at 18-18.

Inu soon tried to win it with a field-goal attempt that went wide. And Declan Patton also attempted a one-pointer before Dean was penalised for offside, allowing Inu to seal the win with a penalty just a minute from the final hooter.

It was the end of Warrington's eight-match winning league run.

St Helens went clear at the top of the table straight after that match as they hammered a young Wigan side 42-0.

Umyla Hanley, Sam Halsall, James McDonnell, Harry Rushton, Kai Pearce-Paul and Ben Kilner were all on debut in a side captained by 20-year-old Harry Smith, who, prior to the 2020 season, had only played one game off the bench for the Warriors' first team.

Saints, on the other hand, were not appearing in the Challenge Cup semi-finals and they hadn't had a game the previous weekend, so their coach Kristian Woolf had no need to rest any of his players, although halfback Lewis Dodd did make his debut off the bench. Another Saints young gun, Jack Welsby, finished with two tries, as did winger Regan Grace.

Huddersfield played a genuine home game and beat Hull KR 32-22.

The Covid-19 crisis provided another twist, pushing the kick-off time back 90 minutes only a few hours prior to the match beginning.

Four coronavirus cases were reported by the Giants early in the afternoon, two of them non-players and the other two players who were not involved in the game against Castleford the previous week and were not scheduled to take part against Hull KR.

However, after conversations with Public Health England the kick-off was moved. It caused all sorts of problems for the Robins, whose travel arrangements were thrown out.

Unsurprisingly, Hull KR found themselves 18-0 down at half-time at the John

Hull KR's Matt Parcell crashes past Tom Holmes for one of his three tries against Huddersfield

Smith's Stadium, though they rallied in the second half against a Giants team that had now registered three wins in a row. Aidan Sezer masterminded the four-try first-half rout, creating two tries for Jermaine McGillvary with boot and hand.

A Matt Parcell hat-trick brought Rovers back into it, although Chris McQueen dotted down a Sezer grubber before Parcell's third, and Jake Wardle and Will Tate swapped late tries.

McGillvary's two tries saw him break into the competition's record books. The Giants winger was now the ninth-highest try scorer in Super League history after his double put him on 169 tries, moving him above David Hodgson and Rob Burrow into ninth place. (Luke Dorn was in eighth position and just one try ahead of the England winger on 170, while Leon Pryce currently occupied seventh place on 173 tries).

On the same night at rainy Headingley, winger Tom Davies scored a hat-trick in Catalans' 34-6 win over a youthful Leeds side.

Leeds gave seven debuts to rising stars. Winger Liam Tindall shone, with one breathtaking run just after the break when he beat a posse of grasping defenders until downed a metre short by Josh Drinkwater.

Jarrod O'Connor, in the unfamiliar role of hooker, made a game-high 54 tackles; Sam Walters and James Harrison were in the mid-40s, whilst there was a great cameo from Corey Hall. Loui McConnell and Jack Broadbent also made their senior debuts. Callum McClelland had his most influential game in blue and amber.

Clearly, the youngsters were massively assisted by Adam Cuthbertson, the skipper for the night, on the back of his announcement of joining York in 2021, along with Bodene Thompson and Brett Ferres.

The Rhinos' ceaseless efforts were not rewarded on the scoreline, which blew out at the end, with the Catalans posting two tries in the closing five minutes.

Fouad Yaha's 51st-minute try score whilst Sam Kasiano was in the sin bin for a professional foul settled it for the Dragons.

September

Castleford played their first post-lockdown home game on the Thursday night, actually the first day of October, when Hull FC edged a thoroughly entertaining contest by 32-28.

The Tigers mounted a terrific comeback from 26-16 down after Ben McNamara went over for a debut try and thought they had it won when Gareth O'Brien converted Michael Shenton's 75th-minute try from Paul McShane's deft kick.

But there was time for one late twist. Jake Connor leapt highest for the kick-off to win the ball back. On tackle three, Marc Sneyd kicked early towards the post and Connor got there first to score what would prove to be the winning try.

Castleford attempted a short kick-off of their own but Connor claimed that too and Hull hung on.

A third successive Super League defeat for Daryl Powell's men left their chances of reaching the top four all but over.

BETFRED SUPER LEAGUE
Thursday 1st October

	P	W	D	L	F	A	D	Win %
St Helens	12	9	0	3	345	135	210	75.00
Warrington Wolves	13	9	0	4	276	168	108	69.23
Wigan Warriors	13	9	0	4	295	240	55	69.23
Leeds Rhinos	11	7	0	4	261	224	37	63.64
Catalans Dragons	10	6	0	4	278	205	73	60.00
Huddersfield Giants	13	7	0	6	254	269	-15	53.85
Hull FC	13	6	0	7	286	358	-72	46.15
Castleford Tigers	13	5	0	8	260	279	-19	38.46
Salford Red Devils	11	4	0	7	214	293	-79	36.36
Wakefield Trinity	11	2	0	9	160	309	-149	18.18
Hull Kingston Rovers	12	2	0	10	204	353	-149	16.67

OCTOBER
A rising challenge

Challenge Cup Semi-finals

Salford Red Devils reached Wembley for the first time in 51 years with a stunning late 24-22 win over holders Warrington.

Salford had defied the odds to reach the previous year's Super League Grand Final under coach Ian Watson but in the light of the fact that six of that side had left for pastures new, the Red Devils' latest accomplishment was more than impressive.

Watson welcomed back Kris Welham and Kevin Brown, whilst Dan Sarginson's two-match ban for a high tackle on Jamie Shaul in the 28-22 over Hull FC was downgraded to no matches, making him available to fill in for the injured Niall Evalds at fullback.

Only Danny Walker remained in Steve Price's first-team squad from the one that lost the midweek league fixture to Salford, with Blake Austin named at loose forward but playing alongside Gareth Widdop in the halves, as Stefan Ratchford – on his 250th Warrington appearance - took the number 13 role.

On a wet and cold Saturday at the Totally Wicked Stadium in St Helens, a BBC TV audience were treated to a highly-entertaining and typical cup-tie between two determined and committed sides.

Enthusiastic Salford defence managed to keep their opponents at bay for the opening exchanges, despite Matty Ashton coming close. But the Red Devils were down to twelve men in the eleventh minute as Tyrone McCarthy was given a yellow card for a dangerous-looking cannonball tackle on Ratchford, although he escaped suspension later in the week.

With a man advantage, Warrington were able to exploit the extra space as Toby King dived over in the corner. Ratchford converted for a 6-0 lead. That became 8-0 when Ratchford opted to keep the scoreboard ticking over when Salford were caught offside.

But on 23 minutes, against the run of play and as McCarthy prepared to come back on, a neat Tui Lolohea grubber fooled Wire fullback Ashton, with Kallum Watkins on hand to superbly ground the ball. Krisnan Inu converted to bring Salford back to within two points.

The next ten minutes were full of errors and it was a Sarginson dropped ball that paved the way for Warrington to hit double figures. As the Salford defence scrambled to the right, Austin stepped off his left foot to break through and score. With Ratchford taking a breather, Widdop took over the kicking duties to make it 14-6, four minutes before half-time.

An inventive short kick-off fell into Salford hands and, after the Wolves were adjudged to be offside, Inu reduced the deficit to six with a penalty goal. It was the two points which, effectively, sent Salford to Wembley.

Powerhouse winger Inu was at the top of his game and he delivered an early blow in the second half, leaping magnificently to take a pin-point Brown kick with less than 42 minutes on the clock. However, he missed the conversion and Salford remained two points behind at 14-12.

Salford's Krisnan Inu finds himself isolated against the Warrington defence

Then it was Warrington's turn to apply pressure as Widdop's kick forced a repeat set but Jake Mamo dropped the swirling Inu drop-out. Mamo's blushes were saved when Greg Burke lost the ball just a tackle later. Things finally settled down when Widdop added another two points for a Salford infringement as the clock hit 50 minutes.

Austin almost sent Ashton away as the Red Devils appeared to creak but the flying fullback couldn't hold the offload. But Salford were on the rocks and, following another Sarginson fumble, Warrington stretched their lead just after the hour mark, Ben Murdoch-Masila taking an inside pass to swat aside two defenders and crash over. Widdop added the goal to make it 22-12.

But Widdop let the Salford kick-off go dead and on the last tackle of the next set Kevin Brown's brilliant kick through was grounded by James Greenwood on 66 minutes. Inu's conversion brought Salford back to within four points.

Salford smelt their chance and an Austin kick that shanked into touch on the full gave them the field position they needed for Joey Lussick to score his trademark try out of dummy-half. Inu's conversion sent the Red Devils into the lead for the first time with six minutes left.

1969 was the last time Salford got to Wembley, when they lost 11-6 to Castleford. But in 2020 there would be no-one allowed inside the stadium to cheer them on, though a petition was set up to allow fans inside. It fell on deaf ears.

Leeds Rhinos would be Salford's Wembley opponents. In the first game of the Saturday double header they produced a wet-weather masterclass to beat Wigan 26-12, two late Warriors tries making the scoreline respectable.

Richie Myler had reinvented himself as a fullback and was one of several crucial players who supported Luke Gale's inch-perfect kicking game all afternoon.

Rhyse Martin broke the deadlock after 14 minutes with a penalty. Three minutes later, a superb 40/20 from Gale beat Joe Burgess to the line and, from that, Robert Lui's inside ball gave Martin space to cut through on the angle, with the backrower converting his own try to make it 8-0.

Leeds' Rhyse Martin is mobbed by Luke Gale after scoring against Wigan

Another penalty from the boot of Martin four minutes later extended the lead and already at that stage Wigan were in trouble. They needed to get a foothold in the game fast. Instead, they conceded another ten points and by half-time, were practically out of the tie.

Six minutes before half-time, they fell further behind when a high kick caused chaos and Myler's scooped pass over the top sent Ash Handley in, with Martin again nailing the conversion to make it 16-0. And while Martin missed on the stroke of half-time after Konrad Hurrell's magnificent pass sent Tom Briscoe over, 20-0 in Leeds' favour looked conclusive.

Wigan had to strike early after half-time to convince the Rhinos they were a credible threat but they just couldn't muster the attacking gusto needed to break down a resolute Leeds defence.

They thought they had done so nine minutes after the break when Dom Manfredi crossed but replays showed that Tommy Leuluai had knocked on in the build-up.

At the other end, it felt like we were all just waiting for the moment when the Rhinos finally put the tie to bed. Hurrell looked to have done that when he profited from Gale's final pass before play was pulled back for offside. But Leeds fans wouldn't have long to wait.

As the game entered the final quarter, the Rhinos struck decisively when Liam Sutcliffe's pass as he headed out of play found its way to Handley, who went over for his second try.

Three minutes later, another penalty from Martin opened up a five-score lead, before Wigan at least avoided the ignominy of being nilled with two tries of their own in the final five minutes. First, substitute Harry Smith raced the length of the field to open Wigan's account before, on the following set, Zak Hardaker crossed against his former club, converting both tries.

It was a personal triumph for coach Richard Agar, who in 2019 inherited the Leeds squad following two dismal seasons and his first game in charge saw the Rhinos suffer a humiliating Challenge Cup defeat at Bradford.

Wakefield's Jacob Miller, Bill Tupou and Tom Johnstone close down Catalans' Israel Folau

Round 16

On the Sunday of the semi-finals, Catalans recorded a comprehensive 40-8 win in Perpignan against a weary-looking Wakefield, leaving Trinity rooted to the bottom of the table on points difference from Hull KR.

Wakefield were in charge the first 35 minutes. Jacob Miller orchestrated a series of attacks, with Joe Westerman and Kelepi Tanginoa tormenting the 5,000 home supporters who had expected an early Dragons rout. But a Bill Tupou try from Miller's grubber into the corner and two Tony Gigot goals were all the visitors had to show for some impressive graft before the interval and a dominant second half had the French supporters singing.

A try against the run of play from Matt Whitley, quickly followed by a powerful touchdown on half-time for Israel Folau, put Catalans in the driving seat at half-time. Sam Kasiano's introduction into the game after half an hour was crucial, his powerful surges wreaking havoc in the Wakefield defence.

Trinity were never in it after the break. Six minutes in, David Mead collected Josh Drinkwater's looping pass to score on the left. Almost straight from the restart, Kasiano scored the try of the match. The giant prop burst through the middle on a 30-metre dash and found Sam Tomkins who returned the favour for Kasiano to finish the move in the left corner. James Maloney's touchline conversion put the Dragons 22-8 ahead. Kasiano gratefully accepted immediate substitution after his epic sprint.

Tomkins then profited from some interplay with Folau down the right, picking up a return pass and shooting in beside the posts, Maloney adding the goal. Following a penalty for a high tackle on Tom Davies, Julian Bousquet forced his way over to the left of the posts, Maloney adding his fifth conversion of the game.

Whitley went close to grounding a Drinkwater grubber, then Tomkins found Mead on the left, the winger crossing with ease for his second try and improving the conversion angle for Maloney.

Wakefield were allowed some possession and position in the final quarter as referee James Child penalised the home team for a series of offences. But the Dragons held firm.

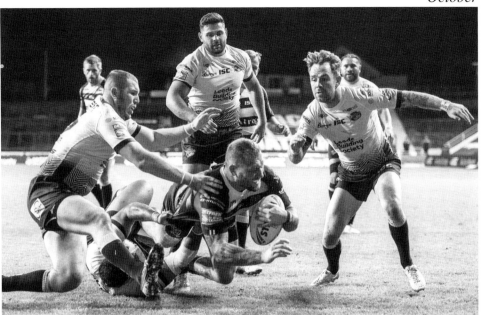

Leeds' Cameron Smith and Richie Myler can't stop Hull FC's Josh Griffin from scoring

Round 15

There was more Covid-disruption going into round 15, due to be played on the Thursday and Friday night at Headingley, when Castleford were hit with Covid-19 issues and had to pull out of their fixture with Leeds.

Hull FC, due a bye round, stepped into the breach with less than 24 hours' notice and gave a good account of themselves, in what was technically a round 18 game on the Thursday, before succumbing to a 40-22 defeat to the Rhinos.

Winger Ash Handley scored a hat-trick and fullback Jack Walker staked his Challenge Cup Final claim on his comeback from a long-term ankle injury with two tries and an assist as Richard Agar's team eventually overcame the late stand-ins.

Hull's interim coach Andy Last was without 13 of his own players for a variety of reasons but his side defied the odds to take an early 10-0 lead, with tries from Mahe Fonua and Andre Savelio.

Walker then stepped forward with two tries and the assist for Handley's first to give the Rhinos a 16-10 half-time lead and Leeds secured victory with an efficient second-half display.

Handley scored a second after the break following James Donaldson's try and it was 28-10. Tries from Josh Griffin and Jack Brown got Hull back to 28-22 before Liam Sutcliffe made it safe on 67 minutes, Handley completing his hat-trick four minutes from time.

The first game that night saw Salford end the winning run of Huddersfield's interim coach Luke Robinson with a 24-16 comeback victory.

Krisnan Inu, playing on the left wing, scored 20 of the Red Devils' 24 points with a hat-trick of tries and four goals, inspiring his side to a victory that looked unlikely when they were 12-0 down with a quarter of the game gone, Leroy Cudjoe and Aidan Sezer crossing for the Giants.

The Giants came into the game looking for their fourth victory under Robinson, which would have kept up the momentum towards a top-four spot. Robinson was able to bring back Lee Gaskell, after a lengthy absence with a broken thumb, to partner captain Sezer at halfback.

October

Salford were without Kevin Brown, as well as Sebastine Ikahihifo and Oliver Roberts, both unable to play against their parent club. Mark Flanagan was rested from the side that defeated Warrington in the Cup, with Luke Yates back after suspension and Chris Atkin starting at scrum-half alongside Tui Lolohea.

Atkin's intercept try and two Inu goals reduced the arrears to 12-8 at half-time. And Inu took control after the break, using his power and size out wide to score three tries in the corner. Sezer had scored in between for the Giants.

Wakefield also suffered Covid losses later in the week but felt compelled to go ahead with their fixture against leaders St Helens on the Friday. One positive case resulted in another seven players being stood down. As a result, coach Chris Chester had just 17 players to pick from. A massacre was expected but that never materialised as Wakefield produced a pugnacious display before going down 20-16.

It wasn't unusual post-lockdown for Trinity to take an early lead before falling badly away. And they did again, tries to Alex Walker and Craig Kopczak, both converted by Ryan Hampshire, had them 12-0 ahead until the half-hour mark.

Up till then Saints had produced a mistake-ridden display but when Louie McCarthy-Scarsbrook burst through for a try, just after the injury-withdrawal of hooker Josh Wood who had been the centre of Wakefield's defensive effort, a Saints comeback looked inevitable. And within five minutes, the arrears were down to two. An orchestrated attack down the Saints' left saw Lachlan Coote put Josh Simm away. The young centre appeared to have been dragged on his back into touch but, somehow, he produced an offload for Coote to grab the four-pointer. But Coote couldn't convert, leaving Saints two points behind at half-time.

The second half was much more efficient from Saints, while Wakefield continued to finish their sets and end them well from the boot of Hampshire. They ended the game with a completion rate above 90 per cent.

It wasn't until they suffered some misfortune that Wakefield finally cracked. Josh Wood took another knock to the head, which left him on the floor. Wood was treated and was adjudged to be fit enough to continue but from ten out Jonny Lomax produced a lofted cut-out ball to Regan Grace, who stepped inside Innes Senior and finished expertly. Saints were ahead.

Then, off the back of a quick Kevin Naiqama play-the-ball, James Roby arced through a gap and offloaded to Lomax, who put Coote away for his second under the sticks.

In the blink of an eye, Saints had established an eight-point lead.

Wakefield continued to ask questions of Saints and reaped their reward in the last minute as David Fifita, back in the side after more than a month, dunked an offload into Matty Ashurst to bring the deficit to four points.

It gave Wakefield a chance at a miracle play to win the game. However, they couldn't pull a final rabbit out of the hat.

Tommy Makinson returned for Saints after a five-match suspension, though there was no James Graham, who had been forced into a 14-day self-isolation period from a family contact.

Over in Perpignan, Catalans Dragons rose to third in the Super League table, following a clinical 34-4 demolition of Hull Kingston Rovers.

The solitary Robins supporter who battled travel restrictions to sit alone in the Puig Aubert Stand only had reason to stand up once, when Harvey Livett scored a second-half consolation try, because it was one-way traffic from start to finish.

Former Robins skipper Joel Tomkins tormented his old team-mates with a hat-trick of tries and Tom Davies scored two. The irrepressible Davies forced his way over the line for his first try just before half-time to put the game to bed at 22-0.

The round's finale at Headingley saw Wigan edge Warrington 18-14, the Wolves falling out of the top-four.

Salford's Kris Welham halted by Huddersfield's Lee Gaskell and Sam Hewitt

The game had been expected to be a stage rehearsal for the following weekend's Challenge Cup Final. As it was, both teams were coming off the back of defeats in the Cup semi-finals and a high-quality game unfolded.

After going 12-0 down early, the Warriors were able to turn the game on its head and take the lead for the first and only time when Liam Farrell ran in Harry Smith's pass with four minutes to go, capping off a mountain of pressure built up in the final quarter.

Warrington had taken an early lead thanks to a penalty try after Matty Ashton was taken out by Dom Manfredi. Chris Hill crashed over soon after to extend Wire's lead but Wigan's Joe Greenwood touched down moments later.

It took Wigan only five minutes to equalise in the second half. A grubber-kick from Jackson Hastings sat up perfectly for Zak Hardaker, who motored on to it and dived in behind the posts, making his job as goal-kicker an easy one.

Warrington responded. Wigan were caught offside and the Wolves took the chance to nudge ahead in the game once again, 14-12, through Stefan Ratchford's penalty.

Entering the final quarter of the game, Warrington went close to stretching their lead when Anthony Gelling attempted to ground in the Wigan in-goal but the centre lost the ball as he neared the line. That moment swung the momentum firmly in favour of the Warriors as they piled on the pressure.

Smith, on the field in place of Sam Powell and operating on the left with Hastings moved to hooker, made an instant impact, forcing a goal-line drop-out. Although nothing came of it, due to a poor pass from Farrell, Wigan kept coming and the pressure finally told with four minutes remaining. Smith timed his pass to Farrell to perfection, allowing the backrower to score the matchwinner, which was converted by Hardaker.

October

Round 16

Round 16 week, with all five fixtures to be played at Warrington on the Tuesday and Thursday, was reduced to four games when the highly anticipated Thursday-night match-up, a re-arranged round 10 game, between Wigan and Catalans was postponed for the second time because of a virus outbreak, this time at the Warriors.

Three games were played on the Tuesday, with Hull KR getting their first win in five league games against a Salford side that featured ten players who would not play the following Saturday in the Challenge Cup Final.

Jamie Ellis's last-gasp penalty goal secured the Robins a 24-22 win after the Red Devils clawed back deficits four times.

Rovers' young halfback Mikey Lewis played at fullback and got two tries, including a 64th-minute penalty try when he was pushed in the back by on-loan Olly Ashall-Bott chasing a kick into the in-goal.

That made it 18-12 but it was all-square again within a few short minutes when Ashall-Bott dodged, ducked, dipped and dived through defenders to score a superb solo try. Ed Chamberlain again converted to make it 18-all with 12 minutes to play.

Salford were behind again within a minute. Pauli Pauli dropped the ball on the next set and Jordan Abdull, starting at centre, jumped into dummy-half, wrapped around, received an offload from Weller Hauraki and scored. Ellis pulled the conversion wide.

Salford still did not accept defeat and with four minutes to play levelled for a fourth time.

After Ellis dropped the ball, following a break created by Abdull, Salford countered and another right-edge move saw Ashall-Bott's looping pass find Chamberlain, who dived in. Crucially, Chamberlain could not convert from the touchline, leaving the game all square with two minutes to play.

Salford couldn't get within striking distance for a field-goal attempt. But Hull KR could. Matt Parcell was tackled high by Pauli, giving Ellis the chance to win the game from 35 metres out with a penalty from in front of the sticks. He obliged.

Next up, Hull FC didn't leave it quite so late. There was still five minutes left when Marc Sneyd kicked the penalty goal that gave Hull FC an 18-16 win over Huddersfield.

The game was tightly contested throughout. Although Hull's final margin of victory was only two points, there was never any point in the game when the Giants were in the lead, which reflected the broad degree of control exercised by the Black and Whites.

Hull dominated the first half hour but only had a well-worked seventh-minute Ratu Naulago try to show for it. And as the final ten minutes of the first half approached, the Giants began to come more into the game following a great run out of defence by on-Giants-debut Brandon Moore, on loan from Halifax. They then got a six-again and Lee Gaskell's kick won a goal-line drop-out.

A minute later Jermaine McGillvary was in at the right corner after Leroy Cudjoe brilliantly caught a pass from Gaskell above his head before expertly flicking it on to his winger. Aidan Sezer couldn't add the conversion and Hull re-took the lead when Mahe Fonua was in from a smart Josh Griffin pass.

As the second half started, Tevita Satae knocked on going over the line in a Matty English tackle and then English himself scored, going over under the posts after expertly collecting a pinpoint Sezer kick. Sezer's goal levelled the scores at 10-10 and everything was to play for.

The Giants attacked again and Sezer launched a bomb that was well taken by Bureta Faraimo, which was followed by a great break out of his own half by Jamie Shaul, who passed the ball on to Joe Cator. Forty-five seconds later Faraimo was in on the left from another smart Griffin pass after McGillvary was drawn away from the touchline. Sneyd kicked another touchline goal to restore a six-point lead for Hull.

But they couldn't shake off the Giants, and they weren't helped by conceding three

penalties in quick succession. Sezer went through a large gap that appeared in the Hull defence to touch down near the posts to level it at 16-16, guaranteeing the exciting finish.

The Giants had the first chance to claim the points but Sezer skewed his field-goal attempt under pressure with seven minutes remaining

The decisive action was taken by referee Scott Mikalauskas shortly afterwards, when he penalised Kenny Edwards for not standing square. Sneyd inevitably made no mistake in sending the kick through the posts.

Like their Wembley opponents, Leeds rested a host of players and the team that fell to a 32-6 defeat to Warrington included only one player, prop Adam Cuthbertson, who was to appear the following Saturday.

Warrington, who were looking for their first win in four games, were without Blake Austin, Mike Cooper, Jake Mamo and Joe Philbin but they had more than adequate replacements, with Declan Patton, Matty Ashton, Ellis Robson and Danny Walker coming into the starting line-up, while key man Daryl Clark started from the bench.

It was Clark's introduction after 48 minutes that turned the game in Warrington's favour and three Wolves tries in the final 18 minutes proved too much for Leeds.

When the Wolves opened the scoring after just five minutes as Toby King timed his run perfectly to pluck Patton's high, cross-field kick out of the air to cross for a try in his 100th game for the club. Stefan Ratchford converted and most people thought that would open the floodgates. But the young Rhinos repelled everything the Wolves threw at them, strong enough in defence to force their more experienced counterparts into numerous errors.

And for that, Leeds got their reward on 15 minutes when Jack Broadbent stole the ball in a one-on-one with Josh Charnley to set up a fresh attack that ended with Sam Walters beating Robson and Ratchford to crash over. Jarrod O'Connor levelled with the conversion before Warrington found themselves down to twelve men for the final ten minutes of a very even first half when Sitaleki Akauola was sin-binned for a dangerous throw on James Harrison. Akauola was subsequently banned for three games. A Ratchford penalty gave the Wolves an 8-6 half-time lead.

Warrington still couldn't break the resolute Rhinos down in the opening stages of the second half. But that all changed with Daryl Clark's introduction from the bench. The hooker added more speed and gave an extra dimension to the Wolves' creativity and he was soon at the heart of the action as the breakthrough came. His perfect pass from dummy-half found Gareth Widdop before the ball passed through the hands of Ratchford, Ben Currie and King, with Ashton finishing off a fast and fluid move in the corner.

Ratchford missed with the conversion, but was on target ten minutes later as the Wolves' dominance began to grow and they further extended their lead. King beat Liam Tindall to claim another Patton kick, before quickly getting the ball out to Currie, who threw a dummy to race in.

With the young Leeds side starting to tire, mistakes were starting to creep in and when Patton was taken out as he attempted to chase his own kick, Ratchford was on target again to increase the Wolves lead.

Two further Warrington tries came in the final ten minutes, with Daryl Clark claiming the first from dummy-half. Then, as King and Tindall challenged for another Patton kick, the ball ricocheted into the hands of Ashton for his second of the night.

Round 9

On the Thursday night at the same venue, beleaguered Wakefield faced leaders St Helens for the second time in six days in a game postponed from round nine, and fell to a resounding 48-6 defeat.

Tommy Makinson scored a finisher's hat-trick as St Helens took another step towards a third League Leaders' Shield in a row with an accomplished win against a

St Helens' James Roby gets a pass away against Wakefield

Wakefield Trinity side now on a ten-game losing streak.

The England winger touched down three times in the space of 24 first-half minutes as Kristian Woolf's side produced two scoring bursts to ease past Trinity. It was 30-0 by half-time.

James Roby contributed a double of his own to reach 100 Super League tries, while Alex Walmsley continued his remarkable scoring run and Lachlan Coote provided the glue for everything in attack.

It proved more than enough to account for a Wakefield side that had pushed Saints all the way just a week earlier and Trinity's only reward came when on-loan Giants winger Innes Senior intercepted in the second half and beat Regan Grace in a 90-metre foot race.

In a Round 9 catch-up game the following Sunday, Hull FC were back at their KCOM Stadium home for the first time since lockdown and they celebrated in style with a 48-6 hammering of Castleford.

It was a second victory in five days for the Airlie Birds and a sweet moment for interim coach Andy Last, in his first game at home since he took over from Lee Radford.

With Jake Connor and Marc Sneyd working well at halfback and Andre Savelio outstanding in the pack, Hull were too hot to handle all afternoon. They were 24-0 up at half-time after a lightning start that featured four tries from Ratu Naulago, Savelio, Connor and Bureta Faraimo, all converted by Sneyd.

Hull continued the second half in similar style to the first, with Naulago breaking away for an unstoppable seventy-metre effort after collecting a Danny Richardson kick deep within Hull's half. Then a 40/20 from Connor set up position for Danny Houghton to go in under the posts through a huge hole in the Tigers line.

The Tigers avoided a nilling when Jaques O'Neill went over with eight minutes to play. But it was a blip. Carlos Tuimavave stepped his way over before, with the very last play of the game, Manu Ma'u scored in the corner.

Hull's chances of making the top-four play-offs looked remote but they had to win all of their four remaining games to have any chance.

Challenge Cup Final

Leeds recorded their 14th Challenge Cup triumph after a spine-tingling Wembley final, thrilling despite the game being played behind closed doors because of the coronavirus, which they edged 17-16 thanks to a 76th-minute field goal from Luke Gale.

Gale's second one-pointer attempt snatched victory away from a gallant Salford Red Devils, who had taken a 16-12 lead just before the hour mark after being 12-6 down at half-time.

'I thought we were gone when they took the lead in the second half,' admitted Rhinos coach Richard Agar after the game.

'I just felt that our spirit got us through in the end. We had great energy, particularly in those last-ditch moments and Luke came up with a play to win the game, just as we know he can.'

Agar reckoned that Gale winning the game wearing the number 7 shirt that was worn for so many years by Leeds icon Rob Burrow, who was currently struggling with Motor Neurone Disease, was highly symbolic. He also paid tribute to Lance Todd Trophy winner Richie Myler, whose future at Leeds had looked highly uncertain earlier in the year. Myler gained exactly half of the 24 votes cast by members of the Rugby League Writers' Association, with Gale his nearest rival for the award, Myler gaining 12 votes, Gale eight, Salford fullback Niall Evalds two and two-try Leeds winger Ash Handley two.

Myler was solid defensively and creative on attack and he didn't let one huge and potentially disastrous error knock him off his stride when he couldn't take a high Tui Lolohea kick that ended with James Greenwood going over for the converted try that put Salford 16-12 ahead with 21 minutes to go. He also played a key part in both of Handley's tries.

It was a tremendous story of perseverance from Myler, as it had become clear at the start of 2020 that Gale and Robert Lui would be Leeds' first-choice halfbacks. Myler remained with the Rhinos, knuckled down and, following an injury to Jack Walker, stepped into the fullback role impressively. He was rewarded with a new two-year Leeds contract in August.

Leeds' other try came from right winger Tom Briscoe, the 2015 Lance Todd Trophy winner, who broke a Wembley record with his seventh try in Challenge Cup finals.

From the off, Leeds were dominant territorially. Salford, missing Dan Sarginson who had tested positive for Covid-19, were struggling to get out of their own 20-metre area, while the Rhinos were starting their sets on halfway.

It was therefore little surprise when Briscoe opened the scoring on twelve minutes, with a beautiful offload from Konrad Hurrell allowing Briscoe to tiptoe into the right corner, five years on from his five-try haul against Hull KR that wrote his name into the competition's history books. Rhyse Martin's touchline conversion went in via the far upright.

Leeds continued to have the upper hand and Gale's kicking game meant Salford couldn't start in good positions. But they got back into it with a long-range effort against the run of play.

It wasn't just a stroke of good fortune. A high Gale kick to the left corner was

CORAL CHALLENGE CUP FINAL

Saturday 17th October 2020

LEEDS RHINOS 17 SALFORD RED DEVILS 16

RHINOS: 16 Richie Myler; 2 Tom Briscoe; 4 Konrad Hurrell; 15 Liam Sutcliffe; 5 Ash Handley; 6 Robert Lui; 7 Luke Gale (C); 8 Ava Seumanufagai; 9 Kruise Leeming; 19 Mikolaj Oledzki; 11 Alex Mellor; 12 Rhyse Martin; 10 Matt Prior. Subs (all used): 14 Brad Dwyer; 17 Adam Cuthbertson; 25 James Donaldson; 26 Alex Sutcliffe.
Tries: T Briscoe (12), Handley (31, 65); **Goals:** Martin 2/3;
Field goal: Gale (76).
RED DEVILS: 1 Niall Evalds; 22 Rhys Williams; 32 Kallum Watkins; 3 Kris Welham; 5 Krisnan Inu; 6 Tui Lolohea; 7 Kevin Brown; 8 Lee Mossop (C); 9 Joey Lussick; 10 Gil Dudson; 13 Tyrone McCarthy; 21 James Greenwood; 19 Mark Flanagan. Subs (all used): 12 Pauli Pauli; 14 Sebastine Ikahihifo; 16 Greg Burke; 17 Luke Yates.
Tries: Williams (19), Pauli (53), Greenwood (58); **Goals:** Inu 2/3.
Rugby Leaguer & League Express Men of the Match:
Rhinos: Luke Gale; *Red Devils:* Kallum Watkins.
Penalty count: 6-5; **Half-time:** 12-6; **Referee:** Liam Moore.
(at Wembley Stadium).

Leeds' Robert Lui is brought down short of the Salford line by Kevin Brown and Joey Lussick

wonderfully taken by former Leeds captain Kallum Watkins. Not only did he claim it, he managed to offload to Evalds as he fell to the ground, which allowed the fullback to immediately send Rhys Williams charging down the wing for a fairytale score by the posts. Krisnan Inu's conversion meant that Salford were level.

Leeds' response was good, even though subs Luke Yates and Sebastine Ikahihifo gave Salford a bit more in the pack battle.

But, eventually, Leeds got on top again. When they did, they capitalised. A quick movement of the ball to the left, the penultimate pass a lightning catch-and-pass from Myler, saw Handley stroll in at the corner, Martin again converting to give Leeds a 12-6 advantage at the break.

There was a general feeling that the first ten minutes of the second half would be pivotal. Salford, late in the half, looked fatigued after their backs-to-the-wall job. But there was almost a sense of inevitability they would pounce when Leeds presented them with a chance.

A high kick to the corner was dropped by Briscoe, who had to go off with a head injury assessment after a fall to the ground. Alex Sutcliffe came on in his place, resulting in a swap of personnel on the edges.

Suspecting vulnerability, Salford pounced on the following set, Pauli Pauli's 22-stone frame too big for Gale to stop as he powered ten metres through the right channel off Lolohea's pass to score. Crucially, Inu couldn't convert.

A few short minutes later Salford went ahead. Lolohea's hoisted kick was shallow, it left Myler needing to stride forward to claim it but he didn't get there in time. Instead, the ball fell into Yates's hands and James Greenwood was in support of Joey Lussick to score to the left of the posts, with Inu's conversion giving the Red Devils a four-point lead with 23 minutes to play.

By now impact hooker Brad Dwyer was on and his dart got Leeds in front of the Salford sticks. The ball was spread left and Myler made amends for his costly error as he joined the attacking line, offloading superbly under pressure to put Handley in for his second. Martin missed for the first time, leaving the scores all level with 15 minutes to play.

Gale had become the master of the match-winning field goal, though he sliced his first effort in the 71st minute.

Salford never got their chance for the one-pointer. They thought they would when they won a penalty for a ball steal on their own 20-metre line but, from the tap on halfway, Pauli gave away a penalty for an improper play the ball. Then, with four minutes and 35 seconds to play, Gale slotted over the winning point.

If there had been a crowd present, it would have raised the roof.

Round 17

Hull FC's away fixture at Catalans, scheduled for the Thursday, was cancelled. Five Catalans players and two members of their backroom staff received positive tests for Covid-19 on the Wednesday, following tests conducted on Tuesday, meaning a shutdown of up to five days to allow further 'antigen' testing. They were also unable to play Warrington the following Monday.

As such, it made Hull's chances of making the top four less likely. And for the Dragons, sitting in fourth with a win percentage of 66.67 per cent, it was a potential hammer blow because of the minimum play-of qualification of 15 games. They had played only 12, following the earlier postponement of fixtures at home to Leeds and away against Wigan, with time running out on the season.

Leeds, six days after their Challenge Cup victory, missed their chance to improve their win percentage when they lost 40-8 to St Helens at the Totally Wicked Stadium.

It was no surprise, as Rhinos coach Richard Agar chose to make 13 changes and field a host of reserve players, only James Donaldson, Mikolaj Oledzki, Brad Dwyer and Alex Sutcliffe being asked to back up from the Wembley-winning side.

The young side lacked the experience across the board to really trouble St Helens, especially in the first half, although they dominated the third quarter of the game. However, they were 22 points down by that stage, with Saints having taken a stranglehold with four tries, three of them by robust centre Josh Simm.

Simm, the grandson of former Saints favourite Geoff Pimblett, the first man to win both the Lance Todd Trophy and Harry Sunderland Trophy, opened the scoring on only three minutes when he took a Zeb Taia offload, sped down the left wing and swerved inside fullback Jack Walker.

The lead was doubled when James Roby spotted some lax defenders on the fifth tackle on the 30-metre line, ran from dummy-half to split Leeds open and found the supporting Taia for the try.

Simm got his second despite a tremendous attempted try-saving tackle from Callum McLelland and he had a treble by half-time after finishing good handling following a Regan Grace break the play before. That made it 22-0 at the break and at that stage there were fears the score could blow right out.

Instead, Leeds dominated the third quarter, deservedly winning it 4-0 after taking the game to their opponents. Cameron Smith scored the try, running a great line to McLelland's pass to crash over, although he couldn't convert his own effort.

Wigan's Bevan French races clear against Salford

Then Saints stepped the pace up again with two tries in three eye-catching minutes. Theo Fages scored the first from a brilliant Matty Lees break and offload. Then Kevin Naiqama first produced a sublime flick pass to release Tommy Makinson down the right touchline before supporting him on the inside to touch down.

Still the Rhinos kept coming forward and they scored a second when winger Liam Tindall took Sam Walters' smart pass and finished in the corner, before Saints had the final word with a try to substitute hooker Aaron Smith, who broke from dummy-half 30 metres out and worked a one-two with Fages.

On the same night at the same place, Wembley runners-up Salford made fewer changes to Leeds but they were on the end of a 58-12 hammering by Wigan.

Wigan fullback Bevan French scored a brilliant hat-trick of tries featuring speed, skill and footwork and he was complemented by two tries each from Liam Farrell, Sam Powell and Oliver Gildart as the Warriors took advantage of Salford's evident hangover after their Challenge Cup defeat.

Wigan, on the other hand, had two weeks to prepare their troops for the trip to the Totally Wicked Stadium. Their game in the previous week against Catalans had been postponed and there was a fresh look and feel to the Warriors. The Reds were behind without touching the ball when Powell dived over from dummy-half and Zak Hardaker kicked the conversion.

Salford were forced into several changes, two of which were made within an hour of kick-off. Niall Evalds and Gil Dudson were both scheduled to play but Olly Ashall-Bott and Mark Flanagan, who would both leave the field with head knocks and not return, were drafted in at the last minute to join Chris Atkin, Elliot Kear, Andy Ackers and Oliver Roberts.

Wigan made four changes to the side that won their last game against Warrington.

Sean O'Loughlin, Harry Smith, Dom Manfredi and Joe Shorrocks all made way for the return of Gildart, Joe Burgess, Ben Flower and Tony Clubb, who was making his first post-lockdown appearance.

French's second in the 35th minute was a beauty when he caught Chris Atkin's kick in his own '30' before splitting Salford's defence on the right. Faced with Krisnan Inu and Tui Lolohea, French made his way superbly between the two to saunter over for a sensational try, which Hardaker improved to make the score 30-6 at the interval.

Salford got the start to the second half they needed when Atkin made a break and offloaded to Ackers, who gave the ball to Lolohea for their second try, which Inu converted. But Wigan quickly regained the ascendancy only three minutes later when Hastings, Willie Isa and French combined to set up a try for Hastings, with Hardaker adding two more points from the boot.

Another try came for Wigan moments later when French broke and gave the ball to Gildart on his left. Hardaker was unable to convert from the touchline, which was his only miss of the game.

Sixteen minutes into the second half and Wigan had their eighth score. Salford couldn't maintain control of the ruck and so Powell was able to easily send Farrell strolling over to complete his double near the play-the-ball.

There was still time for two more tries for the Warriors. More brilliant stepping from French, this time standing up Tyrone McCarthy, saw him score his hat-trick before Hastings' grubber set up Gildart for his second try of the game with only two minutes to play.

The night before, the two-match programme at St Helens was delayed by an hour from its intended 5.30pm kick-off time because of an accident on the M62, which caused the Castleford and Hull KR teams to be diverted from the Saddleworth intersection on top of the Pennines.

The Tigers came into the game on the back of a 48-6 hammering against Hull FC four days earlier, while the Robins had nine days to recover from their last outing, when they had beaten Salford by two points at the Halliwell Jones Stadium. But they were without their coach Tony Smith, who had gone into isolation for two weeks earlier in the day, leaving his assistant David Hodgson in charge of the team.

The Tigers ran out 38-24 winners, with a Greg Eden hat-trick the highlight, having a 24-nil lead in as many minutes after Danny Richardson converted four tries, from Jacques O'Neill, Alex Foster, Adam Milner and Eden.

But Castleford lost Nathan Massey to a rib injury early on and O'Neill limped off on 27 minutes with a knee injury. Three tries from Robbie Mulhern, Elliot Minchella and Shaun Kenny-Dowall, all converted by Will Dagger, followed as Rovers regained the momentum.

Debut Tigers prop Brad Martin impressed before his night ended with a head knock but two more Eden tries took Castleford home, despite Matt Parcell getting one in between for the Robins. Eden's third try on 74 minutes, combined with the subsequent Hull KR kick-off that didn't travel ten metres, sealed the Robins' fate.

In the second game, Wakefield ended their losing run at ten matches with a tenacious 18-14 win over Huddersfield.

The build-up to the game centred around a report in the Daily Star newspaper, with an unnamed source claiming coach Chris Chester had lost the dressing room. Gamestar Jacob Miller dedicated the victory to Chester following the game.

Huddersfield shifted Jake Wardle to the wing because of the absence of Jermaine McGillvary, with Louis Senior taking the fullback position vacated by Ashton Golding's absence. As for Trinity, captain Miller came back into the side alongside Kyle Wood, giving them back two of their key pivots.

Wakefield enjoyed plenty of territory early in the game and were rewarded with an early try on 17 minutes. Miller was the key, stabbing a kick through from close-range that

October

Matty Ashurst was able to reach first for the opening score of the game.

Huddersfield hit back quickly, however, through their own captain Aidan Sezer. The Australian went through easily, collecting the ball from Lee Gaskell, waiting for his dummy-runner to suck in a defender and gliding through the gap presented. Gaskell, who was on kicking duties ahead of Sezer, converted to make it six apiece.

Wakefield had conceded often in the final ten minutes of the first half and the same happened six minutes before the break.

Sezer was involved again but the credit went to Jake Wardle, who out-jumped Ben Jones-Bishop and then superbly threw the ball wide to Jordan Turner to score. Gaskell missed the conversion.

It didn't look like that would particularly matter when Sam Wood scored in the 51st minute on the right edge. One-on-one with Tom Johnstone he sent him flat on his back with a devastating hand-off to score out wide. But Gaskell missed again and the Giants only held an eight-point lead.

Wakefield countered quickly. Four minutes later Johnstone got the better of Wood, receiving a cut-out ball and scorching down the wing to go in at the corner. Ryan Hampshire's second conversion meant there were just two points in it.

Wakefield thought they had hit the front when Ben Jones-Bishop crossed on 69 minutes but the try was, somewhat controversially, ruled out for an offside. But they weren't to be denied. The video referee was consulted again when Johnstone crossed for his second. It came after a big hit from Miller which dislodged the ball from Wood's grasp ten metres from the Huddersfield line. Miller picked up and gave to Johnstone to finish.

It was checked for a possible shoulder charge but the tackle was deemed legitimate and, as a result, Wakefield finally had a win to celebrate.

Round 18

Wakefield backed up in style the following Sunday, in their first post-lockdown game at home, when they beat Hull KR by 48-18 to leap off the bottom of the table and above the Robins.

Whereas Thursday's win against Huddersfield had been hard-earned, gritty and filled with character this win was flamboyant and extravagant, with nine stunning tries proving enough to defeat Hull KR in the battle to avoid the wooden spoon.

There was a magnificent hat-trick scored by Ben Jones-Bishop and inspired play from his centre partner Reece Lyne and left winger Tom Johnstone.

Lyne's first and Jones-Bishop's second try were both the result of length-of-the-field moves started by Johnstone on the left and superb handling.

Leading 26-0 at half-time following a dominant display, undisputedly Trinity's best of the season so far, the job felt done by the interval and, unsurprisingly, Trinity did dip in the second half.

But Hull KR, who were still without coach Tony Smith due to self-isolation, improved after half-time themselves - Jordan Abdull, Jamie Ellis and Ben Crooks scoring tries - but the disastrous first half did for them.

Trinity scored four more tries after the break though. Their ninth and last try was in keeping with the theme of the day. Ryan Hampshire collected his chip-and-chase and his flick pass to Eddie Battye was superb, allowing the prop to finish in style.

The day after, on the Monday night, St Helens fielded a shadow team that gave Salford an almighty battle before succumbing to a 12-10 defeat.

Alex Walmsley, who was due to serve a two-match ban (later reduced to one match on appeal) for dangerous contact, Aaron Smith and James Graham were the only first-team regulars in a side captained by 19-year old Jack Welsby.

There were five debutants - Tom Nisbet, Ben Davies, Nico Rizzelli, Matty Foster and Jake Wingfield - in the 17-man squad, with twelve players in total who had graduated from

Wakefield's Adam Tangata leaves the Hull KR defence in his wake

the Saints Academy. Many of them were playing their first game since March.

It turned out to be a hard-fought game that was only decided right at the end when Krisnan Inu converted his own try from the touchline.

The young Saints team started off the game like a house on fire, with the outstanding Dominique Peyroux breaking through the Salford defence and handing the ball on to Josh Eaves for the young hooker's first try for the club.

Lewis Dodd, starting in his favoured scrum-half position, added the conversion and kicked two more penalties in the first half. The first came from a strip by Tyrone McCarthy in the tenth minute and the second in the 18th minute when Ben Thaler awarded Saints a penalty for obstruction.

That ten-point margin lasted almost until half-time but, with 75 seconds of the first half remaining, Pauli Pauli took a pass from Tui Lolohea near the line and carried a posse of Saints defenders over the line to score, with Inu's goal getting the Red Devils into the game for the first time.

As the second half unfolded, Salford fullback Dan Sarginson dealt with everything Saints could throw at him, making several try-saving tackles. But the best chance of the half fell to St Helens' young winger Nisbet, who was put into space by Welsby. But when he dived he lost control of the ball just before reaching the line.

After that, although Walmsley and James Graham returned to the fray, Salford gradually began to gain field position. It was no real surprise when Pauli offloaded out of four tacklers and Elliot Kear delivered a brilliant pass to Inu, who forced his way over the line near the corner, having the temperament to seal victory with his conversion

It only remained for Sarginson to tackle Josh Simm, snuffing out Saints' last chance to win the game.

The rest of the games in round 18 had been played earlier in the season.

Leeds' Richie Myler clashes with Castleford's Oliver Holmes

Round 15

Also on the Monday night at Headingley, Leeds edged Castleford 28-24.

The Tigers played 50 minutes with twelve men after the dismissal of Oliver Holmes. The back-rower was dismissed for lightly kicking Richie Myler in a petulant offence. Holmes acted in retaliation after being elbowed by Myler as he tried to get a quick play-the-ball. The following Monday both players received a caution from the RFL Match Review Panel.

The Tigers had taken the lead through Liam Watts, back in the side after a calf injury. He raced on to Danny Richardson's threaded grubber to score by the posts. Richardson's conversion made it 6-0. But the scores were soon level as form prop Ava Seumanufagai, excellent throughout, scored with a powerful drive to the line despite the efforts of three Castleford defenders.

On 29 minutes came the Holmes dismissal, a decision both coaches thought was harsh even if, by the letter of the law, referee Tom Grant was correct to dismiss him.

Luke Gale dived over to edge Leeds ahead soon after, though Castleford would be level by the break. An unprepared play saw Cameron Smith kick for Leeds and Tom Briscoe brought the ball down. But his offload was snapped up by Greg Eden, who scorched 70 metres to score.

Eden put Castleford ahead with a delightful finish in the corner shortly after the break, displaying superb balance and awareness to touch down while at full pace and on the spin close to the corner.

Leeds then enjoyed a significant spell of possession but were held over the line a staggering four times in ten minutes, with last-ditch tackles and pugnacious defence keeping them at bay. But a score seemed inevitable and, eventually, they breached the Tigers' defence.

Liam Sutcliffe was the scorer, running a nice line that Richie Myler opened up with a short pass. Rhyse Martin's missed kick meant Leeds were still behind.

A big error let them back in. Gareth O'Brien received a kick return and passed to winger Derrell Olpherts but he spilt the ball cold. Leeds claimed it and shifted to the right edge. With Castleford still retreating, Tom Briscoe dived home.

A third try in eleven minutes followed as Martin's arcing run and subsequent conversion opened up a ten-point lead. Castleford cut the deficit when Cheyse Blair was awarded a penalty try after being taken out by Konrad Hurrell off the ball. But the Tigers ran out of time.

Hull FC's Mahe Fonua offloads under pressure from Hull KR's Mikey Lewis

Round 19

Another round was thrown into disorder when both Salford and Castleford had to cancel their fixtures scheduled to be played at St Helens on the last Friday of October.

Salford were down to 13 players and forfeited their fixture with Warrington. A 24-0 result against them was recorded. The Tigers, due to play Huddersfield, revealed 12 positive Covid-19 tests within the club.

Warrington and the Giants played their round 21 game on the Friday instead.

Castleford's previous opponents, Leeds, confirmed their game with Wakefield would go ahead on the Thursday, despite four track and trace flags, which ruled out Richie Myler, Tom Briscoe, Konrad Hurrell and Matt Prior. The Rhinos came off second best, losing 30-6 to a Trinity side registering their third win in a row.

Wakefield came out of the blocks and established an early dominance with two thrilling tries by their fullback Max Jowitt, with a rejuvenated David Fifita adding another and Jowitt grabbing his hat-trick try on the stroke of half-time to give them an almost unassailable 20-0 lead at that point.

There was no scoring by either side during the third quarter of the game, before Ash Handley's try on 62 minutes gave the Rhinos some hope.

But when Fifita brilliantly prevented Mikolaj Oledzki from touching down by the upright and Alex Mellor was sin-binned soon afterwards for leading with a shoulder to the head of Ryan Hampshire, the game was up for Leeds and Trinity finished with two late tries by loanee Innes Senior. Mellor copped a two-match penalty notice the following Monday.

The two sides were due to meet again three days later at Belle Vue in a postponed round 11 game.

Later that night there was a unique occasion, with St Helens hosting the Hull derby, with Hull FC winning 31-16.

October

The Robins were struggling, with their head coach Tony Smith still in isolation. Hull's left edge ran riot throughout from the point when Bureta Faraimo went on a marauding run that saw him bump off and ride a number of defenders over 40 metres. Once he was eventually hauled down, Hull moved the ball to the middle and Josh Bowden dived over. Marc Sneyd converted.

The Robins responded inside six minutes. A neat one-two between Jordan Abdull and Kane Linnett saw the former give the ball to Dean Hadley, who stepped inside and dived through to score. Will Dagger converted to level the game up.

The Hull FC left-edge would soon conjure up another score. This time Faraimo was the scorer, with Jake Connor the creator. A bobbling pass from Jordan Johnstone was well picked up by Connor who, under pressure from Nick Rawsthorne, provided a precise kick to allow the USA international to score in the corner. Sneyd added the two points.

Hull KR hit back again on 29 minutes. The Abdull-Linnett partnership came up trumps again with Abdull's bullet, cut-out pass from dummy-half finding the run of the centre, who had the power to ground the ball under pressure from two defenders. Dagger goaled to level again before Abdull came off soon afterwards with a leg injury.

Ben Crooks dropped the ball on the next set, giving Hull FC a chance to strike. And strike they did. Connor was the architect again, seamlessly joining the attacking line from fullback and putting Ratu Naulago in at the corner for a diving effort.

Four minutes before the break, Connor was creating another try. Faraimo passed back inside to Connor, who darted through a gap, sidestepped another and superbly offloaded to Ligi Sao for his first Hull FC try. Sneyd's conversion made in 22-12 at half-time.

Connor's fourth try-assist of the night came two minutes after half-time. Another cut-out pass this time found Faraimo, who from five metres out put the bumpers up and crashed over Rawsthorne to ground the ball. Hull's lead was now 16.

The sixth try of the night was too easy. A nice shift to the right was easy on the eye, but the Robins' willingness to retreat gave their rivals too much space, and eventually, Tuimavave put Naulago in for his double.

Sneyd's missed conversions meant the deficit was 18 points but within minutes he extended the gap to four scores with a scruffy field goal from ten yards out.

The Robins, whose effort couldn't be questioned, grabbed a consolation try twelve minutes from time as Crooks dived home untouched from Hadley's pass.

On the Friday night, Wigan leapfrogged St Helens to the top of the table with an 18-6 derby victory at Totally Wicked Stadium after a high-octane contest.

With half-an-hour gone, the two sides were deadlocked following 30 minutes of rip-roaring, tenacious and gripping entertainment - until Lachlan Coote strode over.

There looked to be nothing on but Jonny Lomax stepped out of an attempted tackle by Willie Isa and Thomas Leuluai on the Warriors' 30-metre line and drew fullback Bevan French before offloading to Coote, who stormed under the posts and also converted for a 6-0 lead.

But that seemed to spur Wigan on and, following a rampaging Joe Greenwood break, the Warriors were on the scoresheet just four minutes later. A neat grubber down the line by Zak Hardaker should have been dealt with by Lomax but Jake Bibby somehow grabbed it and won the race to touch down. Hardaker's conversion was wayward to leave Saints with a two-point advantage going into the break.

The Warriors were full of vim and vigour and they finally hit the front in the 53rd minute when Leuluai powered through three defenders in a show of raw strength. Hardaker, however, failed to convert as the Warriors now led by two points.

The first penalty of the game came on 56 minutes as Saints' James Bentley was found guilty of interference at the ruck. The hosts had a penalty of their own moments later but a dropped ball by Zeb Taia let Wigan off.

From that mistake, a superb set had the Warriors charging down the field and

Warrington's Jack Hughes looks for a way past Huddersfield's Lee Gaskell and Jake Wardle

they registered their third try with 17 minutes remaining. A suspicious-looking pass from Leuluai handed Isa the space to offload to the sprinting French. The Australian flyer sped around Coote and Regan Grace like they weren't there. Hardaker missed the conversion though to leave Saints just a converted try behind.

Wigan were not going to let this one go, however, and a one-two with Greenwood had Jackson Hastings crossing the line through the left centre after throwing a big dummy. Hardaker, with his most difficult attempt of the night, converted for the first time to make it 18-6 with ten minutes to go.

What had been boiling throughout the match finally spilled over when Matty Lees was taken high by Greenwood with the final hooter not far away. It should have been a red-card offence but referee Chris Kendall sent the Wigan forward to the sin bin. Greenwood copped a two-game ban

Round 21

Daryl Clark scored two tries in the Wolves' 19-12 win over Huddersfield in what was a fourth narrow defeat on a row for the Giants. It was also a second win of the day for the Wolves, as their previous opponents Salford had forfeited.

Warrington had the better of the opening exchanges and deservedly took the lead after only six minutes when Clark ran out of dummy-half close to the Giants line and dummied over by the posts. Stefan Ratchford converted.

The Wolves thought they had doubled their lead on 14 minutes when Ratchford floated across the line and passed to a charging Gareth Widdop but referee Robert Hick ruled that Ratchford's pass was forward.

Then Josh Charnley went close for the Wire but Lee Gaskell did well to hold up the Warrington winger. In the process, Charnley dislocated his shoulder and was followed off the field by Gaskell, who succumbed to a quad injury. Then Jason Clark landed awkwardly and failed a subsequent head-injury assessment.

The Giants managed to draw level with three minutes to play in the first half. Aidan Sezer's pinpoint kick to the left corner was knocked down in his own in-goal by Anthony Gelling and Jake Wardle was quickest to react, collecting the ball and grounding it. Sezer converted well.

97

October

The Wolves were able to edge in front on the hooter. Joe Wardle compounded a fumble in possession by lifting Toby King's legs in the tackle, resulting in a penalty 40 metres out, to the left of the uprights, which Ratchford converted to give Warrington an 8-6 lead at the interval.

The Giants got the start to the second half they needed when prop James Gavet powered his way through Chris Hill's tackle after only two minutes. Sezer converted the try, giving the Giants a four-point advantage.

But they couldn't hang on to their lead for long. A great short-side play from Warrington involving Ben Currie and King saw Josh Thewlis race away down the left. On his inside he found Ratchford, who tipped the ball on to try-scorer Daryl Clark. Ratchford converted, gaining the lead back for Warrington.

And only a few minutes later, when Joe Wardle obstructed Warrington defenders as the Giants came away from their own line, Huddersfield came under more Wire pressure, which resulted in the Wolves' third try. Blake Austin lobbed the ball over the top to Gelling, who twisted away from Darnell McIntosh and did well to keep hold of the ball and ground it. Ratchford couldn't convert, keeping the Giants six points behind and still in with a shout.

But those chances looked to fade when Sezer was sin-binned for delaying a restart with seven minutes left on the clock. A kick from McIntosh was just too long for the chasing captain and, in frustration, Sezer booted the ball away, drawing the yellow card from referee Robert Hicks.

On the next set, Warrington set up the field goal and Widdop did the rest. The kicker then almost got himself a brilliant try after regathering his own chip but Ashton Golding did superbly to hold up the halfback.

BETFRED SUPER LEAGUE
Friday 30th October

	P	W	D	L	F	A	D	Win %
Wigan Warriors	16	12	0	4	389	272	117	75.00
St Helens	17	12	0	5	469	195	274	70.59
Warrington Wolves	17	12	0	5	365	204	161	70.59
Catalans Dragons	12	8	0	4	352	217	135	66.67
Leeds Rhinos	16	9	0	7	349	372	-23	56.25
Hull FC	17	9	0	8	405	436	-31	52.94
Huddersfield Giants	17	7	0	10	312	348	-36	41.18
Castleford Tigers	16	6	0	10	328	379	-51	37.50
Salford Red Devils	16	6	0	10	284	425	-141	37.50
Wakefield Trinity	17	5	0	12	286	455	-169	29.41
Hull Kingston Rovers	17	3	0	14	290	526	-236	17.65

NOVEMBER
Change of plan

The first week in November 2020 proved to be a pivotal one for the Game.

On the Monday Super League's board, which consisted of the eleven competing clubs plus one representative each of the Rugby Football League and the Super League executive, met to decide on Toronto's application to re-join the competition in 2021. By a majority of eight to four they rejected the application.

The following morning, the fixture planners were hit with the double whammy of two clubs having their seasons brought to a premature end by Covid-19, which was experiencing a second wave of infection throughout most of the world. In the UK a second lockdown was announced from November 5th until December 2nd, although elite sport was to be allowed to continue without crowds.

That didn't matter to Castleford and Hull KR, who couldn't play out the rest of the season. The Tigers' next two fixtures, against Leeds Rhinos the following Friday and Salford Red Devils the Monday after were cancelled when four more players tested positive for the virus during the latest round of testing. Castleford's game against Huddersfield scheduled for the previous Friday had been cancelled after 13 players received positive results.

Hull Kingston Rovers's squad was tested on Monday 2nd November, revealing numerous positive results within the playing bubble. Additionally, a number of both players and staff would have to self-isolate in line with track and trace procedures. 'Naturally, the club are disappointed we will not be able to fulfil our remaining fixtures and will finish our season early,' read a club statement. 'However, the health of our players and coaching staff remains of paramount concern.'

Neither club could make the top four and, with the punishing schedule of games, another remodelling of the season's structure was in the best interests of all in the sport.

Towards the end of October, Super League's fixtures working group had begun exploring the possibility of shortening the season and adding additional teams to the play-offs. Currently, there were two weekends scheduled for the play-offs, but five, six and eight team formats thought likely options were all based on four weekends of action.

In the end a six-team play-off over three weeks was announced, with the regular season wrapped up within the next four days, with two straight knockout games between third to sixth and fourth and fifth taking place the following week.

The winners would then face first and second in the semi-finals on November 19th and 20th, at their home venues, to determine who played in the Grand Final on Friday November 27th at the KCOM Stadium, Hull.

The previous requirement for a club to complete a minimum of 15 games to reach the play-offs was removed - Catalans had only managed 13 games. Their round 20 game that week at home to St Helens was cancelled 'with both teams having already qualified for the top six, and due to the imminent national lockdown and heightened concerns over international travel', according to the statement from Super League.

Two games in November had already been played before the announcement and two more remained in place for the weekend after it, with Wakefield to play Salford and Wigan

against Huddersfield in round 20 games. The Wigan-Giants game was set up to determine if the Warriors would finish with the League Leaders Shield, Wigan having climbed above St Helens with the previous Friday's derby win. They would drop to third if they lost.

The Salford game was presumably staged to decide which side would finish seventh and therefore become the team on standby should any of the play-off sides drop out because of Covid-19. When the announcement of the re-structure was made, the Red Devils were level with Huddersfield on 41.8 per cent, the Giants having a much better points difference.

However, late on the Tuesday, the RFL announced that Salford had been deducted three wins following the club's failure to meet the terms of a financial commitment agreed to in 2013.

That commitment related to the transfer of ownership to Dr Marwan Koukash that kept the Salford club alive. A condition of the January 2013 membership application was that the club, Salford City Reds (2013), fund the CVA of the old company, Salford Football Club (1914) Limited. If the CVA was not met, the RFL would dock six points.

On 22nd October a certificate of non-compliance was issued by an insolvency practitioner, leading to the sanction. It meant that Ian Watson's side dropped from eighth to 10th in the Super League table and no longer had an outside chance of qualifying for the play-offs, as they could no longer finish seventh.

The Super League clubs voted against allowing Toronto Wolfpack back into the competition for 2021 by eight votes to four with one abstention.

In the midst of the Covid-19 crisis, Toronto had resigned from the 2020 competition in July after former owner David Argyle withdrew, stating he could no longer fund the club. Unable to play games in Canada because of the global pandemic, seeing its stars left in limbo in England because of visa issues and without the financial underpinning of TV distribution monies, the Wolfpack didn't have much option.

The prospective new owner, Toronto-based Carlo LiVolsi, offered to underwrite the club's losses and to make good the players' unpaid wages. He promised to cover estimated losses of 3.5 million pounds over the next three years. Contingency planning was put forward to complete the 2021 season entirely in the UK. But his plans were rejected.

Super League executive chairman Robert Elstone admitted the decision would 'divide the game's fans' but that the evidence presented meant allowing the club to return 'would not be right for the development of the competition'.

Before the crunch meeting, Elstone had produced a report which stated that running a team in the north American market would be 'non-strategic' and 'added no material incremental revenue to Super League in the short or medium term'.

'In general, the Committee considered Super League expansion in Canada would not make strategic sense unless it was backed by long term strategic and financial commitment by the IRL (International Rugby League) to Canada. In that regard, the Committee noted that the IRL has no strategic focus on Canada, or current commitment to Canadian expansion.'

It continued: 'The Committee considers that it is highly unlikely that operating in Canada will deliver incremental financial benefits to Super League.'

The report to the clubs failed to acknowledge Australia had been scheduled to play the Wolfpack as a warm-up for their eventually abandoned Test series in England. Toronto also sent a 28-page strategy, produced by Canada Rugby League, detailing plans for the growth of the game. It acknowledged the Wolfpack's good home attendances but questioned the legitimacy of the numbers, as well as how many were paying fans, though it showed no proof to back up those claims.

'Our review of the club's recent submission identified a number of areas of concern, particularly regarding the aggressive revenue targets on which the financial forecasts are based. Separately, it was also apparent that no assessment of the scale and accessibility of the commercial growth that might accrue to the sport from entering the Canadian

market was ever completed prior to the club's first entry into the sport.'

Elstone strongly urged the clubs to reject Toronto's application. There was still a feeling that enough clubs would go against his advice but the vote against the Wolfpack being readmitted was decisive. There were four votes in favour of their readmission - from the RFL, Leeds, St Helens and Catalans. The rest, including the Super League executive, voted against, except for Warrington, who abstained.

Part of LiVolsi's plan involved one of his brands, Wolf Grooming, a men's cosmetics line to be launched in the UK, which he promised would bring money into both the Toronto franchise and Super League. 'This brand itself will help catapult the league into a marketing machine,' he'd promised. But he also made it clear that the Wolfpack should receive equal TV distribution to the other eleven clubs, when in 2020 they had received none.

The rejection ended the Super League dream of the Wolfpack, who had climbed from League 1 into the top tier within just three seasons of starting up. There had been a media frenzy when they brought cross-code star Sonny Bill Williams. But that left them short on the salary cap, particularly as they could not stage home matches because of the harsh early season Toronto climate. They had failed to win a league game, all played in England, before the lockdown, although they did win a Challenge Cup tie at Huddersfield.

The far-reaching decision by the Super League clubs called into question the governance of the game, with clubs bound to be influenced by self interest while deciding the fate of a fellow club.

For Toronto players, it was a hammer blow, with little prospect of their contracts being paid, although most of them were fully behind Rugby League's spread into North America.

Club captain Josh McCrone had written an open letter to that effect before the fateful meeting: 'If we do get the green light from the authorities, I would be proud to pull on the Wolfpack jersey and lead my club through the season in 2021. I feared this opportunity might not arise, but under our new ownership I really hope it does, and that the decision made by our fellow clubs will be a positive one. I understand both the Super League and the RFL have to do their due diligence to ensure we never find ourselves in this same situation again,' he wrote. 'However this remains a unique opportunity to grow the greatest game in the world, in one of the greatest cities in the world.'

After the vote, Wolfpack's Australian prop Darcy Lussick tweeted: 'No wonder the game here is 25 years behind the one on the other side of the world.'

Coach Brian McDermott said the rejection was 'the biggest mistake the game has made'. He continued: 'Our decision that was voted on Monday should never have included so many elements in the game, an independent inquiry that wasn't really independent, that said something really woolly with no real evidence...we had a chance to be what we hope the sport would be - ambitious, expansionist, brave and willing to go and do something....if the game is going to recover from this it will take a number of years.'

The day after, the Super League Board voted unanimously in favour of admitting a 12th team into the competition in 2021.

Given the shortness of the Championship season in 2020, the selection process was not going to be easy and at the time of announcement had clearly not been fully thought through.

There was, unsurprisingly, no shortage of Championship clubs, eight in total and Newcastle from League 1, applying to be included, even though Super League clubs had already decided the promoted club would get a much lower amount of distribution money.

Elstone survived a call from Leeds Rhinos chief executive Gary Hetherington and St Helens owner Eamonn McManus for him to be removed from his position. All the other clubs rejected the motion.

Leeds' Rhyse Martin looks to break free against Wakefield

There were four regular season games played in November.

Round 11

On the Sunday 1st November Wakefield and Leeds met again, this time at Belle Vue, three days after Trinity had beaten the Rhinos at St Helens.

While the result may have had little significance on the end-of-season shake-up, the 20-18 win was important for the Rhinos with their possible inclusion in the play-offs in mind. Brad Dwyer was the matchwinner, darting over from dummy-half from ten metres with 14 minutes remaining.

That was the fourth time the lead had changed hands after a nip-and-tuck game which finished with a compelling final two minutes when Wakefield turned down a shot at goal inside the Leeds half, albeit with a swirling wind in their face, before the Rhinos dug deep to deny a David Fifita offload near their own line to claim a much-needed victory.

Dwyer was among Leeds' best performers on the day, as was stand-in captain Ash Handley, who scored two tries as well as creating another for centre partner Liam Sutcliffe.

Dwyer was one of three Leeds players making their fourth appearance in nine days, with Bodene Thompson and Mikolaj Oledzki the others. Wakefield had five also doing the same: Ryan Hampshire, Kelepi Tanginoa, Kyle Wood, David Fifita and Tinirau Arona.

Trinity gave a debut to promising hooker Harry Bowes and there was an impressive performance from young winger Lee Kershaw, including a 90-metre interception try early in the first half.

Catalans' Tom Davies on the charge as Salford's Gil Dudson gives chase

Round 9

The day after, on the Monday afternoon, Salford put the cleaners through Catalans at the AJ Bell Stadium, emerging with a 42-24 victory, left-winger Krisnan Inu finishing with a hat-trick of tries.

It was an amazing turnaround. The Dragons, having not played in close to a month, looked fresh and raring to go and opened up a comfortable 12-0 lead in almost as many minutes and comfortably controlled the first half to lead by 12 points. However, the Red Devils were able to produce a sensational second half to score 36 straight points to turn the game on its head.

James Maloney's brilliant short pass found back row forward Paul Seguier for the Dragons' first try, which Maloney converted. Then, on the next set, Seguier's offload helped Israel Folau break the line on the right. The centre passed to Tom Davies, who stopped his run and stepped inside Inu, making Maloney's conversion an easy one.

Inu's first try, which he converted himself brilliantly from the touchline, got Salford on the board. But just as they closed the gap, they gifted the Dragons their third score. Chris Atkin initially did well to clean up Josh Drinkwater's chip but, under pressure from the kicker, Atkin lost the ball and substitute Sam Kasiano picked up a gift of a try, which Maloney improved for an 18-6 half-time lead.

After the break, however, Salford were on the board after only two minutes when Kallum Watkins brilliantly brought Rhys Williams back on the angle for a try, converted by Inu, as all of Salford's tries were. They drew level after eight minutes of the half when Tui Lolohea's pass gave Kris Welham the space to send Inu over and the try-scorer rounded under the posts to make his conversion a formality.

Huddersfield's James Gavet and Brandon Moore close down Wigan's Oliver Partington

Soon, the Red Devils were in front. A break down the right from Watkins was finished by Lolohea. And from there, Salford pulled away at a canter. Superb offloading from Pauli Pauli saw Watkins over for the Red Devils' fourth try of the half before an offload from Tyrone McCarthy brought the same result for Lolohea.

And, for Salford's last trick, Luke Yates' break and offload to Atkin eventually found Inu on the left for his hat-trick try. There was still time in the final minute for Mead to score a brilliant chip-and-chase consolation, converted by Arthur Mourgue.

Round 20

In the wake of the announcement on the season's restructuring, St Helens scheduled game in Perpignan was cancelled. Both France and the UK were back in country-wide lockdowns.

Castleford could not fulfil their round 20 fixture with Leeds, likewise Hull KR with Warrington. That left two games, which were both played at Headingley on the Friday.

BETFRED SUPER LEAGUE
Final table - Friday 6th November

	P	W	D	L	F	A	D	Win %
Wigan Warriors	17	13	0	4	408	278	117	76.47
St Helens	17	12	0	5	469	195	274	70.59
Warrington Wolves	17	12	0	5	365	204	161	70.59
Catalans Dragons	13	8	0	5	376	259	117	61.54
Leeds Rhinos	17	10	0	7	369	390	-21	58.82
Hull FC	17	9	0	8	405	436	-31	52.94
Huddersfield Giants	18	7	0	11	318	367	-36	38.89
Castleford Tigers	16	6	0	10	328	379	-51	37.50
Salford Red Devils	18	8	0	10	354	469	-123	27.78
Wakefield Trinity	19	5	0	14	324	503	-171	26.32
Hull Kingston Rovers	17	3	0	14	290	526	-236	17.65

Wigan had overtaken St Helens at the top of the table with their 18-6 win over the reigning champions the previous Friday and needed to beat Huddersfield to win the League Leaders' Shield.

They did but the 19-6 victory was by no means an easy ride. Sam Powell crossed early on for Wigan with a trademark try under the posts, Zak Hardaker converting. And the score stayed at 6-0 until two minutes before the half-time hooter when Sam Wood touched down under the other posts for the Giants, after Bevan French couldn't take Aidan Sezer's kick. Sezer levelled with the conversion.

It was evenly balanced in the second half, although Wigan looked like they had scored before Jermaine McGillvary somehow managed to prevent Oliver Gildart grounding in the left corner.

The impasse lasted until the 61st minute when Jackson Hastings burst over from

Salford's Krisnan Inu claims a high ball against Wakefield

dummy-half by the upright to score Wigan's second try. Within three minutes the game and the League Leaders' Shield were wrapped up. Hastings put in a deft grubber and Zak Hardaker raced through to pounce and secure Adrian Lam's first piece of silverware as Wigan coach.

Hastings' late field goal confirmed the win but the Giants - who handed a debut to Irishman Ronan Michael in the second half - now remained on standby for the upcoming Super League play-offs, having finished seventh.

It was Wigan's fifth League Leaders' Shield, the first since 2012.

In the first game of the evening Salford finished their season with another win, this time claiming a 28-20 victory against Wakefield. It meant they finished ninth, leapfrogging Trinity, although after the Giants' defeat and if they hadn't had wins deducted by the RFL they would have finished seventh and been on stand-by for the play-offs.

Salford owed their win to a brilliant first half. Krisnan Inu, playing on the right wing, touched down inside two minutes as the Red Devils moved the ball wide superbly. A similar move saw Inu put clear and he unselfishly passed inside to Niall Evalds, who was in his last appearance for Salford before joining Castleford.

Ben Jones-Bishop touched down when he chased a Ryan Hampshire kick that bounced favourably to get Trinity on the scoreboard, or so they thought. But the video-referee backed referee Liam Moore's decision that there had been a marginal offside, even though the evidence didn't appear to be conclusive from the video replay.

Before too long, Ed Chamberlain hacked on from his own 30-metre area and scored as Wakefield made a total hash of spreading the ball wide.

Ryan Hampshire pulled one back supporting a long-range break by Reece Lyne. But then Andy Ackers broke from half way and sent Tui Lolohea in on his inside.

A half-time deficit of 22-4 looked too much for Wakefield but they managed to pull back to 22-20 with fourteen minutes to go, Kelepi Tanginoa scoring twice either side of another Hampshire try, this time supporting Innes Senior's dash down the left touchline.

However, with eight minutes left, Senior spilled the ball from Lolohea's grubber kick. Tyrone McCarthy reacted quickly to ground the ball and end Salford's campaign with a third consecutive win, while Wakefield finished in tenth spot in the table. They had the honour of playing more games, 19 of the 22, than any other club.

SUPER LEAGUE PLAY-OFFS
Jack's the lad

Elimination Play-off

Sixth-placed Hull FC moved within 80 minutes of a Grand Final - set for their home venue on 27th November - with a 27-14 Thursday-night win over Warrington at the Halliwell Jones Stadium.

The Airlie Birds had won three games in a row to propel themselves into the now six-team play-off system and they bulldozed their way past a Wolves side who, after impressing in the opening sections of the game, looked tired and devoid of ideas in the second half.

The momentum switched several times, with the final and crucial moment the huge effort of Bureta Faraimo and Josh Griffin to push Stefan Ratchford behind his own line to force a goal-line drop-out. From that, Hull earned a penalty through Chris Hill's high tackle and extended their lead to two-scores with ten minutes to go.

Warrington badly missed form prop Mike Cooper, with no reason given for his absence from the squad but Josh Charnley played on the wing, despite having dislocated his shoulder in the win over the Giants less than two weeks before.

For Hull, Jake Connor played fullback, with Carlos Tuimavave moving to stand-off to partner Marc Sneyd and Mahe Fonua coming in at centre. The selection worked brilliantly, particularly for Connor. He played a key role to set Faraimo free to score the first try and then supplied the kick into the Warrington in-goal for their second try from Joe Cator, before Sneyd added a field goal to give Hull a 13-8 lead at half-time.

The Wolves had battled back from Fairamo's opening score, with two outstanding tries, first of all Matty Ashton touching down in the corner from a smart Toby King pass and then when Gareth Widdop landed a kick that was superbly positioned for Anthony Gelling to catch and touch down on the half-hour mark.

Three minutes after the turnaround, Connor drifted across the Warrington defensive line before giving a perfectly judged pass to put Tevita Satae through a gap to score Hull's third try.

The introduction of Satae and Ligi Sao from the bench in the first half played a big part in Hull gaining the momentum. Along with Manu Ma'u the pair ran with real ferocity. Added to Sneyd's almost perfect kicking game and Connor's unpredictability, the Airlie Birds looked hard to beat.

With Sneyd's conversion it was 19-8 though two errors from Hull coming away from their own end allowed Warrington to bring themselves back into the game. Blake Austin's cut-out pass gave Ashton his second of the game and Ratchford's conversion brought the difference back to only five points. And the Wolves were close to taking the lead when Gelling grubber-kicked down the touchline and Charnley grounded the ball. However, the ball had scraped the touchline on its way into the in-goal.

Good footwork from Scott Taylor drew the penalty from Hill and Sneyd's successful penalty made it 21-14.

The lead was increased in the final minutes of the game. Warrington were desperate

and when Ben Currie was pushed back into his own in-goal, Gareth Widdop stripped his own team-mate of the ball. Somehow Connor ended up with it and he simply dropped to the turf and grounded. Sneyd converted and Hull had won the right to challenge League Leaders Wigan the following week.

Elimination Play-off

Catalans were too strong for Leeds at the Halliwell Jones Stadium the night after, winning the right to challenge champions St Helens with a 26-14 victory over the Rhinos.

The Dragons played with aggression down the middle, complementing it with flair and composure through Sam Tomkins and James Maloney. They got themselves 18-0 up by the half-hour mark and with the Rhinos losing props Ava Seumanufagai and Mikolaj Oledzki to concussion, they were left chasing a lost cause.

After just two minutes, Sam Tomkins broke from dummy-half through a gaping hole in the Leeds defence. As Ash Handley made ground on the fullback, Tomkins had Tom Davies on his shoulder and the winger had the pace to score his 13th try of the season.

The Dragons' second try came on eleven minutes. Sam Tomkins was the craftsman again, with a scheming grubber. Tom Briscoe hesitated, Samisoni Langi didn't, and the centre grounded the ball in-goal. Maloney again converted.

Leeds prop Matt Prior got over the line but a try was ruled out, rightfully, for obstruction, Prior scooting from close range, using team-mate Kruise Leeming to evade the defence.

A well-weighted Sam Tomkins kick was wonderfully caught by Israel Folau and, somehow, he managed to keep his arm free to extend the ball just far enough for it to graze the whitewash. Maloney's third conversion made it 18-0 and the game appeared beyond Leeds already.

The Rhinos gave themselves a glimmer of hope with a try just before the break. Liam Sutcliffe found a chink in the Dragons armour from a drop-off play and offloaded to Luke Gale, who sent Alex Sutcliffe to the line for a converted score that cut the half-time deficit to 12 points.

That was soon cut to eight. A David Mead error in midfield put Leeds in position and, though Konrad Hurrell lost his footing as he went on a marauding run across the field, he got a pass away to Gale. Catalans' numbers were wrong and Liam Sutcliffe went over, though Martin couldn't convert.

In the 63rd minute it was all over as Mead intercepted an offload 30 metres out. He went on to sidestep Hurrell and race in at the corner to extend the lead. Maloney, crucially, nailed the conversion, giving Catalans a 14-point, three-score advantage.

Leeds shifted the ball from left to right through a string of offloads. Eventually they stretched the Dragons' defence and Prior put Konrad Hurrell into the corner. Rhyse Martin missed from the touchline, leaving them ten behind with 13 minutes left.

But Leeds, who had been through a gruelling post-lockdown period after their Challenge Cup triumph, simply couldn't muster a fightback. Catalans remained solid and a ball steal on Leeds' '40' allowed Maloney to add another penalty goal.

The passage to the semi-finals cost the Dragons dear. Hooker Michael McIlorum was given a one-match penalty notice for a careless high tackle on Brad Dwyer, a swinging arm that was clearly seen on TV but unpenalised on the field. McIlorum was also given a four-match ban for 'other contrary behaviour' as he picked up the prostrate Dwyer who was visibly injured. And his high tackle ban was increased on appeal to two games, meaning his total ban would be six matches.

Second-rower Joel Tomkins was also found guilty of 'other contrary behaviour' which consisted of 'inappropriate contact' on the backside of Leeds full-back Richie Myler.

Tomkins' offence was adjudged to be Grade F, the most serious, and the eight-game ban was the minimum sentence that could be imposed.

Super League Play-offs
Semi-final

League Leaders Wigan became the first team to go through to the Grand Final after a commanding 29-2 Thursday-night win over Hull FC at the DW Stadium.

Wigan's two changes saw captain Sean O'Loughlin, who had announced he would retire at the end of the season, come in, as well as young half Harry Smith, with Sam Powell dropping out of the 21-man squad, with no public explanation. Jackson Hastings was named at hooker while Thomas Leuluai and Smith made up the halfback pairing. Hull were unchanged after their impressive win over Warrington in the first round of the play-offs.

It was a blood and thunder first 25 minutes with the Airlie Birds in a deserved 2-0 lead from Marc Sneyd's 13th minute penalty goal from in front of the sticks when Smith was penalised for slowing Andre Savelio at the play-the-ball.

Hull thought they had the first try of the game on 23 minutes when Bevan French dropped Sneyd's chip kick and Bureta Faraimo went over. But Sneyd had pushed Zak Hardaker in the back in the build-up.

The Airlie Birds had also showed their defensive commitment when Savelio did wonders to prevent Joe Burgess touching down in the corner and then held Oliver Partington up over their line.

That commitment continued when Scott Taylor and Ligi Sao dislodged the ball from Willie Isa in his own half and earned a big chance to attack the Wigan line.

But during the wild celebrations of the tackle, Josh Griffin made his way through the pack to pick out Partington and childishly pat him on the head. Instead of a handover, a penalty came from referee Chris Kendall as a needless melee ensued.

If ever there was a single turning point in a game that was it. Within two-and-a-half minutes Burgess was in at the left corner after a Hardaker break down the right and six minutes later Smith scored Wigan's second try following up a kick by Burgess after the young halfback had switched play to the blindside on halfway. With Hardaker's two conversions and a Smith field goal it was 13-2 by the break.

Hull captain Danny Houghton had come off the bench on the half hour but it made no difference as the Warriors totally dominated the second half. After only four minutes, French drifted to the right, attracting the attention of Sneyd, who over-chased, presenting Hardaker with a huge gap on the inside. He flew through and sauntered over under the sticks to make his own conversion a formality.

Hull came close to pulling a try back on two separate occasions heading into the final ten minutes. A clever kick over the top from Sneyd to Griffin in midfield saw the latter break and the kicker was in support but he had to reach behind to collect the pass, throwing him off balance and allowing French to cover and bring him down, with the ball spilling out.

Then Houghton thought he'd scored after Jake Connor's kick came back towards him but the video-referee ruled that it had been knocked on by Ratu Naulago in his tussle with Burgess for the ball.

Wigan finished off their opponents in the remaining minutes as a brilliant French cut-out pass for Jake Bibby put him clear into the right corner. And in the final minute, after picking up a stray pass from a teammate, Oliver Gildart broke between Houghton and Sao and found the supporting French. Hardaker converted as Wigan celebrated reaching their eleventh Grand Final.

Semi-final

The night after, there was an even more one-sided semi-final as St Helens beat Catalans 48-2 at the Totally Wicked Stadium.

The Dragons were without hooker Michael McIlorum and backrower Joel Tomkins, starting their lengthy suspensions. But their absence was not the reason for a heavy defeat. Saints were right at the top of their game.

Catalans Dragons' Jason Baitieri and Mickael Simon bring down St Helens' Regan Grace

Like Hull the night before, Catalans took an early two-point lead, with a penalty by James Maloney, following a high tackle by Alex Walmsley on Rémi Casty.

But then Maloney was sin-binned for a blatant high tackle on Regan Grace in the eleventh minute and almost immediately Lachlan Coote was scoring St Helens' first try from a James Roby dummy and pass from acting halfback.

Soon afterwards the Dragons conceded another penalty and two points for not complying with the shot-clock at a restart play-the-ball, only having one marker, and it started to look ominous.

Another piece of indiscipline cost the Dragons dear when Samisoni Langi was penalised for catching Coote high as he slid to collect a kick. Soon after, a nice one-two between Kevin Naiqama and Tommy Makinson down the right saw the Fiji international get the first try of his hat-trick.

Coote again added the goal but, only 14-2 down at the break, Catalans could still get something from the game if they cleaned up their discipline.

After the re-start, though, it was all Saints and Naiqama soon got his second, not through nifty passing but through fancy footwork. Coote beat the Dragons' chasers to gather a Theo Fages last-tackle kick and instantly kicked it through for the supporting Tommy Makinson and Naiqama. Makinson toe-poked the ball into the path of Naiqama, who touched it down.

Coote was unable to keep up his 100 per cent record with the boot when his attempted conversion ricocheted off the upright. But it was now a damage-limitation exercise for Catalans as two further tries increased the hosts' lead.

Zeb Taia patted a pass from Fages inside into the hands of Coote for his second, before Coote and Jack Welsby combined to give Jonny Lomax a clear run to the line.

Coote converted both to put Saints 30-2 up, but they weren't done yet and they took full advantage of being a man up after Ben Garcia became the second Dragons player to be sent to the sin bin. The French side had been warned about the number of high tackles they were committing, Garcia took Lomax out high and off the ball and referee Liam Moore brandished the yellow card again.

In the time Garcia was off the field, Saints scored their final three tries. The first came from a Roby break, with his offload to James Bentley giving the young forward an easy score. Then came two length-of-the-field efforts, first from Naiqama, intercepting a Maloney pass to complete his hat-trick, before Regan Grace gathered a Maloney chip kick to race 95 metres. Coote added all three conversions to make it 48-2.

Super League Grand Final

St Helens won the 2020 Grand Final, snatching an 8-4 victory from Wigan Warriors at the moment the final hooter sounded behind locked doors at Hull's KCOM Stadium.

A minute earlier the Super League trophy looked to be heading in the opposite direction, as Wigan centre Zak Hardaker lined up a 48-metre penalty goal attempt which if he'd kicked would have given his side a 6-4 victory. But the ball dropped to the right of the posts, allowing Saints one last chance to launch an attack.

Jonny Lomax caught the kick and ran the ball out 30 metres. Three more drives, including a penetrative surge from Kevin Naiqama had Saints just about in field-goal range. Theo Fages, who'd already missed with one effort, shaped for the kick but he was closed down and made a dash down the right instead on tackle four. And on the last tackle, dummy-half James Roby found Tommy Makinson, who launched a huge drop kick from 38 metres which headed for the posts. But the ball hit the right upright, bounced almost straight down in front of the crossbar and bounced back over it back into the in-goal.

Wigan fullback Bevan French, who'd been immaculate under a barrage of high kicks all night, hesitated and by the time he had decided what to do, teenage centre Jack Welsby was by his side and pounced to grab the ball and ground it before his feet swung into dead.

No-one could quite believe it, apart from referee Chris Kendall, who sent the try upstairs to verify his decision of a try. Welsby had timed his run perfectly and was onside. He had collected the ball cleanly and had grounded. And his right foot was in the air as he touched down.

Amid chaotic scenes of celebration, Saints didn't bother with the conversion. The Super League title was their's for the second year running, emulating the achievement of the 1999 and 2000 sides.

Roby was named Harry Sunderland Trophy winner as man of the match for the second time, adding to the one he won in Saints' 14-6 win over Wigan in 2014, the last time the two arch rivals had met in the Grand Final. That was a dramatic match - the Ben Flower send-off final - but it had nothing on this year's decider.

The try was reward for a fantastic effort by 19-year old Welsby - who probably would not have been in the side had Mark Percival not suffered a long-term calf injury in the Cup defeat by Warrington in September - after 80 minutes of high-intensity defence from both teams.

On a cold night, Sam Powell and Joe Greenwood returned for Wigan in place of Flower, ruled out with a hamstring injury picked up in the semi-final win over Hull FC, and Harry Smith. George Burgess was left out. Sean O'Loughlin featured for his 459th, and final, Wigan appearance. Saints had an unchanged squad from the previous week. James Graham, who passed concussion protocols, and Zeb Taia made their final appearances before retiring.

O'Loughlin had won the toss and chosen to kick, giving an indication of his side's tactics. Right from Hardaker's first kick-off the tackling was brutal. But it was obvious that discipline would be key. Liam Farrell caught James Bentley with a high tackle after only two minutes, allowing Saints to set up early camp on the Wigan line.

Roby was stopped inches short of the line after a Graham offload under the sticks. Fages went close. French just got back in time to knock Roby's grubber dead before Walmsley pounced.

Kicking to the corners was a key part of both sides' gameplans because neither could find much space out wide, such was the organisation and commitment of both defences. Another five minutes of St Helens pressure yielded no points. French scooped up Lomax's grubber. Makinson was in touch as the ball was moved wide, more in hope than expectation. And then on a repeat set Makinson rode high and batted back Fages' kick and Naiqama collected but was bundled into touch.

Tommy Makinson launches the field goal attempt that led to St Helens' winning try against Wigan

Twenty minutes had passed before Wigan launched their first attack, although they were starting to look the most likely to find space down the edges from Jackson Hastings' superb flat passes to Oliver Gildart. On one such attack, Bentley was adjudged guilty of pulling a supporting Hastings back. A repeat set followed and ended when Saints scrambled to regain Hastings' kick to the left corner.

But within minutes Wigan moved the ball left again and Hardaker looked a certain scorer in the corner. But he was held up by the Saints scramble, with Lachlan Coote, beaten by Hardaker's initial sidestep somehow getting under the ball.

Then a Hastings' clearing kick was misjudged by Coote who knocked on. But O'Loughlin, just off the bench, mis-timed a pass and Wigan handed the ball back on the first.

And just as it looked like being a scoreless first half, Morgan Smithies took Coote late with a shoulder charge after he launched a kick and Coote kicked a penalty goal from 20 metres out and ten in to give St Helens a 2-0 lead at the break - after the lowest scoring first half for a Grand Final in its 23-year history.

There was no relenting after the turnaround. Hastings' kick into in-goal trapped Coote for Wigan's first goal-line drop out and the attack ended when French's pass to the right went behind Bibby.

Hastings' face caught Naiqama's studs just before French was trapped in-goal by Coote's grubber and then Hastings was trapped from Lomax's grubber. Saints looked like they had ended the try-drought when Taia grounded Roby's deflected grubber. But the video referee called Taia offside and didn't bother checking if he had got to the ball before it went dead.

Almost immediately Willie Isa passed forward to Joe Bullock and, on the last, Roby was stopped short by Bullock and French.

But a penalty for Dominique Peyroux tackling Joe Burgess in the air relieved the pressure and gave Wigan some momentum. A Thomas Leuluai bomb saw Fages carried in-goal and Bibby was given some space by French but lost his footing with a chance of making the line.

But within three minutes the same move saw Bibby speed into the right corner after Coote's clearance kick was charged down under pressure from Isa. Wigan had struck gold but Hardaker's touchline conversion hit the crossbar and came out and the lead was only two points.

Saints just needed a penalty goal to level and they got it as Wigan came under pressure themselves. Farrell was penalised for a high tackle on Fages on the 40-metre line. Coote pondered having a go with the long kick at goal but thought better of it.

It was a good decision, as almost immediately Fages was hit high again, on the call of the touch judge, this time by Hastings, and Coote slotted the goal from 18 metres out and almost straight in front.

It was field-goal time, A one-pointer would have been dramatic enough and Fages was the first to try one from long range in the 78th minute. It was too low and went dead, giving Wigan a seven-tackle 20-metre restart.

They used it wisely with O'Loughlin, back on for the last five minutes, leading the charge downfield. And when Leuluai darted from dummy half over the halfway, Fages conceded a set restart for not getting square at marker before Peyroux was harshly penalised for holding Leuluai down as he played the ball.

Up stepped Hardaker to win the Grand Final but he didn't have quite the range or the direction to the relief of every one in St Helens. There was 50 seconds of the game left when Lomax caught the ball by the upright. The first golden-point Grand Final was less than a minute away.

But Saints had other ideas and Welsby was prepared to give one last drop of energy to produce the most breathtaking of finishes in living memory.

BETFRED SUPER LEAGUE GRAND FINAL

Friday 27th November 2020

ST HELENS 8 WIGAN WARRIORS 4

SAINTS: 1 Lachlan Coote; 2 Tommy Makinson; 3 Kevin Naiqama; 22 Jack Welsby; 5 Regan Grace; 6 Jonny Lomax; 7 Theo Fages; 8 Alex Walmsley; 9 James Roby (C); 32 James Graham; 11 Zeb Taia; 20 James Bentley; 14 Morgan Knowles. Subs (all used): 12 Dominique Peyroux; 13 Louie McCarthy-Scarsbrook; 15 Matty Lees; 16 Kyle Amor.
Try: Welsby (80);
Goals: Coote 2/2 *(last conversion attempt not taken).*
WARRIORS: 6 Bevan French; 23 Jake Bibby; 1 Zak Hardaker; 4 Oliver Gildart; 5 Joe Burgess; 7 Thomas Leuluai; 31 Jackson Hastings; 19 Joe Bullock; 9 Sam Powell; 38 Brad Singleton; 11 Willie Isa; 12 Liam Farrell; 17 Oliver Partington. Subs (all used): 8 Tony Clubb; 13 Sean O'Loughlin (C); 15 Joe Greenwood; 16 Morgan Smithies.
Try: Bibby (66); **Goals:** Hardaker 0/2.
Rugby Leaguer & League Express Men of the Match: *Saints:* James Roby; *Warriors:* Oliver Partington.
Penalty count: 6-6; **Half-time:** 2-0; **Referee:** Chris Kendall. *(at KCOM Stadium, Hull).*

2020 SEASON
IN COLOUR

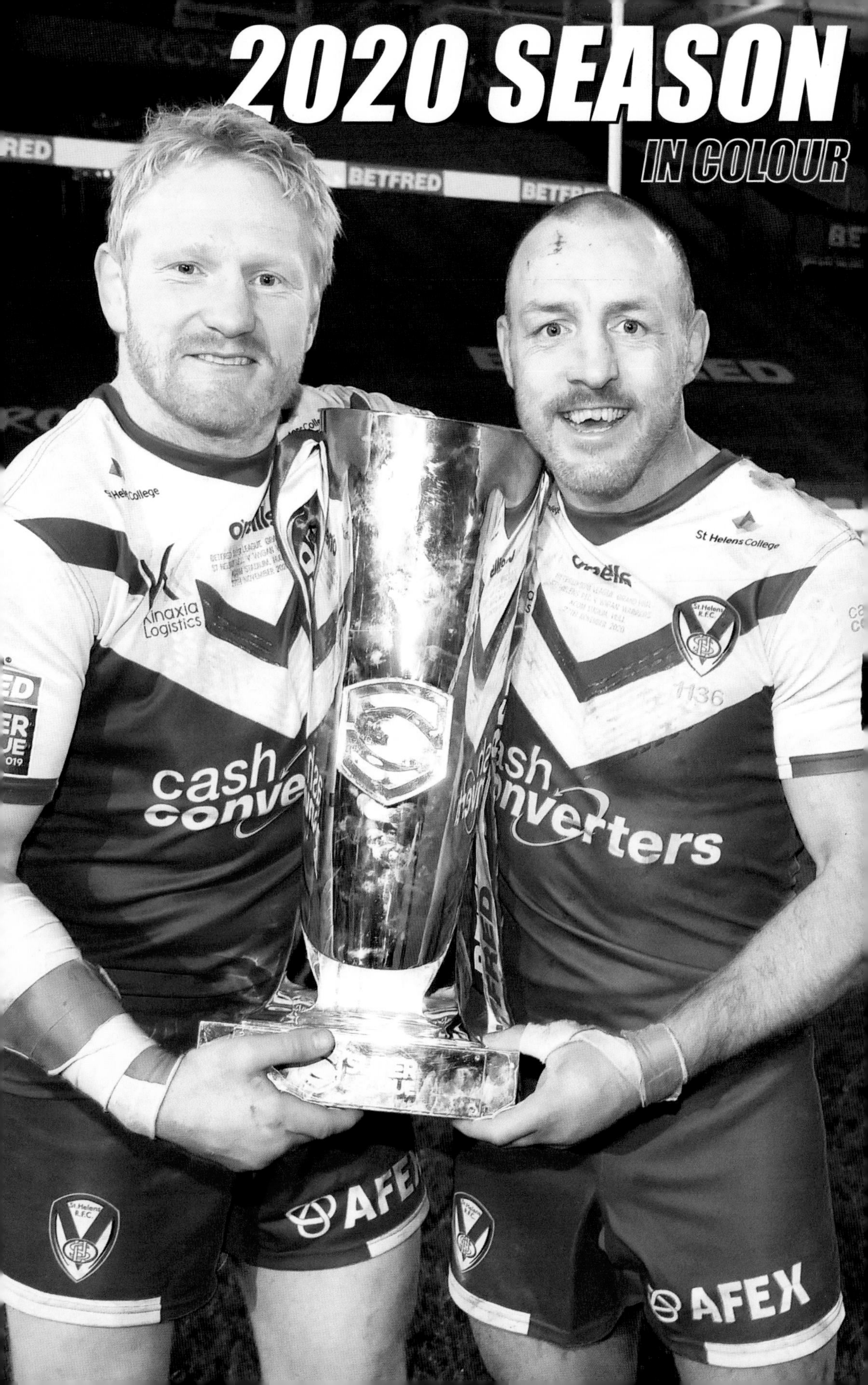

ROUND 1

ABOVE: Hull FC's Ratu Naulago is mobbed by teammates after scoring against Leeds

BETFRED SUPER LEAGUE

BELOW: Hull FC's Jake C... holds off Hull KR... Kane Linnett to...

LEFT: Wigan's Jackson Hastings looks to escape the clutches of Warrington's Danny Walker

RIGHT: Toronto Wolfpack debutant Sonny Bill Williams gets a pass away under pressure from Castleford's Jake Trueman

ROUND 2

ROUND

LEFT: Wakefield's Matty Ashurst ha... against Warrington

ABOVE: Sydney Roosters' Joseph Manu beats St Helens' Lonny Lomax to score

BELOW: Theo Fages looks for a way past Sio Siua Taukeiaho as Angus Crichton gives chase

LEFT: Luke Keary *(left)* and Kyle Flanagan *(right)* celebrate the Roosters' victory

ROUND 4

ROUND

LEFT: Leeds' Brad Dwyer shows his delight after scoring against Warrington

ABOVE: Wigan's Jake Bibby looks for a way past Hull FC's Jake Connor

RIGHT: St Helens' Dominique Peyroux brought down by Huddersfield's Kenny Edwards and Paul Clough

BELOW: Castleford's Peter Mata'utia looks to break free from St Helens' Regan Grace and Jonny Lomax

ROUND 6

ROUND 7

ROUND 2

ROUND 4

ABOVE: St Helens' Lachlan Coote reaches for the Catalans Dragons tryline despite the attentions of Arthur Mourgue

LEFT: Leeds' Konrad Hurrell races away from Huddersfield's Tom Holmes

BETFRED SUPER LEAGUE

ROUND 9

RIGHT: Ben Murdoch-Masila leads the support for the Black Lives Matter movement before Warrington's game with Huddersfield

LEFT: Wigan's Zak Hardaker crosses to score against Wakefield

RIGHT: St Helens' Louie McCarthy-Scarsbrook is tackled by Castleford's Liam Watts

ROUND 8

ROUND 16

ROUND 10

BELOW: Hull KR's Matt Parcell crashes past St Helens' Lachlan Coote for a try

BETFRE
SUPER LEAG

BELOW: Hull KR's Greg Minikin takes on Wigan's Zak Hardaker and Harry Smith

ROUND 18

ABOVE: Wigan's Liam Farrell congratulated by Bevan French after scoring against Castleford

ROUND 11

LEFT: Castleford's Junior Moors halte Salford's Greg Burk and Andy Ackers

LEFT: Wakefield's Kelepi Tanginoa looks for support as Hull FC's Connor Wynne tries to bring him down

BELOW: Reece Lyne and Jermaine McGillvary greet each other before Wakefield's clash with Huddersfield

ROUND 12

ROUND 7

ABOVE: Warrington's Matty Ashton breaks through the Castleford defensive line

ROUND 13

HT: Catalans Dragons' el Folau goes past rington's Daryl Clark

ABOVE: Hull FC's Danny Houghton closes down Salford's Kallum Watkins

ROUND 14

LEFT: St Helens' Regan Grace evades the challenge of Wigan's Umyla Hanley

BELOW: Leeds' Mikolaj Oledzki charges at Hull FC's Brad Fash and Jordan Johnstone

ROUND 15

ABOVE: St Helens' Tommy Makinson claims a high ball against Wakefield

ROUND 18

ROUND 16

BELOW: Catalans Dragons fans celebrate as Sam Kasiano heads for the Wakefield tryline

ROUND 16

RIGHT: Salford's Oliver Roberts gets to grips with Hull KR's Weller Hauraki

BELOW: Castleford's Jake Trueman can't stop Hull FC's Andre Savelio from scoring

ROUND 9

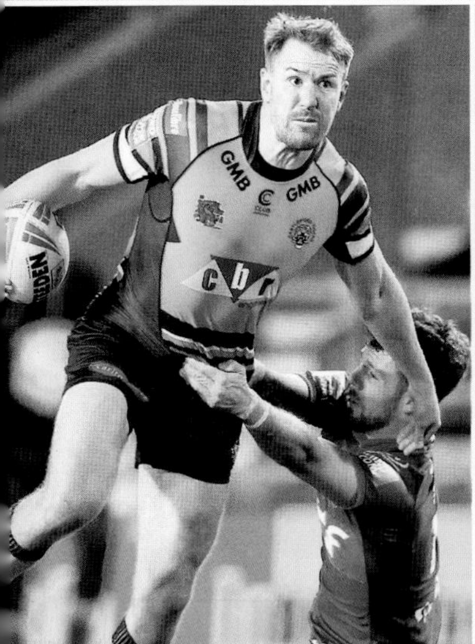

ROUND 17

ABOVE: Castleford's Michael Shenton takes on Hull KR's Will Dagger

BETFRED SUPER LEAGUE

ABOVE: Huddersfield's Brandon Moore and Michael Lawrence combine to halt Wakefield's Ryan Hampshire

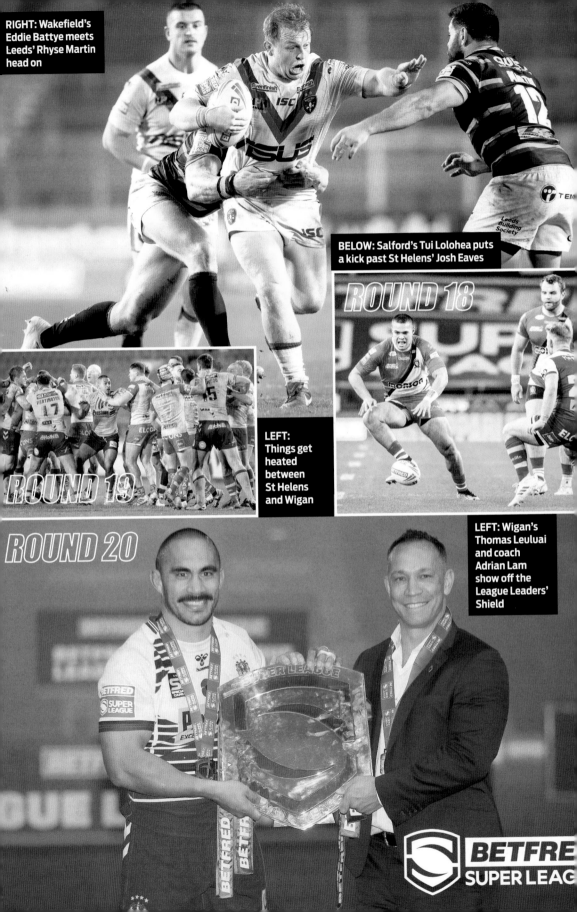

RIGHT: Wakefield's Eddie Battye meets Leeds' Rhyse Martin head on

BELOW: Salford's Tui Lolohea puts a kick past St Helens' Josh Eaves

ROUND 18

ROUND 19

LEFT: Things get heated between St Helens and Wigan

ROUND 20

LEFT: Wigan's Thomas Leuluai and coach Adrian Lam show off the League Leaders' Shield

BETFRE
SUPER LEAG

ABOVE:
Catalans Dragons' Samisoni Langi shows his delight at scoring against Leeds

LEFT: Joel Tomkins clashes with Richie Myler and Luke Gale

RIGHT: Hull FC celebrate Joe Cator's try against Warrington

LEFT: Josh Griffin tackled by Blake Austin and Anthony Gelling

RIGHT: St Helens' James Bentley holds off Catalans Dragons' Julian Bousquet to score

BELOW: Hat-trick hero Kevin Naiqama congratulated by Tommy Makinson

RIGHT: Wigan's Zak Hardaker and Hull FC's Marc Sneyd chase a loose ball

LEFT: Joe Burgess celebrates a try with Harry Smith and Liam Farrell

BETFRED SUPER LEAGUE GRAND FINAL

ABOVE: Jack Welsby beats Wigan's Bevan French to win the Super League title for St Helens

BELOW: St Helens players and staff celebrate Jack Welsby's last-gasp try

VE: Bevan French
ped up by Theo Fages,
es Bentley and
y Lees

LEFT: Jake Bibby reflects on a heartbreaking defeat

RIGHT: Retiring legends James Graham and Sean O'Loughlin meet at full-time

ROUND 5

LEFT: Toronto Wolfpack's Josh McCrone looks for support under pressure from Huddersfield's Sam Wood

ROUND 6

BELOW: Wakefield's Jacob Miller dives over for a try against Catalans Dragons

QUARTER FINALS

BELOW: Salford Dan Sarginson hauls down Catalans Dragon Josh Drinkwater

BELOW: Leeds' Ava Seumanufagai drives forward as Wigan's Jackson Hastings closes in

BELOW: Warrington's Matty Ashton feels the force of Salford's Sebastine Ikahihifo

CORAL CHALLENGE CUP

SEMI-FINALS

BELOW: The victorious Leeds Rhinos show off the Challenge Cup

BOTTOM LEFT: Salford's Rhys Williams away to score a spectacular try

BOTTOM RIGHT: Leeds' Luke Gale the game's crucial field goal

GRAND FINAL

ABOVE: Melbourne Storm celebrate their NRL Grand Final triumph

RIGHT: Penrith Panthers winger Brian To'o looks to break free

LEFT: Ryan Papenhuyzen away from Nathan Cleary Tyrone May on the way to scoring and (inset) shows the Clive Churchill Medal

4
CHAMPIONSHIP, LEAGUE 1 & WOMEN 2020

CHAMPIONSHIP & LEAGUE 1
Ready, steady, stop!

For Championship and League 1 clubs, the season was over almost as soon as it had started.

Only five weeks of the Championship campaign and two rounds of League 1 were fulfilled before the Covid-19 pandemic saw the country enter lockdown.

A number of games had also been postponed due to Storm Ciara, meaning that London Skolars and Rochdale Hornets only played one league game all year.

A large period of the year was spent focusing on ways for the two lower-league competitions to follow their Super League counterparts and return to the field following the lockdown.

However, there were strong disagreements between clubs as to how it could be delivered, indeed whether it was realistic at all.

The big sticking point was the fact games would have to be played behind closed doors. The inability to have supporters at games meant a return to the field would bring substantial costs and no revenue.

During the lockdown, clubs were able to make use of the government's furlough scheme, while overhead costs were reduced too. All the while, they were still receiving their share of central funding.

Returning to the field would have meant taking players and staff off furlough, paying for the cost of Covid-testing and paying for the use of stadiums for clubs who didn't own their own grounds.

Additionally, many clubs were using public gyms, which weren't suitable for return-to-train protocols.

The counter-argument was that clubs had effectively profited during the lockdown and that would help cover the costs incurred from returning to competition, helping fulfil obligations to supporters and sponsors who had paid for season tickets and commercial partnerships.

Ultimately, a decision was made on July 20th to null and void the 2020 season after the government confirmed, at the time, crowds would not be allowed back in at least until October.

As it turned out, the second wave of the virus meant fans would not be allowed into grounds through all of 2020, and many clubs were thankful the correct decision was made.

The generosity and passion of the Rugby League fanbase were then showcased as more than 80 per cent of supporters across the two divisions decided to donate the refunds they were due back on season tickets, helping safeguard their club's futures.

It prompted many clubs to recruit heavily for the 2021 season, though it was still unclear when that would be able to commence. As of November, it was hoped the season

Dewsbury's Sonny Esslemont looks for a gap against Halifax

would start in March, with 1895 Cup matches, as well as a Challenge Cup round, to fill the first month of the season. The regular season had been pencilled in to start on Good Friday, when it was hoped fans would be allowed back in grounds.

The cancellation of the season robbed fans of what was promising to be an unpredictable and exciting campaign at both tiers two and three.

In the Championship, Toulouse Olympique, Leigh Centurions and Featherstone Rovers looked set for a pulsating race for the top spot, all 'ending' the season unbeaten.

All three teams had recruited aggressively in the off-season, with Frank Winterstein, Danny Addy and Brett Ferres joining the three respective sides.

Further competition was set to come from the relegated London Broncos, who had also started impressively with four wins from five games. Dewsbury Rams were the early surprise package as victories over Halifax and Widnes Vikings saw them win three of their opening four.

Bradford Bulls and Halifax both had 50 per cent records while Batley Bulldogs, Swinton Lions, Sheffield Eagles and Oldham all registered one win each.

After finishing third in 2019, York City Knights endured a difficult start as they lost four consecutive games, while newly promoted Whitehaven recorded five straight defeats.

League 1 had far less time to get going but Hunslet, Barrow Raiders and Newcastle Thunder had set the pace with two wins from two.

Rochdale were unbeaten but had only played one game following their relegation from the Championship.

Workington and North Wales had both got their season on track with a win apiece, while London Skolars, Keighley, Coventry and West Wales were winless.

During the extended year of inactivity, there were some coaching changes too. Tim Sheens resigned from his post at Widnes and was replaced by Newcastle Thunder head coach Simon Finnigan.

Clubs started their recruitment early for 2021 as a result of the season ending prematurely. A number made eye-catching acquisitions. Leigh benefitted from the demise

of Toronto Wolfpack to sign a number of their players, including winger Matty Russell, while Toulouse acquired St Helens duo Joseph Paulo and Dominique Peyroux.

Featherstone signed Kris Welham from Salford, while Bradford signed one of the game's all-time great point scorers in Danny Brough.

In League 1, West Wales assembled an interesting halfback partnership in the shape of former Man of Steel Rangi Chase and the Welsh rugby union international Gavin Henson.

Ottawa Aces, set to enter League 1 in 2021, had also recruited a strong-looking squad, however, it was confirmed in November that their entry would be deferred due to the ongoing uncertainty of the pandemic.

Meanwhile, seven clubs - Bradford, Featherstone, Halifax, Leigh, London, Toulouse, Widnes and York - were all invited to apply for Super League entry for the 2021 season following the demise of the Wolfpack. A decision was due to be made in December.

TABLES & LEADING SCORERS

(at suspension of the season)

CHAMPIONSHIP

	P	W	D	L	BP	F	A	D	Pts
Toulouse Olympique	5	5	0	0	0	180	48	132	10
Leigh Centurions	4	4	0	0	0	162	40	122	8
Featherstone Rovers	4	4	0	0	0	137	74	63	8
London Broncos	5	4	0	1	0	120	92	28	8
Widnes Vikings	5	3	0	2	0	128	92	36	6
Dewsbury Rams	4	3	0	1	0	72	66	6	6
Bradford Bulls	4	2	0	2	0	90	60	30	4
Halifax	4	2	0	2	0	82	73	9	4
Batley Bulldogs	5	1	0	4	1	82	133	-51	3
Swinton Lions	3	1	0	2	0	48	55	-7	2
Sheffield Eagles	5	1	0	4	0	60	148	-88	2
Oldham	5	1	0	4	0	46	158	-112	2
York City Knights	4	0	0	4	0	26	102	-76	0
Whitehaven	5	0	0	5	0	54	146	-92	0

LEAGUE 1

	P	W	D	L	BP	F	A	D	Pts
Hunslet	2	2	0	0	0	79	16	63	4
Barrow Raiders	2	2	0	0	0	82	28	54	4
Newcastle Thunder	2	2	0	0	0	58	30	28	4
Doncaster	2	1	0	1	0	72	42	30	2
Rochdale Hornets	1	1	0	0	0	29	14	15	2
Workington Town	2	1	0	1	0	46	36	10	2
North Wales Crusaders	2	1	0	1	0	46	45	1	2
London Skolars	1	0	0	1	0	16	40	-24	0
Keighley Cougars	2	0	0	2	0	20	53	-33	0
Coventry Bears	2	0	0	2	0	14	78	-64	0
West Wales Raiders	2	0	0	2	0	20	100	-80	0

CHAMPIONSHIP TRIES

1	Paul Marcon	Toulouse Olympique	7
2	Greg Worthington	Featherstone Rovers	5
	Adam Higson	Leigh Centurions	5
4	Matty Dawson-Jones	Bradford Bulls	4
	James Harrison	Featherstone Rovers	4
	Jodie Broughton	Halifax	4
	Cameron Scott	Leigh Centurions	4
	James Bell	Toulouse Olympique	4
	Joe Bretherton	Toulouse Olympique	4
	Deon Cross	Widnes Vikings	4
	Jack Owens	Widnes Vikings	4

CHAMPIONSHIP GOALS

1	Ben Reynolds	Leigh Centurions	24
2	Mark Kheirallah	Toulouse Olympique	20
3	Jack Owens	Widnes Vikings	18
4	Paul Sykes	Dewsbury Rams	16
5	Kieran Dixon	London Broncos	15

CHAMPIONSHIP POINTS

			T	G	FG	Pts
1	Jack Owens	Widnes Vikings	4	18	0	52
	Ben Reynolds	Leigh Centurions	1	24	0	52
3	Mark Kheirallah	Toulouse Olympique	1	20	0	44
4	Kieran Dixon	London Broncos	2	15	0	38
5	Paul Sykes	Dewsbury Rams	0	16	0	32

LEAGUE 1 TRIES

1	Sam Doherty	Doncaster	5
2	Kiedan Hartley	Hunslet	4
	Elliot Hall	Workington Town	4
4	Shane Toal	Barrow Raiders	3
	Kieran Gill	Newcastle Thunder	3

LEAGUE 1 GOALS

1	Jamie Dallimore	Barrow Raiders	13
2	Matty Beharrell	Doncaster	10
3	Dom Brambani	Hunslet	9
	Tommy Johnson	North Wales Crusaders	9
5	Reece Dean	Newcastle Thunder	7

LEAGUE 1 POINTS

			T	G	FG	Pts
1	Jamie Dallimore	Barrow Raiders	2	13	0	34
2	Dom Brambani	Hunslet	2	9	1	27
3	Matty Beharrell	Doncaster	0	10	0	20
	Sam Doherty	Doncaster	5	0	0	20
5	Reece Dean	Newcastle Thunder	1	7	0	18
	Tommy Johnson	North Wales Crusaders	0	9	0	18

WOMEN
World Cup the focus

Unsurprisingly the Covid-19 pandemic also played havoc with the women's game.

After a hugely successful year in 2019, which saw Leeds Rhinos complete a league and cup double, with both finals shown live on TV, 2020 failed to materialise and build on that success.

The season had been due to kick off again at the end of March, just days after the whole country went into a national lockdown in an attempt to beat the coronavirus.

Although hopes were high across the game in the coming months that teams and players would return to action at some stage, those were extinguished at the end of August when it was announced that the Betfred Super League season was to be cancelled. The Coral Challenge Cup, which was still only in the early stages, would also not restart.

The year wasn't a complete washout though as the country's leading players did see some action as part of the pre-season Origin Series.

England head coach Craig Richards, looking to build on the many positives from the previous Autumn's tour to Papua New Guinea, named 39 players in a National Performance Squad for 2020. Players from that squad made up the teams in the three-match Yorkshire v Lancashire series.

It was the Red Rose of Lancashire that emerged 2-0 winners overall after winning the first contest 15-8 before recording a 23-0 victory in the final game. The second game had ended in a 12-12 draw.

Those matches were arranged with a specific focus on World Cup preparations and experimental rules were used to try and get as much information on the squad as possible.

Games lasted 30 minutes each half and each try was followed by two conversion attempts worth one point each - to allow the coaching staff to assess the qualities of several options in that role going forward.

Following those games, the squad was split into a 29-woman Performance Squad, with seven of the rest, plus three further players making up the inaugural Women's Knights squad, coached by new Rhinos coach and Women's Rugby League legend Lois Forsell.

It wasn't until September that the Performance Squad got back together. Working through a six-week staged Return to Playing programme, the Performance Squad was split into North West and Yorkshire groups and the players worked on their skills in small bubbles, before stepping up to full contact sessions in larger groups. The whole group returned to training together in October.

'We've done a lot of online work with the girls, but it was a relief to have the full squad and coaching staff together again,' said Richards after that session. 'It has been difficult to get to this point, but we've had great guidance the whole way on what we need to do. The reward of all that hard word was being out there again together. It was a really good session and the enthusiasm from the girls shone through.'

Away from the International set-up, the game was rocked in the build-up to the season that never was by the tragic death of former England forward Natalie Harrowell at the age of 29.

Women

The Featherstone Rovers favourite passed away in hospital in December 2019 after contracting a serious strain of influenza. She was eight weeks pregnant with her second child when she passed away, leaving her daughter Olivia, partner Phil, step-daughter Ruby and family devastated.

As is always the case in Rugby League the game rallied together and an emotional memorial game took place in pre-season which saw Featherstone take on Harrowell's home-town club, West Hull.

Featherstone were hoping for a big season in her memory but coronavirus put paid to that.

Whenever the Women's game returns, they will have some top class support from the very top, with newly-appointed RFL President Clare Balding having publicly stated her desire to help the game grow.

5
SEASON DOWN UNDER

NRL
Southern smiles

Just like the rest of the world, the year 2020 was like no other in the NRL Premiership.

Australasia may not have seen the number of cases or the various peaks of the coronavirus pandemic experienced in Europe but the competition was affected nonetheless.

The season started with one full round of capacity crowds in mid-March, which featured the much anticipated opening of North Queensland Cowboys' new stadium in Townsville. But then the second round was played behind closed doors before the season was suspended indefinitely.

But, after being derided for restarting fixtures on May 28th, initially behind closed doors, the NRL were largely praised as one of the first competitions to restart, with Peter V'Landys, Chairman of the Australian Rugby League Commission and his 'Project Apollo' team deserving the plaudits that came their way.

The team's objective was to restart the season as soon and as risk-free as possible and they achieved that and more.

There were changes to the competition when it returned, however. Now, there was only one referee on the field and, in a revolutionary move, the referee was able to wipe the tackle count back to one for ruck infringements, instead of blowing for a penalty, in an attempt to speed the game up. It was a rule adopted by Super League when it returned three months later, although scrums took place as normal in the NRL.

Compared to Europe, Australia had largely been Covid-free since the outbreak. The NRL did encounter problems along the way, however, with a large-scale outbreak in Melbourne and the state of Victoria. But the competition and the Storm reacted quickly, moving out of the state immediately and continuing to play out of a base on the Sunshine Coast in Queensland.

Melbourne got their rewards with a deserved Premiership, their fourth as a club if one excludes those taken away due to salary cap breaches.

The Storm's sacrifices and hardship clearly made them closer as a group and it showed on Grand Final day when a crowd of 40,000 was able to be in attendance at ANZ Stadium to watch their impressive performance against Minor Premiers Penrith Panthers.

The NRL took their bio-security rules incredibly seriously, with a bubble formed around each squad and, in the case of both the Storm and New Zealand Warriors, that didn't always include the players' families.

The Warriors made the biggest sacrifice of them all to ensure the competition continued, enabling the NRL to honour contracts with major broadcast partners. New Zealand travelled to Australia, quarantined for two weeks, as per the country's rules and were ready to start the season after only a week or so on the Central Coast, their new base for the year.

Without their families, the Warriors did brilliantly to not only compete but finish in a commendable tenth place in the table, even though some of the players returned home early because of the unbearable strain of life away from home.

It was quite incredible that out of such chaos and uncertainty earlier in the year, so

Josh Addo-Carr and Cameron Smith celebrate Melbourne Storm's NRL Grand Final victory

much joy came out of the NRL season. Penrith were a shining example. Their young side sensationally won 17 straight games, losing only one before the Grand Final, to make the showpiece event in Sydney.

Unfortunately for them, they found themselves 26-0 down to the Storm at ANZ Stadium early in the second half but their quality managed to set up a grandstand finish, although they were unable to finish the job, coming up six points short.

A penalty try for centre Justin Olam, as well as scores from Suliasi Vunivalu and Cameron Smith, who also nailed two penalties in the first half, had the Storm comfortably ahead 22-0 at the interval, with Penrith making uncharacteristic errors throughout the first half which stopped them converting possession into points.

Ryan Papenhuyzen's special effort at the start of the second half increased Melbourne's lead further and earned him the Clive Churchill Medal as Man of the Match in the Grand Final.

The Panthers did respond well in the second half. Tries for Brian To'o, Stephen Crichton, Josh Mansour and Nathan Cleary, in the final minute, gave Penrith only three seconds to find one more try after declining the last conversion. But the experienced Storm held firm.

As was the nature of 2020, each team within the NRL had their ups and downs. Here's how they all got on in a crazy season.

MELBOURNE STORM (Premiers/2nd)
Top pointscorer: Cameron Smith (184); Top tryscorer: Josh Addo-Carr (16)

Some things never change. Melbourne fielding a top-quality Rugby League team was one of them.

There was such upheaval and the Storm was subject to more than most during 2020. The first half of the season saw them hang around the upper echelons of the table without being overly impressive. But as the season wore on and ironically, as they were turfed out of their homes and moved hundreds of miles north to Queensland due to the outbreak of Covid-19, their performances and results gradually became incredibly consistent.

So by October, they were unstoppable, even up against the Panthers in the Grand Final who hadn't lost in 17 straight games.

Led once again by their talismanic captain Cameron Smith, the Storm picked up their fourth Premiership after finishing second in the regular season table.

After the final, the question still remained whether Smith would go round one more time.

PENRITH PANTHERS (Runners-up/Minor Premiers)
Top pointscorer: Nathan Cleary (208); Top tryscorer: Stephen Crichton (17)

Penrith were the benchmark for such a long time in 2020. But unfortunately for them, the phrase 'you've got to lose one to win one' caught up with the Panthers.

The Panthers hadn't been in a Grand Final since 2003 and a young team weren't able to turn their seriously impressive form into a Premiership.

But they could still be incredibly happy with their season. They were deserved Minor Premiers, finishing top of the table after the regular season.

And a look at their squad and the ages next to each player made it clear that the Panthers were going to be a force for quite some time. Losing a Grand Final was considered to only improve their chances the next year. The hurt of losing the Grand Final, by 26 points to 20 should help fuel their fire under coach Ivan Cleary, who was awarded Coach of the Year at the Dally M awards ceremony.

The club's top tryscorer, Stephen Crichton, only turned 20 during the latter stages of the campaign and reminded everyone of a younger and slightly more slender Greg Inglis in his left-centre role.

Penrith's halfback partnership also impressed. Nathan Cleary, still only 22 through the season, led the side brilliantly and his partner, Jarome Luai, must go down as one of the most improved players of the season, a good omen for Samoa come the World Cup in 2021.

PARRAMATTA EELS (3rd)
Top pointscorer: Mitchell Moses (127); Top tryscorer: Maika Sivo (15)

Parramatta's season offered so much but in the end produced very little.

You see it with champion teams, they time their run to the final perfectly so they are firing on all cylinders come the big games. However, the Eels weren't playing their finest Rugby League in the second half of the season.

They had the required quality to maintain their position in the top four with some key wins against some of the lower-league opposition but the Finals saw the Eels lose both games and bow out of the competition at the semi-final stage.

They most certainly had the potential to win the competition, as we saw very early on in the year when they beat eventual Minor Premiers Penrith Panthers.

But a combination of injuries and poor form saw them not able to compete with both Melbourne and then South Sydney Rabbitohs in the knockout stages.

Captain Clint Gutherson was the Eels' standout performer at fullback. He led by example. He wasn't above having a cross word or two with the referee but he was an inspiration to the players around him.

SYDNEY ROOSTERS (4th)
Top pointscorer: Kyle Flanagan (198); Top tryscorer: Brett Morris (12)

The year 2020 was definitely a year of transition for Sydney Roosters.

Without Cooper Cronk, the club brought in Kyle Flanagan to the halfback spot to fill some rather big shoes. The young half played a key role in taking the Roosters to the play-offs but by then end of the year he was moved on and joined the Bulldogs.

In general, the Roosters suffered quite severely with injuries throughout 2020, with several key members like Victor Radley missing large chunks of the campaign.

They were still, however, able to finish in the top four and the Morris twins were arguably the story of their season.

Back playing together, with Josh Morris signing during lockdown from Cronulla Sharks, both twins rolled back the years with some impressive performances, particularly early on in the campaign.

Their season, however, came to an end at the semi-finals stage after defeats to both Penrith Panthers and Canberra Raiders, in a 2019 Grand Final rematch, in the Finals.

CANBERRA RAIDERS (5th)
Top pointscorer: Jarrod Croker (162); Top tryscorer: Nick Cotric (14)

The Grand Final year of 2019 was a special one for the Raiders and they'd have done well to replicate it. Nonetheless, they still produced another excellent season.

The highlight was the crowning of Jack Wighton as the Dally M Medalist. The stand-off beat off stiff competition from the likes of Nathan Cleary at Penrith Panthers and Clint Gutherson at Parramatta Eels to become only the third Raiders player to win the accolade after Laurie Daley in 1995 and Wighton's coach, Ricky Stuart in 1993.

The season was also a good maiden campaign for former Wigan star George Williams. Halfbacks have generally struggled to have an impact in the NRL after moving from Super League in recent years but Williams' short kicking game and deadly running of the ball helped him establish himself as one of the best Raiders players of the season.

Canberra eventually succumbed to Melbourne Storm after Finals victories against both Cronulla Sharks and Sydney Roosters. The Storm were on top form in the Preliminary Final and blew the Raiders away in an incredible first-half performance.

SOUTH SYDNEY RABBITOHS (6th)
Top pointscorer: Adam Reynolds (221); Top tryscorer: Alex Johnston (23)

South Sydney took a good few months to warm to the task but ended up being one of the form teams in the competition at just the right time. They made it all the way to the Preliminary Finals stage of the season before narrowly losing out to Penrith Panthers.

Because of their slow start to the campaign, they were only able to finish sixth on the ladder but their left-winger Alex Johnston topped the try-scoring charts both after the regular season and the conclusion of the Grand Final. He scored an incredible five tries in the final round of the competition as the Bunnies humiliated their city rivals Sydney Roosters.

Their halfback, Adam Reynolds, was also in great form with the boot, taking the league's top pointscorer award.

Towards the end of the season, however, some unsavoury allegations were made by the ex-wife of former player and coach Sam Burgess which cast a shadow over the team's great form in the Finals.

NRL

NEWCASTLE KNIGHTS (7th)

Top pointscorer: Kalyn Ponga (132); Top tryscorer: Enari Tuala (11)

A season that once again promised so much but in the end produced very little for Newcastle Knights.

A seventh-place finish was a decent return during the regular season but they were easily ousted from the Finals by South Sydney, despite starting the game strongly.

As has been the case for the past couple of years, Kalyn Ponga is the key to any success the Knights hope to have and 2020 wasn't one of his best years, with injury causing him problems.

A big boost for Newcastle was the emergence of Bradman Best in the centres. Still only a teenager, Best is a big player physically and possesses all the skill to become a quality centre in the future.

It was a good start to the head-coaching career of Adam O'Brien. Up until the end of 2019, he was assistant with Sydney Roosters and deserved a chance to step up into the top role. He certainly showed promise, leading his side into the Finals in a difficult season.

CRONULLA SHARKS (8th)

Top pointscorer: Shaun Johnson (120); Top tryscorer: Sione Katoa (16)

A place in the Finals was a pretty good effort in the end for John Morris's men. Their centres Bronson Xerri and Josh Morris were lost to the squad very early on, with the latter joining the Roosters and Xerri, who would have likely been their star man in 2020 suspended after a positive drugs test.

The Sharks relied heavily on Shaun Johnson in the halves and when he pulled up with injury only a few weeks out from the end of the season, their challenge ended and they were dumped out of the Finals by Canberra in the first round.

Senior players such as Josh Dugan and Andrew Fifita weren't able to find their very best form but a highlight for Cronulla was the form of winger Sione Katoa who quite clearly just loves to entertain, diving in at the corners under no pressure to wow the fans, when they were allowed back in the stadium. Braden Hamlin-Uele, meanwhile, was the shining light in the pack.

The Sharks would have to improve significantly if they want to challenge once again for the Premiership in 2021.

GOLD COAST TITANS (9th)

Top pointscorer: Ash Taylor (84); Top tryscorer: Anthony Don (10)

The year 2020 will go down as a huge success for Gold Coast Titans and their head coach, Justin Holbrook.

Holbrook joined the Titans ahead of the season after winning the Super League with St Helens and, after a slow start, he was able to turn around the fortunes of the Titans.

Gold Coast had been bottom dwellers in the NRL for a good few years and, with a similar squad, Holbrook was able to turn his charges into one of the form teams by the end of the campaign.

They finished the season winning their last five games, including victories over fellow Queenslanders Brisbane Broncos and a massive 36-6 win over Finals-bound Newcastle Knights, scoring some quality tries along the way.

Ash Taylor had a year to forget in 2019 but 2020 was different and his combination with Jamal Fogarty in the halves was a real bonus for the Titans. They were also led ably by young forward Moeaki Fotuaika.

NEW ZEALAND WARRIORS (10th)
Top pointscorer: Chanel Harris-Tavita (62); Top tryscorer: Peta Hiku (8)

The Warriors definitely deserved extra praise after the 2020 season.

With the NRL season in doubt, the whole playing squad and coaching staff made the sacrifice of leaving their families behind and travelling to Australia to help the season continue. With the season done, the whole Rugby League community appreciated how tough that must have been, and the club was awarded the Provan Summons Medal at the end of the year. They and all the other teams gave us all so many great moments.

It was hugely impressive that they managed to secure a tenth-place finish amid all the disruption.

Playing out of the Central Coast, the Warriors were once again led brilliantly by Roger Tuivasa-Sheck as their captain but also had to undergo a switch in coach halfway through the season.

Stephen Kearney was sacked in June, with Todd Payten taking over until the end of the season.

The job Payten did was so impressive, he would take the permanent role at North Queensland Cowboys in 2021.

WESTS TIGERS (11th)
Top pointscorer: Moses Mbye (74); Top tryscorer: David Nofoaluma (17)

Wests Tigers had another season stuck in the middle between the play-offs and the bottom end of the table, without really threatening to finish in either.

The Tigers signed young hooker Harry Grant on loan from Melbourne at the start of the year and that was perhaps the best bit of business by any club in the NRL.

Grant finished the season as Rookie of the Year and was included in the Queensland State of Origin squad.

But Wests did suffer on the playmaking side of things too. Benji Marshall spent his final season with the club in 2020 while both Luke Brooks and Josh Reynolds failed to live up to expectations.

Winger David Nofoaluma meanwhile was perhaps only second to Grant in his performances for the Tigers. He won some games single-handedly, scoring an impressive 17 tries in the regular season.

ST GEORGE ILLAWARRA DRAGONS (12th)
Top pointscorer: Zac Lomax (178); Top tryscorer: Zac Lomax/Matt Dufty/Mikaele Ravalawa (13)

Another poor season for St George Illawarra Dragons.

Head coach Paul McGregor had been at the helm for a good number of years before he left the role in August.

Dean Young did a decent job in caretaker charge in the final months of the season but the club moved to bring in Anthony Griffin ahead of the 2021 season on a two-year deal.

The Dragons have plenty of good young players at their disposal. Not least the pair of Zac Lomax and Matt Dufty. The former was called up into the New South Wales squad at the end of the year after scoring a big proportion of his side's points in 2020, while Dufty blossomed in his role at fullback.

Tyson Frizell was set to join Newcastle Knights for next season, a huge loss for the Dragons.

MANLY SEA EAGLES (13th)

Top pointscorer: Reuben Garrick (98); Top tryscorer: Jorge Taufua (7)

Tom Trbojevic's shoulder injury cost the Sea Eagles a place in the Finals.

The Sea Eagles were flying high early in the season as they looked to make it into the top eight for the second season in a row under Des Hasler but Trbojevic's injury in September saw them slide down the table and comfortably out of the play-off picture.

Daly Cherry-Evans was a good captain but without their fullback they struggled to conjure up the required amount of punch to see off their fellow NRL teams.

Dylan Walker also had various issues throughout the year which didn't help matters.

Joel Thompson signed for St Helens in 2021, a big loss for the Sea Eagles, as was Addin Fonua-Blake, off to New Zealand Warriors.

NORTH QUEENSLAND COWBOYS (14th)

Top pointscorer: Kyle Feldt (122); Top tryscorer: Kyle Feldt (19)

It promised to be a season full of potential for North Queensland Cowboys. But it fell very flat.

The season started off with the opening of their brand new stadium, the North Queensland Stadium but unfortunately Brisbane spoiled the party with a victory against their state rivals and, from there, the club never really recovered.

Head coach Paul Green left the club in July, to be replaced by assistant Josh Hannay as an interim and then by Todd Payten for 2021.

The issue for the Cowboys is that big-money players like Jason Taumalolo, Michael Morgan and Valentine Holmes, fresh from his spell in the NFL, were either not living up to their salaries or were not on the pitch at all.

Morgan was a huge part of the Cowboys side that won the Premiership in 2015 but barely took to the field, while Taumalolo was still important but not playing his best.

CANTERBURY BULLDOGS (15th)

Top pointscorer: Nick Meaney (68); Top tryscorer: Nick Meaney/Raymond Faitala-Mariner (6)

The Bulldogs were probably the one side in the bottom four who couldn't grumble too much about their season.

Many had them down as wooden spooners at the start of the year but they managed to avoid that fate with a couple of well-placed wins towards the end of the season, leaving Brisbane to take that honour.

Trent Barrett will take charge of the side as head coach in 2021 as he departs his job as assistant to Ivan Cleary at Penrith. Head coach Dean Pay resigned in July, with Steve Georgallis winning two games while in temporary charge of the Bulldogs in the second half of the season.

Luke Thompson joined the Bulldogs midway through the season from St Helens after winning the Harry Sunderland Trophy in the Super League Grand Final in 2019. While he managed to hold down a spot in Canterbury's side, he was uninspiring and will be looking to improve alongside the rest of his pack teammates.

BRISBANE BRONCOS (16th)

Top pointscorer: Kotoni Staggs (76); Top tryscorer: Kotoni Staggs (10)

It couldn't have been any worse for Brisbane Broncos.

Nobody predicted the Broncos to finish bottom of the table with the size of the club and the players at their disposal and they looked impressive in the first two games of

NRL ROUND-UP

NRL PREMIERSHIP FINALS SERIES

QUALIFYING FINALS
Friday 2nd October 2020

Penrith Panthers 29.. Sydney Roosters 28

Saturday 3rd October 2020

Melbourne Storm 36 ....Parramatta Eels 24

ELIMINATION FINALS
Saturday 3rd October 2020

Canberra Raiders 32...Cronulla Sharks 20

Sunday 4th October 2020

South Sydney Rabbitohs 46 .... Newcastle Knights 20

SEMI-FINALS
Friday 9th October 2020

Sydney Roosters 18 ....Canberra Raiders 22

Saturday 10th October 2020

Parramatta Eels 24 ....South Sydney Rabbitohs 38

PRELIMINARY FINALS
Friday 16th October 2020

Melbourne Storm 30 .... Canberra Raiders 10

Saturday 17th October 2020

Penrith Panthers 20 .... South Sydney Rabbitohs 16

NRL GRAND FINAL

Sunday 25th October 2020

MELBOURNE STORM 26 PENRITH PANTHERS 20

STORM: 1 Ryan Papenhuyzen; 2 Suliasi Vunivalu; 3 Brenko Lee; 4 Justin Olam; 5 Josh Addo-Carr; 6 Cameron Munster; 7 Jahrome Hughes; 8 Jesse Bromwich; 9 Cameron Smith (C); 10 Christian Welch; 11 Felise Kaufusi; 12 Kenny Bromwich; 13 Nelson Asofa-Solomona. Subs: 14 Brandon Smith; 15 Tino Faasuamaleaui; 16 Dale Finucane; 17 Nicho Hynes (not used).
Tries: Olam (4, pen), Vunivalu (31), C Smith (40), Papenhuyzen (46);
Goals: C Smith 5/6.
Sin bin: Hughes (71) - professional foul; B Smith (80) - professional foul.
PANTHERS: 1 Dylan Edwards; 2 Josh Mansour; 4 Stephen Crichton; 14 Tyrone May; 5 Brian To'o; 6 Jarome Luai; 7 Nathan Cleary; 8 James Tamou (C); 9 Apisai Koroisau; 10 James Fisher-Harris; 11 Viliame Kikau; 12 Liam Martin; 13 Isaah Yeo. Subs (all used): 3 Brent Naden; 15 Kurt Capewell; 16 Moses Leota; 17 Zane Tetevano.
Tries: To'o (54), Crichton (69), Mansour (73), Cleary (80);
Goals: Cleary 2/3 *(last conversion attempt declined)*.
On report: Fisher-Harris (27) - alleged late challenge on B Smith.
Clive Churchill Medal: Ryan Papenhuyzen (Melbourne Storm).
Rugby Leaguer & League Express Men of the Match:
Storm: Ryan Papenhuyzen; *Panthers:* Nathan Cleary.
Half-time: 22-0; **Referee:** Gerard Sutton;
Attendance: 37,303 *(at ANZ Stadium, Sydney)*.

NRL PREMIERSHIP - FINAL TABLE

	P	W	L	D	F	A	D	Pts
Penrith Panthers	20	18	1	1	537	238	299	37
Melbourne Storm	20	16	4	0	534	276	258	32
Parramatta Eels	20	15	5	0	392	288	104	30
Sydney Roosters	20	14	6	0	552	322	230	28
Canberra Raiders	20	14	6	0	445	317	128	28
South Sydney Rabbitohs	20	12	8	0	521	352	169	24
Newcastle Knights	20	11	8	1	421	374	47	23
Cronulla Sharks	20	10	10	0	480	480	0	20
Gold Coast Titans	20	9	11	0	346	463	-117	18
New Zealand Warriors	20	8	12	0	343	458	-115	16
Wests Tigers	20	7	13	0	440	505	-65	14
St George Illawarra Dragons	20	7	13	0	378	452	-74	14
Manly Sea Eagles	20	7	13	0	375	509	-134	14
North Queensland Cowboys	20	5	15	0	368	520	-152	10
Canterbury Bulldogs	20	3	17	0	282	504	-222	6
Brisbane Broncos	20	3	17	0	268	624	-356	6

LEADING POINTSCORERS

Adam Reynolds	South Sydney Rabbitohs	221
Nathan Cleary	Penrith Panthers	208
Kyle Flanagan	Sydney Roosters	198
Cameron Smith	Melbourne Storm	184
Zac Lomax	St George Illawarra Dragons	178

TOP TRYSCORERS

Alex Johnston	South Sydney Rabbitohs	23
Kyle Feldt	North Queensland Cowboys	19
Stephen Crichton	Penrith Panthers	17
David Nofoaluma	Wests Tigers	17
Josh Addo-Carr	Melbourne Storm	16
Sione Katoa	Cronulla Sharks	16

NRLW GRAND FINAL *(Women's Premiership)*
Sunday 25th October 2020

Brisbane Broncos 20... Sydney Roosters 10
(at ANZ Stadium, Sydney)

DALLY M AWARDS

Dally M Medal (Player of the Year): Jack Wighton (Canberra Raiders)
Provan Summons Medal (People's Choice): New Zealand Warriors
Coach of the Year: Ivan Cleary (Penrith Panthers)
Captain of the Year: Roger Tuivasa-Sheck (New Zealand Warriors)
Rookie of the Year: Harry Grant (Wests Tigers/Melbourne Storm)
Female Player of the Year: Ali Brigginshaw (Brisbane Broncos)

the season before lockdown. But after the game restarted in May, they were only able to beat Canterbury Bulldogs once, with every other game lost.

Anthony Seibold left the club late in August after a season of turmoil and will be replaced by Kevin Walters who left his role as Queensland head coach to take up the job.

There are plenty of young players with the Broncos who will hopefully learn from their dreadful season. Kotoni Staggs was named in the NRL team of the year at centre and it was also a breakout year for Wigan-born Herbie Farnworth and Queenslander Xavier Coates in the backs

Too much pressure was applied to Payne Haas this year, the young forward was expected to carry the Brisbane pack.

Darius Boyd played his last season in the NRL in 2020, retiring at the end of the year.

STATE OF ORIGIN
Maroons defy odds

Queensland won the 40th State of Origin series, beating New South Wales 20-14 in a mesmerising decider at Suncorp Stadium in Brisbane.

The series was staged at the end of the season for the first time due to the disruption caused by the coronavirus. And it was the 20th time in its 40-year history that State of Origin had come down to a decider.

The opening clash staged at the Adelaide Oval was a high-intensity affair, with NSW leading 10-0 at half-time before the Maroons gained the momentum early in the second half and hung on for an 18-14 win.

Queensland captain Daly Cherry-Evans was the man of the match while centres Dane Gagai and Kurt Capewell, usually a back-rower and carrying a hamstring strain through the game, were stand-outs.

The second game, in Sydney a week later, saw the Maroons draw first blood before the Blues hit them with six tries, Penrith halfback Nathan Cleary playing a blinder in a 34-10 win.

In the history of Origin, Queensland have never shied away from being underdogs, former Blues great Paul Gallen labelling the team the worst ever to represent the state. Most people expected New South Wales, with a wealth of star talent all the way through the team, to win all three games.

Things looked like they were going to script by half-time at the Adelaide Oval in game one, with NSW 10-0 up, a lead that could have been bigger. But new Queensland coach Wayne Bennett rallied his troops brilliantly at the break, inspiring them to score 18 straight points and turn the game on its head.

Bennett had been appointed at the start of October, after Kevin Walters took the Brisbane Broncos job, his fourth stint as Queensland coach. He had nine players on debut. AJ Brimson, Xavier Coates, Kurt Capewell, who was playing in the centres in the absence of Brenko Lee, Christian Welch, Jake Friend, Tino Faasuamaleaui, Lindsay Collins, Phillip Sami and Jaydn Su'A all made their first appearance in the Maroon jersey.

Blues coach Brad Fittler gave three debuts - Clint Gutherson, playing in the centres instead of his fullback role, Luke Keary and Junior Paulo making their first

NEW SOUTH WALES 14 QUEENSLAND 18

NEW SOUTH WALES: 1 James Tedesco (Sydney Roosters); 2 Daniel Tupou (Sydney Roosters); 3 Clint Gutherson (Parramatta Eels); 4 Jack Wighton (Canberra Raiders); 5 Josh Addo-Carr (Melbourne Storm); 6 Luke Keary (Sydney Roosters); 7 Nathan Cleary (Penrith Panthers); 8 Daniel Saifiti (Newcastle Knights); 9 Damien Cook (South Sydney Rabbitohs); 10 Junior Paulo (Parramatta Eels); 11 Boyd Cordner (Sydney Roosters) (C); 12 Tyson Frizell (St George Illawarra Dragons); 13 Jake Trbojevic (Manly Sea Eagles). Subs (all used): 14 Cody Walker (South Sydney Rabbitohs); 15 Payne Haas (Brisbane Broncos); 16 Cameron Murray (South Sydney Rabbitohs); 17 Angus Crichton (Sydney Roosters).
Tries: Cook (16), Addo-Carr (21, 76); **Goals:** Cleary 1/3.
QUEENSLAND: 1 AJ Brimson (Gold Coast Titans); 2 Xavier Coates (Brisbane Broncos); 4 Dane Gagai (South Sydney Rabbitohs); 18 Kurt Capewell (Penrith Panthers); 5 Phillip Sami (Gold Coast Titans); 6 Cameron Munster (Melbourne Storm); 7 Daly Cherry-Evans (Manly Sea Eagles) (C); 8 Christian Welch (Melbourne Storm); 9 Jake Friend (Sydney Roosters); 10 Josh Papalii (Canberra Raiders); 11 Felise Kaufusi (Melbourne Storm); 12 Coen Hess (North Queensland Cowboys); 13 Tino Faasuamaleaui (Melbourne Storm). Subs (all used): 14 Ben Hunt (St George Illawarra Dragons); 15 Lindsay Collins (Sydney Roosters); 16 Jai Arrow (Gold Coast Titans); 17 Jaydn Su'A (South Sydney Rabbitohs).
Tries: Brimson (50), Coates (54), Munster (66); **Goals:** Cherry-Evans 3/4.
Sin bin: Kaufusi (80) - professional foul.
Rugby Leaguer & League Express Men of the Match:
New South Wales: Josh Addo-Carr; *Queensland:* Daly Cherry-Evans.
Penalty count: 3-2; **Half-time:** 10-0; **Referee:** Gerard Sutton;
Attendance: 25,218 *(at Adelaide Oval).*

Queensland's Valentine Holmes dives past New South Wales' Clint Gutherson to score in the State of Origin decider

starts for their state. Dally M Medal winner Jack Wighton, as he did in the previous year's series, made the switch from stand-off to centre.

After an early wobble, which saw Damien Cook drop the kick-off, NSW worked their way into the ascendancy and fired a warning shot after three minutes when Josh Addo-Carr dived in at the right corner. But good defensive work from Brimson and Sami kept the Blues scoreless.

Queensland responded well and had the chance to take the lead when Daniel Saifiti was caught offside in midfield. Cherry-Evans took the kick but pushed it wide. And the Maroons were punished on 16 minutes as the Blues scored their first try. A swift set saw them motor upfield. Cook put in a grubber kick which ricocheted off Faasuamaleaui back into the hands of the hooker and he swivelled to score. Cleary added the conversion.

Quickly, NSW scored their second. A move to the right finished with Gutherson tipping a pass on to Addo-Carr, who stepped off his right foot to beat the covering Brimson. Cleary's kick drifted wide from the tee.

The Blues again went close eight minutes before the break when Daniel Tupou had

space on the left wing after Coates' slip but Gagai tackled the Roosters star into touch.

The Maroons came out after the break with renewed energy. A dominant opening ten minutes eventually saw them strike with their first points. Capewell pushed away from Gutherson and broke down the left, kicked inside off his right foot over James Tedesco and into the path of the racing Brimson. Cherry-Evans converted the try.

Then, only a few moments later, Ben Hunt's offload gave Gagai space on the right and he dummied and flew through New South Wales' line. He had Tedesco to beat and he dummied, stepped and timed his pass perfectly to Coates, who had the pace to beat the diving Tupou. Cherry-Evans' conversion gave the Maroons the lead for the first time.

Queensland continued to dominate and the pressure got to Tupou and New South Wales as the winger's offload hit the deck and was toed on by Cameron Munster. He gathered the ball and showed speed and strength to fend away from the chasing Cook. Cherry-Evans improved the try, giving the Maroons a handy eight-point cushion.

They needed that buffer as, with four minutes to play, NSW shifted the ball from left to right and Gutherson again provided a try for Addo-Carr in the corner. But Cleary's conversion attempt missed, allowing the Maroons to commit penalty after penalty in the final few minutes to halt any momentum the Blues could generate. Felise Kaufusi was sent to the sin bin in the final minute for a professional foul as Queensland held on for a deserved lead in the series.

A week later at the ANZ Stadium in Sydney, it was a different story as the Blues blew away their opponents 34-10. In Adelaide, halfback Cleary was outshone by opposite number Cherry-Evans. But on home turf, the Blues scrum-half was all over the game, showcasing his superb kicking and dangerous running game.

Cleary was ably assisted by new captain Tedesco - with regular skipper Boyd Cordner sitting out the rest of the series with a head injury – and Cook, who schemed well from dummy-half after spending a night in hospital in the lead up to the game with a boil on his leg.

Bennett made three changes to his Queensland side, with Brimson (foot injury), Welch (head) and the dropped Coen Hess missing out in favour of props Dunamis Lui and Moeaki Fotuaika, both making their Origin debuts. Valentine Holmes returned for his sixth Origin appearance.

Fittler also made three changes for the Blues. Isaah Yeo and Nathan Brown, both debutants, were joined on the bench by Dale Finucane. The injured pair, Cordner and Cameron Murray - who came off the bench in Adelaide and injured a hamstring with his first hit-up of the match - were out. And Luke Keary made way for Cody Walker.

Queensland started the game on the front foot, despite the very early loss of halfback Munster to a head knock from which he didn't return. The Maroons opened the scoring on eight minutes when they found numbers on the right that allowed Gagai to pass to Coates, who swallow-dived in at the corner. Holmes was unable to convert from the touchline.

Indiscipline was hurting the Blues early on but after surviving two successive

STATE OF ORIGIN - GAME II

Wednesday 11th November 2020

NEW SOUTH WALES 34 QUEENSLAND 10

NEW SOUTH WALES: 1 James Tedesco (Sydney Roosters) (C); 2 Daniel Tupou (Sydney Roosters); 3 Clint Gutherson (Parramatta Eels); 4 Jack Wighton (Canberra Raiders); 5 Josh Addo-Carr (Melbourne Storm); 6 Cody Walker (South Sydney Rabbitohs); 7 Nathan Cleary (Penrith Panthers); 8 Daniel Saifiti (Newcastle Knights); 9 Damien Cook (South Sydney Rabbitohs); 10 Payne Haas (Brisbane Broncos); 11 Angus Crichton (Sydney Roosters); 12 Tyson Frizell (St George Illawarra Dragons); 13 Jake Trbojevic (Manly Sea Eagles). Subs (all used): 14 Dale Finucane (Melbourne Storm); 15 Junior Paulo (Parramatta Eels); 16 Nathan Brown (Parramatta Eels); 17 Isaah Yeo (Penrith Panthers).
Tries: Walker (18), Tedesco (23), Addo-Carr (38, 65), Wighton (43), Tupou (53); **Goals:** Cleary 5/7.
Sin bin: Haas (57) - fighting.
QUEENSLAND: 1 Valentine Holmes (North Queensland Cowboys); 2 Xavier Coates (Brisbane Broncos); 3 Kurt Capewell (Penrith Panthers); 4 Dane Gagai (South Sydney Rabbitohs); 5 Phillip Sami (Gold Coast Titans); 6 Cameron Munster (Melbourne Storm); 7 Daly Cherry-Evans (Manly Sea Eagles) (C); 8 Dunamis Lui (Canberra Raiders); 9 Jake Friend (Sydney Roosters); 10 Josh Papalii (Canberra Raiders); 11 Felise Kaufusi (Melbourne Storm); 12 Jaydn Su'A (South Sydney Rabbitohs); 13 Tino Faasuamaleaui (Melbourne Storm). Subs (all used): 14 Ben Hunt (St George Illawarra Dragons); 15 Lindsay Collins (Sydney Roosters); 16 Jai Arrow (Gold Coast Titans); 17 Moeaki Fotuaika (Gold Coast Titans).
Tries: Coates (8), Papalii (63); **Goals:** Holmes 1/2.
Sin bin: Faasuamaleaui (57) - fighting.
Rugby Leaguer & League Express Men of the Match:
New South Wales: Nathan Cleary; *Queensland:* Jake Friend.
Penalty count: 5-3; **Half-time:** 18-4; **Referee:** Gerard Sutton;
Attendance: 36,212 *(at ANZ Stadium, Sydney).*

offside penalties, the game turned as three interventions from referee Gerard Sutton switched the momentum in favour of the hosts. And NSW were able to level the game with Walker's try on 18 minutes and take the lead when Nathan Cleary converted.

The Blues were quick to extend that lead. Cleary's kick early in the tackle count forced a goal-line drop-out thanks to a solid chase from Addo-Carr. On the next set, Tedesco spotted a gap between Hunt and Felise Kaufusi and strolled through it, stepping off his right foot. Cleary converted once again.

The pressure kept coming from New South Wales as errors started to creep into the Maroons' game. And they were made to pay with two minutes to play until the break. After Coates dropped a high kick from Cleary, a scrum play saw Addo-Carr gain space on the right and step back inside both Sami and Hunt to score. Cleary converted to give the Blues a commanding 18-4 lead at the break.

The lead inflated during the opening exchanges of the second half when Wighton got the better of Gagai only three minutes in, with Cleary adding the conversion. And ten minutes later Queensland were opened up by yet another scrum play, which resulted in Tupou flying in on the left untouched. Cleary was unable to convert this time but New South Wales had a commanding 24-point lead.

Tempers briefly flared at the mid-point in the half when Nathan Brown's effort to kick the ball away infuriated Jake Friend and Payne Haas and Faasuamaleaui were at the centre of the disruption. Both were sent to cool down for ten minutes. Later, Bennett criticised the media for focusing in the lead-up on a feisty battle between the two in a schoolboy game three years earlier.

During the pair's stint in the sin bin, Cherry-Evans laid on a try for Josh Papalii with a short ball and Holmes added the conversion for Queensland. But the Blues quickly regained control when Walker grubbered in behind Sami for Addo-Carr's second. Cleary couldn't improve the try but he did have the final say in the game, kicking a penalty with two minutes to play after Tedesco was tackled in the air by Hunt.

The deciding game in Brisbane was Origin at its brilliant best with Queensland emerging 20-14 victors, preventing New South Wales from securing their third consecutive series win. The fact that a capacity was allowed into the stadium - the largest attendance that had gathered for a sporting event in the world since the pandemic was declared in March - made it a special occasion. And the almost wholly partisan home crowd spurred the Maroons on to a win they thoroughly deserved.

Queensland dominated much of the game after they opened the scoring in only the fourth minute but they couldn't shake off NSW's stoic effort which culminated in a thrilling and frantic final few minutes as they sought an equalising score.

The Blues suffered the serious blow of losing their captain Tedesco to a head injury in only the 19th minute and, with only forwards on the bench, were forced to bring on second-rower Yeo to play centre, with Gutherson moving to fullback.

Melbourne stand-off Munster was in inspired form and was awarded the Wally Lewis Medal as man of the series after the final whistle, despite missing nearly all the second game after an early head knock.

Debutant Harry Grant, preferred by Bennett to Ben Hunt, impressed for the Maroons after coming off the bench in the 25th minute and his 63rd minute try allowed Valentine Holmes to kick his fourth goal and make it a three-score game.

Holmes had a number one on his back but played on the left wing, with debutant Souths' Corey Allan at the back. Brenko Lee also debuted in the right centre, with Gagai switching to the left, allowing Capewell to play his usual back-row position. Edrick Lee also made a debut on the right wing after Coates failed a fitness test on a groin injury. Prop Christian Welch was back after missing the second game with concussion.

Brad Fittler fielded the same squad that had seen off the Maroons so convincingly in Sydney.

On the back of an early penalty, Holmes dived into the left corner and grounded

one-handed on the end of a well-worked move involving Munster and Allan, with Gagai the decoy. Holmes converted majestically from the touchline.

But within five minutes the Blues were right back in it as Cleary put his first bomb into the in-goal. Allan looked to have taken it safely to defuse the kick but the ball came out of his grasp, Cherry-Evans hesitated because he was in an offside position and Tedesco gratefully put a hand on it. Cleary converted the try and it was 6-6 after only ten minutes.

A high-scoring game didn't ensue though with some wonderful defence from both sides. Tedesco took an accidental knee from Papalii as he slid to take a kick and the skipper looked highly unlikely to return as he was groggily helped off.

Queensland started to have the better of the territory but great defence from the Blues kept them at bay - until three minutes before the half-time hooter when Edrick Lee benefitted from two miracle plays from Munster. First Munster dribbled a kick through down the left wing, chased, collected and kicked through again, all at top speed, before Tupou lost possession on his own line.

From the play-the-ball, Munster spotted acres of open space to the right and measured a kick. Brenko Lee couldn't hold it but the ball went back to Edrick who collected and went over. Holmes' second touchline conversion made it 12-6 at the break.

Two minutes after the turnaround, Grant made a lightning break but Holmes couldn't control a kick through before the ball went dead. Not long after, Grant launched another attack down the right that should have reaped a try but, when the ball was moved left, Holmes couldn't take Gagai's pass off his toes as he went over the line. But Holmes did convert a penalty to make it 14-6 on 57 minutes after NSW were offside from a ricocheted grubber.

Queensland were spreading the ball with great skill and it paid off when Grant squirmed and reached out to the line from Welch's offload. Holmes converted and at 20-6 with 15 minutes left, the series looked done and dusted.

It wasn't. After a short restart and two penalties that came quickly, Gutherson was putting Tupou clear into the corner for Cleary to convert.

And when Holmes dropped a Gagai pass that put him clear a metre out, it looked like the rugby gods were favouring the Blues again. Two minutes later Cleary made it 20-14 with a penalty goal from under the sticks as Grant slowed Daniel Saifiti's play the ball down. He was lucky not to get ten minutes for a professional foul.

After Walker was knocked out and medi-cabbed off, Allan was sin-binned for checking Addo-Carr as he chased his hack into the in-goal. And as the game entered the final minute Cleary forced a goal-line drop-out for a thrilling last attack.

The Blues' chances of levelling seemed to have fizzled out as Junior Paulo spilled the ball in a tackle under the Queensland sticks. Friend picked up and trotted into dead as the hooter sounded. A 'captain's challenge' went in which proved successful as Friend had knocked down Paulo's offload. However, there was no time left to set a scrum and the 2020 series was Queensland's.

STATE OF ORIGIN - GAME III

Wednesday 18th November 2020

QUEENSLAND 20 NEW SOUTH WALES 14

QUEENSLAND: 5 Corey Allan (South Sydney Rabbitohs); 1 Valentine Holmes (North Queensland Cowboys); 4 Dane Gagai (South Sydney Rabbitohs); 21 Brenko Lee (Melbourne Storm); 19 Edrick Lee (Newcastle Knights); 6 Cameron Munster (Melbourne Storm); 7 Daly Cherry-Evans (Manly Sea Eagles) (C); 8 Christian Welch (Melbourne Storm); 9 Jake Friend (Sydney Roosters); 10 Josh Papalii (Canberra Raiders); 3 Kurt Capewell (Penrith Panthers); 11 Felise Kaufusi (Melbourne Storm); 13 Tino Faasuamaleaui (Melbourne Storm). Subs (all used): 12 Jaydn Su'A (South Sydney Rabbitohs); 14 Harry Grant (Wests Tigers); 15 Lindsay Collins (Sydney Roosters); 16 Jai Arrow (Gold Coast Titans).
Tries: Holmes (4), E Lee (37), Grant (63); **Goals:** Holmes 4/4.
Sin bin: Allan (77) - professional foul.
NEW SOUTH WALES: 1 James Tedesco (Sydney Roosters) (C); 2 Daniel Tupou (Sydney Roosters); 3 Clint Gutherson (Parramatta Eels); 4 Jack Wighton (Canberra Raiders); 5 Josh Addo-Carr (Melbourne Storm); 6 Cody Walker (South Sydney Rabbitohs); 7 Nathan Cleary (Penrith Panthers); 8 Daniel Saifiti (Newcastle Knights); 9 Damien Cook (South Sydney Rabbitohs); 10 Payne Haas (Brisbane Broncos); 11 Angus Crichton (Sydney Roosters); 12 Tyson Frizell (St George Illawarra Dragons); 13 Jake Trbojevic (Manly Sea Eagles). Subs (all used): 14 Dale Finucane (Melbourne Storm); 15 Junior Paulo (Parramatta Eels); 16 Nathan Brown (Parramatta Eels); 17 Isaah Yeo (Penrith Panthers).
Tries: Tedesco (9), Tupou (66); **Goals:** Cleary 3/3.
Rugby Leaguer & League Express Men of the Match:
Queensland: Cameron Munster; *New South Wales:* Nathan Cleary.
Penalty count: 6-7; **Half-time:** 12-6; **Referee:** Gerard Sutton;
Attendance: 49,155 *(at Suncorp Stadium, Brisbane).*

Wally Lewis Medal (Man of the Series):
Cameron Munster (Queensland)

6
STATISTICAL REVIEW

SUPER LEAGUE PLAYERS
1996-2020

PLAYER	CLUB	YEAR	APP	TRIES	GOALS	FG	PTS
Jordan Abdull	Hull KR	2020	10(1)	3	1	0	14
	London	2019	25(2)	10	1	0	42
	Hull	2014-16, 2018	32(20)	9	7	0	50
Carl Ablett	Leeds	2004, 2006-18	238(37)	63	0	0	252
	London	2005	3(2)	0	0	0	0
Darren Abram	Oldham	1996-97	25(2)	11	0	0	44
Mitch Achurch	Leeds	2013-16	25(50)	14	0	0	56
Andy Ackers	Salford	2020	2(7)	1	0	0	4
	Toronto	2020	5	1	0	0	4
Jamie Acton	Leigh	2017	11(4)	4	0	0	16
Brad Adams	Bradford	2014	1(1)	0	0	0	0
Darren Adams	Paris	1996	9(1)	1	0	0	4
Guy Adams	Huddersfield	1998	1(2)	0	0	0	0
Luke Adamson	Salford	2006-07, 2009-12	73(39)	11	1	0	46
Matt Adamson	Leeds	2002-04	54(8)	9	0	0	36
Phil Adamson	St Helens	1999	(1)	0	0	0	0
Toby Adamson	Salford	2010	(1)	0	0	0	0
Danny Addy	Hull KR	2019	9(10)	2	0	0	8
	Bradford	2010-14	49(42)	13	7	0	66
Ade Adebisi	London	2004	(1)	0	0	0	0
Sadiq Adebiyi	London	2019	6(7)	3	0	0	12
Patrick Ah Van	Widnes	2012-18	99	73	56	0	404
	Bradford	2011	26	9	87	0	210
Jamie Ainscough	Wigan	2002-03	30(2)	18	0	0	72
Shaun Ainscough	Bradford	2011-12	27	15	0	0	60
	Wigan	2009-10	12	13	0	0	52
	Castleford	2010	7	4	0	0	16
Glen Air	London	1998-2001	57(13)	27	0	1	109
Paul Aiton	Catalans	2016-18	30(11)	3	0	0	12
	Leeds	2014-15	36(6)	2	0	0	8
	Wakefield	2012-13	43(2)	7	0	0	28
Makali Aizue	Hull KR	2007-09	18(32)	4	0	0	16
Sitaleki Akauola	Warrington	2018-20	9(37)	6	0	0	24
Darren Albert	St Helens	2002-05	105	77	0	0	308
Lucas Albert	Catalans	2015-20	35(10)	7	23	0	74
Wellington Albert	Leeds	2019	2(2)	0	0	0	0
	Widnes	2018	(11)	2	0	0	8
Paul Alcock	Widnes	2003, 2005	1(7)	1	0	0	4
Neil Alexander	Salford	1998	(1)	0	0	0	0
Malcolm Alker	Salford	1997-2002, 2004-07, 2009-10	271(2)	40	0	1	161
Danny Allan	Leeds	2008-09	2(5)	0	0	0	0
Chris Allen	Castleford	1996	(1)	0	0	0	0
Dave Allen	Widnes	2012-14	50(13)	5	0	0	20
	Wigan	2003, 2005	6(15)	2	0	0	8
Gavin Allen	London	1996	10	0	0	0	0
John Allen	Workington	1996	20(1)	6	0	0	24
Ray Allen	London	1996	5(3)	3	0	0	12
Mitch Allgood	Wakefield	2017	6(2)	0	0	0	0
	Hull KR	2015-16	27(2)	5	0	0	20
Richard Allwood	Gateshead	1999	(4)	0	0	0	0
Sean Allwood	Gateshead	1999	3(17)	1	0	0	4
David Alstead	Warrington	2000-02	23(10)	3	0	0	12
Luke Ambler	Harlequins	2011	5(17)	1	0	0	4
	Leeds	2010	1(8)	1	0	0	4
Asa Amone	Halifax	1996-97	32(7)	10	0	0	40
Kyle Amor	St Helens	2014-16	100(68)	17	0	0	68
	Wakefield	2011-13	51(23)	9	0	0	36
	Leeds	2010	(3)	0	0	0	0
Thibaut Ancely	Catalans	2011	(2)	0	0	0	0
Grant Anderson	Castleford	1996-97	15(6)	3	0	0	12
Louis Anderson	Catalans	2012-18	86(41)	32	0	0	128
	Warrington	2008-11	92	18	0	0	72
Paul Anderson	St Helens	2005-06	48(5)	7	1	0	30
	Bradford	1997-2004	74(104)	30	0	0	120
	Halifax	1996	5(1)	1	0	0	4
Paul Anderson	Sheffield	1999	3(7)	1	0	0	4
	St Helens	1996-98	2(28)	4	1	0	18
Scott Anderson	Wakefield	2014-16	25(18)	2	0	0	8
Vinnie Anderson	Salford	2011-12	33(3)	14	0	0	56
	Warrington	2007-10	57(19)	22	0	0	88
	St Helens	2005-06	28(14)	17	0	0	68
Phil Anderton	St Helens	2004	1	0	0	0	0
Chris Annakin	Wakefield	2013-19	7(62)	1	0	0	4
Eric Anselme	Leeds	2008	2(2)	2	0	0	8
	Halifax	1997	(2)	0	0	0	0
Mark Applegarth	Wakefield	2004-07	20(5)	3	0	0	12
Graham Appo	Warrington	2002-05	60(13)	35	80	0	300
	Huddersfield	2001	7	4	0	0	16
Guy Armitage	London	2019	(2)	0	0	0	0
Anthony Armour	London	2005	11(7)	1	0	0	4
Colin Armstrong	Workington	1996	11(2)	1	0	0	4
Tom Armstrong	Widnes	2017	11	1	0	0	4
	St Helens	2009-11	10(5)	9	0	0	36
Richard Armswood	Workington	1996	5(1)	1	0	0	4
Danny Arnold	Salford	2001-02	26(13)	13	0	0	52
	Huddersfield	1998-2000	55(7)	26	0	0	104
	Castleford	2000	(4)	0	0	0	0
	St Helens	1996-97	40(1)	33	0	0	132
Tinirau Arona	Wakefield	2016-20	73(37)	6	0	0	24
Joe Arundel	Wakefield	2015-20	73(9)	20	4	0	88
	Bradford	2014	9(3)	5	0	0	20
	Hull	2013-14	16	7	1	0	30
	Castleford	2008, 2010-12	35(4)	14	2	0	60
Craig Ashall	St Helens	2006	1	1	0	0	4
Olly Ashall-Bott	Salford	2020	3	1	0	0	4
	Widnes	2018	5	1	0	0	4
Nathan Ashe	St Helens	2011-13	6(4)	0	0	0	0
Chris Ashton	Wigan	2005-07	44(2)	25	2	0	104
Matty Ashton	Warrington	2020	8(3)	9	0	0	36
Matty Ashurst	Wakefield	2015-20	109(4)	18	0	0	72
	Salford	2012-14	65(7)	11	0	0	44
	St Helens	2009-11	12(39)	8	0	0	32
Jack Ashworth	St Helens	2015-16, 2018-20	6(37)	4	0	0	16
Roy Asotasi	Warrington	2014-15	16(37)	5	1	0	22
Connor Aspey	Salford	2020	(1)	0	0	0	0
Peter Aspinall	Huddersfield	2013	1(1)	0	0	0	0
Martin Aspinwall	Hull	2012	12(15)	0	0	0	0
	Castleford	2011	12(6)	2	0	0	8
	Huddersfield	2006-10	72(8)	22	0	0	88
	Wigan	2001-05	85(13)	27	0	0	108
Cory Aston	Castleford	2019	8	3	0	0	12
Mark Aston	Sheffield	1996-99	67(6)	6	243	6	516
Paul Atcheson	Widnes	2002-04	16(35)	4	0	0	16
	St Helens	1998-2000	58(4)	18	0	0	72
	Oldham	1996-97	40	21	0	0	84
Chris Atkin	Salford	2020	10(1)	2	0	0	8
	Hull KR	2018-19	28(20)	7	1	3	33
David Atkins	Huddersfield	2001	26(1)	4	0	0	16
Jordan Atkins	London	2014	13(1)	4	0	0	16
Ryan Atkins	Wakefield	2006-09, 2019-20	90(2)	47	0	0	188
	Warrington	2010-19	235(2)	139	0	0	556
Josh Atkinson	Castleford	2012	2	0	0	0	0
Brad Attwood	Halifax	2003	(3)	0	0	0	0
Blake Austin	Warrington	2019-20	43	25	0	5	105
Yusuf Aydin	Wakefield	2020	1(2)	0	0	0	0
Warren Ayres	Salford	1999	2(9)	1	2	0	8
Jerome Azema	Paris	1997	(1)	0	0	0	0
Marcus Bai	Bradford	2006	24	9	0	0	36
	Leeds	2004-05	57	42	0	0	168
David Baildon	Hull	1998-99	26(2)	4	0	0	16
Jean-Philippe Baile	Catalans	2008-14	62(16)	23	0	0	92
Andy Bailey	Hull	2004-05	2(8)	1	0	0	4
Chris Bailey	Huddersfield	2014-15	17(17)	5	0	0	20
	London	2012-13	41	14	0	0	56
	Harlequins	2011	24	3	0	0	12
Connor Bailey	Wakefield	2020	3(2)	0	0	0	0
Julian Bailey	Huddersfield	2003-04	47	13	0	0	52
Phil Bailey	Wigan	2007-10	84(4)	13	0	0	52
Ricky Bailey	St Helens	2015, 2017	2	0	0	0	0
Ryan Bailey	Warrington	2016	1(11)	0	0	0	0
	Castleford	2015	3(2)	0	0	0	0
	Hull KR	2015	(1)	1	0	0	4
	Leeds	2002-14	171(102)	17	0	0	68
Jason Baitieri	Catalans	2011-20	135(79)	20	0	0	80
Simon Baldwin	Salford	2004-06	20(29)	3	0	0	12
	Sheffield	1999	7(15)	2	0	0	8
	Halifax	1996-98	41(15)	16	0	1	65
Jordan Baldwinson	Wakefield	2018	(4)	0	0	0	0
	Leeds	2013, 2016-17	4(9)	1	0	0	4
	Bradford	2014	2(4)	0	0	0	0
Rob Ball	Wigan	1998-2000	3(4)	0	0	0	0
Paul Ballard	Celtic	2009	2	0	0	0	0
	Widnes	2005	3(1)	2	0	0	8
Darren Bamford	Salford	2005	2(1)	0	0	0	0
Michael Banks	Bradford	1998	(1)	0	0	0	0
Steve Bannister	Harlequins	2007	(6)	0	0	0	0
	St Helens	2006-07	(3)	0	0	0	0
Frederic Banquet	Paris	1996	16(2)	7	4	0	36
Ben Barba	St Helens	2017-18	31	31	0	0	124
Lee Bardauskas	Castleford	1996-97	(2)	0	0	0	0
Harry Bardle	Hull KR	2019	(1)	0	0	0	0
Craig Barker	Workington	1996	(2)	0	0	0	0
Dwayne Barker	Harlequins	2008	5(5)	1	0	0	4
	London	2004	3	1	0	0	4
	Hull	2003	(1)	0	0	0	0

PLAYER	CLUB	YEAR	APP	TRIES	GOALS	FG	PTS
Mark Barlow	Wakefield	2002	(1)	0	0	0	0
Danny Barnes	Halifax	1999	2	0	0	0	0
Richie Barnett	Salford	2007	7	4	0	0	16
	Warrington	2006-07	26(10)	15	0	0	60
	Hull	2004-05	21(5)	21	0	0	84
	Widnes	2005	4	2	0	0	8
Richie Barnett	Hull	2003-04	31(1)	17	0	0	68
	London	2001-02	31(4)	13	0	0	52
David Barnhill	Leeds	2000	20(8)	5	0	0	20
Trent Barrett	Wigan	2007-08	53(1)	22	0	4	92
Paul Barrow	Warrington	1996-97	1(10)	1	0	0	4
Scott Barrow	St Helens	1997-2000	9(13)	1	0	0	4
Steve Barrow	London	2000	2	0	0	0	0
	Hull	1998-99	4(17)	1	0	0	4
	Wigan	1996	(8)	3	0	0	12
William Barthau	Catalans	2010, 2012-14	13(3)	2	15	0	38
Ben Barton	Huddersfield	1998	1(6)	1	0	0	4
Danny Barton	Salford	2001	1	0	0	0	0
Wayne Bartrim	Castleford	2002-03	41(2)	9	157	0	350
Greg Barwick	London	1996-97	30(4)	21	110	2	306
David Bastian	Halifax	1996	(2)	0	0	0	0
James Batchelor	Wakefield	2016-20	32(16)	6	13	0	50
Joe Batchelor	St Helens	2019-20	3(5)	0	0	0	0
Ashley Bateman	Celtic	2009	1	0	0	0	0
John Bateman	Wigan	2014-18	110(8)	31	0	0	124
	Bradford	2011-13	25(5)	7	0	0	28
David Bates	Castleford	2001-02	(4)	0	0	0	0
	Warrington	2001	1(2)	0	0	0	0
Sam Bates	Bradford	2014	(2)	0	0	0	0
Nathan Batty	Wakefield	2001	1(1)	0	0	0	0
Eddie Battye	Wakefield	2020	2(6)	1	0	0	4
	London	2019	19(10)	3	0	0	12
Andreas Bauer	Hull KR	2007	10(2)	5	0	0	20
Russell Bawden	London	1996-97, 2002-04	50(49)	15	0	0	60
Neil Baxter	Salford	2001	1	0	0	0	0
Neil Baynes	Salford	1999-2002, 2004	84(19)	10	0	0	40
	Wigan	1996-98	(10)	1	0	0	4
Chris Beasley	Celtic	2009	15(5)	2	0	0	8
Chris Beattie	Catalans	2006	22(5)	3	0	0	12
Richard Beaumont	Hull KR	2011-13	1(16)	1	0	0	4
Robbie Beazley	London	1997-99	48(15)	13	0	0	52
Robbie Beckett	Halifax	2002	27	15	0	0	60
Matty Beharrell	Hull KR	2013	1	0	0	0	0
Dean Bell	Leeds	1996	1	1	0	0	4
Ian Bell	Hull	2003	(1)	0	0	0	0
Mark Bell	Wigan	1998	22	12	0	0	48
Paul Bell	Leeds	2000	1	0	0	0	0
Steven Bell	Catalans	2009-10	43	14	0	0	56
Troy Bellamy	Paris	1997	5(10)	2	0	0	8
Adrian Belle	Huddersfield	1998	10(2)	0	0	0	0
	Oldham	1996	19	8	0	0	32
Lambert Belmas	Catalans	2017-20	3(11)	0	0	0	0
Jamie Benn	Castleford	1998, 2000	3(8)	1	15	0	34
Andy Bennett	Warrington	1996	6(5)	1	0	0	4
Mike Bennett	St Helens	2000-08	74(70)	15	0	0	60
Gavin Bennion	Salford	2018	1(1)	0	0	0	0
Andrew Bentley	Catalans	2007-10	9(15)	1	0	0	4
James Bentley	St Helens	2018-20	24(12)	7	0	0	28
John Bentley	Huddersfield	1999	13(4)	3	0	0	12
	Halifax	1996, 1998	22(3)	24	0	0	96
Kane Bentley	Catalans	2007-10	11(19)	5	0	0	20
Phil Bergman	Paris	1997	20(1)	14	0	0	56
Shaun Berrigan	Hull	2008-10	60(8)	12	0	0	48
Joe Berry	Huddersfield	1998-99	25(14)	3	0	0	12
David Berthezene	Salford	2007	9(1)	0	0	0	0
	Catalans	2006-07	5(14)	0	0	0	0
Colin Best	Hull	2003-04	57	34	0	0	136
Roger Best	London	1997-98	1(5)	1	0	0	4
Bob Beswick	Wigan	2004-05	5(14)	2	0	0	8
Monty Betham	Wakefield	2006	26	2	0	0	8
Mike Bethwaite	Workington	1996	17(3)	1	0	0	4
Denis Betts	Wigan	1998-2001	82(24)	33	0	0	132
Cliff Beverley	Salford	2004-05	47(1)	14	0	0	56
Kyle Bibb	Wakefield	2008-10	1(24)	0	0	0	0
	Harlequins	2010	(2)	0	0	0	0
	Hull KR	2009	(2)	0	0	0	0
Jake Bibby	Wigan	2020	18	5	0	0	20
	Salford	2016-19	65(3)	32	0	0	128
Adam Bibey	Widnes	2004	(1)	0	0	0	0
Ricky Bibey	Wakefield	2007-09	32(25)	1	0	0	4
	St Helens	2004	4(14)	0	0	0	0
	Wigan	2001-03	5(29)	0	0	0	0
Lewis Bienek	Hull	2018, 2020	(8)	0	0	0	0
Chris Birchall	Halifax	2002-03	24(22)	4	0	0	16
	Bradford	2000	(1)	0	0	0	0

PLAYER	CLUB	YEAR	APP	TRIES	GOALS	FG	PTS
Deon Bird	Castleford	2006	17(6)	5	0	0	20
	Widnes	2003-04	39(6)	9	0	0	36
	Wakefield	2002	10(1)	1	0	0	4
	Hull	2000-02	37(22)	20	0	0	80
	Gateshead	1999	19(3)	13	0	0	52
	Paris	1996-97	30	12	2	0	52
Greg Bird	Catalans	2009, 2017-19	68(6)	11	3	0	50
Mike Bishay	London	2013-14	7(11)	2	2	0	12
Nathan Blacklock	Hull	2005-06	44(3)	33	0	0	132
Ben Blackmore	Huddersfield	2013-14	3	4	0	0	16
	Castleford	2012	1	0	0	0	0
Richie Blackmore	Leeds	1997-2000	63	25	0	0	100
Anthony Blackwood							
	Crusaders	2010	1	0	0	0	0
	Celtic	2009	25	5	0	0	20
Jack Blagbrough	Huddersfield	2013	(1)	0	0	0	0
Cheyse Blair	Castleford	2019-20	28(1)	7	0	0	28
Maurice Blair	Hull KR	2015-16, 2018	62(3)	10	1	0	42
Luke Blake	Wakefield	2009	(2)	0	0	0	0
Matthew Blake	Wakefield	2003-04	1(5)	0	0	0	0
Steve Blakeley	Salford	1997-2002	103(5)	26	241	2	588
	Warrington	2000	4(3)	1	9	0	22
Richard Blakeway	Castleford	2002-04	1(14)	0	0	0	0
Damien Blanch	Catalans	2011-13	70	42	0	0	168
	Wakefield	2008-10	44(3)	31	0	0	124
	Castleford	2006	3(2)	0	0	0	0
Matt Blaymire	Wakefield	2007-11	96(3)	26	0	1	105
Ian Blease	Salford	1997	(1)	0	0	0	0
Jamie Bloem	Huddersfield	2003	18(4)	3	11	0	34
	Halifax	1998-2002	82(25)	25	100	2	302
Vea Bloomfield	Paris	1996	4(14)	3	0	0	12
Matty Blythe	Warrington	2007-12, 2017	30(28)	12	0	0	48
	Bradford	2013-14	24(6)	8	0	0	32
Ben Bolger	London	2012	2(7)	1	0	0	4
	Harlequins	2010-11	4(15)	0	0	0	0
Pascal Bomati	Paris	1996	17(1)	10	0	0	40
Simon Booth	Hull	1998-99	5(9)	2	0	0	8
	St Helens	1996-97	10(4)	1	0	0	4
Steve Booth	Huddersfield	1998-99	16(4)	2	3	0	14
Alan Boothroyd	Halifax	1997	2(3)	0	0	0	0
Thomas Bosc	Catalans	2006-17	199(21)	48	483	12	1170
John Boslem	Paris	1996	(5)	0	0	0	0
Liam Bostock	St Helens	2004	1	0	0	0	0
Liam Botham	Wigan	2005	5	0	0	0	0
	Leeds	2003-05	2(11)	4	0	0	16
	London	2004	6(2)	3	7	0	26
Frano Botica	Castleford	1996	21	5	84	2	190
Matthew Bottom	Leigh	2005	(1)	0	0	0	0
Hadj Boudebza	Paris	1996	(2)	0	0	0	0
John Boudebza	Hull KR	2015-16	13(17)	2	0	0	8
David Boughton	Huddersfield	1999	26(1)	4	0	0	16
Amir Bourouh	Wigan	2019-20	1(3)	0	0	0	0
Julian Bousquet	Catalans	2012-20	66(108)	18	0	0	72
David Bouveng	Halifax	1997-99	66(2)	19	0	0	76
Josh Bowden	Hull	2012-20	64(86)	13	0	0	52
Matt Bowen	Wigan	2014-15	43	21	31	0	146
Harry Bowes	Wakefield	2020	1(1)	0	0	0	0
Tony Bowes	Huddersfield	1998	3(2)	0	0	0	0
Radney Bowker	London	2004	3	1	0	0	4
	St Helens	2001	(1)	0	0	0	0
David Boyle	Bradford	1999-2000	36(13)	15	0	1	61
Ryan Boyle	Castleford	2006, 2008-09, 2013-16	12(60)	5	0	0	20
	Salford	2010-13	57(14)	3	0	0	12
Andy Bracek	Crusaders	2011	(2)	0	0	0	0
	Warrington	2005-08	7(49)	7	0	0	28
	St Helens	2004	(1)	0	0	0	0
David Bradbury	Hudds-Sheff	2000	21(2)	1	0	0	4
	Salford	1997-99	23(10)	6	0	0	24
	Oldham	1996-97	19(6)	9	0	0	36
John Braddish	St Helens	2001-02	1(1)	0	3	0	6
Graeme Bradley	Bradford	1996-98	62(1)	29	0	0	116
Nick Bradley-Qalilawa							
	Harlequins	2006	27	6	0	0	24
	London	2005	28	19	0	0	76
Darren Bradstreet	London	1999-2000	1(3)	0	0	0	0
Dominic Brambani	Castleford	2004	2(2)	0	0	0	0
Keanan Brand	Warrington	2020	3	0	0	0	0
	Widnes	2018	1	0	0	0	0
Joe Bretherton	Wigan	2016-17	2(13)	1	0	0	4
Liam Bretherton	Wigan	1999	(5)	2	0	0	8
	Warrington	1997	(2)	1	0	0	4
Johnny Brewer	Halifax	1996	4(2)	2	0	0	8
Chris Bridge	Widnes	2016-17	28(1)	4	11	0	38
	Warrington	2005-15	186(17)	89	248	1	853
	Bradford	2003-04	2(14)	4	6	0	28

153

Super League Players 1996-2020

PLAYER	CLUB	YEAR	APP	TRIES	GOALS	FG	PTS
Danny Bridge	Bradford	2014	4(4)	0	0	0	0
	Warrington	2013	(2)	0	0	0	0
Ryan Brierley	Hull KR	2020	10	3	8	0	28
	Huddersfield	2016-17	19(1)	6	2	0	28
Lee Briers	Warrington	1997-2013	365(12)	130	810	70	2210
	St Helens	1997	3	0	11	0	22
Carl Briggs	Salford	1999	8(5)	3	0	1	13
	Halifax	1996	5(3)	1	0	0	4
Kyle Briggs	Bradford	2011	6	4	0	0	16
	Harlequins	2011	3	0	0	0	0
Mike Briggs	Widnes	2002	1(2)	1	0	0	4
Kriss Brining	Salford	2017	2(20)	4	0	0	16
Luke Briscoe	Leeds	2014, 2016, 2018-20	27(5)	11	0	0	44
	Wakefield	2014	2	0	0	0	0
Shaun Briscoe	Widnes	2012-13	11(2)	4	0	0	16
	Hull KR	2008-11	92	27	0	0	108
	Hull	2004-07	83(9)	50	0	0	200
	Wigan	2002-03	23(5)	11	0	0	44
Tom Briscoe	Leeds	2014-20	132	56	0	0	224
	Hull	2008-13	131(3)	83	0	0	332
Darren Britt	St Helens	2002-03	41	3	0	0	12
Gary Broadbent	Salford	1997-2002	117(2)	22	0	0	88
Jack Broadbent	Leeds	2020	3	0	0	0	0
Paul Broadbent	Wakefield	2002	16(5)	0	0	0	0
	Hull	2000-01	40(9)	3	0	0	12
	Halifax	1999	26(1)	2	0	0	8
	Sheffield	1996-98	63(1)	6	0	0	24
Robin Brochon	Catalans	2018-19	2	0	0	0	0
Andrew Brocklehurst	Salford	2004-07	34(23)	5	0	0	20
	London	2004	12(6)	2	0	0	8
	Halifax	2001-03	37(8)	2	0	0	8
Justin Brooker	Wakefield	2001	25	9	0	0	36
	Bradford	2000	17(4)	11	0	0	44
Sam Brooks	Widnes	2016-17	1(3)	1	0	0	4
Danny Brough	Wakefield	2008-10, 2019-20	74(1)	16	247	9	567
	Huddersfield	2010-18	220(4)	45	721	20	1642
	Castleford	2006	10	1	31	2	68
	Hull	2005-06	25(12)	3	85	1	183
Jodie Broughton	Catalans	2016-19	48	34	0	0	136
	Huddersfield	2014-15	30	16	0	0	64
	Salford	2010-13	93	53	0	0	212
	Hull	2008-09	9(3)	6	0	0	24
Alex Brown	Hull KR	2013	16	9	0	0	36
	Huddersfield	2009	1	0	0	0	0
Darren Brown	Salford	1999-2001	47(9)	11	6	0	56
Gavin Brown	Leeds	1996-97	5(2)	1	2	0	8
Jack Brown	Hull	2019-20	1(9)	3	0	0	12
Kevin Brown	Salford	2020	8	3	0	0	12
	Warrington	2017-18	41(1)	9	0	0	36
	Widnes	2013-16	80	37	1	1	151
	Huddersfield	2006-12	156	43	0	1	173
	Wigan	2003-06	46(18)	27	0	0	108
Lee Brown	Hull	1999	(1)	0	0	0	0
Michael Brown	Huddersfield	2008	(1)	0	0	0	0
Michael Brown	London	1996	(2)	0	0	0	0
Mitch Brown	Warrington	2018	10(1)	2	0	0	8
	Leigh	2017	21	4	0	0	16
Todd Brown	Paris	1996	8(1)	2	0	0	8
Adrian Brunker	Wakefield	1999	17	6	0	0	24
Lamont Bryan	Harlequins	2008-11	9(22)	2	0	0	8
Justin Bryant	Paris	1996	4(1)	0	0	0	0
	London	1996	7(8)	1	0	0	4
Mark Bryant	London	2012-13	16(36)	3	1	0	14
	Crusaders	2010-11	42(8)	1	0	0	4
	Celtic	2009	23(3)	0	0	0	0
Austin Buchanan	Wakefield	2005-06	6	2	0	0	8
	London	2003	3(1)	2	0	0	8
Jack Buchanan	Widnes	2016-17	29(2)	2	0	0	8
Kieran Buchanan	Hull	2019-20	10(3)	3	0	0	12
Owen Buckley	Widnes	2018	4	3	0	0	12
Danny Buderus	Leeds	2009-11	57(14)	14	0	0	56
Neil Budworth	Celtic	2009	8(19)	0	0	0	0
	Harlequins	2006	2(19)	0	0	0	0
	London	2002-05	59(11)	4	1	0	18
Joe Bullock	Wigan	2019-20	20(16)	3	0	0	12
James Bunyan	Huddersfield	1998-99	8(7)	2	0	0	8
Andy Burgess	Salford	1997	3(12)	0	0	0	0
George Burgess	Wigan	2020	2(6)	1	0	0	4
Joe Burgess	Wigan	2013-15, 2017-20	115	91	0	0	364
Luke Burgess	Salford	2018	3(8)	0	0	0	0
	Catalans	2017	3(2)	0	0	0	0
	Leeds	2008-11	10(63)	6	0	0	24
	Harlequins	2007	(3)	0	0	0	0
Sam Burgess	Bradford	2006-09	46(34)	14	5	0	66
Tom Burgess	Bradford	2011-12	1(41)	3	0	0	12
Greg Burke	Salford	2018-20	19(27)	1	0	0	4
	Widnes	2016-18	22(12)	1	0	0	4
	Wigan	2013-14, 2016	13(26)	1	0	0	4
	Hull KR	2015	9(5)	0	0	0	0
	Bradford	2014	(1)	0	0	0	0
Joe Burke	Crusaders	2011	(1)	0	0	0	0
Mike Burnett	Harlequins	2011	16(4)	1	0	0	4
	Hull	2008-10	13(21)	3	0	0	12
Darren Burns	Warrington	2002-04	66(6)	19	0	0	76
Gary Burns	Oldham	1996	6	1	0	0	4
Paul Burns	Workington	1996	5(2)	1	0	0	4
Travis Burns	St Helens	2015-16	27(2)	4	28	0	72
	Hull KR	2013-14	46	8	81	2	196
Lachlan Burr	Leigh	2017	5(14)	1	0	0	4
Luther Burrell	Warrington	2019-20	2(6)	1	0	0	0
Rob Burrow	Leeds	2001-17	313(116)	168	131	5	939
Dean Busby	Warrington	1999-2002	34(34)	7	0	0	28
	Hull	1998	8(6)	0	0	0	0
	St Helens	1996-98	1(7)	0	0	0	0
Tom Bush	Leeds	2010	3(1)	1	0	0	4
Chester Butler	Huddersfield	2019	(1)	0	0	0	0
Rob Butler	London	2019	17(7)	2	0	0	8
Ikram Butt	London	1996	5(1)	0	0	0	0
Reiss Butterworth	Huddersfield	2020	1(1)	0	0	0	0
Liam Byrne	Wigan	2019-20	8(17)	2	0	0	8
Shane Byrne	Huddersfield	1998-99	1(5)	0	0	0	0
Todd Byrne	Hull	2008-09	20	4	0	0	16
Didier Cabestany	Paris	1996-97	20(6)	2	0	0	8
Hep Cahill	Widnes	2012-18	106(13)	4	0	0	16
	Crusaders	2011	16	2	0	0	8
Joel Caine	Salford	2004	24	8	13	0	58
	London	2003	6	4	1	0	18
Mark Calderwood	Harlequins	2011	13	2	0	0	8
	Hull	2009-10	23	6	0	0	24
	Wigan	2006-08	64	23	0	0	92
	Leeds	2001-05	117(9)	88	0	0	352
Mike Callan	Warrington	2002	(4)	0	0	0	0
Matt Calland	Huddersfield	2003	2	0	0	0	0
	Hull	1999	1	0	0	0	0
	Bradford	1996-98	44(5)	24	0	0	96
Dean Callaway	London	1999-2000	26(24)	12	0	0	48
Laurent Cambres	Paris	1996	(1)	0	0	0	0
Chris Campbell	Warrington	2000	7(1)	2	0	0	8
Liam Campbell	Wakefield	2005	(1)	0	0	0	0
Logan Campbell	Hull	1998-99, 2001	70(13)	14	0	0	56
	Castleford	2000	14(2)	3	0	0	12
	Workington	1996	7(1)	1	0	0	4
Terry Campese	Hull KR	2015-16	19(1)	2	4	0	16
Blake Cannova	Widnes	2002	(1)	0	0	0	0
Phil Cantillon	Widnes	2002-03	27(21)	18	0	0	72
	Leeds	1997	(1)	0	0	0	0
Liam Carberry	Widnes	2014-15	2(5)	0	0	0	0
Damien Cardace	Catalans	2012, 2014-15	23	14	0	0	56
Daryl Cardiss	Warrington	2003-04	23(2)	3	4	0	20
	Halifax	1999-2003	91(8)	39	4	0	164
	Wigan	1996-98	12(6)	4	0	0	16
Dale Cardoza	Warrington	2002	5	1	0	0	4
	Halifax	2001	3	1	0	0	4
	Huddersfield	2000-01	20(9)	11	0	0	44
	Sheffield	1998-99	11(7)	3	0	0	12
Paul Carige	Salford	1999	24(1)	7	0	0	28
Dane Carlaw	Catalans	2008-10	58(15)	9	0	0	36
Keal Carlile	Hull KR	2012-15	6(28)	1	0	0	4
	Huddersfield	2009, 2011	2(1)	1	0	0	4
	Bradford	2008	(1)	0	0	0	0
Jim Carlton	Huddersfield	1999	3(11)	2	0	0	8
George Carmont	Wigan	2008-12	136	71	0	0	284
Brian Carney	Warrington	2009	4	2	0	0	8
	Wigan	2001-05	91(10)	42	1	0	170
	Hull	2000	13(3)	7	0	0	28
	Gateshead	1999	3(2)	2	0	0	8
Justin Carney	Hull KR	2018	14	3	0	0	12
	Salford	2016-17	28	12	0	0	48
	Castleford	2013-15	58	56	0	0	224
Martin Carney	Warrington	1997	(1)	0	0	0	0
Todd Carney	Hull KR	2018	(1)	0	0	0	0
	Salford	2017	9(5)	0	7	0	14
	Catalans	2015-16	32	9	4	1	45
Omari Caro	Hull KR	2013-14	21	20	0	0	80
	London	2012	11	4	0	0	16
Paul Carr	Sheffield	1996-98	45(5)	15	0	0	60
Bernard Carroll	London	1996	2(1)	1	0	0	4
Mark Carroll	London	1998	15(3)	1	0	0	4

PLAYER	CLUB	YEAR	APP	TRIES	GOALS	FG	PTS
Tonie Carroll	Leeds	2001-02	42(2)	30	0	0	120
Darren Carter	Workington	1996	10(3)	0	1	0	2
Steve Carter	Widnes	2002	14(7)	4	0	0	16
John Cartwright	Salford	1997	9	0	0	0	0
Garreth Carvell	Castleford	2014	1(4)	1	0	0	4
	Hull	2001-08, 2014	75(84)	22	0	0	88
	Warrington	2009-13	77(40)	13	0	0	52
	Leeds	1997-2000	(4)	0	0	0	0
	Gateshead	1999	4(4)	1	0	0	4
Garen Casey	Salford	1999	13(5)	3	23	0	58
Ray Cashmere	Salford	2009-11	63(3)	5	0	0	20
Mick Cassidy	Widnes	2005	24	0	0	0	0
	Wigan	1996-2004	184(36)	30	0	0	120
Remi Casty	Catalans	2006-13, 2015-20	207(97)	26	0	0	104
Ned Catic	Castleford	2008	7(7)	3	0	0	12
	Wakefield	2006-07	17(29)	4	0	0	16
Mason Caton-Brown							
	Wakefield	2017-19	34	27	0	0	108
	Salford	2014-16	28	10	0	0	40
	London	2013-14	19	15	0	0	60
Joe Cator	Hull	2020	9(2)	1	0	0	4
	Hull KR	2016, 2018	2(3)	0	0	0	0
Chris Causey	Warrington	1997-99	(18)	1	0	0	4
Jason Cayless	St Helens	2006-09	62(9)	7	0	0	28
Arnaud Cervello	Paris	1996	4	4	0	0	16
Marshall Chalk	Celtic	2009	13	4	0	0	16
Ed Chamberlain	Salford	2018-20	10(1)	3	21	0	54
	Widnes	2016-18	16(1)	2	7	0	22
Gary Chambers	Warrington	1996-2000	65(28)	2	0	0	8
Pierre Chamorin	Paris	1996-97	27(3)	8	3	0	38
Alex Chan	Catalans	2006-08	59(19)	11	0	0	44
Jason Chan	Hull KR	2014	5(1)	3	0	0	12
	Huddersfield	2012-14	46(12)	9	0	0	36
	Crusaders	2010-11	48(1)	10	0	0	40
	Celtic	2009	17(6)	3	0	0	12
Joe Chandler	Leeds	2008	(1)	0	0	0	0
Michael Channing	Castleford	2013-15	27(2)	8	0	0	32
	London	2012-13	15(3)	2	0	0	8
Jay Chapelhow	Widnes	2016-18	23(15)	4	0	0	16
Ted Chapelhow	Widnes	2016-18	7(13)	0	0	0	0
Chris Chapman	Leeds	1999	(1)	0	0	0	0
Damien Chapman	London	1998	6(2)	3	4	1	21
David Chapman	Castleford	1996-98	24(6)	8	0	0	32
Jaymes Chapman	Halifax	2002-03	5(8)	1	0	0	4
Richard Chapman	Sheffield	1996	1	2	0	0	8
Chris Charles	Salford	2004-06	59(16)	6	140	0	304
	Castleford	2001	1(4)	1	0	0	4
Olivier Charles	Catalans	2007	2	2	0	0	8
Josh Charnley	Warrington	2018-20	66	37	0	0	148
	Wigan	2010-16	151(2)	141	77	0	718
	Hull KR	2010	5	5	0	0	20
Lewis Charnock	St Helens	2013, 2015	4(1)	2	6	0	20
Rangi Chase	Widnes	2017	6	0	0	0	0
	Castleford	2009-13, 2016-17	122(12)	39	0	3	159
	Salford	2014-15	37	10	13	2	68
Andy Cheetham	Huddersfield	1998-99	30	11	0	0	44
Kris Chesney	London	1998	1(2)	0	0	0	0
Chris Chester	Hull KR	2007-08	28(6)	4	0	0	16
	Hull	2002-06	67(25)	13	0	0	52
	Wigan	1999-2001	21(22)	5	0	0	20
	Halifax	1996-99	47(14)	16	15	1	95
Lee Chilton	Workington	1996	10(3)	6	0	0	24
Dane Chisholm	Hull KR	2015	1	0	0	0	0
Gary Christie	Bradford	1996-97	4(7)	1	0	0	4
James Clare	Castleford	2012-15, 2018-20	90(1)	48	0	0	192
Daryl Clark	Warrington	2015-20	136(13)	34	0	0	136
	Castleford	2011-14	34(51)	31	0	0	124
Dean Clark	Leeds	1996	11(2)	3	0	0	12
Des Clark	St Helens	1999	4	0	0	0	0
	Halifax	1998-99	35(13)	6	0	0	24
Jason Clark	Warrington	2019-20	21(22)	2	0	0	8
Mitch Clark	Wigan	2020	(8)	0	0	0	0
	Castleford	2018-19	(24)	3	0	0	12
Greg Clarke	Halifax	1997	1(1)	0	0	0	0
John Clarke	Oldham	1996-97	27(4)	5	0	0	20
Jon Clarke	Widnes	2012-14	59(1)	5	0	0	20
	Warrington	2001-11	217(25)	56	2	0	228
	London	2000-01	19(11)	2	0	0	8
	Wigan	1997-99	13(10)	3	0	0	12
Chris Clarkson	Castleford	2019	11(8)	4	0	0	16
	Hull KR	2016, 2018	38(2)	4	0	0	16
	Widnes	2015	17(1)	4	0	0	16
	Leeds	2010-14	61(39)	9	0	0	36
Adam Clay	Salford	2011	2	3	0	0	12
Ryan Clayton	Castleford	2004, 2008-10	36(24)	5	0	0	20
	Salford	2006	3(8)	2	0	0	8
	Huddersfield	2005	4(6)	0	0	0	0
	Halifax	2000, 2002-03	28(12)	6	0	0	24
Gavin Clinch	Salford	2004	21(1)	1	0	1	5
	Halifax	1998-99, 2001-02	88(2)	26	45	5	199
	Hudds-Sheff	2000	18(2)	5	0	1	21
	Wigan	1999	10(2)	4	12	0	40
Joel Clinton	Hull KR	2010-12	42(14)	2	0	0	8
John Clough	Salford	2004-06	1(16)	0	0	0	0
Paul Clough	Huddersfield	2017-20	35(43)	3	0	0	12
	Widnes	2014	4(8)	1	0	0	4
	St Helens	2005-13	53(113)	16	0	0	64
Tony Clubb	Wigan	2014-20	71(72)	20	0	0	80
	London	2012-13	24(8)	7	0	0	28
	Harlequins	2006-11	100(11)	29	0	0	116
Bradley Clyde	Leeds	2001	7(5)	1	0	0	4
Michael Coady	Leeds	2010	1	0	0	0	0
Evan Cochrane	Wigan	1996	5(1)	1	0	0	4
Ben Cockayne	Hull KR	2007-11, 2014-16	125(30)	38	18	0	188
	Wakefield	2012-13	54	28	2	0	116
Liam Colbon	Hull	2014	8	1	0	0	4
	London	2012-13	22	5	0	0	20
	Hull KR	2009-11	51	20	0	0	80
	Wigan	2004-05, 2007-08	37(14)	15	0	0	60
Anthony Colella	Huddersfield	2003	5(1)	2	0	0	8
Liam Coleman	Leigh	2005	1(4)	0	0	0	0
Andy Coley	Wigan	2008-11	100(11)	8	0	0	32
	Salford	2001-02, 2004-07	112(34)	34	0	0	136
Richard Colley	Bradford	2004	1	0	0	0	0
Steve Collins	Hull	2000	28	17	0	0	68
	Gateshead	1999	20(4)	13	0	0	52
Wayne Collins	Leeds	1997	21	3	0	0	12
Dean Collis	Wakefield	2012-15	64	28	0	0	112
Aurelien Cologni	Catalans	2006	4(1)	3	0	0	12
Gary Connolly	Widnes	2005	20	4	1	0	18
	Wigan	1996-2002, 2004	168(10)	70	5	0	290
	Leeds	2003-04	27	6	0	0	24
Jake Connor	Hull	2017-20	78(13)	24	70	2	238
	Huddersfield	2013-16	47(1)	21	2	0	88
Nathan Conroy	Bradford	2013-14	(4)	0	0	0	0
Matt Cook	Castleford	2008, 2015-20	22(88)	13	0	0	52
	London	2012-14	50(7)	8	0	0	32
	Hull KR	2010-11	9(16)	7	0	0	28
	Bradford	2005-09	11(52)	4	0	0	16
Mick Cook	Sheffield	1996	9(10)	2	0	0	8
Paul Cook	Huddersfield	1998-99	11(6)	2	13	0	34
	Bradford	1996-97	14(8)	7	38	1	105
Peter Cook	St Helens	2004	(1)	0	0	0	0
Paul Cooke	Wakefield	2010	16(1)	3	36	1	85
	Hull KR	2007-10	54(5)	8	76	2	186
	Hull	1999-2007	177(27)	32	333	4	798
Ben Cooper	Leigh	2005	25(1)	5	0	0	20
	Huddersfield	2000-01, 2003-04	28(12)	3	0	0	12
Mike Cooper	Warrington	2006-13, 2017-20	114(88)	16	0	0	64
	Castleford	2010	1(5)	2	0	0	8
Lachlan Coote	St Helens	2019-20	39	24	176	1	449
Ged Corcoran	Halifax	2003	1(11)	0	0	0	0
Wayne Corcoran	Halifax	2003	4(2)	0	0	0	0
Jamie Cording	Huddersfield	2011-13	4(21)	5	0	0	20
Josh Cordoba	Hull	2009	8	1	0	0	4
Mark Corvo	Salford	2002	7(5)	0	0	0	0
Matthew Costello	St Helens	2018-20	22(2)	6	0	0	24
Neville Costigan	Hull KR	2014	24	3	0	0	12
Brandon Costin	Huddersfield	2001, 2003-04	69	42	93	3	357
	Bradford	2002	20(1)	8	0	0	32
Wes Cotton	London	1997-98	12	3	0	0	12
Phil Coussons	Salford	1997	7(2)	3	0	0	12
Alex Couttet	Paris	1997	1	0	0	0	0
Nick Couttet	Paris	1997	1	0	0	0	0
Jamie Coventry	Castleford	1996	1	0	0	0	0
Jimmy Cowan	Oldham	1996-97	2(8)	0	0	0	0
Will Cowell	Warrington	1998-2000	6(8)	1	0	0	4
Neil Cowie	Wigan	1996-2001	116(27)	10	0	1	41

PLAYER	CLUB	YEAR	APP	TRIES	GOALS	FG	PTS
Danny Cowling	Wakefield	2012-13	2	0	0	0	0
Jordan Cox	Warrington	2016	(16)	0	0	0	0
	Hull KR	2011-15	17(44)	4	0	0	16
	Huddersfield	2015	(2)	0	0	0	0
Mark Cox	London	2003	(3)	0	0	0	0
James Coyle	Wigan	2005	2(3)	1	0	0	4
Thomas Coyle	Wigan	2008	2(1)	0	0	0	0
Eorl Crabtree	Huddersfield	2001, 2003-16	180(167)	52	0	0	208
Andy Craig	Halifax	1999	13(7)	1	3	0	10
	Wigan	1996	5(5)	2	0	0	8
Owen Craigie	Widnes	2005	15	7	0	2	30
Scott Cram	London	1999-2002	65(7)	4	0	0	16
Danny Craven	Widnes	2012-15, 2017-18	53(17)	13	6	3	67
Steve Craven	Hull	1998-2003	53(42)	4	0	0	16
Nicky Crellin	Workington	1996	(2)	0	0	0	0
Jason Critchley	Wakefield	2000	7(1)	4	0	0	16
	Castleford	1997-98	27(3)	11	0	0	44
Jack Croft	Wakefield	2019-20	8	0	0	0	0
Jason Croker	Catalans	2007-09	56(2)	11	0	1	45
Martin Crompton	Salford	1998-2000	30(6)	11	6	2	58
	Oldham	1996-97	36(1)	16	0	3	67
Paul Crook	Widnes	2005	2(2)	0	5	1	11
Paul Crook	Oldham	1996	4(9)	0	3	0	6
Jason Crookes	Hull	2013-14	15(1)	5	0	0	20
	Bradford	2009-12	25(1)	7	0	0	28
Ben Crooks	Hull KR	2018-20	37	21	0	0	84
	Leigh	2017	19	6	0	0	24
	Castleford	2016	24(2)	5	1	0	22
	Hull	2012-14	42(3)	23	0	0	166
Lee Crooks	Castleford	1996-97	27(2)	2	14	0	36
Dominic Crosby	Leeds	2018	(2)	0	0	0	0
	Warrington	2017-18	(16)	0	0	0	0
	Wigan	2012-16	57(35)	6	0	0	24
Alan Cross	St Helens	1997	(2)	0	0	0	0
Ben Cross	Widnes	2012-13	27(1)	2	0	0	8
	Wigan	2011	(4)	0	0	0	0
	Leeds	2011	1(9)	0	0	0	0
Steve Crossley	Castleford	2015	(6)	0	0	0	0
	Bradford	2010-11	(9)	1	0	0	4
Garret Crossman	Hull KR	2008	8(18)	0	0	0	0
Steve Crouch	Castleford	2004	4(1)	2	0	0	8
Kevin Crouthers	Warrington	2001-03	12(1)	4	0	0	16
	London	2000	6(4)	1	0	0	4
	Wakefield	1999	4(4)	1	0	0	4
	Bradford	1997-98	3(9)	2	0	0	8
Jordan Crowther	Wakefield	2014-20	29(17)	2	0	0	8
Matt Crowther	Hull	2001-03	48	20	166	0	412
	Hudds-Sheff	2000	10(4)	5	22	0	64
	Sheffield	1996-99	43(4)	22	10	0	108
Heath Cruckshank	Halifax	2003	19(1)	0	0	0	0
	St Helens	2001	1(12)	0	0	0	0
Leroy Cudjoe	Huddersfield	2008-20	261(1)	102	57	1	523
Paul Cullen	Warrington	1996	19	3	0	0	12
Francis Cummins	Leeds	1996-2005	217(13)	120	26	2	534
James Cunningham							
	Toronto	2020	2(1)	0	0	0	0
	London	2014, 2019	34(8)	3	0	0	12
	Hull	2012, 2014-15	(9)	0	0	0	0
Keiron Cunningham							
	St Helens	1996-2010	357(24)	138	0	0	552
Liam Cunningham	Hull	2010	(1)	0	0	0	0
Ben Currie	Warrington	2012-20	125(31)	57	0	0	228
Andy Currier	Warrington	1996-97	(2)	1	0	0	4
Peter Cusack	Hull	2008-10	34(22)	3	0	0	12
Adam Cuthbertson	Leeds	2015-20	91(39)	30	0	0	120
Alrix Da Costa	Catalans	2016-20	24(32)	3	0	0	12
Will Dagger	Hull KR	2018-20	24(2)	2	12	0	32
	Warrington	2017	3	0	0	0	0
Joe Dakuitoga	Sheffield	1996	6(3)	0	0	0	0
Matty Dale	Hull	2006, 2008	(7)	1	0	0	4
	Wakefield	2008	1(1)	0	0	0	0
Brett Dallas	Wigan	2000-06	156	89	0	0	356
Mark Dalle Cort	Celtic	2009	23	4	0	0	16
Paul Darbyshire	Warrington	1997	(6)	0	0	0	0
James Davey	Wakefield	2009-11	3(14)	1	0	0	4
Maea David	Hull	1998	1	0	0	0	0
Alex Davidson	Salford	2011, 2013	(3)	0	0	0	0
Paul Davidson	Halifax	2001-03	22(30)	10	0	0	40
	London	2000	6(10)	4	0	0	16
	St Helens	1998-99	27(16)	7	0	0	28
	Oldham	1996-97	17(18)	14	0	1	57
Ben Davies	St Helens	2020	0	0	0	0	0
Ben Davies	Castleford	2011, 2013	3(4)	2	0	0	8
	Widnes	2012-13	10(15)	3	0	0	12
	Wigan	2010	(5)	0	0	0	0
Gareth Davies	Warrington	1996-97	1(6)	0	0	0	0
Geraint Davies	Celtic	2009	(7)	0	0	0	0
John Davies	Castleford	2010-12	1(6)	1	0	0	4
Jordan Davies	Salford	2013	2(3)	0	0	0	0
Macauley Davies	Wigan	2016	(1)	0	0	0	0
Matthew Davies	London	2019	(1)	0	0	0	0
Olly Davies	St Helens	2016	(1)	0	0	0	0
Tom Davies	Catalans	2020	10	13	0	0	52
	Wigan	2017-19	57	27	0	0	108
Wes Davies	Wigan	1998-2001	22(22)	11	0	0	44
Brad Davis	Castleford	1997-2000, 2004, 2006	102(3)	31	43	10	220
	Wakefield	2001-03	51(12)	15	22	5	109
Matt Davis	Warrington	2019-20	5(21)	2	0	0	8
	London	2019	4	0	0	0	0
Sam Davis	London	2019	2(1)	0	0	0	0
Matty Dawson-Jones							
	Hull	2019	1	1	0	0	4
	Leigh	2017	23	12	0	0	48
	St Helens	2014-16	46(1)	15	0	0	60
	Huddersfield	2012-13	4	0	0	0	0
Brad Day	Castleford	2014	(1)	0	0	0	0
Matt Daylight	Hull	2000	17(1)	7	0	0	28
	Gateshead	1999	30	25	0	0	100
Michael De Vere	Huddersfield	2005-06	36	6	74	0	172
Paul Deacon	Wigan	2010-11	32(11)	4	14	0	44
	Bradford	1998-2009	258(43)	72	1029	23	2369
	Oldham	1997	(2)	0	0	0	0
Chris Dean	Widnes	2012-18	115(6)	23	0	0	92
	Wakefield	2011	20	8	0	0	32
	St Helens	2007-10	18(3)	9	0	0	36
Craig Dean	Halifax	1996-97	25(11)	12	1	1	51
Gareth Dean	London	2002	(4)	0	0	0	0
Riley Dean	Warrington	2019-20	2	1	0	0	4
Yacine Dekkiche	Hudds-Sheff	2000	11(3)	3	0	0	12
Brett Delaney	Leeds	2010-18	151(30)	23	0	0	92
Jason Demetriou	Wakefield	2004-10	174(3)	50	2	0	204
	Widnes	2002-03	47(1)	15	1	0	62
Martin Dermott	Warrington	1997	1	0	0	0	0
David Despin	Paris	1996	(1)	0	0	0	0
Fabien Devecchi	Paris	1996-97	17(10)	2	0	0	8
Paul Devlin	Widnes	2002-04	32	16	0	0	64
Jordan Dezaria	Catalans	2016-17	3(2)	0	0	0	0
Stuart Dickens	Salford	2005	4(5)	0	4	0	8
Tyler Dickinson	Huddersfield	2016-18	(17)	1	0	0	4
Matt Diskin	Bradford	2011-14	64(16)	11	0	0	44
	Leeds	2001-10	195(37)	40	0	0	160
Andrew Dixon	Toronto	2020	1(1)	0	0	0	0
	Salford	2013-14	34(2)	8	0	0	32
	St Helens	2009-12	19(41)	12	0	0	48
Kieran Dixon	London	2012-14, 2019	76(1)	42	77	0	322
	Hull KR	2015-16	23(4)	21	9	0	102
Kirk Dixon	Castleford	2008-14	143(2)	63	267	0	786
	Hull	2004-06	13(4)	7	4	0	36
Paul Dixon	Sheffield	1996-97	5(9)	1	0	0	4
Nabil Djalout	Catalans	2017	1	0	0	0	0
Gareth Dobson	Castleford	1998-2000	(10)	0	0	0	0
Michael Dobson	Salford	2015-17	58(1)	14	77	1	211
	Hull KR	2008-13	142	51	500	11	1215
	Wigan	2006	14	5	61	0	142
	Catalans	2006	10	4	31	1	79
Michael Docherty	Hull	2000-01	(6)	0	0	0	0
Lewis Dodd	St Helens	2020	1(2)	1	3	0	10
Mitchell Dodds	Warrington	2016	(2)	0	0	0	0
Erjon Dollapi	London	2013-14	(18)	4	0	0	16
Sid Domic	Hull	2006-07	39(4)	15	0	0	60
	Wakefield	2004-05	48	30	0	0	120
	Warrington	2002-03	41(4)	17	0	0	68
Scott Donald	Leeds	2006-10	131	77	0	0	308
James Donaldson	Leeds	2019-20	4(33)	4	0	0	16
	Hull KR	2015-16, 2018	12(30)	4	0	0	16
	Bradford	2009-14	38(35)	4	0	0	16
Glen Donkin	Hull	2002-03	(10)	1	0	0	4
Stuart Donlan	Castleford	2008	20	8	0	0	32
	Huddersfield	2004-06	59(3)	15	0	0	60
	Halifax	2001-03	65(2)	22	0	0	88
Jason Donohue	Bradford	1996	(4)	0	0	0	0
Jeremy Donougher	Bradford	1996-99	40(21)	13	0	0	52
Justin Dooley	London	2000-01	37(18)	2	0	0	8
Dane Dorahy	Halifax	2003	20	7	45	0	118
	Wakefield	2000-01	16(2)	4	19	1	55
Jamie Doran	Wigan	2014	(2)	0	0	0	0
Luke Dorn	Castleford	2008, 2014-16	78(2)	60	0	0	240
	London	2005, 2012-13	58(8)	42	0	0	168
	Harlequins	2006, 2009-11	83(1)	57	0	0	228
	Salford	2007	19(8)	11	0	0	44

PLAYER	CLUB	YEAR	APP	TRIES	GOALS	FG	PTS
Eribe Doro	Warrington	2020	(2)	0	0	0	0
Brandon Douglas	Castleford	2016	(1)	0	0	0	0
Luke Douglas	St Helens	2017-18	23(32)	5	0	0	20
Ewan Dowes	Hull	2003-11	169(51)	10	0	0	40
	Leeds	2001-03	1(9)	0	0	0	0
Jack Downs	Hull	2015-18	5(15)	1	0	0	4
Adam Doyle	Warrington	1998	9(3)	4	0	0	16
Rod Doyle	Sheffield	1997-99	52(10)	10	0	0	40
Brad Drew	Huddersfield	2005-07, 2010	78(13)	18	13	1	99
	Wakefield	2008-09	27(9)	7	14	1	57
Josh Drinkwater	Catalans	2018, 2020	31	8	53	0	138
	Hull KR	2019	29	4	6	0	28
	Leigh	2017	19	1	12	1	29
	London	2014	23(1)	5	54	0	128
Damien Driscoll	Salford	2001	23(1)	1	0	0	4
James Duckworth	London	2014	3	0	0	0	0
	Leeds	2013	2	1	0	0	4
Gil Dudson	Salford	2019-20	39(2)	2	0	0	8
	Widnes	2015-18	57(11)	1	0	0	4
	Wigan	2012-14	26(16)	2	0	0	8
	Crusaders	2011	3(7)	0	0	0	0
	Celtic	2009	(1)	0	0	0	0
Jason Duffy	Leigh	2005	3(1)	0	0	0	0
John Duffy	Leigh	2005	21	6	0	0	24
	Salford	2000	3(11)	0	1	1	3
	Warrington	1997-99	12(12)	0	0	0	0
Tony Duggan	Celtic	2009	4	3	0	0	12
Andrew Duncan	London	1997	2(4)	2	0	0	8
	Warrington	1997	(1)	0	0	0	0
Andrew Dunemann							
	Salford	2006	25	1	0	2	6
	Leeds	2003-05	76(4)	11	0	2	46
	Halifax	1999-2002	68	19	0	1	77
Matt Dunford	London	1997-98	18(20)	3	0	1	13
Vincent Duport	Catalans	2007-09, 2011-18	156(16)	75	0	0	300
Jamie Durbin	Widnes	2005	1	0	0	0	0
	Warrington	2003	(1)	0	0	0	0
Scott Dureau	Catalans	2011-15	88(1)	29	315	10	756
James Durkin	Paris	1997	(5)	0	0	0	0
Bernard Dwyer	Bradford	1996-2000	65(10)	14	0	0	56
Brad Dwyer	Leeds	2018-20	34(23)	12	0	1	49
	Warrington	2012-17	12(63)	11	0	0	44
	Huddersfield	2013	(6)	0	0	0	0
Luke Dyer	Crusaders	2010	23(1)	5	0	0	20
	Celtic	2009	21	6	0	0	24
	Hull KR	2007	26	13	0	0	52
	Castleford	2006	17(2)	5	0	0	20
Adam Dykes	Hull	2008	12	1	0	2	6
Jim Dymock	London	2001-04	94(1)	15	0	1	61
Leo Dynevor	London	1996	8(11)	5	7	0	34
Jason Eade	Paris	1997	9	4	0	0	16
Michael Eagar	Hull	2004-05	12	4	0	0	16
	Castleford	1999-2003	130(2)	60	0	0	240
	Warrington	1998	21	6	0	0	24
Kyle Eastmond	St Helens	2007-11	46(20)	35	117	3	377
Greg Eastwood	Leeds	2010	5(12)	1	0	0	4
Barry Eaton	Widnes	2002	25	2	49	4	110
	Castleford	2000	1(4)	0	3	0	6
Josh Eaves	St Helens	2019-20	1(2)	1	0	0	4
Greg Ebrill	Salford	2002	15(6)	1	0	0	4
Cliff Eccles	Salford	1997-98	30(5)	1	0	0	4
Chris Eckersley	Warrington	1996	1	0	0	0	0
Greg Eden	Castleford	2011, 2017-20	75	78	0	0	312
	Hull KR	2013-14	37	23	0	0	92
	Salford	2014	4	1	0	0	4
	Huddersfield	2012	24	8	0	0	32
Steve Edmed	Sheffield	1997	15(1)	0	0	0	0
Mark Edmondson	Salford	2007	10(2)	0	0	0	0
	St Helens	1999-2005	27(75)	10	0	0	40
Diccon Edwards	Castleford	1996-97	10(5)	1	0	0	4
Grant Edwards	Castleford	2006	(2)	0	0	0	0
Kenny Edwards	Huddersfield	2020	11(5)	0	0	0	0
	Catalans	2018-19	14(18)	10	0	0	40
Max Edwards	Harlequins	2010	1	0	0	0	0
Peter Edwards	Salford	1997-98	35(2)	4	0	0	16
Shaun Edwards	London	1997-2000	32(8)	16	1	0	66
	Bradford	1998	8(2)	4	0	0	16
	Wigan	1996	17(3)	12	1	0	50
Tuoyo Egodo	Castleford	2017-19	10(4)	11	0	0	44
Danny Ekis	Halifax	2001	(1)	0	0	0	0
Abi Ekoku	Bradford	1997-98	21(4)	6	0	0	24
	Halifax	1996	15(1)	5	0	0	20
Shane Elford	Huddersfield	2007-08	26(1)	7	0	0	28

PLAYER	CLUB	YEAR	APP	TRIES	GOALS	FG	PTS
Olivier Elima	Catalans	2008-10, 2013-16	99(35)	34	0	0	136
	Bradford	2011-12	37(3)	12	0	0	48
	Wakefield	2003-07	40(47)	13	0	0	52
	Castleford	2002	(1)	1	0	0	4
Abderazak Elkhalouki							
	Paris	1997	(1)	0	0	0	0
George Elliott	Leeds	2011	1	0	0	0	0
Andy Ellis	Wakefield	2012	10	0	0	0	0
	Harlequins	2010-11	26(11)	8	0	0	32
Gareth Ellis	Hull	2013-17, 2019-20	96(16)	19	0	0	76
	Leeds	2005-08	109	24	1	0	98
	Wakefield	1999-2004	86(17)	21	2	0	88
Jamie Ellis	Hull KR	2020	7	1	18	0	40
	Castleford	2012-14, 2018-19	58(8)	12	150	2	350
	Huddersfield	2015-16	37(3)	14	31	3	121
	Hull	2012	4(5)	1	0	0	4
	St Helens	2009	1(2)	0	1	0	2
Danny Ellison	Castleford	1998-99	7(16)	6	0	0	24
	Wigan	1996-97	15(1)	13	0	0	52
Andrew Emelio	Widnes	2005	22(2)	8	0	0	32
Jake Emmitt	Salford	2013	5(10)	0	0	0	0
	Castleford	2011-13	32(17)	0	0	0	0
	St Helens	2008-10	1(16)	1	0	0	4
Anthony England	Wakefield	2016-19	68(11)	2	0	0	8
	Warrington	2014-15	12(21)	3	0	0	12
Matty English	Huddersfield	2017-20	26(21)	5	0	0	20
Patrick Entat	Paris	1996	22	2	0	0	8
Jason Erba	Sheffield	1997	1(4)	0	0	0	0
Morgan Escare	Wakefield	2019	5	1	0	0	4
	Wigan	2017-19	23(22)	14	39	2	136
	Catalans	2013-16	83	58	1	2	236
Ryan Esders	Harlequins	2009-10	9(11)	3	0	0	12
	Hull KR	2009	(1)	0	0	0	0
Sonny Esslemont	Hull KR	2014-15	(5)	0	0	0	0
Niall Evalds	Salford	2013-20	119(11)	88	0	0	352
Ben Evans	Warrington	2014-15	3(16)	2	0	0	8
	Bradford	2013	3(12)	1	0	0	4
James Evans	Castleford	2009-10	26(1)	13	0	0	52
	Bradford	2007-08	43(5)	20	0	0	80
	Wakefield	2006	6	3	0	0	12
	Huddersfield	2004-06	51	22	0	0	88
Paul Evans	Paris	1997	18	8	0	0	32
Rhys Evans	Leeds	2020	4(1)	1	0	0	4
	Warrington	2010-17	87(7)	37	0	0	148
Wayne Evans	London	2002	11(6)	2	0	0	8
Toby Everett	London	2014	(2)	0	0	0	0
Richie Eyres	Warrington	1997	2(5)	0	0	0	0
	Sheffield	1997	2(3)	0	0	0	0
Henry Fa'afili	Warrington	2004-07	90(1)	70	0	0	280
David Fa'alogo	Huddersfield	2010-12	38(16)	13	0	0	52
Sala Fa'alogo	Widnes	2004-05	8(15)	2	0	0	8
Richard Fa'aoso	Castleford	2006	10(15)	5	0	0	20
Maurie Fa'asavalu	St Helens	2004-10	5(137)	29	0	0	116
Bolouagi Fagborun	Huddersfield	2004-06	4(2)	1	0	0	4
Theo Fages	St Helens	2016-20	91(25)	32	0	1	129
	Salford	2013-15	57(5)	18	4	0	80
Esene Faimalo	Salford	1997-99	23(25)	2	0	0	8
	Leeds	1996	3(3)	0	0	0	0
Joe Faimalo	Salford	1998-2000	23(47)	7	0	0	28
	Oldham	1996-97	37(5)	7	0	0	28
Jacob Fairbank	Huddersfield	2011-15	12(3)	0	0	0	0
	Wakefield	2014	1(3)	0	0	0	0
	London	2013	4(1)	1	0	0	4
	Bradford	2013	(2)	0	0	0	0
Karl Fairbank	Bradford	1996	17(2)	4	0	0	16
David Fairleigh	St Helens	2001	26(1)	8	0	0	32
David Faiumu	Huddersfield	2008-14	38(108)	13	0	0	52
Jamal Fakir	Bradford	2014	3(8)	1	0	0	4
	Catalans	2006-14	55(100)	13	0	0	52
Jim Fallon	Leeds	1996	10	5	0	0	20
Beau Falloon	Leeds	2016	8(2)	0	0	0	0
Bureta Faraimo	Hull	2018-20	64	32	4	0	136
Owen Farnworth	Widnes	2017-18	1(4)	0	0	0	0
Ben Farrar	London	2014	22	1	0	0	4
	Catalans	2011	13	3	0	0	12
Danny Farrar	Warrington	1998-2000	76	13	0	0	52
Andy Farrell	Wigan	1996-2004	230	77	1026	16	2376
Anthony Farrell	Widnes	2002-03	24(22)	4	1	0	18
	Leeds	1997-2001	99(13)	18	0	0	72
	Sheffield	1996	14(5)	5	0	0	20
Connor Farrell	Widnes	2016	3(9)	3	0	0	12
	Wigan	2014-15	1(8)	0	0	0	0
Craig Farrell	Hull	2000-01	1(3)	0	0	0	0

Super League Players 1996-2020

PLAYER	CLUB	YEAR	APP	TRIES	GOALS	FG	PTS
Izaac Farrell	Huddersfield	2019	2	0	4	0	8
Liam Farrell	Wigan	2010-20	189(50)	93	0	0	372
Brad Fash	Hull	2015, 2017-20	7(72)	2	0	0	8
Abraham Fatnowna							
	London	1997-98	7(2)	2	0	0	8
	Workington	1996	5	2	0	0	8
Sione Faumuina	Castleford	2009	18	1	0	0	4
	Hull	2005	3	1	0	0	4
Vince Fawcett	Wakefield	1999	13(1)	2	0	0	8
	Warrington	1998	4(7)	1	0	0	4
	Oldham	1997	5	3	0	0	12
Danny Fearon	Huddersfield	2001	(1)	0	0	0	0
	Halifax	1999-2000	5(6)	0	0	0	0
Chris Feather	Castleford	2009	1(23)	0	0	0	0
	Bradford	2007-08	7(20)	1	0	0	4
	Leeds	2003-04, 2006	16(35)	6	0	0	24
	Wakefield	2001-02, 2004-05	29(32)	9	0	0	36
Dom Feaunati	Leigh	2005	4	1	0	0	4
	St Helens	2004	10(7)	7	0	0	28
Adel Fellous	Hull	2008	1(2)	0	0	0	0
	Catalans	2006-07	16(22)	4	0	0	16
Luke Felsch	Hull	2000-01	46(6)	7	0	0	28
	Gateshead	1999	28(1)	2	0	0	8
Leon Felton	Warrington	2002	4(2)	0	0	0	0
	St Helens	2001	1(1)	0	0	0	0
Dale Ferguson	Huddersfield	2011-13, 2017-19	61(23)	16	0	0	64
	Bradford	2014	3(3)	0	0	0	0
	Hull KR	2013	3(1)	1	0	0	4
	Wakefield	2007-11	40(14)	12	0	0	48
Brett Ferres	Leeds	2016-20	52(16)	11	0	0	44
	Huddersfield	2012-15	72	27	0	0	108
	Castleford	2009-12	78(5)	26	0	0	104
	Wakefield	2007-08	36(2)	6	5	0	34
	Bradford	2005-06	18(17)	11	2	0	48
David Ferriol	Catalans	2007-12	72(55)	8	0	0	32
Jason Ferris	Leigh	2005	4	1	0	0	4
Callum Field	Wigan	2017-18	(8)	0	0	0	0
Jamie Field	Wakefield	1999-2006	133(59)	19	0	0	76
	Huddersfield	1998	15(5)	0	0	0	0
	Leeds	1996-97	3(11)	0	0	0	0
Mark Field	Wakefield	2003-07	28(7)	3	0	0	12
Jamie Fielden	London	2003	(1)	0	0	0	0
	Huddersfield	1998-2000	4(8)	0	0	0	0
Stuart Fielden	Huddersfield	2013	8(1)	0	0	0	0
	Wigan	2006-12	105(24)	2	0	0	8
	Bradford	1998-2006	142(78)	41	0	0	164
David Fifita	Wakefield	2016-20	51(38)	16	0	0	64
Lafaele Filipo	Workington	1996	15(4)	3	0	0	12
Salesi Finau	Warrington	1996-97	16(15)	8	0	0	32
Brett Finch	Wigan	2011-12	49(3)	16	0	0	64
Vinny Finigan	Bradford	2010	4(1)	4	0	0	16
Liam Finn	Widnes	2018	1	0	0	0	0
	Wakefield	2004, 2016-18	71(4)	5	220	0	460
	Castleford	2014-15	45(2)	8	5	2	44
	Halifax	2002-03	16(5)	2	30	1	69
Lee Finnerty	Halifax	2003	18(2)	5	2	0	24
Phil Finney	Warrington	1998	1	0	0	0	0
Simon Finnigan	Widnes	2003-05, 2012	56(24)	21	0	0	84
	Huddersfield	2009-10	22(5)	6	0	0	24
	Bradford	2008	14(13)	8	0	0	32
	Salford	2006-07	50	17	0	0	68
Matt Firth	Halifax	2000-01	12(2)	0	0	0	0
Andy Fisher	Wakefield	1999-2000	31(8)	4	0	0	16
Ben Fisher	London	2013	8(12)	1	0	0	4
	Catalans	2012	9(5)	1	0	0	4
	Hull KR	2007-11	78(46)	18	0	0	72
Craig Fitzgibbon	Hull	2010-11	42(1)	9	8	0	52
Daniel Fitzhenry	Hull KR	2008-09	36(11)	14	0	0	56
Karl Fitzpatrick	Salford	2004-07, 2009-10	89(11)	33	2	0	136
Conor Fitzsimmons							
	Castleford	2016	(2)	0	0	0	0
Mark Flanagan	Salford	2016-20	62(27)	8	0	0	32
	St Helens	2012-15	40(39)	9	0	0	36
	Wigan	2009	3(7)	1	0	0	4
Chris Flannery	St Helens	2007-12	108(11)	32	0	0	128
Darren Fleary	Leigh	2005	24	1	0	0	4
	Huddersfield	2003-04	43(8)	4	0	0	16
	Leeds	1997-2002	98(9)	3	0	0	12
Dan Fleming	Castleford	2013-14, 2020	(16)	1	0	0	4
Greg Fleming	London	1999-2001	64(1)	40	2	0	164
Matty Fleming	London	2019	12(1)	6	0	0	24
	Leigh	2017	5	1	0	0	4
	St Helens	2015-17	17	7	0	0	28
Adam Fletcher	Castleford	2006, 2008	16(7)	11	0	0	44
Bryan Fletcher	Wigan	2006-07	47(2)	14	0	0	56
Richard Fletcher	Castleford	2006	13(5)	3	4	0	20
	Hull	1999-2004	11(56)	5	0	0	20
Greg Florimo	Halifax	2000	26	6	4	0	32
	Wigan	1999	18(2)	7	1	0	30
Ben Flower	Wigan	2012-20	131(37)	21	0	0	84
	Crusaders	2010-11	10(23)	2	0	0	8
	Celtic	2009	2(15)	0	0	0	0
Jason Flowers	Salford	2004	6(1)	0	0	0	0
	Halifax	2002	24(4)	4	0	0	16
	Castleford	1996-2001	119(19)	33	0	1	133
Stuart Flowers	Castleford	1996	(3)	0	0	0	0
Adrian Flynn	Castleford	1996-97	19(2)	10	0	0	40
Paddy Flynn	Castleford	2016	9(1)	6	0	0	24
	Widnes	2012-15	72	41	0	0	164
Wayne Flynn	Sheffield	1997	3(5)	0	0	0	0
Adam Fogerty	Warrington	1998	4	0	0	0	0
	St Helens	1996	13	1	0	0	4
Israel Folau	Catalans	2020	13	5	0	0	20
Mahe Fonua	Hull	2016-17, 2020	64(3)	31	0	0	124
Liam Foran	Salford	2013	10(3)	1	0	0	4
Carl Forber	Leigh	2005	4	1	0	0	4
	St Helens	2004	1(1)	0	6	0	12
Paul Forber	Salford	1997-98	19(12)	4	0	0	16
Byron Ford	Hull KR	2007	13	6	0	0	24
James Ford	Castleford	2009	3(5)	1	0	0	4
Mike Ford	Castleford	1997-98	25(12)	5	0	3	23
	Warrington	1996	3	0	0	0	0
Jim Forshaw	Salford	1999	(1)	0	0	0	0
Mike Forshaw	Warrington	2004	20(1)	5	0	0	20
	Bradford	1997-2003	162(7)	32	0	0	128
	Leeds	1996	11(3)	5	0	0	20
Carl Forster	Salford	2015-16	5(7)	1	0	0	4
	St Helens	2011-12, 2014	(4)	0	0	0	0
	London	2014	2(3)	0	0	0	0
Mark Forster	Warrington	1996-2000	102(1)	40	0	0	160
Liam Forsyth	Wigan	2017-18	11(2)	3	0	0	12
Alex Foster	Castleford	2017-20	34(13)	9	0	0	36
	London	2014	20	3	0	0	12
	Leeds	2013	(8)	1	0	0	4
David Foster	Halifax	2000-01	4(9)	0	0	0	0
Jamie Foster	Huddersfield	2016	3	2	5	0	18
	Bradford	2013-14	32	12	111	0	270
	Hull	2012	9	5	45	0	110
	St Helens	2010-12	44(3)	30	201	0	522
Matthew Foster	St Helens	2020	(1)	0	0	0	0
Peter Fox	Wakefield	2007, 2012-14	85	44	0	0	176
	Hull KR	2008-11	95	52	0	0	208
Matty Fozard	London	2019	7(16)	3	0	0	12
	St Helens	2014	1	0	0	0	0
Nick Fozzard	Castleford	2011	7(10)	0	0	0	0
	St Helens	2004-08, 2010	100(25)	7	0	0	28
	Hull KR	2009	18(4)	1	0	0	4
	Warrington	2002-03	43(11)	2	0	0	8
	Huddersfield	1998-2000	24(8)	2	0	0	8
	Leeds	1996-97	6(16)	3	0	0	12
David Fraisse	Workington	1996	8	0	0	0	0
Daniel Frame	Widnes	2002-05	100(6)	24	0	0	96
Paul Franze	Castleford	2006	2(1)	0	0	0	0
Matt Frawley	Huddersfield	2019	19(2)	4	0	0	16
Laurent Frayssinous							
	Catalans	2006	14(2)	3	32	0	76
Bevan French	Wigan	2019-20	22(5)	21	0	0	84
Andrew Frew	Halifax	2003	17	5	0	0	20
	Wakefield	2002	21	8	0	0	32
	Huddersfield	2001	26	15	0	0	60
Dale Fritz	Castleford	1999-2003	120(4)	9	0	0	36
Gareth Frodsham	St Helens	2008-09	1(9)	0	0	0	0
Liam Fulton	Huddersfield	2009	12(3)	4	0	0	16
David Furner	Leeds	2003-04	45	8	23	0	78
	Wigan	2001-02	51(2)	21	13	0	110
David Furness	Castleford	1996	(1)	0	0	0	0
Matt Gafa	Harlequins	2006-09	81	26	16	0	136
Luke Gale	Leeds	2020	15	6	13	3	53
	Castleford	2015-18	100	32	402	15	947
	Bradford	2012-14	56(2)	13	108	4	272
	Harlequins	2009-11	56(12)	18	86	3	247
Ben Galea	Hull	2013	12(2)	3	0	0	12
	Hull KR	2008-12	115(2)	33	0	0	132
Danny Galea	Widnes	2014-15	38(4)	5	0	0	20
Tommy Gallagher	Hull KR	2007	1(7)	0	0	0	0
	Widnes	2004	(6)	0	0	0	0
	London	2003	1(9)	1	0	0	4

PLAYER	CLUB	YEAR	APP	TRIES	GOALS	FG	PTS
Keith Galloway	Leeds	2016-17	28(4)	1	0	0	4
Mark Gamson	Sheffield	1996	3	0	0	0	0
Jim Gannon	Hull KR	2007	7(16)	1	0	0	4
	Huddersfield	2003-06	79(14)	11	0	0	44
	Halifax	1999-2002	83(4)	14	0	0	56
Josh Ganson	Wigan	2017-18	1(6)	2	0	0	8
Mitch Garbutt	Hull KR	2019-20	5(22)	5	0	0	20
	Leeds	2015-18	36(25)	7	0	0	28
Steve Garces	Salford	2001	(1)	0	0	0	0
Benjamin Garcia	Catalans	2013-20	81(46)	20	0	0	80
Jean-Marc Garcia	Sheffield	1996-97	35(3)	22	0	0	88
Ade Gardner	Hull KR	2014	18	7	0	0	28
	St Helens	2002-13	236(12)	146	0	0	584
Matt Gardner	Harlequins	2009	6(3)	2	0	0	8
	Huddersfield	2006-07	22(3)	7	0	0	28
	Castleford	2004	1	1	0	0	4
Steve Gartland	Oldham	1996	1(1)	0	1	0	2
Daniel Gartner	Bradford	2001-03	74(1)	26	0	0	104
Dean Gaskell	Warrington	2002-05	58(1)	10	0	0	40
Lee Gaskell	Huddersfield	2017-20	81	22	30	0	148
	Bradford	2014	21	5	0	0	20
	Salford	2013	17	8	2	0	36
	St Helens	2010-13	33(9)	14	12	1	81
George Gatis	Huddersfield	2008	5(5)	1	0	0	4
James Gavet	Huddersfield	2020	3(12)	2	0	0	8
Richard Gay	Castleford	1996-2002	94(16)	39	0	0	156
Andrew Gee	Warrington	2000-01	33(1)	4	0	0	16
Matty Gee	Hull KR	2020	6(5)	0	0	0	0
	London	2019	14(8)	5	0	0	20
	Salford	2015	(2)	0	0	0	0
Anthony Gelling	Warrington	2020	11	6	0	0	24
	Wigan	2012-17	101(1)	52	0	0	208
Stanley Gene	Hull KR	2007-09	37(17)	9	0	0	36
	Bradford	2006	5(16)	8	0	0	32
	Huddersfield	2001, 2003-05	70(6)	27	0	0	108
	Hull	2000-01	5(23)	6	0	0	24
Steve Georgallis	Warrington	2001	5(1)	2	0	0	8
Luke George	Bradford	2014	9(1)	3	0	0	12
	Huddersfield	2012-13	28(2)	18	0	0	72
	Hull KR	2013	4	2	0	0	8
	Wakefield	2007-11	38(3)	24	0	0	96
Shaun Geritas	Warrington	1997	(5)	1	0	0	4
Alex Gerrard	Widnes	2012-18	48(40)	4	0	0	16
Anthony Gibbons	Leeds	1996	9(4)	2	0	1	9
David Gibbons	Leeds	1996	3(4)	2	0	0	8
Scott Gibbs	St Helens	1996	9	3	0	0	12
Ashley Gibson	Wakefield	2016-17	9	4	0	0	16
	Castleford	2014-15	27	9	0	0	36
	Salford	2010-13	77(4)	41	0	0	164
	Leeds	2005-09	25(7)	13	9	0	70
Damian Gibson	Castleford	2003-04	40(3)	5	0	0	20
	Salford	2002	28	3	0	0	12
	Halifax	1998-2001	104(1)	39	0	0	156
	Leeds	1997	18	3	0	0	12
Kurt Gidley	Warrington	2016-17	44	11	97	0	238
Matt Gidley	St Helens	2007-10	105	40	6	0	172
Tony Gigot	Wakefield	2020	6(1)	1	6	0	16
	Toronto	2020	2(1)	0	0	0	0
	Catalans	2010-11, 2015-19	117(13)	43	51	12	286
	London	2014	2	0	4	0	8
Ian Gildart	Oldham	1996-97	31(7)	0	0	0	0
Oliver Gildart	Wigan	2015-20	114(2)	54	0	0	216
	Salford	2015	3	1	0	0	4
Chris Giles	Widnes	2003-04	35	12	0	0	48
	St Helens	2002	(1)	0	0	0	0
Kieran Gill	Castleford	2017-18	4	4	0	0	16
Peter Gill	London	1996-99	75(6)	20	0	0	80
Carl Gillespie	Halifax	1996-99	47(36)	13	0	0	52
Michael Gillett	London	2001-02	23(21)	12	2	0	52
Simon Gillies	Warrington	1999	28	6	0	0	24
Tom Gilmore	Salford	2020	2	1	0	0	4
	Widnes	2012-18	38(1)	11	51	3	149
Lee Gilmour	Wakefield	2014	10(3)	2	0	0	8
	Castleford	2013	10(2)	0	0	0	0
	Huddersfield	2010-12	71(1)	17	0	0	68
	St Helens	2004-09	149(3)	41	0	0	164
	Bradford	2001-03	44(31)	20	0	0	80
	Wigan	1997-2000	44(39)	22	0	0	88
Marc Glanville	Leeds	1998-99	43(3)	5	0	0	20
Eddie Glaze	Castleford	1996	1	0	0	0	0
Paul Gleadhill	Leeds	1996	4	0	0	0	0
Ben Gledhill	Salford	2012-13	3(10)	1	0	0	4
	Wakefield	2010-11	(16)	0	0	0	0
Mark Gleeson	Warrington	2000-08	38(102)	12	0	0	48
Martin Gleeson	Salford	2013-14	26(1)	4	0	0	16
	Hull	2011	6	4	0	0	16
	Wigan	2009-11	46(1)	19	0	0	76
	Warrington	2005-09	110(1)	44	0	0	176
	St Helens	2002-04	56(1)	25	0	0	100
	Huddersfield	1999-2001	47(9)	18	0	0	72
Sean Gleeson	Hull KR	2013	6	0	0	0	0
	Salford	2011-12	35	14	0	0	56
	Wakefield	2007-10	67(6)	20	0	0	80
	Wigan	2005-06	3(3)	0	0	0	0
Jon Goddard	Hull KR	2007	20	2	0	0	8
	Castleford	2000-01	(2)	0	0	0	0
Richard Goddard	Castleford	1996-97	11(3)	2	10	0	28
Brad Godden	Leeds	1998-99	47	15	0	0	60
Pita Godinet	Wakefield	2014-15	18(19)	10	0	0	40
Wayne Godwin	Salford	2011-13, 2015	43(8)	6	0	0	24
	Bradford	2008-10	16(44)	9	0	0	36
	Hull	2007	3(13)	1	0	0	4
	Wigan	2005-06	9(38)	6	0	0	24
	Castleford	2001-04	30(33)	18	56	0	184
Jason Golden	London	2012	7(2)	1	0	0	4
	Harlequins	2009-11	34(12)	3	0	0	12
	Wakefield	2007-08	26(5)	1	0	0	4
Marvin Golden	Widnes	2003	4	1	0	0	4
	London	2001	17(2)	1	0	0	4
	Halifax	2000	20(2)	5	0	0	20
	Leeds	1996-99	43(11)	19	0	0	76
Ashton Golding	Huddersfield	2020	11	2	0	0	8
	Leeds	2014-18	42(9)	5	14	0	48
Brett Goldspink	Halifax	2000-02	64(5)	2	0	0	8
	Wigan	1999	6(16)	1	0	0	4
	St Helens	1998	19(4)	2	0	0	8
	Oldham	1997	13(2)	0	0	0	0
Lee Gomersall	Hull KR	2008	1	0	0	0	0
Bryson Goodwin	Warrington	2018-19	52	20	29	0	138
Luke Goodwin	London	1998	9(2)	3	1	1	15
	Oldham	1997	16(4)	10	17	2	76
Grant Gore	Widnes	2012-15	6(11)	1	0	0	4
Aaron Gorrell	Catalans	2007-08	23	6	14	0	52
Andy Gorski	Salford	2001-02	(2)	0	0	0	0
Cyrille Gossard	Catalans	2006-12	54(30)	5	0	0	20
Mickael Goudemand	Catalans	2018-20	7(27)	1	0	0	4
Bobbie Goulding	Salford	2001-02	31(1)	2	56	4	124
	Wakefield	2000	12	3	25	3	65
	Huddersfield	1998-99	27(1)	3	65	4	146
	St Helens	1996-98	42(2)	9	210	4	460
Bobbie Goulding (Jnr)	Wakefield	2013	1(2)	0	1	0	2
Darrell Goulding	Hull KR	2015	8	1	0	0	4
	Wigan	2005-14	129(24)	68	0	0	272
	Salford	2009	9	5	0	0	20
Mick Govin	Leigh	2005	5(6)	4	0	0	16
Craig Gower	London	2012-13	40	7	24	0	76
David Gower	Salford	2006-07	(16)	0	0	0	0
Regan Grace	St Helens	2017-20	101	57	0	0	228
Shane Grady	London	2013	5(4)	1	2	0	8
Brad Graham	Castleford	2020	1	0	0	0	0
James Graham	St Helens	2003-11, 2020	143(63)	48	0	0	192
Nathan Graham	Bradford	1996-98	17(28)	4	0	1	17
Nick Graham	Wigan	2003	13(1)	2	0	0	8
Dalton Grant	Crusaders	2011	(1)	0	0	0	0
Jon Grayshon	Harlequins	2007-09	10(32)	4	0	0	16
	Huddersfield	2003-06	7(43)	5	0	0	20
Blake Green	Wigan	2013-14	42(1)	15	0	0	60
	Hull KR	2011-12	35	14	0	0	56
Brett Green	Gateshead	1999	10(2)	0	0	0	0
Chris Green	Wakefield	2019-20	3(10)	0	0	0	0
	Hull	2012-19	33(92)	7	0	0	28
James Green	Castleford	2018	1(3)	0	0	0	0
	Leigh	2017	4(5)	0	0	0	0
	Hull KR	2012-16	8(64)	3	0	0	12
Toby Green	Huddersfield	2001	3(1)	1	0	0	4
Craig Greenhill	Castleford	2004	21(4)	1	0	0	4
	Hull	2002-03	56	3	2	0	16
Clint Greenshields	Catalans	2007-12	137	81	0	0	324
Brandon Greenwood	Halifax	1996	1	0	0	0	0
Gareth Greenwood	Halifax	2003	(1)	0	0	0	0
	Halifax	2002	1	0	0	0	0
James Greenwood	Salford	2015, 2020	7(2)	1	0	0	4
	Hull KR	2015-16, 2018-19	29(23)	7	0	0	28
	Wigan	2013, 2015	(2)	0	0	0	0
	London	2014	10(5)	3	0	0	12

159

Super League Players 1996-2020

PLAYER	CLUB	YEAR	APP	TRIES	GOALS	FG	PTS
Joe Greenwood	Wigan	2018-20	23(16)	12	0	0	48
	St Helens	2012-17	40(28)	26	0	0	104
Lee Greenwood	Huddersfield	2005	7	3	0	0	12
	London	2004-05	30(2)	19	0	0	76
	Halifax	2000-03	38(2)	17	0	0	68
	Sheffield	1999	1(1)	0	0	0	0
Nick Gregson	Wigan	2016-19	5(9)	1	0	0	4
James Grehan	Castleford	2012	2(2)	0	0	0	0
Maxime Greseque	Wakefield	2007	2(1)	0	0	0	0
Mathieu Griffi	Catalans	2006-08	1(25)	0	0	0	0
Darrell Griffin	Salford	2013-15	31(27)	1	0	0	4
	Leeds	2012	8(19)	2	0	0	8
	Huddersfield	2007-11	65(60)	13	0	0	52
	Wakefield	2003-06	55(37)	9	3	0	42
George Griffin	Castleford	2020	13	0	0	0	0
	Salford	2015-19	69(22)	16	0	0	64
	Wakefield	2015	5	0	0	0	0
	London	2014	(19)	1	0	0	4
	Hull KR	2012-13	11(7)	0	0	0	0
Josh Griffin	Hull	2017-20	85(5)	27	3	0	114
	Salford	2014-16	42	23	77	0	246
	Castleford	2012	20	13	1	0	54
	Wakefield	2011	17	5	21	0	62
	Huddersfield	2009	2	0	0	0	0
Jonathan Griffiths	Paris	1996	(4)	1	0	0	4
Andrew Grima	Workington	1996	2(9)	2	0	0	8
Tony Grimaldi	Hull	2000-01	56(1)	14	0	0	56
	Gateshead	1999	27(2)	10	0	0	40
Danny Grimley	Sheffield	1996	4(1)	1	0	0	4
Scott Grix	Huddersfield	2010-16, 2019	141(11)	53	32	0	276
	Wakefield	2008-09, 2017-18	81(3)	32	0	0	128
Simon Grix	Warrington	2006-14	133(25)	42	0	0	168
	Halifax	2003	2(4)	0	0	0	0
Brett Grogan	Gateshead	1999	14(7)	3	0	0	12
Brent Grose	Warrington	2003-07	134(1)	55	0	0	220
David Guasch	Catalans	2010	1	0	0	0	0
Joan Guasch	Catalans	2014-15	(6)	0	0	0	0
Renaud Guigue	Catalans	2006	14(4)	3	0	0	12
Jerome Guisset	Catalans	2006-10	102(23)	9	0	0	36
	Wigan	2005	20(2)	3	0	0	12
	Warrington	2000-04	59(65)	21	0	0	84
Awen Guttenbeil	Castleford	2008	19	0	0	0	0
Reece Guy	Oldham	1996	3(4)	0	0	0	0
Josh Guzdek	Hull KR	2013, 2015	2	1	0	0	4
Titus Gwaze	Wakefield	2019-20	(5)	0	0	0	0
Tom Haberecht	Castleford	2008	2(2)	1	0	0	4
Dean Hadley	Hull KR	2019-20	14(4)	3	0	0	12
	Hull	2013-16, 2018-19	55(26)	10	0	0	40
	Wakefield	2017	14(7)	2	0	0	8
Gareth Haggerty	Harlequins	2008-09	8(28)	6	0	0	24
	Salford	2004-07	1(93)	15	0	0	60
	Widnes	2002	1(2)	1	0	0	4
Kurt Haggerty	Widnes	2012	6(8)	2	0	0	8
Andy Haigh	St Helens	1996-98	20(16)	11	0	0	44
Scott Hale	St Helens	2011	(3)	1	0	0	4
Michael Haley	Leeds	2008	(1)	0	0	0	0
Carl Hall	Leeds	1996	7(2)	3	0	0	12
Corey Hall	Leeds	2020	(2)	0	0	0	0
Craig Hall	Hull KR	2011-14, 2018-19	102(3)	51	65	2	336
	Wakefield	2015-16	35	14	30	0	116
	Hull	2007-10	59(9)	39	11	0	178
Glenn Hall	Bradford	2010	7(18)	2	0	0	8
Martin Hall	Halifax	1998	2(10)	0	0	0	0
	Hull	1999	7	0	0	0	0
	Castleford	1998	4	0	0	0	0
	Wigan	1996-97	31(5)	7	6	0	40
Ryan Hall	Leeds	2007-18	278(13)	196	0	0	784
Sam Hall	Castleford	2020	(1)	0	0	0	0
Steve Hall	Widnes	2004	1	0	0	0	0
	London	2002-03	35(3)	10	0	0	40
	St Helens	1999-2001	36(22)	19	0	0	76
Graeme Hallas	Huddersfield	2001	1	0	0	0	0
	Hull	1998-99	30(10)	6	39	1	103
	Halifax	1996	11(4)	5	0	0	20
Sam Hallas	Leeds	2016	2(1)	0	0	0	0
Macauley Hallett	Hull KR	2014	2	3	0	0	12
Dave Halley	Bradford	2007-10	63(12)	20	0	0	80
	Wakefield	2009	5	4	0	0	16
Danny Halliwell	Salford	2007	2(3)	0	0	0	0
	Leigh	2005	5	3	0	0	12
	Halifax	2000-03	17(8)	4	0	0	16
	Warrington	2002	9(1)	8	0	0	32
	Wakefield	2002	3	0	0	0	0
Colum Halpenny	Wakefield	2003-06	103(1)	36	0	0	144
	Halifax	2002	22	12	0	0	48
Sam Halsall	Wigan	2020	1	0	0	0	0
Jon Hamer	Bradford	1996	(1)	0	0	0	0
Andrew Hamilton	London	1997, 2003	1(20)	3	0	0	12
John Hamilton	St Helens	1998	3	0	0	0	0
Gabe Hamlin	Wigan	2018-19	6(18)	3	0	0	12
Karle Hammond	Halifax	2002	10(2)	2	14	0	36
	Salford	2001	2(3)	1	0	0	4
	London	1999-2000	47	23	2	3	99
	St Helens	1996-98	58(8)	28	0	4	116
Ryan Hampshire	Wakefield	2018-20	63(5)	22	119	2	328
	Leigh	2017	12(1)	3	0	0	12
	Castleford	2016	19(2)	8	0	0	32
	Wigan	2013-15	20(5)	8	24	0	80
Rhys Hanbury	Widnes	2012-18	153	71	99	1	483
	Crusaders	2010-11	26(1)	14	0	0	56
Anthony Hancock	Paris	1997	8(6)	1	0	0	4
Michael Hancock	Salford	2001-02	12(24)	7	0	0	28
Jordan Hand	Wakefield	2015	(2)	0	0	0	0
	St Helens	2013-14	(3)	0	0	0	0
Gareth Handford	Castleford	2001	7(2)	0	0	0	0
	Bradford	2000	1(1)	0	0	0	0
Paul Handforth	Castleford	2006	2(15)	2	1	0	10
	Wakefield	2000-04	17(44)	10	13	0	66
Ash Handley	Leeds	2014-20	105(3)	66	0	0	264
Paddy Handley	Leeds	1996	1(1)	2	0	0	8
Dean Hanger	Warrington	1999	7(11)	3	0	0	12
	Huddersfield	1998	20(1)	5	0	0	20
Chris Hankinson	Wigan	2018-20	18(4)	4	19	0	54
Umyla Hanley	Wigan	2020	1	0	0	0	0
Josh Hannay	Celtic	2009	17	2	24	0	56
Harrison Hansen	Widnes	2018	1	1	0	0	4
	Leigh	2017	19(2)	1	0	0	4
	Salford	2014-15	41(2)	7	0	0	28
	Wigan	2004-13	155(62)	39	0	0	156
Lee Hansen	Wigan	1997	10(5)	0	0	0	0
Shontayne Hape	Bradford	2003-08	123(2)	79	0	0	316
Lionel Harbin	Wakefield	2001	(1)	0	0	0	0
Zak Hardaker	Wigan	2019-20	48	15	159	1	379
	Castleford	2017	28	12	1	0	50
	Leeds	2011-16	135	57	43	1	315
Ian Hardman	Hull KR	2007	18	4	0	0	16
	St Helens	2003-07	32(11)	9	5	0	46
Jeff Hardy	Hudds-Sheff	2000	20(5)	6	0	1	25
	Sheffield	1999	22(4)	7	0	0	28
Spencer Hargrave	Castleford	1996-99	(6)	0	0	0	0
Bryn Hargreaves	Bradford	2011-12	45(5)	1	0	0	4
	St Helens	2007-10	53(44)	7	0	0	28
	Wigan	2004-06	16(12)	1	0	0	4
Lee Harland	Castleford	1996-2004	148(35)	20	0	0	80
Neil Harmon	Halifax	2003	13(3)	0	0	0	0
	Salford	2001	6(5)	0	0	0	0
	Bradford	1998-2000	15(13)	2	0	0	8
	Huddersfield	1998	12	1	0	0	4
	Leeds	1996	10	1	0	0	4
Ben Harris	Bradford	2005-07	70(4)	24	0	0	96
Iestyn Harris	Bradford	2004-08	109(11)	35	87	2	316
	Leeds	1997-2001	111(7)	57	490	6	1214
	Warrington	1996	16	4	63	2	144
Liam Harris	Hull	2018	9(2)	3	0	0	12
Ben Harrison	Wakefield	2016	3	0	0	0	0
	Warrington	2007-15	125(59)	14	0	0	56
James Harrison	Leeds	2020	2(2)	0	0	0	0
Karl Harrison	Hull	1999	26	2	0	0	8
	Halifax	1996-98	60(2)	2	0	0	8
Owen Harrison	Hull KR	2019-20	3(6)	0	0	0	0
Andrew Hart	London	2004	12(1)	2	0	0	8
Tim Hartley	Harlequins	2006	2	1	0	0	4
	Salford	2004-05	6(7)	5	0	0	20
Carlos Hassan	Bradford	1996	6(4)	2	0	0	8
Phil Hassan	Wakefield	2002	9(1)	0	0	0	0
	Halifax	2000-01	25(4)	3	0	0	12
	Salford	1998	15	2	0	0	8
	Leeds	1996-97	38(4)	12	0	0	48
James Hasson	Wakefield	2017	(4)	0	0	0	0
	Salford	2017	4(1)	0	0	0	0
Jackson Hastings	Wigan	2020	19	9	0	1	37
	Salford	2018-19	34	11	4	0	52
Tom Haughey	Castleford	2006	2(2)	0	0	0	4
	London	2003-04	10(8)	1	0	0	4
	Wakefield	2001-02	5(11)	0	0	0	0
Simon Haughton	Wigan	1996-2002	63(46)	32	0	0	128
Solomon Haumono	Harlequins	2006	10(9)	6	0	0	24
	London	2005	24(5)	8	0	0	32

PLAYER	CLUB	YEAR	APP	TRIES	GOALS	FG	PTS
Weller Hauraki	Hull KR	2019-20	34(4)	5	0	0	20
	Widnes	2018	7	0	0	0	0
	Salford	2015-18	45(12)	8	0	0	32
	Castleford	2013-14	50(2)	9	0	0	36
	Leeds	2011-12	18(17)	6	0	0	24
	Crusaders	2010	26(1)	11	0	0	44
Ethan Havard	Wigan	2019-20	5(5)	0	0	0	0
Richie Hawkyard	Bradford	2007	1(2)	1	0	0	4
Andy Hay	Widnes	2003-04	50(2)	7	0	0	28
	Leeds	1997-2002	112(27)	43	0	0	172
	Sheffield	1996-97	17(3)	5	0	0	20
Adam Hayes	Hudds-Sheff	2000	2(1)	0	0	0	0
Joey Hayes	Salford	1999	9	2	0	0	8
	St Helens	1996-98	11(6)	7	0	0	28
James Haynes	Hull KR	2009	1	0	0	0	0
Callum Hazzard	St Helens	2019	(1)	0	0	0	0
Mathew Head	Hull	2007	9(1)	1	0	1	5
Mitch Healey	Castleford	2001-03	68(1)	10	16	0	72
Daniel Heckenberg	Harlequins	2006-09	31(39)	4	0	0	16
Andrew Heffernan	Hull KR	2018	7	2	0	0	8
Chris Heil	Hull KR	2012-13	4	2	0	0	8
Ben Hellewell	London	2019	2	0	0	0	0
Ricky Helliwell	Salford	1997-99	(2)	0	0	0	0
Tom Hemingway	Huddersfield	2005-09	7(7)	1	17	0	38
Bryan Henare	St Helens	2000-01	4(12)	1	0	0	4
Richard Henare	Warrington	1996-97	28(2)	24	0	0	96
Andrew Henderson	Castleford	2006, 2008	44(11)	4	0	0	16
Ian Henderson	Catalans	2011-15	118(9)	12	0	0	48
	Bradford	2005-07	33(37)	13	0	0	52
Kevin Henderson	Wakefield	2005-11	52(68)	9	0	0	36
	Leigh	2005	(1)	0	0	0	0
Adam Henry	Bradford	2014	23(1)	5	0	0	20
Mark Henry	Salford	2009-11	67	22	0	0	88
Brad Hepi	Castleford	1999, 2001	9(21)	3	0	0	12
	Salford	2000	3(5)	0	0	0	0
	Hull	1998	15(1)	3	0	0	12
Tyla Hepi	Castleford	2020	3(4)	0	0	0	0
	Hull KR	2013	(4)	0	0	0	0
Jon Hepworth	Castleford	2003-04	19(23)	7	8	0	44
	Leeds	2003	(1)	0	0	0	0
	London	2002	(2)	0	0	0	0
Marc Herbert	Bradford	2011	20	4	2	0	20
Aaron Heremaia	Widnes	2015-18	44(41)	7	0	0	28
	Hull	2012-14	27(37)	12	0	0	48
Maxime Herold	London	2014	(2)	0	0	0	0
Ian Herron	Hull	2000	9	1	17	0	38
	Gateshead	1999	25	4	105	0	226
Jason Hetherington	London	2001-02	37	9	0	0	36
Gareth Hewitt	Salford	1999	2(1)	0	0	0	0
Sam Hewitt	Huddersfield	2018-20	8(13)	1	0	0	4
Andrew Hick	Hull	2000	9(9)	1	0	0	4
	Gateshead	1999	12(5)	2	0	0	8
Jarrad Hickey	Wakefield	2011	(8)	2	0	0	8
Chris Hicks	Warrington	2008-10	72	56	119	0	462
Paul Hicks	Wakefield	1999	(1)	0	0	0	0
Darren Higgins	London	1998	5(6)	2	0	0	8
Iain Higgins	London	1997-98	1(7)	2	0	0	8
Liam Higgins	Wakefield	2011	4(12)	0	0	0	0
	Castleford	2008-10	42(32)	2	0	0	8
	Hull	2003-06	1(34)	0	0	0	0
Jack Higginson	Wigan	2016	2(1)	1	0	0	4
Micky Higham	Leigh	2017	11(1)	2	0	0	8
	Warrington	2009-15	73(78)	34	0	0	136
	Wigan	2006-08	61(28)	13	0	0	52
	St Helens	2001-05	43(56)	32	0	0	128
Chris Highton	Warrington	1997	1(1)	0	0	0	0
David Highton	London	2004-05	21(24)	2	0	0	8
	Salford	2002	4(5)	2	0	0	8
	Warrington	1998-2001	18(14)	2	0	0	8
Paul Highton	Salford	1998-2002, 2004-07	114(80)	14	0	0	56
	Halifax	1996-97	12(18)	2	0	0	8
Adam Higson	Leigh	2017	13	2	0	0	8
Peta Hiku	Warrington	2017	4	1	0	0	4
Andy Hill	Huddersfield	1999	(4)	0	0	0	0
	Castleford	1999	4(4)	0	0	0	0
Chris Hill	Warrington	2012-20	224(10)	26	0	0	104
	Leigh	2005	(1)	0	0	0	0
Danny Hill	Wigan	2006-07	1(10)	0	0	0	0
	Hull KR	2007	2	0	0	0	0
	Hull	2004-06	4(6)	0	0	0	0
Howard Hill	Oldham	1996-97	22(12)	4	0	0	16
John Hill	St Helens	2003	(1)	0	0	0	0
	Halifax	2003	1(2)	0	0	0	0
	Warrington	2001-02	(4)	0	0	0	0

PLAYER	CLUB	YEAR	APP	TRIES	GOALS	FG	PTS
Scott Hill	Harlequins	2007-08	41(2)	13	0	0	52
Mark Hilton	Warrington	1996-2000, 2002-06	141(40)	7	0	0	28
Ryan Hinchcliffe	Huddersfield	2016-18	70(11)	11	0	0	44
Daniel Hindmarsh	London	2019	(6)	0	0	0	0
Ian Hindmarsh	Catalans	2006	25	3	0	0	12
Keegan Hirst	Wakefield	2017-19	17(44)	1	0	0	4
Jy Hitchcox	Castleford	2016-18	25(1)	21	0	0	84
Brendan Hlad	Castleford	2008	(3)	0	0	0	0
Andy Hobson	Widnes	2004	5(13)	0	0	0	0
	Halifax	1998-2003	51(85)	8	0	0	32
Gareth Hock	Leigh	2017	12(1)	3	0	0	12
	Salford	2014-15	15(1)	4	0	0	16
	Widnes	2013	15(2)	9	1	0	38
	Wigan	2003-09, 2011-12	126(43)	38	0	0	152
Tommy Hodgkinson	St Helens	2006	(1)	0	0	0	0
Andy Hodgson	Wakefield	1999	14(2)	2	1	0	10
	Bradford	1997-98	8(2)	4	0	0	16
Bailey Hodgson	Castleford	2020	1	0	0	0	0
Brett Hodgson	Warrington	2011-13	66	33	268	1	669
	Huddersfield	2009-10	45	13	166	0	384
David Hodgson	Hull KR	2012-14	51	31	0	0	124
	Huddersfield	2008-11	84	59	0	0	236
	Salford	2005-07	81	30	47	0	214
	Wigan	2000-04	90(19)	43	0	0	172
	Halifax	1999	10(3)	5	0	0	20
Elliot Hodgson	Huddersfield	2009	1	0	0	0	0
Josh Hodgson	Hull KR	2010-14	98(29)	35	0	0	140
	Hull	2009	(2)	0	0	0	0
Ryan Hoffman	Wigan	2011	28(1)	11	0	0	44
Darren Hogg	London	1996	(1)	0	0	0	0
Michael Hogue	Paris	1997	5(7)	0	0	0	0
Lance Hohaia	St Helens	2012-15	67(9)	21	0	1	85
Chris Holden	Warrington	1996-97	2(1)	0	0	0	0
Daniel Holdsworth	Hull	2013	19	2	28	2	66
	Salford	2010-12	71	18	183	1	439
Stephen Holgate	Halifax	2000	1(10)	0	0	0	0
	Hull	1999	1	0	0	0	0
	Wigan	1997-98	11(26)	2	0	0	8
	Workington	1996	19	3	0	0	12
Stephen Holker	Hull KR	2015-16	(4)	0	0	0	0
Martyn Holland	Wakefield	2000-03	52(3)	6	0	0	24
Oliver Holmes	Castleford	2010-20	161(34)	36	0	0	144
Tim Holmes	Widnes	2004-05	15(4)	0	0	0	0
Tom Holmes	Huddersfield	2019-20	12(5)	0	0	0	0
	Castleford	2015-17	7(8)	3	0	0	12
Graham Holroyd	Huddersfield	2003	3(5)	0	0	0	0
	Salford	2000-02	40(11)	8	75	5	187
	Halifax	1999	24(2)	3	74	5	165
	Leeds	1996-98	40(26)	22	101	8	298
Tom Holroyd	Leeds	2018-20	3(8)	0	0	0	0
Dallas Hood	Wakefield	2003-04	18(9)	1	0	0	4
Liam Hood	Leigh	2017	8(5)	3	0	0	12
	Salford	2015	2(15)	0	0	0	0
	Leeds	2012	1(4)	3	0	0	12
Jason Hooper	St Helens	2003-07	89(6)	35	30	0	200
Will Hope	Salford	2013	1(2)	0	0	0	0
Lee Hopkins	Harlequins	2006-07	44(3)	11	0	0	44
	London	2005	29	6	0	0	24
Sam Hopkins	Leigh	2017	3(17)	6	0	0	24
Sean Hoppe	St Helens	1999-2002	69(16)	32	0	0	128
Graeme Horne	Hull KR	2012-16	81(18)	21	0	0	84
	Huddersfield	2010-11	23(17)	11	0	0	44
	Hull	2003-09	49(74)	24	0	0	96
Richard Horne	Hull	1999-2014	341(16)	115	12	6	490
Justin Horo	Wakefield	2018-19	22(14)	6	0	0	24
	Catalans	2016-17	34(1)	12	0	0	48
John Hough	Warrington	1996-97	9	2	0	0	8
Danny Houghton	Hull	2007-20	280(53)	41	0	0	164
Sylvain Houles	Wakefield	2003, 2005	8(1)	1	0	0	4
	London	2001-02	17(10)	11	0	0	44
	Hudds-Sheff	2000	5(2)	1	0	0	4
Chris Houston	Widnes	2016-18	58(1)	5	0	0	20
Harvey Howard	Wigan	2001-02	25(27)	1	0	0	4
	Bradford	1998	4(2)	1	0	0	4
	Leeds	1996	8	0	0	0	0
Kim Howard	London	1997	4(5)	0	0	0	0
Stuart Howarth	Wakefield	2011, 2015-16	30(5)	4	0	0	16
	Hull	2015	2(3)	0	0	0	0
	Salford	2012-14	25(12)	1	0	0	4
	St Helens	2013	14(1)	0	0	0	0
Stuart Howarth	Workington	1996	(2)	0	0	0	0
David Howell	London	2012-13	24	5	0	0	20
	Harlequins	2008-11	76	26	0	0	104

Super League Players 1996-2020

PLAYER	CLUB	YEAR	APP	TRIES	GOALS	FG	PTS
Chris Joynt	St Helens	1996-2004	201(14)	68	0	0	272
Benjamin Jullien	Catalans	2018-20	40(10)	9	0	0	36
	Warrington	2016-17	19(7)	4	0	0	16
Gregory Kacala	Paris	1996	7	1	0	0	4
Andy Kain	Castleford	2004, 2006	9(7)	3	10	0	32
Sam Kasiano	Catalans	2019-20	3(32)	5	0	0	20
Antonio Kaufusi	Huddersfield	2014	15(2)	1	0	0	4
	Bradford	2014	4	0	0	0	0
	London	2012-13	44(5)	5	0	0	20
Mal Kaufusi	London	2004	1(3)	0	0	0	0
Ben Kavanagh	Hull KR	2018	13(8)	0	0	0	0
	Wakefield	2015	6(3)	0	0	0	0
	Widnes	2012-15	18(33)	0	0	0	0
Liam Kay	Wakefield	2012-13, 2020	7	6	0	0	24
	Toronto	2020	6	1	0	0	4
Ben Kaye	Harlequins	2009-10	2(13)	0	0	0	0
	Leeds	2008	2(2)	1	0	0	4
Elliot Kear	Salford	2020	8(1)	1	0	0	4
	London	2019	26	3	0	0	12
	Bradford	2012-14	53(2)	17	0	0	68
	Crusaders	2010-11	16(1)	4	0	0	16
	Celtic	2009	3	0	0	0	0
Brett Kearney	Bradford	2010-14	107	55	0	0	220
Stephen Kearney	Hull	2005	22(2)	5	0	0	20
Damon Keating	Wakefield	2002	7(17)	1	0	0	4
Kris Keating	Hull KR	2014	23	5	0	0	20
Shaun Keating	London	1996	1(3)	0	0	0	0
Mark Keenan	Workington	1996	3(4)	1	0	0	4
Jimmy Keinhorst	Hull KR	2019-20	23(3)	7	0	0	28
	Leeds	2012-18	46(23)	25	0	0	100
	Widnes	2018	3	1	0	0	4
	Wakefield	2014	7	1	0	0	4
Albert Kelly	Hull	2017-20	63(2)	39	0	1	157
	Hull KR	2015-16	37	21	3	0	90
Tony Kemp	Wakefield	1999-2000	15(5)	2	0	1	9
	Leeds	1996-98	23(2)	5	0	2	22
Damien Kennedy	London	2003	5(11)	1	0	0	4
Ian Kenny	St Helens	2004	(1)	0	0	0	0
Sean Kenny	Salford	2016	(4)	0	0	0	0
Shaun Kenny-Dowall	Hull KR	2020	17	3	0	0	12
Jason Kent	Leigh	2005	23	1	0	0	4
Liam Kent	Hull	2012-13	1(5)	0	0	0	0
Shane Kenward	Wakefield	1999	28	6	0	0	24
	Salford	1998	1	0	0	0	0
Jason Keough	Paris	1997	2	1	0	0	4
Keiran Kerr	Widnes	2005	6	2	0	0	8
Lee Kershaw	Wakefield	2019-20	6	2	0	0	8
Martin Ketteridge	Halifax	1996	7(5)	0	0	0	0
Ronnie Kettlewell	Warrington	1996	(1)	0	0	0	0
Joe Keyes	Hull KR	2020	4(1)	0	0	0	0
	London	2014	7	5	0	0	20
Younes Khattabi	Catalans	2006-08	24(4)	10	0	0	40
Samy Kibula	Warrington	2020	(2)	0	0	0	0
	Wigan	2018	(1)	0	0	0	0
David Kidwell	Warrington	2001-02	14(12)	9	0	0	36
Ben Kilner	Wigan	2020	(1)	0	0	0	0
Andrew King	London	2003	23(1)	15	0	0	60
Dave King	Huddersfield	1998-99	11(17)	2	0	0	8
George King	Hull KR	2020	2(2)	0	0	0	0
	Wakefield	2019-20	8(19)	0	0	0	0
	Warrington	2014-18	12(68)	1	0	0	4
James King	Leigh	2005	5(7)	0	0	0	0
Kevin King	Wakefield	2005	8(1)	2	0	0	8
	Castleford	2004	(1)	0	0	0	0
Matt King	Warrington	2008-11	91	58	0	0	232
Paul King	Wakefield	2010-11	10(19)	0	0	1	1
	Hull	1999-2009	136(93)	20	0	1	81
Toby King	Warrington	2014-20	85(7)	27	0	0	108
Jon Luke Kirby	Huddersfield	2019	(3)	0	0	0	0
Andy Kirk	Wakefield	2005	6(3)	1	0	0	4
	Salford	2004	20	5	0	0	20
	Leeds	2001-02	4(4)	0	0	0	0
Ian Kirke	Wakefield	2015	2(2)	1	0	0	4
	Leeds	2006-14	52(132)	10	0	0	40
John Kirkpatrick	London	2004-05	18(1)	5	0	0	20
	St Helens	2001-03	10(11)	10	0	0	40
	Halifax	2003	4	1	0	0	4
Danny Kirmond	Wakefield	2010, 2012-20	147(15)	42	0	0	168
	Huddersfield	2008-11	18(31)	9	0	0	36
Wayne Kitchin	Workington	1996	11(6)	3	17	1	47
Sione Kite	Widnes	2012	6(8)	1	0	0	4
Ian Knott	Leigh	2005	8(1)	2	0	0	8
	Wakefield	2002-03	34(5)	7	79	0	186
	Warrington	1996-2001	68(41)	24	18	0	132
Matt Knowles	Wigan	1996	(3)	0	0	0	0
Michael Knowles	Castleford	2006	(1)	0	0	0	0
Morgan Knowles	St Helens	2016-20	72(48)	19	0	0	76
Phil Knowles	Salford	1997	1	0	0	0	0
Simon Knox	Halifax	1999	(6)	0	0	0	0
	Salford	1998	1(1)	0	0	0	0
	Bradford	1996-98	9(19)	7	0	0	28
Toa Kohe-Love	Warrington	1996-2001, 2005-06	166(3)	90	0	0	360
	Bradford	2004	1(1)	0	0	0	0
	Hull	2002-03	42	19	0	0	76
Paul Koloi	Wigan	1997	1(2)	1	0	0	4
Craig Kopczak	Wakefield	2019-20	25(15)	3	0	0	12
	Salford	2016-18	39(27)	11	0	0	44
	Huddersfield	2013-15	48(37)	6	0	0	24
	Bradford	2006-12	32(83)	10	0	0	40
Michael Korkidas	Wakefield	2003-06, 2009-11	133(36)	15	0	0	60
	Huddersfield	2009	4(1)	1	0	0	4
	Castleford	2008	15(6)	1	0	0	4
	Salford	2007	26(1)	1	0	0	4
Nick Kouparitsas	Harlequins	2011	2(13)	1	0	0	4
Olsi Krasniqi	London	2012-14, 2019	36(35)	3	0	0	12
	Salford	2015-17	8(29)	1	0	0	4
	Harlequins	2010-11	3(20)	1	0	0	4
David Krause	London	1996-97	22(1)	7	0	0	28
Ben Kusto	Huddersfield	2001	21(4)	9	0	1	37
Anthony Laffranchi	St Helens	2012-14	50(18)	19	0	0	76
James Laithwaite	Warrington	2013-15	23(22)	1	0	0	4
	Hull KR	2012	1(2)	1	0	0	4
Adrian Lam	Wigan	2001-04	105(2)	40	1	9	171
Brock Lamb	London	2019	6	3	0	1	13
Callum Lancaster	Hull	2014-16	7	9	0	0	36
Jordan Lane	Hull	2018-20	21(21)	7	0	0	28
Mark Lane	Paris	1996	(2)	0	0	0	0
Allan Langer	Warrington	2000-01	47	13	4	0	60
Kevin Langer	London	1996	12(4)	2	0	0	8
Junior Langi	Salford	2005-06	27(7)	7	0	0	28
Samisoni Langi	Catalans	2018-20	59	12	0	0	48
	Leigh	2017	3	1	0	0	4
Chris Langley	Huddersfield	2000-01	18(1)	3	0	0	12
Gareth Langley	St Helens	2006	1	1	3	0	10
Jamie Langley	Hull KR	2014	6(5)	1	0	0	4
	Bradford	2002-13	182(57)	36	0	0	144
Ryan Lannon	Salford	2015-20	33(29)	6	0	0	24
	Hull KR	2019	1(5)	1	0	0	4
Kevin Larroyer	Castleford	2017	2(4)	0	0	0	0
	Hull KR	2014-16	34(13)	9	0	0	36
	Catalans	2012-13	9(10)	6	0	0	24
Andy Last	Hull	1999-2005	16(10)	4	0	0	16
Leilani Latu	Warrington	2020	3	1	0	0	4
Sam Latus	Hull KR	2010-13	34(3)	13	0	0	52
Epalahame Lauaki	Wigan	2012-13	14(16)	2	0	0	8
	Hull	2009-11	3(50)	4	0	0	16
Dale Laughton	Warrington	2002	15(1)	0	0	0	0
	Huddersfield	2000-01	36(2)	4	0	0	16
	Sheffield	1996-99	48(22)	5	0	0	20
Ali Lauitiiti	Wakefield	2012-15	46(31)	16	0	0	64
	Leeds	2004-11	64(117)	58	0	0	232
Quentin Laulu-Togaga'e	Castleford	2018	8(1)	6	0	0	24
Jason Laurence	Salford	1997	1	0	0	0	0
Graham Law	Wakefield	1999-2002	34(30)	6	40	0	104
Neil Law	Wakefield	1999-2002	83	39	0	0	156
	Sheffield	1998	1(1)	1	0	0	4
Dean Lawford	Widnes	2003-04	17(1)	5	2	4	28
	Halifax	2001	1(1)	0	0	0	0
	Leeds	1997-2000	15(8)	2	3	0	14
	Huddersfield	1999	6(1)	0	6	1	13
	Sheffield	1996	9(5)	2	1	1	11
George Lawler	Hull KR	2016, 2018-20	48(8)	3	0	0	12
Johnny Lawless	Halifax	2001-03	73(1)	10	0	0	40
	Hudds-Sheff	2000	19(6)	3	0	0	12
	Sheffield	1996-99	76(4)	11	0	0	44
Michael Lawrence	Huddersfield	2007-20	223(49)	46	0	0	184
Adam Lawton	Salford	2019	1(1)	0	0	0	0
	Widnes	2013-14	2(10)	5	0	0	20
Charlie Leaeno	Wakefield	2010	7(3)	2	0	0	8
Mark Leafa	Castleford	2008	5(9)	1	0	0	4
	Leigh	2005	28	2	0	0	8
Leroy Leapai	London	1996	2	2	0	0	8
Jim Leatham	Hull	1998-99	20(18)	4	0	0	16
	Leeds	1997	(1)	0	0	0	0
Andy Leathem	Warrington	1999	2(8)	1	0	0	4
	St Helens	1996-98	20(1)	1	0	0	4

Super League Players 1996-2020

PLAYER	CLUB	YEAR	APP	TRIES	GOALS	FG	PTS
Danny Lee	Gateshead	1999	16(2)	0	0	0	0
Jason Lee	Halifax	2001	10(1)	2	0	0	8
Mark Lee	Salford	1997-2000	25(11)	1	0	4	8
Robert Lee	Hull	1999	4(3)	0	0	0	0
Tommy Lee	Hull KR	2018-19	24(6)	2	0	0	8
	St Helens	2017	9(9)	0	0	0	0
	Salford	2014-16	37(5)	4	0	0	16
	London	2013	16(4)	2	0	0	8
	Huddersfield	2012	11(7)	3	0	0	12
	Wakefield	2011	25	6	0	0	24
	Crusaders	2010	3(9)	0	0	0	0
	Hull	2005-09	44(27)	6	0	0	24
Kruise Leeming	Leeds	2020	8(3)	0	0	0	0
	Huddersfield	2013-19	49(67)	15	0	0	60
Matty Lees	St Helens	2017-20	22(39)	2	0	0	8
Matthew Leigh	Salford	2000	(6)	0	0	0	0
Chris Leikvoll	Warrington	2004-07	72(18)	4	0	0	16
Jim Lenihan	Huddersfield	1999	19(1)	10	0	0	40
Mark Lennon	Celtic	2009	10(3)	1	8	0	20
	Hull KR	2007	11(4)	5	7	0	34
	Castleford	2001-03	30(21)	10	21	0	82
Tevita Leo-Latu	Wakefield	2006-10	28(49)	10	0	0	40
Gary Lester	Hull	1998-99	46	17	0	0	68
Stuart Lester	Wigan	1997	1(3)	0	0	0	0
Heath L'Estrange	Bradford	2010-13	56(35)	7	0	0	28
Afi Leuila	Oldham	1996-97	17(3)	2	0	0	8
Kylie Leuluai	Leeds	2007-15	182(45)	20	0	0	80
Macgraff Leuluai	Widnes	2012-18	52(64)	5	0	0	20
Phil Leuluai	Salford	2007, 2009-10	7(47)	3	0	0	12
Thomas Leuluai	Wigan	2007-12, 2017-20	269(2)	63	0	1	253
	Harlequins	2006	15(2)	6	0	0	24
	London	2005	20	13	0	0	52
Ricky Leutele	Toronto	2020	6	0	0	0	0
Mikey Lewis	Hull KR	2019-20	5(2)	2	2	0	12
Simon Lewis	Castleford	2001	4	3	0	0	12
Paul Leyland	St Helens	2006	1	0	0	0	0
Jon Liddell	Leeds	2001	1	0	0	0	0
Jason Lidden	Castleford	1997	15(1)	7	0	0	28
Jordan Lilley	Leeds	2015-18	21(11)	2	42	0	92
Danny Lima	Wakefield	2007	(3)	0	0	0	0
	Salford	2006	7(2)	0	0	0	0
	Warrington	2004-06	15(47)	9	0	0	36
Jeff Lima	Catalans	2014-15	37(7)	3	1	0	14
	Wigan	2011-12	24(29)	4	0	0	16
Tom Lineham	Warrington	2016-20	102	67	0	0	268
	Hull	2012-15	61(1)	50	0	0	200
Kane Linnett	Hull KR	2019-20	38(1)	10	0	0	40
Jez Litten	Hull KR	2019-20	6(5)	0	0	0	0
	Hull	2017-19	(17)	1	0	0	4
Harry Little	London	2013	2	0	0	0	0
Jack Littlejohn	Salford	2018	15(3)	3	1	0	14
Craig Littler	St Helens	2006	1	1	0	0	4
Stuart Littler	Salford	1998-2002, 2004-07, 2009-10	217(30)	65	0	0	260
Harvey Livett	Hull KR	2019-20	8(5)	3	0	0	12
	Warrington	2017-19	23(15)	13	21	0	94
Peter Livett	Workington	1996	3(1)	0	0	0	0
Rhodri Lloyd	Wigan	2012-13, 2015	3(4)	0	0	0	0
	Widnes	2014	(4)	0	0	0	0
	London	2013	2	0	0	0	0
Garry Lo	Castleford	2018	1	1	0	0	4
Kevin Locke	Wakefield	2015	3	0	0	0	0
	Salford	2014-15	13	6	11	0	46
Jack Logan	Hull	2014-16, 2018-19	36(2)	15	0	0	60
Scott Logan	Wigan	2006	10(11)	0	0	0	0
	Hull	2001-03	27(20)	5	0	0	20
Jamahl Lolesi	Huddersfield	2007-10	75(9)	27	0	0	108
Filimone Lolohea	Harlequins	2006	3(6)	0	0	0	0
	London	2005	8(15)	0	0	0	0
Tui Lolohea	Salford	2019-20	30	13	29	0	110
	Leeds	2019	15	2	19	0	46
David Lomax	Huddersfield	2000-01	45(9)	4	0	0	16
	Paris	1997	19(2)	1	0	0	4
Jonny Lomax	St Helens	2009-20	218(2)	103	84	2	582
Dave Long	London	1999	(1)	0	0	0	0
Karl Long	London	2003	(1)	0	0	0	0
	Widnes	2002	4	1	0	0	4
Sean Long	Hull	2010-11	22	6	0	0	24
	St Helens	1997-2009	263(8)	126	826	20	2176
	Wigan	1996-97	1(5)	0	0	0	0
Davide Longo	Bradford	1996	1(3)	0	0	0	0
Ellis Longstaff	Warrington	2020	1(1)	0	0	0	0
Gary Lord	Oldham	1996-97	28(12)	3	0	0	12
Paul Loughlin	Huddersfield	1998-99	34(2)	4	4	0	24
	Bradford	1996-97	36(4)	15	8	0	76
Rhys Lovegrove	Hull KR	2007-14	75(74)	19	0	0	76
Karl Lovell	Hudds-Sheff	2000	14	5	0	0	20
	Sheffield	1999	22(4)	8	0	0	32
Will Lovell	London	2012-14, 2019	26(23)	5	0	0	20
James Lowes	Bradford	1996-2003	205	84	2	2	342
Laurent Lucchese	Paris	1996	13(5)	2	0	0	8
Robert Lui	Leeds	2019-20	23	6	0	0	24
	Salford	2016-19	84(3)	26	33	0	170
Zebastian Luisi	Harlequins	2006-07	23(2)	4	0	0	16
	London	2004-05	21(1)	7	0	0	28
Keith Lulia	Bradford	2012-13	50	19	0	0	76
Shaun Lunt	Leeds	2012, 2019	15(10)	7	0	0	28
	Hull KR	2015-16, 2018-19	25(18)	11	0	0	44
	Huddersfield	2009-15	73(39)	60	0	0	240
Peter Lupton	Crusaders	2010-11	37(9)	10	0	0	40
	Celtic	2009	16(4)	4	0	0	16
	Castleford	2006, 2008	40	11	0	0	44
	Hull	2003-06	19(26)	10	3	0	46
	London	2000-02	10(15)	2	2	0	12
Joey Lussick	Salford	2019-20	27(21)	15	4	0	68
Andy Lynch	Castleford	1999-2004, 2014-17	157(54)	17	0	0	68
	Hull	2012-13	39(14)	3	0	0	12
	Bradford	2005-11	159(29)	46	0	0	184
Reece Lyne	Wakefield	2013-20	168(1)	52	0	0	208
	Hull	2010-11	11(1)	2	0	0	8
Jamie Lyon	St Helens	2005-06	54(1)	39	172	0	500
Iliess Macani	London	2013-14	12(3)	4	0	0	16
Duncan MacGillivray	Wakefield	2004-08	75(18)	6	0	0	24
Brad Mackay	Bradford	2000	24(2)	8	0	0	32
Graham Mackay	Hull	2002	27	18	24	0	120
	Bradford	2001	16(3)	12	1	0	50
	Leeds	2000	12(8)	10	2	0	44
Keiron Maddocks	Leeds	2005	1(3)	0	0	0	0
Steve Maden	Leeds	2005	23	9	0	0	36
	Warrington	2002	3	0	0	0	0
Mateaki Mafi	Warrington	1996-97	7(8)	7	0	0	28
Shaun Magennis	St Helens	2010-12	7(19)	3	0	0	12
Brendan Magnus	London	2000	3	1	0	0	4
Mark Maguire	London	1996-97	11(4)	7	13	0	54
Adam Maher	Hull	2000-03	88(4)	24	0	0	96
	Gateshead	1999	21(5)	3	0	0	12
Lee Maher	Leeds	1996	4(1)	0	0	0	0
Will Maher	Hull KR	2020	6(6)	0	0	0	0
	Castleford	2014-15	5(30)	1	0	0	4
Shaun Mahony	Paris	1997	5	0	0	0	0
Hutch Maiava	Hull	2007	(19)	1	0	0	4
David Maiden	Hull	2000-01	32(10)	11	0	0	44
	Gateshead	1999	5(16)	8	0	0	32
Craig Makin	Salford	1999-2001	24(20)	2	0	0	8
Tommy Makinson	St Helens	2011-20	219(5)	126	116	1	737
Brady Malam	Wigan	2000	5(20)	1	0	0	4
Dominic Maloney	Hull	2009	(7)	0	0	0	0
Francis Maloney	Castleford	1998-99, 2003-04	71(7)	24	33	3	165
	Salford	2001-02	45(1)	26	5	0	114
	Wakefield	2000	11	1	1	0	6
	Oldham	1996-97	39(2)	12	91	2	232
James Maloney	Catalans	2020		2	61	0	130
Jake Mamo	Warrington	2019-20	22(6)	11	0	0	44
	Huddersfield	2017-18	23	17	0	0	68
Dom Manfredi	Wigan	2013-16, 2018-20	70	54	0	0	216
	Salford	2014	1	2	0	0	8
George Mann	Warrington	1997	14(5)	1	0	0	4
	Leeds	1996	11(4)	2	0	0	8
Dane Manning	Leeds	2009	(1)	0	0	0	0
Josh Mantellato	Hull KR	2015-16	26	16	88	0	240
Misili Manu	Widnes	2005	1	0	0	0	0
Sika Manu	Hull	2016-19	90(4)	10	0	0	40
Willie Manu	St Helens	2013-14	35(11)	9	0	0	36
	Hull	2007-14	133(18)	33	0	0	132
	Castleford	2006	19(4)	9	0	0	36
Manase Manuokafoa	Widnes	2015-17	3(54)	3	0	0	12
	Bradford	2012-14	49(21)	3	0	0	12
Darren Mapp	Celtic	2009	9(2)	1	0	0	4
David March	Wakefield	1999-2007	164(23)	34	126	0	388
Paul March	Wakefield	1999-2001, 2007	42(31)	17	23	0	114
	Huddersfield	2003-06	71(19)	17	36	1	141

PLAYER	CLUB	YEAR	APP	TRIES	GOALS	FG	PTS
Nick Mardon	London	1997-98	14	2	0	0	8
Thibaut Margalet	Catalans	2013-18	1(22)	0	0	0	0
Remy Marginet	Catalans	2011	2	0	9	0	18
Antoni Maria	Catalans	2012-16, 2018-20	10(57)	0	0	0	0
	Hull KR	2019	2(3)	0	0	0	0
	Leigh	2017	2(6)	0	0	0	0
Frankie Mariano	Castleford	2014-16	14(21)	8	0	0	32
	Wakefield	2011-13	41(12)	20	0	0	80
	Hull KR	2010	(3)	0	0	0	0
Oliver Marns	Halifax	1996-2002	54(19)	23	0	0	92
Paul Marquet	Warrington	2002	23(2)	0	0	0	0
Callum Marriott	Salford	2011	(1)	0	0	0	0
Iain Marsh	Salford	1998-2001	1(4)	0	0	0	0
Lee Marsh	Salford	2001-02	3(4)	0	0	0	0
Matty Marsh	Hull KR	2015-16, 2018	18(4)	3	0	0	12
Stefan Marsh	Widnes	2012-18	122	56	21	0	266
	Wigan	2010-11	12	3	0	0	12
Liam Marshall	Wigan	2017-20	73	58	5	0	242
Richard Marshall	Leigh	2005	4(16)	0	0	0	0
	London	2002-03	33(11)	1	0	0	4
	Huddersfield	2000-01	35(14)	1	0	0	4
	Halifax	1996-99	38(34)	2	0	0	8
Brad Martin	Castleford	2020	(1)	0	0	0	0
Charlie Martin	Castleford	2013	(6)	0	0	0	0
Jason Martin	Paris	1997	15(2)	3	0	0	12
Rhyse Martin	Leeds	2019-20	20(2)	4	81	0	178
Scott Martin	Salford	1997-99	32(18)	8	0	0	32
Tony Martin	Hull	2012	10	1	0	0	4
	Crusaders	2010-11	40(1)	14	1	0	58
	Wakefield	2008-09	33	10	33	0	106
	London	1996-97, 2001-03	97(1)	36	170	1	485
Ugo Martin	Catalans	2018	1	0	0	0	0
Mick Martindale	Halifax	1996	(4)	0	0	0	0
Sebastien Martins	Catalans	2006, 2009-11	(21)	2	0	0	8
Tommy Martyn	St Helens	1996-2003	125(20)	87	63	12	486
Dean Marwood	Workington	1996	9(6)	0	22	0	44
Martin Masella	Warrington	2001	10(14)	5	0	0	20
	Wakefield	2000	14(8)	4	0	0	16
	Leeds	1997-1999	59(5)	1	0	0	4
Colin Maskill	Castleford	1996	8	1	1	0	6
Mose Masoe	Hull KR	2018-19	28(18)	6	0	0	24
	St Helens	2014-15	17(39)	10	0	0	40
Keith Mason	Castleford	2006, 2013	11(6)	0	0	0	0
	Huddersfield	2006-12	118(14)	4	0	0	16
	St Helens	2003-05	33(23)	4	0	0	16
	Wakefield	2000-01	5(17)	0	0	0	0
Nathan Mason	London	2019	5(10)	1	0	0	4
	Huddersfield	2013, 2015-17	3(26)	3	0	0	12
Willie Mason	Catalans	2016	6(8)	1	0	0	4
	Hull KR	2011	6	1	0	0	4
Samy Masselot	Wakefield	2011	(1)	0	0	0	0
Nathan Massey	Castleford	2008-20	161(66)	10	0	0	40
Suaia Matagi	Huddersfield	2018-20	39(9)	3	0	0	12
Nesiasi Mataitonga	London	2014	11(1)	1	0	0	4
Peter Mata'utia	Castleford	2018-20	46	6	54	1	133
Vila Matautia	St Helens	1996-2001	31(68)	9	0	0	36
Feleti Mateo	London	2005	4(10)	1	0	0	4
Barrie-Jon Mather	Castleford	1998, 2000-02	50(12)	21	0	0	84
Richard Mathers	Wakefield	2012-14	71	24	0	0	96
	Castleford	2011	21(1)	7	0	0	28
	Warrington	2002, 2009-10	42(3)	11	0	0	44
	Wigan	2008-09	23(1)	2	0	0	8
	Leeds	2002-06	85(2)	26	0	0	104
Jamie Mathiou	Leeds	1997-2001	31(82)	3	0	0	12
Masi Matongo	Hull	2015, 2017-20	16(38)	3	0	0	12
Terry Matterson	London	1996-98	46	15	90	6	246
Manu Ma'u	Hull	2020	11	3	0	0	12
Vic Mauro	Salford	2013	1(7)	1	0	0	4
Luke May	Harlequins	2009-10	(3)	0	0	0	0
Casey Mayberry	Halifax	2000	1(1)	0	0	0	0
Chris Maye	Halifax	2003	3(4)	0	0	0	0
Judah Mazive	Wakefield	2016	2	1	0	0	4
Joe Mbu	Harlequins	2006-09	33(20)	3	0	0	12
	London	2003-05	29(19)	4	0	0	16
Danny McAllister	Gateshead	1999	3(3)	1	0	0	4
	Sheffield	1996-97	33(7)	10	0	0	40
John McAtee	St Helens	1996	2(1)	0	0	0	0
Nathan McAvoy	Bradford	1998-2002, 2007	83(31)	46	0	0	184
	Wigan	2006	15(2)	5	0	0	20
	Salford	1997-98, 2004-05	57(4)	18	0	0	72

PLAYER	CLUB	YEAR	APP	TRIES	GOALS	FG	PTS
Tyrone McCarthy	Salford	2017-20	41(20)	8	2	0	36
	Hull KR	2015	20(1)	4	0	0	16
	Warrington	2009-13	12(24)	2	0	0	8
	Wakefield	2011	2(5)	1	0	0	4
Louie McCarthy-Scarsbrook	St Helens	2011-20	133(137)	55	0	0	220
	Harlequins	2006-10	41(50)	17	0	0	68
Dave McConnell	London	2003	(4)	0	0	0	0
	St Helens	2001-02	3(2)	4	0	0	16
Loui McConnell	Leeds	2020	(2)	0	0	0	0
Robbie McCormack	Wigan	1998	24	2	0	0	8
Josh McCrone	Toronto	2020	6	1	0	0	4
Steve McCurrie	Leigh	2005	7(3)	1	0	0	4
	Widnes	2002-04	55(22)	10	0	0	40
	Warrington	1998-2001	69(26)	31	0	0	124
Barrie McDermott	Leeds	1996-2005	163(69)	28	0	0	112
Brian McDermott	Bradford	1996-2002	138(32)	33	0	0	132
Ryan McDonald	Widnes	2002-03	6(4)	0	0	0	0
Wayne McDonald	Huddersfield	2005-06	11(23)	1	0	0	4
	Wigan	2005	(4)	0	0	0	0
	Leeds	2002-05	34(47)	14	0	0	56
	St Helens	2001	7(11)	4	0	0	16
	Hull	2000	5(8)	4	0	0	16
	Wakefield	1999	9(17)	8	0	0	32
James McDonnell	Wigan	2020	1	0	0	0	0
Shannon McDonnell	St Helens	2014-16	28	15	0	0	60
	Hull	2013	19	2	0	0	8
	Hull KR	2012	21	6	0	0	24
Craig McDowell	Huddersfield	2003	(1)	0	0	0	0
	Warrington	2002	(1)	0	0	0	0
	Bradford	2000	(1)	0	0	0	0
Wes McGibbon	Halifax	1999	1	0	0	0	0
Jermaine McGillvary	Huddersfield	2010-20	244	170	0	0	680
Dean McGilvray	Salford	2009-10	14	4	0	0	16
	St Helens	2006-08	5(1)	1	0	0	4
Billy McGinty	Workington	1996	1	0	0	0	0
Ryan McGoldrick	Salford	2013	19(1)	3	0	1	13
	Hull	2012	8	1	0	0	4
	Castleford	2006, 2008-12	129(5)	24	11	0	118
Kevin McGuinness	Salford	2004-07	63(3)	11	0	0	44
Casey McGuire	Catalans	2007-10	87(4)	27	0	0	108
Danny McGuire	Hull KR	2018-19	36	9	1	3	41
	Leeds	2001-17	331(39)	238	0	6	958
Gary McGuirk	Workington	1996	(4)	0	0	0	0
Michael McIlorum	Catalans	2018-20	49	5	0	0	20
	Wigan	2007-17	156(54)	22	0	0	88
Darnell McIntosh	Huddersfield	2017-20	82(1)	41	12	0	188
Richard McKell	Castleford	1997-98	22(7)	2	0	0	8
Chris McKenna	Bradford	2006-07	40(7)	7	0	0	28
	Leeds	2003-05	65(4)	18	0	0	72
Phil McKenzie	Workington	1996	4	0	0	0	0
Chris McKinney	Oldham	1996-97	4(9)	2	0	0	8
Wade McKinnon	Hull	2012	10	4	0	0	16
Callum McLelland	Leeds	2019-20	7(1)	0	0	0	0
Mark McLinden	Harlequins	2006-08	46(1)	20	0	1	81
	London	2005	22(3)	8	0	0	32
Mike McMeeken	Castleford	2015-20	118(13)	30	0	0	120
	London	2012-14	25(9)	5	0	0	20
Shayne McMenemy	Hull	2003-07	80(8)	12	0	0	48
	Halifax	2001-03	63	11	0	0	44
Andy McNally	London	2004	5(3)	0	0	0	0
	Castleford	2001, 2003	2(5)	1	0	0	4
Gregg McNally	Leigh	2017	9	3	0	0	12
	Huddersfield	2011	1	0	6	0	12
Ben McNamara	Hull	2020	2(2)	1	0	0	4
Steve McNamara	Huddersfield	2001, 2003	41(9)	3	134	1	281
	Wakefield	2000	15(2)	2	32	0	72
	Bradford	1996-99	90(3)	14	348	7	759
Paul McNicholas	Hull	2004-05	28(12)	4	0	0	16
Neil McPherson	Salford	1997	(1)	0	0	0	0
Shannan McPherson	Salford	2012-14	20(11)	0	0	0	0
Chris McQueen	Huddersfield	2020	9	2	0	0	8
Duncan McRae	London	1996	11(2)	3	0	1	13
Paul McShane	Castleford	2015-20	119(22)	20	39	0	158
	Wakefield	2014-15	39(9)	5	0	0	20
	Leeds	2009-13	17(38)	12	0	0	48
	Widnes	2012	6(5)	3	4	0	20
	Hull	2010	(4)	0	0	0	0
Derek McVey	St Helens	1996-97	28(4)	6	1	0	26
Dallas Mead	Warrington	1997	2	0	0	0	0

Super League Players 1996-2020

PLAYER	CLUB	YEAR	APP	TRIES	GOALS	FG	PTS
David Mead	Catalans	2018-20	51	23	0	0	92
James Meadows	London	2019	1	0	0	0	0
Robbie Mears	Leigh	2005	8(6)	0	0	0	0
	Leeds	2001	23	6	0	0	24
Paul Medley	Bradford	1996-98	6(35)	9	0	0	36
Francis Meli	Salford	2014	16	11	0	0	44
	St Helens	2006-13	194(1)	122	0	0	488
Vince Mellars	Wakefield	2012-13	21(5)	4	0	0	16
	Crusaders	2010-11	46	17	0	0	68
Chris Melling	London	2012-13	25(12)	5	2	0	24
	Harlequins	2007-11	100(11)	33	6	0	144
	Wigan	2004-05	8(2)	1	3	0	10
Alex Mellor	Leeds	2020	9(1)	2	0	0	8
	Huddersfield	2017-19	65(10)	19	0	0	76
	Bradford	2013-14	(10)	0	0	0	0
Joe Mellor	Toronto	2020	2	0	0	0	0
	Widnes	2012-18	134(1)	46	0	1	185
	Wigan	2012	1(1)	1	0	0	4
	Harlequins	2011	(1)	0	0	0	0
Paul Mellor	Castleford	2003-04	36(3)	18	0	0	72
James Mendeika	London	2013	4(2)	2	0	0	8
Craig Menkins	Paris	1997	4(5)	0	0	0	0
Luke Menzies	Hull KR	2008	(1)	0	0	0	0
Steve Menzies	Catalans	2011-13	61(6)	30	0	0	120
	Bradford	2009-10	52(1)	24	1	0	98
Gary Mercer	Castleford	2002	(1)	0	0	0	0
	Leeds	1996-97, 2001	40(2)	9	0	0	36
	Warrington	2001	18	2	0	0	8
	Halifax	1998-2001	73(2)	16	0	0	64
Trent Merrin	Leeds	2019	27	4	0	0	16
Tony Mestrov	London	1996-97, 2001	59(8)	4	0	0	16
	Wigan	1998-2000	39(39)	3	0	0	12
Keiran Meyer	London	1996	4	1	0	0	4
Brad Meyers	Bradford	2005-06	40(11)	13	0	0	52
Ronan Michael	Huddersfield	2020	(1)	0	0	0	0
Steve Michaels	Hull	2015-17	68(1)	26	0	0	104
Gary Middlehurst	Widnes	2004	(2)	0	0	0	0
Simon Middleton	Castleford	1996-97	19(3)	8	0	0	32
Constantine Mika	Hull KR	2012-13	45(4)	9	0	0	36
Daryl Millard	Catalans	2011-14	91	38	1	0	154
	Wakefield	2010-11	21(1)	11	0	0	44
Shane Millard	Wigan	2007	19(6)	3	0	0	12
	Leeds	2006	6(21)	3	0	0	12
	Widnes	2003-05	69	23	0	0	92
	London	1998-2001	72(14)	11	1	0	46
Jack Miller	Huddersfield	2013	1	0	1	0	2
Jacob Miller	Wakefield	2015-20	134(3)	46	17	6	224
	Hull	2013-14	20	6	9	0	42
Grant Millington	Castleford	2012-20	146(73)	31	0	0	124
David Mills	Harlequins	2006-07, 2010	25(32)	2	0	0	8
	Hull KR	2008-09	20(11)	1	0	0	4
	Widnes	2002-05	17(77)	8	0	0	32
Lewis Mills	Celtic	2009	(4)	0	0	0	0
Adam Milner	Castleford	2010-20	155(85)	36	1	0	146
Lee Milner	Halifax	1999	5(1)	1	0	0	4
Rowan Milnes	Hull KR	2020	2(1)	0	0	0	0
Hakim Miloudi	Toronto	2020	5(1)	1	0	0	4
	Hull	2018-19	13(2)	5	1	0	22
Elliot Minchella	Hull KR	2020	8(7)	3	0	0	12
	Leeds	2013-14	(6)	1	0	0	0
Mark Minichiello	Hull	2015-19	118(4)	20	0	0	80
Greg Minikin	Hull KR	2020	10	6	0	0	24
	Castleford	2016-19	89(2)	39	0	0	156
Thomas Minns	Hull KR	2016, 2018	24(1)	14	0	0	56
	London	2014	23	6	0	0	24
	Leeds	2013	2(1)	1	0	0	4
John Minto	London	1996	13	4	0	0	16
Lee Mitchell	Castleford	2012	13(10)	2	0	0	8
	Warrington	2007-11	8(27)	4	0	0	16
	Harlequins	2011	11(1)	1	0	0	4
Sam Moa	Catalans	2017-20	68(6)	6	0	0	24
	Hull	2009-12	29(44)	6	0	0	24
Martin Moana	Salford	2004	6(3)	1	0	0	4
	Halifax	1996-2001, 2003	126(22)	62	0	1	249
	Wakefield	2002	19(2)	10	0	0	40
	Huddersfield	2001	3(3)	2	0	0	8
Adam Mogg	Catalans	2007-10	74	19	0	1	77
Jon Molloy	Wakefield	2013-16	25(18)	5	0	0	20
	Huddersfield	2011-12	2(1)	0	0	0	0
Steve Molloy	Huddersfield	2000-01	26(20)	3	0	0	12
	Sheffield	1998-99	32(17)	3	0	0	12
Chris Molyneux	Huddersfield	2000-01	1(18)	0	0	0	0
	Sheffield	1999	1(2)	0	0	0	0
Joel Monaghan	Castleford	2016-17	29(3)	13	0	0	52
	Warrington	2011-15	127	125	2	0	504
Michael Monaghan	Warrington	2008-14	143(28)	31	0	4	128
Joel Moon	Leeds	2013-18	136(1)	61	0	0	244
	Salford	2012	17	9	0	0	36
Adrian Moore	Huddersfield	1998-99	1(4)	0	0	0	0
Brandon Moore	Huddersfield	2020	4	0	0	0	0
Danny Moore	London	2000	7	0	0	0	0
	Wigan	1998-99	49(3)	18	0	0	72
Gareth Moore	Wakefield	2011	5	1	14	1	33
Jason Moore	Workington	1996	(5)	0	0	0	0
Richard Moore	Wakefield	2007-10, 2014	52(57)	10	0	0	40
	Leeds	2012-13	3(27)	1	0	0	4
	Crusaders	2011	11(10)	1	0	0	4
	Leigh	2005	2(5)	0	0	0	0
	Bradford	2002-04	1(26)	0	0	0	0
	London	2002, 2004	5(9)	2	0	0	8
Scott Moore	Wakefield	2015-16	12(2)	0	0	0	0
	Castleford	2008, 2015	24(6)	2	0	0	8
	London	2014	26	3	0	0	12
	Huddersfield	2009, 2012	29(7)	9	0	0	36
	Widnes	2012	3(3)	0	0	0	0
	St Helens	2004-07, 2010-11	29(37)	9	0	0	36
Junior Moors	Castleford	2015-20	46(63)	18	0	0	72
Dennis Moran	Wigan	2005-06	39	17	1	1	71
	London	2001-04	107(2)	74	2	5	305
Kieran Moran	Hull KR	2016	(5)	0	0	0	0
Pat Moran	Warrington	2019	(1)	0	0	0	0
Ryan Morgan	London	2019	21	5	0	0	20
	St Helens	2017-18	46	22	0	0	88
Willie Morganson	Sheffield	1997-98	18(12)	5	3	0	26
Paul Moriarty	Halifax	1996	3(2)	0	0	0	0
Adrian Morley	Salford	2014-15	31(14)	2	0	0	8
	Warrington	2007-13	135(21)	8	0	0	32
	Bradford	2005	2(4)	0	0	0	0
	Leeds	1996-2000	95(14)	25	0	0	100
Chris Morley	Salford	1999	3(5)	0	0	0	0
	Warrington	1998	2(8)	0	0	0	0
	St Helens	1996-97	21(16)	4	0	0	16
Frazer Morris	Wakefield	2016	(1)	0	0	0	0
Glenn Morrison	Wakefield	2010-11	43(1)	9	0	0	36
	Bradford	2007-09	48(2)	19	0	0	76
Iain Morrison	Hull KR	2007	5(6)	1	0	0	4
	Huddersfield	2003-05	11(23)	0	0	0	0
	London	2001	(1)	0	0	0	0
Daniel Mortimer	Leigh	2017	3	0	0	0	0
Dale Morton	Wakefield	2009-11	22(3)	8	5	0	42
Gareth Morton	Hull KR	2007	7(4)	3	23	0	58
	Leeds	2001-02	1(1)	0	0	0	0
Kieren Moss	Hull KR	2018	2(1)	4	0	0	16
Lee Mossop	Salford	2017-20	58(3)	6	0	0	24
	Wigan	2008-13, 2015-16	80(65)	11	0	0	44
	Huddersfield	2009	1(4)	1	0	0	4
Aaron Moule	Salford	2006-07	45	17	0	0	68
	Widnes	2004-05	29	12	0	0	48
Bradley Moules	Wakefield	2016	(1)	0	0	0	0
Wilfried Moulinec	Paris	1996	1	0	0	0	0
Gregory Mounis	Catalans	2006-16	149(105)	27	19	0	146
Arthur Mourgue	Catalans	2018-20	4(2)	2	1	0	10
Mark Moxon	Huddersfield	1998-2001	20(5)	1	0	1	5
Robbie Mulhern	Hull KR	2016, 2018-20	43(27)	4	0	0	16
	Leeds	2014-15	(5)	0	0	0	0
Anthony Mullally	Toronto	2020	2(4)	0	0	0	0
	Leeds	2016-18	10(48)	9	0	0	36
	Wakefield	2015	(2)	0	0	0	0
	Huddersfield	2013-15	12(24)	5	0	0	20
	Bradford	2014	1(5)	0	0	0	0
	Widnes	2012	(9)	0	0	0	0
Jake Mullaney	Salford	2014	12	2	24	0	56
Craig Mullen	Wigan	2018	1(1)	0	0	0	0
Brett Mullins	Leeds	2001	5(3)	1	0	0	4
Damian Munro	Widnes	2002	8(2)	1	0	0	4
	Halifax	1996-97	9(6)	8	0	0	32
Matt Munro	Oldham	1996-97	26(5)	8	0	0	32
Ben Murdoch-Masila	Warrington	2018-20	23(35)	13	0	0	52
	Salford	2016-17	46(1)	15	0	0	60
Craig Murdock	Salford	2000	(2)	0	0	0	0
	Hull	1998-99	21(6)	8	0	2	34
	Wigan	1996-98	18(17)	14	0	0	56
Aaron Murphy	Huddersfield	2012-20	169(6)	71	0	0	284
	Wakefield	2008-11	57(2)	12	0	0	48
Jack Murphy	Wigan	2012, 2014	3	1	0	0	4
	Salford	2013	10	3	1	0	14

PLAYER	CLUB	YEAR	APP	TRIES	GOALS	FG	PTS
Jamie Murphy	Crusaders	2011	(2)	0	0	0	0
Jobe Murphy	Bradford	2013	(4)	0	0	0	0
Justin Murphy	Catalans	2006-08	59	49	0	0	196
	Widnes	2004	5	1	0	0	4
Daniel Murray	Hull KR	2019-20	15(8)	0	0	0	0
	Salford	2017-19	14(14)	2	0	0	8
Doc Murray	Warrington	1997	(2)	0	0	0	0
	Wigan	1997	6(2)	0	0	0	0
Scott Murrell	Hull KR	2007-12	114(24)	24	26	1	149
	Leeds	2005	(1)	0	0	0	0
	London	2004	3(3)	2	0	0	8
Muizz Mustapha	Leeds	2020	(2)	0	0	0	0
David Mycoe	Sheffield	1996-97	12(13)	1	0	0	4
Richie Myler	Leeds	2018-20	55(4)	18	6	1	85
	Catalans	2016-17	40	21	2	0	88
	Warrington	2010-15	127(4)	69	1	1	279
	Salford	2009	18	11	0	0	44
Rob Myler	Oldham	1996-97	19(2)	6	0	0	24
Stephen Myler	Salford	2006	4(8)	1	15	0	34
	Widnes	2003-05	35(14)	8	74	0	180
Vinny Myler	Salford	2004	(4)	0	0	0	0
	Bradford	2003	(1)	0	0	0	0
Matt Nable	London	1997	2(2)	1	0	0	4
Kevin Naiqama	St Helens	2019-20	46	26	0	0	104
Brad Nairn	Workington	1996	14	4	0	0	16
Ben Nakubuwai	Salford	2018-19	7(28)	2	0	0	8
Frank Napoli	London	2000	14(6)	2	0	0	8
Carlo Napolitano	Salford	2000	(3)	1	0	0	4
Stephen Nash	Castleford	2012	3(4)	0	0	0	0
	Salford	2007, 2009	2(18)	1	0	0	4
	Widnes	2005	4(1)	0	0	0	0
Curtis Naughton	Leigh	2017	5	3	0	0	12
	Hull	2015-16	26	13	1	0	54
	Bradford	2013	1	0	0	0	0
Ratu Naulago	Hull	2019-20	30	20	0	0	80
Romain Navarrete	Wakefield	2020	3(7)	0	0	0	0
	Wigan	2017-19	36(20)	0	0	0	0
	Catalans	2016-17	1(12)	0	0	0	0
Jim Naylor	Halifax	2000	7(6)	2	0	0	8
Scott Naylor	Salford	1997-98, 2004	30(1)	9	0	0	36
	Bradford	1999-2003	127(1)	51	0	0	204
Adam Neal	Salford	2010-13	17(28)	0	0	0	0
Mike Neal	Salford	1998	(1)	0	0	0	0
	Oldham	1996-97	6(4)	3	0	0	12
Jonathan Neill	Huddersfield	1998-99	20(11)	0	0	0	0
	St Helens	1996	1	0	0	0	0
Chris Nero	Salford	2011-13	31(16)	7	0	0	28
	Bradford	2008-10	65(5)	24	0	0	96
	Huddersfield	2004-07	97(8)	38	0	0	152
Jason Netherton	Hull KR	2007-14	60(74)	4	0	0	16
	London	2003-04	6	0	0	0	0
	Halifax	2002	2(3)	0	0	0	0
	Leeds	2001	(3)	0	0	0	0
Kirk Netherton	Castleford	2009-10	5(23)	3	0	0	12
	Hull KR	2007-08	9(15)	2	0	0	8
Paul Newlove	Castleford	2004	5	1	0	0	4
	St Helens	1996-2003	162	106	0	0	424
Richard Newlove	Wakefield	2003	17(5)	8	0	0	32
Harry Newman	Leeds	2017-20	35	6	0	0	24
Clint Newton	Hull KR	2008-11	90(3)	37	0	0	148
Terry Newton	Wakefield	2010	(2)	0	0	0	0
	Bradford	2006-09	83(6)	26	0	0	104
	Wigan	2000-05	157(9)	62	0	0	248
	Leeds	1996-1999	55(14)	4	0	0	16
Gene Ngamu	Huddersfield	1999-2000	29(2)	9	67	0	170
Danny Nicklas	Hull	2010, 2012	2(8)	0	0	0	0
Sonny Nickle	St Helens	1999-2002	86(18)	14	0	0	56
	Bradford	1996-98	25(16)	9	0	0	36
Jason Nicol	Salford	2000-02	52(7)	11	0	0	44
Tawera Nikau	Warrington	2000-01	51	7	0	0	28
Tom Nisbet	St Helens	2020	1	0	0	0	0
Rob Nolan	Hull	1998-99	20(11)	6	0	0	24
Paul Noone	Harlequins	2006	5(2)	0	0	0	0
	Warrington	2000-06	60(59)	12	20	0	88
Chris Norman	Halifax	2003	13(3)	2	0	0	8
Dan Norman	Widnes	2018	(1)	0	0	0	0
Paul Norman	Oldham	1996	(1)	0	0	0	0
Andy Northey	St Helens	1996-97	8(17)	2	0	0	8
Danny Nutley	Castleford	2006	28	3	0	0	12
	Warrington	1998-2001	94(1)	3	0	0	12
Tony Nuttall	Oldham	1996-97	1(7)	0	0	0	0
Frank-Paul Nuuausala							
	Wigan	2016-18	34(8)	2	0	0	8
Levy Nzoungou	Hull	2019	(1)	0	0	0	0
	Salford	2018	(3)	0	0	0	0

PLAYER	CLUB	YEAR	APP	TRIES	GOALS	FG	PTS
Will Oakes	Hull KR	2016, 2018-19	12	5	0	0	20
Adam O'Brien	Huddersfield	2017-20	50(31)	15	0	0	60
	Bradford	2011-14	12(29)	6	0	0	24
Clinton O'Brien	Wakefield	2003	(2)	0	0	0	0
Gareth O'Brien	Castleford	2013, 2020	10	3	7	2	28
	Toronto	2020	4	1	2	0	8
	Salford	2016-18	49(3)	12	105	2	260
	Warrington	2011-15	48(3)	16	69	3	205
	St Helens	2013	7	0	25	0	50
	Widnes	2012	4	0	15	0	30
Sam Obst	Hull	2011	17(6)	6	0	0	24
	Wakefield	2005-11	100(28)	40	7	0	174
Jamie O'Callaghan	London	2012-14	44(2)	4	0	0	16
	Harlequins	2008-11	54(3)	12	0	0	48
Eamon O'Carroll	Widnes	2012-17	58(11)	3	0	0	12
	Hull	2012	1(9)	0	0	0	0
	Wigan	2006-11	2(59)	3	0	0	12
Jarrod O'Connor	Leeds	2020	2(2)	0	2	0	4
Matt O'Connor	Paris	1997	11(4)	1	26	2	58
Terry O'Connor	Widnes	2005	25	2	0	0	8
	Wigan	1996-2004	177(45)	9	0	0	36
Jarrod O'Doherty	Huddersfield	2003	26	3	0	0	12
David O'Donnell	Paris	1997	21	3	0	0	12
Luke O'Donnell	Huddersfield	2011-13	22(2)	2	0	0	8
Martin Offiah	Salford	2000-01	41	20	0	2	82
	London	1996-99	29(3)	21	0	0	84
	Wigan	1996	8	7	0	0	28
Jacob Ogden	London	2019	2	0	0	0	0
Mark O'Halloran	London	2004-05	34(3)	10	0	0	40
Ryan O'Hara	Hull KR	2012	8(7)	1	0	0	4
	Crusaders	2010-11	41(8)	3	0	0	12
	Celtic	2009	27	3	0	0	12
Hefin O'Hare	Huddersfield	2001, 2003-05	72(10)	27	0	0	108
Edwin Okanga-Ajwang							
	Salford	2013	2	0	0	0	0
Hitro Okesene	Hull	1998	21(1)	0	0	0	0
Anderson Okiwe	Sheffield	1997	1	0	0	0	0
Tom Olbison	Toronto	2020	3(3)	0	0	0	0
	Widnes	2017-18	18(22)	4	0	0	16
	Bradford	2009-14	55(26)	11	0	0	44
Michael Oldfield	Catalans	2014-15	41	28	0	0	112
Mikolaj Oledzki	Leeds	2017-20	26(30)	6	0	0	24
Jamie Olejnik	Paris	1997	11	8	0	0	32
Aaron Ollett	Hull KR	2013-15	5(16)	1	0	0	4
Kevin O'Loughlin	Halifax	1997-98	2(4)	0	0	0	0
	St Helens	1997	(3)	0	0	0	0
Sean O'Loughlin	Wigan	2002-20	371(32)	71	3	2	292
Derrell Olpherts	Castleford	2020	14	8	0	0	32
	Salford	2018-19	35	11	0	0	44
Mark O'Meley	Hull	2010-13	70(13)	13	0	0	52
Jacques O'Neill	Castleford	2019-20	1(21)	3	0	0	12
Jules O'Neill	Widnes	2003-05	57(3)	14	158	7	379
	Wakefield	2005	10(2)	2	4	0	16
	Wigan	2002-03	29(1)	12	72	0	192
Julian O'Neill	Widnes	2002-05	57(39)	3	0	0	12
	Wakefield	2001	24(1)	2	0	0	8
	St Helens	1997-2000	95(8)	5	0	0	20
Mark O'Neill	Hull KR	2007	17	5	0	0	20
	Leeds	2006	1(8)	0	0	0	0
Steve O'Neill	Gateshead	1999	1(1)	0	0	0	0
Tom O'Reilly	Warrington	2001-02	8(6)	1	0	0	4
Matt Orford	Bradford	2010	12	3	31	2	76
Jack Ormondroyd	Salford	2020	4(1)	0	0	0	0
	Leeds	2017-18	3(9)	0	0	0	0
Gene Ormsby	Huddersfield	2016-17	8	4	0	0	16
	Warrington	2014-16	37	26	0	0	104
Chris Orr	Huddersfield	1998	19(3)	2	0	0	8
Danny Orr	Castleford	1997-2003, 2011-12	197(23)	75	308	3	919
	Harlequins	2007-10	90(4)	13	96	0	244
	Wigan	2004-06	66(2)	18	12	0	96
Gareth Owen	Salford	2010, 2012-13	4(32)	6	0	0	24
Nick Owen	Leigh	2005	8(1)	1	11	0	26
Richard Owen	Wakefield	2014-15	29(1)	9	0	0	36
	Castleford	2008-14	109(3)	57	0	0	228
Jack Owens	St Helens	2016-17	31	8	14	0	60
	Widnes	2012-15	53(1)	26	103	0	310
Lopini Paea	Wakefield	2015	1(3)	0	0	0	0
	Catalans	2011-14	41(41)	9	0	0	36
Mickey Paea	Hull	2014-15, 2018-19	78(18)	9	0	0	36
	Hull KR	2012-13	34(17)	5	0	0	20
Liam Paisley	Wigan	2018-19	6(2)	2	0	0	8
Mathias Pala	Catalans	2011-15	28(1)	4	0	0	16

167

Super League Players 1996-2020

PLAYER	CLUB	YEAR	APP	TRIES	GOALS	FG	PTS
Iafeta Palea'aesina	Hull	2014-16	(47)	1	0	0	4
	Salford	2011-12	4(37)	3	0	0	12
	Wigan	2006-10	55(77)	16	0	0	64
Jason Palmada	Workington	1996	12	2	0	0	8
Junior Paramore	Castleford	1996	5(5)	3	0	0	12
Matt Parcell	Hull KR	2019-20	13(2)	7	0	0	28
	Leeds	2017-19	50(16)	27	0	0	108
Paul Parker	Hull	1999-2002	23(18)	9	0	0	36
Rob Parker	Castleford	2011	4(2)	2	0	0	8
	Salford	2009-11	23(14)	4	0	0	16
	Warrington	2006-08	10(56)	6	0	0	24
	Bradford	2000, 2002-05	19(76)	14	0	0	56
	London	2001	9	1	0	0	4
Wayne Parker	Halifax	1996-97	12(1)	0	0	0	0
Ian Parry	Warrington	2001	(1)	0	0	0	0
Jules Parry	Paris	1996	10(2)	0	0	0	0
Oliver Partington	Wigan	2018-20	30(13)	3	0	0	12
Regis Pastre-Courtine	Paris	1996	4(3)	4	0	0	16
Cory Paterson	Leigh	2017	13	2	0	0	8
	Salford	2015	14(1)	7	6	0	40
	Hull KR	2013	15	7	0	0	28
Andrew Patmore	Oldham	1996	8(5)	3	0	0	12
Larne Patrick	Castleford	2016-17	14(7)	1	0	0	4
	Huddersfield	2009-14, 2016	30(107)	30	0	0	120
	Wigan	2015	7(20)	4	0	0	16
Luke Patten	Salford	2011-12	53	16	0	0	64
Dec Patton	Warrington	2015-20	69(18)	11	105	6	260
Henry Paul	Harlequins	2006-08	60(1)	8	94	2	222
	Bradford	1999-2001	81(5)	29	350	6	822
	Wigan	1996-98	60	37	23	0	194
Junior Paul	London	1996	3	1	0	0	4
Robbie Paul	Salford	2009	2(24)	2	0	0	8
	Huddersfield	2006-07	44(8)	7	0	0	28
	Bradford	1996-2005	198(31)	121	3	0	490
Pauli Pauli	Salford	2019-20	5(16)	4	0	0	16
	Wakefield	2018-19	14(30)	10	0	0	40
Joseph Paulo	St Helens	2019-20	6(25)	1	0	0	4
Jason Payne	Castleford	2006	1(1)	0	0	0	0
Lewis Peachey	Castleford	2019-20	(4)	0	0	0	0
Danny Peacock	Bradford	1997-99	32(2)	15	0	0	60
Jamie Peacock	Leeds	2006-15	234(16)	24	0	0	96
	Bradford	1999-2005	163(25)	38	0	0	152
Kai Pearce-Paul	Wigan	2020	(1)	0	0	0	0
Martin Pearson	Wakefield	2001	21(1)	3	60	3	135
	Halifax	1997-98, 2000	55(6)	24	181	0	458
	Sheffield	1999	17(6)	9	36	2	110
Jacques Pech	Paris	1996	16	0	0	0	0
Mike Pechey	Warrington	1998	6(3)	2	0	0	8
Bill Peden	London	2003	21(3)	7	0	0	28
Adam Peek	Crusaders	2010-11	5(22)	1	0	0	4
	Celtic	2009	5(12)	3	0	0	12
Eloi Pelissier	London	2019	7(6)	1	0	0	4
	Leigh	2017	4(16)	0	0	0	0
	Catalans	2011-16	38(104)	23	0	1	93
Dimitri Pelo	Catalans	2007-10	79	37	0	0	148
Sean Penkywicz	Huddersfield	2004-05	21(11)	7	0	0	28
	Halifax	2000-03	29(27)	8	0	0	32
Julian Penni	Salford	1998-99	4	0	0	0	0
Kevin Penny	Warrington	2006-09, 2014-17	83(1)	52	0	0	208
	Wakefield	2011	5	1	0	0	4
	Harlequins	2010	5	3	0	0	12
Lee Penny	Warrington	1996-2003	140(5)	54	0	0	216
Paul Penrice	Workington	1996	11(2)	2	0	0	8
Chris Percival	Widnes	2002-03	26	6	0	0	24
Mark Percival	St Helens	2013-20	146(2)	76	223	0	750
Apollo Perelini	St Helens	1996-2000	103(16)	27	0	0	108
Ugo Perez	Catalans	2015, 2017-18	2(5)	0	0	0	0
Mark Perrett	Halifax	1996-97	15(4)	4	0	0	16
Josh Perry	St Helens	2011-13	32(9)	2	0	0	8
Shane Perry	Catalans	2009	8(8)	1	0	0	4
Adam Peters	Paris	1997	16(3)	0	0	0	0
Dominic Peters	London	1998-2003	58(11)	12	0	0	48
Mike Peters	Warrington	2000	2(12)	1	0	0	4
	Halifax	2000	1	0	0	0	0
Willie Peters	Widnes	2004	9	3	0	2	14
	Wigan	2000	29	15	5	6	76
	Gateshead	1999	27	11	1	6	52
Dave Petersen	Hull KR	2012	2(2)	1	0	0	4
Matt Petersen	Wakefield	2008-09	14	3	0	0	12
Nathaniel Peteru	Hull KR	2020	5(3)	0	0	0	0
	Leeds	2018-19	15(6)	0	0	0	0
Adrian Petrie	Workington	1996	(1)	0	0	0	0
Eddy Pettybourne	Wigan	2014	1(15)	0	0	0	0
Dominique Peyroux	St Helens	2016-20	88(25)	16	0	0	64
Cameron Phelps	Widnes	2012-15	66(1)	23	2	0	96
	Hull	2011	19	2	0	0	8
	Wigan	2008-10	43(1)	14	4	0	64
Joe Philbin	Warrington	2014-20	22(92)	10	0	0	40
Rowland Phillips	Workington	1996	22	1	0	0	4
Nathan Picchi	Leeds	1996	(1)	0	0	0	0
Ian Pickavance	Hull	1999	4(2)	2	0	0	8
	Huddersfield	1999	3(14)	0	0	0	0
	St Helens	1996-98	12(44)	6	0	0	24
James Pickering	Castleford	1999	1(19)	0	0	0	0
Steve Pickersgill	Widnes	2012-13	27(8)	1	0	0	4
	Warrington	2005-09	1(36)	0	0	0	0
Nick Pinkney	Salford	2000-02	64	29	0	0	116
	Halifax	1999	26(2)	13	0	0	52
	Sheffield	1997-98	33	10	0	0	40
Mikhail Piskunov	Paris	1996	1(1)	1	0	0	4
Darryl Pitt	London	1996	2(16)	4	0	1	17
Jay Pitts	Wakefield	2008-09, 2020	21(8)	3	0	0	12
	London	2019	27	7	0	0	28
	Bradford	2014	15(1)	3	0	0	12
	Hull	2012-14	18(30)	1	0	0	4
	Leeds	2009-12	10(15)	2	0	0	8
Andy Platt	Salford	1997-98	20(3)	1	0	0	4
Michael Platt	Salford	2001-02, 2014	4(1)	1	0	0	4
	Bradford	2007-13	121(6)	44	0	0	176
	Castleford	2006	26	7	0	0	28
Willie Poching	Leeds	2002-06	58(73)	44	0	0	176
	Wakefield	1999-2001	65(4)	20	0	0	80
Ben Pomeroy	Warrington	2017-18	3(7)	1	0	0	4
	Catalans	2014-15	44	10	0	0	40
Quentin Pongia	Wigan	2003-04	15(10)	0	0	0	0
Justin Poore	Hull KR	2014	7	0	0	0	0
	Wakefield	2013	23	1	0	0	4
Dan Potter	Widnes	2002-03	34(2)	6	0	0	24
	London	2001	1(3)	1	0	0	4
Craig Poucher	Hull	1999-2002	31(5)	5	0	0	20
Andy Powell	Wigan	2013	2(3)	1	0	0	4
Bryn Powell	Salford	2004	1(1)	0	0	0	0
Daio Powell	Sheffield	1999	13(1)	2	0	0	8
	Halifax	1997-98	30(3)	17	0	0	68
Daryl Powell	Leeds	1998-2000	49(30)	12	0	2	50
Sam Powell	Wigan	2012-20	140(49)	32	4	4	140
Karl Pratt	Bradford	2003-05	35(19)	18	0	0	72
	Leeds	1999-2002	62(12)	33	0	0	132
Paul Prescott	Wigan	2004-13	49(75)	4	0	0	16
Steve Prescott	Hull	1998-99, 2001-03	99	46	191	3	569
	Wakefield	2000	22(1)	3	13	0	38
	St Helens	1996-97	32	15	17	0	94
Lee Prest	Workington	1996	(1)	0	0	0	0
Gareth Price	Salford	2002	(2)	0	0	0	0
	London	2002	2(2)	3	0	0	12
	St Helens	1999	(11)	2	0	0	8
Gary Price	Wakefield	1999-2001	55(13)	11	0	0	44
Richard Price	Sheffield	1996	1(2)	0	0	0	0
Tony Priddle	Paris	1997	11(7)	3	0	0	12
Matt Prior	Leeds	2020	13	0	0	0	0
Frank Pritchard	Hull	2016	10(13)	4	0	0	16
Karl Pryce	Bradford	2003-06, 2012	47(19)	46	1	0	186
	Harlequins	2011	11(7)	12	0	0	48
	Wigan	2009-10	11(2)	12	0	0	48
Leon Pryce	Hull	2015-16	32(2)	8	0	0	32
	Catalans	2012-14	72(2)	15	0	0	60
	St Helens	2006-11	133(3)	64	0	0	256
	Bradford	1998-2005	159(29)	86	0	0	344
Waine Pryce	Wakefield	2007	10(2)	4	0	0	16
	Castleford	2000-06	97(12)	49	0	0	196
Tony Puletua	Hull KR	2015	7	0	0	0	0
	Salford	2014	16(9)	3	0	0	12
	St Helens	2009-13	108(18)	39	0	0	156
Andrew Purcell	Castleford	2000	15(5)	3	0	0	12
	Hull	1999	27	4	0	0	16
Rob Purdham	Harlequins	2006-11	112(3)	18	131	1	335
	London	2002-05	53(15)	16	2	1	69
Adrian Purtell	Bradford	2012-14	45(1)	16	0	0	64
Luke Quigley	Catalans	2007	16(1)	1	0	0	4
Adam Quinlan	Hull KR	2018-20	35	19	0	0	76
	St Helens	2015	11	6	0	0	24
Damien Quinn	Celtic	2009	20(1)	4	12	0	40

PLAYER	CLUB	YEAR	APP	TRIES	GOALS	FG	PTS
Scott Quinnell	Wigan	1996	6(3)	1	0	0	4
Florian Quintilla	Catalans	2008-09	1(4)	0	0	0	0
Lee Radford	Hull	1998, 2006-12	138(30)	23	1	0	94
	Bradford	1999-2005	79(65)	18	12	0	96
Kris Radlinski	Wigan	1996-2006	236(1)	134	1	0	538
Sebastien Raguin	Catalans	2007-12	103(22)	28	0	0	112
Adrian Rainey	Castleford	2002	4(7)	1	0	0	4
Andy Raleigh	Wakefield	2012-14	42(21)	9	0	0	36
	Huddersfield	2006-11	74(46)	13	0	0	52
Jean-Luc Ramondou							
	Paris	1996	1(1)	1	0	0	4
Chad Randall	London	2012-13	29(9)	4	0	0	16
	Harlequins	2006-11	141(2)	37	0	1	149
Craig Randall	Halifax	1999	8(11)	4	0	0	16
	Salford	1997-98	12(18)	4	0	0	16
Tyler Randall	Wakefield	2017-19	37(8)	9	1	0	38
Jordan Rankin	Castleford	2019-20	29(2)	10	19	0	78
	Huddersfield	2017-18	39	3	9	0	30
	Hull	2014-15	41(6)	20	43	0	166
Scott Ranson	Oldham	1996-97	19(2)	7	0	0	28
Aaron Raper	Castleford	1999-2001	48(4)	4	2	1	21
Sam Rapira	Huddersfield	2016-17	29(19)	3	0	0	12
Steve Rapira	Salford	2014	5(13)	0	0	0	0
Stefan Ratchford	Warrington	2012-20	211(10)	73	329	2	952
	Salford	2007, 2009-11	65(5)	23	20	0	132
Mike Ratu	Hull KR	2010	5	1	0	0	4
	Leeds	2007, 2009	1(5)	1	0	0	4
Paul Rauhihi	Warrington	2006-09	67(20)	10	0	0	40
Ben Rauter	Wakefield	2001	15(6)	4	0	0	16
Nick Rawsthorne	Hull KR	2020	5	0	0	0	0
	Leigh	2017	1	1	0	0	4
	Hull	2017	3	2	2	0	12
Gareth Raynor	Bradford	2011	18	4	0	0	16
	Crusaders	2010	7	4	0	0	16
	Hull	2001-09	186	102	0	0	408
	Leeds	2000	(3)	0	0	0	0
Tony Rea	London	1996	22	4	0	0	16
Stuart Reardon	Crusaders	2011	25	11	0	0	44
	Bradford	2003-05, 2010	78(11)	37	0	0	148
	Warrington	2006-08	48	12	0	0	48
	Salford	2002	7(1)	3	0	0	12
Mark Reber	Wigan	1999-2000	9(9)	5	0	0	20
Alan Reddicliffe	Wakefield	2001	1	0	0	0	0
Tahi Reihana	Bradford	1997-98	17(21)	0	0	0	0
Paul Reilly	Wakefield	2008	5(2)	1	0	0	4
	Huddersfield	1999-2001, 2003-07	150(8)	35	1	0	142
Robert Relf	Widnes	2002-04	68(2)	5	0	0	20
Steve Renouf	Wigan	2000-01	55	40	0	0	160
Steele Retchless	London	1998-2004	177(6)	13	0	0	52
Ben Reynolds	Wakefield	2019	5	1	0	0	4
	Leigh	2017	16	6	48	0	120
	Castleford	2013-14	1(3)	0	0	0	0
Scott Rhodes	Hull	2000	2	0	0	0	0
Phillipe Ricard	Paris	1996-97	2	0	0	0	0
Andy Rice	Huddersfield	2000-01	2(13)	1	0	0	4
Basil Richards	Huddersfield	1998-99	28(17)	1	0	0	4
Craig Richards	Oldham	1996	1	0	0	0	0
Greg Richards	London	2019	5(15)	0	0	0	0
	Leigh	2017	(1)	0	0	0	0
	St Helens	2013-17	19(49)	1	0	0	4
Pat Richards	Catalans	2016	19	9	69	0	174
	Wigan	2006-13	199	147	759	4	2110
Andy Richardson	Hudds-Sheff	2000	(2)	0	0	0	0
Danny Richardson	Castleford	2020	15	2	52	1	113
	St Helens	2017-19	52(2)	9	158	8	360
Sean Richardson	Widnes	2002	2(18)	1	0	0	4
	Wakefield	1999	5(1)	0	0	0	0
	Castleford	1996-97	3(8)	1	0	0	4
Mark Riddell	Wigan	2009-10	45(11)	5	2	0	24
Martyn Ridyard	Huddersfield	2017	7	1	26	0	56
	Leigh	2017	4	0	2	0	4
Neil Rigby	St Helens	2006	(1)	0	0	0	0
Shane Rigon	Bradford	2001	14(11)	12	0	0	48
Craig Rika	Halifax	1996	2	0	0	0	0
Chris Riley	Wakefield	2014-15	44	16	0	0	64
	Warrington	2005-14	146(10)	102	0	0	408
	Harlequins	2011	3	2	0	0	8
Glenn Riley	Warrington	2013-14	(15)	0	0	0	0
Peter Riley	Workington	1996	7(5)	0	0	0	0
Julien Rinaldi	London	2012	4(16)	1	0	0	4
	Wakefield	2002, 2010-11	27(9)	6	0	0	24
	Bradford	2009	(7)	1	0	0	4
	Harlequins	2007-08	4(43)	9	0	0	36
	Catalans	2006	16(6)	3	1	0	14

PLAYER	CLUB	YEAR	APP	TRIES	GOALS	FG	PTS
Dean Ripley	Castleford	2004	3(4)	1	0	0	4
Leroy Rivett	Warrington	2002	9	1	0	0	4
	Hudds-Sheff	2000	5(1)	1	0	0	4
	Leeds	1996-2000	39(15)	21	0	0	84
Nico Rizzelli	St Helens	2020	1	0	0	0	0
Jason Roach	Warrington	1998-99	29(7)	15	0	0	60
	Castleford	1997	7	4	0	0	16
Ben Roarty	Castleford	2006	11(6)	2	0	0	8
	Huddersfield	2003-05	52	5	0	0	20
Amos Roberts	Wigan	2009-11	47(2)	27	5	0	118
Ben Roberts	Castleford	2015-19	60(15)	20	0	2	82
Luis Roberts	Salford	2020	2	0	0	0	0
Mark Roberts	Wigan	2003	(3)	0	0	0	0
Oliver Roberts	Salford	2020	7(1)	0	0	0	0
	Huddersfield	2016-19	40(43)	13	0	0	52
	Bradford	2013-14	(5)	0	0	0	0
Robert Roberts	Huddersfield	2001	(1)	0	0	0	0
	Halifax	2000	(3)	0	0	0	0
	Hull	1999	24(2)	4	13	4	46
Tyrone Roberts	Warrington	2018	28	5	32	1	85
Michael Robertson	London	2012-13	35	17	0	0	68
Stan Robin	Catalans	2015-16	5(2)	1	0	0	4
Chad Robinson	Harlequins	2009	13(1)	2	0	0	8
Connor Robinson	Hull KR	2014-15	(2)	0	0	0	0
Craig Robinson	Wakefield	2005	(1)	0	0	0	0
Jason Robinson	Wigan	1996-2000	126(1)	87	0	1	349
Jeremy Robinson	Paris	1997	10(3)	1	21	0	46
John Robinson	Widnes	2003-04	7	1	0	0	4
Luke Robinson	Huddersfield	2008-15	191(18)	45	4	0	188
	Salford	2005-07	79	28	10	2	134
	Wigan	2002-04	17(25)	9	6	1	49
	Castleford	2004	9	4	3	0	22
Will Robinson	Hull	2000	22	4	0	0	16
	Gateshead	1999	28	9	0	0	36
Ash Robson	Castleford	2015	3	1	0	0	4
Ellis Robson	Warrington	2020	2(2)	0	0	0	0
James Roby	St Helens	2004-20	297(123)	100	1	1	403
Mike Roby	St Helens	2004	(1)	0	0	0	0
Colton Roche	Huddersfield	2018-19	1(7)	0	0	0	0
Carl Roden	Warrington	1997	1	0	0	0	0
Shane Rodney	London	2012-13	28	3	12	0	36
Matt Rodwell	Warrington	2002	10	3	0	0	12
Nathan Roebuck	Warrington	2020	1	1	0	0	4
Darren Rogers	Castleford	1999-2004	162(1)	81	0	0	324
	Salford	1997-98	42	16	0	0	64
Arthur Romano	Catalans	2017, 2019-20	17	3	0	0	12
Adam Rooks	Hull KR	2019	(4)	0	0	0	0
Jamie Rooney	Wakefield	2003-09	113(7)	60	321	21	903
	Castleford	2001	2(1)	0	6	0	12
Jonathan Roper	Castleford	2001	13	7	12	0	52
	Salford	2000	1(4)	1	3	0	10
	London	2000	4	0	0	0	0
	Warrington	1996-2000	75(8)	33	71	0	274
Scott Roskell	London	1996-97	30(2)	16	0	0	64
Steve Rosolen	London	1996-98	25(9)	10	0	0	40
Adam Ross	London	1996	(1)	0	0	0	0
Paul Round	Castleford	1996	(3)	0	0	0	0
Steve Rowlands	Widnes	2004-05	18(3)	2	15	0	38
	St Helens	2003	(1)	0	0	0	0
Paul Rowley	Leigh	2005	15(7)	3	0	0	12
	Huddersfield	2001	24	3	0	0	12
	Halifax	1996-2000	107(3)	27	1	3	113
Nigel Roy	London	2001-04	100	39	0	0	156
Nicky Royle	Widnes	2004	13	7	0	0	28
Shad Royston	Bradford	2011	17(1)	10	0	0	40
Chris Rudd	Warrington	1996-98	31(17)	10	16	0	72
Sean Rudder	Catalans	2006	22(1)	6	0	0	24
	Castleford	2004	9(3)	2	0	0	8
Charly Runciman	Widnes	2016-18	68	9	0	0	36
James Rushforth	Halifax	1997	(4)	0	0	0	0
Harry Rushton	Wigan	2020	1	0	0	0	0
Danny Russell	Huddersfield	1998-2000	50(13)	8	0	0	32
Ian Russell	Oldham	1997	1(3)	1	0	0	4
	Paris	1996	3	0	0	0	0
Matty Russell	Toronto	2020	6	2	0	0	8
	Warrington	2014-18	77(4)	22	0	0	88
	Hull	2012	6	0	0	0	0
	Wigan	2012	2	3	0	0	12
Oliver Russell	Huddersfield	2018-20	23(4)	2	55	4	122
Richard Russell	Castleford	1996-98	37(4)	2	0	0	8
Robert Russell	Salford	1998-99	2(1)	0	1	0	2
Sean Rutgerson	Salford	2004-06	60(9)	4	0	0	16
Chris Ryan	London	1998-99	44(3)	17	10	0	88
Ethan Ryan	Hull KR	2020	4	3	0	0	12
Matt Ryan	Wakefield	2014-15	28(12)	7	0	0	28

Super League Players 1996-2020

PLAYER	CLUB	YEAR	APP	TRIES	GOALS	FG	PTS
Sean Ryan	Castleford	2004	11(5)	2	0	0	8
	Hull	2002-03	53	8	0	0	32
Justin Ryder	Wakefield	2004	19(3)	11	0	0	44
Jason Ryles	Catalans	2009	19(2)	2	0	0	8
Setaimata Sa	Widnes	2016	7(5)	3	0	0	12
	Hull	2014-15	18(6)	6	0	0	24
	Catalans	2010-12	58(5)	21	0	0	84
Teddy Sadaoui	Catalans	2006	7	0	0	0	0
Liam Salter	Hull KR	2012-16, 2018	83(3)	17	0	0	68
Matt Salter	London	1997-99	14(34)	0	0	0	0
Ben Sammut	Hull	2000	20	4	67	0	150
	Gateshead	1999	26(2)	6	17	0	58
Jarrod Sammut	Wigan	2019	6(6)	2	0	0	8
	Wakefield	2014-15	19(1)	9	52	0	140
	Bradford	2012-13	35(3)	28	47	1	207
	Crusaders	2010-11	17(16)	17	0	0	68
Dean Sampson	Castleford	1996-2003	124(28)	24	0	0	96
Paul Sampson	London	2004	1(2)	1	0	0	4
	Wakefield	2000	17	8	0	0	32
Jack Sanderson	Castleford	2020	3	1	0	0	4
Lee Sanderson	London	2004	1(5)	1	7	0	18
Chris Sandow	Warrington	2015-16	27(1)	11	26	1	97
Jason Sands	Paris	1996-97	28	0	0	0	0
Ligi Sao	Hull	2020	11(5)	1	0	0	4
Mitchell Sargent	Castleford	2008-10	37(21)	6	0	0	24
Dan Sarginson	Salford	2020	10	2	0	0	8
	Wigan	2014-16, 2018-19	112(2)	30	0	0	120
	London	2012-13	35(1)	10	0	0	40
	Harlequins	2011	8	5	0	0	20
Matt Sarsfield	Salford	2016	2(2)	1	0	0	4
Tevita Satae	Hull	2019-20	3(17)	2	0	0	8
Junior Sa'u	Salford	2014-19	115	46	0	0	184
	Wakefield	2019	3	0	0	0	0
Andre Savelio	Hull	2019-20	10(8)	6	0	0	24
	Warrington	2017	3(14)	4	0	0	16
	Castleford	2016	6(1)	1	0	0	4
	St Helens	2014-16	12(25)	2	0	0	8
Lokeni Savelio	Halifax	2000	2(11)	0	0	0	0
	Salford	1997-98	18(20)	0	0	0	0
Tom Saxton	Salford	2007	5	0	0	0	0
	Wakefield	2006	9(6)	2	0	0	8
	Hull	2005	19(8)	3	0	0	12
	Castleford	2002-04	37(12)	11	0	0	44
Jonathan Scales	Halifax	2000	1	0	0	0	0
	Bradford	1996-98	46(4)	24	0	0	96
Andrew Schick	Castleford	1996-98	45(13)	10	0	0	40
Clinton Schifcofske							
	Crusaders	2010-11	44	5	115	0	250
Garry Schofield	Huddersfield	1998	(2)	0	0	0	0
Gary Schubert	Workington	1996	(1)	0	0	0	0
Matt Schultz	Hull	1998-99	23(9)	2	0	0	8
	Leeds	1996	2(4)	0	0	0	0
John Schuster	Halifax	1996-97	31	9	127	3	293
Cameron Scott	Hull	2018-20	11	1	0	0	4
Nick Scruton	Hull KR	2018	7(10)	0	0	0	0
	Wakefield	2014-16	62(3)	9	0	0	36
	Bradford	2009-14	70(27)	5	0	0	20
	Leeds	2002, 2004-08	11(53)	3	0	0	12
	Hull	2004	2(16)	3	0	0	12
Danny Sculthorpe	Huddersfield	2009	5(8)	0	0	0	0
	Wakefield	2007-09	14(28)	1	0	0	4
	Castleford	2006	18(1)	4	0	1	17
	Wigan	2002-05	13(49)	7	0	0	28
Paul Sculthorpe	St Helens	1998-2008	223(4)	94	356	7	1095
	Warrington	1996-97	40	6	0	0	24
Mick Seaby	London	1997	3(2)	1	0	0	4
Danny Seal	Halifax	1996-99	8(17)	3	0	0	12
Matt Seers	Wakefield	2003	11(1)	2	0	0	8
James Segeyaro	Leeds	2016	1	1	0	0	4
Paul Seguier	Catalans	2016-17, 2020	1(11)	1	0	0	4
Anthony Seibold	London	1999-2000	33(19)	5	0	0	20
Jesse Sene-Lefao	Castleford	2017-19	58(28)	15	0	0	60
Innes Senior	Wakefield	2020	7	4	0	0	16
	Huddersfield	2018-19	25	8	0	0	32
Keith Senior	Leeds	1999-2011	319(2)	159	0	0	636
	Sheffield	1996-99	90(4)	40	0	0	160
Louis Senior	Huddersfield	2018-20	23	14	0	0	56
Fili Seru	Hull	1998-99	37(1)	13	0	0	52
Ava Seumanufagai	Leeds	2019-20	26(2)	3	0	0	12
Anthony Seuseu	Halifax	2003	1(11)	1	0	0	4
Jerry Seuseu	Wigan	2005-06	29(9)	1	0	0	4
Brett Seymour	Hull	2012-13	26(2)	7	0	0	28
Aidan Sezer	Huddersfield	2020	16	7	38	1	105
Will Sharp	Hull	2011-12	27(8)	10	0	0	40
	Harlequins	2008-10	65(1)	19	0	0	76

PLAYER	CLUB	YEAR	APP	TRIES	GOALS	FG	PTS
Jamie Shaul	Hull	2013-20	163	86	0	1	345
Darren Shaw	Salford	2002	5(9)	1	0	0	4
	London	1996, 2002	22(8)	3	0	0	12
	Castleford	2000-01	50(6)	1	0	0	4
	Sheffield	1998-99	51(1)	3	0	1	13
Mick Shaw	Halifax	1999	5	1	0	0	4
	Leeds	1996	12(2)	7	0	0	28
Ryan Shaw	Hull KR	2016, 2018-19	44(1)	19	125	0	326
	London	2013	2	1	2	0	8
Phil Shead	Paris	1996	3(2)	0	0	0	0
Richard Sheil	St Helens	1997	(1)	0	0	0	0
Kelly Shelford	Warrington	1996-97	25(3)	4	0	2	18
Kyle Shelford	Warrington	2020	(1)	0	0	0	0
	Wigan	2016	(1)	0	0	0	0
Michael Shenton	Castleford	2004, 2006, 2008-10, 2013-20	261(2)	108	0	0	432
	St Helens	2011-12	51	15	0	0	60
Ryan Sheridan	Castleford	2004	2	0	0	0	0
	Widnes	2003	14(3)	2	0	0	8
	Leeds	1997-2002	123(7)	46	0	1	185
	Sheffield	1996	9(3)	5	0	1	21
Louis Sheriff	Hull KR	2011-12	8	3	0	0	12
Rikki Sheriffe	Bradford	2009-10	51	14	0	0	56
	Harlequins	2006-08	35(1)	16	0	0	64
	Halifax	2003	6(1)	3	0	0	12
Ian Sherratt	Oldham	1996	5(3)	1	0	0	4
Brent Sherwin	Catalans	2010	12	1	0	1	5
	Castleford	2008-10	48(1)	4	0	3	19
Peter Shiels	St Helens	2001-02	44(3)	11	0	0	44
Gary Shillabeer	Huddersfield	1999	(2)	0	0	0	0
Mark Shipway	Salford	2004-05	30(12)	3	0	0	12
Jake Shorrocks	Wigan	2016-17, 2019-20	9(19)	2	8	0	24
	Salford	2018	10	0	1	0	2
Joe Shorrocks	Wigan	2019-20	(6)	0	0	0	0
Ian Sibbit	Bradford	2011-12	11(7)	0	0	0	0
	Salford	2005-07, 2009-10	64(17)	11	0	0	44
	Warrington	1999-2001, 2003-04	63(18)	24	0	0	96
Mark Sibson	Huddersfield	1999	2	2	0	0	8
Adam Sidlow	Toronto	2020	3(3)	0	0	0	0
	Bradford	2013-14	20(22)	8	0	0	32
	Salford	2009-12	34(44)	14	0	0	56
Harry Siejka	Wakefield	2014	6(3)	1	0	0	4
Jordan Sigismeau	Catalans	2015-16	11	3	0	0	12
Josh Simm	St Helens	2019-20	7	3	0	0	12
Jon Simms	St Helens	2002	(1)	0	0	0	0
Craig Simon	Hull	2000	23(2)	8	0	0	32
	Gateshead	1999	25(4)	6	0	0	24
Mickael Simon	Catalans	2010-14, 2017-20	55(76)	3	0	0	12
	Wakefield	2015-16	15(22)	3	0	0	12
Darren Simpson	Huddersfield	1998-99	17(1)	5	0	0	20
Jamie Simpson	Huddersfield	2011	8(1)	0	0	0	0
Jared Simpson	Huddersfield	2015-18	12	4	0	0	16
Robbie Simpson	London	1999	6(7)	0	0	0	0
Ashton Sims	Warrington	2015-17	69(11)	5	0	0	20
Kevin Sinfield	Leeds	1997-2015	425(29)	70	1566	31	3443
Matt Sing	Hull	2007-08	41	14	0	0	56
Wayne Sing	Paris	1997	18(1)	2	0	0	8
Brad Singleton	Wigan	2020	5(1)	0	0	0	0
	Toronto	2020	3(1)	1	0	0	4
	Leeds	2011-19	92(61)	17	0	0	68
	Wakefield	2013	(1)	0	0	0	0
Fata Sini	Salford	1997	22	7	0	0	28
Ken Sio	Salford	2019-20	29(1)	21	13	0	110
	Hull KR	2015-16	42	23	13	0	118
Michael Sio	Wakefield	2015-17	25(14)	6	0	0	24
John Skandalis	Huddersfield	2007-08	37(5)	4	0	0	16
Dylan Skee	Harlequins	2008-09	(3)	0	0	0	0
Ben Skerrett	Castleford	2003	(1)	0	0	0	0
Kelvin Skerrett	Halifax	1997-99	31(6)	2	0	0	8
	Wigan	1996	1(8)	0	0	0	0
Troy Slattery	Wakefield	2002-03	33(5)	4	0	0	16
	Huddersfield	1999	3	1	0	0	4
Mick Slicker	Huddersfield	2001, 2003-05	17(48)	2	0	0	8
	Sheffield	1999	(3)	1	0	0	4
	Halifax	1997	2(5)	0	0	0	0
Nick Slyney	London	2014	20(4)	3	0	0	12
Ian Smales	Castleford	1996-97	10(8)	5	0	0	20
Aaron Smith	St Helens	2018-20	11(18)	8	0	0	32
	Hull KR	2018	3(1)	0	0	0	0
Aaron Smith	Castleford	2006	(2)	0	0	0	0
	Bradford	2003-04	12(1)	3	0	0	12

170

PLAYER	CLUB	YEAR	APP	TRIES	GOALS	FG	PTS
Andy Smith	Harlequins	2007	6(3)	3	0	0	12
	Bradford	2004-06	9(9)	4	0	0	16
	Salford	2005	4	1	0	0	4
Byron Smith	Castleford	2004	(9)	0	0	0	0
	Halifax	2003	6(1)	0	0	0	0
Cameron Smith	Leeds	2016-20	18(32)	6	1	0	26
Chris Smith	Hull	2001-02	12	3	0	0	12
	St Helens	1998-2000	62(9)	26	0	0	104
	Castleford	1996-97	36(1)	12	0	0	48
Craig Smith	Wigan	2002-04	77(3)	10	0	0	40
Damien Smith	St Helens	1998	21(1)	8	0	0	32
Daniel Smith	Castleford	2019-20	11(18)	1	0	0	4
	Huddersfield	2015-18	9(38)	5	0	0	20
	Wakefield	2014-15	21(15)	6	0	0	24
Danny Smith	Paris	1996	10(2)	1	15	0	34
	London	1996	2(1)	1	0	0	4
Darren Smith	St Helens	2003	25(1)	14	0	0	56
Gary Smith	Castleford	2001	(1)	0	0	0	0
Harry Smith	Wigan	2019-20	6(10)	4	1	2	20
Hudson Smith	Bradford	2000	8(22)	2	0	0	8
	Salford	1999	23(2)	5	0	0	20
James Smith	Salford	2000	23(3)	6	0	0	24
Jamie Smith	Hull	1998-99	24(6)	6	12	0	48
	Workington	1996	5(3)	0	1	0	2
Jason Smith	Hull	2001-04	61(3)	17	0	1	69
Jeremy Smith	Wakefield	2011	9(1)	1	0	0	4
	Salford	2009-10	27(17)	2	0	0	8
Kris Smith	London	2001	(1)	0	0	0	0
	Halifax	2001	(1)	0	0	0	0
Lee Smith	Wakefield	2012-13, 2015	30(4)	16	54	2	174
	Leeds	2005-12	125(10)	60	34	1	309
Leigh Smith	Workington	1996	9	4	0	0	16
Mark Smith	Widnes	2005	12(15)	4	0	0	16
	Wigan	1999-2004	35(77)	8	0	0	32
Martyn Smith	Harlequins	2010	(2)	0	0	0	0
Matty Smith	Warrington	2019	4(1)	0	0	0	0
	Catalans	2019	16	0	0	1	1
	St Helens	2006-08, 2010, 2017-18	38(9)	5	10	4	44
	Wigan	2012-16	122(3)	17	279	25	651
	Salford	2010-12	67(4)	13	6	1	65
	Celtic	2009	15(1)	3	2	1	17
Michael Smith	Hull KR	2007	(3)	1	0	0	4
	Castleford	1998, 2001-04	86(33)	32	0	0	128
	Hull	1999	12(6)	3	0	0	12
Morgan Smith	London	2019	15(1)	1	1	2	8
	Warrington	2016-18	(18)	1	1	0	6
Paul Smith	Huddersfield	2004-06	52(17)	13	0	0	52
Paul Smith	Warrington	2001	(1)	0	0	0	0
	Castleford	1997-2000	6(37)	3	0	0	12
Paul Smith	London	1997	7(1)	2	0	0	8
Peter Smith	Oldham	1996	2	0	0	0	0
Richard Smith	Wakefield	2001	8(1)	1	0	0	4
	Salford	1997	(1)	1	0	0	4
Tim Smith	Wakefield	2012-15	79	11	0	0	44
	Salford	2014	12	2	7	0	22
	Wigan	2008-09	13(8)	2	0	0	8
Tony Smith	Hull	2001-03	43(5)	26	0	0	104
	Wigan	1997-2000	66(5)	46	0	0	184
	Castleford	1996-97	18(2)	10	0	0	40
Tony Smith	Workington	1996	9	1	0	0	4
Tyrone Smith	Harlequins	2006-07	49(3)	13	0	0	52
	London	2005	20(4)	11	0	0	44
Morgan Smithies	Wigan	2019-20	17(23)	1	0	0	4
Rob Smyth	Leigh	2005	15(1)	4	0	0	16
	Warrington	2000-03	65	35	20	0	180
	London	1998-2000	32(2)	9	15	0	66
	Wigan	1996	11(5)	16	0	0	64
Marc Sneyd	Hull	2015-20	142	19	498	31	1103
	Castleford	2014	25(1)	6	100	2	226
	Salford	2010-13	33(12)	4	61	3	141
Steve Snitch	Castleford	2010-12	38(18)	10	0	0	40
	Wakefield	2002-05, 2009	33(55)	9	0	0	36
	Huddersfield	2006-08	24(35)	12	0	0	48
Bright Sodje	Wakefield	2000	15	4	0	0	16
	Sheffield	1996-99	54	34	0	0	136
Iosia Soliola	St Helens	2010-14	83(24)	27	0	0	108
David Solomona	Warrington	2010-12	8(49)	16	1	0	66
	Bradford	2007-09	44(9)	19	0	0	76
	Wakefield	2004-06	73(3)	26	0	0	104
Denny Solomona	Castleford	2015-16	42	58	0	0	232
	London	2014	19(1)	8	0	0	32
Alfred Songoro	Wakefield	1999	8(5)	4	0	0	16
Romain Sort	Paris	1997	(1)	0	0	0	0
Paul Southern	Salford	1997-2002	79(33)	6	13	0	50
	St Helens	2002	1(1)	0	1	0	0
Steve Southern	Wakefield	2012	7(8)	3	0	0	12
Cain Southernwood							
	Bradford	2010	2	0	0	0	0
Roy Southernwood							
	Wakefield	1999	1	0	0	0	0
	Halifax	1996	2	0	0	0	0
Jason Southwell	Huddersfield	2004	(1)	0	0	0	0
Waisale Sovatabua							
	Wakefield	2001-03	44(3)	19	0	0	76
	Hudds-Sheff	2000	23(1)	8	0	0	32
	Sheffield	1996-99	56(17)	19	0	1	77
Jamie Soward	London	2013	6(1)	4	21	0	58
Yusef Sozi	London	2000-01	(5)	0	0	0	0
Scott Spaven	Hull KR	2010	(2)	0	0	0	0
Andy Speak	Castleford	2001	4(4)	0	0	0	0
	Wakefield	2000	6(5)	2	0	0	8
	Leeds	1999	4	1	0	0	4
Dom Speakman	St Helens	2013	(1)	0	0	0	0
Tim Spears	Castleford	2003	(3)	0	0	0	0
Jake Spedding	St Helens	2016-18	3(1)	0	0	0	0
Ady Spencer	London	1996-99	8(36)	5	0	0	20
Jack Spencer	Salford	2009-11	(7)	0	0	0	0
Tom Spencer	Wigan	2012-13	(7)	0	0	0	0
Rob Spicer	Wakefield	2002-05	28(18)	4	0	0	16
Russ Spiers	Wakefield	2011	(2)	0	0	0	0
Gadwin Springer	Toronto	2020	4(1)	0	0	0	0
	Castleford	2015-18	15(41)	3	0	0	12
	Catalans	2014-15	(3)	1	0	0	4
Stuart Spruce	Widnes	2002-03	45(4)	19	0	0	76
	Bradford	1996-2001	107(2)	57	0	0	228
Lee St Hilaire	Castleford	1997	4(2)	0	0	0	0
Marcus St Hilaire	Bradford	2006-07	34(1)	12	0	0	48
	Huddersfield	2003-05	72(2)	30	0	0	120
	Leeds	1996-2002	59(33)	31	0	0	124
Cyril Stacul	Catalans	2007-12	61(1)	18	0	0	72
Dylan Stainton	Workington	1996	2(3)	0	0	0	0
Mark Stamper	Workington	1996	(1)	0	0	0	0
John Stankevitch	Widnes	2005	17(5)	0	0	0	0
	St Helens	2000-04	74(40)	25	0	0	100
Gareth Stanley	Bradford	2000	1	1	0	0	4
Craig Stapleton	Salford	2009	24	2	0	0	8
	Leigh	2005	27(1)	4	0	0	16
Graham Steadman	Castleford	1996-97	11(17)	5	0	0	20
Jon Steel	Hull KR	2007-08	18	6	0	0	24
Jamie Stenhouse	Warrington	2000-01	9(3)	3	0	0	12
Gareth Stephens	Sheffield	1997-99	23(6)	2	0	0	8
David Stephenson	Hull	1998	11(7)	3	0	0	12
	Oldham	1997	10(8)	2	0	0	8
Francis Stephenson							
	London	2002-05	42(34)	5	0	0	20
	Wigan	2001	2(9)	0	0	0	0
	Wakefield	1999-2000	50(1)	6	0	0	24
Paul Sterling	Leeds	1997-2000	79(12)	50	0	0	200
Paul Stevens	Oldham	1996	2(1)	0	0	0	0
	London	1996	(1)	0	0	0	0
Warren Stevens	Leigh	2005	4(14)	1	0	0	4
	Warrington	1996-99, 2002-05	17(66)	1	0	0	4
	Salford	2001	(8)	0	0	0	0
Anthony Stewart	Harlequins	2006	4	0	0	0	0
	Salford	2004-06	51(2)	15	0	0	60
	St Helens	1997-2003	93(23)	44	0	0	176
Glenn Stewart	Leigh	2017	15	0	0	0	0
	Catalans	2016	28	3	0	0	12
Troy Stone	Widnes	2002	18(6)	1	0	0	4
	Huddersfield	2001	12(1)	1	0	0	4
Matthew Storton	Hull KR	2020	9(1)	0	0	0	0
James Stosic	Wakefield	2009	8(10)	1	0	0	4
Lynton Stott	Wakefield	1999	21	4	6	1	29
	Sheffield	1996-98	40(4)	15	0	0	60
Mitchell Stringer	Salford	2005-06	12(4)	0	0	0	0
	London	2004-05	10(19)	0	0	0	0
Graham Strutton	London	1996	9(1)	2	0	0	8
Matt Sturm	Leigh	2005	8(19)	3	0	0	12
	Warrington	2002-04	1(18)	0	0	0	0
	Huddersfield	1998-99	46	8	0	0	32
Anthony Sullivan	St Helens	1996-2001	137(2)	105	0	0	420
Michael Sullivan	Warrington	2006-07	21(16)	8	1	0	34
Phil Sumner	Warrington	1996	(5)	0	0	0	0
Alex Sutcliffe	Leeds	2017, 2019-20	6(4)	1	0	0	4
Liam Sutcliffe	Leeds	2013-20	121(32)	49	168	2	534
	Bradford	2014	3(1)	1	0	0	4
Ryan Sutton	Wigan	2014-18	38(65)	10	0	0	40
Simon Svabic	Salford	1998-2000	13(5)	3	19	0	50

171

Super League Players 1996-2020

PLAYER	CLUB	YEAR	APP	TRIES	GOALS	FG	PTS
Luke Swain	Salford	2009-10	54	3	0	0	12
Richard Swain	Hull	2004-07	89	5	0	0	20
Anthony Swann	Warrington	2001	3	1	0	0	4
Logan Swann	Warrington	2005-06	49(1)	17	0	0	68
	Bradford	2004	25	6	0	0	24
Willie Swann	Warrington	1996-97	25(2)	6	0	0	24
Adam Swift	Hull	2020	5	3	0	0	12
	St Helens	2012-19	120	80	0	0	320
Nathan Sykes	Castleford	1996-2004	158(52)	3	0	0	12
Paul Sykes	Wakefield	2012-14	59(1)	12	135	6	324
	Bradford	1999-2002, 2008-12	99(4)	35	64	2	270
	Harlequins	2006-07	31(2)	15	47	1	155
	London	2001-05	95(1)	26	219	3	545
Wayne Sykes	London	1999	(2)	0	0	0	0
Tom Symonds	Huddersfield	2016-18	6(1)	3	0	0	12
Ukuma Ta'ai	Huddersfield	2013-20	118(63)	43	0	0	172
Semi Tadulala	Wakefield	2004-07,2011	92	37	0	0	148
	Bradford	2008-09	49	30	0	0	120
Whetu Taewa	Sheffield	1997-98	33(7)	8	0	0	32
Zeb Taia	St Helens	2017-20	96(3)	22	0	0	88
	Catalans	2013-15	75	35	0	0	140
Alan Tait	Leeds	1996	3(3)	1	0	0	4
Fetuli Talanoa	Hull	2014-18	115(1)	54	0	0	216
Willie Talau	Salford	2009-10	22	4	0	0	16
	St Helens	2003-08	130(1)	50	0	0	200
Ian Talbot	Wakefield	1999	9(5)	2	31	0	70
	Wigan	1997	3	1	0	0	4
Albert Talipeau	Wakefield	2004	2(3)	0	0	0	0
Gael Tallec	Halifax	2000	5(19)	3	0	0	12
	Castleford	1998-99	19(21)	3	0	0	12
	Wigan	1996-97	8(12)	3	0	0	12
Joe Tamani	Bradford	1996	11(3)	4	0	0	16
Ryan Tandy	Hull KR	2007	8(4)	2	0	0	8
Adam Tangata	Wakefield	2019-20	2(14)	1	0	0	4
Andrew Tangata-Toa	Huddersfield	1999	15	2	0	0	8
David Tangata-Toa	Celtic	2009	1(18)	4	0	0	16
	Hull KR	2007	(17)	3	0	0	12
Kelepi Tanginoa	Wakefield	2019-20	28(5)	7	0	0	28
Jordan Tansey	Huddersfield	2016	2	1	1	0	6
	Wakefield	2015	4	1	0	0	4
	Castleford	2013-15	44(1)	15	0	0	60
	Crusaders	2011	14(4)	5	0	0	20
	Hull	2009-10	30	9	0	0	36
	Leeds	2006-08	18(32)	19	3	0	82
Lama Tasi	Warrington	2019	9(8)	0	0	0	0
	Salford	2014-15, 2017-18	55(26)	4	0	0	16
	St Helens	2016	9(8)	0	0	0	0
Kris Tassell	Wakefield	2002	24	10	0	0	40
	Salford	2000-01	35(10)	12	0	0	48
Will Tate	Hull KR	2020	4	1	0	0	4
Shem Tatupu	Wigan	1996	(3)	0	0	0	0
Tony Tatupu	Wakefield	2000-01	20	2	0	0	8
	Warrington	1997	21(1)	6	0	0	24
Taulima Tautai	Wigan	2015-19	7(111)	4	0	0	16
	Wakefield	2013-14	6(19)	2	0	0	8
Dave Taylor	Catalans	2016	20(4)	8	0	0	32
James Taylor	Leigh	2005	(4)	0	0	0	0
Joe Taylor	Paris	1997	9(5)	2	0	0	8
Lawrence Taylor	Sheffield	1996	(1)	0	0	0	0
Scott Taylor	Hull	2016-20	108(10)	16	0	0	64
	Salford	2015	23	5	0	0	20
	Wigan	2013-14	18(29)	6	0	0	24
	Hull KR	2009-12	21(29)	8	0	0	32
Frederic Teixido	Sheffield	1999	(4)	0	0	0	0
	Paris	1996-97	2(3)	1	0	0	4
Lionel Teixido	Catalans	2006-07	11(3)	3	0	0	12
Karl Temata	London	2005, 2012	1(8)	1	0	0	4
	Harlequins	2006-11	94(22)	7	0	0	28
Jason Temu	Hull	1998	13(2)	1	0	0	4
	Oldham	1996-97	25(3)	1	0	0	4
Paul Terry	London	1997	(1)	0	0	0	0
Anthony Thackeray	Castleford	2008	3(6)	0	0	0	0
	Hull	2007	2	0	0	0	0
Jamie Thackray	Crusaders	2010	1(16)	2	0	0	8
	Hull	2005-06, 2008-09	37(45)	6	0	0	24
	Leeds	2006-07	5(27)	7	0	0	28
	Castleford	2003-04	7(11)	3	0	0	12
	Halifax	2000-02	10(38)	3	0	0	12
Adam Thaler	Castleford	2002	(1)	0	0	0	0
Josh Thewlis	Warrington	2019-20	4	2	0	0	8
Gareth Thomas	Crusaders	2010-11	27(1)	6	0	0	24
Giles Thomas	London	1997-99	1(2)	0	0	0	0
Oscar Thomas	London	2014	4(2)	0	1	0	2
Rob Thomas	Harlequins	2011	(2)	0	0	0	0
Steve Thomas	London	2004	4(2)	0	0	0	0
	Warrington	2001	2	0	0	0	0
Alex Thompson	Warrington	2009	(1)	1	0	0	4
Alex Thompson	Sheffield	1997	4(11)	0	0	0	0
Bobby Thompson	Salford	1999	28	5	2	0	24
Bodene Thompson	Leeds	2020	11	0	0	0	0
	Toronto	2020	4(1)	1	0	0	4
	Warrington	2018	7	0	0	0	0
Corey Thompson	Widnes	2016-17	48	36	9	0	162
David Thompson	Leigh	2017	1	0	0	0	0
	Hull KR	2016	1	0	0	0	0
Jordan Thompson	Hull	2014-17, 2019	27(81)	12	0	0	48
	Leeds	2018	1	0	0	0	0
	Castleford	2009-13	47(24)	25	0	0	100
Luke Thompson	St Helens	2013-20	100(54)	28	0	0	112
Sam Thompson	Harlequins	2009	(2)	0	0	0	0
	St Helens	2008	(5)	0	0	0	0
Chris Thorman	Hull	2009	19(2)	1	0	0	4
	Huddersfield	2000-01, 2005-08	126(20)	51	320	3	847
	London	2003	26(1)	7	81	1	191
	Sheffield	1999	5(13)	2	8	1	25
Tony Thorniley	Warrington	1997	(5)	0	0	0	0
Andy Thornley	Salford	2009	(1)	1	0	0	4
Iain Thornley	Catalans	2017-18	31(1)	7	0	0	28
	Hull KR	2016	21	10	0	0	40
	Wigan	2012-14	40	25	0	0	100
Danny Tickle	Hull KR	2018	14(3)	4	20	0	56
	Leigh	2017	10(13)	4	0	0	16
	Castleford	2016	6(3)	0	1	0	2
	Widnes	2014-15	33(1)	3	88	0	188
	Hull	2007-13	159(5)	45	528	1	1237
	Wigan	2002-06	94(36)	34	200	2	538
	Halifax	2000-02	25(17)	10	91	2	224
Kris Tickle	Warrington	2001	(1)	0	0	0	0
Lewis Tierney	Catalans	2017-20	52	15	0	0	60
	Wigan	2013-17	35	17	0	0	68
James Tilley	St Helens	2013-14	(3)	0	0	0	0
Dane Tilse	Hull KR	2015-16	29(1)	1	0	0	4
John Timu	London	1998-2000	57(3)	11	0	0	44
Liam Tindall	Leeds	2020	3	1	0	0	4
Kerrod Toby	Hull	1997	2(2)	0	0	0	0
Tulsen Tollett	London	1996-2001	105(5)	38	49	1	251
Joel Tomkins	Catalans	2020	10	4	0	0	16
	Hull KR	2018-19	27	7	0	0	28
	Wigan	2005-11, 2014-16	161(51)	60	0	0	240
Logan Tomkins	Salford	2014-19	85(31)	6	0	0	24
	Wigan	2012-15	9(32)	1	0	0	4
Sam Tomkins	Catalans	2019-20	36	14	78	1	213
	Wigan	2009-13, 2016-18	177(6)	129	125	7	773
Glen Tomlinson	Wakefield	1999-2000	41(5)	8	0	0	32
	Hull	1998	5	1	0	0	4
	Bradford	1996-97	27(13)	12	0	0	48
Willie Tonga	Leigh	2017	3	0	0	0	0
	Catalans	2015	18	6	0	0	24
Ryan Tongia	Wakefield	2011	4	2	0	0	8
Ian Tonks	Castleford	1996-2001	32(50)	11	13	0	70
Tony Tonks	Huddersfield	2012	1	0	0	0	0
Motu Tony	Wakefield	2011-12	7(3)	1	0	0	4
	Hull	2005-09	76(20)	25	0	0	100
	Castleford	2004	8(1)	1	0	0	4
Mark Tookey	Harlequins	2006	12(14)	1	0	0	4
	London	2005	13(14)	5	0	0	20
	Castleford	2004	2(8)	1	0	0	4
Clinton Toopi	Leeds	2006-08	40(3)	9	0	0	36
David Tootill	Harlequins	2008	(4)	0	0	0	0
Paul Topping	Oldham	1996-97	23(10)	1	19	0	42
Patrick Torreilles	Paris	1996	9(1)	1	25	0	54
Albert Torrens	Huddersfield	2006	7	5	0	0	20
Mat Toshack	London	1998-2004	120(21)	24	0	0	96
Julien Touxagas	Catalans	2006-11	14(45)	4	0	0	16
Darren Treacy	Salford	2002	24(1)	6	1	0	26
Dean Treister	Hull	2003	16(1)	3	0	0	12
Rocky Trimarchi	Crusaders	2010	16(8)	0	0	0	0
Steve Trindall	London	2003-05	40(20)	3	0	0	12
Shane Tronc	Wakefield	2000	8(3)	2	0	0	8
Kyle Trout	Hull KR	2019-20	1(14)	0	0	0	0
	Wakefield	2012-15	6(17)	3	0	0	12
Owen Trout	Huddersfield	2020	(6)	1	0	0	4
	Leeds	2019	1(1)	0	0	0	0
George Truelove	Wakefield	2002	2	1	0	0	4
	London	2000	5	1	0	0	4

PLAYER	CLUB	YEAR	APP	TRIES	GOALS	FG	PTS
Jake Trueman	Castleford	2017-20	69(2)	19	0	1	77
Va'aiga Tuigamala	Wigan	1996	21	10	3	0	46
Fereti Tuilagi	St Helens	1999-2000	43(15)	21	0	0	84
	Halifax	1996-98	55(3)	27	0	0	108
Carlos Tuimavave	Hull	2016-20	104(6)	35	0	0	140
Evarn Tuimavave	Hull KR	2013	11(12)	2	0	0	8
Sateki Tuipulotu	Leeds	1996	6(3)	1	2	0	8
Anthony Tupou	Wakefield	2016	12(9)	4	0	0	16
Bill Tupou	Wakefield	2015-20	101(3)	37	0	0	148
Tame Tupou	Bradford	2007-08	10(7)	8	0	0	32
Jansin Turgut	Salford	2019	8(2)	1	0	0	4
	Hull	2015-18	10(18)	3	0	0	12
Neil Turley	Leigh	2005	6(3)	2	20	1	49
Calum Turner	Castleford	2018-20	7(6)	4	10	0	36
Darren Turner	Huddersfield	2000-01, 2003-04	42(13)	13	0	0	52
	Sheffield	1996-99	41(29)	15	0	0	60
Ian Turner	Paris	1996	1(1)	1	0	0	4
Jordan Turner	Huddersfield	2017-20	66(2)	10	0	1	41
	St Helens	2013-16	106(4)	44	13	3	205
	Hull	2010-12	62(5)	28	0	0	112
	Salford	2006-07, 2009	22(10)	4	1	0	18
Chris Tuson	Hull	2014	10(1)	0	0	0	0
	Wigan	2008, 2010-13	24(49)	13	0	0	52
	Castleford	2010	3(5)	0	0	0	0
Gregory Tutard	Paris	1996	1(1)	0	0	0	0
Brendon Tuuta	Warrington	1998	18(2)	4	0	0	16
	Castleford	1996-97	41(1)	3	0	0	12
Steve Tyrer	Salford	2010	20	6	9	0	42
	Celtic	2009	8	2	5	0	18
	St Helens	2006-08	17(3)	12	42	0	132
Bobby Tyson-Wilson	Hull	2015	(1)	0	0	0	0
Harry Tyson-Wilson	Hull	2014	(1)	0	0	0	0
Akuila Uate	Huddersfield	2019	12	5	0	0	20
Wayne Ulugia	Hull KR	2014	3	1	0	0	4
Mike Umaga	Halifax	1996-97	38(1)	16	5	0	74
Kava Utoikamanu	Paris	1996	6(3)	0	0	0	0
Frederic Vaccari	Catalans	2010-11, 2013-16	50	26	0	0	104
David Vaealiki	Wigan	2005-07	67(1)	17	0	0	68
Joe Vagana	Bradford	2001-08	176(44)	17	0	0	68
Nigel Vagana	Warrington	1997	20	17	0	0	68
Tevita Vaikona	Bradford	1998-2004	145(2)	89	0	0	356
Lesley Vainikolo	Bradford	2002-07	132(4)	136	1	0	546
Junior Vaivai	Hull KR	2018-19	22(1)	8	0	0	32
Eric Van Brussell	Paris	1996	2	0	0	0	0
Jace Van Dijk	Celtic	2009	19	1	1	0	6
Richard Varkulis	Warrington	2004	4(1)	3	0	0	12
Marcus Vassilakopoulos	Sheffield	1997-99	15(11)	3	10	2	34
	Leeds	1996-97	1(3)	0	0	0	0
Manu Vatuvei	Salford	2017	7	5	0	0	20
Atelea Vea	Leigh	2017	19(1)	5	0	0	20
	St Helens	2015-16	19(17)	10	0	0	40
	London	2014	19(3)	2	0	0	8
Josh Veivers	Salford	2012	5	2	0	0	8
	Wakefield	2011	10(2)	2	22	0	52
Phil Veivers	Huddersfield	1998	7(6)	1	0	0	4
	St Helens	1996	(1)	1	0	0	4
Michael Vella	Hull KR	2007-11	111(5)	13	0	0	52
Bruno Verges	Catalans	2006	25	6	0	0	24
Eric Vergniol	Paris	1996	14(1)	6	0	0	24
Gray Viane	Salford	2007	9	2	0	0	8
	Castleford	2006	20(7)	14	0	0	56
	Widnes	2005	20	13	0	0	52
	St Helens	2004	4	1	0	0	4
Joe Vickery	Leeds	2013	9	1	0	0	4
Daniel Vidot	Salford	2016	5(1)	5	0	0	20
Adrian Vowles	Castleford	1997-2001, 2003	125(1)	29	1	1	119
	Wakefield	2002-03	24(3)	6	1	0	26
	Leeds	2002	14(3)	2	0	0	8
Michael Wainwright	Castleford	2008-10	70	22	0	0	88
	Wakefield	2004-05	21(10)	8	0	0	32
Mike Wainwright	Salford	2000-02, 2007	75(3)	9	0	0	36
	Warrington	1996-99, 2003-07	168(14)	23	0	0	92
Shannon Wakeman	Huddersfield	2017-18	16(13)	3	0	0	12

PLAYER	CLUB	YEAR	APP	TRIES	GOALS	FG	PTS
Adam Walker	Salford	2019	9(14)	4	0	0	16
	Wakefield	2017	5(1)	0	0	0	0
	St Helens	2017	(9)	1	0	0	4
	Hull KR	2013-16	60(27)	6	0	0	24
	Huddersfield	2010-12	1(5)	0	0	0	0
Alex Walker	Wakefield	2020	7	1	0	0	4
	London	2014, 2019	28	6	0	0	24
Anthony Walker	Wakefield	2015-17	1(11)	1	0	0	4
	St Helens	2013-14	9(7)	2	0	0	8
Ben Walker	Leeds	2002	23(1)	8	100	0	232
Brad Walker	Wakefield	2020	1(2)	0	0	0	0
	Widnes	2016-18	3(5)	0	0	0	0
Chev Walker	Bradford	2011-14	44(22)	5	0	0	20
	Hull KR	2008-09	24(7)	5	0	0	20
	Leeds	1999-2006	142(19)	77	0	0	308
Chris Walker	Catalans	2010	11	6	2	0	28
Danny Walker	Warrington	2019-20	8(17)	2	0	0	8
	Widnes	2017-18	3(16)	2	0	0	8
Jack Walker	Leeds	2017-20	52(4)	18	0	0	72
Jonathan Walker	Hull KR	2014	2(6)	0	0	0	0
	Castleford	2010-13	17(31)	4	0	0	16
Jonny Walker	Wigan	2010	(1)	0	0	0	0
Matt Walker	Huddersfield	2001	3(6)	0	0	0	0
Anthony Wall	Paris	1997	9	3	3	0	18
Blake Wallace	Toronto	2020	5(1)	0	7	0	14
Jon Wallace	London	2014	4(12)	0	0	0	0
Mark Wallace	Workington	1996	14(1)	3	0	0	12
Elliot Wallis	Hull KR	2018	4	2	0	0	8
Alex Walmsley	St Helens	2013-20	113(72)	35	0	0	140
Adam Walne	Huddersfield	2018-20	4(9)	0	0	0	0
	Salford	2012-17	15(50)	2	0	0	8
Jordan Walne	Hull KR	2018	(6)	0	0	0	0
	Salford	2013-17	20(32)	3	0	0	12
Joe Walsh	Huddersfield	2009	1(1)	1	0	0	4
	Harlequins	2007-08	1(4)	0	0	0	0
Liam Walsh	Widnes	2017	(1)	0	0	0	0
Luke Walsh	Catalans	2017-18	23	2	71	4	154
	St Helens	2014-16	56(2)	14	188	9	441
Lucas Walshaw	Wakefield	2011-14	15(6)	3	0	0	12
Josh Walters	Leeds	2014-18	15(36)	9	0	0	36
Kerrod Walters	Gateshead	1999	10(12)	2	1	0	10
Kevin Walters	Warrington	2001	1	0	0	0	0
Sam Walters	Leeds	2020	4	1	0	0	4
Jason Walton	Wakefield	2016	7(8)	0	0	0	0
	Salford	2009, 2014-15	7(19)	1	0	0	4
Barry Ward	St Helens	2002-03	20(30)	4	0	0	16
Danny Ward	Harlequins	2008-11	89(7)	4	0	0	16
	Hull KR	2007	11(9)	0	0	0	0
	Castleford	2006	18(7)	2	0	0	8
	Leeds	1999-2005	70(48)	9	0	1	37
Robbie Ward	Leeds	2014-15	5(3)	1	0	0	4
Stevie Ward	Leeds	2012-20	86(29)	19	0	0	76
Joe Wardill	Hull KR	2016, 2018	6(2)	1	0	0	4
Jake Wardle	Huddersfield	2018-20	38	12	5	0	58
Joe Wardle	Huddersfield	2011-16, 2019-20	151(1)	64	0	0	256
	Castleford	2018	15(2)	1	0	0	4
	Bradford	2010	1(1)	0	0	0	0
Phil Waring	Salford	1997-99	6(8)	2	0	0	8
Brett Warton	London	1999-2001	49(7)	14	133	0	322
Kyle Warren	Castleford	2002	13(14)	3	0	0	12
Danny Washbrook	Hull	2005-11, 2016-19	136(71)	19	0	0	76
	Wakefield	2012-15	93(8)	12	0	0	48
Adam Watene	Wakefield	2006-08	45(8)	5	0	0	20
	Bradford	2006	(4)	0	0	0	0
Frank Watene	Wakefield	1999-2001	24(31)	6	0	0	24
Trent Waterhouse	Warrington	2012-14	65(5)	15	0	0	60
Luke Waterworth	Wigan	2016	1	0	0	0	0
Kallum Watkins	Salford	2020	5	2	0	0	8
	Leeds	2008-19	215(7)	110	85	0	610
Dave Watson	Sheffield	1998-99	41(4)	4	0	0	16
Ian Watson	Salford	1997, 2002	24(17)	8	3	5	43
	Workington	1996	4(1)	1	15	0	34
Kris Watson	Warrington	1996	11(2)	2	0	0	8
Anthony Watts	Widnes	2012	(1)	0	0	0	0
Brad Watts	Widnes	2005	6	3	0	0	12
Liam Watts	Castleford	2018-20	62(1)	5	0	0	20
	Hull	2012-18	116(19)	9	0	0	36
	Hull KR	2008, 2010-12	31(26)	6	0	0	24
Michael Watts	Warrington	2002	3	0	0	0	0
Brent Webb	Catalans	2013-14	10	2	0	0	8
	Leeds	2007-12	137(1)	73	0	0	292
Jason Webber	Salford	2000	25(1)	10	0	0	40

PLAYER	CLUB	YEAR	APP	TRIES	GOALS	FG	PTS
Ian Webster	St Helens	2006	1	0	0	0	0
Jake Webster	Castleford	2013-18	103(12)	45	0	0	180
	Hull KR	2008-12	95(1)	34	7	0	150
James Webster	Hull	2008	1	0	0	0	0
	Hull KR	2007-08	36	2	0	2	10
Pat Weisner	Hull KR	2007	(2)	0	0	0	0
	Harlequins	2006	10(6)	3	0	0	12
Taylor Welch	Warrington	2008	1	0	0	0	0
Kris Welham	Salford	2017-20	85(1)	27	0	0	108
	Hull KR	2007-15	164(2)	90	1	0	362
Paul Wellens	St Helens	1998-2015	399(40)	199	34	1	865
Calvin Wellington	St Helens	2016	1	0	0	0	0
Jack Wells	Wigan	2016-17, 2020	5(12)	1	0	0	4
	Toronto	2020	(2)	1	0	0	4
Jon Wells	Harlequins	2006-09	66	10	0	0	40
	London	2004-05	42(2)	19	0	0	76
	Wakefield	2003	22(1)	1	0	0	4
	Castleford	1996-2002	114(14)	49	0	0	196
Jack Welsby	St Helens	2018-20	24(3)	12	0	0	48
Dwayne West	St Helens	2000-02	8(16)	6	0	0	24
	Wigan	1999	1(1)	0	0	0	0
Joe Westerman	Wakefield	2020	15	3	0	0	12
	Hull	2011-15, 2018-19	135(13)	36	52	1	249
	Warrington	2016-17	45(1)	12	0	0	48
	Castleford	2008-10	68(7)	29	151	0	418
Craig Weston	Widnes	2002, 2004	23(9)	2	1	2	12
	Huddersfield	1998-99	46(1)	15	15	0	90
Dayne Weston	Leigh	2017	6(5)	1	0	0	4
Ben Westwood	Warrington	2002-19	363(29)	112	64	0	576
	Wakefield	1999-2002	31(7)	8	1	0	34
Michael Weyman	Hull KR	2014	22(1)	7	0	0	28
Andrew Whalley	Workington	1996	(2)	0	0	0	0
Paul Whatuira	Huddersfield	2008-10	59	23	0	0	92
Scott Wheeldon	Castleford	2014-15	14(23)	5	0	0	20
	London	2012-13	27(4)	3	0	0	12
	Hull KR	2009-12	30(42)	4	0	0	16
	Hull	2006-08	2(60)	4	0	0	16
Gary Wheeler	Toronto	2020	(2)	2	0	0	8
	Warrington	2015-16	6(4)	4	0	0	16
	St Helens	2008-14	48(10)	17	13	0	94
Matt Whitaker	Castleford	2006	8(2)	0	0	0	0
	Widnes	2004-05	10(20)	9	0	0	36
	Huddersfield	2003-04	3(14)	0	0	0	0
Ben White	Leeds	2014	1	0	0	0	0
David White	Wakefield	2000	(1)	0	0	0	0
Josh White	Salford	1998	18(3)	5	5	1	31
	London	1997	14(2)	8	0	1	33
Lloyd White	Widnes	2012-18	72(43)	27	24	1	157
	Crusaders	2010-11	13(11)	8	0	0	32
	Celtic	2009	6	1	0	0	4
Paul White	Salford	2009	1	1	0	0	4
	Wakefield	2006-07	24(12)	12	0	0	48
	Huddersfield	2003-05	11(32)	17	16	0	100
Elliott Whitehead	Catalans	2013-15	64(1)	30	0	0	120
	Bradford	2009-13	90(10)	30	0	0	120
Harvey Whiteley	Leeds	2017, 2020	(3)	0	0	0	0
Richard Whiting	Hull	2004-15	163(72)	69	19	2	316
Matt Whitley	Catalans	2019-20	36(2)	12	0	0	48
	Widnes	2015-18	50(27)	13	0	0	52
Emmerson Whittel	Bradford	2014	(1)	0	0	0	0
Danny Whittle	Warrington	1998	(2)	0	0	0	0
David Whittle	St Helens	2002	1(2)	0	0	0	0
	Warrington	2001	1(2)	0	0	0	0
Jon Whittle	Wakefield	2006	8(2)	3	0	0	12
	Widnes	2005	13	2	0	0	8
	Wigan	2003	1	0	0	0	0
Joel Wicks	London	2013-14	3(10)	0	0	0	0
Dean Widders	Castleford	2009-11	25(32)	23	0	0	92
Gareth Widdop	Warrington	2020	13	5	7	1	35
Stephen Wild	Salford	2011-13	71	4	0	0	16
	Huddersfield	2006-10	116(12)	33	0	0	132
	Wigan	2001-05	67(20)	24	0	0	96
Sam Wilde	Widnes	2017-18	14(7)	2	0	0	8
	Warrington	2015-17	3(15)	1	0	0	4
Matty Wildie	Wakefield	2010-14	13(26)	3	0	0	12
Brayden Wiliame	Catalans	2017-19	64	25	0	0	100
Oliver Wilkes	Wakefield	2008-09, 2012-13	55(47)	10	0	0	40
	Harlequins	2010-11	39(13)	4	0	0	16
	Wigan	2006	1(5)	0	0	0	0
	Leigh	2005	13(1)	1	0	0	4
	Huddersfield	2000-01	1(6)	0	0	0	0
	Sheffield	1998	(1)	0	0	0	0
Jon Wilkin	Toronto	2020	5	1	0	0	4
	St Helens	2003-18	350(30)	78	0	2	314
Alex Wilkinson	Hull	2003-04	11(4)	1	0	0	4
	Huddersfield	2003	8	4	0	0	16
	London	2002	5(1)	0	0	0	0
	Bradford	2000-01	3(3)	1	0	0	4
Bart Williams	London	1998	5(3)	1	0	0	4
Connor Williams	Salford	2016	(1)	0	0	0	0
Daley Williams	Salford	2006-07	9(2)	4	0	0	16
Danny Williams	Harlequins	2006	9(13)	4	0	0	16
	London	2005	1(16)	0	0	0	0
Danny Williams	Bradford	2014	7	2	0	0	8
	Salford	2011-14	54	31	0	0	124
	Leeds	2006, 2008	13(2)	7	0	0	28
	Hull	2008	3	0	0	0	0
Dave Williams	Harlequins	2008-11	1(17)	0	0	0	0
Desi Williams	Wigan	2004	2	0	0	0	0
George Williams	Wigan	2013-19	149(13)	55	56	1	333
Jonny Williams	London	2004	(4)	0	0	0	0
Lee Williams	Crusaders	2011	1(7)	0	0	0	0
Rhys Williams	Salford	2013, 2020	20	7	0	0	28
	London	2019	29	13	0	0	52
	Warrington	2010-13	23(1)	15	0	0	60
	Castleford	2012	8	4	0	0	16
	Crusaders	2011	6	3	0	0	12
Sam Williams	Wakefield	2017	17(5)	4	26	0	68
	Catalans	2014	11(1)	4	21	0	58
Sonny Bill Williams	Toronto	2020	4(1)	0	0	0	0
Luke Williamson	Harlequins	2009-10	39	6	0	0	24
John Wilshere	Salford	2006-07, 2009	72(2)	32	142	0	412
	Leigh	2005	26	8	6	0	44
	Warrington	2004	5	2	0	0	8
Craig Wilson	Hull	2000	2(16)	1	0	1	5
	Gateshead	1999	17(11)	5	0	1	21
George Wilson	Paris	1996	7(2)	3	0	0	12
John Wilson	Catalans	2006-08	69	23	0	0	92
Oliver Wilson	Huddersfield	2019-20	2(15)	0	0	0	0
Richard Wilson	Hull	1998-99	(13)	0	0	0	0
Scott Wilson	Warrington	1998-99	23(2)	6	0	0	24
Johan Windley	Hull	1999	2(2)	1	0	0	4
Jake Wingfield	St Helens	2020	(1)	0	0	0	0
Paul Wingfield	Warrington	1997	5(3)	6	1	0	26
Frank Winterstein	Widnes	2012-13	37(9)	16	0	0	64
	Crusaders	2010-11	26(19)	4	0	0	16
	Wakefield	2009	(5)	0	0	0	0
Lincoln Withers	Hull KR	2012-13	18(22)	10	0	0	40
	Crusaders	2010-11	47	4	0	0	16
	Celtic	2009	21	6	0	0	24
Michael Withers	Wigan	2007	6(1)	1	0	0	4
	Bradford	1999-2006	156(6)	94	15	4	410
Michael Witt	London	2012-13	37	10	89	1	219
	Crusaders	2010-11	39	13	47	4	150
Jeff Wittenberg	Huddersfield	1998	18(1)	1	0	0	4
	Bradford	1997	8(9)	4	0	0	16
Josh Wood	Wakefield	2020	6(4)	1	0	0	4
	Salford	2015-19	19(17)	2	0	0	8
Kyle Wood	Wakefield	2012-13, 2017-20	59(81)	26	0	0	104
	Huddersfield	2011, 2013-16	39(33)	7	0	0	28
	Castleford	2010	1(4)	0	0	0	0
Martin Wood	Sheffield	1997-98	24(11)	4	18	2	54
Mikey Wood	Huddersfield	2016-17	1(1)	0	0	0	0
Nathan Wood	Warrington	2002-05	90	38	0	3	155
	Wakefield	2002	11	2	0	0	8
Paul Wood	Warrington	2000-14	138(171)	40	0	0	160
Phil Wood	Widnes	2004	2(1)	0	0	0	0
Sam Wood	Bradford	2013-14	7(1)	0	0	0	0
Sam Wood	Huddersfield	2016-18, 2020	28(5)	8	4	0	40
James Woodburn-Hall	London	2013-14	9(4)	2	0	0	8
Darren Woods	Widnes	2005	(1)	0	0	0	0
David Woods	Halifax	2002	18(2)	8	0	0	32
Josh Woods	Wigan	2017-18	10(1)	1	4	1	13
Simon Worrall	Leeds	2008-09	5(16)	1	0	0	4
Michael Worrincy	Bradford	2009-10	12(34)	12	0	0	48
	Harlequins	2006-08	20(12)	10	0	0	40
Rob Worrincy	Castleford	2004	1	0	0	0	0
Greg Worthington	Toronto	2020	(1)	0	0	0	0
James Worthington	Wigan	2017	1	2	0	0	8
Troy Wozniak	Widnes	2004	13(7)	1	0	0	4
Matthew Wray	Wakefield	2002-03	13(3)	2	0	0	8
Connor Wrench	Warrington	2020	1	0	0	0	0
David Wrench	Wakefield	2002-06	28(52)	6	0	0	24
	Leeds	1999-2001	7(17)	0	0	0	0
Callum Wright	Wigan	2014	(2)	0	0	0	0

PLAYER	CLUB	YEAR	APP	TRIES	GOALS	FG	PTS
Craig Wright	Castleford	2000	1(9)	0	0	0	0
Nigel Wright	Huddersfield	1999	4(6)	1	0	0	4
	Wigan	1996-97	5(5)	2	0	1	9
Ricky Wright	Sheffield	1997-99	2(13)	0	0	0	0
Vincent Wulf	Paris	1996	13(4)	4	0	0	16
Connor Wynne	Hull	2019-20	6(1)	3	0	0	12
Andrew Wynyard	London	1999-2000	34(6)	4	0	0	16
Bagdad Yaha	Paris	1996	4(4)	2	4	0	16
Fouad Yaha	Catalans	2015-20	83	52	0	0	208
Malakai Yasa	Sheffield	1996	1(3)	0	0	0	0
Andy Yates	Wakefield	2016	(7)	0	0	0	0
	Leeds	2015	(9)	1	0	0	4
Luke Yates	Salford	2020	12(5)	3	0	0	12
	London	2019	28	2	0	0	8
Kirk Yeaman	Hull	2001-16, 2018	322(18)	159	0	0	636
Dominic Young	Huddersfield	2019-20	2	0	0	0	0
Grant Young	London	1998-99	22(2)	2	0	0	8
Nick Youngquest	Castleford	2011-12	37	28	0	0	112
	Crusaders	2010	26(1)	9	0	0	36
Ronel Zenon	Paris	1996	(4)	0	0	0	0
Nick Zisti	Bradford	1999	6(1)	0	0	0	0
Freddie Zitter	Catalans	2006	1	0	0	0	0

NEW FACES - Players making their Super League debuts in 2020

PLAYER	CLUB	DEBUT vs	ROUND	DATE
Andy Ackers	Toronto	Castleford (h)	1	2/2/20
		(club debut: Leigh (a), Ch1, 4/2/18)		
Matty Ashton	Warrington	Wigan (a)	1	30/1/20
Connor Aspey	Salford	Hull KR (a)	16	13/10/20
Yusuf Aydin	Wakefield	Hull FC (a)	12	10/9/20
Connor Bailey	Wakefield	Hull FC (a)	12	10/9/20
Harry Bowes	Wakefield	Leeds (h)	11	1/11/20
Jack Broadbent	Leeds	Catalans (h)	14	30/9/20
George Burgess	Wigan	Warrington (h)	1	30/1/20
Reiss Butterworth	Huddersfield	St Helens (h)	11	4/9/20
Ben Davies	St Helens	Salford (a)	18	26/10/20
Lewis Dodd	St Helens	Wigan (h)	14	29/9/20
Eribe Doro	Warrington	Castleford (a)	12	10/9/20
Israel Folau	Catalans	Castleford (h)	3	15/2/20
Matthew Foster	St Helens	Salford (a)	18	26/10/20
James Gavet	Huddersfield	Catalans (a)	1	1/2/20
Brad Graham	Castleford	Hull FC (a)	9	18/10/20
Corey Hall	Leeds	Catalans (h)	14	30/9/20
Sam Hall	Castleford	Wigan (h)	2	7/2/20
Sam Halsall	Wigan	St Helens (h)	14	29/9/20
Umyla Hanley	Wigan	St Helens (h)	14	29/9/20
James Harrison	Leeds	Catalans (h)	14	30/9/20
Bailey Hodgson	Castleford	Hull KR (h)	17	22/10/20
Connor Jones	Salford	Toronto (h)	2	8/2/20
Shaun Kenny-Dowall	Hull KR	Wakefield (a)	1	31/1/20
Ben Kilner	Wigan	St Helens (h)	14	29/9/20
Leilani Latu	Warrington	Hull FC (h)	11	4/9/20
Ricky Leutele	Toronto	Castleford (h)	1	2/2/20
		(club debut: York (a), Ch1, 3/2/19)		
Ellis Longstaff	Warrington	Hull FC (h)	11	4/9/20
James Maloney	Catalans	Huddersfield (h)	1	1/2/20
Brad Martin	Castleford	Hull KR (h)	17	22/10/20
Manu Ma'u	Hull FC	Leeds (a)	1	2/2/20
Loui McConnell	Leeds	Catalans (h)	14	30/9/20
Josh McCrone	Toronto	Castleford (h)	1	2/2/20
		(club debut: Leigh (a), Ch1, 4/2/18)		
James McDonnell	Wigan	St Helens (h)	14	29/9/20
Ben McNamara	Hull FC	Castleford (a)	14	1/10/20
Chris McQueen	Huddersfield	Leeds (a)	12	11/9/20
Ronan Michael	Huddersfield	Wigan (a)	20	6/11/20
Rowan Milnes	Hull KR	Catalans (a)	15	9/10/20
Brandon Moore	Huddersfield	Hull FC (a)	16	13/10/20
Muizz Mustapha	Leeds	Catalans (h)	14	30/9/20
		(club debut: Workington (h), CC5, 12/4/19)		
Tom Nisbet	St Helens	Salford (a)	18	26/10/20
Jarrod O'Connor	Leeds	Catalans (h)	14	30/9/20
Kai Pearce-Paul	Wigan	St Helens (h)	14	29/9/20
Matt Prior	Leeds	Hull FC (h)	1	2/2/20
Nico Rizzelli	St Helens	Salford (a)	18	26/10/20
Luis Roberts	Salford	Warrington (h)	14	29/9/20
Ellis Robson	Warrington	Hull FC (h)	11	4/9/20
Nathan Roebuck	Warrington	Salford (a)	14	29/9/20
Harry Rushton	Wigan	St Helens (h)	14	29/9/20
Ethan Ryan	Hull KR	Wigan (a)	6	8/3/20
Jack Sanderson	Castleford	Huddersfield (h)	13	24/9/20
Ligi Sao	Hull FC	Leeds (a)	1	2/2/20
Aidan Sezer	Huddersfield	Catalans (a)	1	1/2/20
Matthew Storton	Hull KR	Wakefield (h)	1	31/1/20
Will Tate	Hull KR	Leeds (h)	13	24/9/20
Liam Tindall	Leeds	Catalans (h)	14	30/9/20
Blake Wallace	Toronto	Castleford (h)	1	2/2/20
		(club debut: Siddal (a), CC3, 25/2/17)		
Sam Walters	Leeds	Catalans (h)	14	30/9/20
Gareth Widdop	Warrington	Wakefield (a)	3	16/2/20
Sonny Bill Williams	Toronto	Castleford (h)	1	2/2/20
Jake Wingfield	St Helens	Salford (a)	18	26/10/20
Greg Worthington	Toronto	Warrington (a)	4	21/2/20
		(club debut: Siddal (a), CC3, 25/2/17)		
Connor Wrench	Warrington	Salford (a)	14	29/9/20

Players making their club debuts in other competitions in 2020

Sosaia Feki	Castleford	Hull FC (h)	CC6	13/9/20

All totals in 'Super League Players 1996-2020' include play-off games & Super League Super 8s from 2015-2018. Super 8s (Qualifiers) not included.

Toronto Wolfpack games from 2020 season also included.

OLD FACES - Players making their Super League debuts for new clubs in 2020

PLAYER	CLUB	DEBUT vs	ROUND	DATE
Jordan Abdull	Hull KR	Wakefield (h) (D2)	1	31/1/20
Andy Ackers	Salford	Castleford (h)	11	3/9/20
Olly Ashall-Bott	Salford	Warrington (h)	14	29/9/20
Chris Atkin	Salford	Leeds (h)	4	22/2/20
Eddie Battye	Wakefield	Huddersfield (h)	7	17/9/20
Jake Bibby	Wigan	Warrington (h)	1	30/1/20
Keanan Brand	Warrington	Leeds (a)	5	28/2/20
Ryan Brierley	Hull KR	Wakefield (h)	1	31/1/20
Kevin Brown	Salford	St Helens (a)	1	31/1/20
Joe Cator	Hull FC	Wakefield (a)	6	6/3/20
Mitch Clark	Wigan	Toronto (h)	3	13/2/20
James Cunningham	Toronto	Castleford (h)	1	2/2/20
Tom Davies	Catalans	St Helens (a)	4	2/8/20
Andrew Dixon	Toronto	Castleford (h)	1	2/2/20
(club debut: Siddal (a), CC3, 25/2/17)				
Josh Drinkwater	Catalans	Huddersfield (h) (D2)	1	1/2/20
Kenny Edwards	Huddersfield	Catalans (a)	1	1/2/20
Jamie Ellis	Hull KR	Wakefield (h) (D2)	1	31/1/20
Rhys Evans	Leeds	St Helens (h)	8	9/8/20
Brett Ferres	Leeds	Huddersfield (h) (D2)	12	11/9/20
Dan Fleming	Castleford	Huddersfield (h) (D2)	13	24/9/20
Mahe Fonua	Hull FC	Hull KR (h) (D2)	2	7/2/20
Luke Gale	Leeds	Hull FC (h)	1	2/2/20
Matty Gee	Hull KR	Castleford (h)	5	27/2/20
Anthony Gelling	Warrington	Wigan (a)	1	30/1/20
Tony Gigot	Toronto	Warrington (a)	4	21/2/20
Tony Gigot	Wakefield	Wigan (h)	8	9/8/20
Tom Gilmore	Wakefield	Warrington (h)	14	29/9/20
Ashton Golding	Huddersfield	Leeds (h)	2	2/8/20
James Graham	St Helens	Catalans (h) (D2)	4	2/8/20
James Greenwood	Salford	St Helens (a) (D2)	1	31/1/20
George Griffin	Castleford	Toronto (a)	1	2/2/20
Jackson Hastings	Wigan	Warrington (h)	1	30/1/20
Tyla Hepi	Castleford	Toronto (a)	1	2/2/20
Sebastine Ikahihifo	Salford	St Helens (h)	1	31/1/20
Jordan Johnstone	Hull FC	Leeds (a)	1	2/2/20
Josh Jones	Hull FC	Leeds (a)	1	2/2/20
Liam Kay	Toronto	Castleford (h)	1	2/2/20
(club debut: London Skolars (a), L1-1, 4/3/17)				
Liam Kay	Wakefield	Wigan (h) (D2)	8	9/8/20
Elliot Kear	Salford	Catalans (a)	6	7/3/20
Joe Keyes	Hull KR	Huddersfield (h)	4	21/2/20
Samy Kibula	Warrington	Wakefield (h)	10	30/8/20
George King	Hull KR	Catalans (a)	15	9/10/20
Kruise Leeming	Leeds	Huddersfield (a)	2	2/8/20
Harvey Livett	Hull KR	Wakefield (h) (D2)	1	31/1/20
Will Maher	Hull KR	Wakefield (h)	1	31/1/20
Alex Mellor	Leeds	Hull FC (h)	1	2/2/20
Joe Mellor	Toronto	Castleford (h)	1	2/2/20
(club debut: York (a), Ch1, 3/2/19)				
Hakim Miloudi	Toronto	Castleford (h)	1	2/2/20
(club debut: Sheffield (h), Ch9, 6/4/19)				
Elliot Minchella	Hull KR	Wakefield (h)	1	31/1/20
Greg Minikin	Hull KR	Wakefield (h)	1	31/1/20
Anthony Mullally	Toronto	Castleford (h)	1	2/2/20
(club debut: Leigh (a), Ch4, 24/2/19)				
Romain Navarrete	Wakefield	Hull KR (a)	1	31/1/20
Gareth O'Brien	Toronto	Wigan (a)	3	13/2/20
(club debut: Rochdale (a), Ch7, 23/3/18)				
Gareth O'Brien	Castleford	St Helens (a) (D2)	16	16/8/20
Tom Olbison	Toronto	Castleford (h)	1	2/2/20
(club debut: York (a), Ch1, 3/2/19)				
Derrell Olpherts	Castleford	Toronto (a)	1	2/2/20
Jack Ormondroyd	Salford	Hull FC (a)	13	24/9/20
Pauli Pauli	Salford	St Helens (a) (D2)	1	31/1/20
Nathaniel Peteru	Hull KR	Warrington (a)	8	8/8/20
Jay Pitts	Wakefield	Hull KR (a) (D2)	1	31/1/20
Nick Rawsthorne	Hull KR	Leeds (h)	13	24/9/20
(club debut: Leigh (h), CC5, 15/3/20)				
Danny Richardson	Castleford	Toronto (a)	1	2/2/20
Oliver Roberts	Salford	Leeds (h)	4	22/2/20
Matty Russell	Toronto	Castleford (h)	1	2/2/20
(club debut: Toulouse (h), Ch14, 19/5/18)				
Dan Sarginson	Salford	St Helens (a)	1	31/1/20
Innes Senior	Wakefield	Warrington (a)	10	30/8/20
(club debut: Catalans (a), CC6, 22/8/20)				
Kyle Shelford	Warrington	Salford (a)	14	29/9/20
Adam Sidlow	Toronto	Castleford (h)	1	2/2/20
(club debut: Siddal (a), CC3, 25/2/17)				
Brad Singleton	Toronto	Castleford (h)	1	2/2/20
Brad Singleton	Wigan	Warrington (a)	15	9/10/20
Gadwin Springer	Toronto	Castleford (h)	1	2/2/20
(club debut: Widnes (h), Ch3, 16/2/19)				
Adam Swift	Hull FC	Hull KR (h)	2	7/2/20
Bodene Thompson	Toronto	Salford (a)	2	8/2/20
(club debut: York (a), Ch1, 3/2/19)				
Bodene Thompson	Leeds	Wigan (a)	9	16/8/20
Joel Tomkins	Catalans	Huddersfield (h)	1	1/2/20
Owen Trout	Huddersfield	St Helens (h)	11	4/9/20
Alex Walker	Wakefield	Salford (a)	5	1/3/20
Brad Walker	Wakefield	Hull KR (h)	18	25/10/20
Kallum Watkins	Salford	Hull FC (a)	13	24/9/20
(club debut: Catalans (a), CCQF, 18/9/20)				
Jack Wells	Toronto	St Helens (h)	5	29/2/20
Joe Westerman	Wakefield	Hull KR (a)	1	31/1/20
Gary Wheeler	Toronto	Castleford (h)	1	2/2/20
(club debut: London Skolars (a), L1-1, 4/3/17)				
Jon Wilkin	Toronto	Castleford (h)	1	2/2/20
(club debut: York (a), Ch1, 3/2/19)				
Rhys Williams	Salford	St Helens (a) (D2)	1	31/1/20
Josh Wood	Wakefield	Hull KR (a)	1	31/1/20
Luke Yates	Salford	St Helens (a)	1	31/1/20

SUPER LEAGUE XXV
Club by Club

KEY DATES

5th December 2019 - halfback Jamie Ellis released to join Hull KR.

26th December 2019 - 20-14 home Boxing Day friendly defeat to Bradford.

19th January 2020 - 16-10 home friendly defeat to Toronto in Michael Shenton Testimonial.

2nd February 2020 - 28-10 round-one, away victory over Toronto at Headingley.

4th February 2020 - Peter Mata'utia gets two-match penalty notice for dangerous contact.

7th February 2020 - 16-12 home win over Wigan.

15th February 2020 - 36-18 defeat at Catalans.

21st February 2020 - wingers James Clare and Derrell Olpherts score try-braces in 32-15 home win over Wakefield.

27th February 2020 - Liam Watts ruptures finger ligament in 28-8 win at Hull KR.

6th March 2020 - Jesse Sene-Lefao comes back from pre-season quad injury as late Blake Austin field goal means 9-8 defeat at Warrington.

7th March 2020 - young utility back Jack Sanderson joins from Hull FC.

15th March 2020 - Liam Watts back from finger injury as Derrell Olpherts scores two tries in commanding 28-14 home win over St Helens.

16th March 2020 - season suspended until April 3rd because of coronavirus crisis.

12th May 2020 - Niall Evalds signs from Salford on initial one-year contract.

25th May 2020 - Jordan Rankin released from contract on compassionate grounds and joins Parramatta.

14th July 2020 - first team squad and backroom staff return for first round of Covid-19 testing.

5th August 2020 - Matt Cook to leave at end of season to join Widnes

8th August 2020 - 40-14 round-8 defeat by Catalans at Headingley in first post-covid game.

10th August 2020 - Toronto Wolfpack fullback Gareth O'Brien joins on loan until end of 2020 season. Halifax prop Dan Fleming re-joins on one-month trial.

12th August 2020 - positive Covid-19 tests at Hull FC lead to fixture re-arrangements, with Cas now to face St Helens the following Sunday. Sixth round Challenge Cup tie with Hull FC, scheduled for Saturday week postponed

16th August 2020 - Jake Trueman out with back injury as late Theo Fages try means 10-0 defeat at St Helens.

25th August 2020 - bye weekend switched after positive Covid-19 results at Catalans Dragons with round 18 fixture with Wigan brought forward for following weekend.

29th August 2020 - 30-22 defeat to Wigan at Warrington. James Clare stretchered off with neck injury as Morgan Smithies sin-binned for crusher tackle after just three minutes.

3rd September 2020 - 37-30 win over Salford at Headingley, after trailing 18-0.

5th September 2020 - hooker Jacques O'Neill signs one-year contract extension.

10th September 2020 - late Matty Ashton try means 12-10 defeat to Warrington at St Helens.

13th September 2020 - 29-16 Challenge Cup sixth-round defeat to Hull FC at St Helens.

24th September 2020 - Jack Sanderson scores on debut in 31-19 defeat to Huddersfield at Warrington.

1st October 2020 - last-minute Jake Connor try means 32-28 defeat to Hull FC in first post-lockdown game at Mend-a-Hose Jungle.

8th October 2020 - Tigers withdraw from fixture with Leeds after three positive coronavirus tests, with six squad members stood down through track-and-trace protocols.

14th October 2020 - prop Grant Millington signs one-year contract extension.

15th October 2020 - assistant coach Danny Orr to leave at end of season.

18th October 2020 - 48-6 defeat at Hull FC. Young threequarter Brad Graham makes debut.

22nd October 2020 - Greg Eden scores hat-trick in 38-24 win over Hull KR at St Helens. Fullback Bailey Hodgson and prop Brad Martin make debuts.

26th October 2020 - Oliver Holmes sent off in 29th minute of 28-24 defeat to Leeds.

28th October 2020 - twelve positive Covid-19 tests in club mean Friday fixture with Huddersfield postponed.

2nd November 2020 - Oliver Holmes receives caution for kicking Richie Myler, who gets caution for striking.

2nd November 2020 - four more players test positive for Covid-19. Fixtures against Leeds and Salford called off.

3rd November 2020 - League-wide regular season brought to a halt. Tigers finish in eighth spot.

6th November 2020 - option taken up to extend contract of forward Tyla Hepi until end of 2021.

15th November 2020 - on-loan Gareth O'Brien signs three-year deal until end of 2023

19th November 2020 - Bailey Hodgson to join Newcastle Knights on three-year contract. Undisclosed fee agreed.

CLUB RECORDS

Highest score:
106-0 v Rochdale, 9/9/2007
Highest score against:
12-76 v Leeds, 14/8/2009
Record attendance:
25,449 v Hunslet, 9/3/35

MATCH RECORDS

Tries:
5 Derek Foster v Hunslet, 10/11/72
John Joyner v Millom, 16/9/73
Steve Fenton v Dewsbury, 27/1/78
Ian French v Hunslet, 9/2/86
St John Ellis v Whitehaven, 10/12/89
Greg Eden v Warrington, 11/6/2017
Goals: 17 Sammy Lloyd v Millom, 16/9/73
Points: 43 Sammy Lloyd v Millom, 16/9/73

SEASON RECORDS

Tries: 42 Denny Solomona 2016
Goals: 158 Sammy Lloyd 1976-77
Points: 355 Luke Gale 2017

CAREER RECORDS

Tries: 206 Alan Hardisty 1958-71
Goals: 875 Albert Lunn 1951-63
Points: 1,870 Albert Lunn 1951-63
Appearances: 613 John Joyner 1973-92

CASTLEFORD TIGERS

DATE	FIXTURE	RESULT	SCORERS	LGE	ATT
2/2/20	Toronto (a) ●	W10-28	t:Eden,Millington,Milner,Shenton,Mata'utia g:Richardson(4)	5th	N/A
7/2/20	Wigan (h)	W16-12	t:Olpherts,Blair g:Richardson(4)	2nd	8,848
15/2/20	Catalans Dragons (a)	L36-18	t:Olpherts,Blair,Clare g:Richardson(3)	5th	8,886
21/2/20	Wakefield (h)	W32-15	t:Blair,Olpherts(2),Clare(2),Holmes g:Richardson(4)	3rd	7,202
27/2/20	Hull KR (a)	W8-28	t:Shenton,Richardson,Clare,McMeeken g:Richardson(6)	2nd	7,464
6/3/20	Warrington (a)	L9-8	t:Turner g:Richardson(2)	3rd	9,228
15/3/20	St Helens (h)	W28-14	t:Mata'utia,Olpherts(2),Blair,Trueman g:Richardson(4)	2nd	7,268
8/8/20	Catalans Dragons (h) ●	L14-40	t:Shenton(2) g:Richardson(3)	6th	N/A
16/8/20	St Helens (a)	L10-0		7th	N/A
29/8/20	Wigan (a) ●●	L30-22	t:O'Brien,Massey,Olpherts,Shenton g:Richardson(3)	6th	N/A
3/9/20	Salford (a) ●	W30-37	t:Richardson,Shenton,McShane(2),McMeeken,Millington g:Richardson(6) fg:Richardson	6th	N/A
10/9/20	Warrington (h) ●●●	L10-12	t:O'Brien,Olpherts g:Richardson	6th	N/A
13/9/20	Hull FC (h) (CCR6) ●●●	L16-29	t:Griffin,Holmes,Mata'utia g:Richardson(2)	N/A	N/A
24/9/20	Huddersfield (h) ●●	L19-31	t:O'Brien,Eden,Sanderson g:O'Brien(3) fg:O'Brien	7th	N/A
1/10/20	Hull FC (h)	L28-32	t:McMeeken(2),Eden,Millington,Shenton g:O'Brien(4)	8th	N/A
18/10/20	Hull FC (a)	L48-6	t:O'Neill g:Richardson	9th	N/A
22/10/20	Hull KR (h) ●●●	W38-24	t:O'Neill,Foster,Milner,Eden(3) g:Richardson(7)	8th	N/A
26/10/20	Leeds (a)	L28-24	t:Watts,Eden(2),Blair g:Richardson(4)	9th	N/A

● *Played at Emerald Headingley, Leeds*
●● *Played at Halliwell Jones Stadium, Warrington*
●●● *Played at Totally Wicked Stadium, St Helens*

Huddersfield (a) (R19), Leeds (h) (R20), Salford (h) (R21) and Wakefield (a) (R22) games were cancelled

Toronto (a) (R1) game was later expunged from the Super League table (Player stats from this fixture are included in 'All' columns below)

		APP		TRIES		GOALS		FG		PTS	
	D.O.B.	ALL	SL	ALL	SL	ALL	SL	ALL	SL	ALL	SL
Cheyse Blair	18/1/92	12(1)	10(1)	5	5	0	0	0	0	20	20
James Clare	13/4/91	12	11	4	4	0	0	0	0	16	16
Matt Cook	14/11/86	(2)	(2)	0	0	0	0	0	0	0	0
Greg Eden	14/11/90	8	7	8	7	0	0	0	0	32	28
Sosaia Feki	9/5/91	1	0	0	0	0	0	0	0	0	0
Dan Fleming	8/7/92	(1)	(1)	0	0	0	0	0	0	0	0
Alex Foster	25/9/93	6(2)	6(2)	1	1	0	0	0	0	4	4
Brad Graham	1/9/01	1	1	0	0	0	0	0	0	0	0
George Griffin	26/6/92	14	12	1	1	0	0	0	0	4	4
Sam Hall	8/5/02	(1)	(1)	0	0	0	0	0	0	0	0
Tyla Hepi	15/6/93	3(5)	3(3)	0	0	0	0	0	0	0	0
Bailey Hodgson	5/9/02	1	1	0	0	0	0	0	0	0	0
Oliver Holmes	7/8/92	11(1)	10(1)	2	1	0	0	0	0	8	4
Brad Martin	6/2/01	(1)	(1)	0	0	0	0	0	0	0	0
Nathan Massey	11/7/89	13(2)	13(1)	1	1	0	0	0	0	4	4
Peter Mata'utia	2/11/90	9	7	3	1	0	0	0	0	12	4
Mike McMeeken	10/5/94	14(2)	13(2)	4	4	0	0	0	0	16	16
Paul McShane	19/11/89	18	16	2	2	0	0	0	0	8	8
Grant Millington	1/11/86	5(11)	4(10)	3	2	0	0	0	0	12	8
Adam Milner	19/12/91	6(7)	5(6)	2	1	0	0	0	0	8	4
Junior Moors	30/7/86	2(4)	2(4)	0	0	0	0	0	0	0	0
Gareth O'Brien	31/10/91	8	8	3	3	7	7	1	1	27	27
Jacques O'Neill	8/5/99	2(10)	1(9)	2	2	0	0	0	0	8	8
Derrell Olpherts	7/1/92	15	13	8	8	0	0	0	0	32	32
Lewis Peachey	25/3/01	(3)	(3)	0	0	0	0	0	0	0	0
Jordan Rankin	17/12/91	7	6	0	0	0	0	0	0	0	0
Danny Richardson	2/9/96	16	14	2	2	54	48	1	1	117	105
Jack Sanderson	18/3/98	3	3	1	1	0	0	0	0	4	4
Jesse Sene-Lefao	8/12/89	1(8)	1(8)	0	0	0	0	0	0	0	0
Michael Shenton	22/7/86	17	15	7	6	0	0	0	0	28	24
Daniel Smith	20/3/93	3(7)	3(6)	0	0	0	0	0	0	0	0
Jake Trueman	16/2/99	11	10	1	1	0	0	0	0	4	4
Calum Turner	29/4/99	2(2)	2(1)	1	1	0	0	0	0	4	4
Liam Watts	8/7/90	13	11	1	1	0	0	0	0	4	4

Paul McShane

'SL' totals include Super League games only; 'All' totals also include Challenge Cup

24th October 2019 - Dragons fined £27,500, and Warrington Wolves £15,000, for after-match trouble at fixture in Perpignan on August 3rd.

31st October 2019 - halfback Josh Drinkwater re-signs on two-year contract.

7th November 2019 - Wigan winger Tom Davies joins on two-year contract.

2nd December 2019 - prop Jordan Dezaria and centre Gavin Marguerite sign from Toulouse.

5th December 2019 - halfback Matty Smith released.

18th January 2020 - Lewis Tierney suffers facial fracture in 22-10 friendly win over Toulouse in Carcassonne.

27th January 2020 - Sam Moa undergoes second operation on broken radius.

28th January 2020 - Israel Folau signs on one-year contract.

1st February 2020 - 32-12 round-one, home defeat to Huddersfield.

9th February 2020 - round-two game at Wakefield postponed because of Storm Ciara.

15th February 2020 - Sam Tomkins scores hat-trick and Israel Folau scores on debut in 36-18 home win over Castleford.

1st March 2020 - late James Maloney try secures 34-29 win at Hull FC after being 28-10 down.

6th March 2020 - prop Julian Bousquet signs new three-year contract to end of 2023.

7th March 2020 - Matt Whitley scores two tries in 30-14 home win over Salford.

9th March 2020 - Sam Tomkins gets two-match penalty notice for tripping offence in Salford win.

13th March 2020 - home game with Leeds, due to be played next day behind closed doors, postponed as Rhinos player suspected of carrying coronavirus.

16th March 2020 - French Government announce all non-essential locations must close. SL season suspended until April 3rd because of coronavirus crisis.

3rd July 2020 - Israel Folau signs new one-year contract for 2021.

9th July 2020 - prop Mickael Simon to retire at end of season.

17th July 2020 - prop Antoni Maria to leave at end of season.

KEY DATES

2nd August 2020 - 34-6 defeat to St Helens at Headingley as Super League restarts.

8th August 2020 - Tom Davies scores try-double in 40-14 round-8 win over Castleford at Headingley.

15th August 2020 - Matt Whitley and Tom Davies score hat-tricks in 58-0 thrashing of Wakefield at St Helens. Sam Moa banned for two games for high tackle and Sam Tomkins one game for tripping.

22nd August 2020 - David Mead scores hat-trick in 36-24 Challenge Cup round five win over Wakefield at Huddersfield.

25th August 2020 - fixture against Wigan, scheduled for Saturday, postponed after three Dragons players and member of non-playing staff return positive tests in routine Covid-19 testing.

27th August 2020 - Super League fixture against Leeds scheduled for Monday 7th September, postponed.

12th September 2020 - lacklustre 28-12 defeat by Wigan in first match at Gilbert Brutus for six months, with capped attendance of 5,000.

18th September 2020 - 22-18 golden-point try defeat to Salford in Challenge Cup sixth round.

25th September 2020 - 30-16 defeat at Warrington.

30th September 2020 - Tom Davies scores hat-trick and Fouad Yaha two tries in 34-6 win at Leeds.

4th October 2020 - Sam Kasiano stars in 40-8 win over Wakefield, after trailing 8-0 on 35 minutes.

9th October 2020 - Joel Tomkins and Tom Davies score doubles in 34-4 home win over Hull KR. Samisoni Langi tears hamstring.

14th October 2020 - round-16 game against Wigan at Warrington postponed due to positive Covid tests at Wigan club.

21st October 2020 - five Catalans players and two members of backroom staff test positive for Covid-19. Round-17 home fixture with Hull FC cancelled.

24th October 2020 - fixture with Warrington on 26th October cancelled.

28th October 2020 - Covid results all negative and training resumes.

2nd November 2020 - 42-24 Monday afternoon defeat at Salford.

3rd November 2020 - League-wide regular season brought to a halt. Dragons finish fourth and enter re-modelled six-team play-offs.

13th November 2020 - 26-14 defeat of Leeds at Warrington sets up semi-final at St Helens.

17th November 2020 - Michael McIlorum banned for six games, two for high tackle, four for lifting injured player off floor. Joel Tomkins banned for eight games for 'inappropriate contact' on the backside of Leeds fullback Richie Myler.

20th November 2020 - 48-2 defeat at St Helens in play-off semi-final ends season.

CLUB RECORDS

Highest score: 92-8 v York, 12/5/2013
Highest score against:
0-62 v Hull FC, 12/5/2017
Record attendance: 31,555 v Wigan, 18/5/2019 *(Barcelona)*
11,856 v Wigan, 2/7/2016 *(Stade Gilbert Brutus)*

MATCH RECORDS

Tries:
4 Justin Murphy v Warrington, 13/9/2008
Damien Cardace v Widnes, 31/3/2012
Kevin Larroyer v York, 12/5/2013
Jodie Broughton v St Helens, 14/4/2016
Fouad Yaha v Salford, 21/7/2018
David Mead v Huddersfield, 29/9/2018
Fouad Yaha v Leeds, 23/3/2019
Brayden Wiliame v Doncaster, 11/5/2019
Goals:
11 Thomas Bosc v Featherstone, 31/3/2007
Thomas Bosc v Batley, 29/5/2010
Scott Dureau v Widnes, 31/3/2012
Points:
26 Thomas Bosc v Featherstone, 31/3/2007

SEASON RECORDS

Tries: 29 Morgan Escare 2014
Goals: 134 Scott Dureau 2012
Points: 319 Scott Dureau 2012

CAREER RECORDS

Tries: 87 Vincent Duport 2007-2009; 2011-2018
Goals:
579 *(inc 14fg)* Thomas Bosc 2006-2017
Points: 1,380 Thomas Bosc 2006-2017
Appearances:
337 Remi Casty 2006-2013; 2015-2020

CATALANS DRAGONS

DATE	FIXTURE	RESULT	SCORERS	LGE	ATT
1/2/20	Huddersfield (h)	L12-32	t:Yaha,S Tomkins g:Maloney(2)	10th	8,259
15/2/20	Castleford (h)	W36-18	t:S Tomkins(3),Folau,Langi,Yaha g:Maloney(6)	8th	8,886
1/3/20	Hull FC (a)	W29-34	t:Jullien(2),Yaha,Drinkwater,Langi,Maloney g:Maloney(5)	6th	12,003
7/3/20	Salford (h)	W30-14	t:McIlorum,Whitley(2),Yaha,Tierney g:Maloney(5)	6th	7,940
2/8/20	St Helens (a) ●	L34-6	t:Maloney g:Maloney	7th	N/A
8/8/20	Castleford (a) ●	W14-40	t:Davies(2),Da Costa,Folau,Garcia,J Tomkins,Baitieri g:Maloney(6)	5th	N/A
15/8/20	Wakefield (a) ●●	W0-58	t:Whitley(3),Langi(2),Davies(3),Bousquet,Yaha g:Maloney(7),S Tomkins(2)	3rd	N/A
22/8/20	Wakefield (h) (CCR6) ●●●	W36-24	t:Mead(3),Yaha,Garcia,Whitley g:Maloney(6)	N/A	N/A
12/9/20	Wigan (h)	L12-28	t:Bousquet,Yaha g:Maloney(2)	5th	5,000
18/9/20	Salford (h) (CCQF) ●●	L18-22 (aet)	t:Yaha,Maloney,Whitley g:Maloney(3)	N/A	N/A
25/9/20	Warrington (a)	L30-16	t:Davies,Langi,Yaha g:Maloney(2)	5th	N/A
30/9/20	Leeds (a)	W6-34	t:Davies(3),Yaha(2),Mourgue g:Maloney(5)	5th	N/A
4/10/20	Wakefield (h)	W40-8	t:Whitley,Folau,Mead(2),Kasiano,S Tomkins,Bousquet g:Maloney(6)	4th	5,000
9/10/20	Hull KR (h)	W34-4	t:J Tomkins(3),Davies(2),Folau g:Maloney(5)	3rd	5,000
2/11/20	Salford (h)	L42-24	t:Seguier,Davies,Kasiano,Mead g:Maloney(3),Mourgue	4th	N/A
13/11/20	Leeds (h) (EPO) ●●●●	W26-14	t:Davies,Langi,Folau,Mead g:Maloney(5)	N/A	N/A
20/11/20	St Helens (a) (SF)	L48-2	g:Maloney	N/A	N/A

● *Played at Emerald Headingley, Leeds*
●● *Played at Totally Wicked Stadium, St Helens*
●●● *Played at John Smith's Stadium, Huddersfield*
●●●● *Played at Halliwell Jones Stadium, Warrington*

Leeds (h) (R7), Wigan (a) (R10), Hull FC (h) (R17), Warrington (h) (R18), St Helens (h) (R20), Hull KR (a) (R21) and Huddersfield (a) (R22) games were cancelled

	D.O.B.	APP		TRIES		GOALS		FG		PTS	
		ALL	SL	ALL	SL	ALL	SL	ALL	SL	ALL	SL
Lucas Albert	4/7/98	1	1	0	0	0	0	0	0	0	0
Jason Baitieri	2/7/89	(16)	(14)	1	1	0	0	0	0	4	4
Lambert Belmas	11/8/97	(1)	(1)	0	0	0	0	0	0	0	0
Julian Bousquet	18/7/91	11(4)	10(4)	3	3	0	0	0	0	12	12
Remi Casty	5/2/85	16(1)	14(1)	0	0	0	0	0	0	0	0
Alrix Da Costa	2/10/97	2(2)	2(2)	1	1	0	0	0	0	4	4
Tom Davies	11/1/97	11	10	13	13	0	0	0	0	52	52
Josh Drinkwater	15/6/92	16	14	1	1	0	0	0	0	4	4
Israel Folau	3/4/89	15	13	5	5	0	0	0	0	20	20
Benjamin Garcia	5/4/93	17	15	2	1	0	0	0	0	8	4
Mickael Goudemand	9/3/96	(7)	(5)	0	0	0	0	0	0	0	0
Benjamin Jullien	1/3/95	5(6)	5(5)	2	2	0	0	0	0	8	8
Sam Kasiano	21/9/90	(16)	(14)	2	2	0	0	0	0	8	8
Samisoni Langi	11/6/93	15	14	6	6	0	0	0	0	24	24
James Maloney	15/6/86	17	15	3	2	70	61	0	0	152	130
Antoni Maria	21/3/87	1(3)	(3)	0	0	0	0	0	0	0	0
Michael McIlorum	10/1/88	14	12	1	1	0	0	0	0	4	4
David Mead	4/11/88	8	7	7	4	0	0	0	0	28	16
Sam Moa	14/6/86	9(2)	8(2)	0	0	0	0	0	0	0	0
Arthur Mourgue	2/5/99	3(2)	2(2)	1	1	1	1	0	0	6	6
Arthur Romano	17/8/97	2	2	0	0	0	0	0	0	0	0
Paul Seguier	8/9/97	1(4)	1(4)	1	1	0	0	0	0	4	4
Mickael Simon	2/4/87	(2)	(2)	0	0	0	0	0	0	0	0
Lewis Tierney	20/10/94	5	4	1	1	0	0	0	0	4	4
Joel Tomkins	21/3/87	11	10	4	4	0	0	0	0	16	16
Sam Tomkins	23/3/89	13	12	5	5	2	2	0	0	24	24
Matt Whitley	20/1/96	15	13	8	6	0	0	0	0	32	24
Fouad Yaha	19/8/96	13	11	11	9	0	0	0	0	44	36

James Maloney

'SL' totals include regular season & play-offs; 'All' totals also include Challenge Cup

24th October 2019 - Scott Grix leaves to join Halifax.

1st November 2019 - Sebastine Ikahihifo joins Salford.

26th November 2019 - backrower Owen Trout signs from Leeds on four-year contract, with Kruise Leeming going the other way.

28th November 2019 - halfback Aidan Sezer signs from Canberra Raiders on two-year deal.

4th December 2019 - Matt Frawley released and returns to Australia.

8th January 2020 - 19-year-old prop Ronan Michael joins Canberra Raiders under-20s for 2020 season after signing extended contract with Giants.

9th January 2020 - Aidan Sezer appointed club captain.

24th January 2020 - Ashton Golding sustains long-term hamstring injury in 16-4 win at Wakefield in pre-season friendly.

1st February 2020 - Aidan Sezer stars as Jermaine McGillvary scores two tries in 32-12 round-one win at Catalans.

9th February 2020 - round-two home fixture v Leeds postponed because of Storm Ciara.

14th February 2020 - late Aidan Sezer penalty clinches 12-10 win at Salford.

18th February 2020 - second-row forward Oliver Roberts joins Salford on loan deal with immediate effect.

21st February 2020 - 22-4 win at Hull KR puts Giants top of table.

1st March 2020 - 42-10 home defeat to Wigan as Giants concede four tries while Aidan Sezer is in sin bin.

4th March 2020 - hooker Reiss Butterworth joins York City Knights on month loan

6th March 2020 - 12-10 victory at reigning champions St Helens.

11th March 2020 - 18-0 home Challenge Cup fifth-round exit at hands of Toronto Wolfpack.

12th March 2020 - back row Chester Butler has surgery on groin injury.

16th March 2020 - season suspended until April 3rd because of coronavirus crisis.

10th May 2020 - Sam Hewitt and Jon-Luke Kirby sign contract extensions to end of 2022.

15th May 2020 - Louis and Innes Senior both sign one-year contract extensions to end of 2021.

22nd May 2020 - Jake Wardle signs contract extension to end of 2023.

29th May 2020 - Akuila Uate released from contract, due to expire at end of 2021, and returns to Australia.

KEY DATES

12th June 2020 - halfback Oliver Russell signs new two-year contract.

19th June 2020 - Oliver Roberts loan at Salford extended for 2021 season.

3rd July 2020 - Lee Gaskell extends contract to end of 2021 season.

11th July 2020 - Giants first club to return to training.

2nd August 2020 - Ashton Golding makes debut and Darnell McIntosh scores hat-trick in 27-26 golden-point defeat at Leeds, after leading 26-6 with 15 minutes left.

7th August 2020 - teenage threequarter Dominic Young signs three-year contract with Newcastle Knights from 2021.

15th August 2020 - Aidan Sezer suffers hamstring strain and Ukuma Ta'ai bad ankle injury as late Blake Austin field goal means 19-18 defeat by Warrington at St Helens.

17th August 2020 - prop Paul Clough released and joins Widnes.

18th August 2020 - Innes Senior joins Wakefield on one-month loan.

30th August 2020 - 31-12 defeat by Hull FC at Warrington.

4th September 2020 - injury-hit side falls to 54-6 defeat to St Helens at Headingley.

4th September 2020 - former Origin forward Chris McQueen arrives from Wests Tigers on three-month trial.

11th September 2020 - Luke Gale field goal five minutes from time means 13-12 defeat to Leeds at St Helens. Adam O'Brien suffers season-ending neck injury.

13th September 2020 - head coach Simon Woolford to leave at end of season.

16th September 2020 - Simon Woolford leaves by mutual agreement. Luke Robinson takes interim charge.

17th September 2020 - Aidan Sezer stars in 29-6 win over Wakefield in first game back at John Smith's Stadium.

24th September 2020 - Halifax hooker Brandon Moore joins on loan until the end of the season.

24th September 2020 - Jermaine McGillvary scores hat-trick in 31-19 win over Castleford at Warrington.

30th September 2020 - 32-22 home win over Hull KR in game delayed by 90 minutes after positive Covid-19 tests in Giants camp.

8th October 2020 - Lee Gaskell returns in 24-16 defeat by Salford at Headingley.

13th October 2020 - late Marc Sneyd penalty goal means 18-16 defeat to Hull FC at Warrington.

22nd October 2020 - late Tom Johnstone try means 18-14 defeat to Wakefield at St Helens.

28th October 2020 - Friday fixture at St Helens with Castleford cancelled due to Covid outbreak at Tigers. Giants to face Warrington instead.

30th October 2020 - Leroy Cudjoe makes 300th career appearance in 19-12 defeat by Warrington at St Helens.

2nd November 2020 - Leroy Cudjoe signs one-year contract extension.

3rd November 2020 - League-wide regular season brought to a halt. Giants finish seventh and are on stand-by for re-modelled six-team play-offs.

6th November 2020 - 19-6 defeat to Wigan at Headingley.

8th November 2020 - Toronto Wolfpack hooker James Cunningham signs on two-year contract.

11th November 2020 - Chris McQueen signs one-year contract after short-term trial.

19th November 2020 - Salford coach Ian Watson appointed head coach on three-year deal from 1 December.

CLUB RECORDS

Highest score:
142-4 v Blackpool, 26/11/94
Highest score against:
12-94 v Castleford, 18/9/88
Record attendance:
32,912 v Wigan, 4/3/50 *(Fartown)*
15,629 v Leeds, 10/2/2008
*(McAlpine/Galpharm/
John Smith's Stadium)*

MATCH RECORDS

Tries:
10 Lionel Cooper v Keighley, 17/11/51
Goals: 18 Major Holland
v Swinton Park, 28/2/1914
Points: 39 Major Holland
v Swinton Park, 28/2/1914

SEASON RECORDS

Tries: 80 Albert Rosenfeld 1913-14
Goals: 156 *(inc 2fg)* Danny Brough 2013
Points: 346 Danny Brough 2013

CAREER RECORDS

Tries: 420 Lionel Cooper 1947-55
Goals: 958 Frank Dyson 1949-63
Points: 2,072 Frank Dyson 1949-63
Appearances: 485 Douglas Clark 1909-29

HUDDERSFIELD GIANTS

DATE	FIXTURE	RESULT	SCORERS	LGE	ATT
1/2/20	Catalans Dragons (a)	W12-32	t:Joe Wardle,McGillvary(2),Sezer,Senior g:Sezer(6)	3rd	8,259
14/2/20	Salford (a)	W10-12	t:O'Brien,Senior g:Sezer(2)	3rd	3,350
21/2/20	Hull KR (a)	W4-22	t:Senior,Gaskell,Clough,Matagi g:Sezer(3)	1st	7,350
1/3/20	Wigan (h)	L10-42	t:O'Brien g:Sezer(3)	5th	6,574
6/3/20	St Helens (a)	W10-12	t:O'Brien,Jake Wardle g:Sezer(2)	4th	10,418
11/3/20	Toronto (a) (CCR5) ●	L18-0		N/A	1,488
2/8/20	Leeds (h) ●●	L26-27			
		(aet)	t:Senior(2),McIntosh(3) g:Sezer(3)	4th	N/A
15/8/20	Warrington (h) ●●●	L18-19	t:Ta'ai,McGillvary,Russell g:Sezer(2),Russell	5th	N/A
30/8/20	Hull FC (h) ●●●●	L12-31	t:Golding,Turner g:Russell(2)	7th	N/A
4/9/20	St Helens (h) ●●	L6-54	t:Trout g:Russell	7th	N/A
11/9/20	Leeds (a) ●●●	L13-12	t:English g:Russell(4)	8th	N/A
17/9/20	Wakefield (a) ●	W6-29	t:McQueen,Matagi,Gavet,Sezer,Jake Wardle g:Sezer(4) fg:Turner	7th	N/A
24/9/20	Castleford (a) ●●●●	W19-31	t:McGillvary(3),Jake Wardle,Sezer g:Sezer(5) fg:Sezer	6th	N/A
30/9/20	Hull KR (h)	W32-22	t:Golding,McGillvary(2),Cudjoe,McQueen,Jake Wardle g:Sezer,Russell(3)	6th	N/A
8/10/20	Salford (h) ●●	L16-24	t:Cudjoe,Sezer(2) g:Sezer(2)	6th	N/A
13/10/20	Hull FC (h) ●●●●	L18-16	t:McGillvary,English,Sezer g:Sezer(2)	6th	N/A
22/10/20	Wakefield (h) ●●●	L14-18	t:Sezer,Turner,Wood g:Gaskell	7th	N/A
30/10/20	Warrington (a) ●●●	L19-12	t:Jake Wardle,Gavet g:Sezer(2)	7th	N/A
6/11/20	Wigan (a) ●●	L19-6	t:Wood g:Sezer	7th	N/A

● Played at John Smith's Stadium
●● Played at Emerald Headingley, Leeds
●●● Played at Totally Wicked Stadium, St Helens
●●●● Played at Halliwell Jones Stadium, Warrington

Castleford (h) (R19) and Catalans Dragons (h) (R22) games were cancelled

		APP		TRIES		GOALS		FG		PTS	
	D.O.B.	ALL	SL	ALL	SL	ALL	SL	ALL	SL	ALL	SL
Reiss Butterworth	7/12/98	1(1)	1(1)	0	0	0	0	0	0	0	0
Paul Clough	27/9/87	2(4)	1(4)	1	1	0	0	0	0	4	4
Leroy Cudjoe	7/4/88	12	12	2	2	0	0	0	0	8	8
Kenny Edwards	13/9/89	12(5)	11(5)	0	0	0	0	0	0	0	0
Matty English	14/11/97	11(2)	11(2)	2	2	0	0	0	0	8	8
Lee Gaskell	28/10/90	10	10	1	1	1	1	0	0	6	6
James Gavet	19/10/89	4(12)	3(12)	2	2	0	0	0	0	8	8
Ashton Golding	4/9/96	11	11	2	2	0	0	0	0	8	8
Sam Hewitt	29/4/99	3(6)	3(5)	0	0	0	0	0	0	0	0
Tom Holmes	2/3/96	7(5)	6(5)	0	0	0	0	0	0	0	0
Michael Lawrence	12/4/90	17(1)	17	0	0	0	0	0	0	0	0
Suaia Matagi	23/3/88	12(2)	11(2)	2	2	0	0	0	0	8	8
Jermaine McGillvary	16/5/88	17	16	9	9	0	0	0	0	36	36
Darnell McIntosh	5/7/97	13	12	3	3	0	0	0	0	12	12
Chris McQueen	8/3/87	9	9	2	2	0	0	0	0	8	8
Ronan Michael	3/7/00	(1)	(1)	0	0	0	0	0	0	0	0
Brandon Moore	27/7/96	4	4	0	0	0	0	0	0	0	0
Aaron Murphy	26/11/88	5(2)	4(2)	0	0	0	0	0	0	0	0
Adam O'Brien	11/7/93	10(1)	10	3	3	0	0	0	0	12	12
Oliver Russell	21/9/98	5(4)	4(4)	1	1	11	11	0	0	26	26
Louis Senior	30/5/00	8	8	5	5	0	0	0	0	20	20
Aidan Sezer	24/6/91	17	16	7	7	38	38	1	1	105	105
Ukuma Ta'ai	17/1/87	3(6)	3(6)	1	1	0	0	0	0	4	4
Owen Trout	15/10/99	(6)	(6)	1	1	0	0	0	0	4	4
Jordan Turner	9/1/89	12(2)	11(2)	2	2	0	0	1	1	9	9
Adam Walne	3/10/90	(1)	(1)	0	0	0	0	0	0	0	0
Jake Wardle	18/11/98	17	16	5	5	0	0	0	0	20	20
Joe Wardle	22/9/91	11(1)	11(1)	1	1	0	0	0	0	4	4
Oliver Wilson	22/3/98	2(8)	2(7)	0	0	0	0	0	0	0	0
Sam Wood	11/6/97	11(5)	10(5)	2	2	0	0	0	0	8	8
Dominic Young	9/8/01	1	1	0	0	0	0	0	0	0	0

Jermaine McGillvary

'SL' totals include Super League games only; 'All' totals also include Challenge Cup

17th January 2020 - prop Lewis Bienek and centre Cameron Scott join Leigh on season-long loan. Scott signs two-year contract extension with Hull to end of 2022.

19th January 2020 - 38-6 friendly win at Batley.

23rd January 2020 - Matty Dawson-Jones released to join Bradford.

2nd February 2020 - Manu Ma'u and Gareth Ellis pick up injuries in dominant 30-4 round-one victory over Leeds at Headingley.

7th February 2020 - Adam Swift makes club debut and Mahe Fonua returns off bench in 25-16 home win over Hull KR.

10th February 2020 - Tevita Satae banned for three games for late hit, reduced to two on appeal.

16th February 2020 - 32-18 home defeat to St Helens after leading at half-time.

23rd February 2020 - 26-12 defeat at Wigan.

25th February 2020 - halfback Liam Harris joins Halifax on initial one-month loan deal.

1st March 2020 - 34-29 home defeat to Catalans after leading 28-10.

6th March 2020 - Joe Cator makes debut as golden-point Marc Sneyd field goal secures 27-26 win at Wakefield.

12th March 2020 - coach Lee Radford sacked immediately after 38-4 home defeat to Warrington. Assistant Andy Last takes interim charge,

16th March 2020 - season suspended until April 3rd because of coronavirus crisis.

19th May 2020 - winger Ratu Naulago to leave at end of season to join rugby union club.

11th June 2020 - halfback Albert Kelly to return home to Australia with his family at end of season.

9th August 2020 - 54-18 defeat by Salford in first game back from lockdown.

12th August 2020 - six Hull players test positive for Covid-19. That increases to nine players and three non-playing staff. All at club self-isolate. League game with Castleford on following Sunday and Challenge Cup tie against same side week later, also postponed.

30th August 2020 - 31-12 win over Huddersfield at Halliwell Jones Stadium, Marc Sneyd suffers ankle injury.

4th September 2020 - 37-12 defeat by Warrington at Headingley.

HULL F.C.
EST. 1865

KEY DATES

10th September 2020 - Adam Swift and Jordan Lane score try-doubles in 26-23 win over Wakefield at St Helens.

11th September 2020 - outside-back Kieran Buchanan to join Batley at end of season.

13th September 2020 - Carlos Tuimavave signs new four-year contract to end of 2024 season.

13th September 2020 - Carlos Tuimavave stars with try brace in 29-16 Challenge Cup sixth round win over Castleford at St Helens.

19th September 2020 - 36-4 defeat to Wigan at Salford means Challenge Cup quarter-final exit.

24th September 2020 - Jamie Shaul scores 100th career try in 28-22 defeat by Salford at Warrington.

1st October 2020 - Ben McNamara scores try on debut in 32-28 win at Castleford.

8th October 2020 - 40-22 defeat at Leeds as Hull fill in at short notice for Covid-hit Castleford.

13th October 2020 - late Marc Sneyd penalty goal secures 18-16 win over Huddersfield at Warrington.

18th October 2020 - Ratu Naulago scores try-double in 48-6 demolition of Castleford on return to KCOM Stadium. Jamie Shaul suffers ACL injury.

21st October 2020 - scheduled round-17 fixture at Catalans cancelled due to positive Covid tests in Dragons camp.

29th October 2020 - Albert Kelly gains early release from contract to return to Australia after confirmation of season-ending hamstring injury.

29th October 2020 - Jake Connor makes 100th club appearance and stars in 31-16 win over Hull KR in derby played at St Helens.

3rd November 2020 - League-wide regular season brought to a halt. Hull finish sixth and enter re-modelled six-team play-offs.

12th November 2020 - 27-14 win at Warrington sets up semi-final at league leaders Wigan.

18th November 2020 - Danny Houghton signs two-year contract extension.

19th November 2020 - 29-2 defeat at Wigan means play-off semi-final exit.

24th November 2020 - back-rower Jordan Lane signs new two-year contract to end of 2022 season.

25th November 2020 - former Warrington and Huddersfield fullback Brett Hodgson appointed head coach on three-year contract.

CLUB RECORDS

Highest score: 88-0 v Sheffield, 2/3/2003
Highest score against:
10-80 v Warrington, 30/8/2018
Record attendance:
28,798 v Leeds, 7/3/36 *(The Boulevard)*
23,004 v Hull KR, 2/9/2007 *(KC Stadium)*

MATCH RECORDS

Tries: 7 Clive Sullivan v Doncaster, 15/4/68
Goals: 14 Jim Kennedy v Rochdale, 7/4/21
Sammy Lloyd v Oldham, 10/9/78
Matt Crowther v Sheffield, 2/3/2003
Points: 36 Jim Kennedy v Keighley, 29/1/21

SEASON RECORDS

Tries: 52 Jack Harrison 1914-15
Goals: 170 Sammy Lloyd 1978-79
Points: 369 Sammy Lloyd 1978-79

CAREER RECORDS

Tries: 250 Clive Sullivan 1961-74; 1981-85
Goals: 687 Joe Oliver 1928-37; 1943-45
Points: 1,842 Joe Oliver 1928-37; 1943-45
Appearances: 500 Edward Rogers 1906-25

HULL F.C.

HULL F.C.

DATE	FIXTURE	RESULT	SCORERS	LGE	ATT
2/2/20	Leeds (a)	W4-30	t:Tuimavave,Naulago(2),Bowden,Shaul g:Sneyd(5)	2nd	19,700
7/2/20	Hull KR (h)	W25-16	t:Connor,Houghton,Sneyd,Griffin g:Sneyd(4) fg:Sneyd	1st	19,599
16/2/20	St Helens (h)	L18-32	t:Tuimavave(2),Shaul g:Sneyd(3)	4th	12,399
23/2/20	Wigan (a)	L26-12	t:Swift,Griffin g:Sneyd(2)	7th	12,005
1/3/20	Catalans Dragons (h)	L29-34	t:Fonua(2),Tuimavave,Shaul,Ma'u g:Sneyd(4) fg:Sneyd	7th	12,003
6/3/20	Wakefield (a)	W26-27		7th	5,528
		(aet)	t:Fonua,Shaul,Buchanan,Kelly g:Sneyd(5) fg:Sneyd	8th	10,214
12/3/20	Warrington (h)	L4-38	t:Buchanan	8th	N/A
9/8/20	Salford (a) ●	L54-18	t:Kelly,Ma'u,Shaul g:Sneyd(3)	8th	N/A
30/8/20	Huddersfield (a) ●●	W12-31	t:Kelly,Sneyd,Griffin,Brown,Fonua g:Sneyd(2),Griffin(3) fg:Shaul	8th	N/A
4/9/20	Warrington (a) ●	L37-12	t:Griffin,Tuimavave g:Connor(2)	8th	N/A
10/9/20	Wakefield (h) ●●●	W26-23	t:Lane(2),Swift(2),Savelio g:Connor(3)	7th	N/A
13/9/20	Castleford (a) (CCR6) ●●●	W16-29	t:Tuimavave(2),Kelly,Naulago g:Connor(6) fg:Connor	N/A	N/A
19/9/20	Wigan (h) (CCQF) ●●●	L4-36	t:Fonua	N/A	N/A
24/9/20	Salford (h) ●●	L22-28	t:Shaul(2),Savelio,Lane g:Connor(3)	8th	N/A
1/10/20	Castleford (a)	W28-32	t:Scott,Johnstone,Satae,McNamara,Connor g:Sneyd(6)	7th	N/A
8/10/20	Leeds (h) ●●●	L22-40	t:Fonua,Savelio,Griffin,Brown g:Sneyd(3)	7th	N/A
13/10/20	Huddersfield (h) ●●	W18-16	t:Naulago,Fonua,Faraimo g:Sneyd(3)	7th	N/A
18/10/20	Castleford (h)	W48-6	t:Naulago(2),Savelio,Connor,Faraimo,Houghton,Tuimavave,Ma'u g:Sneyd(7),Connor	6th	N/A
29/10/20	Hull KR (a) ●●●	W16-31	t:Bowden,Faraimo(2),Naulago(2),Sao g:Sneyd(3) fg:Sneyd	6th	N/A
12/11/20	Warrington (a) (EPO)	W14-27	t:Faraimo,Cator,Satae,Connor g:Sneyd(5) fg:Sneyd	N/A	N/A
19/11/20	Wigan (a) (SF)	L29-2	g:Sneyd	N/A	N/A

● *Played at Emerald Headingley, Leeds*
●● *Played at Halliwell Jones Stadium, Warrington*
●●● *Played at Totally Wicked Stadium, St Helens*
●●●● *Played at AJ Bell Stadium, Salford*

Catalans Dragons (a) (R17), St Helens (a) (R21) and Wigan (h) (R22) games were cancelled

		APP		TRIES		GOALS		FG		PTS	
	D.O.B.	ALL	SL	ALL	SL	ALL	SL	ALL	SL	ALL	SL
Lewis Bienek	11/4/98	(1)	(1)	0	0	0	0	0	0	0	0
Josh Bowden	14/1/92	11(6)	11(6)	2	2	0	0	0	0	8	8
Jack Brown	25/6/00	1(8)	1(7)	2	2	0	0	0	0	8	8
Kieran Buchanan	26/1/98	4(2)	4(2)	2	2	0	0	0	0	8	8
Joe Cator	15/6/98	11(2)	9(2)	1	1	0	0	0	0	4	4
Jake Connor	18/10/94	17(1)	15(1)	4	4	15	9	1	0	47	34
Gareth Ellis	3/5/81	6(2)	5(2)	0	0	0	0	0	0	0	0
Bureta Faraimo	16/7/90	15	13	5	5	0	0	0	0	20	20
Brad Fash	24/1/96	7(10)	5(10)	0	0	0	0	0	0	0	0
Mahe Fonua	24/12/92	15(4)	14(3)	7	6	0	0	0	0	28	24
Josh Griffin	9/5/90	18	16	5	5	3	3	0	0	26	26
Danny Houghton	25/9/88	9(8)	9(6)	2	2	0	0	0	0	8	8
Jordan Johnstone	24/5/97	12(5)	10(5)	1	1	0	0	0	0	4	4
Josh Jones	12/5/93	7	7	0	0	0	0	0	0	0	0
Albert Kelly	21/3/91	8	7	4	3	0	0	0	0	16	12
Jordan Lane	20/10/97	11(2)	9(2)	3	3	0	0	0	0	12	12
Masi Matongo	15/5/96	1(4)	(4)	0	0	0	0	0	0	0	0
Manu Ma'u	24/8/88	13	11	3	3	0	0	0	0	12	12
Ben McNamara	18/12/01	2(2)	2(2)	1	1	0	0	0	0	4	4
Ratu Naulago	8/6/91	11	10	8	7	0	0	0	0	32	28
Ligi Sao	11/10/92	11(7)	11(5)	1	1	0	0	0	0	4	4
Tevita Satae	22/10/92	2(16)	2(14)	2	2	0	0	0	0	8	8
Andre Savelio	21/3/95	10(2)	10(2)	4	4	0	0	0	0	16	16
Cameron Scott	7/10/99	4	4	1	1	0	0	0	0	4	4
Jamie Shaul	1/7/92	14	13	7	7	0	0	1	1	29	29
Marc Sneyd	9/2/91	17	16	2	2	56	56	5	5	125	125
Adam Swift	20/2/93	5	5	3	3	0	0	0	0	12	12
Scott Taylor	27/2/91	11	11	0	0	0	0	0	0	0	0
Carlos Tuimavave	10/1/92	18(1)	16(1)	8	6	0	0	0	0	32	24
Connor Wynne	15/1/01	2(1)	1(1)	0	0	0	0	0	0	0	0

Carlos Tuimavave

'SL' totals include regular season & play-offs; 'All' totals also include Challenge Cup

24th October 2019 - halfbacks Joe Keyes and Rowan Milnes, back-rowers Elliot Minchella and Matthew Storton and prop Anesu Mudoti all sign from Bradford on three-year deals.

25th October 2019 - prop Daniel Murray signs one-year permanent deal.

12th November 2019 - outside backs Elliot Wallis join York and Will Oakes Dewsbury on season-long loans.

28th November 2019 - centre Jimmy Keinhorst joins York on season-long loan.

5th December 2019 - Jamie Ellis re-signs from Castleford and Ryan Brierley from Toronto on one-year deals.

10th December 2019 - Adam Rooks and Rowan Milnes go on season-long loans at Bradford.

12th January 2020 - Mose Masoe suffers career-ending spinal injury in 18-6 friendly defeat at Wakefield. Weller Hauraki sustains ankle injury that requires surgery.

19th January 2020 - Dean Hadley suffers thumb injury in 16-14 home friendly win over Featherstone.

31st January 2020 - Ben Crooks scores four tries in 30-12 round-one home win over Wakefield.

8th February 2020 - Ben Crooks scores spectacular team try but can't prevent 25-16 defeat at Hull FC. Adam Quinlan suffers ankle injury.

14th February 2020 - Jamie Ellis picks up injury in warm-up before 52-10 round-three hammering at Leeds.

21st February 2020 - Matt Parcell suffers ankle injury as Joe Keyes makes debut in 22-4 home defeat to Huddersfield.

25th February 2020 - chief executive Mike Smith to step down from his position after decade in the role.

27th February 2020 - Ben Crooks sustains neck injury in injury-hit 28-8 home defeat to Castleford

8th March 2020 - Ethan Ryan scores on debut as Matty Storton and Robbie Mulhern suffer knee injuries from 'cannonballs' in gutsy 30-16 defeat at leaders Wigan.

11th March 2020 - prop forward Nathaniel Peteru, released by Leeds, signs for 2020 season.

15th March 2020 - debutant Nick Rawsthorne scores late try to snatch 22-19 home Challenge Cup win over Leigh. Adam Quinlan and Weller Hauraki return from injury

16th March 2020 - season suspended until April 3rd because of coronavirus crisis.

7th June 2020 - Wakefield prop George King signs for 2021.

8th August 2020 - 40-10 round-8 defeat by Warrington at Headingley in first post-covid-lockdown game.

24th August 2020 - Neil Hudgell to step down as chairman after 16 years on 1st December 2020.

KEY DATES

30th August 2020 - 32-18 defeat to St Helens at Warrington is seventh straight Super League defeat.

3rd September 2020 - Jordan Abdull returns and stars as shock 34-18 win over Wigan at Headingley ends seven-game losing run.

3rd September 2020 - Jimmy Keinhorst (York) and Rowan Milnes (Bradford) recalled from loans.

3rd September 2020 - Jamie Ellis to re-join Leigh for 2021.

11th September 2020 - 21-20 golden-point defeat to St Helens at Totally Wicked Stadium.

17th September 2020 - Jordan Abdull suspended for two matches after being found guilty of grabbing testicles of Saints back-rower James Bentley.

17th September 2020 - Will Dagger signs one-year contract extension.

18th September 2020 - 48-18 Challenge Cup quarter-final defeat by Leeds at St Helens.

24th September 2020 - Will Tate makes debut at fullback as much-changed side hammered 41-16 by Leeds at Warrington.

27th September 2020 - George King signs from Wakefield Trinity until 2022 with immediate effect.

28th September 2020 - hooker Matt Parcell extends contract by one year, with option for further year.

30th September 2020 - 32-22 defeat at Huddersfield as kick-off delayed by 90 minutes by coronavirus cases in Giants camp. Matt Parcell scores hat-trick.

1st October 2020 - Ben Crooks signs one year contract extension.

5th October 2020 - Matty Gee to join Leigh at end of season.

9th October 2020 - Rowan Milnes and George King make debuts in 34-4 defeat to Catalans Dragons in Perpignan.

13th October 2020 - last-minute Jamie Ellis penalty seals 24-22 win over Salford at Warrington to end four-match losing run.

15th October 2020 - Adam Quinlan signs one-year contract extension.

19th October 2020 - Mitch Garbutt, moving to Toulouse Olympique in 2021, ruled out for remainder of season with elbow injury.

22nd October 2020 - head coach Tony Smith self-isolating for 14 days after coming into contact with someone subsequently tested positive for Covid-19.

22nd October 2020 - 38-24 defeat by Castleford at St Helens in game delayed for an hour because of M62 closure.

25th October 2020 - 48-18 defeat at Wakefield means wooden spoon.

27th October 2020 - Tony Smith tests negative in two covid tests but must isolate.

29th October 2020 - 31-16 defeat to Hull FC in derby played at St Helens.

30th October 2020 - Ryan Brierley to join Leigh at season end.

2nd November 2020 - nine players ruled out following coronavirus testing. Rovers unable to fulfil remaining three fixtures.

3rd November 2020 - League-wide regular season brought to a halt. Rovers finish eleventh and bottom of table.

4th November 2020 - Danny McGuire to become assistant first-team coach at Hull KR in 2021, alongside head of recruitment role.

12th November 2020 - prop forward Albert Vete signs from Melbourne Storm on two-year contract.

14th November 2020 - England winger Ryan Hall signs from Sydney Roosters until end of 2022 season.

17th November 2020 - Muizz Mustapha signs from Leeds on season-long loan for 2021.

19th November 2020 - Korbin Sims signs on two-year contract, subject to visa.

CLUB RECORDS

Highest score:
100-6 v Nottingham City, 19/8/90
Highest score against:
6-84 v Wigan, 1/4/2013
Record attendance:
27,670 v Hull FC, 3/4/53 *(Boothferry Park)*
12,100 v Hull FC, 1/2/2019 *(Craven Park)*

MATCH RECORDS

Tries: 11 George West
v Brooklands Rovers, 4/3/1905
Goals:
14 Alf Carmichael v Merthyr, 8/10/1910
Mike Fletcher v Whitehaven, 18/3/90
Colin Armstrong v Nottingham City, 19/8/90
Damien Couturier v Halifax, 23/4/2006
Points: 53 George West
v Brooklands Rovers, 4/3/1905

SEASON RECORDS

Tries: 45 Gary Prohm 1984-85
Goals: 199 Mike Fletcher 1989-90
Points: 450 Mike Fletcher 1989-90

CAREER RECORDS

Tries: 207 Roger Millward 1966-80
Goals: 1,268 Mike Fletcher 1987-98
Points: 2,760 Mike Fletcher 1987-98
Appearances: 489 Mike Smith 1975-91

HULL KINGSTON ROVERS

DATE	FIXTURE	RESULT	SCORERS	LGE	ATT
31/1/20	Wakefield (h)	W30-12	t:Crooks(4),Minikin,Brierley g:Ellis(3)	4th	8,492
7/2/20	Hull FC (a)	L25-16	t:Livett,Quinlan,Crooks g:Ellis(2)	6th	19,599
14/2/20	Leeds (a)	L52-10	t:Minikin,Abdull g:Brierley	10th	11,057
21/2/20	Huddersfield (h)	L4-22	t:Crooks	11th	7,350
27/2/20	Castleford (h)	L8-28	t:Crooks g:Brierley(2)	11th	7,464
8/3/20	Wigan (a)	L30-16	t:Ryan,Minikin,Brierley g:Brierley(2)	11th	11,511
15/3/20	Leigh (h) (CCR5)	W22-19	t:Linnett,Kenny-Dowall,Dagger,Rawsthorne g:Lewis(3)	N/A	2,620
8/8/20	Warrington (a) ●	L40-10	t:Crooks,Quinlan g:Brierley	11th	N/A
30/8/20	St Helens (h) ●●	L18-32	t:Quinlan,Ryan,Parcell g:Ellis(3)	11th	N/A
3/9/20	Wigan (h) ●	W34-18	t:Minchella(2),Minikin(3),Hadley g:Lewis(2),Dagger(2),Abdull	11th	N/A
11/9/20	St Helens (a)	L21-20			
		(aet)	t:Hadley,Kenny-Dowall,Ryan g:Dagger(4)	11th	N/A
18/9/20	Leeds (h) (CCQF) ●●●	L18-48	t:Ellis(2),Litten g:Ellis(3)	N/A	N/A
24/9/20	Leeds (h) ●●	L16-41	t:Keinhorst,Brierley,Kenny-Dowall g:Brierley(2)	10th	N/A
30/9/20	Huddersfield (a)	L32-22	t:Parcell(3),Tate g:Ellis(3)	11th	N/A
9/10/20	Catalans Dragons (a)	L34-4	t:Livett	10th	5,000
13/10/20	Salford (h) ●●	W24-22	t:Lewis(2),Crooks,Abdull g:Ellis(4)	10th	N/A
22/10/20	Castleford (a) ●●●	L38-24	t:Mulhern,Minchella,Kenny-Dowall,Parcell g:Dagger(4)	10th	N/A
25/10/20	Wakefield (a)	L48-18	t:Abdull,Ellis,Crooks g:Ellis(3)	11th	N/A
29/10/20	Hull FC (h) ●●●	L16-31	t:Hadley,Linnett,Crooks g:Dagger(2)	11th	N/A

● *Played at Emerald Headingley, Leeds*
●● *Played at Halliwell Jones Stadium, Warrington*
●●● *Played at Totally Wicked Stadium, St Helens*

Warrington (h) (R20), Catalans Dragons (h) (R21) and Salford (a) (R22) games were cancelled

		APP		TRIES		GOALS		FG		PTS	
	D.O.B.	ALL	SL	ALL	SL	ALL	SL	ALL	SL	ALL	SL
Jordan Abdull	5/2/96	11(1)	10(1)	3	3	1	1	0	0	14	14
Ryan Brierley	12/3/92	10	10	3	3	8	8	0	0	28	28
Ben Crooks	15/6/93	12	12	11	11	0	0	0	0	44	44
Will Dagger	21/2/99	12	10	1	0	12	12	0	0	28	24
Jamie Ellis	4/10/89	8	7	3	1	21	18	0	0	54	40
Mitch Garbutt	18/4/89	3(5)	3(5)	0	0	0	0	0	0	0	0
Matty Gee	12/12/94	6(7)	6(5)	0	0	0	0	0	0	0	0
Dean Hadley	5/8/92	10(3)	9(3)	3	3	0	0	0	0	12	12
Owen Harrison	10/4/99	1(3)	1(2)	0	0	0	0	0	0	0	0
Weller Hauraki	18/2/85	11	9	0	0	0	0	0	0	0	0
Jimmy Keinhorst	14/7/90	1	1	1	1	0	0	0	0	4	4
Shaun Kenny-Dowall	23/1/88	19	17	4	3	0	0	0	0	16	12
Joe Keyes	17/9/95	4(1)	4(1)	0	0	0	0	0	0	0	0
George King	24/2/95	2(2)	2(2)	0	0	0	0	0	0	0	0
George Lawler	1/9/95	12(1)	12(1)	0	0	0	0	0	0	0	0
Mikey Lewis	4/7/01	6(2)	4(2)	2	2	5	2	0	0	18	12
Kane Linnett	11/1/89	17	15	2	1	0	0	0	0	8	4
Jez Litten	10/3/98	6(3)	6(1)	1	0	0	0	0	0	4	0
Harvey Livett	4/1/97	8(2)	7(2)	2	2	0	0	0	0	8	8
Will Maher	4/11/95	6(6)	6(6)	0	0	0	0	0	0	0	0
Rowan Milnes	1/9/97	2(1)	2(1)	0	0	0	0	0	0	0	0
Elliot Minchella	28/1/96	9(7)	8(7)	3	3	0	0	0	0	12	12
Greg Minikin	29/3/95	11	10	6	6	0	0	0	0	24	24
Robbie Mulhern	18/10/94	6(7)	5(7)	1	1	0	0	0	0	4	4
Daniel Murray	21/3/96	7(7)	6(6)	0	0	0	0	0	0	0	0
Matt Parcell	30/10/92	9(2)	8(2)	5	5	0	0	0	0	20	20
Nathaniel Peteru	1/1/92	5(4)	5(3)	0	0	0	0	0	0	0	0
Adam Quinlan	13/11/92	5	4	3	3	0	0	0	0	12	12
Nick Rawsthorne	30/9/95	6	5	1	0	0	0	0	0	4	0
Ethan Ryan	12/5/96	6	4	3	3	0	0	0	0	12	12
Matthew Storton	10/3/99	10(1)	9(1)	0	0	0	0	0	0	0	0
Will Tate	20/12/01	4	4	1	1	0	0	0	0	4	4
Kyle Trout	1/3/91	(11)	(10)	0	0	0	0	0	0	0	0

Shaun Kenny-Dowall

'SL' totals include Super League games only; 'All' totals also include Challenge Cup

24th October 2019 - prop Nathaniel Peteru leaves by mutual consent two years into three-year deal.

6th November 2019 - out-of-contract Brett Ferres joins Featherstone.

22nd November 2019 - Brad Singleton signs for Toronto for undisclosed fee.

27th November 2019 - England Knights hooker Kruise Leeming signs from Huddersfield on two-year deal.

29th November 2019 - NSW State of Origin prop Matt Prior signs from Cronulla Sharks on two-year contract.

22nd December 2019 - Stevie Ward appointed club captain.

26th December 2019 - 30-4 home win over Wakefield in Wetherby Whaler Challenge.

2nd January 2020 - Bradford centre Rhys Evans joins on season-long loan.

12th January 2020 - 19,560 crowd attend Jamie Jones-Buchanan Testimonial which he shares with Rob Burrow, after his MND diagnosis.

14th January 2020 - Jamie Jones-Buchanan appointed assistant coach.

1st February 2020 - captain Stevie Ward and Konrad Hurrell both suffer concussion in 30-4 round-one home defeat to Hull FC.

9th February 2020 - round-two game at Huddersfield postponed because of Storm Ciara.

14th February 2020 - Cameron Smith and Harry Newman both score two tries in 52-10 home win over Hull KR.

21st February 2020 - hooker Kruise Leeming has knee surgery.

22nd February 2020 - 22-unanswered points secure 22-8 win at Salford.

25th February 2020 - England international Joe Greenwood joins on two-month loan from Wigan.

27th February 2020 - captain Stevie Ward stood down indefinitely because of concussion suffered in opening round of season.

28th February 2020 - Jack Walker injures ankle as sub Richie Myler stars in 36-0 home win over Warrington.

5th March 2020 - Rob Lui and Luke Gale, on 300th career appearance, both score try-braces in 66-12 home win over Toronto Wolfpack.

11th March 2020 - Cameron Smith signs new three-year contract to end of 2023

13th March 2020 - Rhinos refuse to fly to play Catalans, already to be played behind closed doors, after unnamed player suspected of contracting coronavirus.

14th March 2020 - unnamed player cleared of coronavirus.

16th March 2020 - season suspended until April 3rd because of coronavirus crisis.

4th May 2020 - on-loan Joe Greenwood returns to Wigan without making appearance.

KEY DATES

22nd May 2020 - no disciplinary action taken by RFL for Leeds' withdrawal from Catalans fixture.

13th July 2020 - Liam Sutcliffe makes transfer request.

30th July 2020 - hooker Brad Dwyer agrees new two-year contract to end of 2022 season.

2nd August 2020 - skipper Luke Gale kicks golden-point field goal to seal 27-26 comeback win against Huddersfield.

9th August 2020 - Rhys Evans makes debut in 48-0 defeat by St Helens at Headingley.

13th August 2020 - back row Bodene Thompson signs from Toronto Wolfpack for rest of season.

16th August 2020 - Bodene Thompson makes debut in 28-10 defeat to Wigan at St Helens.

27th August 2020 - fixture at Catalans, scheduled for Monday 7 September, postponed due to Covid in Dragons camp.

29th August 2020 - hat-tricks from Ash Handley and Richie Myler help secure 50-12 win over Salford at Halliwell Jones Stadium.

30th August 2020 - Featherstone Rovers pair James Harrison and Brett Ferres join on loan deals.

11th September 2020 - late Luke Gale field goal seals 13-12 win over Huddersfield at St Helens.

14th September 2020 - Alex Sutcliffe, two matches for dangerous contact, and Brad Dwyer, one for shoulder charge, suspended

18th September 2020 - 48-18 win over Hull KR in Challenge Cup quarter final at St Helens.

24th September 2020 - Ash Handley scores brace in 41-16 win over Hull KR at Warrington. Harry Newman suffers double break to lower leg.

27th September 2020 - Adam Cuthbertson to join York for 2010 season.

30th September 2020 - seven debutants in 34-6 defeat by Catalans at Headingley.

3rd October 2020 - Ash Handley scores brace in 26-12 Challenge Cup semi-final win over Wigan at St Helens.

8th October 2020 - Jack Walker returns in 40-22 win over Hull FC at Headingley after scheduled opponents Castleford have positive Covid-19 tests.

13th October 2020 - weakened side suffers 32-6 defeat by Warrington at Halliwell Jones Stadium.

14th October 2020 - winger Tom Briscoe extends contract until end of 2022 season.

17th October 2020 - late field goal from Luke Gale secures 17-16 Challenge Cup Final win behind closed doors at Wembley. Fullback Richie Myler wins Lance Todd trophy.

23rd October 2020 - 40-8 defeat by St Helens for youthful Rhinos side at St Helens.

26th October 2020 - Sean Long to join as assistant coach in 2021.

26th October 2020 - 28-24 win over Castleford at Headingley.

29th October 2020 - four players stood down through Covid protocols before 30-6 defeat by Wakefield at St Helens.

1st November 2020 - Brad Dwyer scores late try to secure 20-18 win at Wakefield, in fourth game in nine days.

2nd November 2020 - Alex Mellor gets two-game ban for striking in defeat by Wakefield at St Helens.

2nd November 2020 - Friday fixture with Castleford cancelled as four more Tigers players test positive for Covid-19.

3rd November 2020 - League-wide regular season brought to a halt. Rhinos finish fifth and enter re-modelled six-team play-offs.

6th November 2020 - prop Mikolaj Oledzki signs new four-year contract.

13th November 2020 - 26-14 elimination defeat by Catalans at Warrington ends season. Richard Agar misses game because of self-isolation.

19th November 2020 - Bodene Thompson signs two-year contract to end of 2022 season.

CLUB RECORDS

Highest score:
106-10 v Swinton, 11/2/2001
Highest score against:
6-74 v Wigan, 20/5/92
Record attendance:
40,175 v Bradford, 21/5/47

MATCH RECORDS

Tries:
8 Fred Webster v Coventry, 12/4/1913
Eric Harris v Bradford, 14/9/31
Goals:
17 Iestyn Harris v Swinton, 11/2/2001
Points:
42 Iestyn Harris v Huddersfield, 16/7/99

SEASON RECORDS

Tries: 63 Eric Harris 1935-36
Goals: 173 *(inc 5fg)* Kevin Sinfield 2012
Points: 431 Lewis Jones 1956-57

CAREER RECORDS

Tries: 391 Eric Harris 1930-39
Goals:
1,831 *(inc 39fg)* Kevin Sinfield 1997-2015
Points: 3,967 Kevin Sinfield 1997-2015
Appearances: 625 John Holmes 1968-89

LEEDS RHINOS

DATE	FIXTURE	RESULT	SCORERS	LGE	ATT
2/2/20	Hull FC (h)	L4-30	t:Handley	11th	19,700
14/2/20	Hull KR (h)	W52-10	t:Newman(2),Smith(2),Walker,Handley,Hurrell,Donaldson,Myler g:Gale(8)	6th	11,057
22/2/20	Salford (a)	W8-22	t:Gale,L Briscoe,Oledzki,Walker g:Gale(3)	5th	4,757
28/2/20	Warrington (h)	W36-0	t:Walker,Myler,Dwyer,Hurrell,Seumanufagai,Handley g:Martin(6)	4th	12,134
5/3/20	Toronto (h)	W66-12	t:Dwyer,Myler,Gale(2),Lui(2),Handley,Smith,Oledzki,Cuthbertson,Hurrell g:Martin(11)	2nd	12,143
2/8/20	Huddersfield (a) ●	W26-27 (aet)	t:Hurrell(2),Gale,L Briscoe,Mellor g:Martin(3) fg:Gale	1st	N/A
9/8/20	St Helens (h)	L0-48		4th	N/A
16/8/20	Wigan (a) ●●	L28-10	t:T Briscoe,L Sutcliffe g:Martin	6th	N/A
29/8/20	Salford (h) ●●●	W50-12	t:Handley(3),Myler(3),Gale,Lui,Oledzki g:Martin(7)	5th	N/A
11/9/20	Huddersfield (h) ●●	W13-12	t:Hurrell,T Briscoe g:Gale(2) fg:Gale	4th	N/A
18/9/20	Hull KR (a) (CCQF) ●●	W18-48	t:Seumanufagai,Handley,T Briscoe,Newman,Leeming(2),L Briscoe,Martin g:Martin(8)	N/A	N/A
24/9/20	Hull KR (a) ●●●	W16-41	t:Martin,Handley(2),Donaldson,Myler,Mellor,L Briscoe g:Martin(6) fg:Gale	4th	N/A
30/9/20	Catalans Dragons (h)	L6-34	t:Evans g:O'Connor	4th	N/A
3/10/20	Wigan (CCSF) ●●	W26-12	t:Martin,Handley(2),T Briscoe g:Martin(5)	N/A	N/A
8/10/20	Hull FC (a) ●	W22-40	t:Walker(2),Handley(3),Donaldson,L Sutcliffe g:Martin(6)	4th	N/A
13/10/20	Warrington (a)	L32-6	t:Walters g:O'Connor	5th	N/A
17/10/20	Salford (CCF) ●●●●	W17-16	t:T Briscoe,Handley(2) g:Martin(2) fg:Gale	N/A	N/A
23/10/20	St Helens (a)	L40-8	t:Smith,Tindall	5th	N/A
26/10/20	Castleford (h)	W28-24	t:Seumanufagai,Gale,L Sutcliffe,T Briscoe,Martin g:Martin(4)	5th	N/A
29/10/20	Wakefield (h) ●●	L6-30	t:Handley g:Martin	5th	N/A
1/11/20	Wakefield (a)	W18-20	t:Handley(2),L Sutcliffe,Dwyer g:L Sutcliffe,Martin	5th	N/A
13/11/20	Catalans Dragons (a) (EPO) ●●●	L26-14	t:A Sutcliffe,L Sutcliffe,Hurrell g:Martin	N/A	N/A

● *Played at Emerald Headingley*
●● *Played at Totally Wicked Stadium, St Helens*
●●● *Played at Halliwell Jones Stadium, Warrington*
●●●● *Played at Wembley Stadium*

Catalans Dragons (a) (R7), Castleford (a) (R20) and Wigan (h) (R21) games were cancelled

Toronto (h) (R6) game was later expunged from the Super League table (Player stats from this fixture are included in 'All' columns below)

		APP		TRIES		GOALS		FG		PTS	
	D.O.B.	ALL	SL	ALL	SL	ALL	SL	ALL	SL	ALL	SL
Luke Briscoe	11/3/94	12(2)	11(1)	4	3	0	0	0	0	16	12
Tom Briscoe	19/3/90	11	8	6	3	0	0	0	0	24	12
Jack Broadbent	1/11/01	3	3	0	0	0	0	0	0	0	0
Adam Cuthbertson	24/2/85	4(10)	4(8)	1	0	0	0	0	0	4	0
James Donaldson	14/9/91	2(14)	2(10)	3	3	0	0	0	0	12	12
Brad Dwyer	28/4/93	9(9)	8(7)	3	2	0	0	0	0	12	8
Rhys Evans	30/10/92	4(1)	4(1)	1	1	0	0	0	0	4	4
Brett Ferres	17/4/86	2(2)	2(2)	0	0	0	0	0	0	0	0
Luke Gale	22/6/88	18	14	6	4	13	13	4	3	54	45
Corey Hall	7/8/02	(2)	(2)	0	0	0	0	0	0	0	0
Ash Handley	16/2/96	19	15	20	14	0	0	0	0	80	56
James Harrison	15/6/96	2(2)	2(2)	0	0	0	0	0	0	0	0
Tom Holroyd	9/2/01	3(6)	3(4)	0	0	0	0	0	0	0	0
Konrad Hurrell	5/8/91	12(1)	9(1)	7	6	0	0	0	0	28	24
Kruise Leeming	7/9/95	11(3)	8(3)	2	0	0	0	0	0	8	0
Robert Lui	23/2/90	16	12	3	1	0	0	0	0	12	4
Rhyse Martin	1/3/93	15(1)	11(1)	4	2	62	36	0	0	140	80
Loui McConnell	21/11/99	(2)	(2)	0	0	0	0	0	0	0	0
Callum McLelland	16/9/99	6(2)	6	0	0	0	0	0	0	0	0
Alex Mellor	24/9/94	12(1)	8(1)	2	2	0	0	0	0	8	8
Muizz Mustapha	3/4/00	(2)	(2)	0	0	0	0	0	0	0	0
Richie Myler	21/5/90	11(4)	7(4)	7	6	0	0	0	0	28	24
Harry Newman	19/2/00	12	10	3	2	0	0	0	0	12	8
Jarrod O'Connor	20/7/01	2(2)	2(2)	0	0	2	2	0	0	4	4
Mikolaj Oledzki	8/11/98	14(6)	10(6)	3	2	0	0	0	0	12	8
Matt Prior	27/5/87	16	12	0	0	0	0	0	0	0	0
Ava Seumanufagai	4/6/91	17	13	3	2	0	0	0	0	12	8
Cameron Smith	7/11/98	6(9)	6(7)	4	3	0	0	0	0	16	12
Alex Sutcliffe	21/1/99	5(4)	5(3)	1	1	0	0	0	0	4	4
Liam Sutcliffe	25/11/94	13(1)	10(1)	5	5	1	1	0	0	22	22
Bodene Thompson	1/8/88	11	11	0	0	0	0	0	0	0	0
Liam Tindall	27/9/01	3	3	1	1	0	0	0	0	4	4
Jack Walker	8/8/99	10	10	5	5	0	0	0	0	20	20
Sam Walters	25/12/00	4	4	1	1	0	0	0	0	4	4
Stevie Ward	17/11/93	1	1	0	0	0	0	0	0	0	0
Harvey Whiteley	26/9/98	(2)	(2)	0	0	0	0	0	0	0	0

Ash Handley

'SL' totals include regular season & play-offs; 'All' totals also include Challenge Cup

25th October 2019 - on-loan prop Ryan Lannon returns on permanent basis.

4th November 2019 - Huddersfield Giants prop Sebastine Ikahihifo joins on season-long loan.

5th January 2020 - comfortable 52-4 victory in pre-season derby fixture against Swinton.

23rd January 2020 - 26-10 friendly defeat at Warrington.

29th January 2020 - head coach Ian Watson signs two-year contract extension to 2022.

31st January 2020 - 48-8 round-one defeat at St Helens.

8th February 2020 - Niall Evalds scores try in 150th Salford appearance in 24-16 home win over Toronto.

14th February 2020 - last-second Aidan Sezer penalty from under sticks means 12-10 home defeat by Huddersfield.

18th February 2020 - Ireland international back row Oliver Roberts joins on season-long loan from Huddersfield.

20th February 2020 - prop Adam Walker leaves club with immediate effect.

22nd February 2020 - Oliver Roberts makes debut in 22-8 home defeat to Leeds.

1st March 2020 - Ken Sio scores try-brace in 22-12 home defeat to Wakefield.

3rd March 2020 - Ed Chamberlain joins London Broncos on one-month loan deal.

6th March 2020 - coach Ian Watson gets 'nominal fine' for comments on match official after Leeds defeat.

7th March 2020 - Elliot Kear makes debut as Ken Sio scores try-brace in 30-14 defeat at Catalans.

10th March 2020 - prop Gil Dudson to join Catalans in 2021.

13th March 2020 - second-half brace from Niall Evalds seals 18-14 comeback home win over leaders Wigan.

16th March 2020 - season suspended until April 3rd because of coronavirus crisis.

12th May 2020 - Niall Evalds signs for Castleford for 2021.

21st May 2020 - captain Lee Mossop signs two-year contract extension to end of 2022 season.

22nd May 2020 - prop Luke Yates signs two-year contract extension to end of 2022 season.

4th June 2020 - hooker Andy Ackers joins from Toronto Wolfpack with immediate effect.

19th June 2020 - forward Oliver Roberts extends loan from Huddersfield to end of 2021.

KEY DATES

14th July 2020 - Morgan Escaré signs on three-year contract from 2021.

20th July 2020 - Red Devils return to training.

9th August 2020 - Tui Lolohea stars in 54-18 win over Hull FC in first game back, at Headingley.

11th August 2020 - training cancelled after some Hull FC players test positive for Covid-19.

12th August 2020 - weekend fixture with Catalans Dragons postponed. 11 players required to self-isolate after the track and trace analysis carried out by the RFL, despite no positive tests.

29th August 2020 - Ken Sio suffers early season-ending knee injury in 50-12 defeat by Leeds at Warrington.

3rd September 2020 - Niall Evalds sustains calf injury in 37-30 defeat by Castleford at Headingley after leading 18-0.

6th September 2020 - England centre Kallum Watkins signs on three-year deal and arrives for remainder of season.

19th September 2020 - Dan Sarginson scores golden point try in 22-18 Challenge Cup quarter-final win over Catalans as Kallum Watkins makes debut.

24th September 2020 - 28-22 win over Hull FC in Warrington.

25th September 2020 - Tom Gilmore joins on loan from Halifax and Olly Ashall-Bott from London Broncos for month.

29th September 2020 - Luke Yates banned for one match for dangerous contact. Dan Sarginson two-game ban for high tackle reduced to no games on appeal.

29th September 2020 - on-loan Tom Gilmore scores try on debut in 20-18 win over Warrington at AJ Bell Stadium.

3rd October 2020 - late Joey Lussick try seals 24-22 Challenge Cup semi-final win over Warrington at St Helens.

8th October 2020 - second-half hat-trick from Krisnan Inu in fifth consecutive victory, by 24-16 over Huddersfield.

13th October 2020 - last-minute Jamie Ellis penalty seals 24-22 defeat by Hull KR for weakened team at Warrington.

16th October 2020 - Dan Sarginson and Jack Ormondroyd ruled out of Cup Final after testing positive for Covid-19.

17th October 2020 - late field goal from Luke Gale means 17-16 Challenge Cup Final defeat behind closed doors at Wembley.

23rd October 2020 - 58-12 defeat to Wigan at St Helens.

24th October 2020 - Kris Welham to join Featherstone at season end.

26th October 2020 - Krisnan Inu try and touchline goal secures 12-10 win at St Helens.

28th October 2020 - Red Devils down to last 13 players and unable to fulfil fixture with Warrington, 24-0 defeat awarded.

2nd November 2020 - Krisnan Inu scores hat-trick in 42-24 home win over Catalans after trailing 18-6 at half-time.

3rd November 2020 - League-wide regular season brought to a halt.

3rd November 2020 - three wins deducted for failure to meet terms of commitment to fund CVA of old company, Salford Football Club (1914) Limited in 2013.

6th November 2020 - 28-20 win over Wakefield at Headingley. Red Devils finish in ninth.

9th November 2020 - head coach Ian Watson leaves with immediate effect to join another Super League club. Compensation agreed between all parties.

13th November 2020 - Sebastine Ikahihifo loan deal from Huddersfield extended for 2021.

19th November 2020 - Dan Sarginson signs two-year contract extension to end of 2023.

CLUB RECORDS
Highest score: 100-12 v Gateshead, 23/3/2003 **Highest score against:** 16-96 v Bradford, 25/6/2000 **Record attendance:** 26,470 v Warrington, 13/2/37 *(The Willows)* 7,102 v Wakefield, 16/2/2014 *(AJ Bell Stadium)*
MATCH RECORDS
Tries: 6 Frank Miles v Lees, 5/3/1898 Ernest Bone v Goole, 29/3/1902 Jack Hilton v Leigh, 7/10/39 **Goals:** 14 Steve Blakeley v Gateshead, 23/3/2003 **Points:** 39 Jim Lomas v Liverpool City, 2/2/1907
SEASON RECORDS
Tries: 46 Keith Fielding 1973-74 **Goals:** 221 David Watkins 1972-73 **Points:** 493 David Watkins 1972-73
CAREER RECORDS
Tries: 297 Maurice Richards 1969-83 **Goals:** 1,241 David Watkins 1967-79 **Points:** 2,907 David Watkins 1967-79 **Appearances:** 498 Maurice Richards 1969-83

SALFORD RED DEVILS

DATE	FIXTURE	RESULT	SCORERS	LGE	ATT
31/1/20	St Helens (a)	L48-8	t:Sio g:Lolohea(2)	12th	12,008
8/2/20	Toronto (h)	W24-16	t:Brown,Lolohea,Williams,Sarginson,Evalds g:Lolohea(2)	8th	4,593
14/2/20	Huddersfield (h)	L10-12	t:Sio,Sarginson g:Lolohea	11th	3,350
22/2/20	Leeds (h)	L8-22	t:Evalds,Lolohea	10th	4,757
1/3/20	Wakefield (h)	L12-22	t:Lolohea,Sio(2)	10th	3,801
7/3/20	Catalans Dragons (a)	L30-14	t:Evalds,Sio(2) g:Lolohea	10th	7,940
13/3/20	Wigan (h)	W18-14	t:Evalds(2),Brown g:Lolohea(3)	10th	4,796
9/8/20	Hull FC (h) ●	W54-18	t:Sio(2),Lolohea(2),Williams(2),Atkin,Yates,Welham,Evalds g:Lolohea(7)	10th	N/A
29/8/20	Leeds (a) ●●	L50-12	t:Evalds(2) g:Lolohea(2)	9th	N/A
3/9/20	Castleford (h) ●	L30-37	t:Brown,Evalds,Lussick,Yates,Williams g:Inu(5)	9th	N/A
18/9/20	Catalans Dragons (a) (CCQF) ●●●	W18-22 (aet)	t:Sarginson(2),Inu,Greenwood g:Inu(3)	N/A	N/A
24/9/20	Hull FC (a) ●●	W22-28	t:Inu(2),Lussick,Williams,Ackers g:Inu(4)	9th	N/A
29/9/20	Warrington (h)	W20-18	t:Williams,Kear,Gilmore g:Inu(4)	9th	N/A
3/10/20	Warrington (CCSF) ●●●	W24-22	t:Watkins,Inu,Greenwood,Lussick g:Inu(4)	N/A	N/A
8/10/20	Huddersfield (a) ●	W16-24	t:Atkin,Inu(3) g:Inu(4)	8th	N/A
13/10/20	Hull KR (a) ●●	L24-22	t:Jones,Yates,Ashall-Bott,Chamberlain g:Chamberlain(3)	9th	N/A
17/10/20	Leeds (CCF) ●●●●	L17-16	t:Williams,Pauli,Greenwood g:Inu(2)	N/A	N/A
23/10/20	Wigan (a) ●●●	L58-12	t:Watkins,Lolohea g:Inu(2)	9th	N/A
26/10/20	St Helens (h) ●	W12-10	t:Pauli,Inu g:Inu(2)	8th	N/A
2/11/20	Catalans Dragons (h)	W42-24	t:Inu(3),Williams,Lolohea(2),Watkins g:Inu(7)	8th	N/A
6/11/20	Wakefield (a) ●	W20-28	t:Inu,Evalds,Chamberlain,Lolohea,McCarthy g:Inu(4)	9th	N/A

● *Played at Emerald Headingley, Leeds*
●● *Played at Halliwell Jones Stadium, Warrington*
●●● *Played at Totally Wicked Stadium, St Helens*
●●●● *Played at Wembley Stadium*

Castleford (a) (R21) and Hull KR (h) (R22) games were cancelled

Warrington (a) (R19) game ruled a 24-0 defeat after being unable to field a team

Toronto (h) (R2) game was later expunged from the Super League table (Player stats from this fixture are included in 'All' columns below)

		APP		TRIES		GOALS		FG		PTS	
	D.O.B.	ALL	SL	ALL	SL	ALL	SL	ALL	SL	ALL	SL
Andy Ackers	25/12/93	2(7)	2(7)	1	1	0	0	0	0	4	4
Olly Ashall-Bott	24/11/97	3	3	1	1	0	0	0	0	4	4
Connor Aspey	16/4/02	(1)	(1)	0	0	0	0	0	0	0	0
Chris Atkin	7/2/93	10(1)	10(1)	2	2	0	0	0	0	8	8
Kevin Brown	2/10/84	11	7	3	2	0	0	0	0	12	8
Greg Burke	12/2/93	7(8)	6(5)	0	0	0	0	0	0	0	0
Ed Chamberlain	8/2/96	3	3	2	2	3	3	0	0	14	14
Gil Dudson	16/6/90	12(2)	8(2)	0	0	0	0	0	0	0	0
Niall Evalds	26/8/93	12	10	10	9	0	0	0	0	40	36
Mark Flanagan	4/12/87	7(6)	4(6)	0	0	0	0	0	0	0	0
Tom Gilmore	2/2/94	2	2	1	1	0	0	0	0	4	4
James Greenwood	17/6/91	9(1)	5(1)	3	0	0	0	0	0	12	0
Sebastine Ikahihifo	27/1/91	4(13)	4(9)	0	0	0	0	0	0	0	0
Krisnan Inu	17/3/87	12	9	12	10	41	32	0	0	130	104
Josh Johnson	25/7/94	1(3)	1(3)	0	0	0	0	0	0	0	0
Connor Jones	26/1/96	7	6	1	1	0	0	0	0	4	4
Elliot Kear	29/11/88	8(1)	8(1)	1	1	0	0	0	0	4	4
Ryan Lannon	11/1/96	6(4)	6(4)	0	0	0	0	0	0	0	0
Tui Lolohea	23/1/95	19	15	9	8	18	16	0	0	72	64
Joey Lussick	28/12/95	13(5)	10(4)	3	2	0	0	0	0	12	8
Tyrone McCarthy	21/4/88	15(3)	11(3)	1	1	0	0	0	0	4	4
Lee Mossop	17/1/89	15	12	0	0	0	0	0	0	0	0
Jack Ormondroyd	7/11/91	4(1)	4(1)	0	0	0	0	0	0	0	0
Pauli Pauli	4/8/94	5(16)	5(12)	2	1	0	0	0	0	8	4
Luis Roberts	24/3/02	2	2	0	0	0	0	0	0	0	0
Oliver Roberts	24/12/94	7(1)	7(1)	0	0	0	0	0	0	0	0
Dan Sarginson	26/5/93	12	9	4	1	0	0	0	0	16	4
Ken Sio	29/10/90	9	8	8	8	0	0	0	0	32	32
Kallum Watkins	12/3/91	8	5	3	2	0	0	0	0	12	8
Kris Welham	12/5/87	16	12	1	1	0	0	0	0	4	4
Rhys Williams	8/12/89	19	15	8	6	0	0	0	0	32	24
Luke Yates	6/3/95	13(6)	12(4)	3	3	0	0	0	0	12	12

Krisnan Inu

'SL' totals include Super League games only; 'All' totals also include Challenge Cup

4th November 2019 - club chairman Eamonn McManus fined £3,000 following comments made about match officials after August's Challenge Cup Final.

26th November 2019 - Jack Welsby signs new four-year deal to end of 2022 season, with club having option for further year.

19th January 2020 - 36-6 home win over London Broncos in Louie McCarthy-Scarsbrook Testimonial.

31st January 2020 - Alex Walmsley, Kevin Naiqama and Jack Welsby score try braces in 48-8 round-one home win over Salford. Lachlan Coote suffers knee injury.

3rd February 2020 - Luke Thompson to join Canterbury Bulldogs at end of season.

6th February 2020 - Alex Walmsley suffers calf injury in warm-up to 19-0 round-two defeat at Warrington.

12th February 2020 - 18-year-old halfback Lewis Dodd signs four-year deal until end 2023.

13th February 2020 - Mark Percival agrees new five-year deal to end of 2024 season and has shoulder surgery.

16th February 2020 - four tries in 12 second-half minutes turns 6-2 half-time deficit into 32-18 win at Hull FC.

22nd February 2020 - Regan Grace, Lachlan Coote and Mark Percival miss 20-12 defeat to Sydney Roosters in World Club Challenge.

29th February 2020 - comfortable 32-0 victory in away game against Toronto Wolfpack on bitterly cold night at Warrington's Halliwell Jones Stadium.

2nd March 2020 - hooker Aaron Smith gets one-match ban for dangerous contact on Adam Sidlow.

6th March 2020 - 12-10 defeat to Huddersfield is first home defeat in regular season since August 2018.

15th March 2020 - 28-14 defeat at Castleford. Lachlan Coote returns from knee injury suffered in round one.

16th March 2020 - season suspended until April 3rd because of coronavirus crisis.

12th June 2020 - Luke Thompson transferred to Canterbury Bulldogs for undisclosed sum with immediate effect.

19th June 2020 - Zeb Taia to leave at end of 2020 season to return home to Australia.

30th June 2020 - James Graham to return from St George-Illawarra with immediate effect on short-term deal until end of 2020 season

2nd August 2020 - James Graham makes second club debut in dominant 34-6 win over Catalans in first post-lockdown game.

KEY DATES

9th August 2020 - Regan Grace scores brilliant hat-trick in 48-0 win over Leeds at Headingley.

12th August 2020 - positive Covid-19 tests at Hull FC mean Saints will play Castleford the following Sunday, not Wakefield as scheduled.

16th August 2020 - late Theo Fages try seals 10-0 win over Castleford at Totally Wicked Stadium in James Roby's 500th career appearance.

19th August 2020 - Tommy Makinson suspended for five matches after admitting to grabbing Liam Watts' genitals during win over Castleford.

30th August 2020 - Theo Fages suffers knee injury in 32-18 victory over Hull KR at Halliwell Jones Stadium.

1st September 2020 - Three un-named players self isolate for 10 days following positive test on one player.

4th September 2020 - Young side beats Huddersfield 54-6 at Headingley.

11th September 2020 - Theo Fages returns from injury and kicks golden-point field goal to secure 21-20 win over Hull KR.

15th September 2020 - Kevin Naiqama banned for two games for high tackle but sentence reduced to fine and no ban on appeal.

19th September 2020 - Mark Percival returns but aggravates hamstring injury in 20-18 Challenge Cup quarter-final defeat to Warrington at Salford.

29th September 2020 - Lewis Dodd makes debut off bench in 42-0 win against young Wigan side at Salford.

9th October 2020 - Tommy Makinson back in 20-16 win over Wakefield at Leeds.

15th October 2020 - Tommy Makinson scores first-half hat-trick and James Roby two in 48-6 win over Wakefield at Warrington.

21st October 2020 - Manly backrower Joel Thompson to join in 2021 on two-year contract.

23rd October 2020 - centre Josh Simm scores first-half hat-trick in 40-8 home win over Leeds.

26th October 2020 - Alex Walmsley banned for two games for dangerous contact on Alex Sutcliffe. Reduced on appeal to one game.

26th October 2020 - late 12-10 home defeat to Salford for side with five - backs Tom Nisbet, Ben Davies and Nico Rizzelli and forwards Matty Foster and Jake Wingfield - on debut.

30th October 2020 - 18-6 home defeat by Wigan sees Warriors leapfrog Saints to top of table.

3rd November 2020 - League-wide regular season brought to a halt. Saints finish second and enter re-modelled six-team play-offs.

6th November 2020 - Morgan Knowles signs new two-year contract until end of 2022.

9th November 2020 - prop Matty Lees signs new contract until end of 2022.

10th November 2020 - Joseph Paulo to leave for Toulouse.

11th November 2020 - Louie McCarthy-Scarsbrook signs new one-year deal.

13th November 2020 - Tongan prop Agnatius Paasi signs from NZ Warriors on two-year deal, with option for third.

17th November 2020 - Kyle Amor signs one-year contract extension. Dominique Peyroux to join Toulouse.

18th November 2020 - 24-year-old backrower Sione Mata'utia signs from Newcastle Knights on two-year contract, with option for third year.

20th November 2020 - Kevin Naiqama scores hat-trick in 48-2 play-off semi-final win over Catalans.

27th November 2020 - dramatic last second Jack Welsby try secures 8-4 Grand Final win over Wigan.

CLUB RECORDS

Highest score:
112-0 v Carlisle, 14/9/86
Highest score against:
6-78 v Warrington, 12/4/1909
Record attendance:
35,695 v Wigan, 26/12/49 *(Knowsley Road)*
17,980 v Wigan, 6/4/2012
v Wigan, 18/4/2014
v South Sydney, 22/2/2015
v Wigan, 30/3/2018
(Langtree Park/Totally Wicked Stadium)

MATCH RECORDS

Tries: 6 Alf Ellaby v Barrow, 5/3/32
Steve Llewellyn v Castleford, 3/3/56
Steve Llewellyn v Liverpool, 20/8/56
Tom van Vollenhoven v Wakefield, 21/12/57
Tom van Vollenhoven v Blackpool, 23/4/62
Frank Myler v Maryport, 1/9/69
Shane Cooper v Hull, 17/2/88
Goals: 16 Paul Loughlin v Carlisle, 14/9/86
Points:
40 Paul Loughlin v Carlisle, 14/9/86

SEASON RECORDS

Tries: 62 Tom van Vollenhoven 1958-59
Goals: 214 Kel Coslett 1971-72
Points: 452 Kel Coslett 1971-72

CAREER RECORDS

Tries: 392 Tom van Vollenhoven 1957-68
Goals: 1,639 Kel Coslett 1962-76
Points: 3,413 Kel Coslett 1962-76
Appearances: 531 Kel Coslett 1962-76

ST HELENS

DATE	FIXTURE	RESULT	SCORERS	LGE	ATT
31/1/20	Salford (h)	W48-8	t:Taia,Walmsley(2),Fages,Naiqama(2),Welsby(2) g:Coote(3),Percival(5)	1st	12,008
6/2/20	Warrington (a)	L19-0		3rd	12,562
16/2/20	Hull FC (a)	W18-32	t:Costello,Thompson,McCarthy-Scarsbrook,Bentley, Smith g:Makinson(6)	1st	12,399
22/2/20	Sydney Roosters (h) (WCC)	L12-20	t:Thompson,Walmsley g:Makinson(2)	N/A	16,108
29/2/20	Toronto (a) ●	W0-32	t:Lomax(2),Bentley,McCarthy-Scarsbrook,Smith g:Makinson(6)	3rd	4,000
6/3/20	Huddersfield (h)	L10-12	t:Thompson,Knowles g:Makinson	5th	10,418
15/3/20	Castleford (a)	L28-14	t:Makinson,Welsby,Thompson g:Makinson	6th	7,268
2/8/20	Catalans Dragons (h) ●●	W34-6	t:Coote(2),Bentley,Taia,Makinson,Walmsley g:Coote(5)	5th	N/A
9/8/20	Leeds (a)	W0-48	t:Graham,Walmsley,Makinson,Grace(3),Fages,Coote g:Coote(8)	2nd	N/A
16/8/20	Castleford (h)	W10-0	t:Fages g:Coote(3)	2nd	N/A
30/8/20	Hull KR (a) ●	W18-32	t:Walmsley,Welsby(2),Naiqama,Smith g:Coote(6)	2nd	N/A
4/9/20	Huddersfield (a) ●●	W6-54	t:Coote(2),Smith,Grace(2),McCarthy-Scarsbrook,Costello,Peyroux, Walmsley g:Coote(9)	1st	N/A
11/9/20	Hull KR (h)	W21-20 *(aet)*	t:Grace,Welsby,Walmsley g:Coote(4) fg:Fages	1st	N/A
19/9/20	Warrington (h) (CCQF) ●●●	L18-20	t:Lomax,Grace,Naiqama g:Coote(3)	N/A	N/A
29/9/20	Wigan (a) ●●●	W0-42	t:Walmsley,Welsby(2),Grace(2),Knowles,Bentley g:Coote(7)	1st	N/A
9/10/20	Wakefield (a) ●●	W16-20	t:McCarthy-Scarsbrook,Coote(2),Grace g:Coote(2)	1st	N/A
15/10/20	Wakefield (h) ●	W48-6	t:Roby(2),Makinson(3),Walmsley,Grace,Dodd,Naiqama g:Coote(6)	1st	N/A
23/10/20	Leeds (h)	W40-8	t:Simm(3),Taia,Fages,Naiqama,Smith g:Coote(6)	1st	N/A
26/10/20	Salford (a) ●●	L12-10	t:Eaves g:Dodd(3)	1st	N/A
30/10/20	Wigan (h)	L6-18	t:Coote g:Coote	2nd	N/A
20/11/20	Catalans Dragons (h) (SF)	W48-2	t:Coote(2),Naiqama(3),Lomax,Bentley,Grace g:Coote(8)	N/A	N/A
27/11/20	Wigan (GF) ●●●●	W8-4	t:Welsby g:Coote(2)	N/A	N/A

● *Played at Halliwell Jones Stadium, Warrington*
●● *Played at Emerald Headingley, Leeds*
●●● *Played at AJ Bell Stadium, Salford*
●●●● *Played at KCOM Stadium, Hull*

Catalans Dragons (a) (R20), Hull FC (h) (R21) and Warrington (h) (R22) games were cancelled

Toronto (a) (R5) game was later expunged from the Super League table (Player stats from this fixture are included in 'All' columns below)

		APP		TRIES		GOALS		FG		PTS	
	D.O.B.	ALL	SL	ALL	SL	ALL	SL	ALL	SL	ALL	SL
Kyle Amor	26/5/87	(16)	(15)	0	0	0	0	0	0	0	0
Jack Ashworth	3/7/95	(4)	(4)	0	0	0	0	0	0	0	0
Joe Batchelor	28/10/94	1(3)	1(3)	0	0	0	0	0	0	0	0
James Bentley	19/10/97	19	16	5	4	0	0	0	0	20	16
Lachlan Coote	6/4/90	16	15	10	10	73	70	0	0	186	180
Matthew Costello	9/4/98	7(1)	6(1)	2	2	0	0	0	0	8	8
Ben Davies	21/4/00	1	1	0	0	0	0	0	0	0	0
Lewis Dodd	27/1/02	1(2)	1(2)	1	1	3	3	0	0	10	10
Josh Eaves	20/10/97	1	1	1	1	0	0	0	0	4	4
Theo Fages	23/8/94	20	17	4	4	0	0	1	1	17	17
Matthew Foster	25/6/01	(1)	(1)	0	0	0	0	0	0	0	0
Regan Grace	12/12/96	20	18	12	11	0	0	0	0	48	44
James Graham	10/9/85	12	11	1	1	0	0	0	0	4	4
Morgan Knowles	5/11/96	18	15	2	2	0	0	0	0	8	8
Matty Lees	4/2/98	8(12)	8(9)	0	0	0	0	0	0	0	0
Jonny Lomax	4/9/90	21	18	4	1	0	0	0	0	16	4
Tommy Makinson	10/10/91	14	12	6	6	16	8	0	0	56	40
Louie McCarthy-Scarsbrook	14/1/86	4(16)	4(13)	4	3	0	0	0	0	16	12
Kevin Naiqama	4/2/89	21	18	9	8	0	0	0	0	36	32
Tom Nisbet	8/10/99	1	1	0	0	0	0	0	0	0	0
Joseph Paulo	2/1/88	1(7)	1(5)	0	0	0	0	0	0	0	0
Mark Percival	29/5/94	5	4	0	0	5	5	0	0	10	10
Dominique Peyroux	21/1/89	8(8)	6(8)	1	1	0	0	0	0	4	4
Nico Rizzelli	28/3/00	1	1	0	0	0	0	0	0	0	0
James Roby	22/11/85	17	14	2	2	0	0	0	0	8	8
Josh Simm	27/2/01	6	6	3	3	0	0	0	0	12	12
Aaron Smith	12/10/96	1(14)	1(11)	5	4	0	0	0	0	20	16
Zeb Taia	11/10/84	18(2)	15(2)	3	3	0	0	0	0	12	12
Luke Thompson	27/4/95	7	5	4	3	0	0	0	0	16	12
Alex Walmsley	10/4/90	20	17	10	9	0	0	0	0	40	36
Jack Welsby	17/3/01	17	14	9	9	0	0	0	0	36	36
Jake Wingfield	1/8/01	(1)	(1)	0	0	0	0	0	0	0	0

Regan Grace

'SL' totals include regular season & play-offs; 'All' totals also include Challenge Cup & World Club Challenge

5th October 2019 - 24-26 home win over Featherstone in Championship Grand Final secures Super League place.

5th November 2019 - Sonny Bill Williams joins on two-year contract.

22nd November 2019 - prop Brad Singleton signs from Leeds, three years, and halfback James Cunningham from London for next two seasons.

26th November 2019 - head coach Brian McDermott signs new five-year contract.

29th November 2019 - winger Liam Kay, prop Adam Sidlow and stand-off Blake Wallace sign new two-year contracts.

2nd December 2019 - Gary Wheeler, Andy Ackers, Gadwin Springer and Chase Stanley all re-sign on two-year deals. Josh McCrone extends for one year.

3rd December 2019 - second-rower Bodene Thompson and utility Hakim Miloudi extend contracts for another season.

19th January 2020 - 18-10 friendly win at Castleford.

2nd February 2020 - 28-10 round-one home defeat to Castleford at Headingley.

8th February 2020 - Gary Wheeler scores twice in 24-16 round-two defeat at Salford.

13th February 2020 - Gareth O'Brien makes seasonal bow, Sonny Bill Williams misses 32-10 defeat at Wigan.

19th February 2020 - Tony Gigot arrives on four-week trial.

20th February 2020 - director of rugby Brian Noble leaves the Wolfpack.

21st February 2020 - 32-22 defeat at Warrington after fighting back to 22-all. Greg Worthington recalled from Featherstone loan.

26th February 2020 - young forwards Ben Kilner and Jack Wells sign from Wigan on one-month loan deals.

29th February 2020 - Jack Wells makes debut during 32-0 defeat to St Helens in home game played at Warrington.

5th March 2020 - 66-12 defeat at Leeds.

10th March 2020 - 20-year-old Canadian Quinn Ngawati re-signs for Wolfpack.

11th March 2020 - Joe Mellor and Chase Stanley return as Ricky Leutele scores two tries in shock 18-0 Challenge Cup win at Huddersfield.

16th March 2020 - season suspended until April 3rd because of coronavirus crisis.

KEY DATES

21st May 2020 - England international centre Kallum Watkins signs on three-year deal, effective immediately, after release by Gold Coast.

4th June 2020 - hooker Andy Ackers joins Salford with immediate effect.

16th July 2020 - Liam Kay joins Wakefield.

16th July 2020 - revised Super League fixture list means no home games staged in Toronto.

20th July 2020 - Wolfpack withdraw from competitions for 2020 and tell players to seek other contracts.

3rd August 2020 - Super League terminates Wolfpack's Super League Participation Agreement for the 2020 season

7th August 2020 - four bids fielded for purchase of club.

13th August 2020 - back row Bodene Thompson signs for Leeds on loan for rest of season.

5th September 2020 - Sonny Bill Williams makes second debut for Sydney Roosters.

5th September 2020 - Blake Wallace leaves Wolfpack for Leigh Centurions.

25th September 2020 - prospective new owner Carlo LiVolsi given four weeks by SLE to re-apply for Super League membership.

2nd November 2020 - Wolfpack's application to re-enter Super League for 2021 season rejected.

2nd November 2020 - Sonny Bill Williams, Chase Stanley, Josh McCrone, Ricky Leutele, Darcy Lussick, Tom Olbison, Andrew Dixon, Adam Sidlow, Ryan Hall, Stevie Ward, Ben Flower and Paul Brearley leave as free agents.

CLUB RECORDS

Highest score: 82-6 v Doncaster, 9/4/2017
Highest score against:
10-66 v Warrington, 13/5/2018;
12-66 v Leeds, 5/3/2020
Record attendance:
9,974 v Featherstone, 5/10/2019

MATCH RECORDS

Tries: 5 Liam Kay v York, 1/7/2017
Goals: 13 Craig Hall v Doncaster, 9/4/2017
Points: 38 Craig Hall v Hemel, 15/7/2017

SEASON RECORDS

Tries:
27 Liam Kay 2017; Matty Russell 2019
Goals: 171 Craig Hall 2017
Points: 442 Craig Hall 2017

CAREER RECORDS

Tries: 66 Liam Kay 2017-2020
Goals:
177 *(inc 2fg)* Gareth O'Brien 2018-2020
Points: 484 Gareth O'Brien 2018-2020
Appearances: 80 Adam Sidlow 2017-2020

TORONTO
WOLFPACK

TORONTO WOLFPACK

DATE	FIXTURE	RESULT	SCORERS	LGE	ATT
2/2/20	Castleford (h) ●	L10-28	t:Kay,Miloudi g:Wallace	9th	N/A
8/2/20	Salford (a)	L24-16	t:Wheeler(2),Singleton g:Wallace(2)	11th	4,593
13/2/20	Wigan (a)	L32-10	t:Russell,Thompson g:Wallace	12th	10,333
21/2/20	Warrington (a)	L32-22	t:Wilkin,Ackers,Russell,O'Brien g:Wallace(3)	12th	11,182
29/2/20	St Helens (h) ●●	L0-32		12th	4,000
5/3/20	Leeds (a)	L66-12	t:McCrone,Wells g:O'Brien(2)	12th	12,143
11/3/20	Huddersfield (h) (CCR5) ●●●	W18-0	t:Leutele(2) g:O'Brien(5)	N/A	1,488

● Played at Emerald Headingley, Leeds
●● Played at Halliwell Jones Stadium, Warrington
●●● Played at John Smith's Stadium

		APP		TRIES		GOALS		FG		PTS	
	D.O.B.	ALL	SL	ALL	SL	ALL	SL	ALL	SL	ALL	SL
Andy Ackers	25/12/93	6	5	1	1	0	0	0	0	4	4
James Cunningham	3/4/94	2(1)	2(1)	0	0	0	0	0	0	0	0
Andrew Dixon	28/2/90	2(1)	1(1)	0	0	0	0	0	0	0	0
Tony Gigot	27/12/90	2(1)	2(1)	0	0	0	0	0	0	0	0
Liam Kay	17/12/91	7	6	1	1	0	0	0	0	4	4
Ricky Leutele	10/4/90	7	6	2	0	0	0	0	0	8	0
Josh McCrone	12/4/87	7	6	1	1	0	0	0	0	4	4
Joe Mellor	28/11/90	3	2	0	0	0	0	0	0	0	0
Hakim Miloudi	26/6/93	6(1)	5(1)	1	1	0	0	0	0	4	4
Anthony Mullally	28/6/91	2(5)	2(4)	0	0	0	0	0	0	0	0
Gareth O'Brien	31/10/91	5	4	1	1	7	2	0	0	18	8
Tom Olbison	20/3/91	4(3)	3(3)	0	0	0	0	0	0	0	0
Matty Russell	6/6/93	6	6	2	2	0	0	0	0	8	8
Adam Sidlow	25/10/87	4(3)	3(3)	0	0	0	0	0	0	0	0
Brad Singleton	29/10/92	3(1)	3(1)	1	1	0	0	0	0	4	4
Gadwin Springer	4/4/93	5(1)	4(1)	0	0	0	0	0	0	0	0
Chase Stanley	31/5/89	1	0	0	0	0	0	0	0	0	0
Bodene Thompson	1/8/88	5(1)	4(1)	1	1	0	0	0	0	4	4
Blake Wallace	18/6/92	5(1)	5(1)	0	0	7	7	0	0	14	14
Jack Wells	21/9/97	(2)	(2)	1	1	0	0	0	0	4	4
Gary Wheeler	30/9/89	(2)	(2)	2	2	0	0	0	0	8	8
Jon Wilkin	11/1/83	5	5	1	1	0	0	0	0	4	4
Sonny Bill Williams	3/8/85	4(1)	4(1)	0	0	0	0	0	0	0	0
Greg Worthington	17/7/90	(1)	(1)	0	0	0	0	0	0	0	0

Sonny Bill Williams

'SL' totals include Super League games only; 'All' totals also include Challenge Cup

KEY DATES

25th October 2019 - Jay Pitts signs from London Broncos on two-year deal.

6th November 2019 - prop Adam Tangata signs season-long loan deal from Halifax.

10th November 2019 - loose forward Brad Walker joins from Widnes on two-year deal.

26th December 2019 - 30-4 defeat at Leeds in Boxing Day friendly.

6th January 2020 - Ben Jones-Bishop set for spell on sidelines with undisclosed medical condition.

27th January 2020 - Wigan prop Romain Navarrete joins on season-long loan.

31st January 2020 - Danny Brough suffers knee injury in 30-12 round-one defeat at Hull KR.

9th February 2020 - round-two home game with Catalans postponed because of Storm Ciara.

16th February 2020 - two tries in last ten minutes secure 18-8 home win over Warrington.

21st February 2020 - Joe Arundel suffers season-ending ACL and Ryan Hampshire broken jaw in 32-15 defeat at Castleford.

1st March 2020 - 22-12 win at Salford.

6th March 2020 - Marc Sneyd golden-point field goal means 27-26 home defeat to Hull FC.

13th March 2020 - Danny Brough and David Fifita return from injury in scratchy 17-14 home Challenge Cup win over Bradford.

16th March 2020 - season suspended until April 3rd because of coronavirus crisis.

7th June 2020 - prop George King signs for Hull KR for 2021 after turning down contract offer.

9th July 2020 - Danny Brough to leave for Bradford at end of 2020 season.

16th July 2020 - Liam Kay re-signs for two years from 2021 and on loan for rest of 2020 season.

23rd July 2020 - winger Lee Kershaw signs one-year contract for 2021.

23rd July 2020 - former Catalans utility back Tony Gigot signs until end of 2021.

9th August 2020 - Tom Johnstone scores wonder try and Liam Kay, on second debut, a late double as late Harry Smith field goal means 23-22 defeat to Wigan at Headingley.

15th August 2020 - 58-0 hammering by Catalans at St Helens.

19th August 2020 - Huddersfield winger Innes Senior joins on one-month loan.

22nd August 2020 - 36-24 Challenge Cup round five defeat by Catalans at Huddersfield.

28th August 2020 - Jay Pitts and Alex Walker self-isolate for 14 days after positive Covid tests in Catalans camp. Liam Kay self isolates due to domestic situation. David Fifita stood down for refusing to wear GPS tracking system.

30th August 2020 - 36-0 round 10 defeat by Warrington at Halliwell Jones.

1st September 2020 - two unnamed players test positive for Covid. Following Thursday fixture against Leeds postponed.

7th September 2020 - results of latest round of squad testing for Covid-19, following recent positive tests, all negative and training resumes.

10th September 2020 - 26-23 defeat to Hull FC at St Helens.

11th September 2020 - prop Eddie Battye joins on loan from London Broncos until end of season.

13th September 2020 - former player Willie Poching to become assistant coach from November 1st.

17th September 2020 - 29-6 defeat in 'home' fixture at Huddersfield Giants.

26th September 2020 - 28-16 defeat to Wigan at Warrington.

4th October 2020 - 40-8 defeat to Catalans in Perpignan after leading 8-0 on 30 minutes.

9th October 2020 - 20-16 defeat to St Helens at Headingley after leading 10-0 on 30 minutes.

15th October 2020 - 48-6 defeat by St Helens at Warrington.

22nd October 2020 - late Tom Johnstone try secures 18-14 win over Huddersfield at St Helens, ending losing league run at ten games.

25th October 2020 - Ben Jones-Bishop scores hat-trick in 48-18 win over Hull KR in first game back at Belle Vue.

29th October 2020 - Max Jowitt gets hat-trick in 30-6 win over Leeds at St Helens.

1st November 2020 - late Brad Dwyer try means 20-18 home defeat to Leeds in fourth game in ten days.

3rd November 2020 - League-wide regular season brought to a halt.

6th November 2020 - 28-20 defeat by Salford at Headingley. Trinity finish in tenth spot.

13th November 2020 - Kelepi Tanginoa signs new contract to end of 2024 season.

25th November 2020 - 26-year-old Samoa stand-off Mason Lino signs from Newcastle Knights on three-year deal.

CLUB RECORDS

Highest score:
90-12 v Highfield, 27/10/92
Highest score against:
0-86 v Castleford, 17/4/95
Record attendance:
30,676 v Huddersfield, 26/2/21

MATCH RECORDS

Tries:
7 Fred Smith v Keighley, 25/4/59
Keith Slater v Hunslet, 6/2/71
Goals:
13 Mark Conway v Highfield, 27/10/92
Points:
36 Jamie Rooney v Chorley, 27/2/2004

SEASON RECORDS

Tries: 38 Fred Smith 1959-60
David Smith 1973-74
Goals: 163 Neil Fox 1961-62
Points: 407 Neil Fox 1961-62

CAREER RECORDS

Tries: 272 Neil Fox 1956-74
Goals: 1,836 Neil Fox 1956-74
Points: 4,488 Neil Fox 1956-74
Appearances:
605 Harry Wilkinson 1930-49

WAKEFIELD TRINITY

DATE	FIXTURE	RESULT	SCORERS	LGE	ATT
31/1/20	Hull KR (a)	L30-12	t:Westerman,J Wood g:Brough,Hampshire	8th	8,492
16/2/20	Warrington (h)	W18-8	t:Ashurst,Johnstone g:Hampshire(5)	9th	5,197
21/2/20	Castleford (a)	L32-15	t:Westerman,Johnstone g:Hampshire(3) fg:Miller	9th	7,202
1/3/20	Salford (a)	W12-22	t:Jowitt,Johnstone,Tupou,Tanginoa g:Jowitt(3)	8th	3,801
6/3/20	Hull FC (h)	L26-27 (aet)	t:Atkins(2),Pitts,Johnstone(2) g:Jowitt(3)	9th	5,528
13/3/20	Bradford (h) (CCR5)	W17-14	t:Westerman,A Walker,Lyne g:Brough(2) fg:Miller	N/A	3,112
9/8/20	Wigan (h) ●	L22-23	t:K Wood,Johnstone,Kay(2) g:Gigot(2),Jowitt	9th	N/A
15/8/20	Catalans Dragons (h) ●●	L0-58		10th	N/A
22/8/20	Catalans Dragons (a) (CCR6) ●●●	L36-24	t:Pitts(2),Arona,Miller g:Hampshire(4)	N/A	N/A
30/8/20	Warrington (a)	L36-0		10th	N/A
10/9/20	Hull FC (a) ●●	L26-23	t:Jowitt(2),Tanginoa(2) g:Hampshire(3) fg:Hampshire	10th	N/A
17/9/20	Huddersfield (h) ●●●	L6-29	t:Tanginoa g:Hampshire	11th	N/A
25/9/20	Wigan (a) ●●●●	L28-16	t:Miller,Arona,Johnstone g:Gigot(2)	11th	N/A
4/10/20	Catalans Dragons (a)	L40-8	t:Tupou g:Gigot(2)	11th	5,000
9/10/20	St Helens (h) ●	L16-20	t:A Walker,Kopczak,Ashurst g:Hampshire(2)	11th	N/A
15/10/20	St Helens (a) ●●●●	L48-6	t:Senior g:Hampshire	11th	N/A
22/10/20	Huddersfield (a) ●●	W14-18	t:Ashurst,Johnstone(2) g:Hampshire(3)	11th	N/A
25/10/20	Hull KR (h)	W48-18	t:Gigot,Lyne(2),Jones-Bishop(3),Tangata,Hampshire,Battye g:Hampshire(6)	10th	N/A
29/10/20	Leeds (a) ●●	W6-30	t:Jowitt(3),Fifita,Senior(2) g:Hampshire(3)	10th	N/A
1/11/20	Leeds (h)	L18-20	t:Kershaw,Westerman,Senior g:Hampshire(3)	10th	N/A
6/11/20	Salford (h) ●	L20-28	t:Hampshire(2),Tanginoa(2) g:Hampshire(2)	10th	N/A

● Played at Emerald Headingley, Leeds
●● Played at Totally Wicked Stadium, St Helens
●●● Played at John Smith's Stadium, Huddersfield
●●●● Played at Halliwell Jones Stadium, Warrington

Castleford (h) (R22) game was cancelled

		APP		TRIES		GOALS		FG		PTS	
	D.O.B.	ALL	SL	ALL	SL	ALL	SL	ALL	SL	ALL	SL
Tinirau Arona	8/5/89	11(1)	9(1)	2	1	0	0	0	0	8	4
Joe Arundel	22/8/91	2	2	0	0	0	0	0	0	0	0
Matty Ashurst	1/11/89	14(1)	12(1)	3	3	0	0	0	0	12	12
Ryan Atkins	7/10/85	4	3	2	2	0	0	0	0	8	8
Yusuf Aydin	13/9/00	1(2)	1(2)	0	0	0	0	0	0	0	0
Connor Bailey	10/10/00	3(2)	3(2)	0	0	0	0	0	0	0	0
James Batchelor	9/4/98	6(3)	6(3)	0	0	0	0	0	0	0	0
Eddie Battye	24/7/91	2(6)	2(6)	1	1	0	0	0	0	4	4
Harry Bowes	7/9/01	1(1)	1(1)	0	0	0	0	0	0	0	0
Danny Brough	15/1/83	2	1	0	0	3	1	0	0	6	2
Jack Croft	21/12/00	6	5	0	0	0	0	0	0	0	0
Jordan Crowther	19/2/97	7(4)	7(3)	0	0	0	0	0	0	0	0
David Fifita	28/6/89	3(8)	2(7)	1	1	0	0	0	0	4	4
Tony Gigot	27/12/90	6(1)	6(1)	1	1	6	6	0	0	16	16
Chris Green	3/1/90	3(7)	3(6)	0	0	0	0	0	0	0	0
Titus Gwaze	8/6/99	(1)	(1)	0	0	0	0	0	0	0	0
Ryan Hampshire	29/12/94	15	14	3	3	37	33	1	1	87	79
Tom Johnstone	13/8/95	14	13	9	9	0	0	0	0	36	36
Ben Jones-Bishop	24/8/88	8	8	3	3	0	0	0	0	12	12
Max Jowitt	6/5/97	14	13	6	6	7	7	0	0	38	38
Liam Kay	17/12/91	3	3	2	2	0	0	0	0	8	8
Lee Kershaw	2/5/99	2	2	1	1	0	0	0	0	4	4
George King	24/2/95	1(2)	1(1)	0	0	0	0	0	0	0	0
Danny Kirmond	11/11/85	(3)	(3)	0	0	0	0	0	0	0	0
Craig Kopczak	20/12/86	12(2)	12(1)	1	1	0	0	0	0	4	4
Reece Lyne	2/12/92	18	17	3	2	0	0	0	0	12	8
Jacob Miller	22/8/92	15	13	2	1	0	0	2	1	10	5
Romain Navarrete	30/6/94	3(8)	3(7)	0	0	0	0	0	0	0	0
Jay Pitts	9/12/89	14	12	3	1	0	0	0	0	12	4
Innes Senior	30/5/00	8	7	4	4	0	0	0	0	16	16
Adam Tangata	17/3/91	(11)	(11)	1	1	0	0	0	0	4	4
Kelepi Tanginoa	1/3/94	17(4)	16(3)	6	6	0	0	0	0	24	24
Bill Tupou	2/7/90	17	15	2	2	0	0	0	0	8	8
Alex Walker	4/9/95	9	7	2	1	0	0	0	0	8	4
Brad Walker	30/1/98	1(2)	1(2)	0	0	0	0	0	0	0	0
Joe Westerman	15/11/89	17	15	4	3	0	0	0	0	16	12
Josh Wood	15/11/95	6(5)	6(4)	1	1	0	0	0	0	4	4
Kyle Wood	18/6/89	8(10)	6(10)	1	1	0	0	0	0	4	4

Kelepi Tanginoa

'SL' totals include Super League games only; 'All' totals also include Challenge Cup

17th November 2019 - England Academy pair Josh Thewlis and Ellis Longstaff agree full-time contracts until November 2022.

9th January 2020 - marquee signing Gareth Widdop to miss start of season after injuring ankle in training.

21st January 2020 - Gold Coast prop forward Leilani Latu joins on two-year deal until November 2021.

23rd January 2020 - 26-10 home win over Salford in Mike Cooper Testimonial.

29th January 2020 - Jack Hughes undergoes double hernia operation.

30th January 2020 - Chris Hill sent off after 23 minutes of 16-10 opening-round defeat at Wigan. Matt Ashton makes impressive debut.

3rd February 2020 - Chris Hill gets three-match penalty notice for high tackle on Sam Powell.

5th February 2020 - Stefan Ratchford agrees new contract to end of 2022 season.

6th February 2020 - 19-0 home win over St Helens.

12th February 2020 - Anthony Gelling suspended after arrest on suspicion of wounding.

16th February 2020 - Gareth Widdop makes debut and Matt Ashton left out of 18-8 defeat at Wakefield.

21st February 2020 - Matty Ashton returns at fullback in 32-22 home win over Toronto but injures hamstring.

28th February 2020 - Chris Hill returns from suspension and Keanan Brand makes debut in 36-0 hammering at Leeds.

5th March 2020 - Matty Ashton undergoes hamstring surgery.

6th March 2020 - late Blake Austin field goal secures 9-8 home win over Castleford.

8th March 2020 - Ben Murdoch-Masila to join NZ Warriors at end of season.

12th March 2020 - Gareth Widdop and Blake Austin both score try-braces in 38-4 round-7 win at Hull FC.

16th March 2020 - season suspended until April 3rd because of coronavirus crisis.

19th May 2020 - Greg Inglis comes out of retirement to sign one-year deal for 2021.

8th August 2020 - 40-10 round-8 win over Hull KR at Headingley in first post-lockdown game.

KEY DATES

15th August 2020 - Blake Austin kicks late field goal to seal 19-18 win over Huddersfield at St Helens.

18th August 2020 - Academy captain Ellis Robson signs for Ottawa Aces for 2021.

30th August 2020 - Blake Austin scores hat-trick in 36-0 defeat of Wakefield at Halliwell Jones.

4th September 2020 - 37-12 win over Hull FC at Headingley, despite seven players stood down due to Covid protocols.

10th September 2020 - spectacular late Matty Ashton try seals 12-10 win over Castleford at St Helens.

13th September 2020 - centre Luther Burrell released after eight appearances since joining from Northampton RUFC midway through 2019 season.

14th September 2020 - Tom Lineham suspended for eight matches after being found guilty of grabbing testicles of opponent in win over Castleford.

19th September 2020 - 20-18 Challenge Cup quarter-final win over St Helens at Salford.

25th September 2020 - 30-16 win over Catalans at Halliwell Jones Stadium.

29th September 2020 - late Krisnan Inu penalty means 20-18 defeat for youthful side at AJ Bell Stadium.

3rd October 2020 - late Joey Lussick try means 24-22 Challenge Cup semi-final defeat to Salford.

9th October 2020 - late Liam Farrell try means 18-14 defeat to Wigan.

13th October 2020 - 32-6 win over weakened Leeds team at Halliwell Jones Stadium regains top-four place in table.

23rd October 2020 - forward Ellis Robson now to stay with Wolves until end of 2022 season.

24th October 2020 - Monday fixture in Perpignan cancelled because of Covid cases in Dragons camp.

28th October 2020 - Salford unable to fulfil Friday fixture with Warrington due to player availability issues. Wolves awarded 24-0 victory. Huddersfield new opponents.

30th October 2020 - Daryl Clark double in 19-12 win over Huddersfield at St Helens. Josh Charnley dislocates shoulder.

3rd November 2020 - League-wide regular season brought to a halt. Wolves finish third and enter re-modelled six-team play-offs.

12th November 2020 - 27-14 Elimination Play-off defeat at home to Hull FC ends season.

24th November 2020 - London Broncos prop Rob Butler signs on two-year contract.

CLUB RECORDS

Highest score:
112-0 v Swinton, 20/5/2011
Highest score against:
12-84 v Bradford, 9/9/2001
Record attendance:
34,404 v Wigan, 22/1/49 *(Wilderspool)*
15,008 v Widnes, 25/3/2016
(Halliwell Jones Stadium)

MATCH RECORDS

Tries:
7 Brian Bevan v Leigh, 29/3/48
Brian Bevan v Bramley, 22/4/53
Goals:
16 Lee Briers v Swinton, 20/5/2011
Points:
44 Lee Briers v Swinton, 20/5/2011

SEASON RECORDS

Tries: 66 Brian Bevan 1952-53
Goals: 170 Steve Hesford 1978-79
Points: 363 Harry Bath 1952-53

CAREER RECORDS

Tries: 740 Brian Bevan 1945-62
Goals: 1,159 Steve Hesford 1975-85
Points: 2,586 Lee Briers 1997-2013
Appearances: 620 Brian Bevan 1945-62

WARRINGTON WOLVES

DATE	FIXTURE	RESULT	SCORERS	LGE	ATT
30/1/20	Wigan (a)	L16-10	t:Murdoch-Masila g:Ratchford(3)	7th	15,040
6/2/20	St Helens (h)	W19-0	t:D Clark,Lineham,Charnley g:Ratchford(3) fg:Austin	5th	12,562
16/2/20	Wakefield (a)	L18-8	t:Ratchford g:Ratchford(2)	7th	5,197
21/2/20	Toronto (h)	W32-22	t:Charnley,Widdop,Lineham,Ashton,Murdoch-Masila g:Ratchford(6)	6th	11,182
28/2/20	Leeds (a)	L36-0		9th	12,134
6/3/20	Castleford (h)	W9-8	t:Lineham g:Ratchford(2) fg:Austin	8th	9,228
12/3/20	Hull FC (a)	W4-38	t:Austin(2),Lineham,Widdop(2),Gelling,Murdoch-Masila g:Ratchford(4),Widdop	4th	10,214
8/8/20	Hull KR (h) ●	W40-10	t:Lineham(2),Akauola,Gelling,Charnley,Widdop,Ratchford g:Ratchford(5),Widdop	3rd	N/A
15/8/20	Huddersfield (a) ●●	W18-19	t:Currie,Widdop,Lineham g:Ratchford(3) fg:Austin	4th	N/A
30/8/20	Wakefield (h)	W36-0	t:King,Austin(3),Charnley,Currie g:Ratchford(6)	3rd	N/A
4/9/20	Hull FC (h) ●	W37-12	t:Cooper,Ashton,Mamo(2),Latu,Austin g:Ratchford(5),Patton fg:Austin	2nd	N/A
10/9/20	Castleford (a) ●●	W10-12	t:Gelling,Ashton g:Ratchford(2)	2nd	N/A
19/9/20	St Helens (a) (CCQF) ●●●	W18-20	t:Gelling,Charnley(2),Ashton g:Ratchford(2)	N/A	N/A
25/9/20	Catalans Dragons (h)	W30-16	t:Gelling,Ashton,Davis,Austin,Walker g:Widdop(5)	1st	N/A
29/9/20	Salford (a)	L20-18	t:Roebuck,Thewlis,Dean g:Patton(3)	2nd	N/A
3/10/20	Salford (CCSF) ●●	W24-22	t:King,Austin,Murdoch-Masila g:Ratchford(2),Widdop(3)	N/A	N/A
9/10/20	Wigan (h) ●	L14-18	t:Ashton,Hill g:Ratchford(3)	5th	N/A
13/10/20	Leeds (h)	W32-6	t:King,Ashton(2),Currie,D Clark g:Ratchford(6)	3rd	N/A
30/10/20	Huddersfield (h) ●●	W19-12	t:D Clark(2),Gelling g:Ratchford(3) fg:Widdop	3rd	N/A
12/11/20	Hull FC (h) (EPO)	L14-27	t:Ashton(2),Gelling g:Ratchford	N/A	N/A

● *Played at Emerald Headingley, Leeds*
●● *Played at Totally Wicked Stadium, St Helens*
●●● *Played at AJ Bell Stadium, Salford*

Catalans Dragons (a) (R18), Hull KR (a) (R20) and St Helens (a) (R22) games were cancelled

Salford (h) (R19) game ruled a 24-0 victory after the Red Devils were unable to field a team

Toronto (h) (R4) game was later expunged from the Super League table (Player stats from this fixture are included in 'All' columns below)

		APP		TRIES		GOALS		FG		PTS	
	D.O.B.	ALL	SL	ALL	SL	ALL	SL	ALL	SL	ALL	SL
Sitaleki Akauola	7/4/92	1(8)	1(8)	1	1	0	0	0	0	4	4
Matty Ashton	28/7/98	10(3)	7(3)	10	8	0	0	0	0	40	32
Blake Austin	1/2/91	18	15	8	7	0	0	4	4	36	32
Keanan Brand	8/1/99	3	3	0	0	0	0	0	0	0	0
Luther Burrell	6/12/87	(5)	(4)	0	0	0	0	0	0	0	0
Josh Charnley	26/6/91	19	16	6	3	0	0	0	0	24	12
Daryl Clark	10/2/93	15(3)	12(3)	4	4	0	0	0	0	16	16
Jason Clark	28/6/89	15(2)	13(1)	0	0	0	0	0	0	0	0
Mike Cooper	15/9/88	17	14	1	1	0	0	0	0	4	4
Ben Currie	15/7/94	19	16	3	3	0	0	0	0	12	12
Matt Davis	5/7/96	1(11)	1(9)	1	1	0	0	0	0	4	4
Riley Dean	10/8/01	1	1	1	1	0	0	0	0	4	4
Eribe Doro	26/3/01	(2)	(2)	0	0	0	0	0	0	0	0
Anthony Gelling	18/10/90	13	11	7	6	0	0	0	0	28	24
Chris Hill	3/11/87	14	12	1	1	0	0	0	0	4	4
Jack Hughes	4/1/92	10	8	0	0	0	0	0	0	0	0
Luis Johnson	20/2/99	1(5)	1(4)	0	0	0	0	0	0	0	0
Samy Kibula	7/8/99	(2)	(2)	0	0	0	0	0	0	0	0
Toby King	9/7/96	19	16	3	2	0	0	0	0	12	8
Leilani Latu	5/2/93	3	3	1	1	0	0	0	0	4	4
Tom Lineham	21/9/91	12	11	7	6	0	0	0	0	28	24
Ellis Longstaff	5/7/02	1(1)	1(1)	0	0	0	0	0	0	0	0
Jake Mamo	6/6/94	9(2)	7(2)	2	2	0	0	0	0	8	8
Ben Murdoch-Masila	7/2/91	9(5)	8(3)	4	2	0	0	0	0	16	8
Dec Patton	23/5/95	3(1)	3(1)	0	0	4	4	0	0	8	8
Joe Philbin	16/11/94	4(12)	3(10)	0	0	0	0	0	0	0	0
Stefan Ratchford	19/7/88	18	15	2	2	58	48	0	0	124	104
Ellis Robson	14/9/98	2(2)	2(2)	0	0	0	0	0	0	0	0
Nathan Roebuck	2/10/99	1	1	1	1	0	0	0	0	4	4
Kyle Shelford	13/9/96	(1)	(1)	0	0	0	0	0	0	0	0
Josh Thewlis	30/4/02	2	2	1	1	0	0	0	0	4	4
Danny Walker	29/6/99	5(11)	5(8)	1	1	0	0	0	0	4	4
Gareth Widdop	12/3/89	14	12	5	4	10	7	1	1	41	31
Connor Wrench	4/10/01	1	1	0	0	0	0	0	0	0	0

Matty Ashton

'SL' totals include regular season & play-offs; 'All' totals also include Challenge Cup

26th October 2019 - Oliver Gildart dislocates shoulder in Great Britain defeat by Tonga.

7th November 2019 - winger Tom Davies leaves to join Catalans.

8th November 2019 - London Broncos' Academy forward Kai Pearce-Paul signs four-year deal

15th November 2019 - Sean O'Loughlin signs one-year contract extension.

3rd December 2019 - Josh Woods and Craig Mullen loaned to Leigh for 2020 season.

5th December 2019 - Jarrod Sammut signs for Leigh.

19th January 2020 - 22-10 home defeat by Leeds in Liam Farrell Testimonial game.

27th January 2020 - prop Liam Byrne signs new four-year deal to end of 2023. Romain Navarrete joins Wakefield on season-long loan.

30th January 2020 - tough 16-10 round-one, home win over Warrington.

4th February 2020 - former prop Gabe Hamlin, sacked in 2019, suspended by WADA for two years for cocaine use.

7th February 2020 - halfback Harry Smith makes first start in 16-12 round-two defeat at Castleford.

13th February 2020 - Mitch Clark makes debut in 32-10 home win over Toronto.

23rd February 2020 - Dom Manfredi scores try on return in 26-12 home win over Hull FC.

25th February 2020 - Joe Greenwood goes to Leeds on two-month loan deal.

26th February 2020 - young forwards Ben Kilner and Jack Wells join Toronto Wolfpack on one-month loan.

1st March 2020 - Liam Marshall scores hat-trick in 42-10 win at unbeaten Huddersfield.

8th March 2020 - Ben Flower sin-binned in return from injury as Jackson Hastings scores brace in hard-fought 30-16 home win over Hull KR.

11th March 2020 - winger Liam Marshall signs contract extension to 2023, with option for 2024.

13th March 2020 - 18-14 defeat at Salford after leading 14-2.

16th March 2020 - season suspended until April 3rd because of coronavirus crisis.

15th June 2020 - Morgan Escaré ends contract by mutual consent and signs for Salford.

3rd July 2020 - John Bateman re-signs from Canberra Raiders for 2021 season on four-year deal with option for fifth year.

9th August 2020 - Harry Smith kicks late field goal to secure 23-22 win over Wakefield at Headingley as season restarts at round 8.

KEY DATES

16th August 2020 - Bevan French nets try-double and Liam Farrell scores 100th try for Wigan in 28-10 win over Leeds at St Helens.

25th August 2020 - round-18 clash with Castleford brought forward after scheduled opponents Catalans report four positive tests in routine Covid-19 testing.

29th August 2020 - winger Liam Marshall suffers season-ending knee injury in 30-22 win over Castleford at Warrington.

31st August 2020 - Morgan Smithies cops two-match penalty notice for head-butting in win over Castleford.

1st September 2020 - Morgan Smithies gets further four-match suspension after pleading guilty to dangerous contact with Tigers' James Clare.

3rd September 2020 - Oliver Gildart makes return from dislocated shoulder for first game of season in 34-18 defeat to Hull KR at Headingley.

8th September 2020 - Ben Flower banned for two matches for dangerous contact with Hull KR's George Lawler. Appeal fails.

12th September 2020 - Joe Burgess scores try-double in 28-12 win in Perpignan in first crowd-attended game since lockdown.

16th September 2020 - young prop Ethan Havard signs new deal until end of 2022, with option for 2023.

17th September 2020 - Toronto Wolfpack prop Brad Singleton signs on three-year deal.

19th September 2020 - try-braces from Bevan French and Liam Farrell in 36-4 Challenge Cup quarter-final win over Hull FC at Salford.

25th September 2020 - Bevan French double in 28-16 win over Wakefield at Warrington, after trailing 12-0.

29th September 2020 - Harry Smith captains side with six debutants in 42-0 defeat by St Helens at Salford.

3rd October 2020 - 26-12 Challenge Cup semi-final defeat to Leeds at rain-soaked St Helens.

8th October 2020 - three unnamed players test positive for Covid-19 and go into self-isolation.

9th October 2020 - late Liam Farrell try secures 18-14 win over Warrington at Leeds. Morgan Smithies returns from suspension. Brad Singleton makes debut.

14th October 2020 - three members of support staff test positive for Covid-19. Scheduled game against Catalans postponed.

23rd October 2020 - Bevan French hat-trick in 58-12 win over Salford at St Helens.

30th October 2020 - 18-6 win at St Helens sees Warriors go top after top quality game.

1st November 2020 - Bevan French signs new one-year contract, with further option for 2022.

2nd November 2020 - Joe Greenwood gets two-match penalty notice for high tackle on St Helens' Matty Lees.

3rd November 2020 - League-wide regular season brought to a halt.

6th November 2020 - 19-6 win over Huddersfield at Headingley. Warriors crowned League Leaders and enter re-modelled six-team play-offs.

9th November 2020 - 23-year-old halfback Jai Field signs from Parramatta on two-year deal

11th November 2020 - Jackson Hastings signs new one-year contract.

13th November 2020 - Sean O'Loughlin confirms he will retire at end of season.

19th November 2020 - 29-2 play-off semi-final win over Hull FC.

27th November 2020 - dramatic last second Jack Welsby try means 8-4 Grand Final defeat by St Helens.

CLUB RECORDS
Highest score: 116-0 v Flimby & Fothergill, 14/2/25 **Highest score against:** 0-75 v St Helens, 26/6/2005 **Record attendance:** 47,747 v St Helens, 27/3/59 *(Central Park)* 25,004 v St Helens, 25/3/2005 *(JJB/DW Stadium)*

MATCH RECORDS
Tries: 10 Martin Offiah v Leeds, 10/5/92 Shaun Edwards v Swinton, 29/9/92 **Goals:** 22 Jim Sullivan v Flimby & Fothergill, 14/2/25 **Points:** 44 Jim Sullivan v Flimby & Fothergill, 14/2/25

SEASON RECORDS
Tries: 62 Johnny Ring 1925-26 **Goals:** 186 Frano Botica 1994-95 **Points:** 462 Pat Richards 2010

CAREER RECORDS
Tries: 478 Billy Boston 1953-68 **Goals:** 2,317 Jim Sullivan 1921-46 **Points:** 4,883 Jim Sullivan 1921-46 **Appearances:** 774 Jim Sullivan 1921-46

WIGAN WARRIORS

DATE	FIXTURE	RESULT	SCORERS	LGE	ATT
30/1/20	Warrington (h)	W16-10	t:French,Powell,Marshall g:Hardaker(2)	6th	15,040
7/2/20	Castleford (a)	L16-12	t:Byrne,J Burgess g:Hardaker(2)	7th	8,848
13/2/20	Toronto (h)	W32-10	t:Smith,French(2),J Burgess,Farrell(2) g:Hardaker(4)	2nd	10,333
23/2/20	Hull FC (h)	W26-12	t:French,Manfredi,Hastings,Isa g:Hardaker(5)	2nd	12,005
1/3/20	Huddersfield (a)	W10-42	t:Isa,Marshall(3),Powell,Manfredi,Partington,G Burgess g:Hardaker(5)	1st	6,574
8/3/20	Hull KR (h)	W30-16	t:Hastings(2),Farrell,Powell,Marshall g:Hardaker(5)	1st	11,511
13/3/20	Salford (a)	L18-14	t:Hastings,Powell g:Hankinson(3)	1st	4,796
9/8/20	Wakefield (a) ●	W22-23	t:Hardaker,French,Marshall,Bibby g:Hardaker(3) fg:Smith	1st	N/A
16/8/20	Leeds (h) ●●	W28-10	t:Farrell,French(2),Manfredi,Bibby g:Hardaker(4)	1st	N/A
29/8/20	Castleford (h) ●●●	W30-22	t:Powell,J Burgess,Flower,Farrell,Bullock g:Hardaker(5)	1st	N/A
3/9/20	Hull KR (a) ●	L34-18	t:Powell,Smith,Hastings g:Hardaker(3)	3rd	N/A
12/9/20	Catalans Dragons (a)	W12-28	t:Gildart,French,J Burgess(2),Powell g:Hardaker(4)	3rd	5,000
19/9/20	Hull FC (a) (CCQF) ●●●●	W4-36	t:Powell,Farrell(2),French(2),J Burgess,Gildart g:Hardaker(4)	N/A	N/A
25/9/20	Wakefield (h) ●●●	W28-16	t:Hastings,French(2),Powell,Gildart g:Hardaker(4)	2nd	N/A
29/9/20	St Helens (h)	L0-42		3rd	N/A
3/10/20	Leeds (CCSF) ●●	L26-12	t:Smith,Hardaker g:Hardaker(2)	N/A	N/A
9/10/20	Warrington (a) ●	W14-18	t:Greenwood,Hardaker,Farrell g:Hardaker(3)	2nd	N/A
23/10/20	Salford (h) ●●	W58-12	t:Powell(2),Farrell(2),French(3),Hastings,Gildart(2) g:Hardaker(9)	2nd	N/A
30/10/20	St Helens (a)	W6-18	t:Bibby,Leuluai,French,Hastings g:Hardaker	1st	N/A
6/11/20	Huddersfield (h) ●	W19-6	t:Powell,Hastings,Hardaker g:Hardaker(3) fg:Hastings	1st	N/A
19/11/20	Hull FC (h) (SF)	W29-2	t:J Burgess,Smith,Hardaker,Bibby,French g:Hardaker(4) fg:Smith	N/A	N/A
27/11/20	St Helens (GF) ●●●●●	L8-4	t:Bibby	N/A	N/A

● *Played at Emerald Headingley, Leeds*
●● *Played at Totally Wicked Stadium, St Helens*
●●● *Played at Halliwell Jones Stadium, Warrington*
●●●● *Played at AJ Bell Stadium, Salford*
●●●●● *Played at KCOM Stadium, Hull*

Catalans Dragons (h) (R10), Leeds (a) (R21) and Hull FC (a) (R22) games were cancelled

Toronto (h) (R3) game was later expunged from the Super League table (Player stats from this fixture are included in 'All' columns below)

		APP		TRIES		GOALS		FG		PTS	
	D.O.B.	ALL	SL	ALL	SL	ALL	SL	ALL	SL	ALL	SL
Jake Bibby	17/6/96	19	17	5	5	0	0	0	0	20	20
Amir Bourouh	5/1/01	1(2)	1(1)	0	0	0	0	0	0	0	0
Joe Bullock	27/11/92	11(5)	11(3)	1	1	0	0	0	0	4	4
George Burgess	21/4/92	2(6)	2(6)	1	1	0	0	0	0	4	4
Joe Burgess	14/10/94	13	10	7	5	0	0	0	0	28	20
Liam Byrne	18/8/99	7(4)	7(4)	1	1	0	0	0	0	4	4
Mitch Clark	13/3/93	(9)	(7)	0	0	0	0	0	0	0	0
Tony Clubb	12/6/87	4(6)	3(6)	0	0	0	0	0	0	0	0
Liam Farrell	2/7/90	21	18	10	6	0	0	0	0	40	24
Ben Flower	19/10/87	2(7)	2(7)	1	1	0	0	0	0	4	4
Bevan French	4/1/96	21	18	17	13	0	0	0	0	68	52
Oliver Gildart	6/8/96	9	8	5	4	0	0	0	0	20	16
Joe Greenwood	2/4/93	2(8)	2(6)	1	1	0	0	0	0	4	4
Sam Halsall	18/8/01	1	1	0	0	0	0	0	0	0	0
Chris Hankinson	30/11/93	3	3	0	0	3	3	0	0	6	6
Umyla Hanley	5/3/02	1	1	0	0	0	0	0	0	0	0
Zak Hardaker	17/10/91	20	17	5	4	72	62	0	0	164	140
Jackson Hastings	14/1/96	21	18	9	9	0	0	1	1	37	37
Ethan Havard	26/10/00	7(4)	5(4)	0	0	0	0	0	0	0	0
Willie Isa	1/1/89	21	18	2	2	0	0	0	0	8	8
Ben Kilner	11/5/99	(1)	(1)	0	0	0	0	0	0	0	0
Thomas Leuluai	22/6/85	19	16	1	1	0	0	0	0	4	4
Dom Manfredi	1/10/93	11	9	3	3	0	0	0	0	12	12
Liam Marshall	9/5/96	10	9	6	6	0	0	0	0	24	24
James McDonnell	12/1/00	1	1	0	0	0	0	0	0	0	0
Sean O'Loughlin	24/11/82	6(2)	3(2)	0	0	0	0	0	0	0	0
Oliver Partington	3/9/98	17	14	1	1	0	0	0	0	4	4
Kai Pearce-Paul	19/2/01	(1)	(1)	0	0	0	0	0	0	0	0
Sam Powell	3/7/92	18	16	12	11	0	0	0	0	48	44
Harry Rushton	13/11/01	1	1	0	0	0	0	0	0	0	0
Jake Shorrocks	26/10/95	1(1)	1(1)	0	0	0	0	0	0	0	0
Joe Shorrocks	25/11/99	(7)	(5)	0	0	0	0	0	0	0	0
Brad Singleton	29/10/92	5(1)	5(1)	0	0	0	0	0	0	0	0
Harry Smith	25/1/00	6(11)	5(9)	4	2	0	0	2	2	18	10
Morgan Smithies	7/11/00	4(12)	4(11)	0	0	0	0	0	0	0	0
Jack Wells	21/9/97	1(1)	1(1)	0	0	0	0	0	0	0	0

Bevan French

'SL' totals include regular season & play-offs; 'All' totals also include Challenge Cup

SUPER LEAGUE XXV
Round by Round

ROUND 1

Thursday 30th January 2020

WIGAN WARRIORS 16 WARRINGTON WOLVES 10

WARRIORS: 6 Bevan French; 2 Liam Marshall; 1 Zak Hardaker; 23 Jake Bibby (D); 5 Joe Burgess; 7 Thomas Leuluai; 31 Jackson Hastings (D); 17 Oliver Partington; 9 Sam Powell; 10 George Burgess (D); 11 Willie Isa; 12 Liam Farrell; 13 Sean O'Loughlin (C). Subs (all used): 20 Liam Byrne; 8 Tony Clubb; 30 Ethan Havard; 16 Morgan Smithies.
Tries: French (18), Powell (23, pen), Marshall (65);
Goals: Hardaker 2/3.
On report: Smithies (29) - alleged eye gouge on Austin.
WOLVES: 26 Matty Ashton (D); 2 Tom Lineham; 3 Anthony Gelling (D); 4 Toby King; 5 Josh Charnley; 6 Blake Austin; 1 Stefan Ratchford; 8 Chris Hill (C); 9 Daryl Clark; 10 Mike Cooper; 11 Ben Currie; 13 Ben Murdoch-Masila; 14 Jason Clark. Subs (all used): 15 Joe Philbin; 18 Sitaleki Akauola; 20 Danny Walker; 23 Luther Burrell.
Try: Murdoch-Masila (14); **Goals:** Ratchford 3/3.
Dismissal: Hill (23) - high tackle on Powell.
Sin bin: Cooper (63) - professional foul.
Rugby Leaguer & League Express Men of the Match:
Warriors: Bevan French; *Wolves:* Matty Ashton.
Penalty count: 6-6; **Half-time:** 12-10;
Referee: Chris Kendall; **Attendance:** 15,040.

Friday 31st January 2020

HULL KINGSTON ROVERS 30 WAKEFIELD TRINITY 12

ROVERS: 1 Adam Quinlan; 5 Greg Minikin (D); 3 Shaun Kenny-Dowall (C) (D); 4 Kane Linnett; 2 Ben Crooks; 30 Jamie Ellis (D2); 31 Ryan Brierley (D); 15 George Lawler; 18 Jez Litten; 16 Daniel Murray; 12 Harvey Livett (D2); 28 Matthew Storton (D); 7 Jordan Abdull (D2). Subs (all used): 8 Robbie Mulhern; 14 Mitch Garbutt; 26 Will Maher (D); 27 Elliot Minchella (D).
Tries: Crooks (8, 48, 62, 67), Minikin (12), Brierley (77);
Goals: Ellis 3/6.
Sin bin: Quinlan (79) - holding down.
TRINITY: 29 Ryan Hampshire; 28 Ryan Atkins; 4 Reece Lyne; 3 Bill Tupou; 2 Tom Johnstone; 6 Jacob Miller (C); 7 Danny Brough; 15 Craig Kopczak; 23 Josh Wood (D); 36 Kelepi Tanginoa; 14 Jay Pitts (D2); 11 Matty Ashurst; 13 Joe Westerman (D). Subs (all used): 12 Danny Kirmond; 37 Romain Navarrete (D); 18 Adam Tangata; 9 Kyle Wood.
Tries: Westerman (23), J Wood (65);
Goals: Brough 1/1, Hampshire 1/1.
Rugby Leaguer & League Express Men of the Match:
Rovers: Ben Crooks; *Trinity:* Joe Westerman.
Penalty count: 10-9; **Half-time:** 10-6;
Referee: Robert Hicks; **Attendance:** 8,492.

ST HELENS 48 SALFORD RED DEVILS 8

SAINTS: 1 Lachlan Coote; 22 Jack Welsby; 3 Kevin Naiqama; 4 Mark Percival; 5 Regan Grace; 6 Jonny Lomax (C); 7 Theo Fages; 8 Alex Walmsley; 20 James Bentley; 10 Luke Thompson; 11 Zeb Taia; 12 Dominique Peyroux; 13 Louie McCarthy-Scarsbrook. Subs (all used): 15 Matty Lees; 17 Jack Ashworth; 18 Joseph Paulo; 19 Aaron Smith.
Tries: Taia (13), Walmsley (19, 74), Fages (38), Naiqama (46, 59), Welsby (65, 71);
Goals: Coote 3/3, Percival 5/5.
RED DEVILS: 1 Niall Evalds; 23 Ken Sio; 3 Kris Welham; 4 Dan Sarginson (D); 22 Rhys Williams (D2); 6 Tui Lolohea; 7 Kevin Brown (D); 8 Lee Mossop (C); 9 Joey Lussick; 10 Gil Dudson; 21 James Greenwood (D2); 13 Tyrone McCarthy; 16 Greg Burke. Subs (all used): 12 Pauli Pauli (D2); 14 Sebastine Ikahihifo (D); 17 Luke Yates (D); 20 Josh Johnson.
Try: Sio (50); **Goals:** Lolohea 2/2.
Rugby Leaguer & League Express Men of the Match:
Saints: Jonny Lomax; *Red Devils:* Niall Evalds.
Penalty count: 10-7; **Half-time:** 18-2;
Referee: Liam Moore; **Attendance:** 12,008.

Saturday 1st February 2020

CATALANS DRAGONS 12 HUDDERSFIELD GIANTS 32

DRAGONS: 29 Sam Tomkins; 22 Arthur Romano; 3 Samisoni Langi; 1 David Mead; 5 Fouad Yaha; 6 James Maloney (D); 7 Josh Drinkwater (D2); 8 Remi Casty (C); 9 Michael Mcllorum; 14 Julian Bousquet; 11 Matt Whitley; 12 Joel Tomkins (D); 13 Benjamin Garcia. Subs (all used): 15 Mickael Simon; 17 Benjamin Jullien; 24 Jason Baitieri; 28 Sam Kasiano.
Tries: Yaha (27), S Tomkins (43); **Goals:** Maloney 2/2.
Sin bin: Garcia (17) - dangerous challenge on Edwards; Maloney (69) - punching O'Brien.
GIANTS: 5 Darnell McIntosh; 2 Jermaine McGillvary; 3 Jake Wardle; 27 Sam Wood; 24 Louis Senior; 6 Lee Gaskell; 7 Aidan Sezer (C) (D); 14 Matty English; 9 Adam O'Brien; 10 Suaia Matagi; 16 Aaron Murphy; 12 Joe Wardle; 13 Michael Lawrence. Subs (all used): 8 James Gavet (D); 11 Kenny Edwards (D); 17 Ukuma Ta'ai; 18 Paul Clough.
Tries: Joe Wardle (7), McGillvary (18, 61), Sezer (35), Senior (58); **Goals:** Sezer 6/7.
Rugby Leaguer & League Express Men of the Match:
Dragons: Benjamin Garcia; *Giants:* Aidan Sezer.
Penalty count: 11-8; **Half-time:** 6-16;
Referee: Scott Mikalauskas; **Attendance:** 8,259.

Sunday 2nd February 2020

TORONTO WOLFPACK 10 CASTLEFORD TIGERS 28

WOLFPACK: 17 Blake Wallace; 5 Liam Kay; 23 Hakim Miloudi; 4 Ricky Leutele; 2 Matty Russell; 6 Joe Mellor; 7 Josh McCrone (C); 8 Adam Sidlow; 9 Andy Ackers; 10 Anthony Mullally; 11 Andrew Dixon; 16 Tom Olbison; 13 Jon Wilkin. Subs (all used): 15 Gadwin Springer; 18 Brad Singleton (D); 20 James Cunningham (D); 21 Sonny Bill Williams (D).
Tries: Kay (4), Miloudi (60); **Goals:** Wallace 1/2.
TIGERS: 1 Jordan Rankin; 2 Derrell Olpherts (D); 3 Peter Mata'utia; 4 Michael Shenton (C); 25 Greg Eden; 6 Jake Trueman; 7 Danny Richardson (D); 8 Liam Watts; 9 Paul McShane; 10 Grant Millington; 16 George Griffin (D); 18 Cheyse Blair; 13 Adam Milner. Subs (all used): 14 Nathan Massey; 19 Daniel Smith; 22 Jacques O'Neill; 24 Tyla Hepi (D).
Tries: Eden (8), Millington (18), Milner (31), Shenton (35), Mata'utia (46); **Goals:** Richardson 4/6.
Rugby Leaguer & League Express Men of the Match:
Wolfpack: Blake Wallace; *Tigers:* Jake Trueman.
Penalty count: 9-6; **Half-time:** 4-22;
Referee: James Child. *(at Emerald Headingley, Leeds)*.

LEEDS RHINOS 4 HULL FC 30

RHINOS: 1 Jack Walker; 3 Harry Newman; 15 Liam Sutcliffe; 4 Konrad Hurrell; 5 Ash Handley; 6 Robert Lui; 7 Luke Gale (D); 19 Mikolaj Oledzki; 14 Brad Dwyer; 10 Matt Prior (D); 12 Rhyse Martin; 13 Stevie Ward (C); 22 Cameron Smith. Subs (all used): 25 James Donaldson; 17 Adam Cuthbertson; 16 Richie Myler; 11 Alex Mellor (D).
Try: Handley (63); **Goals:** Martin 0/1.
HULL FC: 1 Jamie Shaul; 2 Bureta Faraimo; 3 Carlos Tuimavave; 4 Josh Griffin; 33 Ratu Naulago; 6 Jake Connor; 7 Marc Sneyd; 8 Scott Taylor; 16 Jordan Johnstone (D); 13 Ligi Sao (D); 11 Josh Jones (D); 12 Manu Ma'u (D); 29 Gareth Ellis (C). Subs (all used): 10 Tevita Satae; 21 Jordan Lane; 22 Josh Bowden; 23 Andre Savelio.
Tries: Tuimavave (19), Naulago (32, 56), Bowden (35), Shaul (78); **Goals:** Sneyd 5/8.
Rugby Leaguer & League Express Men of the Match:
Rhinos: Harry Newman; *Hull FC:* Tevita Satae.
Penalty count: 11-5; **Half-time:** 0-20;
Referee: Ben Thaler; **Attendance:** 19,700.

ROUND 2

Thursday 6th February 2020

WARRINGTON WOLVES 19 ST HELENS 0

WOLVES: 26 Matty Ashton; 2 Tom Lineham; 3 Anthony Gelling; 4 Toby King; 5 Josh Charnley; 6 Blake Austin; 1 Stefan Ratchford (C); 15 Joe Philbin; 9 Daryl Clark; 10 Mike Cooper; 11 Ben Currie; 13 Ben Murdoch-Masila; 14 Jason Clark. Subs (all used): 19 Matt Davis; 18 Sitaleki Akauola; 20 Danny Walker; 23 Luther Burrell.
Tries: D Clark (31), Lineham (35), Charnley (54);
Goals: Ratchford 3/5; **Field goal:** Austin (40).
SAINTS: 22 Jack Welsby; 3 Kevin Naiqama; 21 Matthew Costello; 4 Mark Percival; 5 Regan Grace; 6 Jonny Lomax (C); 7 Theo Fages; 15 Matty Lees; 20 James Bentley; 10 Luke Thompson; 11 Zeb Taia; 12 Dominique Peyroux; 13 Louie McCarthy-Scarsbrook. Subs (all used): 23 Joe Batchelor; 17 Jack Ashworth; 18 Joseph Paulo; 19 Aaron Smith.
Rugby Leaguer & League Express Men of the Match:
Wolves: Daryl Clark; *Saints:* Luke Thompson.
Penalty count: 10-8; **Half-time:** 13-0;
Referee: Chris Kendall; **Attendance:** 12,562.

Friday 7th February 2020

CASTLEFORD TIGERS 16 WIGAN WARRIORS 12

TIGERS: 1 Jordan Rankin; 2 Derrell Olpherts; 18 Cheyse Blair; 4 Michael Shenton (C); 21 James Clare; 6 Jake Trueman; 7 Danny Richardson; 8 Liam Watts; 9 Paul McShane; 19 Daniel Smith; 11 Oliver Holmes; 10 Grant Millington; 14 Nathan Massey. Subs (all used): 20 Junior Moors; 22 Jacques O'Neill; 27 Lewis Peachey; 32 Sam Hall (D).
Tries: Olpherts (18), Blair (32); **Goals:** Richardson 4/5.
WARRIORS: 6 Bevan French; 2 Liam Marshall; 1 Zak Hardaker; 23 Jake Bibby; 5 Joe Burgess; 28 Harry Smith; 31 Jackson Hastings; 8 Tony Clubb; 7 Thomas Leuluai; 17 Oliver Partington; 11 Willie Isa; 12 Liam Farrell; 13 Sean O'Loughlin (C). Subs (all used): 16 Morgan Smithies; 20 Liam Byrne; 27 Jake Shorrocks; 30 Ethan Havard.
Tries: Byrne (38), J Burgess (79); **Goals:** Hardaker 2/2.
Rugby Leaguer & League Express Men of the Match:
Tigers: Paul McShane; *Warriors:* Harry Smith.
Penalty count: 11-7; **Half-time:** 12-6;
Referee: Marcus Griffiths; **Attendance:** 8,848.

HULL FC 25 HULL KINGSTON ROVERS 16

HULL FC: 1 Jamie Shaul; 33 Ratu Naulago; 3 Carlos Tuimavave; 4 Josh Griffin; 5 Adam Swift (D); 6 Jake Connor; 7 Marc Sneyd; 8 Scott Taylor; 9 Danny Houghton (C); 13 Ligi Sao; 11 Josh Jones; 21 Jordan Lane; 23 Andre Savelio. Subs (all used): 10 Tevita Satae; 16 Jordan Johnstone; 22 Josh Bowden; 24 Mahe Fonua (D2).
Tries: Connor (16), Houghton (32), Sneyd (56), Griffin (63);
Goals: Sneyd 4/4; **Field goal:** Sneyd (78).
ROVERS: 1 Adam Quinlan; 5 Greg Minikin; 3 Shaun Kenny-Dowall (C); 4 Kane Linnett; 2 Ben Crooks; 30 Jamie Ellis; 31 Ryan Brierley; 8 Robbie Mulhern; 18 Jez Litten; 16 Daniel Murray; 12 Harvey Livett; 28 Matthew Storton; 15 George Lawler. Subs (all used): 13 Dean Hadley; 17 Kyle Trout; 26 Will Maher; 27 Elliot Minchella.
Tries: Livett (10), Quinlan (23), Crooks (51); **Goals:** Ellis 2/4.
Rugby Leaguer & League Express Men of the Match:
Hull FC: Marc Sneyd; *Rovers:* Harvey Livett.
Penalty count: 10-9; **Half-time:** 12-10;
Referee: Robert Hicks; **Attendance:** 19,599.

Saturday 8th February 2020

SALFORD RED DEVILS 24 TORONTO WOLFPACK 16

RED DEVILS: 1 Niall Evalds; 23 Ken Sio; 3 Kris Welham; 4 Dan Sarginson; 22 Rhys Williams; 6 Tui Lolohea; 7 Kevin Brown; 8 Lee Mossop (C); 25 Connor Jones (D); 10 Gil Dudson; 13 Tyrone McCarthy; 21 James Greenwood; 16 Greg Burke. Subs (all used): 9 Joey Lussick; 12 Pauli Pauli; 14 Sebastine Ikahihifo; 17 Luke Yates.
Tries: Brown (27), Lolohea (47), Williams (49), Sarginson (74), Evalds (77); **Goals:** Lolohea 2/4, Lussick 0/1.
Sin bin: Welham (37) - high tackle on Wallace.
WOLFPACK: 17 Blake Wallace; 5 Liam Kay; 23 Hakim Miloudi; 4 Ricky Leutele; 2 Matty Russell; 6 Joe Mellor; 7 Josh McCrone (C); 15 Gadwin Springer; 20 James Cunningham; 18 Brad Singleton; 21 Sonny Bill Williams; 16 Tom Olbison; 13 Jon Wilkin. Subs (all used): 8 Adam Sidlow; 10 Anthony Mullally; 12 Bodene Thompson; 19 Gary Wheeler.
Tries: Wheeler (18, 54), Singleton (69); **Goals:** Wallace 2/3.
Sin bin: Miloudi (37) - fighting.
Rugby Leaguer & League Express Men of the Match:
Red Devils: Niall Evalds; *Wolfpack:* Sonny Bill Williams.
Penalty count: 7-9; **Half-time:** 6-4;
Referee: James Child; **Attendance:** 4,593.

ROUND 3

Thursday 13th February 2020

WIGAN WARRIORS 32 TORONTO WOLFPACK 10

WARRIORS: 6 Bevan French; 2 Liam Marshall; 1 Zak Hardaker; 23 Jake Bibby; 5 Joe Burgess; 28 Harry Smith; 31 Jackson Hastings; 8 Tony Clubb; 7 Thomas Leuluai; 17 Oliver Partington; 11 Willie Isa; 12 Liam Farrell; 13 Sean O'Loughlin (C). Subs (all used): 16 Morgan Smithies; 19 Joe Bullock; 22 Mitch Clark (D); 32 Amir Bourouh.
Tries: Smith (27), French (33, 64), J Burgess (59), Farrell (76, 78); **Goals:** Hardaker 4/6.
WOLFPACK: 1 Gareth O'Brien; 5 Liam Kay; 23 Hakim Miloudi; 4 Ricky Leutele; 2 Matty Russell; 17 Blake Wallace; 7 Josh McCrone (C); 15 Gadwin Springer; 9 Andy Ackers; 18 Brad Singleton; 12 Bodene Thompson; 16 Tom Olbison; 20 James Cunningham. Subs (all used): 8 Adam Sidlow; 10 Anthony Mullally; 11 Andrew Dixon; 19 Gary Wheeler.
Tries: Russell (20), Thompson (48); **Goals:** Wallace 1/2.
Sin bin: Miloudi (75) - high tackle on O'Loughlin.
Rugby Leaguer & League Express Men of the Match:
Warriors: Bevan French; *Wolfpack:* Andy Ackers.
Penalty count: 7-8; **Half-time:** 10-4;
Referee: Chris Kendall; **Attendance:** 10,333.

Friday 14th February 2020

LEEDS RHINOS 52 HULL KINGSTON ROVERS 10

RHINOS: 1 Jack Walker; 24 Luke Briscoe; 3 Harry Newman; 4 Konrad Hurrell; 5 Ash Handley; 6 Robert Lui; 7 Luke Gale (C); 8 Ava Seumanufagai; 14 Brad Dwyer; 10 Matt Prior; 11 Alex Mellor; 15 Liam Sutcliffe; 22 Cameron Smith. Subs (all used): 19 Mikolaj Oledzki; 17 Adam Cuthbertson; 25 James Donaldson; 16 Richie Myler.
Tries: Newman (9, 19), Smith (22, 57), Walker (46), Handley (51), Hurrell (68), Donaldson (77), Myler (79);
Goals: Gale 8/10.

ROVERS: 19 Will Dagger; 5 Greg Minikin; 3 Shaun Kenny-Dowall (C); 4 Kane Linnett; 2 Ben Crooks; 7 Jordan Abdull; 31 Ryan Brierley; 16 Daniel Murray; 9 Matt Parcell; 26 Will Maher; 12 Harvey Livett; 13 Dean Hadley; 15 George Lawler. Subs (all used): 8 Robbie Mulhern; 17 Kyle Trout; 27 Elliot Minchella; 28 Matthew Storton.
Tries: Minikin (38), Abdull (65); **Goals:** Brierley 1/2.
Rugby Leaguer & League Express Men of the Match: *Rhinos:* Harry Newman; *Rovers:* George Lawler.
Penalty count: 7-5; **Half-time:** 20-4;
Referee: Tom Grant; **Attendance:** 11,057.

SALFORD RED DEVILS 10 HUDDERSFIELD GIANTS 12

RED DEVILS: 1 Niall Evalds; 23 Ken Sio; 3 Kris Welham; 4 Dan Sarginson; 22 Rhys Williams; 6 Tui Lolohea; 7 Kevin Brown; 8 Lee Mossop (C); 25 Connor Jones; 20 Josh Johnson; 13 Tyrone McCarthy; 21 James Greenwood; 16 Greg Burke. Subs (all used): 9 Joey Lussick; 12 Pauli Pauli; 11 Ryan Lannon; 17 Luke Yates.
Tries: Sio (27), Sarginson (45); **Goals:** Lolohea 1/2.
Sin bin: Brown (76) - use of the head on Turner.
GIANTS: 5 Darnell McIntosh; 2 Jermaine McGillvary; 4 Jordan Turner; 27 Sam Wood; 24 Louis Senior; 6 Lee Gaskell; 7 Aidan Sezer (C); 14 Matty English; 9 Adam O'Brien; 10 Suaia Matagi; 16 Aaron Murphy; 12 Joe Wardle; 13 Michael Lawrence. Subs (all used): 8 James Gavet; 11 Kenny Edwards; 17 Ukuma Ta'ai; 18 Paul Clough.
Tries: O'Brien (18), Senior (54); **Goals:** Sezer 2/3.
Rugby Leaguer & League Express Men of the Match: *Red Devils:* Niall Evalds; *Giants:* Aidan Sezer.
Penalty count: 4-7; **Half-time:** 4-6;
Referee: James Child; **Attendance:** 3,350.

Saturday 15th February 2020

CATALANS DRAGONS 36 CASTLEFORD TIGERS 18

DRAGONS: 29 Sam Tomkins; 2 Lewis Tierney; 3 Samisoni Langi; 4 Israel Folau (D); 5 Fouad Yaha; 6 James Maloney; 7 Josh Drinkwater; 8 Remi Casty (C); 9 Michael Mcllorum; 14 Julian Bousquet; 11 Matt Whitley; 12 Joel Tomkins; 13 Benjamin Garcia. Subs (all used): 17 Benjamin Jullien; 23 Antoni Maria; 24 Jason Baitieri; 28 Sam Kasiano.
Tries: S Tomkins (3, 50, 78), Folau (6), Langi (32), Yaha (61);
Goals: Maloney 6/7.
TIGERS: 1 Jordan Rankin; 2 Derrell Olpherts; 18 Cheyse Blair; 4 Michael Shenton (C); 21 James Clare; 6 Jake Trueman; 7 Danny Richardson; 8 Liam Watts; 9 Paul McShane; 16 George Griffin; 11 Oliver Holmes; 10 Grant Millington; 14 Nathan Massey. Subs (all used): 12 Mike McMeeken; 19 Daniel Smith; 22 Jacques O'Neill; 24 Tyla Hepi.
Tries: Olpherts (14), Blair (39), Clare (65);
Goals: Richardson 3/3.
Sin bin: Olpherts (55) - delaying restart.
Rugby Leaguer & League Express Men of the Match: *Dragons:* Sam Tomkins; *Tigers:* Danny Richardson.
Penalty count: 10-8; **Half-time:** 20-12;
Referee: Gareth Hewer; **Attendance:** 8,886.

Sunday 16th February 2020

HULL FC 18 ST HELENS 32

HULL FC: 1 Jamie Shaul; 33 Ratu Naulago; 3 Carlos Tuimavave; 24 Mahe Fonua; 5 Adam Swift; 6 Jake Connor; 7 Marc Sneyd; 8 Scott Taylor; 9 Danny Houghton (C); 13 Ligi Sao; 11 Josh Jones; 4 Josh Griffin; 29 Gareth Ellis. Subs (all used): 16 Jordan Johnstone; 19 Masi Matongo; 20 Brad Fash; 21 Jordan Lane.
Tries: Tuimavave (29, 65), Shaul (79); **Goals:** Sneyd 3/3.
SAINTS: 22 Jack Welsby; 2 Tommy Makinson; 3 Kevin Naiqama; 21 Matthew Costello; 5 Regan Grace; 6 Jonny Lomax (C); 7 Theo Fages; 8 Alex Walmsley; 20 James Bentley; 10 Luke Thompson; 11 Zeb Taia; 12 Dominique Peyroux; 14 Morgan Knowles. Subs (all used): 13 Louie McCarthy-Scarsbrook; 15 Matty Lees; 18 Joseph Paulo; 19 Aaron Smith.
Tries: Costello (46), Thompson (49), McCarthy-Scarsbrook (52), Bentley (56), Smith (76);
Goals: Makinson 6/7.
Rugby Leaguer & League Express Men of the Match: *Hull FC:* Carlos Tuimavave; *Saints:* Jonny Lomax.
Penalty count: 8-7; **Half-time:** 6-2;
Referee: Liam Moore; **Attendance:** 12,399.

WAKEFIELD TRINITY 18 WARRINGTON WOLVES 8

TRINITY: 21 Max Jowitt; 3 Bill Tupou; 4 Reece Lyne; 20 Joe Arundel; 2 Tom Johnstone; 6 Jacob Miller (C); 29 Ryan Hampshire; 15 Craig Kopczak; 9 Kyle Wood; 36 Kelepi Tanginoa; 14 Jay Pitts; 11 Matty Ashurst; 13 Joe Westerman. Subs (all used): 23 Josh Wood; 18 Adam Tangata; 16 James Batchelor; 37 Romain Navarrete.
Tries: Ashurst (71), Johnstone (74); **Goals:** Hampshire 5/5.
WOLVES: 1 Stefan Ratchford (C); 2 Tom Lineham; 4 Toby King; 17 Jake Mamo; 5 Josh Charnley; 6 Blake Austin; 7 Gareth Widdop (D); 10 Mike Cooper; 9 Daryl Clark; 15 Joe Philbin; 11 Ben Currie; 13 Ben Murdoch-Masila; 14 Jason Clark. Subs (all used): 18 Sitaleki Akauola; 19 Matt Davis; 20 Danny Walker; 23 Luther Burrell.
Try: Ratchford (61); **Goals:** Ratchford 2/2.
Rugby Leaguer & League Express Men of the Match: *Trinity:* Ryan Hampshire; *Wolves:* Stefan Ratchford.
Penalty count: 10-8; **Half-time:** 0-2;
Referee: Marcus Griffiths; **Attendance:** 5,197.

ROUND 4

Friday 21st February 2020

CASTLEFORD TIGERS 32 WAKEFIELD TRINITY 15

TIGERS: 1 Jordan Rankin; 2 Derrell Olpherts; 3 Peter Mata'utia; 4 Michael Shenton (C); 21 James Clare; 6 Jake Trueman; 7 Danny Richardson; 8 Liam Watts; 9 Paul McShane; 16 George Griffin; 11 Oliver Holmes; 18 Cheyse Blair; 14 Nathan Massey. Subs (all used): 10 Grant Millington; 12 Mike McMeeken; 19 Daniel Smith; 22 Jacques O'Neill.
Tries: Blair (14), Olpherts (19, 57), Clare (33, 43), Holmes (55); **Goals:** Richardson 4/8.
TRINITY: 21 Max Jowitt; 3 Bill Tupou; 4 Reece Lyne; 20 Joe Arundel; 2 Tom Johnstone; 6 Jacob Miller (C); 29 Ryan Hampshire; 15 Craig Kopczak; 9 Kyle Wood; 36 Kelepi Tanginoa; 14 Jay Pitts; 11 Matty Ashurst; 13 Joe Westerman. Subs (all used): 16 James Batchelor; 18 Adam Tangata; 23 Josh Wood; 37 Romain Navarrete.
Tries: Westerman (6), Johnstone (26);
Goals: Hampshire 3/4; **Field goal:** Miller (40).
Sin bin: Batchelor (49) - obstruction;
Navarrete (63) - dangerous challenge.
Rugby Leaguer & League Express Men of the Match: *Tigers:* Paul McShane; *Trinity:* Tom Johnstone.
Penalty count: 13-8; **Half-time:** 14-15;
Referee: James Child; **Attendance:** 7,202.

HULL KINGSTON ROVERS 4 HUDDERSFIELD GIANTS 22

ROVERS: 19 Will Dagger; 5 Greg Minikin; 3 Shaun Kenny-Dowall (C); 4 Kane Linnett; 2 Ben Crooks; 24 Joe Keyes (D); 31 Ryan Brierley; 16 Daniel Murray; 9 Matt Parcell; 26 Will Maher; 12 Harvey Livett; 28 Matthew Storton; 13 Dean Hadley. Subs (all used): 8 Robbie Mulhern; 17 Kyle Trout; 27 Elliot Minchella; 14 Mitch Garbutt.
Try: Crooks (69); **Goals:** Brierley 0/1.
GIANTS: 5 Darnell McIntosh; 2 Jermaine McGillvary; 3 Jake Wardle; 27 Sam Wood; 24 Louis Senior; 6 Lee Gaskell; 7 Aidan Sezer (C); 14 Matty English; 9 Adam O'Brien; 10 Suaia Matagi; 16 Aaron Murphy; 12 Joe Wardle; 13 Michael Lawrence. Subs (all used): 8 James Gavet; 11 Kenny Edwards; 17 Ukuma Ta'ai; 18 Paul Clough.
Tries: Senior (2), Gaskell (18), Clough (56), Matagi (59);
Goals: Sezer 3/4.
Rugby Leaguer & League Express Men of the Match: *Rovers:* Matthew Storton; *Giants:* Suaia Matagi.
Penalty count: 11-12; **Half-time:** 0-10;
Referee: Liam Moore; **Attendance:** 7,350.

WARRINGTON WOLVES 32 TORONTO WOLFPACK 22

WOLVES: 26 Matty Ashton; 5 Josh Charnley; 1 Stefan Ratchford (C); 4 Toby King; 2 Tom Lineham; 6 Blake Austin; 7 Gareth Widdop; 15 Joe Philbin; 9 Daryl Clark; 10 Mike Cooper; 11 Ben Currie; 13 Ben Murdoch-Masila; 14 Jason Clark. Subs (all used): 19 Matt Davis; 20 Danny Walker; 22 Luis Johnson; 23 Luther Burrell.
Tries: Charnley (7), Widdop (10), Lineham (23), Ashton (36), Murdoch-Masila (79); **Goals:** Ratchford 6/7.
WOLFPACK: 1 Gareth O'Brien; 5 Liam Kay; 23 Hakim Miloudi; 4 Ricky Leutele; 2 Matty Russell; 17 Blake Wallace; 7 Josh McCrone (C); 10 Anthony Mullally; 9 Andy Ackers; 18 Brad Singleton; 21 Sonny Bill Williams; 12 Bodene Thompson; 13 Jon Wilkin. Subs (all used): 8 Adam Sidlow; 16 Tom Olbison; 22 Greg Worthington; 24 Tony Gigot (D).
Tries: Wilkin (33), Ackers (40), Russell (49), O'Brien (56);
Goals: Wallace 3/4.
Rugby Leaguer & League Express Men of the Match: *Wolves:* Josh Charnley; *Wolfpack:* Jon Wilkin.
Penalty count: 5-8; **Half-time:** 22-12;
Referee: Scott Mikalauskas; **Attendance:** 11,182.

Saturday 22nd February 2020

SALFORD RED DEVILS 8 LEEDS RHINOS 22

RED DEVILS: 1 Niall Evalds; 23 Ken Sio; 3 Kris Welham; 5 Krisnan Inu; 22 Rhys Williams; 6 Tui Lolohea; 18 Chris Atkin (D); 17 Luke Yates; 25 Connor Jones; 10 Gil Dudson (C); 29 Oliver Roberts (D); 12 Pauli Pauli; 13 Tyrone McCarthy. Subs (all used): 9 Joey Lussick; 11 Ryan Lannon; 14 Sebastine Ikahihifo; 19 Mark Flanagan.
Tries: Evalds (20), Lolohea (27);
Goals: Lolohea 0/1, Atkin 0/1.
RHINOS: 1 Jack Walker; 24 Luke Briscoe; 4 Konrad Hurrell; 3 Harry Newman; 5 Ash Handley; 6 Robert Lui; 7 Luke Gale (C); 8 Ava Seumanufagai; 14 Brad Dwyer; 10 Matt Prior; 11 Alex Mellor; 25 James Donaldson; 22 Cameron Smith. Subs (all used): 16 Richie Myler; 17 Adam Cuthbertson; 19 Mikolaj Oledzki; 26 Alex Sutcliffe.
Tries: Gale (39), L Briscoe (51), Oledzki (54), Walker (71);
Goals: Gale 3/5.
Rugby Leaguer & League Express Men of the Match: *Red Devils:* Pauli Pauli; *Rhinos:* Luke Gale.
Penalty count: 8-6; **Half-time:** 8-6;
Referee: Marcus Griffiths; **Attendance:** 4,757.

Sunday 23rd February 2020

WIGAN WARRIORS 26 HULL FC 12

WARRIORS: 6 Bevan French; 21 Dom Manfredi; 1 Zak Hardaker; 23 Jake Bibby; 2 Liam Marshall; 31 Jackson Hastings; 7 Thomas Leuluai (C); 8 Tony Clubb; 9 Sam Powell; 17 Oliver Partington; 11 Willie Isa; 12 Liam Farrell; 16 Morgan Smithies. Subs (all used): 19 Joe Bullock; 20 Liam Byrne; 22 Mitch Clark; 28 Harry Smith.
Tries: French (3), Manfredi (45), Hastings (61), Isa (68);
Goals: Hardaker 5/6.
Sin bin: Farrell (39) - fighting.
HULL FC: 1 Jamie Shaul; 5 Adam Swift; 4 Josh Griffin; 24 Mahe Fonua; 2 Bureta Faraimo; 6 Jake Connor; 7 Marc Sneyd; 8 Scott Taylor; 9 Danny Houghton (C); 13 Ligi Sao; 11 Josh Jones; 21 Jordan Lane; 20 Brad Fash. Subs (all used): 16 Jordan Johnstone; 19 Masi Matongo; 22 Josh Bowden; 29 Gareth Ellis.
Tries: Swift (25), Griffin (74); **Goals:** Sneyd 2/3.
Sin bin: Griffin (39) - fighting.
Rugby Leaguer & League Express Men of the Match: *Warriors:* Bevan French; *Hull FC:* Josh Griffin.
Penalty count: 7-8; **Half-time:** 10-8;
Referee: Robert Hicks; **Attendance:** 12,005.

ROUND 5

Thursday 27th February 2020

HULL KINGSTON ROVERS 8 CASTLEFORD TIGERS 28

ROVERS: 19 Will Dagger; 5 Greg Minikin; 3 Shaun Kenny-Dowall (C); 4 Kane Linnett; 2 Ben Crooks; 24 Joe Keyes; 31 Ryan Brierley; 16 Daniel Murray; 18 Jez Litten; 26 Will Maher; 25 Matty Gee (D); 28 Matthew Storton; 13 Dean Hadley. Subs (all used): 14 Mitch Garbutt; 17 Kyle Trout; 21 Owen Harrison; 27 Elliot Minchella.
Try: Crooks (6); **Goals:** Brierley 2/2.
Sin bin: Brierley (42) - professional foul.
TIGERS: 1 Jordan Rankin; 2 Derrell Olpherts; 3 Peter Mata'utia; 4 Michael Shenton (C); 21 James Clare; 6 Jake Trueman; 7 Danny Richardson; 8 Liam Watts; 9 Paul McShane; 16 George Griffin; 11 Oliver Holmes; 12 Mike McMeeken; 14 Nathan Massey. Subs (all used): 10 Grant Millington; 13 Adam Milner; 18 Cheyse Blair; 19 Daniel Smith.
Tries: Shenton (35), Richardson (49), Clare (55), McMeeken (73); **Goals:** Richardson 6/6.
Rugby Leaguer & League Express Men of the Match: *Rovers:* Ben Crooks; *Tigers:* Paul McShane.
Penalty count: 7-8; **Half-time:** 8-6;
Referee: Chris Kendall; **Attendance:** 7,464.

Friday 28th February 2020

LEEDS RHINOS 36 WARRINGTON WOLVES 0

RHINOS: 1 Jack Walker; 24 Luke Briscoe; 3 Harry Newman; 4 Konrad Hurrell; 5 Ash Handley; 6 Robert Lui; 7 Luke Gale (C); 19 Mikolaj Oledzki; 14 Brad Dwyer; 8 Ava Seumanufagai; 12 Rhyse Martin; 11 Alex Mellor; 10 Matt Prior. Subs (all used): 16 Richie Myler; 17 Adam Cuthbertson; 22 Cameron Smith; 25 James Donaldson.
Tries: Walker (6), Myler (38), Dwyer (45), Hurrell (52), Seumanufagai (57), Handley (59); **Goals:** Martin 6/8.
WOLVES: 1 Stefan Ratchford; 2 Tom Lineham; 24 Keanan Brand (D); 4 Toby King; 5 Josh Charnley; 6 Blake Austin; 7 Gareth Widdop; 8 Chris Hill (C); 9 Daryl Clark; 10 Mike Cooper; 11 Ben Currie; 13 Ben Murdoch-Masila; 14 Jason Clark. Subs (all used): 15 Joe Philbin; 19 Matt Davis; 22 Luis Johnson; 23 Luther Burrell.
Sin bin: Murdoch-Masila (51) - high tackle on Mellor.
Rugby Leaguer & League Express Men of the Match: *Rhinos:* Richie Myler; *Wolves:* Josh Charnley.
Penalty count: 7-9; **Half-time:** 14-0;
Referee: Robert Hicks; **Attendance:** 12,134.

Saturday 29th February 2020

TORONTO WOLFPACK 0 ST HELENS 32

WOLFPACK: 24 Tony Gigot; 5 Liam Kay; 17 Blake Wallace; 4 Ricky Leutele; 2 Matty Russell; 1 Gareth O'Brien; 7 Josh McCrone (C); 8 Adam Sidlow; 9 Andy Ackers; 15 Gadwin Springer; 12 Bodene Thompson; 21 Sonny Bill Williams; 13 Jon Wilkin. Subs (all used): 10 Anthony Mullally; 16 Tom Olbison; 23 Hakim Miloudi; 25 Jack Wells (D).
Dismissal: Thompson (67) - shoulder charge on Lees.
SAINTS: 22 Jack Welsby; 2 Tommy Makinson; 3 Kevin Naiqama; 20 James Bentley; 5 Regan Grace; 6 Jonny Lomax; 7 Theo Fages; 8 Alex Walmsley; 9 James Roby (C); 10 Luke Thompson; 11 Zeb Taia; 12 Dominique Peyroux; 14 Morgan Knowles. Subs (all used): 13 Louie McCarthy-Scarsbrook; 15 Matty Lees; 18 Joseph Paulo; 19 Aaron Smith.
Tries: Lomax (8, 22), Bentley (27), McCarthy-Scarsbrook (56), Smith (68);
Goals: Makinson 6/6.
Rugby Leaguer & League Express Men of the Match:
Wolfpack: Josh McCrone; *Saints:* Jonny Lomax.
Penalty count: 7-20; **Half-time:** 0-20;
Referee: Marcus Griffiths; **Attendance:** 4,000
(at Halliwell Jones Stadium, Warrington).

Sunday 1st March 2020

HUDDERSFIELD GIANTS 10 WIGAN WARRIORS 42

GIANTS: 24 Louis Senior; 2 Jermaine McGillvary; 3 Jake Wardle; 4 Jordan Turner; 27 Sam Wood; 6 Lee Gaskell; 7 Aidan Sezer (C); 14 Matty English; 9 Adam O'Brien; 10 Suaia Matagi; 16 Aaron Murphy; 12 Joe Wardle; 13 Michael Lawrence. Subs (all used): 18 Paul Clough; 11 Kenny Edwards; 8 James Gavet; 17 Ukuma Ta'ai.
Try: O'Brien (29); **Goals:** Sezer 3/3.
Sin bin: Sezer (35) - high tackle on Leuluai.
WARRIORS: 6 Bevan French; 21 Dom Manfredi; 1 Zak Hardaker; 3 Chris Hankinson; 2 Liam Marshall; 7 Thomas Leuluai (C); 31 Jackson Hastings; 8 Tony Clubb; 9 Sam Powell; 17 Oliver Partington; 11 Willie Isa; 12 Liam Farrell; 16 Morgan Smithies. Subs (all used): 19 Joe Bullock; 10 George Burgess; 20 Liam Byrne; 28 Harry Smith.
Tries: Isa (16), Marshall (35, 40, 48), Powell (39), Manfredi (42), Partington (60), G Burgess (78);
Goals: Hardaker 5/8.
Rugby Leaguer & League Express Men of the Match:
Giants: Suaia Matagi; *Warriors:* Liam Marshall.
Penalty count: 6-7; **Half-time:** 10-20;
Referee: James Child; **Attendance:** 6,574.

HULL FC 29 CATALANS DRAGONS 34

HULL FC: 1 Jamie Shaul; 24 Mahe Fonua; 6 Jake Connor; 4 Josh Griffin; 26 Kieran Buchanan; 14 Albert Kelly; 7 Marc Sneyd; 8 Scott Taylor; 9 Danny Houghton (C); 13 Ligi Sao; 21 Jordan Lane; 12 Manu Ma'u; 29 Gareth Ellis. Subs (all used): 3 Carlos Tuimavave; 10 Tevita Satae; 20 Brad Fash; 22 Josh Bowden.
Tries: Fonua (14, 32), Tuimavave (38), Shaul (46), Ma'u (52); **Goals:** Sneyd 4/5; **Field goal:** Sneyd (77).
DRAGONS: 29 Sam Tomkins; 2 Lewis Tierney; 3 Samisoni Langi; 4 Israel Folau; 5 Fouad Yaha; 6 James Maloney; 7 Josh Drinkwater; 8 Remi Casty (C); 9 Michael McIlorum; 14 Julian Bousquet; 11 Matt Whitley; 17 Benjamin Jullien; 13 Benjamin Garcia. Subs (all used): 21 Paul Seguier; 23 Antoni Maria; 24 Jason Baitieri; 28 Sam Kasiano.
Tries: Jullien (23, 62), Yaha (29), Drinkwater (64), Langi (71), Maloney (79); **Goals:** Maloney 5/6.
Rugby Leaguer & League Express Men of the Match:
Hull FC: Manu Ma'u; *Dragons:* Sam Tomkins.
Penalty count: 5-6; **Half-time:** 16-10;
Referee: Gareth Hewer; **Attendance:** 12,003.

SALFORD RED DEVILS 12 WAKEFIELD TRINITY 22

RED DEVILS: 1 Niall Evalds; 23 Ken Sio; 3 Kris Welham; 4 Dan Sarginson; 22 Rhys Williams; 6 Tui Lolohea; 18 Chris Atkin; 8 Lee Mossop (C); 25 Connor Jones; 10 Gil Dudson; 12 Pauli Pauli; 29 Oliver Roberts; 17 Luke Yates. Subs (all used): 9 Joey Lussick; 11 Ryan Lannon; 14 Sebastine Ikahihifo; 19 Mark Flanagan.
Tries: Lolohea (15), Sio (46, 72); **Goals:** Lolohea 0/3.
TRINITY: 1 Alex Walker (D); 3 Bill Tupou; 4 Reece Lyne; 28 Ryan Atkins; 2 Tom Johnstone; 21 Max Jowitt; 6 Jacob Miller (C); 15 Craig Kopczak; 9 Kyle Wood; 37 Romain Navarrete; 11 Matty Ashurst; 14 Jay Pitts; 13 Joe Westerman. Subs (all used): 23 Josh Wood; 17 Chris Green; 36 Kelepi Tanginoa; 19 Jordan Crowther.
Tries: Jowitt (25), Johnstone (52), Tupou (58), Tanginoa (65); **Goals:** Jowitt 3/4.
Rugby Leaguer & League Express Men of the Match:
Red Devils: Pauli Pauli; *Trinity:* Kelepi Tanginoa.
Penalty count: 7-7; **Half-time:** 4-6;
Referee: Liam Moore; **Attendance:** 3,801.

ROUND 6

Thursday 5th March 2020

LEEDS RHINOS 66 TORONTO WOLFPACK 12

RHINOS: 16 Richie Myler; 24 Luke Briscoe; 3 Harry Newman; 4 Konrad Hurrell; 5 Ash Handley; 6 Robert Lui; 7 Luke Gale (C); 19 Mikolaj Oledzki; 14 Brad Dwyer; 8 Ava Seumanufagai; 12 Rhyse Martin; 11 Alex Mellor; 10 Matt Prior. Subs (all used): 22 Cameron Smith; 17 Adam Cuthbertson; 23 Callum McLelland; 25 James Donaldson.
Tries: Dwyer (3), Myler (7), Gale (20, 63), Lui (26, 32), Handley (39), Smith (55), Oledzki (61), Cuthbertson (77), Hurrell (79); **Goals:** Martin 11/11.
WOLFPACK: 24 Tony Gigot; 5 Liam Kay; 23 Hakim Miloudi; 4 Ricky Leutele; 2 Matty Russell; 1 Gareth O'Brien; 7 Josh McCrone (C); 8 Adam Sidlow; 9 Andy Ackers; 15 Gadwin Springer; 21 Sonny Bill Williams; 12 Bodene Thompson; 13 Jon Wilkin. Subs (all used): 10 Anthony Mullally; 16 Tom Olbison; 17 Blake Wallace; 25 Jack Wells.
Tries: McCrone (17), Wells (52); **Goals:** O'Brien 2/2.
Sin bin: McCrone (79) - professional foul.
Rugby Leaguer & League Express Men of the Match:
Rhinos: Luke Gale; *Wolfpack:* Ricky Leutele.
Penalty count: 7-7; **Half-time:** 36-6;
Referee: Liam Moore; **Attendance:** 12,143.

Friday 6th March 2020

ST HELENS 10 HUDDERSFIELD GIANTS 12

SAINTS: 22 Jack Welsby; 2 Tommy Makinson; 3 Kevin Naiqama; 14 Morgan Knowles; 5 Regan Grace; 6 Jonny Lomax; 7 Theo Fages; 8 Alex Walmsley; 9 James Roby (C); 10 Luke Thompson; 11 Zeb Taia; 12 Dominique Peyroux; 13 Louie McCarthy-Scarsbrook. Subs (all used): 15 Matty Lees; 16 Kyle Amor; 18 Joseph Paulo; 21 Matthew Costello.
Tries: Thompson (14), Knowles (22); **Goals:** Makinson 1/2.
GIANTS: 5 Darnell McIntosh; 2 Jermaine McGillvary; 4 Jordan Turner; 3 Jake Wardle; 27 Sam Wood; 6 Lee Gaskell; 7 Aidan Sezer (C); 8 James Gavet; 9 Adam O'Brien; 18 Paul Clough; 11 Kenny Edwards; 12 Joe Wardle; 13 Michael Lawrence. Subs (all used): 15 Oliver Wilson; 16 Aaron Murphy; 17 Ukuma Ta'ai; 22 Tom Holmes.
Tries: O'Brien (7), Jake Wardle (64); **Goals:** Sezer 2/2.
Rugby Leaguer & League Express Men of the Match:
Saints: Luke Thompson; *Giants:* Michael Lawrence.
Penalty count: 8-8; **Half-time:** 10-6;
Referee: Gareth Hewer; **Attendance:** 10,418.

WAKEFIELD TRINITY 26 HULL FC 27
(after golden point extra-time)

TRINITY: 1 Alex Walker; 3 Bill Tupou; 4 Reece Lyne; 28 Ryan Atkins; 2 Tom Johnstone; 6 Jacob Miller (C); 21 Max Jowitt; 17 Chris Green; 19 Jordan Crowther; 36 Kelepi Tanginoa; 14 Jay Pitts; 11 Matty Ashurst; 13 Joe Westerman. Subs (all used): 9 Kyle Wood; 10 Tinirau Arona; 22 George King; 37 Romain Navarrete.
Tries: Atkins (3, 58), Pitts (52), Johnstone (69, 77);
Goals: Jowitt 3/5.
HULL FC: 1 Jamie Shaul; 26 Kieran Buchanan; 4 Josh Griffin; 3 Carlos Tuimavave; 24 Mahe Fonua; 14 Albert Kelly; 7 Marc Sneyd; 8 Scott Taylor; 9 Danny Houghton (C); 22 Josh Bowden; 11 Josh Jones; 12 Manu Ma'u; 15 Joe Cator (D). Subs (all used): 10 Tevita Satae; 13 Ligi Sao; 16 Jordan Johnstone; 29 Gareth Ellis.
Tries: Fonua (9), Shaul (14), Buchanan (23), Kelly (62);
Goals: Sneyd 5/6; **Field goal:** Sneyd (81).
Rugby Leaguer & League Express Men of the Match:
Trinity: Ryan Atkins; *Hull FC:* Jamie Shaul.
Penalty count: 4-5; **Half-time:** 6-20;
Referee: James Child; **Attendance:** 5,528.

WARRINGTON WOLVES 9 CASTLEFORD TIGERS 8

WOLVES: 1 Stefan Ratchford; 2 Tom Lineham; 24 Keanan Brand; 4 Toby King; 5 Josh Charnley; 6 Blake Austin; 7 Gareth Widdop; 8 Chris Hill (C); 20 Danny Walker; 10 Mike Cooper; 11 Ben Currie; 13 Ben Murdoch-Masila; 14 Jason Clark. Subs: 9 Daryl Clark; 15 Joe Philbin; 17 Jake Mamo (not used); 18 Sitaleki Akauola.
Try: Lineham (26); **Goals:** Ratchford 2/3;
Field goal: Austin (79).
TIGERS: 1 Jordan Rankin; 2 Derrell Olpherts; 3 Peter Mata'utia; 4 Michael Shenton (C); 26 Calum Turner; 6 Jake Trueman; 7 Danny Richardson; 19 Daniel Smith; 9 Paul McShane; 16 George Griffin; 18 Cheyse Blair; 12 Mike McMeeken; 14 Nathan Massey. Subs (all used): 10 Grant Millington; 11 Oliver Holmes; 13 Adam Milner; 15 Jesse Sene-Lefao.
Try: Turner (52, pen); **Goals:** Richardson 2/2.
Rugby Leaguer & League Express Men of the Match:
Wolves: Joe Philbin; *Tigers:* Cheyse Blair.
Penalty count: 7-8; **Half-time:** 4-2;
Referee: Robert Hicks; **Attendance:** 9,228.

Saturday 7th March 2020

CATALANS DRAGONS 30 SALFORD RED DEVILS 14

DRAGONS: 29 Sam Tomkins; 2 Lewis Tierney; 3 Samisoni Langi; 4 Israel Folau; 5 Fouad Yaha; 6 James Maloney; 7 Josh Drinkwater; 8 Remi Casty (C); 9 Michael McIlorum; 14 Julian Bousquet; 11 Matt Whitley; 17 Benjamin Jullien; 13 Benjamin Garcia. Subs (all used): 21 Paul Seguier; 23 Antoni Maria; 24 Jason Baitieri; 28 Sam Kasiano.
Tries: McIlorum (6), Whitley (25, 29), Yaha (74), Tierney (77); **Goals:** Maloney 5/7.
RED DEVILS: 1 Niall Evalds; 23 Ken Sio; 3 Kris Welham; 24 Elliot Kear (D); 22 Rhys Williams; 6 Tui Lolohea; 7 Kevin Brown; 8 Lee Mossop (C); 9 Joey Lussick; 10 Gil Dudson; 11 Ryan Lannon; 29 Oliver Roberts; 19 Mark Flanagan. Subs (all used): 12 Pauli Pauli; 13 Tyrone McCarthy; 14 Sebastine Ikahihifo; 17 Luke Yates.
Tries: Evalds (42), Sio (52, 66); **Goals:** Lolohea 1/3.
Rugby Leaguer & League Express Men of the Match:
Dragons: James Maloney; *Red Devils:* Ken Sio.
Penalty count: 8-6; **Half-time:** 18-0;
Referee: Chris Kendall; **Attendance:** 7,940.

Sunday 8th March 2020

WIGAN WARRIORS 30 HULL KINGSTON ROVERS 16

WARRIORS: 6 Bevan French; 21 Dom Manfredi; 1 Zak Hardaker; 23 Jake Bibby; 2 Liam Marshall; 7 Thomas Leuluai (C); 31 Jackson Hastings; 17 Oliver Partington; 9 Sam Powell; 20 Liam Byrne; 11 Willie Isa; 12 Liam Farrell; 16 Morgan Smithies. Subs (all used): 10 George Burgess; 14 Ben Flower; 30 Ethan Havard; 28 Harry Smith.
Tries: Hastings (20, 36), Farrell (25), Powell (56), Marshall (63); **Goals:** Hardaker 5/5.
On report:
Flower (27) - alleged dangerous challenge on Storton.
ROVERS: 19 Will Dagger; 5 Greg Minikin; 3 Shaun Kenny-Dowall (C); 4 Kane Linnett; 23 Ethan Ryan (D); 24 Joe Keyes; 31 Ryan Brierley; 8 Robbie Mulhern; 27 Elliot Minchella; 15 George Lawler; 12 Harvey Livett; 28 Matthew Storton; 25 Matty Gee. Subs (all used): 7 Jordan Abdull; 16 Daniel Murray; 18 Jez Litten; 26 Will Maher.
Tries: Ryan (13), Minikin (34), Brierley (48);
Goals: Brierley 2/3.
Rugby Leaguer & League Express Men of the Match:
Warriors: Liam Farrell; *Rovers:* Elliot Minchella.
Penalty count: 6-8; **Half-time:** 18-12;
Referee: Tom Grant; **Attendance:** 11,511.

ROUND 7

Thursday 12th March 2020

HULL FC 4 WARRINGTON WOLVES 38

HULL FC: 1 Jamie Shaul; 24 Mahe Fonua; 3 Carlos Tuimavave; 4 Josh Griffin; 26 Kieran Buchanan; 14 Albert Kelly; 7 Marc Sneyd; 8 Scott Taylor; 9 Danny Houghton (C); 10 Tevita Satae; 11 Josh Jones; 21 Jordan Lane; 22 Josh Bowden. Subs (all used): 16 Jordan Johnstone; 19 Masi Matongo; 20 Brad Fash; 30 Jack Brown.
Try: Buchanan (80); **Goals:** Sneyd 0/1.
WOLVES: 1 Stefan Ratchford; 5 Josh Charnley; 3 Anthony Gelling; 4 Toby King; 2 Tom Lineham; 6 Blake Austin; 7 Gareth Widdop; 8 Chris Hill (C); 20 Danny Walker; 10 Mike Cooper; 11 Ben Currie; 13 Ben Murdoch-Masila; 14 Jason Clark. Subs (all used): 9 Daryl Clark; 15 Joe Philbin; 17 Jake Mamo; 18 Sitaleki Akauola.
Tries: Austin (4, 71), Lineham (37), Widdop (48, 69), Gelling (57), Murdoch-Masila (59);
Goals: Ratchford 4/6, Widdop 1/1.
Rugby Leaguer & League Express Men of the Match:
Hull FC: Jack Brown; *Wolves:* Ben Murdoch-Masila.
Penalty count: 7-4; **Half-time:** 0-12;
Referee: Chris Kendall; **Attendance:** 10,214.

Friday 13th March 2020

SALFORD RED DEVILS 18 WIGAN WARRIORS 14

RED DEVILS: 1 Niall Evalds; 23 Ken Sio; 3 Kris Welham; 4 Dan Sarginson; 22 Rhys Williams; 6 Tui Lolohea; 7 Kevin Brown; 8 Lee Mossop (C); 9 Joey Lussick; 17 Luke Yates; 11 Ryan Lannon; 29 Oliver Roberts; 13 Tyrone McCarthy. Subs: 12 Pauli Pauli; 14 Sebastine Ikahihifo; 19 Mark Flanagan; 24 Elliot Kear (not used).
Tries: Evalds (59, 65), Brown (72); **Goals:** Lolohea 3/4.
WARRIORS: 6 Bevan French; 21 Dom Manfredi; 3 Chris Hankinson; 23 Jake Bibby; 2 Liam Marshall; 7 Thomas Leuluai (C); 31 Jackson Hastings; 10 George Burgess; 9 Sam Powell; 20 Liam Byrne; 11 Willie Isa; 12 Liam Farrell; 16 Morgan Smithies. Subs (all used): 19 Joe Bullock; 30 Ethan Havard; 22 Mitch Clark; 28 Harry Smith.
Tries: Hastings (21), Powell (36); **Goals:** Hankinson 3/3.

Rugby Leaguer & League Express Men of the Match: *Red Devils:* Dan Sarginson; *Warriors:* Liam Farrell.
Penalty count: 9-5; **Half-time:** 2-14;
Referee: James Child; **Attendance:** 4,796.

Sunday 15th March 2020

CASTLEFORD TIGERS 28 ST HELENS 14

TIGERS: 1 Jordan Rankin; 2 Derrell Olpherts; 3 Peter Mata'utia; 4 Michael Shenton (C); 21 James Clare; 6 Jake Trueman; 7 Danny Richardson; 8 Liam Watts; 9 Paul McShane; 16 George Griffin; 18 Cheyse Blair; 12 Mike McMeeken; 14 Nathan Massey. Subs (all used): 10 Grant Millington; 13 Adam Milner; 15 Jesse Sene-Lefao; 19 Daniel Smith.
Tries: Mata'utia (12), Olpherts (20, 33), Blair (56), Trueman (74); **Goals:** Richardson 4/7.
SAINTS: 1 Lachlan Coote; 2 Tommy Makinson; 3 Kevin Naiqama; 22 Jack Welsby; 5 Regan Grace; 6 Jonny Lomax; 7 Theo Fages; 8 Alex Walmsley; 9 James Roby (C); 10 Luke Thompson; 11 Zeb Taia; 12 Dominique Peyroux; 14 Morgan Knowles. Subs (all used): 13 Louie McCarthy-Scarsbrook; 15 Matty Lees; 16 Kyle Amor; 19 Aaron Smith.
Tries: Makinson (39), Welsby (73), Thompson (78);
Goals: Makinson 1/3.
Sin bin: Lees (30) - high tackle on Rankin; McCarthy-Scarsbrook (44) - high tackle on Richardson.
Rugby Leaguer & League Express Men of the Match: *Tigers:* Paul McShane; *Saints:* Tommy Makinson.
Penalty count: 6-7; **Half-time:** 14-4;
Referee: Liam Moore; **Attendance:** 7,268.

Toronto Wolfpack withdrew from Super League prior to the season restarting, with their results later being expunged from the league table.

ROUND 4

Sunday 2nd August 2020

ST HELENS 34 CATALANS DRAGONS 6

SAINTS: 1 Lachlan Coote; 2 Tommy Makinson; 3 Kevin Naiqama; 4 Mark Percival; 5 Regan Grace; 6 Jonny Lomax; 7 Theo Fages; 8 Alex Walmsley; 9 James Roby (C); 32 James Graham (D2); 11 Zeb Taia; 20 James Bentley; 14 Morgan Knowles. Subs (all used): 13 Louie McCarthy-Scarsbrook; 16 Kyle Amor; 19 Aaron Smith; 23 Joe Batchelor.
Tries: Coote (16, 45), Bentley (26), Taia (33), Makinson (53), Walmsley (71); **Goals:** Coote 5/7.
DRAGONS: 25 Arthur Mourgue; 16 Tom Davies (D); 3 Samisoni Langi; 4 Israel Folau; 5 Fouad Yaha; 6 James Maloney; 7 Josh Drinkwater; 14 Julian Bousquet; 9 Michael Mcllorum; 8 Remi Casty (C); 12 Joel Tomkins; 11 Matt Whitley; 13 Benjamin Garcia. Subs (all used): 10 Sam Moa; 18 Alrix Da Costa; 24 Jason Baitieri; 28 Sam Kasiano.
Try: Maloney (61); **Goals:** Maloney 1/1.
Rugby Leaguer & League Express Men of the Match: *Saints:* Lachlan Coote; *Dragons:* Arthur Mourgue.
Penalty count: 2-4; **Half-time:** 16-0; **Referee:** Ben Thaler. *(at Emerald Headingley, Leeds).*

ROUND 2

Sunday 2nd August 2020

HUDDERSFIELD GIANTS 26 LEEDS RHINOS 27
(after golden point extra-time)

GIANTS: 1 Ashton Golding (D); 24 Louis Senior; 3 Jake Wardle; 4 Jordan Turner; 5 Darnell McIntosh; 6 Lee Gaskell; 7 Aidan Sezer (C); 8 James Gavet; 9 Adam O'Brien; 14 Matty English; 11 Kenny Edwards; 27 Sam Wood; 13 Michael Lawrence. Subs (all used): 22 Tom Holmes; 15 Oliver Wilson; 10 Suaia Matagi; 16 Aaron Murphy.
Tries: Senior (4, 63), McIntosh (16, 22, 45);
Goals: Sezer 3/6.
RHINOS: 16 Richie Myler; 24 Luke Briscoe; 3 Harry Newman; 4 Konrad Hurrell; 5 Ash Handley; 7 Luke Gale (C); 6 Robert Lui; 8 Ava Seumanufagai; 14 Brad Dwyer; 19 Mikolaj Oledzki; 11 Alex Mellor; 12 Rhyse Martin; 10 Matt Prior. Subs (all used): 22 Cameron Smith; 25 James Donaldson; 17 Adam Cuthbertson; 9 Kruise Leeming (D).
Tries: Hurrell (13, 78), Gale (68), L Briscoe (70), Mellor (72);
Goals: Martin 3/5; **Field goal:** Gale (85).
Sin bin: Handley (62) - repeated team offences.
Rugby Leaguer & League Express Men of the Match: *Giants:* Ashton Golding; *Rhinos:* Luke Gale.
Penalty count: 11-7; **Half-time:** 14-6;
Referee: Robert Hicks. *(at Emerald Headingley).*

ROUND 8

Saturday 8th August 2020

CASTLEFORD TIGERS 14 CATALANS DRAGONS 40

TIGERS: 25 Greg Eden; 2 Derrell Olpherts; 3 Peter Mata'utia; 4 Michael Shenton (C); 21 James Clare; 6 Jake Trueman; 7 Danny Richardson; 16 George Griffin; 9 Paul McShane; 10 Grant Millington; 11 Oliver Holmes; 12 Mike McMeeken; 13 Adam Milner. Subs (all used): 15 Jesse Sene-Lefao; 17 Alex Foster; 22 Jacques O'Neill; 24 Tyla Hepi.
Tries: Shenton (8, 10); **Goals:** Richardson 3/3.
Sin bin: Mata'utia (31) - dangerous challenge on Langi.
DRAGONS: 25 Arthur Mourgue; 16 Tom Davies; 3 Samisoni Langi; 4 Israel Folau; 5 Fouad Yaha; 6 James Maloney; 7 Josh Drinkwater; 14 Julian Bousquet; 13 Benjamin Garcia; 10 Sam Moa; 11 Matt Whitley; 12 Joel Tomkins; 8 Remi Casty (C). Subs (all used): 17 Benjamin Jullien; 18 Alrix Da Costa; 24 Jason Baitieri; 28 Sam Kasiano.
Tries: Davies (23, 67), Da Costa (32), Folau (34), Garcia (45), J Tomkins (63), Baitieri (78); **Goals:** Maloney 6/8.
Rugby Leaguer & League Express Men of the Match: *Tigers:* Jake Trueman; *Dragons:* Israel Folau.
Penalty count: 4-7; **Half-time:** 14-16;
Referee: Robert Hicks. *(at Emerald Headingley, Leeds).*

WARRINGTON WOLVES 40
HULL KINGSTON ROVERS 10

WOLVES: 1 Stefan Ratchford; 2 Tom Lineham; 3 Anthony Gelling; 4 Toby King; 5 Josh Charnley; 6 Blake Austin; 7 Gareth Widdop; 8 Chris Hill (C); 9 Daryl Clark; 10 Mike Cooper; 11 Ben Currie; 12 Jack Hughes; 14 Jason Clark. Subs (all used): 15 Joe Philbin; 18 Sitaleki Akauola; 26 Matty Ashton; 20 Danny Walker.
Tries: Lineham (23, 80), Akauola (35), Gelling (45), Charnley (53), Widdop (62), Ratchford (69);
Goals: Ratchford 5/6, Widdop 1/1.
Sin bin: Gelling (12) - dangerous challenge on Gee.
ROVERS: 1 Adam Quinlan; 19 Will Dagger; 3 Shaun Kenny-Dowall; 4 Kane Linnett; 2 Ben Crooks; 31 Ryan Brierley; 30 Jamie Ellis; 32 Nathaniel Peteru (D); 9 Matt Parcell; 15 George Lawler; 25 Matty Gee; 11 Weller Hauraki (C); 13 Dean Hadley. Subs (all used): 27 Elliot Minchella; 16 Daniel Murray; 17 Kyle Trout; 14 Mitch Garbutt.
Tries: Crooks (1), Quinlan (75); **Goals:** Brierley 1/2.
Sin bin: Kenny-Dowall (16) - professional foul.
Rugby Leaguer & League Express Men of the Match: *Wolves:* Daryl Clark; *Rovers:* Matty Gee.
Penalty count: 4-5; **Half-time:** 12-4;
Referee: James Child. *(at Emerald Headingley, Leeds).*

Sunday 9th August 2020

SALFORD RED DEVILS 54 HULL FC 18

RED DEVILS: 1 Niall Evalds; 23 Ken Sio; 3 Kris Welham; 4 Dan Sarginson; 22 Rhys Williams; 6 Tui Lolohea; 18 Chris Atkin; 8 Lee Mossop (C); 9 Joey Lussick; 14 Sebastine Ikahihifo; 11 Ryan Lannon; 13 Tyrone McCarthy; 17 Luke Yates. Subs (all used): 12 Pauli Pauli; 20 Josh Johnson; 19 Mark Flanagan; 24 Elliot Kear.
Tries: Sio (10, 78), Lolohea (21, 25), Williams (30, 68), Atkin (44), Yates (59), Welham (72), Evalds (79);
Goals: Lolohea 7/10.
HULL FC: 1 Jamie Shaul; 33 Ratu Naulago; 3 Carlos Tuimavave; 4 Josh Griffin; 24 Mahe Fonua; 14 Albert Kelly; 7 Marc Sneyd; 29 Gareth Ellis; 9 Danny Houghton (C); 13 Ligi Sao; 11 Josh Jones; 12 Manu Ma'u; 23 Andre Savelio. Subs (all used): 6 Jake Connor; 10 Tevita Satae; 15 Joe Cator; 22 Josh Bowden.
Tries: Kelly (3), Ma'u (38), Shaul (49); **Goals:** Sneyd 3/3.
Sin bin: Naulago (62) - delaying restart.
Rugby Leaguer & League Express Men of the Match: *Red Devils:* Tui Lolohea; *Hull FC:* Albert Kelly.
Penalty count: 2-4; **Half-time:** 22-12;
Referee: Liam Moore. *(at Emerald Headingley, Leeds).*

WAKEFIELD TRINITY 22 WIGAN WARRIORS 23

TRINITY: 39 Tony Gigot (D); 38 Liam Kay (D2); 4 Reece Lyne; 3 Bill Tupou; 2 Tom Johnstone; 6 Jacob Miller (C); 21 Max Jowitt; 15 Craig Kopczak; 23 Josh Wood; 37 Romain Navarrete; 14 Jay Pitts; 36 Kelepi Tanginoa; 10 Tinirau Arona. Subs (all used): 9 Kyle Wood; 8 David Fifita; 12 Danny Kirmond; 18 Adam Tangata.
Tries: K Wood (34), Johnstone (66), Kay (71, 78);
Goals: Gigot 2/4, Jowitt 1/1.
WARRIORS: 6 Bevan French; 21 Dom Manfredi; 1 Zak Hardaker; 23 Jake Bibby; 2 Liam Marshall; 31 Jackson Hastings; 7 Thomas Leuluai (C); 19 Joe Bullock; 9 Sam Powell; 20 Liam Byrne; 11 Willie Isa; 12 Liam Farrell; 30 Ethan Havard. Subs (all used): 10 George Burgess; 22 Mitch Clark; 28 Harry Smith; 16 Morgan Smithies.
Tries: Hardaker (15), French (24), Marshall (37), Bibby (51);
Goals: Hardaker 3/4; **Field goal:** Smith (77).

Rugby Leaguer & League Express Men of the Match: *Trinity:* Kyle Wood; *Warriors:* Zak Hardaker.
Penalty count: 9-4; **Half-time:** 6-16;
Referee: Ben Thaler. *(at Emerald Headingley, Leeds).*

LEEDS RHINOS 0 ST HELENS 48

RHINOS: 5 Ash Handley; 24 Luke Briscoe; 3 Harry Newman; 26 Alex Sutcliffe; 2 Tom Briscoe; 23 Callum McLelland; 7 Luke Gale (C); 8 Ava Seumanufagai; 14 Brad Dwyer; 10 Matt Prior; 11 Alex Mellor; 12 Rhyse Martin; 22 Cameron Smith. Subs (all used): 19 Mikolaj Oledzki; 17 Adam Cuthbertson; 9 Kruise Leeming; 21 Rhys Evans (D).
SAINTS: 1 Lachlan Coote; 2 Tommy Makinson; 3 Kevin Naiqama; 21 Matthew Costello; 5 Regan Grace; 6 Jonny Lomax; 7 Theo Fages; 8 Alex Walmsley; 9 James Roby (C); 32 James Graham; 11 Zeb Taia; 20 James Bentley; 14 Morgan Knowles. Subs (all used): 13 Louie McCarthy-Scarsbrook; 15 Matty Lees; 16 Kyle Amor; 19 Aaron Smith.
Tries: Graham (8), Walmsley (15), Makinson (26), Grace (39, 57, 65), Fages (74), Coote (80); **Goals:** Coote 8/8.
Rugby Leaguer & League Express Men of the Match: *Rhinos:* Alex Sutcliffe; *Saints:* Regan Grace.
Penalty count: 4-5; **Half-time:** 0-24; **Referee:** Ben Thaler.

ROUND 2

Saturday 15th August 2020

WAKEFIELD TRINITY 0 CATALANS DRAGONS 58

TRINITY: 39 Tony Gigot; 38 Liam Kay; 4 Reece Lyne; 3 Bill Tupou; 27 Lee Kershaw; 6 Jacob Miller (C); 29 Ryan Hampshire; 15 Craig Kopczak; 23 Josh Wood; 36 Kelepi Tanginoa; 14 Jay Pitts; 11 Matty Ashurst; 13 Joe Westerman. Subs (all used): 8 David Fifita; 9 Kyle Wood; 18 Adam Tangata; 37 Romain Navarrete.
DRAGONS: 29 Sam Tomkins; 16 Tom Davies; 3 Samisoni Langi; 1 David Mead; 5 Fouad Yaha; 6 James Maloney; 7 Josh Drinkwater; 8 Remi Casty (C); 9 Michael Mcllorum; 10 Sam Moa; 11 Matt Whitley; 12 Joel Tomkins; 13 Benjamin Garcia. Subs (all used): 14 Julian Bousquet; 17 Benjamin Jullien; 24 Jason Baitieri; 28 Sam Kasiano.
Tries: Whitley (8, 64, 69), Langi (11, 76), Davies (17, 27, 41), Bousquet (48), Yaha (56);
Goals: Maloney 7/9, S Tomkins 2/2.
Rugby Leaguer & League Express Men of the Match: *Trinity:* Kyle Wood; *Dragons:* Sam Tomkins.
Penalty count: 5-5; **Half-time:** 0-24;
Referee: Chris Kendall.
(at Totally Wicked Stadium, St Helens).

ROUND 9

Saturday 15th August 2020

HUDDERSFIELD GIANTS 18
WARRINGTON WOLVES 19

GIANTS: 1 Ashton Golding; 2 Jermaine McGillvary; 21 Leroy Cudjoe (C); 3 Jake Wardle; 5 Darnell McIntosh; 22 Tom Holmes; 7 Aidan Sezer; 14 Matty English; 9 Adam O'Brien; 10 Suaia Matagi; 11 Kenny Edwards; 17 Ukuma Ta'ai; 13 Michael Lawrence. Subs (all used): 23 Oliver Russell; 26 Sam Hewitt; 27 Sam Wood; 28 Adam Walne.
Tries: Ta'ai (12), McGillvary (53), Russell (73);
Goals: Sezer 2/3, Russell 1/1.
WOLVES: 1 Stefan Ratchford; 2 Tom Lineham; 4 Toby King; 17 Jake Mamo; 5 Josh Charnley; 6 Blake Austin; 7 Gareth Widdop; 8 Chris Hill (C); 9 Daryl Clark; 10 Mike Cooper; 11 Ben Currie; 13 Ben Murdoch-Masila; 12 Jack Hughes. Subs (all used): 14 Jason Clark; 15 Joe Philbin; 18 Sitaleki Akauola; 20 Danny Walker.
Tries: Currie (24), Widdop (41), Lineham (58);
Goals: Ratchford 3/4; **Field goal:** Austin (75).
Sin bin: Murdoch-Masila (3) - high challenge on English; Austin (19) - trip on O'Brien.
Rugby Leaguer & League Express Men of the Match: *Giants:* Sam Hewitt; *Wolves:* Toby King.
Penalty count: 9-4; **Half-time:** 8-8; **Referee:** Ben Thaler. *(at Totally Wicked Stadium, St Helens).*

ROUND 16

Sunday 16th August 2020

ST HELENS 10 CASTLEFORD TIGERS 0

SAINTS: 1 Lachlan Coote; 2 Tommy Makinson; 3 Kevin Naiqama; 4 Mark Percival; 5 Regan Grace; 6 Jonny Lomax; 7 Theo Fages; 8 Alex Walmsley; 9 James Roby (C); 32 James Graham; 11 Zeb Taia; 20 James Bentley; 14 Morgan Knowles. Subs (all used): 13 Louie McCarthy-Scarsbrook; 15 Matty Lees; 16 Kyle Amor; 19 Aaron Smith.
Try: Fages (77); **Goals:** Coote 3/3.
On report:
Makinson (14) - alleged dangerous contact on Watts.

TIGERS: 34 Gareth O'Brien (D2); 2 Derrell Olpherts; 17 Alex Foster; 4 Michael Shenton (C); 21 James Clare; 9 Paul McShane; 7 Danny Richardson; 8 Liam Watts; 13 Adam Milner; 16 George Griffin; 11 Oliver Holmes; 12 Mike McMeeken; 14 Nathan Massey. Subs (all used): 10 Grant Millington; 26 Calum Turner; 15 Jesse Sene-Lefao; 22 Jacques O'Neill.
Sin bin: Millington (48) - shoulder charge on Lomax.
Rugby Leaguer & League Express Men of the Match: *Saints:* Lachlan Coote; *Tigers:* Oliver Holmes.
Penalty count: 6-1; **Half-time:** 0-0; **Referee:** James Child.

ROUND 9

Sunday 16th August 2020

WIGAN WARRIORS 28 LEEDS RHINOS 10

WARRIORS: 6 Bevan French; 21 Dom Manfredi; 1 Zak Hardaker; 23 Jake Bibby; 2 Liam Marshall; 28 Harry Smith; 31 Jackson Hastings; 19 Joe Bullock; 9 Sam Powell; 20 Liam Byrne; 11 Willie Isa; 12 Liam Farrell (C); 30 Ethan Havard. Subs (all used): 22 Mitch Clark; 15 Joe Greenwood; 33 Joe Shorrocks; 16 Morgan Smithies.
Tries: Farrell (15), French (38, 80), Manfredi (52), Bibby (75); **Goals:** Hardaker 4/6.
RHINOS: 5 Ash Handley; 24 Luke Briscoe; 3 Harry Newman; 4 Konrad Hurrell; 2 Tom Briscoe; 23 Callum McLelland; 7 Luke Gale (C); 28 Tom Holroyd; 9 Kruise Leeming; 10 Matt Prior; 20 Bodene Thompson (D); 12 Rhyse Martin; 17 Adam Cuthbertson. Subs (all used): 14 Brad Dwyer; 19 Mikolaj Oledzki; 15 Liam Sutcliffe; 22 Cameron Smith.
Tries: T Briscoe (21), L Sutcliffe (65); **Goals:** Martin 1/2.
Sin bin: Gale (65) - dangerous challenge on Hastings.
Rugby Leaguer & League Express Men of the Match: *Warriors:* Liam Farrell; *Rhinos:* Ash Handley.
Penalty count: 5-4; **Half-time:** 12-4;
Referee: Robert Hicks.
(at Totally Wicked Stadium, St Helens).

ROUND 18

Saturday 29th August 2020

WIGAN WARRIORS 30 CASTLEFORD TIGERS 22

WARRIORS: 6 Bevan French; 2 Liam Marshall; 1 Zak Hardaker; 23 Jake Bibby; 5 Joe Burgess; 31 Jackson Hastings; 7 Thomas Leuluai (C); 19 Joe Bullock; 9 Sam Powell; 20 Liam Byrne; 11 Willie Isa; 12 Liam Farrell; 30 Ethan Havard. Subs (all used): 10 George Burgess; 14 Ben Flower; 16 Morgan Smithies; 28 Harry Smith.
Tries: Powell (24), J Burgess (26), Flower (35), Farrell (62), Bullock (67); **Goals:** Hardaker 5/6.
Sin bin: Smithies (42) - dangerous challenge on Clare.
TIGERS: 34 Gareth O'Brien; 2 Derrell Olpherts; 17 Alex Foster; 4 Michael Shenton (C); 21 James Clare; 6 Jake Trueman; 7 Danny Richardson; 8 Liam Watts; 9 Paul McShane; 16 George Griffin; 11 Oliver Holmes; 12 Mike McMeeken; 14 Nathan Massey. Subs (all used): 10 Grant Millington; 13 Adam Milner; 15 Jesse Sene-Lefao; 19 Daniel Smith.
Tries: O'Brien (16), Massey (21), Olpherts (44), Shenton (74); **Goals:** Richardson 3/4.
Rugby Leaguer & League Express Men of the Match: *Warriors:* Liam Farrell; *Tigers:* Gareth O'Brien.
Penalty count: 6-1; **Half-time:** 16-12;
Referee: James Child.
(at Halliwell Jones Stadium, Warrington).

ROUND 10

Saturday 29th August 2020

LEEDS RHINOS 50 SALFORD RED DEVILS 12

RHINOS: 16 Richie Myler; 2 Tom Briscoe; 15 Liam Sutcliffe; 3 Harry Newman; 5 Ash Handley; 6 Robert Lui; 7 Luke Gale (C); 8 Ava Seumanufagai; 9 Kruise Leeming; 19 Mikolaj Oledzki; 20 Bodene Thompson; 12 Rhyse Martin; 10 Matt Prior. Subs (all used): 14 Brad Dwyer; 17 Adam Cuthbertson; 26 Alex Sutcliffe; 28 Tom Holroyd.
Tries: Handley (9, 31, 76), Myler (14, 28, 74), Gale (16), Lui (58), Oledzki (62); **Goals:** Martin 7/9.
RED DEVILS: 1 Niall Evalds; 23 Ken Sio; 3 Kris Welham; 24 Elliot Kear; 22 Rhys Williams; 6 Tui Lolohea; 7 Kevin Brown; 14 Sebastine Ikahihifo; 9 Joey Lussick; 10 Gil Dudson; 11 Ryan Lannon; 13 Tyrone McCarthy; 17 Luke Yates. Subs (all used): 12 Pauli Pauli; 18 Chris Atkin; 19 Mark Flanagan (C); 20 Josh Johnson.
Tries: Evalds (47, 52); **Goals:** Lolohea 2/2.
Rugby Leaguer & League Express Men of the Match: *Rhinos:* Richie Myler; *Red Devils:* Niall Evalds.
Penalty count: 4-1; **Half-time:** 26-0;
Referee: Liam Moore.
(at Halliwell Jones Stadium, Warrington).

Sunday 30th August 2020

HULL KINGSTON ROVERS 18 ST HELENS 32

ROVERS: 1 Adam Quinlan; 23 Ethan Ryan; 3 Shaun Kenny-Dowall; 4 Kane Linnett; 5 Greg Minikin; 31 Ryan Brierley; 30 Jamie Ellis; 32 Nathaniel Peteru; 9 Matt Parcell; 15 George Lawler; 25 Matty Gee; 28 Matthew Storton; 11 Weller Hauraki (C). Subs (all used): 13 Dean Hadley; 16 Daniel Murray; 8 Robbie Mulhern; 26 Will Maher.
Tries: Quinlan (24), Ryan (27), Parcell (71); **Goals:** Ellis 3/4.
SAINTS: 1 Lachlan Coote; 22 Jack Welsby; 3 Kevin Naiqama; 21 Matthew Costello; 5 Regan Grace; 6 Jonny Lomax; 7 Theo Fages; 8 Alex Walmsley; 9 James Roby (C); 15 Matty Lees; 11 Zeb Taia; 20 James Bentley; 32 James Graham. Subs (all used): 12 Dominique Peyroux; 13 Louie McCarthy-Scarsbrook; 16 Kyle Amor; 19 Aaron Smith.
Tries: Walmsley (5), Welsby (16, 62), Naiqama (47), Smith (59); **Goals:** Coote 6/6.
Rugby Leaguer & League Express Men of the Match: *Rovers:* Matt Parcell; *Saints:* James Roby.
Penalty count: 4-2; **Half-time:** 12-12;
Referee: Scott Mikalauskas.
(at Halliwell Jones Stadium, Warrington).

HUDDERSFIELD GIANTS 12 HULL FC 31

GIANTS: 1 Ashton Golding; 2 Jermaine McGillvary; 21 Leroy Cudjoe (C); 3 Jake Wardle; 5 Darnell McIntosh; 23 Oliver Russell; 22 Tom Holmes; 14 Matty English; 9 Adam O'Brien; 10 Suaia Matagi; 11 Kenny Edwards; 4 Jordan Turner; 13 Michael Lawrence. Subs (all used): 8 James Gavet; 15 Oliver Wilson; 26 Sam Hewitt; 27 Sam Wood.
Tries: Golding (36), Turner (62); **Goals:** Russell 2/2.
HULL FC: 1 Jamie Shaul; 33 Ratu Naulago; 3 Carlos Tuimavave; 4 Josh Griffin; 2 Bureta Faraimo; 14 Albert Kelly; 7 Marc Sneyd; 29 Gareth Ellis; 16 Jordan Johnstone; 20 Brad Fash; 21 Jordan Lane; 12 Manu Ma'u; 15 Joe Cator. Subs (all used): 9 Danny Houghton (C); 10 Tevita Satae; 24 Mahe Fonua; 30 Jack Brown.
Tries: Kelly (11), Sneyd (17), Griffin (23), Brown (28), Fonua (33); **Goals:** Sneyd 2/3, Griffin 3/3;
Field goal: Shaul (77).
Sin bin: Fonua (64) - dangerous challenge on McIntosh.
Rugby Leaguer & League Express Men of the Match: *Giants:* Kenny Edwards; *Hull FC:* Jordan Johnstone.
Penalty count: 3-8; **Half-time:** 6-28;
Referee: Chris Kendall.
(at Halliwell Jones Stadium, Warrington).

WARRINGTON WOLVES 36 WAKEFIELD TRINITY 0

WOLVES: 1 Stefan Ratchford; 2 Tom Lineham; 4 Toby King; 17 Jake Mamo; 5 Josh Charnley; 6 Blake Austin; 7 Gareth Widdop; 8 Chris Hill (C); 9 Daryl Clark; 10 Mike Cooper; 11 Ben Currie; 12 Jack Hughes; 14 Jason Clark. Subs (all used): 15 Joe Philbin; 19 Matt Davis; 25 Samy Kibula (D); 26 Matty Ashton.
Tries: King (18), Austin (26, 46, 76), Charnley (32), Currie (71); **Goals:** Ratchford 6/6.
TRINITY: 21 Max Jowitt; 40 Innes Senior; 3 Bill Tupou; 39 Tony Gigot; 24 Jack Croft; 6 Jacob Miller (C); 29 Ryan Hampshire; 37 Romain Navarrete; 9 Kyle Wood; 10 Tinirau Arona; 16 James Batchelor; 11 Matty Ashurst; 13 Joe Westerman. Subs (all used): 12 Danny Kirmond; 17 Chris Green; 19 Jordan Crowther; 36 Kelepi Tanginoa.
Rugby Leaguer & League Express Men of the Match: *Wolves:* Blake Austin; *Trinity:* Kelepi Tanginoa.
Penalty count: 4-5; **Half-time:** 18-0;
Referee: Marcus Griffiths.

ROUND 11

Thursday 3rd September 2020

HULL KINGSTON ROVERS 34 WIGAN WARRIORS 18

ROVERS: 19 Will Dagger; 23 Ethan Ryan; 3 Shaun Kenny-Dowall; 4 Kane Linnett; 5 Greg Minikin; 7 Jordan Abdull; 20 Mikey Lewis; 11 Weller Hauraki (C); 18 Jez Litten; 15 George Lawler; 28 Matthew Storton; 13 Dean Hadley; 27 Elliot Minchella. Subs (all used): 12 Harvey Livett; 16 Daniel Murray; 24 Joe Keyes; 32 Nathaniel Peteru.
Tries: Minchella (17, 23), Minikin (20, 40, 45), Hadley (43);
Goals: Lewis 2/3, Dagger 2/3, Abdull 1/1.
Sin bin: Kenny-Dowall (70) - professional foul.
WARRIORS: 6 Bevan French; 21 Dom Manfredi; 1 Zak Hardaker; 4 Oliver Gildart; 23 Jake Bibby; 28 Harry Smith; 31 Jackson Hastings; 20 Liam Byrne; 9 Sam Powell; 14 Ben Flower; 11 Willie Isa; 12 Liam Farrell (C); 17 Oliver Partington. Subs (all used): 15 Joe Greenwood; 22 Mitch Clark; 32 Amir Bourouh; 33 Joe Shorrocks.
Tries: Powell (9), Smith (26), Hastings (71);
Goals: Hardaker 3/3.
Rugby Leaguer & League Express Men of the Match: *Rovers:* Jordan Abdull; *Warriors:* Harry Smith.
Penalty count: 2-2; **Half-time:** 22-12;
Referee: Tom Grant. *(at Emerald Headingley, Leeds).*

SALFORD RED DEVILS 30 CASTLEFORD TIGERS 37

RED DEVILS: 1 Niall Evalds; 5 Krisnan Inu; 3 Kris Welham; 24 Elliot Kear; 22 Rhys Williams; 6 Tui Lolohea; 7 Kevin Brown; 10 Gil Dudson; 9 Joey Lussick; 17 Luke Yates; 21 James Greenwood; 13 Tyrone McCarthy; 19 Mark Flanagan (C). Subs (all used): 12 Pauli Pauli; 14 Sebastine Ikahihifo; 16 Greg Burke; 30 Andy Ackers (D).
Tries: Brown (3), Evalds (7), Lussick (11), Yates (38), Williams (52); **Goals:** Inu 5/5.
TIGERS: 34 Gareth O'Brien; 2 Derrell Olpherts; 17 Alex Foster; 4 Michael Shenton (C); 25 Greg Eden; 3 Peter Mata'utia; 7 Danny Richardson; 8 Liam Watts; 9 Paul McShane; 16 George Griffin; 11 Oliver Holmes; 12 Mike McMeeken; 14 Nathan Massey. Subs: 10 Grant Millington; 13 Adam Milner; 20 Junior Moors; 26 Calum Turner (not used).
Tries: Richardson (18), Shenton (24), McShane (28, 30), McMeeken (47), Millington (72); **Goals:** Richardson 6/6;
Field goal: Richardson (65).
Rugby Leaguer & League Express Men of the Match: *Red Devils:* Luke Yates; *Tigers:* Danny Richardson.
Penalty count: 3-5; **Half-time:** 24-24;
Referee: Robert Hicks. *(at Emerald Headingley, Leeds).*

Friday 4th September 2020

HUDDERSFIELD GIANTS 6 ST HELENS 54

GIANTS: 24 Louis Senior; 2 Jermaine McGillvary; 21 Leroy Cudjoe (C); 4 Jordan Turner; 33 Dominic Young; 23 Oliver Russell; 22 Tom Holmes; 8 James Gavet; 9 Adam O'Brien; 14 Matty English; 26 Sam Hewitt; 12 Joe Wardle; 27 Sam Wood. Subs (all used): 11 Kenny Edwards; 15 Oliver Wilson; 30 Reiss Butterworth (D); 32 Owen Trout (D).
Try: Trout (47); **Goals:** Russell 1/1.
SAINTS: 1 Lachlan Coote; 21 Matthew Costello; 3 Kevin Naiqama; 26 Josh Simm; 5 Regan Grace; 6 Jonny Lomax (C); 22 Jack Welsby; 8 Alex Walmsley; 19 Aaron Smith; 15 Matty Lees; 20 James Bentley; 14 Morgan Knowles; 32 James Graham. Subs (all used): 12 Dominique Peyroux; 13 Louie McCarthy-Scarsbrook; 16 Kyle Amor; 17 Jack Ashworth.
Tries: Coote (4, 62), Smith (13), Grace (25, 56), McCarthy-Scarsbrook (50), Costello (59), Peyroux (69), Walmsley (71); **Goals:** Coote 9/10.
Rugby Leaguer & League Express Men of the Match: *Giants:* Sam Wood; *Saints:* Alex Walmsley.
Penalty count: 2-5; **Half-time:** 0-20;
Referee: Liam Moore. *(at Emerald Headingley, Leeds).*

WARRINGTON WOLVES 37 HULL FC 12

WOLVES: 26 Matty Ashton; 2 Tom Lineham; 3 Anthony Gelling; 17 Jake Mamo; 5 Josh Charnley; 6 Blake Austin; 21 Dec Patton; 16 Leilani Latu (D); 9 Daryl Clark; 10 Mike Cooper (C); 11 Ben Currie; 4 Toby King; 1 Stefan Ratchford. Subs (all used): 20 Danny Walker; 22 Luis Johnson; 27 Ellis Robson (D); 31 Ellis Longstaff (D).
Tries: Cooper (12), Ashton (19), Mamo (36, 45), Latu (60), Austin (78); **Goals:** Ratchford 5/5, Patton 1/1;
Field goal: Austin (39).
HULL FC: 1 Jamie Shaul; 5 Adam Swift; 3 Carlos Tuimavave; 4 Josh Griffin; 2 Bureta Faraimo; 14 Albert Kelly; 6 Jake Connor; 13 Ligi Sao; 16 Jordan Johnstone; 30 Jack Brown; 21 Jordan Lane; 12 Manu Ma'u; 20 Brad Fash. Subs (all used): 9 Danny Houghton (C); 24 Mahe Fonua; 26 Kieran Buchanan; 22 Josh Bowden.
Tries: Griffin (2), Tuimavave (31); **Goals:** Connor 2/2.
Rugby Leaguer & League Express Men of the Match: *Wolves:* Mike Cooper; *Hull FC:* Albert Kelly.
Penalty count: 5-2; **Half-time:** 19-12;
Referee: Ben Thaler. *(at Emerald Headingley, Leeds).*

ROUND 12

Thursday 10th September 2020

HULL FC 26 WAKEFIELD TRINITY 23

HULL FC: 25 Connor Wynne; 5 Adam Swift; 24 Mahe Fonua; 31 Cameron Scott; 2 Bureta Faraimo; 14 Albert Kelly; 6 Jake Connor; 22 Josh Bowden; 9 Danny Houghton (C); 20 Brad Fash; 21 Jordan Lane; 23 Andre Savelio; 15 Joe Cator. Subs (all used): 10 Tevita Satae; 19 Masi Matongo; 26 Kieran Buchanan; 30 Jack Brown.
Tries: Lane (11, 64), Swift (19, 37), Savelio (54);
Goals: Connor 3/5.
Sin bin: Wynne (74) - professional foul.
TRINITY: 21 Max Jowitt; 40 Innes Senior; 3 Bill Tupou; 4 Reece Lyne; 5 Ben Jones-Bishop; 31 Connor Bailey (D); 29 Ryan Hampshire; 15 Craig Kopczak; 19 Jordan Crowther; 22 George King; 14 Jay Pitts (C); 36 Kelepi Tanginoa; 13 Joe Westerman. Subs (all used): 17 Chris Green; 23 Josh Wood; 26 Titus Gwaze; 30 Yusuf Aydin (D).
Tries: Jowitt (24, 26), Tanginoa (71, 76);
Goals: Hampshire 3/4; **Field goal:** Hampshire (40).

Rugby Leaguer & League Express Men of the Match: *Hull FC:* Joe Cator; *Trinity:* Kelepi Tanginoa.
Penalty count: 5-5; **Half-time:** 14-13;
Referee: Marcus Griffiths.
(at Totally Wicked Stadium, St Helens).

CASTLEFORD TIGERS 10 WARRINGTON WOLVES 12

TIGERS: 34 Gareth O'Brien; 2 Derrell Olpherts; 17 Alex Foster; 4 Michael Shenton (C); 25 Greg Eden; 3 Peter Mata'utia; 7 Danny Richardson; 8 Liam Watts; 9 Paul McShane; 16 George Griffin; 11 Oliver Holmes; 12 Mike McMeeken; 14 Nathan Massey. Subs (all used): 10 Grant Millington; 13 Adam Milner; 20 Junior Moors; 22 Jacques O'Neill.
Tries: O'Brien (18), Olpherts (55); **Goals:** Richardson 1/2.
WOLVES: 26 Matty Ashton; 2 Tom Lineham; 3 Anthony Gelling; 17 Jake Mamo; 5 Josh Charnley; 6 Blake Austin; 1 Stefan Ratchford; 16 Leilani Latu; 20 Danny Walker; 10 Mike Cooper (C); 11 Ben Currie; 4 Toby King; 13 Ben Murdoch-Masila. Subs (all used): 21 Dec Patton; 22 Luis Johnson; 27 Ellis Robson; 33 Eribe Doro (D).
Tries: Gelling (39), Ashton (79); **Goals:** Ratchford 2/2.
Sin bin: Mamo (53) - professional foul.
On report:
Lineham (31) - alleged dangerous contact on Foster.
Rugby Leaguer & League Express Men of the Match: *Tigers:* Peter Mata'utia; *Wolves:* Mike Cooper.
Penalty count: 4-3; **Half-time:** 6-6; **Referee:** Robert Hicks.
(at Totally Wicked Stadium, St Helens).

Friday 11th September 2020

ST HELENS 21 HULL KINGSTON ROVERS 20
(after golden point extra-time)

SAINTS: 1 Lachlan Coote; 22 Jack Welsby; 3 Kevin Naiqama; 26 Josh Simm; 5 Regan Grace; 6 Jonny Lomax; 7 Theo Fages; 8 Alex Walmsley; 9 James Roby (C); 32 James Graham; 11 Zeb Taia; 20 James Bentley; 14 Morgan Knowles. Subs (all used): 12 Dominique Peyroux; 15 Matty Lees; 16 Kyle Amor; 19 Aaron Smith.
Tries: Grace (34), Welsby (43), Walmsley (60);
Goals: Coote 4/4; **Field goal:** Fages (83).
Sin bin: Naiqama (78) - high tackle on Linnett.
ROVERS: 19 Will Dagger; 23 Ethan Ryan; 3 Shaun Kenny-Dowall; 4 Kane Linnett; 5 Greg Minikin; 7 Jordan Abdull; 20 Mikey Lewis; 11 Weller Hauraki (C); 18 Jez Litten; 15 George Lawler; 28 Matthew Storton; 13 Dean Hadley; 27 Elliot Minchella. Subs (all used): 9 Matt Parcell; 16 Daniel Murray; 14 Mitch Garbutt; 32 Nathaniel Peteru.
Tries: Hadley (24), Kenny-Dowall (52), Ryan (74);
Goals: Dagger 4/4.
Rugby Leaguer & League Express Men of the Match: *Saints:* Jonny Lomax; *Rovers:* George Lawler.
Penalty count: 6-8; **Half-time:** 8-6; **Referee:** Jack Smith.

LEEDS RHINOS 13 HUDDERSFIELD GIANTS 12

RHINOS: 16 Richie Myler; 2 Tom Briscoe; 3 Harry Newman; 15 Liam Sutcliffe; 5 Ash Handley; 6 Robert Lui; 7 Luke Gale (C); 8 Ava Seumanufagai; 9 Kruise Leeming; 17 Adam Cuthbertson; 20 Bodene Thompson; 26 Alex Sutcliffe; 19 Mikolaj Oledzki. Subs (all used): 4 Konrad Hurrell; 14 Brad Dwyer; 25 James Donaldson; 40 Brett Ferres (D2).
Tries: Hurrell (45), T Briscoe (56); **Goals:** Gale 2/3;
Field goal: Gale (75).
GIANTS: 1 Ashton Golding; 2 Jermaine McGillvary; 21 Leroy Cudjoe; 3 Jake Wardle; 5 Darnell McIntosh; 23 Oliver Russell; 7 Aidan Sezer (C); 14 Matty English; 9 Adam O'Brien; 13 Michael Lawrence; 11 Kenny Edwards; 12 Joe Wardle; 34 Chris McQueen (D). Subs (all used): 8 James Gavet; 15 Oliver Wilson; 22 Tom Holmes; 26 Sam Hewitt.
Try: English (4); **Goals:** Russell 4/4.
Sin bin: English (15) - repeated team offences.
Rugby Leaguer & League Express Men of the Match: *Rhinos:* Brad Dwyer; *Giants:* Michael Lawrence.
Penalty count: 4-7; **Half-time:** 0-10;
Referee: Scott Mikalauskas *(replaced by James Child (20).* *(at Totally Wicked Stadium, St Helens).*

Saturday 12th September 2020

CATALANS DRAGONS 12 WIGAN WARRIORS 28

DRAGONS: 29 Sam Tomkins; 2 Lewis Tierney; 3 Samisoni Langi; 4 Israel Folau; 5 Fouad Yaha; 6 James Maloney; 20 Lucas Albert; 8 Remi Casty (C); 18 Alrix Da Costa; 14 Julian Bousquet; 11 Matt Whitley; 12 Joel Tomkins; 13 Benjamin Garcia. Subs (all used): 17 Benjamin Jullien; 19 Mickael Goudemand; 24 Jason Baitieri; 28 Sam Kasiano.
Tries: Bousquet (72), Yaha (80); **Goals:** Maloney 2/2.
WARRIORS: 6 Bevan French; 21 Dom Manfredi; 1 Zak Hardaker; 4 Oliver Gildart; 5 Joe Burgess; 7 Thomas Leuluai (C); 31 Jackson Hastings; 19 Joe Bullock; 9 Sam Powell; 30 Ethan Havard; 11 Willie Isa; 12 Liam Farrell; 17 Oliver Partington. Subs (all used): 10 George Burgess; 15 Joe Greenwood; 28 Harry Smith; 33 Joe Shorrocks.
Tries: Gildart (7), French (31), J Burgess (38, 53), Powell (69); **Goals:** Hardaker 4/6.
Sin bin: Greenwood (43) - interference.
Rugby Leaguer & League Express Men of the Match: *Dragons:* Sam Tomkins; *Warriors:* Sam Powell.
Penalty count: 10-7; **Half-time:** 0-18;
Referee: Chris Kendall; **Attendance:** 5,000.

ROUND 7

Thursday 17th September 2020

WAKEFIELD TRINITY 6 HUDDERSFIELD GIANTS 29

TRINITY: 21 Max Jowitt; 38 Liam Kay; 4 Reece Lyne; 3 Bill Tupou; 5 Ben Jones-Bishop; 31 Connor Bailey; 29 Ryan Hampshire; 15 Craig Kopczak; 23 Josh Wood; 41 Eddie Battye (D); 14 Jay Pitts (C); 36 Kelepi Tanginoa; 13 Joe Westerman. Subs (all used): 9 Kyle Wood; 19 Jordan Crowther; 37 Romain Navarrete; 39 Tony Gigot.
Try: Tanginoa (69); **Goals:** Hampshire 1/1.
GIANTS: 1 Ashton Golding; 2 Jermaine McGillvary; 21 Leroy Cudjoe; 3 Jake Wardle; 5 Darnell McIntosh; 4 Jordan Turner; 7 Aidan Sezer (C); 15 Oliver Wilson; 30 Reiss Butterworth; 10 Suaia Matagi; 11 Kenny Edwards; 34 Chris McQueen; 13 Michael Lawrence. Subs (all used): 22 Tom Holmes; 27 Sam Wood; 32 Owen Trout; 8 James Gavet.
Tries: McQueen (17), Matagi (21), Gavet (47), Sezer (49), Jake Wardle (56); **Goals:** Sezer 4/5;
Field goal: Turner (39).
Rugby Leaguer & League Express Men of the Match: *Trinity:* Reece Lyne; *Giants:* Aidan Sezer.
Penalty count: 4-5; **Half-time:** 0-13; **Referee:** Jack Smith.
(at John Smith's Stadium).

ROUND 13

Thursday 24th September 2020

HULL KINGSTON ROVERS 16 LEEDS RHINOS 41

ROVERS: 33 Will Tate (D); 22 Nick Rawsthorne; 34 Jimmy Keinhorst; 12 Harvey Livett; 3 Shaun Kenny-Dowall (C); 24 Joe Keyes; 31 Ryan Brierley; 14 Mitch Garbutt; 18 Jez Litten; 26 Will Maher; 25 Matty Gee; 32 Nathaniel Peteru; 8 Robbie Mulhern. Subs (all used): 16 Daniel Murray; 17 Kyle Trout; 21 Owen Harrison; 27 Elliot Minchella.
Tries: Keinhorst (40), Brierley (54), Kenny-Dowall (72);
Goals: Brierley 2/3.
RHINOS: 16 Richie Myler; 2 Tom Briscoe; 3 Harry Newman; 15 Liam Sutcliffe; 5 Ash Handley; 6 Robert Lui; 7 Luke Gale (C); 8 Ava Seumanufagai; 9 Kruise Leeming; 19 Mikolaj Oledzki; 11 Alex Mellor; 12 Rhyse Martin; 10 Matt Prior. Subs (all used): 17 Adam Cuthbertson; 24 Luke Briscoe; 25 James Donaldson; 28 Tom Holroyd.
Tries: Martin (6), Handley (11, 46), Donaldson (24), Myler (36), Mellor (58), L Briscoe (64); **Goals:** Martin 6/7;
Field goal: Gale (78).
Rugby Leaguer & League Express Men of the Match: *Rovers:* Elliot Minchella; *Rhinos:* Kruise Leeming.
Penalty count: 2-4; **Half-time:** 6-24; **Referee:** Jack Smith.
(at Halliwell Jones Stadium, Warrington).

HULL FC 22 SALFORD RED DEVILS 28

HULL FC: 1 Jamie Shaul; 31 Cameron Scott; 24 Mahe Fonua; 4 Josh Griffin; 2 Bureta Faraimo; 3 Carlos Tuimavave; 6 Jake Connor; 10 Tevita Satae; 9 Danny Houghton (C); 22 Josh Bowden; 21 Jordan Lane; 12 Manu Ma'u; 13 Ligi Sao. Subs (all used): 15 Joe Cator; 20 Brad Fash; 23 Andre Savelio; 30 Jack Brown.
Tries: Shaul (11, 52), Savelio (26), Lane (67);
Goals: Connor 3/4.
RED DEVILS: 4 Dan Sarginson; 5 Krisnan Inu; 3 Kris Welham; 32 Kallum Watkins; 22 Rhys Williams; 6 Tui Lolohea; 7 Kevin Brown; 10 Gil Dudson; 9 Joey Lussick; 17 Luke Yates; 29 Oliver Roberts; 26 Jack Ormondroyd (D); 19 Mark Flanagan (C). Subs (all used): 12 Pauli Pauli; 14 Sebastine Ikahihifo; 16 Greg Burke; 30 Andy Ackers.
Tries: Inu (19, 37), Lussick (31), Williams (48), Ackers (55);
Goals: Inu 4/5.
Sin bin: Sarginson (21) - high tackle on Shaul.
Rugby Leaguer & League Express Men of the Match: *Hull FC:* Jamie Shaul; *Red Devils:* Kevin Brown.
Penalty count: 7-6; **Half-time:** 12-18;
Referee: Chris Kendall.
(at Halliwell Jones Stadium, Warrington).

CASTLEFORD TIGERS 19 HUDDERSFIELD GIANTS 31

TIGERS: 21 James Clare; 35 Jack Sanderson (D); 18 Cheyse Blair; 4 Michael Shenton (C); 25 Greg Eden; 34 Gareth O'Brien; 26 Calum Turner; 8 Liam Watts; 9 Paul McShane; 16 George Griffin; 15 Jesse Sene-Lefao; 12 Mike McMeeken; 14 Nathan Massey. Subs (all used): 10 Grant Millington; 22 Jacques O'Neill; 24 Tyla Hepi; 36 Dan Fleming (D2).
Tries: O'Brien (6), Eden (11), Sanderson (42);
Goals: O'Brien 3/5; **Field goal:** O'Brien (39).
GIANTS: 1 Ashton Golding; 2 Jermaine McGillvary; 21 Leroy Cudjoe; 3 Jake Wardle; 5 Darnell McIntosh; 4 Jordan Turner; 7 Aidan Sezer (C); 15 Oliver Wilson; 22 Tom Holmes; 10 Suaia Matagi; 11 Kenny Edwards; 34 Chris McQueen; 13 Michael Lawrence. Subs (all used): 8 James Gavet; 23 Oliver Russell; 27 Sam Wood; 32 Owen Trout.
Tries: McGillvary (17, 61, 79), Jake Wardle (22), Sezer (69);
Goals: Sezer 5/5; **Field goal:** Sezer (68).
Rugby Leaguer & League Express Men of the Match: *Tigers:* Mike McMeeken; *Giants:* Jake Wardle.
Penalty count: 5-7; **Half-time:** 13-12; **Referee:** Liam Moore.
(at Halliwell Jones Stadium, Warrington).

Friday 25th September 2020

WARRINGTON WOLVES 30 CATALANS DRAGONS 16

WOLVES: 26 Matty Ashton; 17 Jake Mamo; 3 Anthony Gelling; 4 Toby King; 5 Josh Charnley; 6 Blake Austin; 7 Gareth Widdop; 8 Chris Hill (C); 9 Daryl Clark; 10 Mike Cooper; 11 Ben Currie; 12 Jack Hughes; 14 Jason Clark. Subs (all used): 13 Ben Murdoch-Masila; 15 Joe Philbin; 19 Matt Davis; 20 Danny Walker.
Tries: Gelling (8), Ashton (39), Davis (45), Austin (56), Walker (76); **Goals:** Widdop 5/5.
DRAGONS: 29 Sam Tomkins; 16 Tom Davies; 3 Samisoni Langi; 4 Israel Folau; 5 Fouad Yaha; 6 James Maloney; 7 Josh Drinkwater; 8 Remi Casty (C); 9 Michael McIlorum; 10 Sam Moa; 11 Matt Whitley; 12 Joel Tomkins; 13 Benjamin Garcia. Subs (all used): 19 Mickael Goudemand; 21 Paul Seguier; 24 Jason Baitieri; 26 Lambert Belmas.
Tries: Davies (24), Langi (33), Yaha (59);
Goals: Maloney 2/3.
Sin bin: Maloney (76) - high tackle on Ashton.
Rugby Leaguer & League Express Men of the Match: *Wolves:* Matty Ashton; *Dragons:* Sam Tomkins.
Penalty count: 7-3; **Half-time:** 12-12;
Referee: Robert Hicks.

WIGAN WARRIORS 28 WAKEFIELD TRINITY 16

WARRIORS: 6 Bevan French; 23 Jake Bibby; 1 Zak Hardaker; 4 Oliver Gildart; 5 Joe Burgess; 31 Jackson Hastings; 7 Thomas Leuluai (C); 14 Ben Flower; 9 Sam Powell; 30 Ethan Havard; 11 Willie Isa; 12 Liam Farrell; 17 Oliver Partington. Subs (all used): 22 Mitch Clark; 28 Harry Smith; 29 Jack Wells; 33 Joe Shorrocks.
Tries: Hastings (25), French (29, 68), Powell (60), Gildart (66); **Goals:** Hardaker 4/5.
TRINITY: 1 Alex Walker; 2 Tom Johnstone; 3 Bill Tupou; 4 Reece Lyne; 5 Ben Jones-Bishop; 6 Jacob Miller (C); 39 Tony Gigot; 15 Craig Kopczak; 19 Jordan Crowther; 10 Tinirau Arona; 36 Kelepi Tanginoa; 14 Jay Pitts; 13 Joe Westerman. Subs (all used): 9 Kyle Wood; 11 Matty Ashurst; 17 Chris Green; 18 Adam Tangata.
Tries: Miller (11), Arona (17), Johnstone (76);
Goals: Gigot 2/3.
Rugby Leaguer & League Express Men of the Match: *Warriors:* Bevan French; *Trinity:* Jacob Miller.
Penalty count: 2-8; **Half-time:** 12-12;
Referee: James Child.
(at Halliwell Jones Stadium, Warrington).

ROUND 14

Tuesday 29th September 2020

SALFORD RED DEVILS 20 WARRINGTON WOLVES 18

RED DEVILS: 34 Olly Ashall-Bott (D); 28 Luis Roberts (D); 5 Krisnan Inu; 24 Elliot Kear; 22 Rhys Williams; 33 Tom Gilmore (D); 18 Chris Atkin; 8 Lee Mossop (C); 25 Connor Jones; 14 Sebastine Ikahihifo; 13 Tyrone McCarthy; 26 Jack Ormondroyd; 16 Greg Burke. Subs (all used): 11 Ryan Lannon; 12 Pauli Pauli; 21 James Greenwood; 30 Andy Ackers.
Tries: Williams (39), Kear (52), Gilmore (71); **Goals:** Inu 4/4.
WOLVES: 29 Josh Thewlis; 18 Sitaleki Akauola; 32 Connor Wrench (D); 24 Keanan Brand; 28 Nathan Roebuck (D); 30 Riley Dean; 21 Dec Patton (C); 16 Leilani Latu; 20 Danny Walker; 22 Luis Johnson; 31 Ellis Longstaff; 27 Ellis Robson; 19 Matt Davis. Subs: 25 Samy Kibula; 33 Eribe Doro; 34 Cole Oakley (not used); 35 Kyle Shelford (D).
Tries: Roebuck (18), Thewlis (30), Dean (35);
Goals: Patton 3/3.
Rugby Leaguer & League Express Men of the Match: *Red Devils:* Olly Ashall-Bott; *Wolves:* Josh Thewlis.
Penalty count: 10-3; **Half-time:** 6-18;
Referee: Scott Mikalauskas.

WIGAN WARRIORS 0 ST HELENS 42

WARRIORS: 39 Umyla Hanley (D); 35 Sam Halsall (D); 3 Chris Hankinson; 36 James McDonnell (D); 23 Jake Bibby; 27 Jake Shorrocks; 28 Harry Smith (C); 19 Joe Bullock; 32

Amir Bourouh; 20 Liam Byrne; 15 Joe Greenwood; 37 Harry Rushton (D); 29 Jack Wells. Subs (all used): 14 Ben Flower; 22 Mitch Clark; 34 Kai Pearce-Paul (D); 40 Ben Kilner (D).
Sin bin: Halsall (14) - late challenge on Coote.
SAINTS: 1 Lachlan Coote; 22 Jack Welsby; 3 Kevin Naiqama; 26 Josh Simm; 5 Regan Grace; 6 Jonny Lomax; 7 Theo Fages; 8 Alex Walmsley; 9 James Roby (C); 15 Matty Lees; 14 Morgan Knowles; 20 James Bentley; 32 James Graham. Subs (all used): 11 Zeb Taia; 13 Louie McCarthy-Scarsbrook; 16 Kyle Amor; 27 Lewis Dodd (D).
Tries: Walmsley (12), Welsby (15, 66), Grace (19, 78), Knowles (52), Bentley (56); **Goals:** Coote 7/7.
Sin bin: Lomax (69) - dangerous challenge on Rushton.
Rugby Leaguer & League Express Men of the Match: *Warriors:* Harry Smith; *Saints:* Regan Grace.
Penalty count: 6-4; **Half-time:** 0-18; **Referee:** Ben Thaler. *(at AJ Bell Stadium, Salford).*

Wednesday 30th September 2020

HUDDERSFIELD GIANTS 32 HULL KINGSTON ROVERS 22

GIANTS: 1 Ashton Golding; 2 Jermaine McGillvary; 3 Jake Wardle; 21 Leroy Cudjoe; 27 Sam Wood; 4 Jordan Turner; 7 Aidan Sezer (C); 14 Matty English; 22 Tom Holmes; 10 Suaia Matagi; 34 Chris McQueen; 11 Kenny Edwards; 13 Michael Lawrence. Subs (all used): 15 Oliver Wilson; 23 Oliver Russell; 26 Sam Hewitt; 32 Owen Trout.
Tries: Golding (13), McGillvary (21, 30), Cudjoe (40), McQueen (57), Jake Wardle (67);
Goals: Sezer 1/3, Russell 3/4.
ROVERS: 2 Ben Crooks; 3 Shaun Kenny-Dowall; 5 Greg Minikin; 22 Nick Rawsthorne; 33 Will Tate; 7 Jordan Abdull; 30 Jamie Ellis; 11 Weller Hauraki (C); 9 Matt Parcell; 15 George Lawler; 4 Kane Linnett; 21 Owen Harrison; 27 Elliot Minchella. Subs (all used): 8 Robbie Mulhern; 17 Kyle Trout; 25 Matty Gee; 32 Nathaniel Peteru.
Tries: Parcell (44, 53, 60), Tate (78); **Goals:** Ellis 3/4.
Sin bin: Parcell (62) - professional foul.
Rugby Leaguer & League Express Men of the Match: *Giants:* Aidan Sezer; *Rovers:* Matt Parcell.
Penalty count: 7-4; **Half-time:** 18-0;
Referee: Marcus Griffiths.

LEEDS RHINOS 6 CATALANS DRAGONS 34

RHINOS: 1 Jack Walker; 38 Liam Tindall (D); 21 Rhys Evans; 26 Alex Sutcliffe; 24 Luke Briscoe; 34 Jack Broadbent (D); 23 Callum McLelland; 17 Adam Cuthbertson (C); 33 Jarrod O'Connor (D); 40 Brett Ferres; 20 Bodene Thompson; 27 Sam Walters (D); 39 James Harrison (D). Subs (all used): 30 Muizz Mustapha; 36 Corey Hall (D); 41 Harvey Whiteley; 43 Loui McConnell (D).
Try: Evans (29); **Goals:** O'Connor 1/1.
DRAGONS: 29 Sam Tomkins; 16 Tom Davies; 22 Arthur Romano; 4 Israel Folau; 5 Fouad Yaha; 6 James Maloney; 7 Josh Drinkwater; 14 Julian Bousquet; 9 Michael McIlorum; 10 Sam Moa; 11 Matt Whitley; 12 Joel Tomkins; 13 Benjamin Garcia. Subs (all used): 24 Jason Baitieri; 28 Sam Kasiano; 8 Remi Casty (C); 25 Arthur Mourgue.
Tries: Davies (19, 25, 39), Yaha (51, 79), Mourgue (75);
Goals: Maloney 5/6.
Sin bin: Kasiano (44) - professional foul.
Rugby Leaguer & League Express Men of the Match: *Rhinos:* Adam Cuthbertson; *Dragons:* Tom Davies.
Penalty count: 10-5; **Half time:** 6-16;
Referee: Robert Hicks.

Thursday 1st October 2020

CASTLEFORD TIGERS 28 HULL FC 32

TIGERS: 21 James Clare; 35 Jack Sanderson; 18 Cheyse Blair; 4 Michael Shenton (C); 25 Greg Eden; 9 Paul McShane; 34 Gareth O'Brien; 16 George Griffin; 13 Adam Milner; 24 Tyla Hepi; 20 Junior Moors; 12 Mike McMeeken; 10 Grant Millington. Subs (all used): 14 Nathan Massey; 22 Jacques O'Neill; 23 Matt Cook; 27 Lewis Peachey.
Tries: McMeeken (6, 71), Eden (13), Millington (56), Shenton (75); **Goals:** O'Brien 4/5.
Sin bin: Cook (36) - late challenge.
HULL FC: 26 Kieran Buchanan; 2 Bureta Faraimo; 24 Mahe Fonua; 3 Carlos Tuimavave; 31 Cameron Scott; 6 Jake Connor; 7 Marc Sneyd; 8 Scott Taylor (C); 16 Jordan Johnstone; 22 Josh Bowden; 21 Jordan Lane; 23 Andre Savelio; 15 Joe Cator. Subs (all used): 10 Tevita Satae; 13 Ligi Sao; 20 Brad Fash; 35 Ben McNamara (D).
Tries: Scott (3), Johnstone (28), Satae (46), McNamara (61), Connor (78); **Goals:** Sneyd 6/7.
Rugby Leaguer & League Express Men of the Match: *Tigers:* Greg Eden; *Hull FC:* Jake Connor.
Penalty count: 5-10; **Half-time:** 12-14; **Referee:** Tom Grant.

ROUND 16

Sunday 4th October 2020

CATALANS DRAGONS 40 WAKEFIELD TRINITY 8

DRAGONS: 29 Sam Tomkins; 16 Tom Davies; 3 Samisoni Langi; 4 Israel Folau; 1 David Mead; 6 James Maloney; 7 Josh Drinkwater; 8 Remi Casty (C); 9 Michael McIlorum; 10 Sam Moa; 11 Matt Whitley; 17 Benjamin Jullien; 13 Benjamin Garcia. Subs (all used): 14 Julian Bousquet; 19 Mickael Goudemand; 24 Jason Baitieri; 28 Sam Kasiano.
Tries: Whitley (37), Folau (40), Mead (46, 63), Kasiano (49), S Tomkins (51), Bousquet (59);
Goals: Maloney 6/7.
TRINITY: 1 Alex Walker; 5 Ben Jones-Bishop; 4 Reece Lyne; 3 Bill Tupou; 2 Tom Johnstone; 6 Jacob Miller (C); 39 Tony Gigot; 36 Kelepi Tanginoa; 19 Jordan Crowther; 10 Tinirau Arona; 11 Matty Ashurst; 14 Jay Pitts; 13 Joe Westerman. Subs (all used): 9 Kyle Wood; 15 Craig Kopczak; 17 Chris Green; 18 Adam Tangata.
Try: Tupou (20); **Goals:** Gigot 2/2.
Rugby Leaguer & League Express Men of the Match: *Dragons:* Sam Tomkins; *Trinity:* Jacob Miller.
Penalty count: 8-11; **Half-time:** 12-8;
Referee: James Child; **Attendance:** 5,000.

ROUND 15

Thursday 8th October 2020

HUDDERSFIELD GIANTS 16 SALFORD RED DEVILS 24

GIANTS: 1 Ashton Golding; 2 Jermaine McGillvary; 21 Leroy Cudjoe (C); 3 Jake Wardle; 5 Darnell McIntosh; 6 Lee Gaskell; 7 Aidan Sezer; 26 Sam Hewitt; 22 Tom Holmes; 10 Suaia Matagi; 11 Kenny Edwards; 34 Chris McQueen; 13 Michael Lawrence. Subs (all used): 8 James Gavet; 12 Joe Wardle; 23 Oliver Russell; 32 Owen Trout.
Tries: Cudjoe (15), Sezer (19, 66); **Goals:** Sezer 2/3.
Sin bin: Edwards (47) - repeated team offences.
RED DEVILS: 4 Dan Sarginson; 22 Rhys Williams; 32 Kallum Watkins; 3 Kris Welham; 5 Krisnan Inu; 6 Tui Lolohea; 18 Chris Atkin; 8 Lee Mossop (C); 9 Joey Lussick; 10 Gil Dudson; 11 Ryan Lannon; 21 James Greenwood; 17 Luke Yates. Subs (all used): 12 Pauli Pauli; 16 Greg Burke; 26 Jack Ormondroyd; 30 Andy Ackers.
Tries: Atkin (30), Inu (47, 59, 72); **Goals:** Inu 4/5.
Sin bin: Sarginson (33) - dangerous contact on Golding.
Rugby Leaguer & League Express Men of the Match: *Giants:* Ashton Golding; *Red Devils:* Krisnan Inu.
Penalty count: 3-6; **Half-time:** 12-8;
Referee: Robert Hicks. *(at Emerald Headingley, Leeds).*

ROUND 18

Thursday 8th October 2020

HULL FC 22 LEEDS RHINOS 40

HULL FC: 6 Jake Connor; 2 Bureta Faraimo; 24 Mahe Fonua; 3 Carlos Tuimavave; 31 Cameron Scott; 35 Ben McNamara; 7 Marc Sneyd (C); 22 Josh Bowden; 16 Jordan Johnstone; 13 Ligi Sao; 4 Josh Griffin; 23 Andre Savelio; 20 Brad Fash. Subs (all used): 10 Tevita Satae; 25 Connor Wynne; 28 Lewis Bienek; 30 Jack Brown.
Tries: Fonua (9), Savelio (17), Griffin (58), Brown (62);
Goals: Sneyd 3/4.
RHINOS: 1 Jack Walker; 2 Tom Briscoe; 15 Liam Sutcliffe; 4 Konrad Hurrell; 5 Ash Handley; 16 Richie Myler; 7 Luke Gale (C); 8 Ava Seumanufagai; 9 Kruise Leeming; 19 Mikolaj Oledzki; 12 Rhyse Martin; 20 Bodene Thompson; 10 Matt Prior. Subs (all used): 14 Brad Dwyer; 25 James Donaldson; 22 Cameron Smith; 28 Tom Holroyd.
Tries: Walker (25, 38), Handley (29, 47, 76), Donaldson (45), L Sutcliffe (67); **Goals:** Martin 6/7.
Sin bin: Myler (16) - professional foul.
Rugby Leaguer & League Express Men of the Match: *Hull FC:* Jake Connor; *Rhinos:* Ash Handley.
Penalty count: 3-4; **Half-time:** 10-16; **Referee:** Ben Thaler. *(at Emerald Headingley).*

ROUND 15

Friday 9th October 2020

WAKEFIELD TRINITY 16 ST HELENS 20

TRINITY: 1 Alex Walker; 40 Innes Senior; 4 Reece Lyne (C); 24 Jack Croft; 2 Tom Johnstone; 21 Max Jowitt; 29 Ryan Hampshire; 15 Craig Kopczak; 23 Josh Wood; 36 Kelepi Tanginoa; 11 Matty Ashurst; 16 James Batchelor; 13 Joe Westerman. Subs (all used): 8 David Fifita; 18 Adam Tangata; 31 Connor Bailey; 41 Eddie Battye.
Tries: A Walker (9), Kopczak (19), Ashurst (80);
Goals: Hampshire 2/3.
SAINTS: 1 Lachlan Coote; 2 Tommy Makinson; 3 Kevin Naiqama; 26 Josh Simm; 5 Regan Grace; 6 Jonny Lomax; 7 Theo Fages; 8 Alex Walmsley; 9 James Roby (C); 15 Matty Lees; 20 James Bentley; 14 Morgan Knowles; 13 Louie McCarthy-Scarsbrook. Subs: 11 Zeb Taia; 12 Dominique Peyroux; 16 Kyle Amor; 22 Jack Welsby (not used).
Tries: McCarthy-Scarsbrook (32), Coote (37, 69), Grace (63);
Goals: Coote 2/4.
Rugby Leaguer & League Express Men of the Match: *Trinity:* Ryan Hampshire; *Saints:* Lachlan Coote.
Penalty count: 6-3; **Half-time:** 12-10;
Referee: Liam Moore. *(at Emerald Headingley, Leeds).*

CATALANS DRAGONS 34 HULL KINGSTON ROVERS 4

DRAGONS: 29 Sam Tomkins; 1 David Mead; 3 Samisoni Langi; 4 Israel Folau; 16 Tom Davies; 6 James Maloney; 7 Josh Drinkwater; 8 Remi Casty (C); 9 Michael McIlorum; 10 Sam Moa; 17 Benjamin Jullien; 12 Joel Tomkins; 13 Benjamin Garcia. Subs (all used): 14 Julian Bousquet; 19 Mickael Goudemand; 24 Jason Baitieri; 28 Sam Kasiano.
Tries: J Tomkins (21, 26, 37), Davies (39, 79), Folau (56);
Goals: Maloney 5/8.
ROVERS: 2 Ben Crooks; 22 Nick Rawsthorne; 3 Shaun Kenny-Dowall; 4 Kane Linnett; 33 Will Tate; 7 Jordan Abdull; 35 Rowan Milnes (D); 11 Weller Hauraki (C); 9 Matt Parcell; 14 Mitch Garbutt; 28 Matthew Storton; 32 Nathaniel Peteru; 15 George Lawler. Subs (all used): 12 Harvey Livett; 17 Kyle Trout; 25 Matty Gee; 36 George King (D).
Try: Livett (67); **Goals:** Rawsthorne 0/1.
Rugby Leaguer & League Express Men of the Match: *Dragons:* Sam Tomkins; *Rovers:* Jordan Abdull.
Penalty count: 10-3; **Half-time:** 22-0;
Referee: Jack Smith; **Attendance:** 5,000.

WARRINGTON WOLVES 14 WIGAN WARRIORS 18

WOLVES: 1 Stefan Ratchford; 17 Jake Mamo; 3 Anthony Gelling; 4 Toby King; 5 Josh Charnley; 6 Blake Austin; 7 Gareth Widdop; 8 Chris Hill (C); 9 Daryl Clark; 10 Mike Cooper; 11 Ben Currie; 12 Jack Hughes; 14 Jason Clark. Subs: 15 Joe Philbin; 19 Matt Davis; 26 Matty Ashton; 27 Ellis Robson (not used).
Tries: Ashton (12, pen), Hill (21); **Goals:** Ratchford 3/3.
WARRIORS: 6 Bevan French; 21 Dom Manfredi; 11 Willie Isa; 1 Zak Hardaker; 23 Jake Bibby; 7 Thomas Leuluai; 31 Jackson Hastings; 19 Joe Bullock; 9 Sam Powell; 17 Oliver Partington; 15 Joe Greenwood; 12 Liam Farrell; 13 Sean O'Loughlin (C). Subs (all used): 16 Morgan Smithies; 28 Harry Smith; 33 Joe Shorrocks; 38 Brad Singleton (D).
Tries: Greenwood (24), Hardaker (44), Farrell (76);
Goals: Hardaker 3/3.
Sin bin: Isa (5) - professional foul.
Rugby Leaguer & League Express Men of the Match: *Wolves:* Stefan Ratchford; *Warriors:* Liam Farrell.
Penalty count: 5-3; **Half-time:** 12-6;
Referee: Chris Kendall. *(at Emerald Headingley, Leeds).*

ROUND 16

Tuesday 13th October 2020

HULL KINGSTON ROVERS 24 SALFORD RED DEVILS 22

ROVERS: 20 Mikey Lewis; 2 Ben Crooks; 4 Kane Linnett; 7 Jordan Abdull; 3 Shaun Kenny-Dowall; 30 Jamie Ellis; 31 Ryan Brierley; 8 Robbie Mulhern; 27 Elliot Minchella; 26 Will Maher; 11 Weller Hauraki (C); 13 Dean Hadley; 14 Mitch Garbutt. Subs (all used): 9 Matt Parcell; 15 George Lawler; 17 Kyle Trout; 25 Matty Gee.
Tries: Lewis (17, 64, pen), Crooks (35), Abdull (69);
Goals: Ellis 4/5.
RED DEVILS: 34 Olly Ashall-Bott; 2 Ed Chamberlain; 25 Connor Jones; 24 Elliot Kear; 28 Luis Roberts; 33 Tom Gilmore; 18 Chris Atkin; 14 Sebastine Ikahihifo; 30 Andy Ackers; 29 Oliver Roberts; 11 Ryan Lannon; 13 Tyrone McCarthy (C); 16 Greg Burke. Subs: 5 Krisnan Inu (not used); 12 Pauli Pauli; 17 Luke Yates; 27 Connor Aspey (D).
Tries: Jones (24), Yates (46), Ashall-Bott (68), Chamberlain (75); **Goals:** Chamberlain 3/4.
Rugby Leaguer & League Express Men of the Match: *Rovers:* Kane Linnett; *Red Devils:* Luke Yates.
Penalty count: 6-6; **Half-time:** 12-6; **Referee:** James Child. *(at Halliwell Jones Stadium, Warrington).*

HULL FC 18 HUDDERSFIELD GIANTS 16

HULL FC: 1 Jamie Shaul; 2 Bureta Faraimo; 24 Mahe Fonua; 3 Carlos Tuimavave; 33 Ratu Naulago; 6 Jake Connor; 7 Marc Sneyd (C); 22 Josh Bowden; 16 Jordan Johnstone; 13 Ligi Sao; 4 Josh Griffin; 23 Andre Savelio; 15 Joe Cator. Subs (all used): 10 Tevita Satae; 20 Brad Fash; 30 Jack Brown; 35 Ben McNamara.
Tries: Naulago (7), Fonua (40), Faraimo (51);
Goals: Sneyd 3/4.

GIANTS: 1 Ashton Golding; 2 Jermaine McGillvary; 21 Leroy Cudjoe; 3 Jake Wardle; 27 Sam Wood; 6 Lee Gaskell; 7 Aidan Sezer (C); 34 Chris McQueen; 37 Brandon Moore (D); 10 Suaia Matagi; 11 Kenny Edwards; 12 Joe Wardle; 13 Michael Lawrence. Subs (all used): 4 Jordan Turner; 14 Matty English; 22 Tom Holmes; 26 Sam Hewitt.
Tries: McGillvary (31), English (46), Sezer (62);
Goals: Sezer 2/3.
Rugby Leaguer & League Express Men of the Match:
Hull FC: Josh Griffin; *Giants:* Aidan Sezer.
Penalty count: 3-7; **Half-time:** 10-4;
Referee: Scott Mikalauskas.
(at Halliwell Jones Stadium, Warrington).

WARRINGTON WOLVES 32 LEEDS RHINOS 6

WOLVES: 1 Stefan Ratchford; 5 Josh Charnley; 3 Anthony Gelling; 4 Toby King; 26 Matty Ashton; 7 Gareth Widdop; 21 Dec Patton; 8 Chris Hill (C); 20 Danny Walker; 27 Ellis Robson; 11 Ben Currie; 12 Jack Hughes; 14 Jason Clark. Subs (all used): 9 Daryl Clark; 18 Sitaleki Akauola; 19 Matt Davis; 22 Luis Johnson.
Tries: King (5), Ashton (51, 78), Currie (62), D Clark (76);
Goals: Ratchford 6/7.
Sin bin: Akauola (29) - dangerous challenge on Harrison.
RHINOS: 1 Jack Walker; 38 Liam Tindall; 21 Rhys Evans; 34 Jack Broadbent; 24 Luke Briscoe; 22 Cameron Smith; 23 Callum McLelland; 17 Adam Cuthbertson (C); 33 Jarrod O'Connor; 28 Tom Holroyd; 20 Bodene Thompson; 27 Sam Walters; 40 Brett Ferres. Subs (all used): 30 Muizz Mustapha; 39 James Harrison; 41 Harvey Whiteley; 43 Loui McConnell.
Try: Walters (15); **Goals:** O'Connor 1/1.
Rugby Leaguer & League Express Men of the Match:
Wolves: Toby King; *Rhinos:* Jack Broadbent.
Penalty count: 6-5; **Half-time:** 8-6;
Referee: Chris Kendall.

ROUND 9

Thursday 15th October 2020

ST HELENS 48 WAKEFIELD TRINITY 6

SAINTS: 1 Lachlan Coote; 2 Tommy Makinson; 3 Kevin Naiqama; 22 Jack Welsby; 5 Regan Grace; 6 Jonny Lomax; 7 Theo Fages; 8 Alex Walmsley; 9 James Roby (C); 15 Matty Lees; 20 James Bentley; 11 Zeb Taia; 14 Morgan Knowles. Subs (all used): 12 Dominique Peyroux; 13 Louie McCarthy-Scarsbrook; 16 Kyle Amor; 27 Lewis Dodd.
Tries: Roby (4, 28), Makinson (16, 35, 40), Walmsley (31), Grace (67), Dodd (72), Naiqama (79); **Goals:** Coote 6/9.
TRINITY: 1 Alex Walker; 40 Innes Senior; 4 Reece Lyne (C); 24 Jack Croft; 2 Tom Johnstone; 21 Max Jowitt; 29 Ryan Hampshire; 15 Craig Kopczak; 23 Josh Wood; 17 Chris Green; 36 Kelepi Tanginoa; 11 Matty Ashurst; 13 Joe Westerman. Subs (all used): 8 David Fifita; 16 James Batchelor; 37 Romain Navarrete; 41 Eddie Battye.
Try: Senior (58); **Goals:** Hampshire 1/1.
Rugby Leaguer & League Express Men of the Match:
Saints: Lachlan Coote; *Trinity:* Matty Ashurst.
Penalty count: 3-5; **Half-time:** 30-0;
Referee: Robert Hicks.
(at Halliwell Jones Stadium, Warrington).

Sunday 18th October 2020

HULL FC 48 CASTLEFORD TIGERS 6

HULL FC: 1 Jamie Shaul; 2 Bureta Faraimo; 4 Josh Griffin; 3 Carlos Tuimavave; 33 Ratu Naulago; 6 Jake Connor; 7 Marc Sneyd; 22 Josh Bowden; 16 Jordan Johnstone; 13 Ligi Sao; 12 Manu Ma'u; 23 Andre Savelio; 15 Joe Cator. Subs (all used): 10 Tevita Satae; 9 Danny Houghton (C); 20 Brad Fash; 30 Jack Brown.
Tries: Naulago (6, 54), Savelio (10), Connor (21), Faraimo (25), Houghton (68), Tuimavave (78), Ma'u (80);
Goals: Sneyd 7/7, Connor 1/1.
TIGERS: 34 Gareth O'Brien; 35 Jack Sanderson; 17 Alex Foster; 4 Michael Shenton (C); 28 Brad Graham (D); 6 Jake Trueman; 7 Danny Richardson; 14 Nathan Massey; 9 Paul McShane; 24 Tyla Hepi; 18 Cheyse Blair; 12 Mike McMeeken; 13 Adam Milner. Subs (all used): 10 Grant Millington; 15 Jesse Sene-Lefao; 22 Jacques O'Neill; 23 Matt Cook.
Try: O'Neill (73); **Goals:** Richardson 1/1.
Rugby Leaguer & League Express Men of the Match:
Hull FC: Andre Savelio; *Tigers:* Jacques O'Neill.
Penalty count: 5-6; **Half-time:** 24-0;
Referee: Marcus Griffiths.

ROUND 17

Thursday 22nd October 2020

CASTLEFORD TIGERS 38 HULL KINGSTON ROVERS 24

TIGERS: 33 Bailey Hodgson (D); 2 Derrell Olpherts; 18 Cheyse Blair; 4 Michael Shenton (C); 25 Greg Eden; 9 Paul McShane; 7 Danny Richardson; 14 Nathan Massey; 22 Jacques O'Neill; 19 Daniel Smith; 20 Junior Moors; 12 Mike McMeeken; 13 Adam Milner. Subs (all used): 15 Jesse Sene-Lefao; 17 Alex Foster; 27 Lewis Peachey; 31 Brad Martin (D).
Tries: O'Neill (8), Foster (11), Milner (21), Eden (24, 44, 74);
Goals: Richardson 7/8.
ROVERS: 19 Will Dagger; 2 Ben Crooks; 3 Shaun Kenny-Dowall; 4 Kane Linnett; 22 Nick Rawsthorne; 7 Jordan Abdull; 35 Rowan Milnes; 15 George Lawler; 9 Matt Parcell; 26 Will Maher; 11 Weller Hauraki (C); 13 Dean Hadley; 27 Elliot Minchella. Subs (all used): 8 Robbie Mulhern; 20 Mikey Lewis; 25 Matty Gee; 36 George King.
Tries: Mulhern (28), Minchella (32), Kenny-Dowall (37), Parcell (65); **Goals:** Dagger 4/4.
Rugby Leaguer & League Express Men of the Match:
Tigers: Greg Eden; *Rovers:* Jordan Abdull.
Penalty count: 5-6; **Half-time:** 26-18;
Referee: Gareth Hewer.
(at Totally Wicked Stadium, St Helens).

HUDDERSFIELD GIANTS 14 WAKEFIELD TRINITY 18

GIANTS: 24 Louis Senior; 3 Jake Wardle; 21 Leroy Cudjoe; 4 Jordan Turner; 27 Sam Wood; 6 Lee Gaskell; 7 Aidan Sezer (C); 14 Matty English; 37 Brandon Moore; 34 Chris McQueen; 11 Kenny Edwards; 12 Joe Wardle; 13 Michael Lawrence. Subs: 8 James Gavet; 10 Suaia Matagi; 17 Ukuma Ta'ai; 23 Oliver Russell (not used).
Tries: Sezer (21), Turner (34), Wood (51); **Goals:** Gaskell 1/3.
TRINITY: 21 Max Jowitt; 5 Ben Jones-Bishop; 4 Reece Lyne; 24 Jack Croft; 2 Tom Johnstone; 6 Jacob Miller (C); 29 Ryan Hampshire; 36 Kelepi Tanginoa; 19 Jordan Crowther; 10 Tinirau Arona; 11 Matty Ashurst; 16 James Batchelor; 41 Eddie Battye. Subs (all used): 8 David Fifita; 9 Kyle Wood; 18 Adam Tangata; 30 Yusuf Aydin.
Tries: Ashurst (17), Johnstone (54, 74);
Goals: Hampshire 3/3.
Rugby Leaguer & League Express Men of the Match:
Giants: Brandon Moore; *Trinity:* Jacob Miller.
Penalty count: 5-5; **Half-time:** 10-6;
Referee: Marcus Griffiths.
(at Totally Wicked Stadium, St Helens).

Friday 23rd October 2020

WIGAN WARRIORS 58 SALFORD RED DEVILS 12

WARRIORS: 6 Bevan French; 5 Joe Burgess; 1 Zak Hardaker; 4 Oliver Gildart; 23 Jake Bibby; 7 Thomas Leuluai (C); 31 Jackson Hastings; 19 Joe Bullock; 9 Sam Powell; 38 Brad Singleton; 11 Willie Isa; 12 Liam Farrell; 17 Oliver Partington. Subs (all used): 8 Tony Clubb; 14 Ben Flower; 15 Joe Greenwood; 16 Morgan Smithies.
Tries: Powell (2, 15), Farrell (17, 56), French (26, 35, 66), Hastings (46), Gildart (51, 78); **Goals:** Hardaker 9/10.
RED DEVILS: 34 Olly Ashall-Bott; 22 Rhys Williams; 32 Kallum Watkins; 24 Elliot Kear; 5 Krisnan Inu; 6 Tui Lolohea; 18 Chris Atkin; 8 Lee Mossop (C); 9 Joey Lussick; 17 Luke Yates; 29 Oliver Roberts; 21 James Greenwood; 13 Tyrone McCarthy. Subs (all used): 12 Pauli Pauli; 16 Greg Burke; 19 Mark Flanagan; 30 Andy Ackers.
Tries: Watkins (30), Lolohea (43); **Goals:** Inu 2/2.
Rugby Leaguer & League Express Men of the Match:
Warriors: Bevan French; *Red Devils:* Joey Lussick.
Penalty count: 4-4; **Half-time:** 30-6;
Referee: Chris Kendall.
(at Totally Wicked Stadium, St Helens).

ST HELENS 40 LEEDS RHINOS 8

SAINTS: 1 Lachlan Coote; 2 Tommy Makinson; 3 Kevin Naiqama; 26 Josh Simm; 5 Regan Grace; 6 Jonny Lomax; 7 Theo Fages; 8 Alex Walmsley; 9 James Roby (C); 15 Matty Lees; 11 Zeb Taia; 20 James Bentley; 14 Morgan Knowles. Subs (all used): 13 Louie McCarthy-Scarsbrook; 16 Kyle Amor; 19 Aaron Smith; 23 Joe Batchelor.
Tries: Simm (3, 21, 37), Taia (15), Fages (63), Naiqama (65), Smith (75); **Goals:** Coote 6/7.
Sin bin: Walmsley (11) - dangerous contact.
RHINOS: 1 Jack Walker; 24 Luke Briscoe; 26 Alex Sutcliffe; 21 Rhys Evans; 38 Liam Tindall; 23 Callum McLelland; 34 Jack Broadbent; 19 Mikolaj Oledzki; 14 Brad Dwyer; 28 Tom Holroyd; 27 Sam Walters; 20 Bodene Thompson; 22 Cameron Smith (C). Subs (all used): 25 James Donaldson; 33 Jarrod O'Connor; 36 Corey Hall; 39 James Harrison.
Tries: Smith (52), Tindall (72); **Goals:** Smith 0/2.
Rugby Leaguer & League Express Men of the Match:
Saints: Josh Simm; *Rhinos:* James Donaldson.
Penalty count: 4-5; **Half-time:** 22-0;
Referee: Liam Moore.

ROUND 18

Sunday 25th October 2020

WAKEFIELD TRINITY 48 HULL KINGSTON ROVERS 18

TRINITY: 21 Max Jowitt; 5 Ben Jones-Bishop; 4 Reece Lyne (C); 3 Bill Tupou; 2 Tom Johnstone; 29 Ryan Hampshire; 39 Tony Gigot; 8 David Fifita; 19 Jordan Crowther; 10 Tinirau Arona; 11 Matty Ashurst; 16 James Batchelor; 25 Brad Walker (D). Subs (all used): 9 Kyle Wood; 18 Adam Tangata; 36 Kelepi Tanginoa; 41 Eddie Battye.
Tries: Gigot (13), Lyne (16, 23), Jones-Bishop (32, 39, 49), Tangata (64), Hampshire (76), Battye (78);
Goals: Hampshire 6/9.
ROVERS: 33 Will Tate; 2 Ben Crooks; 3 Shaun Kenny-Dowall (C); 12 Harvey Livett; 19 Will Dagger; 7 Jordan Abdull; 30 Jamie Ellis; 16 Daniel Murray; 27 Elliot Minchella; 36 George King; 25 Matty Gee; 32 Nathaniel Peteru; 8 Robbie Mulhern. Subs (all used): 13 Dean Hadley; 17 Kyle Trout; 20 Mikey Lewis; 26 Will Maher.
Tries: Abdull (46), Ellis (53), Crooks (61); **Goals:** Ellis 3/3.
Rugby Leaguer & League Express Men of the Match:
Trinity: Reece Lyne; *Rovers:* Ben Crooks.
Penalty count: 3-8; **Half-time:** 26-0;
Referee: Scott Mikalauskas.

ROUND 18

Monday 26th October 2020

SALFORD RED DEVILS 12 ST HELENS 10

RED DEVILS: 4 Dan Sarginson; 22 Rhys Williams; 2 Ed Chamberlain; 24 Elliot Kear; 5 Krisnan Inu; 6 Tui Lolohea; 18 Chris Atkin; 8 Lee Mossop (C); 30 Andy Ackers; 17 Luke Yates; 13 Tyrone McCarthy; 12 Pauli Pauli; 16 Greg Burke. Subs: 9 Joey Lussick; 10 Gil Dudson; 25 Connor Jones (not used); 29 Oliver Roberts.
Tries: Pauli (38), Inu (76); **Goals:** Inu 2/2.
SAINTS: 21 Matthew Costello; 30 Tom Nisbet (D); 33 Ben Davies (D); 26 Josh Simm; 28 Nico Rizzelli (D); 22 Jack Welsby (C); 27 Lewis Dodd; 8 Alex Walmsley; 24 Josh Eaves; 23 Joe Batchelor; 18 Joseph Paulo; 12 Dominique Peyroux; 32 James Graham. Subs (all used): 17 Jack Ashworth; 19 Aaron Smith; 29 Matthew Foster (D); 31 Jake Wingfield (D).
Try: Eaves (4); **Goals:** Dodd 3/3.
Rugby Leaguer & League Express Men of the Match:
Red Devils: Dan Sarginson; *Saints:* Dominique Peyroux.
Penalty count: 4-7; **Half-time:** 6-10; **Referee:** Ben Thaler.
(at Emerald Headingley, Leeds).

ROUND 15

Monday 26th October 2020

LEEDS RHINOS 28 CASTLEFORD TIGERS 24

RHINOS: 16 Richie Myler; 2 Tom Briscoe; 4 Konrad Hurrell; 15 Liam Sutcliffe; 5 Ash Handley; 6 Robert Lui; 7 Luke Gale (C); 10 Matt Prior; 9 Kruise Leeming; 8 Ava Seumanufagai; 11 Alex Mellor; 12 Rhyse Martin; 20 Bodene Thompson. Subs (all used): 14 Brad Dwyer; 22 Cameron Smith; 25 James Donaldson; 19 Mikolaj Oledzki.
Tries: Seumanufagai (12), Gale (35), L Sutcliffe (62), T Briscoe (68), Martin (73); **Goals:** Martin 4/5.
TIGERS: 34 Gareth O'Brien; 2 Derrell Olpherts; 21 James Clare; 18 Cheyse Blair; 25 Greg Eden; 6 Jake Trueman; 7 Danny Richardson; 8 Liam Watts; 9 Paul McShane (C); 24 Tyla Hepi; 17 Alex Foster; 12 Mike McMeeken; 11 Oliver Holmes. Subs: 15 Jesse Sene-Lefao; 19 Daniel Smith; 20 Junior Moors; 27 Lewis Peachey (not used).
Tries: Watts (2), Eden (40, 44), Blair (79, pen);
Goals: Richardson 4/4.
Dismissal: Holmes (29) - kicking Myler.
Rugby Leaguer & League Express Men of the Match:
Rhinos: Ava Seumanufagai; *Tigers:* Greg Eden.
Penalty count: 6-3; **Half-time:** 12-12; **Referee:** Tom Grant.

ROUND 19

Thursday 29th October 2020

LEEDS RHINOS 6 WAKEFIELD TRINITY 30

RHINOS: 1 Jack Walker; 24 Luke Briscoe; 26 Alex Sutcliffe; 15 Liam Sutcliffe; 5 Ash Handley; 6 Robert Lui; 7 Luke Gale (C); 8 Ava Seumanufagai; 9 Kruise Leeming; 19 Mikolaj Oledzki; 11 Alex Mellor; 12 Rhyse Martin; 20 Bodene Thompson. Subs (all used): 14 Brad Dwyer; 22 Cameron Smith; 28 Tom Holroyd; 40 Brett Ferres.
Try: Handley (62); **Goals:** Martin 1/1.
Sin bin: Mellor (71) - late challenge on Hampshire.
On report:
L Briscoe (47) - alleged dangerous challenge on Fifita.
TRINITY: 21 Max Jowitt; 40 Innes Senior; 4 Reece Lyne; 3 Bill Tupou; 2 Tom Johnstone; 29 Ryan Hampshire; 6 Jacob Miller (C); 8 David Fifita; 19 Jordan Crowther; 10 Tinirau Arona; 36 Kelepi Tanginoa; 16 James Batchelor; 13 Joe Westerman. Subs (all used): 9 Kyle Wood; 18 Adam Tangata; 25 Brad Walker; 41 Eddie Battye.

Tries: Jowitt (12, 22, 40), Fifita (29), Senior (74, 79);
Goals: Hampshire 3/6.
Rugby Leaguer & League Express Men of the Match:
Rhinos: Ava Seumanufagai; *Trinity:* Max Jowitt.
Penalty count: 5-5; **Half-time:** 0-20; **Referee:** Ben Thaler.
(at Totally Wicked Stadium, St Helens).

HULL KINGSTON ROVERS 16 HULL FC 31

ROVERS: 19 Will Dagger; 2 Ben Crooks; 3 Shaun Kenny-Dowall; 4 Kane Linnett; 22 Nick Rawsthorne; 7 Jordan Abdull; 20 Mikey Lewis; 15 George Lawler; 9 Matt Parcell; 36 George King; 11 Weller Hauraki (C); 13 Dean Hadley; 27 Elliot Minchella. Subs (all used): 8 Robbie Mulhern; 25 Matty Gee; 26 Will Maher; 35 Rowan Milnes.
Tries: Hadley (14), Linnett (28), Crooks (68);
Goals: Dagger 2/3.
HULL FC: 6 Jake Connor; 2 Bureta Faraimo; 24 Mahe Fonua; 3 Carlos Tuimavave; 33 Ratu Naulago; 35 Ben McNamara; 7 Marc Sneyd; 8 Scott Taylor; 16 Jordan Johnstone; 22 Josh Bowden; 12 Manu Ma'u; 23 Andre Savelio; 15 Joe Cator. Subs (all used): 9 Danny Houghton (C); 10 Tevita Satae; 13 Ligi Sao; 20 Brad Fash.
Tries: Bowden (8), Faraimo (17, 42), Naulago (31, 61), Sao (36); **Goals:** Sneyd 3/6; **Field goal:** Sneyd (65).
Rugby Leaguer & League Express Men of the Match:
Rovers: Dean Hadley; *Hull FC:* Jake Connor.
Penalty count: 5-4; **Half-time:** 12-22;
Referee: Liam Moore.
(at Totally Wicked Stadium, St Helens).

ROUND 21

Friday 30th October 2020

WARRINGTON WOLVES 19 HUDDERSFIELD GIANTS 12

WOLVES: 1 Stefan Ratchford; 29 Josh Thewlis; 3 Anthony Gelling; 4 Toby King; 5 Josh Charnley; 6 Blake Austin; 7 Gareth Widdop; 8 Chris Hill (C); 9 Daryl Clark; 10 Mike Cooper; 11 Ben Currie; 12 Jack Hughes; 14 Jason Clark. Subs (all used): 13 Ben Murdoch-Masila; 15 Joe Philbin; 19 Matt Davis; 20 Danny Walker.
Tries: D Clark (6, 49), Gelling (58); **Goals:** Ratchford 3/4;
Field goal: Widdop (75).
GIANTS: 1 Ashton Golding; 2 Jermaine McGillvary; 3 Jake Wardle; 21 Leroy Cudjoe; 5 Darnell McIntosh; 6 Lee Gaskell; 7 Aidan Sezer (C); 17 Ukuma Ta'ai; 37 Brandon Moore; 26 Sam Hewitt; 34 Chris McQueen; 12 Joe Wardle; 13 Michael Lawrence. Subs (all used): 4 Jordan Turner; 8 James Gavet; 14 Matty English; 15 Oliver Wilson.
Tries: Jake Wardle (37), Gavet (42); **Goals:** Sezer 2/2.
Sin bin: Sezer (73) - dissent.
Rugby Leaguer & League Express Men of the Match:
Wolves: Daryl Clark; *Giants:* Jake Wardle.
Penalty count: 3-5; **Half-time:** 8-6; **Referee:** Robert Hicks.
(at Totally Wicked Stadium, St Helens).

ROUND 19

Friday 30th October 2020

ST HELENS 6 WIGAN WARRIORS 18

SAINTS: 1 Lachlan Coote; 2 Tommy Makinson; 3 Kevin Naiqama; 22 Jack Welsby; 5 Regan Grace; 6 Jonny Lomax; 7 Theo Fages; 32 James Graham; 9 James Roby (C); 15 Matty Lees; 11 Zeb Taia; 20 James Bentley; 14 Morgan Knowles. Subs (all used): 12 Dominique Peyroux; 13 Louie McCarthy-Scarsbrook; 16 Kyle Amor; 18 Joseph Paulo.
Try: Coote (30); **Goals:** Coote 1/1.
WARRIORS: 6 Bevan French; 23 Jake Bibby; 1 Zak Hardaker; 4 Oliver Gildart; 5 Joe Burgess; 31 Jackson Hastings; 7 Thomas Leuluai (C); 19 Joe Bullock; 9 Sam Powell; 38 Brad Singleton; 11 Willie Isa; 12 Liam Farrell; 17 Oliver Partington. Subs (all used): 8 Tony Clubb; 14 Ben Flower; 15 Joe Greenwood; 16 Morgan Smithies.
Tries: Bibby (34), Leuluai (54), French (63), Hastings (70);
Goals: Hardaker 1/4.
Sin bin: Greenwood (79) - high tackle on Lees.
Rugby Leaguer & League Express Men of the Match:
Saints: Jonny Lomax; *Warriors:* Thomas Leuluai.
Penalty count: 3-2; **Half-time:** 6-4; **Referee:** Chris Kendall.

ROUND 11

Sunday 1st November 2020

WAKEFIELD TRINITY 18 LEEDS RHINOS 20

TRINITY: 1 Alex Walker; 5 Ben Jones-Bishop; 24 Jack Croft; 40 Innes Senior; 27 Lee Kershaw; 6 Jacob Miller (C); 29 Ryan Hampshire; 17 Chris Green; 9 Kyle Wood; 10 Tinirau Arona; 36 Kelepi Tanginoa; 13 Joe Westerman; 30 Yusuf Aydin. Subs (all used): 33 Harry Bowes (D); 31 Connor Bailey; 41 Eddie Battye; 8 David Fifita.

Tries: Kershaw (11), Westerman (17), Senior (47);
Goals: Hampshire 3/3.
RHINOS: 1 Jack Walker; 5 Ash Handley (C); 15 Liam Sutcliffe; 21 Rhys Evans; 24 Luke Briscoe; 6 Robert Lui; 23 Callum McLelland; 8 Ava Seumanufagai; 14 Brad Dwyer; 39 James Harrison; 27 Sam Walters; 20 Bodene Thompson; 25 James Donaldson. Subs (all used): 19 Mikolaj Oledzki; 9 Kruise Leeming; 12 Rhyse Martin; 33 Jarrod O'Connor.
Tries: Handley (8, 38), L Sutcliffe (21), Dwyer (66);
Goals: L Sutcliffe 1/2, Martin 1/2.
Rugby Leaguer & League Express Men of the Match:
Trinity: Ryan Hampshire; *Rhinos:* Ash Handley.
Penalty count: 6-6; **Half-time:** 12-14;
Referee: Liam Moore.

ROUND 9

Monday 2nd November 2020

SALFORD RED DEVILS 42 CATALANS DRAGONS 24

RED DEVILS: 4 Dan Sarginson; 22 Rhys Williams; 32 Kallum Watkins; 3 Kris Welham; 5 Krisnan Inu; 6 Tui Lolohea; 18 Chris Atkin; 8 Lee Mossop (C); 9 Joey Lussick; 17 Luke Yates; 26 Jack Ormondroyd; 12 Pauli Pauli; 16 Greg Burke. Subs (all used): 10 Gil Dudson; 13 Tyrone McCarthy; 14 Sebastine Ikahihifo; 30 Andy Ackers.
Tries: Inu (24, 48, 76), Williams (42), Lolohea (51, 62), Watkins (54); **Goals:** Inu 7/7.
DRAGONS: 1 David Mead; 16 Tom Davies; 3 Samisoni Langi; 4 Israel Folau; 5 Fouad Yaha; 6 James Maloney; 7 Josh Drinkwater; 8 Remi Casty (C); 9 Michael Mcllorum; 10 Sam Moa; 21 Paul Seguier; 17 Benjamin Jullien; 13 Benjamin Garcia. Subs (all used): 14 Julian Bousquet; 19 Mickael Goudemand; 25 Arthur Mourgue; 28 Sam Kasiano.
Tries: Seguier (12), Davies (14), Kasiano (29), Mead (80);
Goals: Maloney 3/3, Mourgue 1/1.
Rugby Leaguer & League Express Men of the Match:
Red Devils: Dan Sarginson; *Dragons:* Israel Folau.
Penalty count: 3-2; **Half-time:** 6-18; **Referee:** Jack Smith.

ROUND 20

Friday 6th November 2020

WAKEFIELD TRINITY 20 SALFORD RED DEVILS 28

TRINITY: 29 Ryan Hampshire; 5 Ben Jones-Bishop; 4 Reece Lyne; 3 Bill Tupou; 40 Innes Senior; 9 Kyle Wood; 31 Connor Bailey; 36 Kelepi Tanginoa; 33 Harry Bowes; 15 Craig Kopczak; 16 James Batchelor; 14 Jay Pitts; 10 Tinirau Arona. Subs (all used): 10 David Fifita; 17 Chris Green; 25 Brad Walker; 41 Eddie Battye.
Tries: Hampshire (30, 60), Tanginoa (51, 66);
Goals: Hampshire 2/4.
RED DEVILS: 1 Niall Evalds; 24 Elliot Kear; 32 Kallum Watkins; 2 Ed Chamberlain; 5 Krisnan Inu; 6 Tui Lolohea; 18 Chris Atkin; 8 Lee Mossop (C); 25 Connor Jones; 17 Luke Yates; 26 Jack Ormondroyd; 12 Pauli Pauli; 19 Mark Flanagan. Subs (all used): 13 Tyrone McCarthy; 14 Sebastine Ikahihifo; 16 Greg Burke; 30 Andy Ackers.
Tries: Inu (1), Evalds (9), Chamberlain (24), Lolohea (37), McCarthy (70); **Goals:** Inu 4/5.
Sin bin: Mossop (65) - tripping.
Rugby Leaguer & League Express Men of the Match:
Trinity: Kelepi Tanginoa; *Red Devils:* Krisnan Inu.
Penalty count: 3-4; **Half-time:** 4-22; **Referee:** Liam Moore.
(at Emerald Headingley, Leeds).

WIGAN WARRIORS 19 HUDDERSFIELD GIANTS 6

WARRIORS: 6 Bevan French; 23 Jake Bibby; 1 Zak Hardaker; 4 Oliver Gildart; 5 Joe Burgess; 7 Thomas Leuluai (C); 31 Jackson Hastings; 19 Joe Bullock; 9 Sam Powell; 38 Brad Singleton; 11 Willie Isa; 12 Liam Farrell; 17 Oliver Partington. Subs (all used): 8 Tony Clubb; 10 George Burgess; 14 Ben Flower; 16 Morgan Smithies.
Tries: Powell (5), Hastings (61), Hardaker (64);
Goals: Hardaker 3/3; **Field goal:** Hastings (77).
GIANTS: 1 Ashton Golding; 2 Jermaine McGillvary; 3 Jake Wardle; 21 Leroy Cudjoe; 24 Louis Senior; 23 Oliver Russell; 7 Aidan Sezer (C); 17 Ukuma Ta'ai; 37 Brandon Moore; 13 Michael Lawrence; 34 Chris McQueen; 12 Joe Wardle; 4 Jordan Turner. Subs (all used): 8 James Gavet; 27 Sam Wood; 32 Owen Trout; 36 Ronan Michael (D).
Try: Wood (38); **Goals:** Sezer 1/1.
Rugby Leaguer & League Express Men of the Match:
Warriors: Jackson Hastings; *Giants:* Ashton Golding.
Penalty count: 5-1; **Half-time:** 6-6; **Referee:** Chris Kendall.
(at Emerald Headingley, Leeds).

CANCELLED GAMES

(Due to COVID-19 unless stated)

ROUND 7
Catalans Dragons v Leeds Rhinos

ROUND 10
Wigan Warriors v Catalans Dragons

ROUND 17
Catalans Dragons v Hull FC

ROUND 18
Catalans Dragons v Warrington Wolves

ROUND 19
Huddersfield Giants v Castleford Tigers
Warrington Wolves v Salford Red Devils
(24-0 win awarded to Warrington after Salford not able to field a team)

ROUND 20
Castleford Tigers v Leeds Rhinos
Catalans Dragons v St Helens
Hull Kingston Rovers v Warrington Wolves

ROUND 21
(Remaining games cancelled due to regular season and play-off restructure)
Castleford Tigers v Salford Red Devils
Hull Kingston Rovers v Catalans Dragons
Leeds Rhinos v Wigan Warriors
St Helens v Hull FC

ROUND 22
(Entire round cancelled due to regular season and play-off restructure)
Huddersfield Giants v Catalans Dragons
Hull FC v Wigan Warriors
Salford Red Devils v Hull Kingston Rovers
St Helens v Warrington Wolves
Wakefield Trinity v Castleford Tigers

ELIMINATION PLAY-OFFS

Thursday 12th November 2020

WARRINGTON WOLVES 14 HULL FC 27

WOLVES: 1 Stefan Ratchford; 26 Matty Ashton; 3 Anthony Gelling; 4 Toby King; 5 Josh Charnley; 6 Blake Austin; 7 Gareth Widdop; 8 Chris Hill (C); 9 Daryl Clark; 15 Joe Philbin; 11 Ben Currie; 12 Jack Hughes; 14 Jason Clark. Subs: 13 Ben Murdoch-Masila; 17 Jake Mamo; 19 Matt Davis; 27 Ellis Robson (not used).
Tries: Ashton (24, 52), Gelling (29); **Goals:** Ratchford 1/3.
HULL FC: 6 Jake Connor; 33 Ratu Naulago; 24 Mahe Fonua; 4 Josh Griffin; 2 Bureta Faraimo; 3 Carlos Tuimavave; 7 Marc Sneyd; 8 Scott Taylor; 16 Jordan Johnstone; 22 Josh Bowden; 12 Manu Ma'u; 23 Andre Savelio; 15 Joe Cator. Subs (all used): 9 Danny Houghton (C); 10 Tevita Satae; 13 Ligi Sao; 20 Brad Fash.
Tries: Faraimo (19), Cator (33), Satae (43), Connor (77);
Goals: Sneyd 5/5; **Field goal:** Sneyd (40).
Rugby Leaguer & League Express Men of the Match:
Wolves: Jason Clark; *Hull FC:* Jake Connor.
Penalty count: 1-3; **Half-time:** 8-13; **Referee:** Liam Moore.

Friday 13th November 2020

CATALANS DRAGONS 26 LEEDS RHINOS 14

DRAGONS: 29 Sam Tomkins; 16 Tom Davies; 3 Samisoni Langi; 4 Israel Folau; 1 David Mead; 6 James Maloney; 7 Josh Drinkwater; 8 Remi Casty (C); 9 Michael Mcllorum; 14 Julian Bousquet; 11 Matt Whitley; 12 Joel Tomkins; 13 Benjamin Garcia. Subs: 10 Sam Moa; 21 Paul Seguier (not used); 24 Jason Baitieri; 28 Sam Kasiano.
Tries: Davies (2), Langi (8), Folau (30), Mead (63);
Goals: Maloney 5/5.
RHINOS: 16 Richie Myler; 2 Tom Briscoe; 4 Konrad Hurrell; 15 Liam Sutcliffe; 5 Ash Handley; 6 Robert Lui; 7 Luke Gale (C); 8 Ava Seumanufagai; 9 Kruise Leeming; 19 Mikolaj Oledzki; 20 Bodene Thompson; 12 Rhyse Martin; 10 Matt Prior. Subs (all used): 14 Brad Dwyer; 22 Cameron Smith; 25 James Donaldson; 26 Alex Sutcliffe.
Tries: A Sutcliffe (35), L Sutcliffe (48), Hurrell (67);
Goals: Martin 1/3.
Rugby Leaguer & League Express Men of the Match:
Dragons: Sam Tomkins; *Rhinos:* Matt Prior.
Penalty count: 5-8; **Half-time:** 18-6;
Referee: Chris Kendall.
(at Halliwell Jones Stadium, Warrington).

Wigan's Bevan French looks for a way past Hull FC's Marc Sneyd in the first Super League semi-final

Remi Casty, Samisoni Langi and Alrix Da Costa halt Tommy Makinson as St Helens end Catalans Dragons' season

SEMI-FINALS

Thursday 19th November 2020

WIGAN WARRIORS 29 HULL FC 2

WARRIORS: 6 Bevan French; 23 Jake Bibby; 1 Zak Hardaker; 4 Oliver Gildart; 5 Joe Burgess; 7 Thomas Leuluai; 28 Harry Smith; 19 Joe Bullock; 31 Jackson Hastings; 38 Brad Singleton; 11 Willie Isa; 12 Liam Farrell; 17 Oliver Partington. Subs (all used): 8 Tony Clubb; 13 Sean O'Loughlin (C); 14 Ben Flower; 16 Morgan Smithies. **Tries:** J Burgess (27), Smith (33), Hardaker (45), Bibby (75), French (79); **Goals:** Hardaker 4/5; **Field goal:** Smith (40).
HULL FC: 6 Jake Connor; 33 Ratu Naulago; 24 Mahe Fonua; 4 Josh Griffin; 2 Bureta Faraimo; 3 Carlos Tuimavave; 7 Marc Sneyd; 8 Scott Taylor; 16 Jordan Johnstone; 22 Josh Bowden; 12 Manu Ma'u; 23 Andre Savelio; 15 Joe Cator. Subs (all used): 9 Danny Houghton (C); 10 Tevita Satae; 13 Ligi Sao; 20 Brad Fash. **Goals:** Sneyd 1/1.
Rugby Leaguer & League Express Men of the Match:
Warriors: Jackson Hastings; *Hull FC:* Ligi Sao.
Penalty count: 8-4; **Half-time:** 13-2;
Referee: Chris Kendall.

Friday 20th November 2020

ST HELENS 48 CATALANS DRAGONS 2

SAINTS: 1 Lachlan Coote; 2 Tommy Makinson; 3 Kevin Naiqama; 22 Jack Welsby; 5 Regan Grace; 6 Jonny Lomax; 7 Theo Fages; 8 Alex Walmsley; 9 James Roby (C); 32 James Graham; 11 Zeb Taia; 20 James Bentley; 14 Morgan Knowles. Subs (all used): 12 Dominique Peyroux; 13 Louie McCarthy-Scarsbrook; 15 Matty Lees; 16 Kyle Amor. **Tries:** Coote (14, 51), Naiqama (31, 43, 70), Lomax (55), Bentley (66), Grace (74); **Goals:** Coote 8/9.
DRAGONS: 29 Sam Tomkins; 1 David Mead; 3 Samisoni Langi; 4 Israel Folau; 16 Tom Davies; 6 James Maloney; 7 Josh Drinkwater; 14 Julian Bousquet; 18 Alrix Da Costa; 10 Sam Moa; 11 Matt Whitley; 13 Benjamin Garcia; 8 Remi Casty (C). Subs (all used): 15 Mickael Simon; 21 Paul Seguier; 24 Jason Baitieri; 28 Sam Kasiano. **Goals:** Maloney 1/1.
Sin bin: Maloney (12) - high tackle on Grace; Garcia (65) - late challenge on Lomax.
Rugby Leaguer & League Express Men of the Match:
Saints: Lachlan Coote; *Dragons:* Sam Tomkins.
Penalty count: 7-5; **Half-time:** 14-2; **Referee:** Liam Moore.

GRAND FINAL

Friday 27th November 2020

ST HELENS 8 WIGAN WARRIORS 4

SAINTS: 1 Lachlan Coote; 2 Tommy Makinson; 3 Kevin Naiqama; 22 Jack Welsby; 5 Regan Grace; 6 Jonny Lomax; 7 Theo Fages; 8 Alex Walmsley; 9 James Roby (C); 32 James Graham; 11 Zeb Taia; 20 James Bentley; 14 Morgan Knowles. Subs (all used): 12 Dominique Peyroux; 13 Louie McCarthy-Scarsbrook; 15 Matty Lees; 16 Kyle Amor. **Try:** Welsby (80);
Goals: Coote 2/2 *(last conversion attempt not taken)*.
WARRIORS: 6 Bevan French; 23 Jake Bibby; 1 Zak Hardaker; 4 Oliver Gildart; 5 Joe Burgess; 7 Thomas Leuluai; 31 Jackson Hastings; 19 Joe Bullock; 9 Sam Powell; 38 Brad Singleton; 11 Willie Isa; 12 Liam Farrell; 17 Oliver Partington. Subs (all used): 8 Tony Clubb; 13 Sean O'Loughlin (C); 15 Joe Greenwood; 16 Morgan Smithies. **Try:** Bibby (66); **Goals:** Hardaker 0/2.
Rugby Leaguer & League Express Men of the Match:
Saints: James Roby; *Warriors:* Oliver Partington.
Penalty count: 6-6; **Half-time:** 2-0;
Referee: Chris Kendall. *(at KCOM Stadium, Hull).*

St Helens' Alex Walmsley charges at Wigan's Brad Singleton during the Super League Grand Final

SUPER LEAGUE XXV
Opta Analysis

SUPER LEAGUE XXV TRIES SCORED/CONCEDED

TOTAL TRIES SCORED		SCORED FROM KICKS		TRIES SCORED FROM OWN HALF		TRIES SCORED FROM UNDER 10M	
St Helens	84	Huddersfield Giants	9	Leeds Rhinos	13	St Helens	44
Wigan Warriors	77	Hull FC	8	Hull FC	12	Wigan Warriors	39
Leeds Rhinos	76	Wigan Warriors	8	St Helens	11	Leeds Rhinos	35
Hull FC	69	Salford Red Devils	7	Wakefield Trinity	11	Hull FC	33
Salford Red Devils	68	Hull Kingston Rovers	6	Warrington Wolves	11	Castleford Tigers	32
Catalans Dragons	65	Wakefield Trinity	6	Salford Red Devils	9	Huddersfield Giants	32
Warrington Wolves	60	Castleford Tigers	5	Wigan Warriors	8	Salford Red Devils	32
Castleford Tigers	59	Catalans Dragons	5	Castleford Tigers	7	Wakefield Trinity	30
Wakefield Trinity	57	Warrington Wolves	5	Catalans Dragons	7	Catalans Dragons	27
Huddersfield Giants	54	Leeds Rhinos	4	Hull Kingston Rovers	4	Hull Kingston Rovers	27
Hull Kingston Rovers	52	St Helens	2	Huddersfield Giants	3	Warrington Wolves	18
Toronto Wolfpack	13	Toronto Wolfpack	2	Toronto Wolfpack	2	Toronto Wolfpack	7

TOTAL TRIES CONCEDED		CONCEDED FROM KICKS		TRIES CONCEDED FROM OVER 50M		TRIES CONCEDED FROM UNDER 10M	
Wakefield Trinity	91	Leeds Rhinos	9	Leeds Rhinos	13	Hull Kingston Rovers	45
Hull Kingston Rovers	90	Salford Red Devils	9	Salford Red Devils	12	Hull FC	43
Salford Red Devils	79	Castleford Tigers	8	Wakefield Trinity	11	Wakefield Trinity	41
Hull FC	77	Hull FC	8	Hull Kingston Rovers	10	Leeds Rhinos	34
Leeds Rhinos	70	Huddersfield Giants	7	Castleford Tigers	9	Salford Red Devils	32
Castleford Tigers	64	Wakefield Trinity	7	Catalans Dragons	9	Huddersfield Giants	31
Huddersfield Giants	62	Catalans Dragons	6	Huddersfield Giants	9	Castleford Tigers	29
Wigan Warriors	48	Hull Kingston Rovers	6	Toronto Wolfpack	7	Wigan Warriors	26
Catalans Dragons	44	St Helens	2	Wigan Warriors	6	Warrington Wolves	25
Warrington Wolves	38	Warrington Wolves	2	Hull FC	5	Toronto Wolfpack	19
Toronto Wolfpack	37	Wigan Warriors	2	St Helens	5	Catalans Dragons	18
St Helens	34	Toronto Wolfpack	1	Warrington Wolves	2	St Helens	13

SUPER LEAGUE XXV AVERAGES PER MATCH

TACKLES		OFFLOADS		MISSED TACKLES		ERRORS	
Huddersfield Giants	359.7	Toronto Wolfpack	19.2	Hull Kingston Rovers	42.1	Leeds Rhinos	14.9
Wigan Warriors	359.0	Warrington Wolves	16.7	Huddersfield Giants	36.9	Hull Kingston Rovers	14.8
St Helens	355.4	Hull Kingston Rovers	15.1	Toronto Wolfpack	36.8	Toronto Wolfpack	14.0
Leeds Rhinos	351.4	Hull FC	11.8	Wakefield Trinity	36.6	St Helens	13.6
Wakefield Trinity	348.9	Wakefield Trinity	11.7	Leeds Rhinos	35.4	Catalans Dragons	13.3
Salford Red Devils	346.7	Castleford Tigers	9.9	Salford Red Devils	34.7	Hull FC	13.2
Hull FC	337.5	Catalans Dragons	9.6	Catalans Dragons	34.2	Wakefield Trinity	13.1
Hull Kingston Rovers	337.1	St Helens	9.3	Castleford Tigers	33.3	Warrington Wolves	12.8
Toronto Wolfpack	337.0	Salford Red Devils	9.2	Wigan Warriors	30.1	Castleford Tigers	11.9
Warrington Wolves	326.3	Leeds Rhinos	8.2	Warrington Wolves	29.1	Huddersfield Giants	11.6
Catalans Dragons	326.0	Huddersfield Giants	6.7	St Helens	28.9	Wigan Warriors	11.6
Castleford Tigers	325.1	Wigan Warriors	6.2	Hull FC	28.1	Salford Red Devils	10.9

CLEAN BREAKS		KICKS IN GENERAL PLAY		DEFENDERS BEATEN		PASSES	
St Helens	7.6	Salford Red Devils	20.4	St Helens	41.2	Wigan Warriors	238.6
Leeds Rhinos	7.4	Wigan Warriors	20.2	Hull FC	38.5	St Helens	235.8
Wigan Warriors	7.2	Huddersfield Giants	19.4	Leeds Rhinos	35.6	Hull Kingston Rovers	222.1
Warrington Wolves	6.9	Castleford Tigers	19.3	Wigan Warriors	34.9	Wakefield Trinity	222.1
Catalans Dragons	6.5	Warrington Wolves	18.8	Castleford Tigers	34.5	Castleford Tigers	221.9
Castleford Tigers	6.2	St Helens	18.7	Warrington Wolves	34.4	Leeds Rhinos	221.2
Hull Kingston Rovers	6.1	Wakefield Trinity	18.5	Catalans Dragons	33.5	Toronto Wolfpack	219.3
Hull FC	6.0	Hull Kingston Rovers	17.9	Toronto Wolfpack	32.3	Warrington Wolves	217.6
Salford Red Devils	5.5	Catalans Dragons	17.5	Hull Kingston Rovers	32.0	Catalans Dragons	217.0
Huddersfield Giants	4.8	Hull FC	17.5	Salford Red Devils	31.3	Huddersfield Giants	212.0
Toronto Wolfpack	4.7	Leeds Rhinos	16.4	Wakefield Trinity	30.7	Hull FC	210.4
Wakefield Trinity	4.5	Toronto Wolfpack	12.7	Huddersfield Giants	24.8	Salford Red Devils	202.1

SUPER LEAGUE XXV TOP PERFORMERS

CARRIES

Player	Team	
Jackson Hastings	Wigan	320
Liam Farrell	Wigan	288
Jermaine McGillvary	Huddersfield	277
Rhys Williams	Salford	270
Jonny Lomax	St Helens	262
Ash Handley	Leeds	258
Kelepi Tanginoa	Wakefield	258
Alex Walmsley	St Helens	257
Josh Charnley	Warrington	248
Mike Cooper	Warrington	246

OFFLOADS

Player	Team	
Toby King	Warrington	42
Mike Cooper	Warrington	37
Shaun Kenny-Dowall	Hull KR	34
Ligi Sao	Hull FC	28
Mike McMeeken	Castleford	27
Elliot Minchella	Hull KR	27
Joe Westerman	Wakefield	27
Anthony Gelling	Warrington	26
Kane Linnett	Hull KR	26
Liam Watts	Castleford	26

BREAK PASSES

Player	Team	
Jackson Hastings	Wigan	20
Paul McShane	Castleford	20
Jake Connor	Hull FC	13
James Roby	St Helens	13
Bevan French	Wigan	11
Luke Gale	Leeds	11
Jonny Lomax	St Helens	11
Aidan Sezer	Huddersfield	11
Gareth Widdop	Warrington	11
Jack Welsby	St Helens	10

INITIAL BREAKS

Player	Team	
Bevan French	Wigan	27
Ash Handley	Leeds	24
Regan Grace	St Helens	20
Ben Crooks	Hull KR	19
Liam Farrell	Wigan	19
Jermaine McGillvary	Huddersfield	17
Liam Marshall	Wigan	15
Ken Sio	Salford	15
Kevin Naiqama	St Helens	13
Rhys Williams	Salford	13

METRES

Player	Team	
Ash Handley	Leeds	2541
Liam Farrell	Wigan	2384
Alex Walmsley	St Helens	2242
Regan Grace	St Helens	2163
Bevan French	Wigan	2151
Rhys Williams	Salford	2091
Tommy Makinson	St Helens	1990
Reece Lyne	Wakefield	1977
Jermaine McGillvary	Huddersfield	1947
Josh Griffin	Hull FC	1902

TRY ASSISTS

Player	Team	
Jonny Lomax	St Helens	21
Jackson Hastings	Wigan	18
Aidan Sezer	Huddersfield	18
Jake Connor	Hull FC	14
Lachlan Coote	St Helens	14
Josh Drinkwater	Catalans	14
Danny Richardson	Castleford	13
Luke Gale	Leeds	11
Sam Tomkins	Catalans	11
Richie Myler	Leeds	10

TRY PASSES

Player	Team	
Jonny Lomax	St Helens	20
Lachlan Coote	St Helens	13
Jackson Hastings	Wigan	13
Aidan Sezer	Huddersfield	13
Jake Connor	Hull FC	12
Josh Drinkwater	Catalans	11
Sam Tomkins	Catalans	11
Toby King	Warrington	10
Richie Myler	Leeds	10
Danny Richardson	Castleford	10

TRY KICKS

Player	Team	
Jackson Hastings	Wigan	5
Aidan Sezer	Huddersfield	5
Marc Sneyd	Hull FC	4
Jordan Abdull	Hull KR	3
Josh Drinkwater	Catalans	3
Luke Gale	Leeds	3
Danny Richardson	Castleford	3
Gareth Widdop	Warrington	3
Jake Connor	Hull FC	2
Jacob Miller	Wakefield	2

TACKLES

Player	Team	
Michael Lawrence	Huddersfield	749
Sam Powell	Wigan	705
Liam Farrell	Wigan	676
Luke Yates	Salford	641
James Bentley	St Helens	636
Paul McShane	Castleford	604
Danny Houghton	Hull FC	584
Joey Lussick	Salford	559
Elliot Minchella	Hull KR	538
James Roby	St Helens	533

SUPPORTED BREAKS

Player	Team	
Ash Handley	Leeds	11
Luke Gale	Leeds	7
Jackson Hastings	Wigan	7
Jamie Shaul	Hull FC	7
Tom Lineham	Warrington	6
Tui Lolohea	Salford	6
Lachlan Coote	St Helens	5
Toby King	Warrington	5
Mike McMeeken	Castleford	5
Michael Shenton	Castleford	5

QUICK PLAY THE BALLS

Player	Team	
Carlos Tuimavave	Hull FC	64
Jermaine McGillvary	Huddersfield	62
Alex Walmsley	St Helens	56
Liam Farrell	Wigan	54
Tommy Makinson	St Helens	51
Kevin Naiqama	St Helens	51
Luke Briscoe	Leeds	49
Josh Charnley	Warrington	48
Ash Handley	Leeds	46
Pauli Pauli	Salford	46

MISSED TACKLES

Player	Team	
Tui Lolohea	Salford	77
Jacob Miller	Wakefield	63
Luke Gale	Leeds	60
Morgan Knowles	St Helens	60
James Maloney	Catalans	56
Brad Dwyer	Leeds	52
Bill Tupou	Wakefield	52
Paul McShane	Castleford	50
Shaun Kenny-Dowall	Hull KR	49
Willie Isa	Wigan	48

DEFENDERS BEATEN

Player	Team	
Bevan French	Wigan	101
Alex Walmsley	St Helens	78
Toby King	Warrington	74
Ben Crooks	Hull KR	69
Liam Farrell	Wigan	69
Carlos Tuimavave	Hull FC	68
Zak Hardaker	Wigan	67
Regan Grace	St Helens	66
Ash Handley	Leeds	65
Derrell Olpherts	Castleford	62

PENALTIES CONCEDED

Player	Team	
James Bentley	St Helens	15
Ligi Sao	Hull FC	15
Liam Farrell	Wigan	14
James Maloney	Catalans	14
Paul McShane	Castleford	14
Kenny Edwards	Huddersfield	13
Ryan Hampshire	Wakefield	13
Shaun Kenny-Dowall	Hull KR	13
Louie McCarthy-Scarsbrook	St Helens	13
Danny Richardson	Castleford	13

ERRORS

Player	Team	
Bevan French	Wigan	32
Shaun Kenny-Dowall	Hull KR	28
Ben Crooks	Hull KR	25
Anthony Gelling	Warrington	24
Toby King	Warrington	22
Reece Lyne	Wakefield	21
Pauli Pauli	Salford	21
James Bentley	St Helens	20
Tui Lolohea	Salford	20
Luke Gale	Leeds	19

KICKS IN GENERAL PLAY

Player	Team	
Danny Richardson	Castleford	177
Tui Lolohea	Salford	175
Aidan Sezer	Huddersfield	160
Blake Austin	Warrington	154
Theo Fages	St Helens	153
Marc Sneyd	Hull FC	151
Luke Gale	Leeds	135
Jackson Hastings	Wigan	117
Ryan Hampshire	Wakefield	112
James Maloney	Catalans	95

All statistics in Opta Analysis include Super League regular season only

SUPER LEAGUE XXV PENALTIES

TOTAL PENALTIES AWARDED

Huddersfield Giants	119
Wakefield Trinity	118
Leeds Rhinos	113
Castleford Tigers	112
Hull FC	111
Hull Kingston Rovers	107
St Helens	103
Salford Red Devils	102
Warrington Wolves	99
Wigan Warriors	98
Catalans Dragons	90
Toronto Wolfpack	50

TOTAL PENALTIES CONCEDED

Castleford Tigers	121
Hull Kingston Rovers	115
Wigan Warriors	115
Wakefield Trinity	113
Warrington Wolves	111
St Helens	108
Leeds Rhinos	107
Huddersfield Giants	106
Salford Red Devils	103
Hull FC	94
Catalans Dragons	86
Toronto Wolfpack	43

FOUL PLAY - AWARDED

Castleford Tigers	34
Wakefield Trinity	34
St Helens	33
Huddersfield Giants	32
Hull Kingston Rovers	32
Leeds Rhinos	27
Catalans Dragons	26
Wigan Warriors	23
Hull FC	21
Warrington Wolves	20
Salford Red Devils	17
Toronto Wolfpack	9

FOUL PLAY - CONCEDED

Wigan Warriors	37
Castleford Tigers	34
Wakefield Trinity	32
Leeds Rhinos	31
St Helens	31
Hull FC	27
Catalans Dragons	26
Salford Red Devils	26
Warrington Wolves	26
Hull Kingston Rovers	18
Huddersfield Giants	15
Toronto Wolfpack	5

OFFSIDE - AWARDED

Salford Red Devils	22
Huddersfield Giants	20
Hull Kingston Rovers	19
Wigan Warriors	19
Wakefield Trinity	18
St Helens	17
Warrington Wolves	12
Castleford Tigers	11
Catalans Dragons	11
Leeds Rhinos	11
Hull FC	10
Toronto Wolfpack	3

OFFSIDE - CONCEDED

Huddersfield Giants	21
Wigan Warriors	20
Warrington Wolves	19
Hull Kingston Rovers	18
Salford Red Devils	16
Wakefield Trinity	16
St Helens	15
Hull FC	12
Leeds Rhinos	12
Castleford Tigers	11
Catalans Dragons	9
Toronto Wolfpack	4

INTERFERENCE - AWARDED

Salford Red Devils	33
Hull FC	32
Warrington Wolves	32
Castleford Tigers	30
Wigan Warriors	28
St Helens	24
Wakefield Trinity	23
Leeds Rhinos	21
Catalans Dragons	19
Hull Kingston Rovers	19
Toronto Wolfpack	18
Huddersfield Giants	16

INTERFERENCE - CONCEDED

Warrington Wolves	31
Hull Kingston Rovers	29
Huddersfield Giants	27
St Helens	27
Salford Red Devils	25
Wakefield Trinity	25
Castleford Tigers	24
Toronto Wolfpack	23
Leeds Rhinos	22
Wigan Warriors	22
Catalans Dragons	20
Hull FC	20

OBSTRUCTION - AWARDED

Wakefield Trinity	13
Huddersfield Giants	12
Catalans Dragons	8
Hull Kingston Rovers	8
Warrington Wolves	8
St Helens	7
Castleford Tigers	6
Hull FC	5
Toronto Wolfpack	5
Salford Red Devils	4
Leeds Rhinos	3
Wigan Warriors	3

OBSTRUCTION - CONCEDED

Castleford Tigers	11
St Helens	11
Leeds Rhinos	10
Hull FC	7
Hull Kingston Rovers	7
Wigan Warriors	7
Salford Red Devils	6
Wakefield Trinity	6
Warrington Wolves	6
Huddersfield Giants	5
Catalans Dragons	4
Toronto Wolfpack	2

BALL STEALING - AWARDED

Leeds Rhinos	27
Hull FC	15
Wakefield Trinity	14
Castleford Tigers	13
Hull Kingston Rovers	11
Warrington Wolves	11
Wigan Warriors	11
Huddersfield Giants	10
St Helens	10
Catalans Dragons	9
Salford Red Devils	5
Toronto Wolfpack	4

BALL STEALING - CONCEDED

Wakefield Trinity	17
Castleford Tigers	16
Huddersfield Giants	16
Hull FC	14
Hull Kingston Rovers	14
Salford Red Devils	13
Leeds Rhinos	11
Warrington Wolves	11
Wigan Warriors	10
Catalans Dragons	7
St Helens	6
Toronto Wolfpack	5

OFFSIDE MARKERS - AWARDED

Hull FC	6
Wakefield Trinity	4
Castleford Tigers	3
Huddersfield Giants	3
Hull Kingston Rovers	3
Leeds Rhinos	3
Salford Red Devils	3
St Helens	3
Catalans Dragons	2
Warrington Wolves	2
Toronto Wolfpack	1
Wigan Warriors	1

OFFSIDE MARKERS - CONCEDED

Huddersfield Giants	6
Hull Kingston Rovers	5
Hull FC	4
Castleford Tigers	3
Leeds Rhinos	3
Wakefield Trinity	3
Warrington Wolves	3
Catalans Dragons	2
Wigan Warriors	2
Salford Red Devils	1
St Helens	1
Toronto Wolfpack	1

OFFSIDE FROM KICK - AWARDED

Huddersfield Giants	9
Salford Red Devils	7
Catalans Dragons	5
Hull FC	5
Hull Kingston Rovers	4
Leeds Rhinos	4
Castleford Tigers	3
Wigan Warriors	3
Toronto Wolfpack	2
Wakefield Trinity	2
St Helens	1
Warrington Wolves	1

OFFSIDE FROM KICK - CONCEDED

Castleford Tigers	9
Huddersfield Giants	5
Hull Kingston Rovers	5
Catalans Dragons	4
Hull FC	4
Salford Red Devils	4
St Helens	4
Wakefield Trinity	4
Leeds Rhinos	3
Warrington Wolves	2
Wigan Warriors	2
Toronto Wolfpack	0

DISSENT - AWARDED

Hull Kingston Rovers	4
Castleford Tigers	2
Hull FC	2
Huddersfield Giants	1
Salford Red Devils	1
St Helens	1
Toronto Wolfpack	1
Wakefield Trinity	1
Warrington Wolves	1
Catalans Dragons	0
Leeds Rhinos	0
Wigan Warriors	0

DISSENT - CONCEDED

Wigan Warriors	4
Catalans Dragons	2
Hull FC	2
St Helens	2
Huddersfield Giants	1
Leeds Rhinos	1
Salford Red Devils	1
Wakefield Trinity	1
Castleford Tigers	0
Hull Kingston Rovers	0
Toronto Wolfpack	0
Warrington Wolves	0

CASTLEFORD TIGERS
SUPER LEAGUE XXV LEADERS

CARRIES
Derrell Olpherts	233
Mike McMeeken	192
Grant Millington	184
Michael Shenton	169
Liam Watts	158

OFFLOADS
Mike McMeeken	27
Liam Watts	26
Paul McShane	15
Grant Millington	12
Derrell Olpherts	11

METRES
Derrell Olpherts	1752
Mike McMeeken	1500
James Clare	1245
Paul McShane	1239
Greg Eden	1198

TACKLES
Paul McShane	604
Grant Millington	423
George Griffin	421
Mike McMeeken	401
Liam Watts	360

MISSED TACKLES
Paul McShane	50
Danny Richardson	47
Mike McMeeken	37
Adam Milner	35
Michael Shenton	33

INITIAL BREAKS
Greg Eden	13
Derrell Olpherts	13
James Clare	9
Michael Shenton	9
Gareth O'Brien	8

DEFENDERS BEATEN
Derrell Olpherts	62
Mike McMeeken	41
Paul McShane	41
Peter Mata'utia	38
Jake Trueman	34

TRY ASSISTS
Danny Richardson	13
Paul McShane	8
Jordan Rankin	5
Jake Trueman	4
Peter Mata'utia	3

MARKER TACKLES
George Griffin	109
Paul McShane	108
Oliver Holmes	83
Grant Millington	76
Nathan Massey	72

CATALANS DRAGONS
SUPER LEAGUE XXV LEADERS

CARRIES
Samisoni Langi	184
Benjamin Garcia	163
Sam Tomkins	146
Julian Bousquet	145
Israel Folau	145

OFFLOADS
Israel Folau	15
Sam Tomkins	14
Julian Bousquet	13
Joel Tomkins	13
Benjamin Garcia	12

METRES
Samisoni Langi	1443
Fouad Yaha	1281
Benjamin Garcia	1216
Israel Folau	1213
Tom Davies	1195

TACKLES
Benjamin Garcia	493
Michael McIlorum	389
Matt Whitley	328
Jason Baitieri	314
Remi Casty	278

MISSED TACKLES
James Maloney	56
Michael McIlorum	43
Samisoni Langi	37
Matt Whitley	37
Josh Drinkwater	27

INITIAL BREAKS
Sam Tomkins	13
Tom Davies	12
Israel Folau	12
Fouad Yaha	11
David Mead	6

DEFENDERS BEATEN
Israel Folau	56
Sam Tomkins	52
Samisoni Langi	38
Tom Davies	33
Fouad Yaha	28

TRY ASSISTS
Josh Drinkwater	14
Sam Tomkins	11
Israel Folau	7
James Maloney	6
Samisoni Langi	5

MARKER TACKLES
Benjamin Garcia	90
Jason Baitieri	79
Michael McIlorum	63
Remi Casty	56
Julian Bousquet	51

HUDDERSFIELD GIANTS
SUPER LEAGUE XXV LEADERS

CARRIES
Jermaine McGillvary	277
Michael Lawrence	244
Ashton Golding	202
Aidan Sezer	201
Jake Wardle	169

OFFLOADS
Kenny Edwards	18
James Gavet	18
Leroy Cudjoe	12
Ashton Golding	8
Jake Wardle	8

METRES
Jermaine McGillvary	1947
Michael Lawrence	1602
Jake Wardle	1599
Ashton Golding	1572
Suaia Matagi	1172

TACKLES
Michael Lawrence	749
Joe Wardle	413
Adam O'Brien	396
Kenny Edwards	379
Suaia Matagi	348

MISSED TACKLES
Adam O'Brien	48
Aidan Sezer	42
Jordan Turner	40
Matty English	36
Kenny Edwards	33

INITIAL BREAKS
Jermaine McGillvary	17
Jake Wardle	9
Aidan Sezer	8
Louis Senior	7
Ashton Golding	6

DEFENDERS BEATEN
Ashton Golding	49
Jermaine McGillvary	44
Kenny Edwards	42
Jake Wardle	37
Darnell McIntosh	33

TRY ASSISTS
Aidan Sezer	18
Lee Gaskell	6
Darnell McIntosh	5
Leroy Cudjoe	3
Tom Holmes	3

MARKER TACKLES
Michael Lawrence	191
Adam O'Brien	77
Joe Wardle	75
Kenny Edwards	69
Matty English	62

HULL F.C.
SUPER LEAGUE XXV LEADERS

CARRIES

Josh Griffin	205
Carlos Tuimavave	205
Jamie Shaul	200
Ligi Sao	195
Mahe Fonua	163

OFFLOADS

Ligi Sao	28
Mahe Fonua	26
Manu Ma'u	16
Carlos Tuimavave	14
Josh Griffin	13

METRES

Josh Griffin	1902
Carlos Tuimavave	1875
Jamie Shaul	1387
Ligi Sao	1357
Bureta Faraimo	1346

TACKLES

Danny Houghton	584
Ligi Sao	429
Brad Fash	404
Jordan Johnstone	389
Joe Cator	386

MISSED TACKLES

Danny Houghton	39
Marc Sneyd	39
Ligi Sao	37
Mahe Fonua	31
Jake Connor	28

INITIAL BREAKS

Josh Griffin	13
Carlos Tuimavave	10
Jake Connor	9
Ratu Naulago	8
Jamie Shaul	8

DEFENDERS BEATEN

Carlos Tuimavave	68
Josh Griffin	61
Jamie Shaul	48
Bureta Faraimo	45
Mahe Fonua	42

TRY ASSISTS

Jake Connor	14
Albert Kelly	7
Josh Griffin	6
Jordan Johnstone	6
Marc Sneyd	6

MARKER TACKLES

Danny Houghton	114
Brad Fash	111
Joe Cator	86
Ligi Sao	84
Tevita Satae	76

HULL KINGSTON ROVERS
SUPER LEAGUE XXV LEADERS

CARRIES

Shaun Kenny-Dowall	212
Kane Linnett	206
Ben Crooks	190
George Lawler	169
Greg Minikin	167

OFFLOADS

Shaun Kenny-Dowall	34
Elliot Minchella	27
Kane Linnett	26
Greg Minikin	20
Matt Parcell	14

METRES

Shaun Kenny-Dowall	1581
Ben Crooks	1577
Kane Linnett	1567
George Lawler	1226
Greg Minikin	1186

TACKLES

Elliot Minchella	538
George Lawler	438
Dean Hadley	373
Matt Parcell	350
Robbie Mulhern	316

MISSED TACKLES

Shaun Kenny-Dowall	49
George Lawler	44
Jordan Abdull	36
Mikey Lewis	32
Kane Linnett	32

INITIAL BREAKS

Ben Crooks	19
Greg Minikin	10
Will Dagger	8
Shaun Kenny-Dowall	7
Kane Linnett	7

DEFENDERS BEATEN

Ben Crooks	69
Shaun Kenny-Dowall	61
Will Dagger	39
Matt Parcell	36
Kane Linnett	26

TRY ASSISTS

Jordan Abdull	10
Harvey Livett	5
Kane Linnett	4
Ryan Brierley	3
Shaun Kenny-Dowall	3

MARKER TACKLES

Elliot Minchella	119
Dean Hadley	94
Robbie Mulhern	69
George Lawler	66
Matt Parcell	63

LEEDS RHINOS
SUPER LEAGUE XXV LEADERS

CARRIES

Ash Handley	258
Luke Gale	197
Mikolaj Oledzki	183
Cameron Smith	182
Luke Briscoe	176

OFFLOADS

Adam Cuthbertson	21
Cameron Smith	16
Harry Newman	15
Konrad Hurrell	13
Rhyse Martin	13

METRES

Ash Handley	2541
Mikolaj Oledzki	1605
Luke Briscoe	1398
Konrad Hurrell	1229
Harry Newman	1223

TACKLES

Cameron Smith	508
Mikolaj Oledzki	433
Matt Prior	420
Brad Dwyer	419
Rhyse Martin	357

MISSED TACKLES

Luke Gale	60
Brad Dwyer	52
Rhyse Martin	45
Robert Lui	40
Cameron Smith	37

INITIAL BREAKS

Ash Handley	24
Harry Newman	10
Liam Sutcliffe	10
Luke Briscoe	9
Konrad Hurrell	8

DEFENDERS BEATEN

Ash Handley	65
Konrad Hurrell	57
Harry Newman	53
Richie Myler	41
Luke Briscoe	39

TRY ASSISTS

Luke Gale	11
Richie Myler	10
Liam Sutcliffe	7
Brad Dwyer	6
Ash Handley	5

MARKER TACKLES

Cameron Smith	114
Mikolaj Oledzki	96
Brad Dwyer	95
Adam Cuthbertson	80
Matt Prior	76

SALFORD RED DEVILS
SUPER LEAGUE XXV LEADERS

CARRIES
Rhys Williams	270
Dan Sarginson	217
Luke Yates	184
Kris Welham	180
Pauli Pauli	178

OFFLOADS
Pauli Pauli	16
Elliot Kear	15
Kris Welham	13
Tui Lolohea	12
Dan Sarginson	12

METRES
Rhys Williams	2091
Pauli Pauli	1496
Dan Sarginson	1475
Luke Yates	1430
Kris Welham	1224

TACKLES
Luke Yates	641
Joey Lussick	559
Tyrone McCarthy	439
Lee Mossop	394
Gil Dudson	339

MISSED TACKLES
Tui Lolohea	77
Kris Welham	44
Joey Lussick	43
Tyrone McCarthy	41
Sebastine Ikahihifo	28

INITIAL BREAKS
Ken Sio	15
Rhys Williams	13
Niall Evalds	11
Krisnan Inu	11
Dan Sarginson	7

DEFENDERS BEATEN
Sebastine Ikahihifo	58
Rhys Williams	55
Krisnan Inu	53
Pauli Pauli	52
Tui Lolohea	50

TRY ASSISTS
Tui Lolohea	10
Niall Evalds	9
Kevin Brown	6
Dan Sarginson	5
Chris Atkin	4

MARKER TACKLES
Luke Yates	132
Joey Lussick	106
Tyrone McCarthy	88
Lee Mossop	75
Gil Dudson	73

ST HELENS
SUPER LEAGUE XXV LEADERS

CARRIES
Jonny Lomax	262
Alex Walmsley	257
Regan Grace	245
Zeb Taia	244
Tommy Makinson	230

OFFLOADS
Zeb Taia	25
Alex Walmsley	24
James Graham	13
Jonny Lomax	12
Jack Welsby	11

METRES
Alex Walmsley	2242
Regan Grace	2163
Tommy Makinson	1990
Zeb Taia	1720
Jonny Lomax	1565

TACKLES
James Bentley	636
Morgan Knowles	533
James Roby	533
Zeb Taia	457
Matty Lees	446

MISSED TACKLES
Morgan Knowles	60
Kevin Naiqama	41
James Bentley	38
Jonny Lomax	38
Zeb Taia	38

INITIAL BREAKS
Regan Grace	20
Kevin Naiqama	13
Jack Welsby	12
James Bentley	10
Lachlan Coote	10

DEFENDERS BEATEN
Alex Walmsley	78
Regan Grace	66
Tommy Makinson	54
James Bentley	53
Jonny Lomax	51

TRY ASSISTS
Jonny Lomax	21
Lachlan Coote	14
James Roby	8
Theo Fages	7
Jack Welsby	5

MARKER TACKLES
James Bentley	160
Morgan Knowles	121
Matty Lees	104
James Roby	102
Alex Walmsley	73

TORONTO WOLFPACK
SUPER LEAGUE XXV LEADERS

CARRIES
Hakim Miloudi	89
Liam Kay	88
Matty Russell	83
Ricky Leutele	79
Blake Wallace	77

OFFLOADS
Sonny Bill Williams	23
Hakim Miloudi	16
Adam Sidlow	14
Josh McCrone	13
Ricky Leutele	11

METRES
Ricky Leutele	694
Liam Kay	641
Matty Russell	542
Hakim Miloudi	541
Adam Sidlow	501

TACKLES
Jon Wilkin	234
Adam Sidlow	188
Andy Ackers	177
Brad Singleton	154
Tom Olbison	151

MISSED TACKLES
Jon Wilkin	27
Andy Ackers	26
Bodene Thompson	20
Josh McCrone	16
Gadwin Springer	13

INITIAL BREAKS
Liam Kay	5
Matty Russell	4
Hakim Miloudi	2
Adam Sidlow	2
Brad Singleton	2

DEFENDERS BEATEN
Ricky Leutele	34
Hakim Miloudi	32
Matty Russell	26
Liam Kay	19
Blake Wallace	12

TRY ASSISTS
Ricky Leutele	2
Josh McCrone	2
Hakim Miloudi	2
Gareth O'Brien	2
Jon Wilkin	1

MARKER TACKLES
Jon Wilkin	69
Adam Sidlow	43
Brad Singleton	36
Tom Olbison	32
Bodene Thompson	29

WAKEFIELD TRINITY
SUPER LEAGUE XXV LEADERS

CARRIES
Kelepi Tanginoa	258
Reece Lyne	230
Bill Tupou	221
Joe Westerman	186
Tom Johnstone	176

OFFLOADS
Joe Westerman	27
Reece Lyne	20
David Fifita	15
Bill Tupou	14
Chris Green	13

METRES
Reece Lyne	1977
Kelepi Tanginoa	1901
Bill Tupou	1693
Tom Johnstone	1355
Joe Westerman	1188

TACKLES
Kyle Wood	480
Kelepi Tanginoa	479
Joe Westerman	474
Matty Ashurst	430
Jay Pitts	397

MISSED TACKLES
Jacob Miller	63
Bill Tupou	52
Reece Lyne	41
Kyle Wood	39
Ryan Hampshire	36

INITIAL BREAKS
Tom Johnstone	9
Ben Jones-Bishop	8
Kelepi Tanginoa	8
Reece Lyne	7
Ryan Hampshire	6

DEFENDERS BEATEN
Kelepi Tanginoa	55
Tom Johnstone	54
Reece Lyne	46
Joe Westerman	41
David Fifita	31

TRY ASSISTS
Reece Lyne	8
Jacob Miller	7
Ryan Hampshire	6
Max Jowitt	6
Bill Tupou	3

MARKER TACKLES
Tinirau Arona	92
Joe Westerman	83
Kyle Wood	80
Matty Ashurst	71
Jay Pitts	66

WARRINGTON WOLVES
SUPER LEAGUE XXV LEADERS

CARRIES
Josh Charnley	248
Mike Cooper	246
Toby King	226
Stefan Ratchford	186
Blake Austin	180

OFFLOADS
Toby King	42
Mike Cooper	37
Anthony Gelling	26
Stefan Ratchford	24
Ben Currie	20

METRES
Josh Charnley	1883
Mike Cooper	1776
Toby King	1712
Ben Currie	1428
Stefan Ratchford	1335

TACKLES
Ben Currie	474
Daryl Clark	450
Mike Cooper	447
Jason Clark	347
Danny Walker	333

MISSED TACKLES
Blake Austin	43
Mike Cooper	39
Toby King	37
Daryl Clark	27
Ben Currie	27

INITIAL BREAKS
Josh Charnley	12
Toby King	12
Tom Lineham	12
Blake Austin	11
Matty Ashton	10

DEFENDERS BEATEN
Toby King	74
Blake Austin	55
Daryl Clark	53
Anthony Gelling	47
Stefan Ratchford	38

TRY ASSISTS
Toby King	10
Blake Austin	6
Daryl Clark	6
Ben Currie	6
Gareth Widdop	6

MARKER TACKLES
Matt Davis	96
Danny Walker	85
Daryl Clark	76
Joe Philbin	76
Ben Currie	70

WIGAN WARRIORS
SUPER LEAGUE XXV LEADERS

CARRIES
Jackson Hastings	320
Liam Farrell	288
Bevan French	244
Zak Hardaker	206
Willie Isa	181

OFFLOADS
Bevan French	15
Joe Greenwood	12
Liam Farrell	11
Willie Isa	10
Harry Smith	10

METRES
Liam Farrell	2384
Bevan French	2151
Jackson Hastings	1758
Zak Hardaker	1601
Jake Bibby	1327

TACKLES
Sam Powell	705
Liam Farrell	676
Morgan Smithies	512
Willie Isa	503
Oliver Partington	462

MISSED TACKLES
Willie Isa	48
Harry Smith	39
Oliver Partington	36
Thomas Leuluai	33
Jake Bibby	31

INITIAL BREAKS
Bevan French	27
Liam Farrell	19
Liam Marshall	15
Joe Burgess	11
Zak Hardaker	9

DEFENDERS BEATEN
Bevan French	101
Liam Farrell	69
Zak Hardaker	67
Jackson Hastings	57
Liam Marshall	38

TRY ASSISTS
Jackson Hastings	18
Bevan French	7
Thomas Leuluai	7
Liam Farrell	5
Zak Hardaker	5

MARKER TACKLES
Sam Powell	158
Liam Farrell	127
Morgan Smithies	115
Ethan Havard	79
Oliver Partington	76

CHAMPIONSHIP 2020
Club by Club

BATLEY BULLDOGS

		APP		TRIES		GOALS		FG		PTS	
	D.O.B.	ALL	Ch	ALL	Ch	ALL	Ch	ALL	Ch	ALL	Ch
Jack Blagbrough	18/1/94	1(5)	(5)	0	0	0	0	0	0	0	0
Anthony Bowman	18/3/92	5	5	0	0	0	0	0	0	0	0
James Brown	6/5/88	4	4	1	1	0	0	0	0	4	4
Johnny Campbell	17/7/87	3	2	2	2	0	0	0	0	8	8
Tyler Dickinson	18/8/96	(1)	(1)	0	0	0	0	0	0	0	0
Tyler Dupree	8/2/00	1(3)	(3)	1	0	0	0	0	0	4	0
Toby Everett	22/12/95	6	5	1	1	0	0	0	0	4	4
Lewis Galbraith	1/2/95	6	5	2	2	0	0	0	0	8	8
Luke Hooley	1/8/98	5	4	0	0	3	2	0	0	6	4
Aiden Ineson	16/9/97	1	1	0	0	0	0	0	0	0	0
Alistair Leak	5/4/92	3(3)	2(3)	3	3	0	0	0	0	12	12
Tom Lillycrop	29/11/91	1(1)	1	0	0	0	0	0	0	0	0
Shaun Lunt	15/4/86	3(3)	3(2)	1	1	0	0	0	0	4	4
Dane Manning	15/4/89	6	5	1	1	0	0	0	0	4	4
Dale Morton	31/10/90	4	4	1	1	11	11	0	0	26	26
Shaun Pick	21/9/93	(2)	(2)	0	0	0	0	0	0	0	0
Wayne Reittie	21/1/88	6	5	0	0	0	0	0	0	0	0
Dave Scott	8/6/93	2	1	0	0	0	0	0	0	0	0
George Senior	29/8/99	2	1	1	0	0	0	0	0	4	0
Jo Taira	30/3/89	(1)	0	0	0	0	0	0	0	0	0
Keenen Tomlinson	22/5/97	5	4	0	0	0	0	0	0	0	0
Lucas Walshaw	4/8/92	4	4	1	1	0	0	0	0	4	4
Michael Ward	10/2/91	(5)	(4)	1	1	0	0	0	0	4	4
Ben White	27/10/94	6	5	0	0	0	0	0	0	0	0
Danny Yates	28/5/94	4	4	0	0	0	0	0	0	0	0

Keenen Tomlinson

'Ch' totals include Championship games only; 'All' totals also include Challenge Cup

CLUB RECORDS **MATCH RECORDS**
Highest score: 100-4 v Gateshead, 17/3/2010 **Highest score against:** 9-78 v Wakefield, 26/8/67 **Record attendance:** 23,989 v Leeds, 14/3/25
Tries: 5 Joe Oakland v Bramley, 19/12/1908; Tommy Brannan v Swinton, 17/1/1920; Jim Wale v Bramley, 4/12/26; Jim Wale v Cottingham, 12/2/27; Tommy Oldroyd v Highfield, 6/3/94; Ben Feehan v Halifax, 10/8/2008; Jermaine McGillvary v Whitehaven, 24/5/2009
Goals: 16 Gareth Moore v Gateshead, 17/3/2010 **Points:** 40 Gareth Moore v Gateshead, 17/3/2010
SEASON RECORDS **CAREER RECORDS**
Tries: 30 Johnny Campbell 2010 **Goals:** 144 Barry Eaton 2004 **Points:** 308 Richard Price 1997
Tries: 142 Craig Lingard 1998-2008 **Goals:** 463 Wharton 'Wattie' Davies 1897-1912 **Points:** 1,297 Wharton 'Wattie' Davies 1897-1912
Appearances: 421 Wharton 'Wattie' Davies 1897-1912

BRADFORD BULLS

		APP		TRIES		GOALS		FG		PTS	
	D.O.B.	ALL	Ch	ALL	Ch	ALL	Ch	ALL	Ch	ALL	Ch
Jack Brown	25/6/00	(1)	(1)	0	0	0	0	0	0	0	0
Joe Brown	14/1/99	6	4	0	0	0	0	0	0	0	0
Joe Cator	15/6/98	1	1	1	1	0	0	0	0	4	4
Steve Crossley	28/11/89	6	4	1	1	0	0	0	0	4	4
Matty Dawson-Jones	2/10/90	6	4	4	4	0	0	0	0	16	16
Thomas Doyle	29/6/99	1(4)	(3)	2	2	0	0	0	0	8	8
Anthony England	19/10/86	5	4	0	0	0	0	0	0	0	0
Rhys Evans	30/10/92	2	2	0	0	0	0	0	0	0	0
George Flanagan	8/10/86	1(3)	(2)	1	0	0	0	0	0	4	0
David Foggin-Johnston	19/8/96	2	0	0	0	0	0	0	0	0	0
Bradley Gallagher	28/2/00	6	4	2	2	0	0	0	0	8	8
Sam Hallas	18/10/96	6	4	1	1	0	0	0	0	4	4
Evan Hodgson	14/9/98	(3)	(2)	0	0	0	0	0	0	0	0
Greg Johnson	20/2/90	2	2	0	0	0	0	0	0	0	0
Liam Kirk	26/3/97	4	3	0	0	0	0	0	0	0	0
Jordan Lilley	4/9/96	6	4	3	2	1	1	0	0	14	10
Rowan Milnes	1/9/97	6	4	2	0	18	12	0	0	44	24
Levy Nzoungou	22/1/98	(6)	(4)	1	0	0	0	0	0	4	0
Ross Oakes	12/10/96	6	4	0	0	0	0	0	0	0	0
Brandon Pickersgill	29/3/97	6	4	3	3	0	0	0	0	12	12
Adam Rooks	15/1/99	5	3	1	0	0	0	0	0	4	0
Ebon Scurr	11/5/00	(6)	(4)	0	0	0	0	0	0	0	0
Daniel Waite-Pullan	14/11/98	1(1)	1	0	0	0	0	0	0	0	0

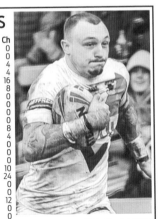

Matty Dawson-Jones

'Ch' totals include Championship games only; 'All' totals also include Challenge Cup

CLUB RECORDS **MATCH RECORDS**
Highest score: 124-0 v West Wales, 6/5/2018 **Highest score against:** 6-84 v Wigan, 21/4/2014 **Record attendance:** 69,429 v Huddersfield, 14/3/53
Tries: 6 Eric Batten v Leeds, 15/9/45; Trevor Foster v Wakefield, 10/4/48; Steve McGowan v Barrow, 8/11/92; Lesley Vainikolo v Hull, 2/9/2005
Goals: 20 Dane Chisholm v West Wales, 6/5/2018 **Points:** 48 Dane Chisholm v West Wales, 6/5/2018
SEASON RECORDS **CAREER RECORDS**
Tries: 63 Jack McLean 1951-52 **Goals:** 213 *(inc 5fg)* Henry Paul 2001 **Points:** 457 Henry Paul 2001
Tries: 261 Jack McLean 1950-56 **Goals:** 1,165 *(inc 25fg)* Paul Deacon 1998-2009 **Points:** 2,605 Paul Deacon 1998-2009
Appearances: 588 Keith Mumby 1973-90; 1992-93

DEWSBURY RAMS

	D.O.B.	APP ALL	Ch	TRIES ALL	Ch	GOALS ALL	Ch	FG ALL	Ch	PTS ALL	Ch
Chris Annakin	30/1/91	5	4	0	0	0	0	0	0	0	0
Tommy Brierley	8/9/96	1	0	0	0	0	0	0	0	0	0
Rhys Davies	9/6/96	(1)	0	0	0	0	0	0	0	0	0
Sam Day	12/6/94	3(3)	3(1)	1	1	0	0	0	0	4	4
Davey Dixon	31/5/97	2(1)	(1)	0	0	0	0	0	0	0	0
Sonny Esslemont	29/12/93	5	4	0	0	0	0	0	0	0	0
Liam Finn	2/11/83	6	4	0	0	5	0	0	0	10	0
Matty Fleming	13/1/96	5	4	0	0	0	0	0	0	0	0
Andy Gabriel	21/12/93	5	4	2	2	0	0	0	0	8	8
Matty Gee	12/12/94	1	1	1	1	0	0	0	0	4	4
Liam Johnson	12/5/97	3(3)	1(3)	0	0	0	0	0	0	0	0
Michael Knowles	2/5/87	4	3	2	1	0	0	0	0	8	4
Jon Magrin	8/10/94	1(5)	(4)	0	0	0	0	0	0	0	0
Joe Martin	28/3/95	5	4	1	1	0	0	0	0	4	4
Frazer Morris	22/2/97	3(1)	1(1)	0	0	0	0	0	0	0	0
Luke Nelmes	7/6/93	2(2)	2(1)	0	0	0	0	0	0	0	0
Will Oakes	27/2/99	6	4	2	1	0	0	0	0	8	4
Morgan Punchard	26/1/99	1	0	0	0	0	0	0	0	0	0
Martyn Reilly	5/1/96	4(1)	3	1	0	0	0	0	0	4	0
Adam Ryder	20/10/89	5	4	2	2	0	0	0	0	8	8
Connor Scott	27/5/93	2(4)	1(3)	3	1	0	0	0	0	12	4
Dom Speakman	22/3/94	3(2)	1(2)	2	0	0	0	0	0	8	0
Paul Sykes	11/8/81	5	4	1	0	21	16	0	0	46	32
James Thornton	30/9/95	1(1)	0	0	0	0	0	0	0	0	0

Connor Scott

'Ch' totals include Championship games only; 'All' totals also include Challenge Cup

CLUB RECORDS	**Highest score:** 90-5 v Blackpool, 4/4/93 **Highest score against:** 0-82 v Widnes, 30/11/86
MATCH RECORDS	**Record attendance:** 26,584 v Halifax, 30/10/1920 *(Crown Flatt)*; 4,068 v Bradford, 6/4/2015 *(Tetley's Stadium)*
	Tries: 8 Dai Thomas v Liverpool, 13/4/1907
	Goals: 13 Greg Pearce v Blackpool Borough, 4/4/93; Francis Maloney v Hunslet, 25/3/2007 **Points:** 32 Les Holliday v Barrow, 11/9/94
SEASON RECORDS	**Tries:** 40 Dai Thomas 1906-07 **Goals:** 169 Barry Eaton 2000 **Points:** 394 Barry Eaton 2000
CAREER RECORDS	**Tries:** 144 Joe Lyman 1913-31 **Goals:** 863 Nigel Stephenson 1967-78; 1984-86 **Points:** 2,082 Nigel Stephenson 1967-78; 1984-86
	Appearances: 454 Joe Lyman 1913-31

FEATHERSTONE ROVERS

	D.O.B.	APP ALL	Ch	TRIES ALL	Ch	GOALS ALL	Ch	FG ALL	Ch	PTS ALL	Ch
Wellington Albert	3/9/93	1(5)	(4)	0	0	0	0	0	0	0	0
Jimmy Beckett	29/8/99	(1)	0	0	0	0	0	0	0	0	0
Ben Blackmore	19/2/93	6	4	5	3	0	0	0	0	20	12
Luke Briscoe	11/3/94	1	1	1	1	0	0	0	0	4	4
Jack Bussey	17/8/92	5(1)	4	2	2	0	0	0	0	8	8
Conor Carey	7/4/95	3(3)	1(3)	1	0	0	0	0	0	4	0
Dane Chisholm	4/7/90	3	2	4	2	15	10	1	1	47	29
Luke Cooper	28/7/94	2(4)	(4)	0	0	0	0	0	0	0	0
Brett Ferres	17/4/86	5(1)	3(1)	0	0	0	0	0	0	0	0
Brandan French	7/3/97	(2)	0	0	0	0	0	0	0	0	0
Gareth Gale	5/6/93	3	2	1	0	0	0	0	0	4	0
Craig Hall	21/2/88	6	4	3	2	13	10	0	0	38	28
Josh Hardcastle	28/8/92	6	4	3	2	0	0	0	0	12	8
James Harrison	15/6/96	6	4	4	4	0	0	0	0	16	16
Tom Holroyd	9/2/01	3	3	0	0	0	0	0	0	0	0
Louis Jouffret	24/5/95	5	3	2	2	0	0	0	0	8	8
James Lockwood	21/3/86	4(1)	3	0	0	0	0	0	0	0	0
Callum McLelland	16/9/99	3	3	1	1	0	0	0	0	4	4
Jarrod O'Connor	20/7/01	1(1)	1(1)	0	0	0	0	0	0	0	0
Sam Ottewell	7/4/97	1	0	1	0	0	0	0	0	4	0
Dean Parata	4/10/91	1(2)	(2)	0	0	0	0	0	0	0	0
Alec Susino	24/5/95	4(2)	3(1)	0	0	0	0	0	0	0	0
Alex Sutcliffe	21/1/99	2	2	0	0	0	0	0	0	0	0
Liam Sutcliffe	25/11/94	1	1	0	0	0	0	0	0	0	0
Jake Sweeting	15/12/99	2	0	2	0	0	0	0	0	8	0
Greg Worthington	17/7/90	4	4	5	5	0	0	0	0	20	20

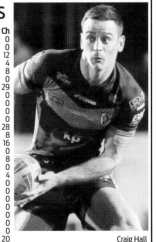

Craig Hall

'Ch' totals include Championship games only; 'All' totals also include Challenge Cup

CLUB RECORDS	**Highest score:** 96-0 v Castleford Lock Lane, 8/2/2004 **Highest score against:** 14-80 v Bradford, 3/4/2005 **Record attendance:** 17,531 v St Helens, 21/3/59
MATCH RECORDS	**Tries:** 6 Mike Smith v Doncaster, 13/4/68; Chris Bibb v Keighley, 17/9/89; Brad Dwyer v Rochdale, 1/7/2018
	Goals: 13 Mark Knapper v Keighley, 17/9/89; Liam Finn v Hunslet Old Boys, 25/3/2012; Liam Finn v Swinton, 12/8/2012
	Points: 40 Martin Pearson v Whitehaven, 26/11/95
SEASON RECORDS	**Tries:** 48 Paul Newlove 1992-93 **Goals:** 183 *(inc 2fg)* Liam Finn 2012 **Points:** 436 Liam Finn 2012
CAREER RECORDS	**Tries:** 162 Don Fox 1953-66 **Goals:** 1,210 Steve Quinn 1975-88 **Points:** 2,654 Steve Quinn 1975-88 **Appearances:** 440 Jim Denton 1921-34

HALIFAX

	D.O.B.	APP ALL	APP Ch	TRIES ALL	TRIES Ch	GOALS ALL	GOALS Ch	FG ALL	FG Ch	PTS ALL	PTS Ch
Ed Barber	26/4/90	1(2)	1(1)	1	1	0	0	0	0	4	4
Paul Brearley	5/2/92	4(1)	3(1)	1	0	0	0	0	0	4	0
Jodie Broughton	9/1/88	4	3	5	4	0	0	0	0	20	16
Will Calcott	16/12/97	2(1)	2	0	0	0	0	0	0	0	0
Keal Carlile	20/3/90	2(1)	2	0	0	0	0	0	0	0	0
Curtis Davies	17/1/97	(3)	(3)	0	0	0	0	0	0	0	0
Jacob Fairbank	4/3/90	4	3	1	0	0	0	0	0	4	0
Dan Fleming	8/7/92	1(4)	1(3)	0	0	0	0	0	0	0	0
Matt Garside	1/10/90	5	4	1	0	0	0	0	0	4	0
Tom Gilmore	2/2/94	2	2	0	0	0	0	0	0	0	0
Scott Grix	1/5/84	5	4	1	1	0	0	0	0	4	4
Sam Hewitt	29/4/99	(1)	(1)	0	0	0	0	0	0	0	0
Keegan Hirst	13/12/88	4(1)	3(1)	0	0	0	0	0	0	0	0
Kevin Larroyer	19/6/89	2(3)	1(3)	0	0	0	0	0	0	0	0
Conor McGrath	14/8/96	1	1	1	1	0	0	0	0	4	4
Brandon Moore	27/7/96	3(1)	2(1)	0	0	0	0	0	0	0	0
Elliot Morris	4/1/96	2	2	0	0	0	0	0	0	0	0
Scott Murrell	5/9/85	5	4	1	1	0	0	0	0	4	4
Oliver Roberts	24/12/94	1	1	1	1	0	0	0	0	4	4
Shaun Robinson	13/7/89	4	3	3	3	0	0	0	0	12	12
James Saltonstall	27/9/93	4(1)	3(1)	1	1	0	0	0	0	4	4
Steve Tyrer	16/3/89	4	3	2	2	8	7	0	0	24	22
Oliver Wilson	22/3/99	(1)	(1)	0	0	0	0	0	0	0	0
James Woodburn-Hall	2/2/95	5	4	1	1	2	2	0	0	8	8

Jodie Broughton

'Ch' totals include Championship games only; 'All' totals also include Challenge Cup

CLUB RECORDS Highest score: 94-4 v Myton, 25/3/2012 Highest score against: 6-88 v Hull KR, 23/4/2006
Record attendance: 29,153 v Wigan, 21/3/59 *(Thrum Hall)*; 9,827 v Bradford, 12/3/2000 *(The Shay)*
MATCH RECORDS Tries: 8 Keith Williams v Dewsbury, 9/11/57 Goals: 14 Bruce Burton v Hunslet, 27/8/72
Points: 32 John Schuster v Doncaster, 9/10/94; Steve Tyrer v Whitehaven, 7/2/2016
SEASON RECORDS Tries: 48 Johnny Freeman 1956-57 Goals: 156 Graham Holroyd 2008 Points: 362 John Schuster 1994-95
CAREER RECORDS Tries: 290 Johnny Freeman 1954-67 Goals: 1,028 Ronnie James 1961-71 Points: 2,191 Ronnie James 1961-71 Appearances: 482 Stan Kielty 1946-58

LEIGH CENTURIONS

	D.O.B.	APP ALL	APP Ch	TRIES ALL	TRIES Ch	GOALS ALL	GOALS Ch	FG ALL	FG Ch	PTS ALL	PTS Ch
Danny Addy	15/1/91	6	4	1	0	0	0	0	0	4	0
Lewis Bienek	11/4/98	(3)	(3)	1	1	0	0	0	0	4	4
Sam Brooks	29/9/93	(1)	0	0	0	0	0	0	0	0	0
Callum Field	7/10/97	(3)	(1)	0	0	0	0	0	0	0	0
Liam Forsyth	23/3/96	1	1	2	2	0	0	0	0	8	8
Alex Gerrard	5/11/91	2(4)	(4)	1	1	0	0	0	0	4	4
Nick Glohe	16/9/92	5(1)	4	1	1	0	0	0	0	4	4
Ben Hellewell	30/1/92	6	4	5	3	0	0	0	0	20	12
Adam Higson	19/5/87	5	3	7	5	0	0	0	0	28	20
Liam Hood	6/1/92	6	4	5	3	0	0	0	0	20	12
Mark Ioane	3/2/90	5	3	0	0	0	0	0	0	0	0
Nathan Mason	8/9/93	4	4	0	0	0	0	0	0	0	0
Gregg McNally	2/1/91	4	3	0	0	1	1	0	0	2	2
Craig Mullen	15/1/98	2	1	0	0	0	0	0	0	0	0
Ben Reynolds	15/1/94	6	4	1	1	33	24	0	0	70	52
Jarrod Sammut	15/2/87	1	1	0	0	0	0	0	0	0	0
Junior Sa'u	18/4/87	6	4	0	0	0	0	0	0	0	0
Cameron Scott	7/10/99	4	4	4	4	0	0	0	0	16	16
Ryan Shaw	27/2/92	2	0	0	0	0	0	0	0	0	0
Tom Spencer	2/1/91	1(2)	1	0	0	0	0	0	0	0	0
Jordan Thompson	4/9/91	1(5)	(4)	0	0	0	0	0	0	0	0
Iain Thornley	11/9/91	6	4	5	3	0	0	0	0	20	12
Matty Wildie	25/10/90	1(5)	(4)	2	2	0	0	0	0	8	8
Josh Woods	13/12/97	4	3	2	2	0	0	1	0	9	8

Liam Hood

'Ch' totals include Championship games only; 'All' totals also include Challenge Cup

CLUB RECORDS Highest score: 92-2 v Keighley, 30/4/86 Highest score against: 4-94 v Workington, 26/2/95
Record attendance: 31,326 v St Helens, 14/3/53 *(Hilton Park)*; 10,556 v Batley, 17/9/2016 *(Leigh Sports Village)*
MATCH RECORDS Tries: 6 Jack Wood v York, 4/10/47; Neil Turley v Workington, 31/1/2001 Goals: 15 Mick Stacey v Doncaster, 28/3/76 Points: 42 Neil Turley v Chorley, 4/4/2004
SEASON RECORDS Tries: 55 Neil Turley 2001 Goals: 187 Neil Turley 2004 Points: 468 Neil Turley 2004
CAREER RECORDS Tries: 189 Mick Martyn 1954-67 Goals: 1,043 Jimmy Ledgard 1948-58 Points: 2,492 John Woods 1976-85; 1990-92 Appearances: 503 Albert Worrall 1920-38

LONDON BRONCOS

	D.O.B.	APP ALL	APP Ch	TRIES ALL	TRIES Ch	GOALS ALL	GOALS Ch	FG ALL	FG Ch	PTS ALL	PTS Ch
Sadiq Adebiyi	8/1/97	(1)	(1)	0	0	0	0	0	0	0	0
Mitch Allgood	27/4/89	1	1	0	0	0	0	0	0	0	0
Guy Armitage	29/11/91	5	4	3	2	0	0	0	0	12	8
Olly Ashall-Bott	24/11/97	1	0	0	0	0	0	0	0	0	0
Cory Aston	1/3/95	6	5	1	1	1	0	0	0	6	4
Eddie Battye	24/7/91	6	5	1	1	0	0	0	0	4	4
Will Blakemore	20/9/98	(1)	0	0	0	0	0	0	0	0	0
Rob Butler	15/5/98	3(2)	3(2)	1	1	0	0	0	0	4	4
Ed Chamberlain	8/2/96	1	1	0	0	0	0	0	0	0	0
Rhys Curran	7/7/89	6	5	3	2	0	0	0	0	12	8
Sam Davis	11/11/98	2(4)	1(4)	0	0	0	0	0	0	0	0
Kieran Dixon	22/8/92	5	5	2	2	15	15	0	0	38	38
Tuoyo Egodo	16/2/97	6	5	4	3	0	0	0	0	16	12
Matty Fozard	3/3/95	6	5	2	2	1	1	0	0	10	10
Daniel Hindmarsh	8/8/98	2(2)	1(2)	2	1	0	0	0	0	8	4
Josh Hodson	15/6/00	1(1)	(1)	0	0	0	0	0	0	0	0
Olsi Krasniqi	26/6/92	3(3)	2(3)	0	0	0	0	0	0	0	0
Will Lovell	10/5/93	3	3	0	0	0	0	0	0	0	0
James Meadows	15/6/99	5	4	0	0	0	0	0	0	0	0
Dan Norman	8/9/97	1(4)	1(3)	0	0	0	0	0	0	0	0
Jacob Ogden	23/1/98	5	4	2	2	0	0	0	0	8	8
Eloi Pelissier	18/6/91	1(2)	1(1)	3	2	0	0	0	0	12	8
Greg Richards	12/7/95	2	2	0	0	0	0	0	0	0	0
Morgan Smith	30/4/98	2	2	0	0	0	0	0	0	0	0
Josh Walters	23/12/94	5(1)	5	3	3	0	0	0	0	12	12
Jordan Williams	4/6/97	(3)	(3)	0	0	0	0	0	0	0	0

Kieran Dixon

'Ch' totals include Championship games only; 'All' totals also include Challenge Cup

CLUB RECORDS	**Highest score:** 82-0 v Highfield, 12/11/95; 82-2 v Barrow, 20/5/2006 **Highest score against:** 6-82 v Warrington, 20/3/2011; 10-82 v Warrington, 8/6/2013
	Record attendance: 15,013 v Wakefield, 15/2/81 *(Craven Cottage)*; 3,051 v Leeds, 1/9/2019 *(Trailfinders Sports Ground)*
MATCH RECORDS	**Tries:** 5 Martin Offiah v Whitehaven, 14/3/99; Sean Morris v Batley, 13/9/2015
	Goals: 13 Rob Purdham v Barrow, 20/5/2006 **Points:** 34 Rob Purdham v Barrow, 20/5/2006; Jarrod Sammut v Sheffield, 13/5/2018
SEASON RECORDS	**Tries:** 43 Mark Johnson 1993-94 **Goals:** 159 John Gallagher 1993-94 **Points:** 384 John Gallagher 1993-94
CAREER RECORDS	**Tries:** 109 Luke Dorn 2005-2006; 2009-2013 **Goals:** 309 Steve Diamond 1981-84 **Points:** 772 Paul Sykes 2001-2007
	Appearances: 202 Steele Retchless 1998-2004

OLDHAM

	D.O.B.	APP ALL	APP Ch	TRIES ALL	TRIES Ch	GOALS ALL	GOALS Ch	FG ALL	FG Ch	PTS ALL	PTS Ch
Harry Aaronson	28/3/98	2	2	0	0	0	0	0	0	0	0
Dan Abram	11/11/95	6	5	2	1	11	9	0	0	30	22
Jimmy Beckett	29/8/99	2(2)	2(2)	1	1	0	0	0	0	4	4
Liam Bent	11/10/97	4	3	0	0	0	0	0	0	0	0
Danny Bridge	4/1/93	5	4	2	2	0	0	0	0	8	8
Adam Brook	29/9/94	2	1	0	0	0	0	0	0	0	0
Lewis Charnock	2/9/94	6	5	0	0	0	0	0	0	0	0
Jack Croft	21/12/00	2	2	0	0	0	0	0	0	0	0
Ben Davies	2/11/89	(3)	(2)	0	0	0	0	0	0	0	0
Matthew Fletcher	15/2/00	1(5)	1(4)	1	1	0	0	0	0	4	4
Titus Gwaze	8/6/99	(4)	(4)	0	0	0	0	0	0	0	0
Dave Hewitt	4/11/95	5(1)	5	0	0	0	0	0	0	0	0
John Hutchings	1/1/99	1(1)	(1)	0	0	0	0	0	0	0	0
Daniel Igbinedion	26/1/95	(1)	(1)	0	0	0	0	0	0	0	0
Ryan Ince	16/9/96	2	2	1	1	0	0	0	0	4	4
Kyran Johnson	23/3/94	4	3	0	0	0	0	0	0	0	0
Phil Joy	4/9/91	6	5	0	0	0	0	0	0	0	0
Dec Kay	24/11/96	5	4	0	0	0	0	0	0	0	0
Lee Kershaw	2/5/99	1	1	0	0	0	0	0	0	0	0
Danny Langtree	18/2/91	6	5	1	0	0	0	0	0	4	0
Cameron Leeming	3/7/95	4	3	0	0	0	0	0	0	0	0
Gareth Owen	3/7/92	6	5	1	1	0	0	0	0	4	4
Jack Spencer	21/12/90	6	5	0	0	0	0	0	0	0	0
Matty Wilkinson	13/6/96	(6)	(5)	0	0	0	0	0	0	0	0
James Worthington	21/5/99	2	2	0	0	0	0	0	0	0	0

Danny Bridge

'Ch' totals include Championship games only; 'All' totals also include Challenge Cup

CLUB RECORDS	**Highest score:** 102-6 v West Wales, 8/7/2018 **Highest score against:** 0-84 v Widnes, 25/7/99
	Record attendance: 28,000 v Huddersfield, 24/2/1912 *(Watersheddings)*; 2,394 v Warrington, 7/5/2016 *(Bower Fold)*
MATCH RECORDS	**Tries:** 7 James Miller v Barry, 31/10/1908 **Goals:** 14 Bernard Ganley v Liverpool City, 4/4/59
	Points: 34 Andy Ballard v London Skolars, 2/5/2009; Chris Baines v Hunslet, 20/9/2009; Lewis Palfrey v Hemel, 9/8/2015
SEASON RECORDS	**Tries:** 49 Reg Farrar 1921-22 **Goals:** 200 Bernard Ganley 1957-58 **Points:** 412 Bernard Ganley 1957-58
CAREER RECORDS	**Tries:** 174 Alan Davies 1950-61 **Goals:** 1,358 Bernard Ganley 1951-61 **Points:** 2,761 Bernard Ganley 1951-61 **Appearances:** 627 Joe Ferguson 1899-1923

SHEFFIELD EAGLES

	D.O.B.	APP ALL	Ch	TRIES ALL	Ch	GOALS ALL	Ch	FG ALL	Ch	PTS ALL	Ch
Connor Bower	18/1/97	5	3	0	0	0	0	0	0	0	0
Blake Broadbent	11/12/98	1(5)	(5)	0	0	0	0	0	0	0	0
Aaron Brown	27/7/92	7	5	2	2	0	0	0	0	8	8
Greg Burns	25/3/95	4	3	0	0	0	0	0	0	0	0
Paddy Burns	15/3/98	(6)	(4)	0	0	0	0	0	0	0	0
James Davey	21/8/89	3(2)	2(1)	0	0	0	0	0	0	0	0
Olly Davies	30/11/95	7	5	3	0	0	0	0	0	12	0
Rory Dixon	17/10/97	4	4	0	0	0	0	0	0	0	0
Izaac Farrell	30/1/98	5	4	1	0	9	6	2	2	24	14
Joel Farrell	15/3/94	7	5	5	2	0	0	0	0	20	8
Josh Guzdek	22/4/95	5	4	2	1	3	1	0	0	14	6
Brad Knowles	31/7/93	6(1)	5	0	0	0	0	0	0	0	0
Corey Makelim	6/1/94	5	3	2	0	0	0	0	0	8	0
Frankie Mariano	10/5/87	1(5)	1(3)	0	0	0	0	0	0	0	0
Zack McComb	9/9/95	7	5	1	1	0	0	0	0	4	4
Ryan Millar	12/5/94	7	5	3	2	0	0	0	0	12	8
Lewis Taylor	15/4/97	(5)	(3)	1	1	0	0	0	0	4	4
Anthony Thackeray	19/2/86	6	4	0	0	0	0	0	0	0	0
Robbie Ward	27/10/95	(4)	(4)	1	1	0	0	0	0	4	4
Scott Wheeldon	23/2/86	5	3	0	0	0	0	0	0	0	0
Rob Worrincy	9/7/85	5	3	1	1	0	0	0	0	4	4
Menzie Yere	24/10/83	1	1	0	0	0	0	0	0	0	0

Joel Farrell

'Ch' totals include Championship games only; 'All' totals also include Challenge Cup

CLUB RECORDS
Highest score: 112-6 v Leigh East, 7/4/2013 **Highest score against:** 0-88 v Hull, 2/3/2003
Record attendance: 10,603 v Bradford, 16/8/97 *(Don Valley Stadium)*; 1,711 v Bradford, 15/2/2019 *(Olympic Legacy Park)*
MATCH RECORDS **Tries:** 5 Daryl Powell v Mansfield, 2/1/89; Menzie Yere v Leigh East, 7/4/2013; Quentin Laulu-Togaga'e v Rochdale, 7/9/2014; Garry Lo v Rochdale, 4/6/2017
Goals: 14 Dominic Brambani v Leigh East, 7/4/2013 **Points:** 32 Roy Rafferty v Fulham, 21/9/86
SEASON RECORDS **Tries:** 46 Menzie Yere 2013 **Goals:** 169 *(inc 1fg)* Dominic Brambani 2013 **Points:** 361 Dominic Brambani 2013
CAREER RECORDS **Tries:** 196 Menzie Yere 2009-2020 **Goals:** 986 Mark Aston 1986-2004 **Points:** 2,142 Mark Aston 1986-2004 **Appearances:** 389 Mark Aston 1986-2004

SWINTON LIONS

	D.O.B.	APP ALL	Ch	TRIES ALL	Ch	GOALS ALL	Ch	FG ALL	Ch	PTS ALL	Ch
Gavin Bennion	31/12/93	5	3	0	0	0	0	0	0	0	0
Billy Brickhill	30/4/97	(2)	(1)	0	0	0	0	0	0	0	0
Louis Brogan	6/5/00	(5)	(3)	0	0	0	0	0	0	0	0
Tayler Brown	16/10/99	(1)	0	0	0	0	0	0	0	0	0
Mike Butt	6/5/95	5	3	9	3	0	0	0	0	36	12
Mitch Cox	15/11/93	5	3	3	2	0	0	0	0	12	8
Rob Fairclough	10/9/97	4	3	1	1	0	0	0	0	4	4
Sam Grant	24/3/99	3	1	1	0	0	0	0	0	4	0
Frankie Halton	18/6/96	5	3	2	1	0	0	0	0	8	4
Jack Hansen	12/1/97	5	3	0	0	10	8	0	0	20	16
Lewis Hatton	14/1/97	5	3	2	1	0	0	0	0	8	4
Ben Heyes	5/10/98	(1)	0	0	0	0	0	0	0	0	0
Will Hope	2/6/93	5	3	2	0	0	0	0	0	8	0
Paddy Jones	7/2/97	(4)	(3)	0	0	0	0	0	0	0	0
Jose Kenga	3/5/95	(3)	(3)	0	0	0	0	0	0	0	0
Richard Lepori	22/10/91	5	3	2	0	0	0	0	0	8	0
Rhodri Lloyd	22/7/93	5	3	0	0	0	0	0	0	0	0
Ben Morris	1/8/97	2(1)	2	0	0	0	0	0	0	0	0
Oscar Thomas	3/1/94	1(3)	(2)	0	0	6	0	0	0	12	0
Luke Waterworth	20/6/96	5	3	0	0	0	0	0	0	0	0
Brandon Wood	31/7/00	5	3	0	0	0	0	0	0	0	0

Mike Butt

'Ch' totals include Championship games only; 'All' totals also include Challenge Cup

CLUB RECORDS
Highest score: 96-4 v Oxford, 12/7/2015 **Highest score against:** 0-112 v Warrington, 20/5/2011
Record attendance: 26,891 v Wigan, 12/2/64 *(Station Road)*; 2,155 v Toulouse, 28/4/2018 *(Heywood Road)*
MATCH RECORDS **Tries:** 6 Mark Riley v Prescot, 11/8/96 **Goals:** 14 Ian Mort v Oxford, 12/7/2015 **Points:** 48 Ian Mort v Oxford, 12/7/2015
SEASON RECORDS **Tries:** 42 John Stopford 1963-64 **Goals:** 128 Albert Blan 1960-61 **Points:** 338 Ian Mort 2011
CAREER RECORDS **Tries:** 197 Frank Evans 1921-31 **Goals:** 970 Ken Gowers 1954-73 **Points:** 2,105 Ken Gowers 1954-73 **Appearances:** 601 Ken Gowers 1954-73

TOULOUSE OLYMPIQUE

	D.O.B.	APP ALL	APP Ch	TRIES ALL	TRIES Ch	GOALS ALL	GOALS Ch	FG ALL	FG Ch	PTS ALL	PTS Ch
Bastien Ader	6/6/91	5	5	1	1	0	0	0	0	4	4
William Barthau	30/1/90	5	5	2	2	6	6	0	0	20	20
James Bell	2/5/94	5	5	4	4	0	0	0	0	16	16
Clement Boyer	27/7/94	2(3)	2(3)	0	0	0	0	0	0	0	0
Joe Bretherton	5/10/95	5	5	4	4	0	0	0	0	16	16
Ben Evans	30/10/92	(4)	(4)	0	0	0	0	0	0	0	0
Johnathon Ford	17/8/89	4	4	0	0	0	0	0	0	0	0
Harrison Hansen	26/10/85	4	4	1	1	0	0	0	0	4	4
Jy Hitchcox	18/8/89	4	4	3	3	0	0	0	0	12	12
Mathieu Jussaume	17/5/99	(1)	(1)	0	0	0	0	0	0	0	0
Mark Kheirallah	15/2/90	5	5	1	1	20	20	0	0	44	44
Pierre-Jean Lima	13/10/00	(1)	(1)	0	0	0	0	0	0	0	0
Paul Marcon	10/7/95	5	5	7	7	0	0	0	0	28	28
Tony Maurel	21/4/93	1	1	0	0	0	0	0	0	0	0
Con Mika	14/9/89	1(2)	1(2)	0	0	0	0	0	0	0	0
Hugo Pezet	20/10/00	1	1	1	1	0	0	0	0	4	4
Maxime Puech	16/3/94	(4)	(4)	0	0	0	0	0	0	0	0
Stan Robin	21/10/90	5	5	3	3	0	0	0	0	12	12
Justin Sangare	7/3/98	(3)	(3)	1	1	0	0	0	0	4	4
Junior Vaivai	18/1/90	4	4	2	2	0	0	0	0	8	8
Paterika Vaivai	14/2/92	5	5	1	1	0	0	0	0	4	4
Lloyd White	9/8/88	(2)	(2)	1	1	0	0	0	0	4	4
Frank Winterstein	17/12/86	4	4	0	0	0	0	0	0	0	0

Paul Marcon

CLUB RECORDS
MATCH RECORDS Highest score: 84-6 v Keighley, 18/6/2016 Highest score against: 10-90 v Featherstone, 3/7/2011 Record attendance: 6,103 v Toronto, 9/3/2019
Tries: 6 Ilias Bergal v Rochdale, 13/7/2019 Goals: 12 Mark Kheirallah v Keighley, 18/6/2016 Points: 40 Mark Kheirallah v Keighley, 18/6/2016
SEASON RECORDS Tries: 36 Kuni Minga 2016 Goals: 171 Mark Kheirallah 2016 Points: 466 Mark Kheirallah 2016
CAREER RECORDS Tries: 92 Mark Kheirallah 2016-2020 Goals: 569 Mark Kheirallah 2016-2020
Points: 1,507 Mark Kheirallah 2016-2020 Appearances: 128 Sebastien Planas 2009-2011; 2016-2018

● *Records only include seasons when the club competed in the British game (2009-2011 & 2016-2020)*

WHITEHAVEN

	D.O.B.	APP ALL	APP Ch	TRIES ALL	TRIES Ch	GOALS ALL	GOALS Ch	FG ALL	FG Ch	PTS ALL	PTS Ch
Dion Aiye	6/11/87	3(2)	2(2)	2	2	0	0	0	0	8	8
Jake Bradley	29/4/01	1(3)	(3)	0	0	0	0	0	0	0	0
Andrew Bulman	4/10/99	5	4	2	1	0	0	0	0	8	4
Brett Carter	9/7/88	3	2	0	0	0	0	0	0	0	0
Kris Coward	1/10/81	4	3	0	0	0	0	0	0	0	0
Karl Dixon	13/9/93	4	4	2	2	1	1	0	0	10	10
Sam Dowsett	2/11/92	1(1)	1	0	0	0	0	0	0	0	0
Sam Forrester	28/6/93	5	4	1	0	0	0	0	0	4	0
Ellis Gillam	6/10/97	4	4	1	1	0	0	0	0	4	4
Connor Holliday	9/6/95	1(2)	(2)	0	0	2	1	0	0	4	2
Ethan Kelly	31/12/94	2(3)	1(3)	0	0	0	0	0	0	0	0
Jake Moore	6/9/96	3(2)	2(2)	0	0	2	1	0	0	4	2
Jason Mossop	12/9/85	6	5	2	1	0	0	0	0	8	4
James Newton	20/12/91	4(1)	3(1)	0	0	4	4	0	0	8	8
Karl Olstrom	21/9/91	(1)	(1)	0	0	0	0	0	0	0	0
Jessie Joe Parker	22/8/85	5	4	0	0	0	0	0	0	0	0
Brett Phillips	25/10/88	4(1)	4	0	0	0	0	0	0	0	0
Callum Phillips	19/2/92	6	5	1	1	0	0	0	0	4	4
Marc Shackley	14/1/89	5	5	0	0	0	0	0	0	0	0
Chris Taylor	25/10/93	1	1	0	0	0	0	0	0	0	0
Jamie Thackray	30/9/79	1(3)	1(2)	0	0	0	0	0	0	0	0
Dave Thompson	13/9/95	5	5	1	0	0	0	0	0	4	0
Tom Walker	25/12/94	(5)	(4)	1	1	0	0	0	0	4	4
Tom Wilkinson	19/4/96	5	5	0	0	0	0	0	0	0	0

'Ch' totals include Championship games only; 'All' totals also include Challenge Cup

Jason Mossop

CLUB RECORDS
MATCH RECORDS Highest score: 86-6 v Highfield, 25/1/95 Highest score against: 8-106 v Wigan, 12/5/2008 Record attendance: 18,500 v Wakefield, 19/3/60
Tries: 6 Vince Gribbin v Doncaster, 18/11/84; Andrew Bulman v Wigan St Patricks, 10/3/2019
Goals: 13 Lee Anderson v Highfield, 25/1/95 Points: 32 Mick Nanyn v Batley, 22/8/2004
SEASON RECORDS Tries: 34 Mike Pechey 1994-95 Goals: 141 John McKeown 1956-57 Points: 398 Mick Nanyn 2004
CAREER RECORDS Tries: 239 Craig Calvert 2004-2017 Goals: 1,050 John McKeown 1948-61 Points: 2,133 John McKeown 1948-61 Appearances: 417 John McKeown 1948-61

WIDNES VIKINGS

	D.O.B.	APP ALL	APP Ch	TRIES ALL	TRIES Ch	GOALS ALL	GOALS Ch	FG ALL	FG Ch	PTS ALL	PTS Ch
Kenny Baker	1/3/92	5(1)	3(1)	3	1	0	0	0	0	12	4
Jay Chapelhow	21/9/95	(3)	(2)	1	1	0	0	0	0	4	4
Ted Chapelhow	21/9/95	7	5	0	0	0	0	0	0	0	0
Danny Craven	21/11/91	4	3	1	0	0	0	0	0	4	0
Deon Cross	30/7/96	6	4	6	4	0	0	0	0	24	16
Connor Dwyer	29/12/93	1(2)	1(1)	0	0	0	0	0	0	0	0
Joe Edge	22/2/00	3(3)	1(3)	2	1	0	0	0	0	8	4
Owen Farnworth	11/2/99	(5)	(4)	0	0	0	0	0	0	0	0
Shane Grady	13/12/89	5(1)	3(1)	2	2	0	0	0	0	8	8
Lewis Hulme	1/7/94	1	0	0	0	0	0	0	0	0	0
Jack Johnson	25/4/96	7	5	5	2	0	0	0	0	20	8
Leilani Latu	5/2/93	(1)	(1)	0	0	0	0	0	0	0	0
MacGraff Leuluai	9/2/90	2(4)	2(2)	1	0	0	0	0	0	4	0
Joe Lyons	16/10/97	3(4)	2(3)	3	2	0	0	0	0	12	8
Jake Mamo	6/6/94	1	1	0	0	0	0	0	0	0	0
Pat Moran	2/4/98	7	5	0	0	0	0	0	0	0	0
Jack Owens	3/6/94	7	5	4	4	30	18	0	0	76	52
Dec Patton	23/5/95	1(1)	1(1)	0	0	0	0	0	0	0	0
Ellis Robson	14/9/98	1	1	1	1	0	0	0	0	4	4
Lloyd Roby	3/1/99	5(1)	4	1	0	0	0	0	0	4	0
Matty Smith	23/7/87	6	4	0	0	0	0	0	0	0	0
Jake Spedding	26/9/96	6	5	4	3	0	0	0	0	16	12
Logan Tomkins	1/8/91	6	5	0	0	0	0	0	0	0	0
Sam Wilde	8/9/95	7	5	4	2	0	0	0	0	16	8
Callum Wood	11/4/99	(2)	(1)	0	0	0	0	0	0	0	0

'Ch' totals include Championship games only; 'All' totals also include Challenge Cup

Sam Wilde

CLUB RECORDS	**Highest score:** 90-4 v Doncaster, 10/6/2007; 90-0 v Coventry, 21/4/2018 **Highest score against:** 6-76 v Catalans Dragons, 31/3/2012
	Record attendance: 24,205 v St Helens, 16/2/61
MATCH RECORDS	**Tries:** 7 Phil Cantillon v York, 18/2/2001 **Goals:** 14 Mark Hewitt v Oldham, 25/7/99; Tim Hartley v Saddleworth, 7/3/2009
	Points: 38 Gavin Dodd v Doncaster, 10/6/2007
SEASON RECORDS	**Tries:** 58 Martin Offiah 1988-89 **Goals:** 161 Mick Nanyn 2007 **Points:** 434 Mick Nanyn 2007
CAREER RECORDS	**Tries:** 234 Mal Aspey 1964-80 **Goals:** 1,083 Ray Dutton 1966-78 **Points:** 2,195 Ray Dutton 1966-78 **Appearances:** 591 Keith Elwell 1970-86

YORK CITY KNIGHTS

	D.O.B.	APP ALL	APP Ch	TRIES ALL	TRIES Ch	GOALS ALL	GOALS Ch	FG ALL	FG Ch	PTS ALL	PTS Ch
Jordan Baldwinson	10/11/94	3(3)	2(2)	1	0	0	0	0	0	4	0
Jason Bass	10/5/96	4	3	3	0	0	0	0	0	12	0
Kriss Brining	16/11/93	(3)	(2)	0	0	0	0	0	0	0	0
Reiss Butterworth	7/12/98	(2)	(1)	1	0	0	0	0	0	4	0
Lewis Carr	11/8/00	1	1	0	0	0	0	0	0	0	0
Chris Clarkson	7/4/90	6	4	1	0	0	0	0	0	4	0
James Green	29/11/90	(5)	(3)	1	0	0	0	0	0	4	0
Brad Hey	4/9/94	2	1	0	0	0	0	0	0	0	0
Ben Johnston	8/3/92	5	3	1	0	0	0	0	0	4	0
Josh Jordan-Roberts	26/8/98	1(1)	1(1)	0	0	0	0	0	0	0	0
Will Jubb	17/9/96	6	4	0	0	0	0	0	0	0	0
Jimmy Keinhorst	14/7/90	5	3	2	1	0	0	0	0	8	4
Matty Marsh	21/4/95	4	4	6	2	0	0	0	0	24	8
Joe Porter	26/1/93	1(1)	1(1)	0	0	0	0	0	0	0	0
Connor Robinson	23/10/94	5	3	2	0	16	3	0	0	40	6
Liam Salter	14/6/93	6	4	0	0	0	0	0	0	0	0
Sam Scott	5/6/90	6	4	0	0	0	0	0	0	0	0
Will Sharp	12/5/86	4	3	2	1	0	0	0	0	8	4
Tim Spears	27/7/84	6	4	0	0	0	0	0	0	0	0
Marcus Stock	1/5/96	1(5)	1(3)	2	1	0	0	0	0	8	4
Jack Teanby	14/5/96	3(3)	1(3)	0	0	0	0	0	0	0	0
Elliot Wallis	10/5/00	3	2	0	0	0	0	0	0	0	0
Danny Washbrook	18/9/85	4(1)	3	0	0	0	0	0	0	0	0

'Ch' totals include Championship games only; 'All' totals also include Challenge Cup

Jason Bass

CLUB RECORDS	**Highest score:** 144-0 v West Wales, 29/4/2018 **Highest score against:** 0-98 v Rochdale, 8/4/2001
	Record attendance: 14,689 v Swinton, 10/2/34 *(Clarence Street)*; 4,221 v Bradford, 18/2/2018 *(Bootham Crescent)*
MATCH RECORDS	**Tries:** 7 Brad Davis v Highfield, 17/9/95; Kieren Moss v West Wales, 29/4/2018
	Goals: 21 Connor Robinson v West Wales, 11/8/2018 **Points:** 56 Chris Thorman v Northumbria University, 6/3/2011
SEASON RECORDS	**Tries:** 35 John Crossley 1980-81 **Goals:** 186 *(inc 4fg)* Connor Robinson 2018 **Points:** 420 Connor Robinson 2018
CAREER RECORDS	**Tries:** 167 Peter Foster 1955-67 **Goals:** 1,060 Vic Yorke 1954-67 **Points:** 2,159 Vic Yorke 1954-67 **Appearances:** 449 Willie Hargreaves 1952-65

BATLEY BULLDOGS

DATE	FIXTURE	RESULT	SCORERS	LGE	ATT
2/2/20	Featherstone (h)	L18-38	t:Galbraith,Leak,Walshaw g:Morton(3)	12th	1,795
9/2/20	Widnes (a)	L32-12	t:Galbraith,Leak g:Hooley(2)	12th	3,577
16/2/20	Swinton (h)	W20-10	t:Campbell(2),Manning,Ward g:Morton(2)	9th	746
21/2/20	Leigh (a) (CCR4)	L36-10	t:Dupree,Senior g:Hooley	N/A	1,586
1/3/20	Sheffield (h)	L18-19			
		(aet)	t:Lunt,Leak,Brown g:Morton(3)	8th	925
7/3/20	Toulouse (a)	L34-14	t:Morton,Everett g:Morton(3)	9th	2,817

BRADFORD BULLS

DATE	FIXTURE	RESULT	SCORERS	LGE	ATT
2/2/20	London Broncos (h)	L14-18	t:Dawson-Jones(2),Doyle g:Lilley	9th	2,637
16/2/20	Featherstone (h)	L22-30	t:Doyle,Lilley,Pickersgill,Dawson-Jones g:Milnes(3)	11th	3,640
23/2/20	Underbank (h) (CCR4)	W22-0	t:Rooks,Flanagan,Nzoungou,Milnes g:Milnes(3)	N/A	1,458
1/3/20	Oldham (a)	W12-26	t:Hallas,Crossley,Pickersgill,Cator g:Milnes(5)	10th	1,189
8/3/20	Sheffield (h)	W28-0	t:Gallagher(2),Pickersgill,Lilley,Dawson-Jones g:Milnes(4)	7th	2,707
13/3/20	Wakefield (a) (CCR5)	L17-14	t:Lilley,Milnes g:Milnes(3)	N/A	3,112

(All home games played at Tetley's Stadium, Dewsbury)

DEWSBURY RAMS

DATE	FIXTURE	RESULT	SCORERS	LGE	ATT
31/1/20	Leigh (h)	L10-36	t:Ryder g:Sykes(3)	13th	1,723
18/2/20	Halifax (a)	W16-18	t:Gee,Gabriel g:Sykes(5)	8th	1,159
1/3/20	Widnes (h)	W20-8	t:Knowles,Day,Ryder g:Sykes(4)	7th	1,043
8/3/20	Oldham (a)	W6-24	t:Gabriel,Scott,Martin,Oakes g:Sykes(4)	6th	684
11/3/20	Whitehaven (a) (CCR4)	W16-22	t:Speakman(2),Scott g:Finn(5)	N/A	427
15/3/20	Newcastle (a) (CCR5)	L38-30	t:Knowles,Sykes,Scott,Reilly,Oakes g:Sykes(5)	N/A	689

FEATHERSTONE ROVERS

DATE	FIXTURE	RESULT	SCORERS	LGE	ATT
2/2/20	Batley (a)	W18-38	t:Worthington,Briscoe,Chisholm(2),Hardcastle,Harrison g:Chisholm(7)	3rd	1,795
16/2/20	Bradford (a)	W22-30	t:McLelland,Harrison,Bussey,Hall,Blackmore g:Hall(5)	4th	3,640
22/2/20	Barrow (h) (CCR4)	W18-16	t:Hall,Parata,Gale g:Hall(3)	N/A	1,120
1/3/20	London Broncos (a)	W10-34	t:Harrison,Blackmore,Bussey,Hall,Jouffret,Hardcastle g:Hall(5)	3rd	1,035
8/3/20	Swinton (h)	W35-24	t:Harrison,Jouffret,Worthington(4),Blackmore g:Chisholm(3) fg:Chisholm	3rd	1,874
13/3/20	Hunslet (h) (CCR5)	W46-6	t:Sweeting(2),Ottewell,Chisholm(2),Hardcastle,Blackmore(2),Carey g:Chisholm(5)	N/A	1,002

HALIFAX

DATE	FIXTURE	RESULT	SCORERS	LGE	ATT
2/2/20	Sheffield (h)	W18-17	t:McGrath,Tyrer,Saltonstall,Roberts g:Tyrer	7th	1,525
18/2/20	Dewsbury (h)	L16-18	t:Murrell,Broughton(2) g:Woodburn-Hall(2)	7th	1,159
22/2/20	Sheffield (a) (CCR4) ●	L20-18	t:Garside,Brearley,Broughton,Fairbank g:Tyrer	N/A	429
1/3/20	York (h)	W28-4	t:Robinson(2),Tyrer,Woodburn-Hall,Grix g:Tyrer(4)	5th	1,430
8/3/20	Leigh (a)	L34-20	t:Broughton(2),Barber,Robinson g:Tyrer(2)	8th	3,095

● Played at Mobile Rocket Stadium, Wakefield

LEIGH CENTURIONS

DATE	FIXTURE	RESULT	SCORERS	LGE	ATT
31/1/20	Dewsbury (a)	W10-36	t:Woods,Scott,Hellewell,Thornley,Reynolds,Higson g:Reynolds(6)	2nd	1,723
8/2/20	Sheffield (h)	W58-10	t:Higson(3),Woods,Thornley,Glohe,Bienek,Wildie,Gerrard,Hellewell,Hood g:Reynolds(6),McNally	1st	3,104
16/2/20	York (h)	W34-0	t:Forsyth(2),Thornley,Hood,Hellewell,Wildie g:Reynolds(5)	1st	2,942
21/2/20	Batley (h) (CCR4)	W36-10	t:Hood,Addy,Thornley(2),Hellewell,Higson g:Reynolds(6)	N/A	1,586
8/3/20	Halifax (h)	W34-20	t:Hood,Scott(3),Higson g:Reynolds(7)	2nd	3,095
15/3/20	Hull KR (a) (CCR5)	L22-19	t:Higson,Hellewell,Hood g:Reynolds(3) fg:Woods	N/A	2,620

LONDON BRONCOS

DATE	FIXTURE	RESULT	SCORERS	LGE	ATT
2/2/20	Bradford (a)	W14-18	t:Armitage,Butler,Walters g:Dixon(3)	6th	2,637
9/2/20	Whitehaven (h)	W36-20	t:Walters,Egodo(2),Ogden,Fozard,Hindmarsh,Dixon g:Dixon(4)	4th	735
16/2/20	Widnes (a)	W12-38	t:Walters,Dixon,Fozard,Battye,Pelissier,Egodo,Aston g:Dixon(4),Fozard	3rd	3,680
23/2/20	York (h) (CCR4)	L22-24	t:Hindmarsh,Egodo,Curran,Pelissier,Armitage g:Aston	N/A	543
1/3/20	Featherstone (h)	L10-34	t:Ogden,Pelissier g:Dixon	4th	1,035
8/3/20	York (a)	W12-18	t:Curran(2),Armitage g:Dixon(3)	4th	1,364

OLDHAM

DATE	FIXTURE	RESULT	SCORERS	LGE	ATT
2/2/20	Widnes (h)	L6-36	t:Beckett g:Abram	14th	1,726
8/2/20	Toulouse (a)	L58-6	t:Fletcher g:Abram	14th	2,318
16/2/20	Whitehaven (a)	W14-16	t:Owen,Abram g:Abram(4)	10th	532
23/2/20	Widnes (a) (CCR4)	L52-12	t:Abram,Langtree g:Abram(2)	N/A	1,564
1/3/20	Bradford (h)	L12-26	t:Bridge(2) g:Abram(2)	12th	1,189
8/3/20	Dewsbury (h)	L6-24	t:Ince g:Abram	12th	684

SHEFFIELD EAGLES

DATE	FIXTURE	RESULT	SCORERS	LGE	ATT
2/2/20	Halifax (a)	L18-17	t:Millar,Ward,J Farrell g:I Farrell(2) fg:I Farrell	8th	1,525
8/2/20	Leigh (a)	L58-10	t:Guzdek,Taylor g:I Farrell	13th	3,104
16/2/20	Toulouse (h) ●	L14-26	t:McComb,J Farrell,Worrincy g:Guzdek	14th	618
22/2/20	Halifax (h) (CCR4) ●●	W20-18	t:Davies(2),J Farrell,Guzdek g:Guzdek(2)	N/A	429
1/3/20	Batley (a)	W18-19 *(aet)*	t:Millar,Brown(2) g:I Farrell(3) fg:I Farrell	11th	925
8/3/20	Bradford (a)	L28-0		11th	2,707
15/3/20	Workington (h) (CCR5) ●●●	W34-18	t:J Farrell(2),Millar,Davies,Makelim(2),I Farrell g:I Farrell(3)	N/A	323

● *Played at Castle Park, Doncaster* ●● *Played at Mobile Rocket Stadium, Wakefield* ●●● *Played at Keepmoat Stadium, Doncaster*

SWINTON LIONS

DATE	FIXTURE	RESULT	SCORERS	LGE	ATT
2/2/20	Whitehaven (a)	W0-14	t:Hatton,Butt g:Hansen(3)	4th	803
16/2/20	Batley (a)	L20-10	t:Cox,Halton g:Hansen	6th	746
22/2/20	Leigh Miners Rangers (h) (CCR4)	W56-0	t:Butt(4),Grant,Cox,Hope(2),Lepori(2),Halton g:Thomas(6)	N/A	622
8/3/20	Featherstone (a)	L35-24	t:Cox,Fairclough,Butt(2) g:Hansen(4)	10th	1,874
15/3/20	Widnes (a) (CCR5)	L32-16	t:Butt(2),Hatton g:Hansen(2)	N/A	1,527

TOULOUSE OLYMPIQUE

DATE	FIXTURE	RESULT	SCORERS	LGE	ATT
1/2/20	York (h)	W22-10	t:Bretherton,Marcon,P Vaivai,J Vaivai g:Kheirallah(3)	5th	3,151
8/2/20	Oldham (h)	W58-6	t:Ader,Bell,Marcon(3),J Vaivai,Bretherton(3),White,Barthau g:Kheirallah(7)	2nd	2,318
16/2/20	Sheffield (a) ●	W14-26	t:Robin(2),Bell,Marcon g:Kheirallah(5)	2nd	618
1/3/20	Whitehaven (a)	W4-40	t:Hitchcox(3),Marcon,Barthau,Bell,Sangare g:Kheirallah(2),Barthau(4)	1st	516
7/3/20	Batley (h)	W34-14	t:Hansen,Marcon,Robin,Kheirallah,Bell,Pezet g:Barthau(2),Kheirallah(3)	1st	2,817

● *Played at Castle Park, Doncaster*

WHITEHAVEN

DATE	FIXTURE	RESULT	SCORERS	LGE	ATT
2/2/20	Swinton (h)	L0-14		11th	803
9/2/20	London Broncos (a)	L36-20	t:Walker,Gillam,C Phillips g:Newton(4)	11th	735
16/2/20	Oldham (h)	L14-16	t:Aiye(2),Mossop g:Moore	12th	532
1/3/20	Toulouse (h)	L4-40	t:Thompson	13th	516
8/3/20	Widnes (a)	L40-16	t:Bulman,Dixon(2) g:Dixon,Holliday	14th	2,977
11/3/20	Dewsbury (h) (CCR4)	L16-22	t:Forrester,Bulman,Mossop g:Moore,Holliday	N/A	427

WIDNES VIKINGS

DATE	FIXTURE	RESULT	SCORERS	LGE	ATT
2/2/20	Oldham (a)	W6-36	t:Johnson(2),Owens,Spedding,Grady,Cross,Wilde g:Owens(4)	1st	1,726
9/2/20	Batley (h)	W32-12	t:Spedding(2),Cross,Baker,Grady,Owens g:Owens(4)	3rd	3,577
16/2/20	London Broncos (h)	L12-38	t:Cross,Owens g:Owens(2)	5th	3,680
23/2/20	Oldham (h) (CCR4)	W52-12	t:Roby,Cross,Wilde(2),Craven,Baker,Johnson(2),Edge g:Owens(8)	N/A	1,564
1/3/20	Dewsbury (a)	L20-8	t:Robson g:Owens(2)	6th	1,043
8/3/20	Whitehaven (h)	W40-16	t:J Chapelhow,Wilde,Lyons(2),Cross,Edge,Owens g:Owens(6)	5th	2,977
15/3/20	Swinton (h) (CCR5)	W32-16	t:Spedding,Johnson,Baker,Leuluai,Cross,Lyons g:Owens(4)	N/A	1,527

YORK CITY KNIGHTS

DATE	FIXTURE	RESULT	SCORERS	LGE	ATT
1/2/20	Toulouse (a)	L22-10	t:Sharp,Stock g:Robinson	10th	3,151
16/2/20	Leigh (a)	L34-0		13th	2,942
23/2/20	London Broncos (a) (CCR4)	W22-24	t:Green,Baldwinson,Stock,Keinhorst g:Robinson(4)	N/A	543
1/3/20	Halifax (a)	L28-4	t:Keinhorst	14th	1,430
8/3/20	London Broncos (h)	L12-18	t:Marsh(2) g:Robinson(2)	13th	1,364
15/3/20	Rochdale (h) (CCR5) ●	W70-12	t:Bass(3),Clarkson,Robinson(2),Marsh(4),Butterworth,Sharp,Johnston g:Robinson(9)	N/A	400

● *Played at LD Nutrition Stadium, Featherstone*

CHAMPIONSHIP 2020
Round by Round

ROUND 1

Friday 31st January 2020

DEWSBURY RAMS 10 LEIGH CENTURIONS 36

RAMS: 1 Joe Martin; 2 Andy Gabriel; 3 Adam Ryder; 4 Matty Fleming; 5 Will Oakes; 6 Paul Sykes; 7 Liam Finn; 16 Connor Scott; 9 Dom Speakman; 17 Martyn Reilly; 19 Sonny Esslemont; 15 Liam Johnson; 13 Chris Annakin. Subs (all used): 14 Sam Day; 18 Davey Dixon; 22 Luke Nelmes; 23 Jon Magrin.
Try: Ryder (26); **Goals:** Sykes 3/3.
CENTURIONS: 1 Gregg McNally; 25 Cameron Scott; 3 Iain Thornley; 4 Junior Sa'u; 5 Adam Higson; 6 Ben Reynolds; 17 Josh Woods; 8 Nathan Mason; 9 Liam Hood; 18 Tom Spencer; 11 Ben Hellewell; 21 Nick Glohe; 13 Danny Addy. Subs (all used): 14 Matty Wildie; 15 Jordan Thompson; 27 Alex Gerrard; 23 Callum Field.
Tries: Woods (18), Scott (36), Hellewell (52), Thornley (58), Reynolds (69), Higson (79);
Goals: Reynolds 6/6.
Rugby Leaguer & League Express Men of the Match: *Rams:* Paul Sykes; *Centurions:* Ben Reynolds.
Penalty count: 10-6; **Half-time:** 10-12;
Referee: Cameron Worsley; **Attendance:** 1,723.

Saturday 1st February 2020

TOULOUSE OLYMPIQUE 22 YORK CITY KNIGHTS 10

OLYMPIQUE: 1 Mark Kheirallah; 2 Jy Hitchcox; 3 Junior Vaivai; 19 Bastien Ader; 5 Paul Marcon; 6 Johnathon Ford; 7 Stan Robin; 16 Harrison Hansen; 30 William Barthau; 17 Paterika Vaivai; 10 Joe Bretherton; 18 Clement Boyer; 13 James Bell. Subs (all used): 14 Lloyd White; 8 Maxime Puech; 15 Ben Evans; 23 Justin Sangare.
Tries: Bretherton (20), Marcon (65), P Vaivai (71), J Vaivai (80); **Goals:** Kheirallah 3/4.
Dismissal: White (60) - kicking Salter.
CITY KNIGHTS: 1 Matty Marsh; 21 Jason Bass; 22 Brad Hey; 4 Liam Salter; 5 Will Sharp; 6 Ben Johnston; 7 Connor Robinson; 19 Jordan Baldwinson; 9 Will Jubb; 16 Chris Clarkson; 11 Danny Washbrook; 12 Sam Scott; 13 Tim Spears. Subs (all used): 10 Jack Teanby; 17 Joe Porter; 20 Marcus Stock; 23 Josh Jordan-Roberts.
Tries: Sharp (10), Stock (49); **Goals:** Robinson 1/2.
On report: Spears (64) - alleged dangerous challenge.
Rugby Leaguer & League Express Men of the Match: *Olympique:* James Bell; *City Knights:* Chris Clarkson.
Penalty count: 7-6; **Half-time:** 6-4;
Referee: Marcus Griffiths; **Attendance:** 3,151.

Sunday 2nd February 2020

BATLEY BULLDOGS 18 FEATHERSTONE ROVERS 38

BULLDOGS: 14 Luke Hooley; 2 Wayne Reittie; 3 Keenen Tomlinson; 4 Lewis Galbraith; 22 Dale Morton; 6 Ben White; 7 Danny Yates; 13 James Brown; 24 Shaun Lunt; 10 Toby Everett; 11 Dane Manning; 12 Lucas Walshaw; 25 Anthony Bowman. Subs (all used): 9 Alistair Leak; 15 Jack Blagbrough; 16 Michael Ward; 17 Shaun Pick.
Tries: Galbraith (23), Leak (27), Walshaw (56);
Goals: Morton 3/3.
ROVERS: 1 Craig Hall; 31 Luke Briscoe; 27 Greg Worthington; 3 Josh Hardcastle; 2 Ben Blackmore; 30 Callum McLelland; 7 Dane Chisholm; 13 James Lockwood; 16 Jack Bussey; 17 Alec Susino; 10 James Harrison; 11 Brett Ferres; 33 Jarrod O'Connor. Subs (all used): 5 Conor Carey; 9 Dean Parata; 15 Luke Cooper; 29 Wellington Albert.
Tries: Worthington (13), Briscoe (35), Chisholm (43, 50), Hardcastle (72), Harrison (74); **Goals:** Chisholm 7/7.
Rugby Leaguer & League Express Men of the Match: *Bulldogs:* Alistair Leak; *Rovers:* Dane Chisholm.
Penalty count: 6-8; **Half-time:** 12-12;
Referee: Tom Grant; **Attendance:** 1,795.

BRADFORD BULLS 14 LONDON BRONCOS 18

BULLS: 1 Brandon Pickersgill; 2 Greg Johnson; 5 Joe Brown; 4 Ross Oakes; 19 Matty Dawson-Jones; 6 Rowan Milnes; 7 Jordan Lilley; 8 Anthony England; 13 Sam Hallas; 10 Steve Crossley; 11 Adam Rooks; 28 Bradley Gallagher; 15 Liam Kirk. Subs (all used): 17 Levy Nzoungou; 29 Ebon Scurr; 18 Evan Hodgson; 9 Thomas Doyle.
Tries: Dawson-Jones (45, 74), Doyle (57); **Goals:** Lilley 1/3.
BRONCOS: 5 Kieran Dixon; 19 Jacob Ogden; 4 Will Lovell; 3 Guy Armitage; 2 Tuoyo Egodo; 17 James Meadows; 6 Cory Aston; 15 Greg Richards; 14 Matty Fozard; 10 Rob Butler; 12 Rhys Curran; 11 Josh Walters; 8 Eddie Battye. Subs (all used): 13 Sadiq Adebiyi; 16 Olsi Krasniqi; 18 Dan Norman; 21 Sam Davis.
Tries: Armitage (14), Butler (19), Walters (54);
Goals: Dixon 3/3.
Rugby Leaguer & League Express Men of the Match: *Bulls:* Rowan Milnes; *Broncos:* James Meadows.
Penalty count: 8-10; **Half-time:** 0-12;
Referee: Aaron Moore; **Attendance:** 2,637.

HALIFAX 18 SHEFFIELD EAGLES 17

HALIFAX: 1 Scott Grix; 18 James Saltonstall; 3 Steve Tyrer; 4 James Woodburn-Hall; 19 Conor McGrath; 6 Scott Murrell; 7 Tom Gilmore; 10 Keegan Hirst; 14 Keal Carlile; 8 Elliot Morris; 11 Matt Garside; 34 Oliver Roberts; 13 Jacob Fairbank. Subs (all used): 15 Paul Brearley; 20 Curtis Davies; 29 Dan Fleming; 31 Kevin Larroyer.
Tries: McGrath (4), Tyrer (54), Saltonstall (74), Roberts (79); **Goals:** Tyrer 1/4.
Sin bin: Larroyer (29) - dangerous contact on J Farrell.
EAGLES: 1 Josh Guzdek; 2 Rob Worrincy; 19 Zack McComb; 18 Connor Bower; 5 Ryan Millar; 24 Izaac Farrell; 6 Corey Makelim; 22 Rory Dixon; 14 Greg Burns; 11 Brad Knowles; 15 Olly Davies; 12 Joel Farrell; 13 Aaron Brown. Subs (all used): 16 Robbie Ward; 17 Frankie Mariano; 20 Blake Broadbent; 21 Paddy Burns.
Tries: Millar (16), Ward (35), J Farrell (59);
Goals: I Farrell 2/3; **Field goal:** I Farrell (71).
Rugby Leaguer & League Express Men of the Match: *Halifax:* Scott Murrell; *Eagles:* Joel Farrell.
Penalty count: 7-7; **Half-time:** 4-10;
Referee: Billy Pearson; **Attendance:** 1,525.

OLDHAM 6 WIDNES VIKINGS 36

OLDHAM: 1 Dan Abram; 2 Dec Kay; 3 James Worthington; 5 Kyran Johnson; 20 Harry Aaronson; 6 Lewis Charnock; 7 Dave Hewitt; 8 Phil Joy; 9 Gareth Owen; 10 Jack Spencer; 11 Danny Langtree; 12 Danny Bridge; 13 Liam Bent. Subs (all used): 30 Daniel Igbinedion; 14 Matty Wilkinson; 28 Matthew Fletcher; 22 Jimmy Beckett.
Try: Beckett (51); **Goals:** Abram 1/1.
Sin bin: Owen (16) - late challenge.
VIKINGS: 1 Jack Owens; 2 Jack Johnson; 4 Lloyd Roby; 3 Jake Spedding; 5 Deon Cross; 17 Matty Smith; 6 Danny Craven; 14 Pat Moran; 9 Logan Tomkins; 10 Ted Chapelhow; 12 Sam Wilde; 15 Kenny Baker; 19 Connor Dwyer. Subs (all used): 25 Joe Edge; 16 Owen Farnworth; 7 Joe Lyons; 11 Shane Grady.
Tries: Johnson (9, 62), Owens (17), Spedding (25), Grady (41), Cross (46), Wilde (76); **Goals:** Owens 4/7.
Rugby Leaguer & League Express Men of the Match: *Oldham:* Jimmy Beckett; *Vikings:* Matty Smith.
Penalty count: 9-6; **Half-time:** 0-16;
Referee: Jack Smith; **Attendance:** 1,726.

WHITEHAVEN 0 SWINTON LIONS 14

WHITEHAVEN: 1 Sam Forrester; 5 Andrew Bulman; 23 Jason Mossop; 3 Chris Taylor; 2 Dave Thompson; 6 Karl Dixon; 13 Dion Aiye; 8 Marc Shackley; 9 Callum Phillips; 10 Kris Coward; 11 Brett Phillips; 12 Jake Moore; 16 Tom Wilkinson. Subs (all used): 18 James Newton; 24 Ethan Kelly; 17 Tom Walker; 20 Jake Bradley.
Sin bin: Bulman (71) - fighting.
LIONS: 1 Mike Butt; 2 Richard Lepori; 3 Ben Morris; 4 Mitch Cox; 5 Brandon Wood; 6 Jack Hansen; 7 Rob Fairclough; 8 Gavin Bennion; 9 Luke Waterworth; 10 Lewis Hatton; 11 Rhodri Lloyd; 12 Frankie Halton; 13 Will Hope. Subs (all used): 20 Oscar Thomas; 18 Louis Brogan; 16 Paddy Jones; 17 Jose Kenga.
Tries: Hatton (4), Butt (46); **Goals:** Hansen 3/3.
Sin bin: Lloyd (71) - use of the elbow; Butt (75) - professional foul.
Rugby Leaguer & League Express Men of the Match: *Whitehaven:* Tom Walker; *Lions:* Jack Hansen.
Penalty count: 10-9; **Half-time:** 0-6;
Referee: Gareth Hewer; **Attendance:** 803.

ROUND 2

Saturday 8th February 2020

LEIGH CENTURIONS 58 SHEFFIELD EAGLES 10

CENTURIONS: 1 Gregg McNally; 25 Cameron Scott; 3 Iain Thornley; 4 Junior Sa'u; 5 Adam Higson; 6 Ben Reynolds; 17 Josh Woods; 8 Nathan Mason; 9 Liam Hood; 10 Mark Ioane; 11 Ben Hellewell; 21 Nick Glohe; 13 Danny Addy. Subs (all used): 14 Matty Wildie; 15 Jordan Thompson; 27 Alex Gerrard; 26 Lewis Bienek.
Tries: Higson (4, 8, 18), Woods (24), Thornley (26), Glohe (42), Bienek (48), Wildie (50), Gerrard (53), Hellewell (60), Hood (80);
Goals: Reynolds 6/9, Woods 0/1, McNally 1/1.
Sin bin: Reynolds (32) - fighting.
EAGLES: 6 Corey Makelim; 19 Zack McComb; 1 Josh Guzdek; 18 Connor Bower; 5 Ryan Millar; 24 Izaac Farrell; 7 Anthony Thackeray; 22 Rory Dixon; 14 Greg Burns; 11 Brad Knowles; 15 Olly Davies; 12 Joel Farrell; 13 Aaron Brown. Subs (all used): 23 Lewis Taylor; 16 Robbie Ward; 20 Blake Broadbent; 21 Paddy Burns.
Tries: Guzdek (67), Taylor (76); **Goals:** I Farrell 1/2.
Rugby Leaguer & League Express Men of the Match: *Centurions:* Danny Addy; *Eagles:* Blake Broadbent.
Penalty count: 11-9; **Half-time:** 26-0;
Referee: Michael Mannifield; **Attendance:** 3,104.

TOULOUSE OLYMPIQUE 58 OLDHAM 6

OLYMPIQUE: 1 Mark Kheirallah; 5 Paul Marcon; 3 Junior Vaivai; 19 Bastien Ader; 2 Jy Hitchcox; 7 Stan Robin; 6 Johnathon Ford; 17 Paterika Vaivai; 30 William Barthau; 16 Harrison Hansen; 10 Joe Bretherton; 12 Frank Winterstein; 13 James Bell. Subs (all used): 14 Lloyd White; 11 Con Mika; 15 Ben Evans; 18 Clement Boyer.
Tries: Ader (11), Bell (18), Marcon (28, 56, 65), J Vaivai (36), Bretherton (44, 52, 75), White (68), Barthau (77);
Goals: Kheirallah 7/11.
OLDHAM: 18 Adam Brook; 2 Dec Kay; 5 Kyran Johnson; 1 Dan Abram; 20 Harry Aaronson; 6 Lewis Charnock; 7 Dave Hewitt; 8 Phil Joy; 9 Gareth Owen; 10 Jack Spencer; 11 Danny Langtree; 13 Liam Bent; 28 Matthew Fletcher. Subs (all used, only three named): 14 Matty Wilkinson; 30 Titus Gwaze; 19 John Hutchings.
Try: Fletcher (63); **Goals:** Abram 1/1.
Rugby Leaguer & League Express Men of the Match: *Olympique:* Joe Bretherton; *Oldham:* Titus Gwaze.
Penalty count: 4-5; **Half-time:** 18-0;
Referee: Aaron Moore; **Attendance:** 2,318.

Sunday 9th February 2020

LONDON BRONCOS 36 WHITEHAVEN 20

BRONCOS: 5 Kieran Dixon; 19 Jacob Ogden; 4 Will Lovell; 11 Josh Walters; 2 Tuoyo Egodo; 6 Cory Aston; 17 James Meadows; 15 Greg Richards; 14 Matty Fozard; 18 Dan Norman; 20 Daniel Hindmarsh; 12 Rhys Curran; 8 Eddie Battye. Subs (all used): 21 Sam Davis; 16 Olsi Krasniqi; 10 Rob Butler; 23 Jordan Williams.
Tries: Walters (22), Egodo (25, 47), Ogden (50), Fozard (60), Hindmarsh (70), Dixon (78); **Goals:** Dixon 4/7.
Sin bin: Butler (36) - fighting.
WHITEHAVEN: 1 Sam Forrester; 2 Dave Thompson; 4 Jessie Joe Parker; 23 Jason Mossop; 5 Andrew Bulman; 13 Dion Aiye; 9 Callum Phillips; 8 Marc Shackley; 18 James Newton; 24 Ethan Kelly; 11 Brett Phillips; 19 Ellis Gillam; 16 Tom Wilkinson. Subs (all used): 12 Jake Moore; 28 Karl Olstrom; 25 Jamie Thackray; 17 Tom Walker.
Tries: Walker (33), Gillam (39), C Phillips (42);
Goals: Newton 4/4.
Rugby Leaguer & League Express Men of the Match: *Broncos:* Josh Walters; *Whitehaven:* Andrew Bulman.
Penalty count: 6-7; **Half-time:** 10-14;
Referee: Matt Rossleigh; **Attendance:** 735.

WIDNES VIKINGS 32 BATLEY BULLDOGS 12

VIKINGS: 1 Jack Owens; 2 Jack Johnson; 4 Lloyd Roby; 3 Jake Spedding; 5 Deon Cross; 6 Danny Craven; 17 Matty Smith; 10 Ted Chapelhow; 9 Logan Tomkins; 14 Pat Moran; 12 Sam Wilde; 11 Shane Grady; 13 MacGraff Leuluai. Subs (all used): 7 Joe Lyons; 25 Joe Edge; 15 Kenny Baker; 16 Owen Farnworth.
Tries: Spedding (2, 39), Cross (13), Baker (47), Grady (51), Owens (80); **Goals:** Owens 4/7.
BULLDOGS: 14 Luke Hooley; 2 Wayne Reittie; 3 Keenen Tomlinson; 4 Lewis Galbraith; 1 Dave Scott; 6 Ben White; 7 Danny Yates; 13 James Brown; 9 Alistair Leak; 10 Toby Everett; 11 Dane Manning; 12 Lucas Walshaw; 25 Anthony Bowman. Subs (all used): 16 Michael Ward; 15 Jack Blagbrough; 24 Shaun Lunt; 17 Shaun Pick.
Tries: Galbraith (24), Leak (26); **Goals:** Hooley 2/2.
Rugby Leaguer & League Express Men of the Match: *Vikings:* Shane Grady; *Bulldogs:* Alistair Leak.
Penalty count: 6-8; **Half-time:** 16-12;
Referee: Tom Grant; **Attendance:** 3,577.

ROUND 3

Sunday 16th February 2020

BATLEY BULLDOGS 20 SWINTON LIONS 10

BULLDOGS: 14 Luke Hooley; 2 Wayne Reittie; 22 Dale Morton; 4 Lewis Galbraith; 5 Johnny Campbell; 6 Ben White; 7 Danny Yates; 10 Toby Everett; 9 Alistair Leak; 13 James Brown; 11 Dane Manning; 12 Lucas Walshaw; 25 Anthony Bowman. Subs (all used): 24 Shaun Lunt; - Tyler Dupree; 16 Michael Ward; 15 Jack Blagbrough.
Tries: Campbell (3, 24), Manning (29), Ward (40);
Goals: Hooley 0/2, Morton 2/2.
Sin bin: Everett (20) - late challenge; Reittie (37) - kicking out.

Championship 2020 - Round by Round

LIONS: 1 Mike Butt; 2 Richard Lepori; 3 Ben Morris; 4 Mitch Cox; 5 Brandon Wood; 7 Rob Fairclough; 6 Jack Hansen; 8 Gavin Bennion; 9 Luke Waterworth; 10 Lewis Hatton; 11 Rhodri Lloyd; 12 Frankie Halton; 13 Will Hope. Subs (all used): 14 Billy Brickhill; 18 Louis Brogan; 16 Paddy Jones; 17 Jose Kenga.
Tries: Cox (63), Halton (73); **Goals:** Hansen 1/2.
Rugby Leaguer & League Express Men of the Match: *Bulldogs:* Danny Yates; *Lions:* Jack Hansen.
Penalty count: 7-10; **Half-time:** 20-0;
Referee: Billy Pearson; **Attendance:** 746.

BRADFORD BULLS 22 FEATHERSTONE ROVERS 30

BULLS: 1 Brandon Pickersgill; 2 Greg Johnson; 5 Joe Brown; 4 Ross Oakes; 19 Matty Dawson-Jones; 6 Rowan Milnes; 7 Jordan Lilley; 8 Anthony England; 13 Sam Hallas; 10 Steve Crossley; 11 Adam Rooks; 28 Bradley Gallagher; 15 Liam Kirk. Subs (all used): 17 Levy Nzoungou; 29 Ebon Scurr; 18 Evan Hodgson; 9 Thomas Doyle.
Tries: Doyle (35), Lilley (43), Pickersgill (65), Dawson-Jones (72); **Goals:** Milnes 3/4.
ROVERS: 1 Craig Hall; 2 Ben Blackmore; 27 Greg Worthington; 3 Josh Hardcastle; 5 Conor Carey; 6 Louis Jouffret; 30 Callum McLelland; 17 Alec Susino; 16 Jack Bussey; 32 Tom Holroyd; 10 James Harrison; 11 Brett Ferres; 13 James Lockwood. Subs (all used): 9 Dean Parata; 15 Luke Cooper; 33 Jarrod O'Connor; 29 Wellington Albert.
Tries: McLelland (14), Harrison (33), Bussey (55), Hall (60), Blackmore (75); **Goals:** Hall 5/5.
Sin bin: Blackmore (21) - fighting; Bussey (34) - professional foul.
Rugby Leaguer & League Express Men of the Match: *Bulls:* Sam Hallas; *Rovers:* Craig Hall.
Penalty count: 8-10; **Half-time:** 6-12;
Referee: Matt Rossleigh; **Attendance:** 3,640.

LEIGH CENTURIONS 34 YORK CITY KNIGHTS 0

CENTURIONS: 1 Gregg McNally; 25 Cameron Scott; 3 Iain Thornley; 4 Junior Sa'u; 20 Liam Forsyth; 6 Ben Reynolds; 17 Josh Woods; 8 Nathan Mason; 9 Liam Hood; 10 Mark Ioane; 11 Ben Hellewell; 21 Nick Glohe; 13 Danny Addy. Subs (all used): 14 Matty Wildie; 15 Jordan Thompson; 26 Lewis Bienek; 27 Alex Gerrard.
Tries: Forsyth (23, 27), Thornley (60), Hood (71), Hellewell (76), Wildie (79); **Goals:** Reynolds 5/6.
CITY KNIGHTS: 5 Will Sharp; 21 Jason Bass; 3 Jimmy Keinhorst; 4 Liam Salter; 24 Elliot Wallis; 6 Ben Johnston; 1 Matty Marsh; 19 Jordan Baldwinson; 9 Will Jubb; 16 Chris Clarkson; 23 Josh Jordan-Roberts; 12 Sam Scott; 13 Tim Spears. Subs (all used): 14 Kriss Brining; 15 James Green; 20 Marcus Stock; 10 Jack Teanby.
Rugby Leaguer & League Express Men of the Match: *Centurions:* Ben Reynolds; *City Knights:* Chris Clarkson.
Penalty count: 9-8; **Half-time:** 10-0;
Referee: Scott Mikalauskas; **Attendance:** 2,942.

SHEFFIELD EAGLES 14 TOULOUSE OLYMPIQUE 26

EAGLES: 1 Josh Guzdek; 2 Rob Worrincy; 19 Zack McComb; 13 Aaron Brown; 5 Ryan Millar; 6 Corey Makelim; 7 Anthony Thackeray; 8 Scott Wheeldon; 9 James Davey; 11 Brad Knowles; 15 Olly Davies; 12 Joel Farrell; 22 Rory Dixon. Subs (all used): 16 Robbie Ward; 17 Frankie Mariano; 20 Blake Broadbent; 23 Lewis Taylor.
Tries: McComb (38), J Farrell (58), Worrincy (79); **Goals:** Guzdek 1/3.
OLYMPIQUE: 1 Mark Kheirallah; 5 Paul Marcon; 19 Bastien Ader; 3 Junior Vaivai; 2 Jy Hitchcox; 11 Con Mika; 7 Stan Robin; 17 Paterika Vaivai; 30 William Barthau; 16 Harrison Hansen; 10 Joe Bretherton; 12 Frank Winterstein; 13 James Bell. Subs (all used): 4 Mathieu Jussaume; 8 Maxime Puech; 15 Ben Evans; 18 Clement Boyer.
Tries: Robin (6, 12), Bell (31), Marcon (70); **Goals:** Kheirallah 5/6.
Sin bin: Hansen (77) - dangerous challenge.
Rugby Leaguer & League Express Men of the Match: *Eagles:* Lewis Taylor; *Olympique:* Stan Robin.
Penalty count: 8-8; **Half-time:** 4-20;
Referee: Aaron Moore; **Attendance:** 618 *(at Castle Park, Doncaster).*

WIDNES VIKINGS 12 LONDON BRONCOS 38

VIKINGS: 1 Jack Owens; 2 Jack Johnson; 4 Lloyd Roby; 3 Jake Spedding; 5 Deon Cross; 31 Dec Patton; 17 Matty Smith; 10 Ted Chapelhow; 9 Logan Tomkins; 14 Pat Moran; 12 Sam Wilde; 11 Shane Grady; 13 MacGraff Leuluai. Subs (all used): 7 Joe Lyons; 25 Joe Edge; 30 Leilani Latu; 16 Owen Farnworth.
Tries: Cross (46), Owens (63); **Goals:** Owens 2/3.
BRONCOS: 17 James Meadows; 5 Kieran Dixon; 19 Jacob Ogden; 3 Guy Armitage; 2 Tuoyo Egodo; 14 Matty Fozard; 6 Cory Aston; 10 Rob Butler; 21 Sam Davis; 16 Olsi Krasniqi; 11 Josh Walters; 12 Rhys Curran; 8 Eddie Battye. Subs (all used): 18 Dan Norman; 20 Daniel Hindmarsh; 9 Eloi Pelissier; 23 Jordan Williams.
Tries: Walters (14), Dixon (20), Fozard (23), Battye (31), Pelissier (37), Egodo (56), Aston (76);
Goals: Dixon 4/6, Fozard 1/1.
Rugby Leaguer & League Express Men of the Match: *Vikings:* Matty Smith; *Broncos:* Matty Fozard.
Penalty count: 6-4; **Half-time:** 2-26;
Referee: Jack Smith; **Attendance:** 3,680.

WHITEHAVEN 14 OLDHAM 16

WHITEHAVEN: 1 Sam Forrester; 2 Dave Thompson; 23 Jason Mossop; 4 Jessie Joe Parker; 22 Brett Carter; 6 Karl Dixon; 9 Callum Phillips; 8 Marc Shackley; 18 James Newton; 10 Kris Coward; 11 Brett Phillips; 19 Ellis Gillam; 16 Tom Wilkinson. Subs (all used): 13 Dion Aiye; 24 Ethan Kelly; 17 Tom Walker; 12 Jake Moore.
Tries: Aiye (45, 59), Mossop (71);
Goals: Moore 1/2, Newton 0/1.
Sin bin: Forrester (56) - trip.
OLDHAM: 1 Dan Abram; 2 Dec Kay; 24 Jack Croft; 4 Cameron Leeming; 5 Kyran Johnson; 6 Lewis Charnock; 7 Dave Hewitt; 8 Phil Joy; 9 Gareth Owen; 10 Jack Spencer; 11 Danny Langtree; 12 Danny Bridge; 13 Liam Bent. Subs (all used): 14 Matty Wilkinson; 22 Jimmy Beckett; 28 Matthew Fletcher; 30 Titus Gwaze.
Tries: Owen (5), Abram (56, pen); **Goals:** Abram 4/4.
Rugby Leaguer & League Express Men of the Match: *Whitehaven:* Dion Aiye; *Oldham:* Dan Abram.
Penalty count: 11-5; **Half-time:** 0-8;
Referee: Michael Mannifield; **Attendance:** 532.

Tuesday 18th February 2020

HALIFAX 16 DEWSBURY RAMS 18

HALIFAX: 1 Scott Grix; 2 Shaun Robinson; 4 James Woodburn-Hall; 12 Ed Barber; 5 Jodie Broughton; 6 Scott Murrell; 7 Tom Gilmore; 29 Dan Fleming; 14 Keal Carlile; 8 Elliot Morris; 11 Matt Garside; 15 Paul Brearley; 31 Kevin Larroyer. Subs (all used): 9 Brandon Moore; 10 Keegan Hirst; 18 James Saltonstall; 34 Oliver Wilson.
Tries: Murrell (44), Broughton (48, 55);
Goals: Woodburn-Hall 2/3.
Dismissal: Grix (38) - punching Speakman.
Sin bin: Larroyer (26) - repeated team offences; Barber (30) - trip.
RAMS: 1 Joe Martin; 2 Andy Gabriel; 3 Adam Ryder; 4 Matty Fleming; 5 Will Oakes; 6 Paul Sykes; 7 Liam Finn; 8 Frazer Morris; 14 Sam Day; 13 Chris Annakin; 19 Sonny Esslemont; 12 Michael Knowles; 31 Matty Gee. Subs (all used): 9 Dom Speakman; 15 Liam Johnson; 16 Connor Scott; 23 Jon Magrin.
Tries: Gee (51), Gabriel (65); **Goals:** Sykes 5/5.
Dismissal: Speakman (38) - use of the knee on Grix.
Rugby Leaguer & League Express Men of the Match: *Halifax:* Keegan Hirst; *Rams:* Adam Ryder.
Penalty count: 7-12; **Half-time:** 0-6;
Referee: Cameron Worsley; **Attendance:** 1,159.

ROUND 4

Sunday 1st March 2020

BATLEY BULLDOGS 18 SHEFFIELD EAGLES 19
(after golden point extra-time)

BULLDOGS: 14 Luke Hooley; 2 Wayne Reittie; 3 Keenen Tomlinson; 4 Lewis Galbraith; 22 Dale Morton; 6 Ben White; 7 Danny Yates; 13 James Brown; 24 Shaun Lunt; 10 Toby Everett; 11 Dane Manning; 12 Lucas Walshaw; 25 Anthony Bowman. Subs (all used): 9 Alistair Leak; 15 Jack Blagbrough; 16 Michael Ward; - Tyler Dupree.
Tries: Lunt (4), Leak (55), Brown (70); **Goals:** Morton 3/3.
EAGLES: 1 Josh Guzdek; 2 Rob Worrincy; 19 Zack McComb; 13 Aaron Brown; 5 Ryan Millar; 24 Izaac Farrell; 7 Anthony Thackeray; 8 Scott Wheeldon; 14 Greg Burns; 11 Brad Knowles; 15 Olly Davies; 12 Joel Farrell; 17 Frankie Mariano. Subs (all used): 9 James Davey; 20 Blake Broadbent; 23 Lewis Taylor; 21 Paddy Burns.
Tries: Millar (31), Brown (45, 51); **Goals:** I Farrell 3/4;
Field goal: I Farrell (88).
Rugby Leaguer & League Express Men of the Match: *Bulldogs:* Dale Morton; *Eagles:* Anthony Thackeray.
Penalty count: 8-7; **Half-time:** 6-4;
Referee: Matt Rossleigh; **Attendance:** 925.

HALIFAX 28 YORK CITY KNIGHTS 4

HALIFAX: 1 Scott Grix; 2 Shaun Robinson; 3 Steve Tyrer; 18 James Saltonstall; 5 Jodie Broughton; 6 Scott Murrell; 4 James Woodburn-Hall; 10 Keegan Hirst; 9 Brandon Moore; 22 Will Calcott; 11 Matt Garside; 15 Paul Brearley; 13 Jacob Fairbank. Subs (all used): 20 Curtis Davies; 29 Dan Fleming; 34 Sam Hewitt; 31 Kevin Larroyer.
Tries: Robinson (15, 21), Tyrer (29), Woodburn-Hall (60), Grix (69); **Goals:** Tyrer 4/5.
CITY KNIGHTS: 1 Matty Marsh; 24 Elliot Wallis; 3 Jimmy Keinhorst; 4 Liam Salter; 36 Lewis Carr; 6 Ben Johnston; 7 Connor Robinson; 16 Chris Clarkson; 9 Will Jubb; 20 Marcus Stock; 11 Danny Washbrook; 12 Sam Scott; 13 Tim Spears. Subs (all used): 10 Jack Teanby; 14 Kriss Brining; 15 James Green; 19 Jordan Baldwinson.
Try: Keinhorst (71); **Goals:** Robinson 0/1.
Rugby Leaguer & League Express Men of the Match: *Halifax:* Scott Grix; *City Knights:* Jimmy Keinhorst.
Penalty count: 5-12; **Half-time:** 18-0;
Referee: Jack Smith; **Attendance:** 1,430.

LONDON BRONCOS 10 FEATHERSTONE ROVERS 34

BRONCOS: 17 James Meadows; 5 Kieran Dixon; 19 Jacob Ogden; 3 Guy Armitage; 2 Tuoyo Egodo; 6 Cory Aston; 7 Morgan Smith; 16 Olsi Krasniqi; 9 Eloi Pelissier; 8 Eddie Battye; 11 Josh Walters; 12 Rhys Curran; 14 Matty Fozard. Subs (all used): 21 Sam Davis; 20 Daniel Hindmarsh; 10 Rob Butler; 27 Josh Hodson.
Tries: Ogden (73), Pelissier (80); **Goals:** Dixon 1/2.
Sin bin: Armitage (57) - dissent.
ROVERS: 1 Craig Hall; 28 Gareth Gale; 27 Greg Worthington; 31 Alex Sutcliffe; 2 Ben Blackmore; 6 Louis Jouffret; 30 Callum McLelland; 13 James Lockwood; 16 Jack Bussey; 32 Tom Holroyd; 11 Brett Ferres; 3 Josh Hardcastle; 10 James Harrison. Subs (all used): 17 Alec Susino; 15 Luke Cooper; 5 Conor Carey; 29 Wellington Albert.
Tries: Harrison (9), Blackmore (20), Bussey (38), Hall (59), Jouffret (63), Hardcastle (65); **Goals:** Hall 5/6.
Rugby Leaguer & League Express Men of the Match: *Broncos:* Sam Davis; *Rovers:* Callum McLelland.
Penalty count: 5-4; **Half-time:** 0-16;
Referee: Scott Mikalauskas; **Attendance:** 1,035.

OLDHAM 12 BRADFORD BULLS 26

OLDHAM: 1 Dan Abram; 21 Ryan Ince; 30 Jack Croft; 4 Cameron Leeming; - Lee Kershaw; 6 Lewis Charnock; 7 Dave Hewitt; 8 Phil Joy; 9 Gareth Owen; 22 Jimmy Beckett; 12 Danny Bridge; 11 Danny Langtree; 10 Jack Spencer. Subs (all used): 14 Matty Wilkinson; 28 Matthew Fletcher; 15 Ben Davies; 24 Titus Gwaze.
Tries: Bridge (57, 67); **Goals:** Abram 2/2.
Sin bin: Langtree (77) - fighting.
BULLS: 1 Brandon Pickersgill; 19 Matty Dawson-Jones; 4 Ross Oakes; 3 Rhys Evans; 5 Joe Brown; 6 Rowan Milnes; 7 Jordan Lilley; 10 Steve Crossley; 13 Sam Hallas; 8 Anthony England; 28 Bradley Gallagher; 20 Daniel Waite-Pullan; 32 Joe Cator. Subs (all used): 17 Levy Nzoungou; 14 George Flanagan; 31 Jack Brown; 29 Ebon Scurr.
Tries: Hallas (3), Crossley (6), Pickersgill (9), Cator (21);
Goals: Milnes 5/5.
Sin bin: Cator (77) - fighting.
Rugby Leaguer & League Express Men of the Match: *Oldham:* Danny Bridge; *Bulls:* Brandon Pickersgill.
Penalty count: 4-6; **Half-time:** 0-24;
Referee: Cameron Worsley; **Attendance:** 1,189.

WHITEHAVEN 4 TOULOUSE OLYMPIQUE 40

WHITEHAVEN: 22 Brett Carter; 2 Dave Thompson; 23 Jason Mossop; 4 Jessie Joe Parker; 5 Andrew Bulman; 6 Karl Dixon; 9 Callum Phillips; 8 Marc Shackley; 18 James Newton; 10 Kris Coward; 12 Jake Moore; 19 Ellis Gillam; 16 Tom Wilkinson. Subs (all used): 13 Dion Aiye; 20 Jake Bradley; 15 Connor Holliday; 25 Jamie Thackray.
Try: Thompson (44); **Goals:** Moore 0/1.
OLYMPIQUE: 1 Mark Kheirallah; 5 Paul Marcon; 19 Bastien Ader; 3 Junior Vaivai; 2 Jy Hitchcox; 6 Johnathon Ford; 7 Stan Robin; 17 Paterika Vaivai; 30 William Barthau; 18 Clement Boyer; 10 Joe Bretherton; 12 Frank Winterstein; 13 James Bell. Subs (all used): 8 Maxime Puech; 15 Ben Evans; 22 Pierre-Jean Lima; 23 Justin Sangare.
Tries: Hitchcox (5, 19, 52), Marcon (10), Barthau (32), Bell (48), Sangare (56); **Goals:** Kheirallah 2/3, Barthau 4/4.
Rugby Leaguer & League Express Men of the Match: *Whitehaven:* Jason Mossop; *Olympique:* James Bell.
Penalty count: 8-10; **Half-time:** 0-22;
Referee: Aaron Moore; **Attendance:** 516.

DEWSBURY RAMS 20 WIDNES VIKINGS 8

RAMS: 1 Joe Martin; 2 Andy Gabriel; 3 Adam Ryder; 4 Matty Fleming; 5 Will Oakes; 6 Paul Sykes; 7 Liam Finn; 17 Martyn Reilly; 14 Sam Day; 22 Luke Nelmes; 19 Sonny Esslemont; 12 Michael Knowles; 13 Chris Annakin. Subs (all used): 8 Frazer Morris; 15 Liam Johnson; 23 Jon Magrin; 16 Connor Scott.
Tries: Knowles (9), Day (29), Ryder (51); **Goals:** Sykes 4/5.
VIKINGS: 1 Jack Owens; 32 Jake Mamo; 3 Jake Spedding; 4 Lloyd Roby; 2 Jack Johnson; 6 Danny Craven; 7 Joe Lyons; 10 Ted Chapelhow; 9 Logan Tomkins; 14 Pat Moran; 12 Sam Wilde; 30 Ellis Robson; 15 Kenny Baker. Subs (all used): 8 Jay Chapelhow; 13 MacGraff Leuluai; 19 Connor Dwyer; 31 Dec Patton.
Try: Robson (21); **Goals:** Owens 2/2.

Rugby Leaguer & League Express Men of the Match:
Rams: Paul Sykes; *Vikings:* Ellis Robson.
Penalty count: 8-6; **Half-time:** 14-8;
Referee: James Vella; **Attendance:** 1,043.

ROUND 5

Saturday 7th March 2020

TOULOUSE OLYMPIQUE 34 BATLEY BULLDOGS 14

OLYMPIQUE: 1 Mark Kheirallah; 21 Tony Maurel; 26
Hugo Pezet; 19 Bastien Ader; 5 Paul Marcon; 7 Stan
Robin; 6 Johnathon Ford; 17 Paterika Vaivai; 30 William
Barthau; 16 Harrison Hansen; 10 Joe Bretherton; 12 Frank
Winterstein; 13 James Bell. Subs (all used): 18 Clement
Boyer; 23 Justin Sangare; 8 Maxime Puech; 11 Con Mika.
Tries: Hansen (17), Marcon (45), Robin (52),
Kheirallah (67), Bell (69), Pezet (78);
Goals: Barthau 2/2, Kheirallah 3/4.
Sin bin: Sangare (59) - fighting; Barthau (64) - dissent.
BULLDOGS: 5 Johnny Campbell; 2 Wayne Reittie; 4
Lewis Galbraith; 18 George Senior; 22 Dale Morton; 6 Ben
White; 27 Aiden Ineson; - Tom Lillycrop; 24 Shaun Lunt;
10 Toby Everett; 11 Dane Manning; 3 Keenen Tomlinson;
25 Anthony Bowman. Subs (all used): - Tyler Dupree; 9
Alistair Leak; 8 Tyler Dickinson; 15 Jack Blagbrough.
Tries: Morton (9), Everett (75); **Goals:** Morton 3/3.
Sin bin: Dupree (59) - fighting.
Rugby Leaguer & League Express Men of the Match:
Olympique: Stan Robin; *Bulldogs:* Dane Manning.
Penalty count: 9-9; **Half-time:** 6-8;
Referee: Cameron Worsley; **Attendance:** 2,817.

Sunday 8th March 2020

FEATHERSTONE ROVERS 35 SWINTON LIONS 24

ROVERS: 1 Craig Hall; 28 Gareth Gale; 33 Liam Sutcliffe;
27 Greg Worthington; 2 Ben Blackmore; 6 Louis Jouffret;
7 Dane Chisholm; 32 Tom Holroyd; 16 Jack Bussey; 17 Alec
Susino; 31 Alex Sutcliffe; 3 Josh Hardcastle; 10 James
Harrison. Subs (all used): 5 Conor Carey; 11 Brett Ferres; 15
Luke Cooper; 29 Wellington Albert.
Tries: Harrison (18), Jouffret (31),
Worthington (40, 44, 56, 77), Blackmore (60);
Goals: Chisholm 3/7; **Field goal:** Chisholm (75).
LIONS: 1 Mike Butt; 2 Richard Lepori; 19 Sam Grant; 4
Mitch Cox; 5 Brandon Wood; 7 Rob Fairclough; 6 Jack
Hansen; 8 Gavin Bennion; 9 Luke Waterworth; 10 Lewis
Hatton; 11 Rhodri Lloyd; 12 Frankie Halton; 13 Will Hope.
Subs (all used): 16 Paddy Jones; 17 Jose Kenga; 18 Louis
Brogan; 20 Oscar Thomas.
Tries: Cox (5), Fairclough (11), Butt (51, 65);
Goals: Hansen 4/5.
Rugby Leaguer & League Express Men of the Match:
Rovers: Greg Worthington; *Lions:* Rob Fairclough.
Penalty count: 8-5; **Half-time:** 16-14;
Referee: Jack Smith; **Attendance:** 1,874.

LEIGH CENTURIONS 34 HALIFAX 20

CENTURIONS: 22 Craig Mullen; 25 Cameron Scott; 3 Iain
Thornley; 4 Junior Sa'u; 5 Adam Higson; 6 Ben Reynolds;
7 Jarrod Sammut; 8 Nathan Mason; 9 Liam Hood; 10 Mark
Ioane; 11 Ben Hellewell; 21 Nick Glohe; 13 Danny Addy.
Subs (all used): 14 Matty Wildie; 15 Jordan Thompson; 26
Lewis Bienek; 27 Alex Gerrard.
Tries: Hood (4), Scott (8, 18, 76), Higson (51);
Goals: Reynolds 7/9.
Dismissal: Sammut (39) - dangerous challenge on Barber.
Sin bin: Higson (35) - late challenge on Tyrer.
On report: Addy (55) - alleged late challenge on Murrell.
HALIFAX: 1 Scott Grix; 2 Shaun Robinson; 3 Steve Tyrer;
18 James Saltonstall; 5 Jodie Broughton; 6 Scott Murrell;
4 James Woodburn-Hall; 10 Keegan Hirst; 9 Brandon
Moore; 22 Will Calcott; 11 Matt Garside; 15 Paul Brearley;
13 Jacob Fairbank. Subs (all used): 12 Ed Barber; 20 Curtis
Davies; 31 Kevin Larroyer; 29 Dan Fleming.
Tries: Broughton (22, 55), Barber (26), Robinson (78);
Goals: Tyrer 2/4.
Sin bin: Larroyer (72) - shoulder charge on Reynolds.
Rugby Leaguer & League Express Men of the Match:
Centurions: Ben Reynolds; *Halifax:* Will Calcott.
Penalty count: 12-9; **Half-time:** 14-10;
Referee: James Vella; **Attendance:** 3,095.

OLDHAM 6 DEWSBURY RAMS 24

OLDHAM: 1 Dan Abram; 21 Ryan Ince; 3 James
Worthington; 4 Cameron Leeming; 2 Dec Kay; 6 Lewis
Charnock; 7 Dave Hewitt; 8 Phil Joy; 9 Gareth Owen; 22
Jimmy Beckett; 12 Danny Bridge; 11 Danny Langtree; 10
Jack Spencer. Subs (all used): 14 Matty Wilkinson; 28
Matthew Fletcher; 15 Ben Davies; 24 Titus Gwaze.
Try: Ince (15); **Goals:** Abram 1/1.

Halifax's Shaun Robinson closed down by Leigh's Adam Higson

RAMS: 1 Joe Martin; 2 Andy Gabriel; 3 Adam Ryder; 4
Matty Fleming; 5 Will Oakes; 6 Paul Sykes; 7 Liam Finn;
17 Martyn Reilly; 14 Sam Day; 22 Luke Nelmes; 19 Sonny
Esslemont; 12 Michael Knowles; 13 Chris Annakin. Subs
(all used): 9 Dom Speakman; 15 Liam Johnson; 16 Connor
Scott; 23 Jon Magrin.
Tries: Gabriel (25), Scott (45), Martin (71), Oakes (79);
Goals: Sykes 4/5.
Rugby Leaguer & League Express Men of the Match:
Oldham: Ryan Ince; *Rams:* Will Oakes.
Penalty count: 6-4; **Half-time:** 6-6;
Referee: Scott Mikalauskas; **Attendance:** 684.

WIDNES VIKINGS 40 WHITEHAVEN 16

VIKINGS: 7 Joe Lyons; 2 Jack Johnson; 25 Joe Edge; 3 Jake
Spedding; 5 Deon Cross; 1 Jack Owens; 17 Matty Smith; 10
Ted Chapelhow; 9 Logan Tomkins; 14 Pat Moran; 12 Sam
Wilde; 11 Shane Grady; 15 Kenny Baker. Subs (all used): 33
Callum Wood; 8 Jay Chapelhow; 13 MacGraff Leuluai; 16
Owen Farnworth.
Tries: J Chapelhow (25), Wilde (39), Lyons (54, 60),
Cross (71), Edge (77), Owens (80); **Goals:** Owens 6/7.
WHITEHAVEN: 1 Sam Forrester; 2 Dave Thompson; 4
Jessie Joe Parker; 23 Jason Mossop; 5 Andrew Bulman;
6 Karl Dixon; 9 Callum Phillips; 8 Marc Shackley; 14 Sam
Dowsett; 25 Jamie Thackray; 11 Brett Phillips; 19 Ellis
Gillam; 16 Tom Wilkinson. Subs (all used): 15 Connor
Holliday; 24 Ethan Kelly; 20 Jake Bradley; 17 Tom Walker.
Tries: Bulman (10), Dixon (34, 68);
Goals: Dixon 1/3, Holliday 1/1.
Rugby Leaguer & League Express Men of the Match:
Vikings: Joe Lyons; *Whitehaven:* Ellis Gillam.
Penalty count: 6-4; **Half-time:** 12-10;
Referee: Billy Pearson; **Attendance:** 2,977.

YORK CITY KNIGHTS 12 LONDON BRONCOS 18

CITY KNIGHTS: 1 Matty Marsh; 5 Will Sharp; 3 Jimmy
Keinhorst; 4 Liam Salter; 21 Jason Bass; 11 Danny
Washbrook; 7 Connor Robinson; 16 Chris Clarkson; 9
Will Jubb; 10 Jack Teanby; 17 Joe Porter; 12 Sam Scott; 13
Tim Spears. Subs (all used): 15 James Green; 19 Jordan
Baldwinson; 20 Marcus Stock; 36 Reiss Butterworth.
Tries: Marsh (32, 40); **Goals:** Robinson 2/2.
BRONCOS: 5 Kieran Dixon; 29 Ed Chamberlain; 4 Will
Lovell; 3 Guy Armitage; 2 Tuoyo Egodo; 6 Cory Aston; 7
Morgan Smith; 26 Mitch Allgood; 14 Matty Fozard; 10 Rob
Butler; 11 Josh Walters; 12 Rhys Curran; 8 Eddie Battye.
Subs (all used): 16 Olsi Krasniqi; 18 Dan Norman; 21 Sam
Davis; 23 Jordan Williams.
Tries: Curran (10, 25), Armitage (14); **Goals:** Dixon 3/3.
Rugby Leaguer & League Express Men of the Match:
City Knights: Matty Marsh; *Broncos:* Rhys Curran.
Penalty count: 7-7; **Half-time:** 12-18;
Referee: Marcus Griffiths; **Attendance:** 1,364.

BRADFORD BULLS 28 SHEFFIELD EAGLES 0

BULLS: 1 Brandon Pickersgill; 5 Joe Brown; 3 Rhys Evans;
4 Ross Oakes; 19 Matty Dawson-Jones; 6 Rowan Milnes; 7
Jordan Lilley; 8 Anthony England; 13 Sam Hallas; 10 Steve
Crossley; 11 Adam Rooks; 28 Bradley Gallagher; 15 Liam
Kirk. Subs (all used): 9 Thomas Doyle; 29 Ebon Scurr; 17
Levy Nzoungou; 14 George Flanagan.
Tries: Gallagher (4, 32), Pickersgill (61), Lilley (66),
Dawson-Jones (73); **Goals:** Milnes 4/5.
EAGLES: 24 Izaac Farrell; 19 Zack McComb; 18 Connor
Bower; 3 Menzie Yere; 5 Ryan Millar; 13 Aaron Brown; 7
Anthony Thackeray; 8 Scott Wheeldon; 9 James Davey;
22 Rory Dixon; 15 Olly Davies; 12 Joel Farrell; 11 Brad
Knowles. Subs (all used): 21 Paddy Burns; 20 Blake
Broadbent; 16 Robbie Ward; 17 Frankie Mariano.
Rugby Leaguer & League Express Men of the Match:
Bulls: Rowan Milnes; *Eagles:* Izaac Farrell.
Penalty count: 8-7; **Half-time:** 10-0;
Referee: Aaron Moore; **Attendance:** 2,707.

LEAGUE 1 2020
Club by Club

BARROW RAIDERS

	D.O.B.	APP		TRIES		GOALS		FG		PTS	
		ALL	L1	ALL	L1	ALL	L1	ALL	L1	ALL	L1
Jake Carter	24/11/98	(1)	(1)	0	0	0	0	0	0	0	0
Bradd Crellin	2/7/89	1	1	1	1	0	0	0	0	4	4
Luke Cresswell	5/5/95	4	2	2	1	0	0	0	0	8	4
Jamie Dallimore	20/8/88	4	2	3	2	20	13	0	0	52	34
Ryan Duffy	13/5/93	1(3)	(2)	3	2	0	0	0	0	12	8
Carl Forster	4/6/92	4	2	0	0	0	0	0	0	0	0
Tom Hopkins	21/12/92	2(2)	1(1)	0	0	0	0	0	0	0	0
Declan Hulme	14/1/93	4	2	0	0	0	0	0	0	0	0
Lee Jewitt	14/2/87	1(1)	1	0	0	0	0	0	0	0	0
Ryan Johnston	16/3/98	4	2	0	0	0	0	0	0	0	0
Carl McBain	30/9/89	1	0	0	0	0	0	0	0	0	0
Danny Morrow	30/4/90	3(1)	1(1)	2	0	0	0	0	0	8	0
Wartovo Puara	24/6/90	4	2	1	0	0	0	0	0	4	0
Theerapol Ritson	7/1/96	4	2	3	1	0	0	0	0	12	4
Perry Singleton	5/1/94	3	1	0	0	0	0	0	0	0	0
Jono Smith	12/11/88	3	2	0	0	0	0	0	0	0	0
Connor Terrill	3/7/01	(1)	0	1	0	0	0	0	0	4	0
Dan Toal	22/9/89	(4)	(2)	2	2	0	0	0	0	8	8
Shane Toal	11/11/95	4	2	3	3	0	0	0	0	12	12
Mark Tyson	31/5/90	1(3)	1(1)	1	1	0	0	0	0	4	4
Jordan Walne	28/12/92	4	2	1	0	0	0	0	0	4	0

'L1' totals include League 1 games only; 'All' totals also include Challenge Cup

Jamie Dallimore

CLUB RECORDS
MATCH RECORDS
SEASON RECORDS
CAREER RECORDS

Highest score: 138-0 v Nottingham City, 27/11/94 **Highest score against:** 0-90 v Leeds, 11/2/90 **Record attendance:** 21,651 v Salford, 15/4/38
Tries: 6 Val Cumberbatch v Batley, 21/11/36; Jim Thornburrow v Maryport, 19/2/38; Steve Rowan v Nottingham City, 15/11/92
Goals: 17 Darren Carter v Nottingham City, 27/11/94 **Points:** 42 Darren Carter v Nottingham City, 27/11/94
Tries: 50 Jim Lewthwaite 1956-57 **Goals:** 135 Joe Ball 1956-57 **Points:** 323 Jamie Rooney 2010
Tries: 352 Jim Lewthwaite 1943-57 **Goals:** 1,099 *(inc 63fg)* Darren Holt 1998-2002; 2004-2009; 2012
Points: 2,403 Darren Holt 1998-2002; 2004-2009; 2012 **Appearances:** 500 Jim Lewthwaite 1943-57

COVENTRY BEARS

	D.O.B.	APP		TRIES		GOALS		FG		PTS	
		ALL	L1	ALL	L1	ALL	L1	ALL	L1	ALL	L1
Ben Bradshaw	18/11/99	(1)	(1)	0	0	0	0	0	0	0	0
Will Budd	19/6/00	(3)	(2)	0	0	0	0	0	0	0	0
Doug Chirnside	18/10/95	1	1	0	0	0	0	0	0	0	0
Brad Clavering	14/3/98	3	2	0	0	1	1	0	0	2	2
Chris Cullimore	13/2/93	2(1)	1(1)	0	0	0	0	0	0	0	0
Hayden Freeman	20/8/97	3	2	1	0	0	0	0	0	4	0
Ben Gray	12/11/95	1(1)	1(1)	0	0	0	0	0	0	0	0
Darius Hamilton	2/12/91	(1)	0	0	0	0	0	0	0	0	0
Leon Harber	24/7/99	1(1)	(1)	0	0	0	0	0	0	0	0
Nathan Hill	13/7/97	3	2	1	1	0	0	0	0	4	4
Harry Kaufman	20/12/91	2	1	0	0	0	0	0	0	0	0
Ryan Langton	16/4/96	2(1)	1(1)	0	0	0	0	0	0	0	0
Sam Moorhouse	24/4/01	(1)	(1)	0	0	0	0	0	0	0	0
Kieran Moran	2/11/96	2	2	0	0	0	0	0	0	0	0
Morgan Punchard	26/1/99	2	2	0	0	0	0	0	0	0	0
Reece Rance	17/7/93	3	2	1	1	0	0	0	0	4	4
Peter Ryan	25/2/95	3	2	0	0	0	0	0	0	0	0
Brad Sheridan	24/3/94	1	0	0	0	0	0	0	0	0	0
Kieran Smith	28/6/96	3	2	0	0	0	0	0	0	0	0
Cameron Stewart	1/3/99	(1)	0	0	0	0	0	0	0	0	0
James Thornton	30/9/95	2	2	0	0	0	0	0	0	0	0
Liam Welham	11/11/88	3	2	1	1	0	0	0	0	4	4
Alex Williams	8/8/93	(1)	0	0	0	0	0	0	0	0	0
Kadeem Williams	23/3/95	2	1	0	0	0	0	0	0	0	0

'L1' totals include League 1 games only; 'All' totals also include Challenge Cup

Nathan Hill

CLUB RECORDS
MATCH RECORDS
SEASON RECORDS
CAREER RECORDS

Highest score: 64-6 v West Wales, 25/7/2018 **Highest score against:** 6-98 v Keighley, 6/5/2018 **Record attendance:** 1,465 v Bradford, 30/6/2018
Tries: 3 *(10 players)* **Goals:** 8 Connor Robinson v Hemel, 19/4/2015; Ben Stead v West Wales, 25/7/2018 **Points:** 22 Dan Parker v London Skolars, 7/6/2015
Tries: 17 Elliot Hall 2019 **Goals:** 61 Ben Stead 2018 **Points:** 138 Brad Delaney 2017
Tries: 37 Hayden Freeman 2016-2020 **Goals:** 61 Ben Stead 2018 **Points:** 148 Hayden Freeman 2016-2020 **Appearances:** 106 Chris Barratt 2015-2019

DONCASTER

	D.O.B.	APP ALL	APP L1	TRIES ALL	TRIES L1	GOALS ALL	GOALS L1	FG ALL	FG L1	PTS ALL	PTS L1
Matty Beharrell	29/3/94	3	2	0	0	12	10	0	0	24	20
Watson Boas	8/11/94	3	1	1	0	0	0	0	0	4	0
Ryan Boyle	17/10/87	3	1	1	1	0	0	0	0	4	4
Danny Bravo	25/10/90	1(1)	1(1)	0	0	0	0	0	0	0	0
Harry Carter	10/2/94	4	2	0	0	0	0	0	0	0	0
Rangi Chase	11/4/86	2	1	0	0	0	0	0	0	0	0
Kieran Cross	18/2/95	1(3)	(2)	2	1	0	0	0	0	8	4
Ryan Dixon	11/8/93	(1)	(1)	0	0	0	0	0	0	0	0
Sam Doherty	14/11/93	4	2	6	5	0	0	0	0	24	20
Brandon Douglas	17/8/97	2(2)	1(1)	1	1	0	0	0	0	4	4
Brad Foster	28/8/95	4	2	1	1	0	0	0	0	4	4
Tom Halliday	2/2/97	1	0	0	0	0	0	0	0	0	0
Alex Holdstock	16/6/01	(1)	0	0	0	0	0	0	0	0	0
Graeme Horne	22/3/85	3	2	0	0	0	0	0	0	0	0
Ben Howe	17/1/01	(1)	0	0	0	0	0	0	0	0	0
Jack Logan	8/9/95	3	2	0	0	4	0	0	0	8	0
Jake McLoughlin	13/3/94	(1)	0	0	0	0	0	0	0	0	0
Aaron Ollett	19/11/92	4	2	1	0	0	0	0	0	4	0
Ross Peltier	24/4/92	(4)	(2)	2	2	0	0	0	0	8	8
Josh Rickett	20/10/97	3	2	1	1	0	0	0	0	4	4
Sam Smeaton	26/10/88	4	2	0	0	0	0	0	0	0	0
Russ Spiers	28/4/91	2(1)	1	0	0	0	0	0	0	0	0
Jason Tali	7/7/89	4	2	3	1	0	0	0	0	12	4
Brandan Wilkinson	7/9/97	1(1)	(1)	0	0	0	0	0	0	0	0

'L1' totals include League 1 games only; 'All' totals also include Challenge Cup

Jason Tali

CLUB RECORDS	**Highest score:** 102-6 v West Wales, 15/7/2018 **Highest score against:** 4-90 v Widnes, 10/6/2007
	Record attendance: 10,000 v Bradford, 16/2/52 *(York Road)*; 6,528 v Castleford, 12/4/2007 *(Keepmoat Stadium)*
MATCH RECORDS	**Tries:** 6 Kane Epati v Oldham, 30/7/2006; Lee Waterman v Sharlston, 24/3/2012
	Goals: 15 Liam Harris v West Wales, 15/7/2018 **Points:** 38 Liam Harris v West Wales, 15/7/2018
SEASON RECORDS	**Tries:** 36 Lee Waterman 2012 **Goals:** 129 Jonny Woodcock 2002 **Points:** 306 Jonny Woodcock 2002
CAREER RECORDS	**Tries:** 112 Mark Roache 1985-97 **Goals:** 850 David Noble 1976-77; 1980-89; 1992 **Points:** 1,751 David Noble 1976-77; 1980-89; 1992
	Appearances: 327 Audley Pennant 1980-83; 1985-97

HUNSLET

	D.O.B.	APP ALL	APP L1	TRIES ALL	TRIES L1	GOALS ALL	GOALS L1	FG ALL	FG L1	PTS ALL	PTS L1
Jack Aldous	3/4/91	(4)	(1)	0	0	0	0	0	0	0	0
Jordan Andrade	24/1/92	(5)	(2)	3	2	0	0	0	0	12	8
Tom Ashton	20/6/92	5	2	1	1	0	0	0	0	4	4
Anthony Boardman	11/11/89	2	0	2	0	0	0	0	0	8	0
Zach Braham	14/1/95	2	0	0	0	0	0	0	0	0	0
Dom Brambani	10/5/85	4	2	3	2	16	9	1	1	45	27
Simon Brown	23/6/89	5	2	0	0	0	0	0	0	0	0
Matty Chrimes	2/11/97	2	0	1	0	0	0	0	0	4	0
Nathan Conroy	6/3/95	1(4)	(2)	1	1	0	0	0	0	4	4
Liam Copland	5/6/93	1	0	0	0	0	0	0	0	0	0
Vila Halafihi	24/1/94	5	2	1	1	0	0	0	0	4	4
Harvey Hallas	14/11/97	1(3)	(2)	0	0	0	0	0	0	0	0
Kiedan Hartley	3/7/00	4	2	6	4	0	0	0	0	24	16
Ben Heaton	12/3/90	4	2	1	0	0	0	0	0	4	0
Harry Kidd	12/6/95	4	2	0	0	0	0	0	0	0	0
Danny King	16/9/97	1(1)	0	0	0	0	0	0	0	0	0
Jack Lee	1/11/88	4	2	1	0	0	0	0	0	4	0
Ben Markland	3/2/01	3	2	1	1	0	0	0	0	4	4
Jack Ray	8/10/98	(2)	(1)	0	0	0	0	0	0	0	0
Alex Rowe	11/3/85	3(1)	2	0	0	0	0	0	0	0	0
Danny Rowse	24/1/90	1	0	0	0	1	0	0	0	2	0
Duane Straugheir	29/9/89	5	2	2	1	0	0	0	0	8	4
Josh Tonks	14/8/91	5	2	2	1	0	0	0	0	8	4
Jimmy Watson	9/9/91	3	2	2	1	0	0	0	0	8	4

'L1' totals include League 1 games only; 'All' totals also include Challenge Cup

Kiedan Hartley

CLUB RECORDS	**Highest score:** 86-0 v West Wales, 27/5/2018; 86-6 v West Wales, 4/8/2018 **Highest score against:** 0-82 v Bradford, 2/3/2003
	Record attendance: 24,700 v Wigan, 15/3/24 *(Parkside)*; 2,454 v Wakefield, 13/4/98 *(South Leeds Stadium)*
MATCH RECORDS	**Tries:** 7 George Dennis v Bradford, 20/1/34 **Goals:** 13 Joe Sanderson v West Wales, 27/5/2018; Joe Sanderson v West Wales, 4/8/2018
	Points: 30 Simon Wilson v Highfield, 21/1/96; Joe Sanderson v West Wales, 27/5/2018
SEASON RECORDS	**Tries:** 34 Alan Snowden 1956-57 **Goals:** 181 Billy Langton 1958-59 **Points:** 380 Billy Langton 1958-59
CAREER RECORDS	**Tries:** 154 Fred Williamson 1943-55 **Goals:** 1,044 Billy Langton 1955-66 **Points:** 2,202 Billy Langton 1955-66 **Appearances:** 579 Geoff Gunney 1951-73

KEIGHLEY COUGARS

	D.O.B.	APP ALL	APP L1	TRIES ALL	TRIES L1	GOALS ALL	GOALS L1	FG ALL	FG L1	PTS ALL	PTS L1
Mo Agoro	29/1/93	3	2	0	0	0	0	0	0	0	0
Matthew Bailey	1/12/91	(2)	(1)	0	0	0	0	0	0	0	0
Jack Coventry	5/3/94	1(2)	1(1)	1	1	0	0	0	0	4	4
Spencer Darley	25/9/98	(1)	0	0	0	0	0	0	0	0	0
Dalton Desmond-Walker	25/4/93	1(1)	(1)	0	0	0	0	0	0	0	0
James Feather	15/4/84	1(2)	1(1)	0	0	0	0	0	0	0	0
Billy Gaylor	30/4/97	2	2	0	0	0	0	0	0	0	0
Macauley Hallett	27/11/95	3	2	0	0	0	0	0	0	0	0
Benn Hardcastle	4/1/90	1	0	0	0	2	0	0	0	4	0
Dan Hawksworth	30/3/93	1(1)	1(1)	0	0	0	0	0	0	0	0
Ritchie Hawkyard	21/1/86	1	1	1	1	0	0	0	0	4	4
Kyle Kesik	3/6/89	2	1	0	0	0	0	0	0	0	0
Aaron Levy	19/12/95	3	2	1	0	0	0	0	0	4	0
Josh Lynam	16/2/93	1	0	1	0	0	0	0	0	4	0
Jack Miller	28/11/94	3	2	1	1	2	2	0	0	8	8
Jason Muranka	4/8/89	2	2	0	0	0	0	0	0	0	0
Dan Parker	11/3/93	3	2	0	0	0	0	0	0	0	0
Taylor Prell	3/7/96	1	1	0	0	0	0	0	0	0	0
Alfie Seeley	30/12/96	3	2	0	0	0	0	0	0	0	0
Louis Sheriff	6/9/92	1(2)	(2)	0	0	0	0	0	0	0	0
Jake Webster	29/10/83	2	2	1	1	0	0	0	0	4	4
Matt Welham	1/2/93	1	0	0	0	0	0	0	0	0	0
Lewis Wray	6/5/98	3	2	0	0	0	0	0	0	0	0
Ryan Wright	28/10/91	(1)	(1)	0	0	0	0	0	0	0	0

Jake Webster

'L1' totals include League 1 games only; 'All' totals also include Challenge Cup

CLUB RECORDS
MATCH RECORDS Highest score: 112-6 v West Wales, 15/9/2018 Highest score against: 2-92 v Leigh, 30/4/86 Record attendance: 14,500 v Halifax, 3/3/51
Tries: 6 Jason Critchley v Widnes, 18/8/96
Goals: 15 John Wasyliw v Nottingham City, 1/11/92; Martyn Wood v Lancashire Lynx, 1/5/2000 Points: 36 John Wasyliw v Nottingham City, 1/11/92
SEASON RECORDS Tries: 45 Nick Pinkney 1994-95 Goals: 187 John Wasyliw 1992-93 Points: 490 John Wasyliw 1992-93
CAREER RECORDS Tries: 155 Sam Stacey 1904-20 Goals: 967 Brian Jefferson 1965-77 Points: 2,116 Brian Jefferson 1965-77
Appearances: 372 Hartley Tempest 1902-15; David McGoun 1925-38

LONDON SKOLARS

	D.O.B.	APP ALL	APP L1	TRIES ALL	TRIES L1	GOALS ALL	GOALS L1	FG ALL	FG L1	PTS ALL	PTS L1
Mike Bishay	8/2/93	2	1	0	0	0	0	0	0	0	0
Lamont Bryan	12/4/88	(1)	(1)	0	0	0	0	0	0	0	0
Ryan Cane	17/1/97	(1)	0	0	0	0	0	0	0	0	0
Costa Charalambous	6/7/92	1(1)	(1)	0	0	0	0	0	0	0	0
Max Clarke	1/1/00	2	1	0	0	0	0	0	0	0	0
Dalton Grant	21/4/90	1	0	0	0	0	0	0	0	0	0
Mike Greenhalgh	8/6/94	2	1	0	0	0	0	0	0	0	0
Charles Hammond	1/2/97	1	0	1	0	0	0	0	0	4	0
Julius Hobbs	24/12/98	(2)	(1)	0	0	0	0	0	0	0	0
Lameck Juma	6/12/90	1	1	1	1	0	0	0	0	4	4
Iliess Macani	6/12/93	2	1	0	0	0	0	0	0	0	0
Shay North	6/10/99	(2)	(1)	0	0	0	0	0	0	0	0
Kameron Pearce-Paul	28/2/97	2	1	0	0	0	0	0	0	0	0
Matt Ross	2/9/92	2	1	0	0	0	0	0	0	0	0
Josh Spearing	7/6/96	(1)	0	0	0	0	0	0	0	0	0
Ben Steele	20/12/95	1	1	0	0	0	0	0	0	0	0
Oscar Stone	4/1/00	1	1	0	0	0	0	0	0	0	0
Jacob Thomas	9/10/93	2	1	1	0	0	0	0	0	4	0
Neil Thorman	4/6/84	2	1	1	0	5	2	0	0	14	4
Richard Wilkinson	26/10/93	2	1	1	1	0	0	0	0	4	4
Jerome Yates	31/10/97	2	1	1	1	0	0	0	0	4	4

Neil Thorman

'L1' totals include League 1 games only; 'All' totals also include Challenge Cup

CLUB RECORDS Highest score: 76-8 v West Wales, 7/4/2018; 76-6 v Hemel, 8/9/2018 Highest score against: 4-98 v Sheffield, 3/8/2003
Record attendance: 1,524 v Toronto, 4/3/2017
MATCH RECORDS Tries: 5 Mark Cantoni v Gateshead, 27/6/2004 Goals: 12 Neil Thorman v West Wales, 7/4/2018 Points: 28 Dylan Skee v South Wales, 29/7/2012
SEASON RECORDS Tries: 20 Mark Cantoni 2004; James Anthony 2013 Goals: 100 Dylan Skee 2013 Points: 248 Dylan Skee 2013
CAREER RECORDS Tries: 57 Austen Aggrey 2004-2012 Goals: 230 *(inc 1fg)* Dylan Skee 2011-2013 Points: 579 Dylan Skee 2011-2013 Appearances: 198 Gareth Honor 2003-2011

NEWCASTLE THUNDER

	D.O.B.	APP ALL	APP L1	TRIES ALL	TRIES L1	GOALS ALL	GOALS L1	FG ALL	FG L1	PTS ALL	PTS L1
Harry Aldous	19/11/95	1(4)	1(1)	1	0	0	0	0	0	4	0
Bob Beswick	8/12/84	4	2	1	0	0	0	0	0	4	0
Sam Blake	5/5/98	1(3)	(2)	3	1	0	0	0	0	12	4
Joe Brown	24/4/87	3(1)	1(1)	2	1	0	0	0	0	8	4
Jed Charlton	14/1/99	1(1)	1	0	0	0	0	0	0	0	0
Rhys Clarke	12/3/91	1(1)	(1)	0	0	0	0	0	0	0	0
Alex Clegg	9/7/99	5	2	3	1	0	0	0	0	12	4
Tyler Craig	4/7/93	1	0	0	0	0	0	0	0	0	0
Reece Dean	30/11/96	5	2	1	1	19	7	0	0	42	18
Alex Donaghy	22/9/01	2	0	0	0	0	0	0	0	0	0
Ashley Gibson	25/9/86	4	2	2	1	0	0	0	0	8	4
Kieran Gill	4/12/95	5	2	6	3	0	0	0	0	24	12
Kieran Hudson	13/6/00	(1)	0	0	0	0	0	0	0	0	0
Quentin Laulu-Togaga'e	1/12/84	5	2	1	0	0	0	0	0	4	0
Adam Lawton	13/6/93	5	2	2	1	0	0	0	0	8	4
Jake Lightowler	22/2/99	(1)	(1)	0	0	0	0	0	0	0	0
Sam Luckley	29/11/95	2(3)	1(1)	1	1	0	0	0	0	4	4
Colton Roche	23/6/93	2(1)	0	1	0	0	0	0	0	4	0
Brenden Santi	5/8/93	5	2	0	0	0	0	0	0	0	0
Evan Simons	11/10/91	2(3)	1(1)	0	0	0	0	0	0	0	0
Brad Walker	30/1/98	1	0	0	0	0	0	0	0	0	0
Mikey Wood	18/4/96	5	2	1	0	0	0	0	0	4	0
Matthew Wright	30/1/91	1	1	0	0	0	0	0	0	0	0
Lewis Young	1/7/95	4	2	1	1	0	0	0	0	4	4

Reece Dean

'L1' totals include League 1 games only; 'All' totals also include Challenge Cup

CLUB RECORDS Highest score: 98-6 v West Wales, 23/9/2018 **Highest score against:** 0-132 v Blackpool Panthers, 16/5/2010
Record attendance: 6,631 v Bradford, 16/5/99 *(Gateshead International Stadium)*; 4,137 v Bradford, 18/5/2018 *(Kingston Park)*
MATCH RECORDS Tries: 5 Andy Walker v London Skolars, 22/6/2003 **Goals:** 12 Rhys Clarke v Coventry, 18/8/2019 **Points:** 28 Benn Hardcastle v Oxford, 18/6/2017
SEASON RECORDS Tries: 28 Kieran Gill 2019 **Goals:** 129 *(inc 1fg)* Dan Russell 2008 **Points:** 293 Dan Russell 2008
CAREER RECORDS Tries: 74 Kevin Neighbour 2001-2006; 2008-2010 **Goals:** 283 *(inc 8fg)* Benn Hardcastle 2013-2017 **Points:** 682 Benn Hardcastle 2013-2017
Appearances: 232 Joe Brown 2005-2006; 2010-2020

NORTH WALES CRUSADERS

	D.O.B.	APP ALL	APP L1	TRIES ALL	TRIES L1	GOALS ALL	GOALS L1	FG ALL	FG L1	PTS ALL	PTS L1
Chris Barratt	7/2/93	4	2	0	0	0	0	0	0	0	0
Brad Billsborough	4/8/98	4	2	1	0	0	0	0	0	4	0
Brad Brennan	18/1/93	4	2	0	0	0	0	0	0	0	0
Jack Cottington	7/4/98	(4)	(2)	0	0	0	0	0	0	0	0
Dave Eccleston	12/9/96	4	2	1	1	0	0	0	0	4	4
Jordy Gibson	11/6/92	4	2	1	0	0	0	0	0	4	0
Jack Holmes	5/1/94	1	0	2	0	0	0	0	0	8	0
Earl Hurst	21/4/89	3	1	1	1	0	0	0	0	4	4
Elliott Jenkins	6/2/99	3(1)	2	2	0	0	0	0	0	8	0
Tommy Johnson	19/4/91	4	2	0	0	22	9	0	0	44	18
Rob Massam	29/11/87	4	2	4	1	0	0	0	0	16	4
Ryan Millington	14/1/87	(4)	(2)	0	0	0	0	0	0	0	0
Dante Morley-Samuels	22/11/98	1	1	0	0	0	0	0	0	0	0
Jordan Penny	26/4/98	3	2	1	1	0	0	0	0	4	4
Matt Reid	16/9/92	2	2	0	0	0	0	0	0	0	0
Gav Rodden	20/12/96	4	2	5	1	0	0	0	0	20	4
Steve Roper	10/11/86	1(2)	(1)	0	0	0	0	0	0	0	0
Kieran Sherratt	15/11/95	2(1)	(1)	2	0	0	0	0	0	8	0
Warren Thompson	24/2/90	4	2	1	1	0	0	0	0	4	4
James Tilley	11/11/93	(3)	(2)	0	0	0	0	0	0	0	0

Tommy Johnson

'L1' totals include League 1 games only; 'All' totals also include Challenge Cup

CLUB RECORDS Highest score: 82-6 v West Hull, 6/4/2013 **Highest score against:** 4-98 v Wigan, 15/4/2012
Record attendance: 1,562 v South Wales, 1/9/2013 *(Racecourse Ground)*; 886 v Bradford, 12/8/2018 *(Queensway Stadium)*
MATCH RECORDS Tries: 5 Rob Massam v Rochdale, 30/6/2013; Jono Smith v Hemel, 16/5/2015
Goals: 11 Tommy Johnson v West Hull, 6/4/2013; Ian Mort v Hemel, 16/5/2015; Ben Stead v West Wales, 19/4/2019
Points: 30 Tommy Johnson v West Hull, 6/4/2013
SEASON RECORDS Tries: 29 Rob Massam 2015 **Goals:** 109 Tommy Johnson 2015 **Points:** 266 Tommy Johnson 2015
CAREER RECORDS Tries: 122 Rob Massam 2012-2016; 2019-2020 **Goals:** 564 Tommy Johnson 2012-2018, 2020 **Points:** 1,352 Tommy Johnson 2012-2018, 2020
Appearances: 170 Tommy Johnson 2012-2018, 2020

ROCHDALE HORNETS

	D.O.B.	APP ALL	L1	TRIES ALL	L1	GOALS ALL	L1	FG ALL	L1	PTS ALL	L1
Shaun Ainscough	27/11/89	2	0	2	0	0	0	0	0	8	0
Dale Bloomfield	24/10/87	4	1	1	0	0	0	0	0	4	0
Ben Calland	24/9/96	4	1	4	0	0	0	0	0	16	0
Adam Carr	24/12/99	(2)	0	0	0	0	0	0	0	0	0
Luke Fowden	1/9/96	(4)	(1)	0	0	0	0	0	0	0	0
Sam Freeman	3/4/99	4	1	2	0	24	6	0	0	56	12
Adam Hesketh	27/11/93	3(1)	(1)	2	0	0	0	0	0	8	0
Jack Higginson	4/4/97	3	1	2	0	0	0	0	0	8	0
Brad Holroyd	15/4/00	2	1	0	0	0	0	0	0	0	0
Sam Hopkins	17/2/90	4	1	2	1	0	0	0	0	8	4
Andy Lea	14/12/92	4	1	2	1	0	0	0	0	8	4
Callum Marriott	30/5/93	2(2)	1	0	0	0	0	0	0	0	0
Ben Moores	6/12/93	2	0	0	0	0	0	0	0	0	0
Quinn Ngawati	15/6/99	(1)	0	0	0	0	0	0	0	0	0
Sean Penkywicz	18/5/82	2	1	0	0	0	0	0	0	0	0
Martyn Ridyard	25/7/86	1	1	0	0	0	0	1	1	1	1
Declan Sheridan	24/2/97	(4)	(1)	0	0	0	0	0	0	0	0
Lewis Sheridan	14/1/94	4	1	3	0	0	0	0	0	12	0
Jordan Syme	14/11/96	4	1	0	0	0	0	0	0	0	0
Jamie Tracey	22/5/94	4	1	4	1	0	0	0	0	16	4
Liam Whalley	27/4/93	2(2)	(1)	1	1	0	0	0	0	4	4
Matt Whitehead	2/8/96	1	0	0	0	0	0	0	0	0	0

'L1' totals include League 1 games only; 'All' totals also include Challenge Cup

Callum Marriott

CLUB RECORDS	Highest score: 120-4 v Illingworth, 13/3/2005 Highest score against: 0-106 v Castleford, 9/9/2007 Record attendance: 26,664 v Oldham, 25/3/22 (*Athletic Grounds*); 8,061 v Oldham, 26/12/89 (*Spotland*)
MATCH RECORDS	Tries: 5 Jack Corsi v Barrow, 31/12/21; Jack Corsi v Broughton Moor, 25/2/22; Jack Williams v St Helens, 4/4/33; Norman Brelsford v Whitehaven, 3/9/73; Marlon Billy v York, 8/4/2001 Goals: 18 Lee Birdseye v Illingworth, 13/3/2005 Points: 44 Lee Birdseye v Illingworth, 13/3/2005
SEASON RECORDS	Tries: 31 Marlon Billy 2001 Goals: 150 Martin Strett 1994-95 Points: 350 Mick Nanyn 2003
CAREER RECORDS	Tries: 103 Jack Williams 1931-37 Goals: 741 Walter Gowers 1922-36 Points: 1,497 Walter Gowers 1922-36; Paul Crook 2010-2016 Appearances: 456 Walter Gowers 1922-36

WEST WALES RAIDERS

	D.O.B.	APP ALL	L1	TRIES ALL	L1	GOALS ALL	L1	FG ALL	L1	PTS ALL	L1
Charlie Bodman	7/12/01	(3)	(2)	0	0	0	0	0	0	0	0
Harry Boots	15/12/96	3	2	0	0	0	0	0	0	0	0
Phil Cowburn	15/10/90	3	2	1	0	0	0	0	0	4	0
Chris Davies	24/12/91	1	0	0	0	0	0	0	0	0	0
Dai Evans	30/7/92	3	2	1	1	0	0	0	0	4	4
Morgan Evans	23/3/92	2	1	1	1	0	0	0	0	4	4
Sam Herron	13/12/93	2(1)	2	0	0	0	0	0	0	0	0
Alex Hicken	4/3/88	(2)	(2)	0	0	0	0	0	0	0	0
Rowland Kaye	27/8/99	2	1	0	0	0	0	0	0	0	0
Jamie Laing	6/2/89	1(1)	1(1)	0	0	0	0	0	0	0	0
Bailey Liu	3/8/96	3	2	0	0	0	0	0	0	0	0
Sam Martin	25/1/96	(1)	0	0	0	0	0	0	0	0	0
Robert Matamosi	23/2/97	2	2	1	1	0	0	0	0	4	4
Emosi Nadaubale	6/11/92	2	2	1	1	0	0	0	0	4	4
Dafydd Phillips	10/8/95	3	2	2	1	0	0	0	0	8	4
Alan Pope	1/4/85	(3)	(2)	0	0	0	0	0	0	0	0
Dan Price	5/10/92	3	2	0	0	2	2	0	0	4	4
Ryan Shallish	25/2/93	2(1)	1(1)	0	0	0	0	0	0	0	0
Mitch Shaw	25/8/98	3	2	0	0	0	0	0	0	0	0
Archie Snook	26/3/99	3	2	0	0	0	0	0	0	0	0
Lewys Thompson	11/9/99	1	0	0	0	0	0	0	0	0	0

'L1' totals include League 1 games only; 'All' totals also include Challenge Cup

Phil Cowburn

CLUB RECORDS	Highest score: 44-16 v Coventry, 20/7/2019 Highest score against: 0-144 v York, 29/4/2018 Record attendance: 826 v Bradford, 9/9/2018
MATCH RECORDS	Tries: 2 (*6 players*) Goals: 6 Phil Cowburn v Coventry, 20/7/2019 Points: 12 Phil Cowburn v Coventry, 20/7/2019
SEASON RECORDS	Tries: 8 Steve Parry 2018 Goals: 22 Phil Cowburn 2019 Points: 52 Phil Cowburn 2019
CAREER RECORDS	Tries: 13 Steve Parry 2018-2019 Goals: 22 Phil Cowburn 2018-2020 Points: 72 Phil Cowburn 2018-2020 Appearances: 45 Archie Snook 2018-2020

WORKINGTON TOWN

	D.O.B.	APP ALL	APP L1	TRIES ALL	TRIES L1	GOALS ALL	GOALS L1	FG ALL	FG L1	PTS ALL	PTS L1
Caine Barnes	22/2/99	5	2	1	0	0	0	0	0	4	0
Russ Bolton	1/3/92	1	0	1	0	0	0	0	0	4	0
Tom Curwen	15/8/89	1(4)	(2)	0	0	0	0	0	0	0	0
Andrew Dawson	12/3/89	4(1)	2	0	0	0	0	0	0	0	0
Hanley Dawson	25/5/96	5	2	2	1	0	0	0	0	8	4
Jamie Doran	8/12/94	5	2	2	1	0	0	0	0	8	4
Gabriel Fell	12/9/95	5	2	1	0	0	0	0	0	4	0
Conor Fitzsimmons	7/5/98	5	2	0	0	0	0	0	0	0	0
Carl Forber	17/3/85	5	2	2	1	15	5	0	0	38	14
Elliot Hall	6/7/97	5	2	6	4	0	0	0	0	24	16
Tyler Lancaster	10/9/99	4	1	0	0	0	0	0	0	0	0
Blain Marwood	23/1/98	(5)	(2)	2	0	0	0	0	0	8	0
Gordon Maudling	9/2/91	(1)	0	0	0	0	0	0	0	0	0
Elliott Miller	14/9/90	3	2	0	0	0	0	0	0	0	0
Fuifui Moimoi	26/9/79	(5)	(2)	1	0	0	0	0	0	4	0
Marcus O'Brien	13/7/93	5	2	1	1	0	0	0	0	4	4
Adam Ramsden	27/8/91	(2)	(1)	0	0	0	0	0	0	0	0
Stevie Scholey	7/1/96	5	2	0	0	0	0	0	0	0	0
Calvin Wellington	10/12/95	2	1	0	0	0	0	0	0	0	0
Ryan Wilson	24/7/91	(2)	(1)	0	0	0	0	0	0	0	0
Alex Young	6/4/99	5	2	2	1	0	0	0	0	8	4

Gabriel Fell

'L1' totals include League 1 games only; 'All' totals also include Challenge Cup

CLUB RECORDS	
MATCH RECORDS	**Highest score:** 94-4 v Leigh, 26/2/95 **Highest score against:** 0-92 v Bradford, 14/2/99 **Record attendance:** 17,741 v Wigan, 3/3/65
	Tries: 7 Ike Southward v Blackpool, 17/9/55 **Goals:** 14 Darren Holt v Gateshead, 12/6/2011
	Points: 42 Dean Marwood v Highfield, 1/11/92; Dean Marwood v Leigh, 26/2/95
SEASON RECORDS	**Tries:** 49 Johnny Lawrenson 1951-52 **Goals:** 186 Lyn Hopkins 1981-82 **Points:** 438 Lyn Hopkins 1981-82
CAREER RECORDS	**Tries:** 274 Ike Southward 1952-68 **Goals:** 814 *(inc 5fg)* Carl Forber 2007-2009; 2012-2020 **Points:** 1,851 Carl Forber 2007-2009; 2012-2020
	Appearances: 419 Paul Charlton 1961-69; 1975-80

BARROW RAIDERS

DATE	FIXTURE	RESULT	SCORERS	LGE	ATT
16/2/20	London Skolars (h) (CCR3)	W38-18	t:Dallimore,Morrow(2),Ritson(2),Puara,Duffy g:Dallimore(5)	N/A	769
22/2/20	Featherstone (a) (CCR4)	L18-16	t:Cresswell,Terrill,Walne g:Dallimore(2)	N/A	1,120
1/3/20	Doncaster (a)	W22-32	t:Duffy(2),Puara,Dallimore,S Toal g:Dallimore(6)	5th	982
8/3/20	Coventry (h)	W50-6	t:S Toal(2),Crellin,Ritson,Tyson,Cresswell,D Toal(2),Dallimore g:Dallimore(7)	2nd	1,253

COVENTRY BEARS

DATE	FIXTURE	RESULT	SCORERS	LGE	ATT
9/2/20	Hunslet (a) (CCR3)	L36-4	t:Freeman	N/A	225
1/3/20	Newcastle (h)	L8-28	t:Rance,Hill	9th	384
8/3/20	Barrow (a)	L50-6	t:Welham g:Clavering	10th	1,253

DONCASTER

DATE	FIXTURE	RESULT	SCORERS	LGE	ATT
8/2/20	Thornhill (a) (CCR3) ●	W20-24	t:Ollett,Cross,Doherty,Boas g:Logan(4)	N/A	N/A
23/2/20	Workington (a) (CCR4)	L22-12	t:Tali(2) g:Beharrell(2)	N/A	612
1/3/20	Barrow (h)	L22-32	t:Boyle,Douglas,Rickett,Tali g:Beharrell(3)	7th	982
8/3/20	West Wales (h)	W50-10	t:Doherty(5),Foster,Peltier(2),Cross g:Beharrell(7)	4th	540

● *Played at Tetley's Stadium, Dewsbury*

HUNSLET

DATE	FIXTURE	RESULT	SCORERS	LGE	ATT
9/2/20	Coventry (h) (CCR3)	W36-4	t:Hartley(2),Straugheir,Chrimes,Andrade,Tonks,Lee g:Brambani(4)	N/A	225
23/2/20	North Wales (a) (CCR4)	W18-22	t:Watson,Boardman(2),Brambani g:Brambani(3)	N/A	249
1/3/20	West Wales (a)	W10-50	t:Watson,Hartley(3),Andrade,Conroy,Tonks,Halafihi,Markland,Ashton g:Brambani(5)	1st	304
8/3/20	North Wales (h)	W29-6	t:Brambani(2),Straugheir,Andrade,Hartley g:Brambani(4) fg:Brambani	1st	501
13/3/20	Featherstone (a) (CCR5)	L46-6	t:Heaton g:Rowse	N/A	1,002

KEIGHLEY COUGARS

DATE	FIXTURE	RESULT	SCORERS	LGE	ATT
15/2/20	Newcastle (h) (CCR3)	L12-16	t:Lynam,Levy g:Hardcastle(2)	N/A	402
1/3/20	Workington (a)	L24-6	t:Coventry g:Miller	8th	887
8/3/20	Rochdale (a)	L29-14	t:Miller,Webster,Hawkyard g:Miller	9th	541

LONDON SKOLARS

DATE	FIXTURE	RESULT	SCORERS	LGE	ATT
16/2/20	Barrow (a) (CCR3)	L38-18	t:Hammond,Thomas,Thorman g:Thorman(3)	N/A	769
1/3/20	North Wales (h)	L16-40	t:Juma,Yates,Wilkinson g:Thorman(2)	10th	223

NEWCASTLE THUNDER

DATE	FIXTURE	RESULT	SCORERS	LGE	ATT
15/2/20	Keighley (a) (CCR3)	W12-16	t:Roche,Gill g:Dean(4)	N/A	402
22/2/20	Siddal (a) (CCR4)	W10-30	t:Clegg,Blake(2),Aldous,Wood,Brown g:Dean(3)	N/A	450
1/3/20	Coventry (a)	W8-28	t:Clegg,Gill,Young,Brown,Luckley,Blake g:Dean(2)	3rd	384
8/3/20	Workington (h)	W30-22	t:Lawton,Gibson,Dean,Gill(2) g:Dean(5)	3rd	1,011
15/3/20	Dewsbury (h) (CCR5)	W38-30	t:Gill(2),Laulu-Togaga'e,Gibson,Beswick,Lawton,Clegg g:Dean(5)	N/A	689

NORTH WALES CRUSADERS

DATE	FIXTURE	RESULT	SCORERS	LGE	ATT
8/2/20	Rochdale Mayfield (a) (CCR3)	W6-64	t:Rodden(4),Jenkins,Sherratt,Massam(2),Billsborough,Holmes(2) g:Johnson(10)	N/A	229
23/2/20	Hunslet (h) (CCR4)	L18-22	t:Sherratt,Jenkins,Massam g:Johnson(3)	N/A	249
1/3/20	London Skolars (a)	W16-40	t:Thompson,Eccleston,Hurst,Rodden,Penny,Gibson g:Johnson(8)	2nd	223
8/3/20	Hunslet (a)	L29-6	t:Massam g:Johnson	7th	501

ROCHDALE HORNETS

DATE	FIXTURE	RESULT	SCORERS	LGE	ATT
16/2/20	York Acorn (h) (CCR3) ●	W54-10	t:Freeman(2),Tracey,L Sheridan,Bloomfield,Ainscough,Calland,Hesketh, Higginson g:Freeman(9)	N/A	200
23/2/20	British Army (h) (CCR4)	W54-10	t:Lea,Calland(3),Hopkins,Ainscough,Tracey(2),Higginson,Hesketh g:Freeman(7)	N/A	400
8/3/20	Keighley (h)	W29-14	t:Lea,Tracey,Whalley,Hopkins g:Freeman(6) fg:Ridyard	5th	541
15/3/20	York (a) (CCR5) ●●	L70-12	t:L Sheridan(2) g:Freeman(2)	N/A	400

● *Played at AJ Bell Stadium, Salford* ●● *Played at LD Nutrition Stadium, Featherstone*

WEST WALES RAIDERS

DATE	FIXTURE	RESULT	SCORERS	LGE	ATT
9/2/20	Underbank (h) (CCR3)	L8-30	t:Cowburn,Phillips	N/A	50
1/3/20	Hunslet (h)	L10-50	t:D Evans,Phillips g:Price	11th	304
8/3/20	Doncaster (a)	L50-10	t:M Evans,Matamosi g:Price	11th	540

WORKINGTON TOWN

DATE	FIXTURE	RESULT	SCORERS	LGE	ATT
16/2/20	West Bowling (h) (CCR3)	W28-22	t:Young,Barnes,Hall,Fell,Bolton g:Forber(4)	N/A	950
23/2/20	Doncaster (h) (CCR4)	W22-12	t:H Dawson,Marwood,Doran,Hall g:Forber(3)	N/A	612
1/3/20	Keighley (h)	W24-6	t:Hall(4),O'Brien g:Forber(2)	4th	887
8/3/20	Newcastle (a)	L30-22	t:H Dawson,Forber,Doran,Young g:Forber(3)	6th	1,011
15/3/20	Sheffield (a) (CCR5) ●	L34-18	t:Forber,Moimoi,Marwood g:Forber(3)	N/A	323

● *Played at Keepmoat Stadium, Doncaster*

LEAGUE 1 2020
Round by Round

ROUND 2

Sunday 1st March 2020

COVENTRY BEARS 8 NEWCASTLE THUNDER 28

BEARS: 1 Nathan Hill; 2 Hayden Freeman; 3 Liam Welham; 4 Kadeem Williams; 5 Reece Rance; 6 Kieran Smith; 7 Morgan Punchard; 14 Kieran Moran; 24 Doug Chirnside; 10 Peter Ryan; 11 Brad Clavering; 12 James Thornton; 13 Ryan Langton. Subs (all used): 8 Sam Moorhouse; 21 Will Budd; 23 Chris Cullimore; 16 Ben Gray. **Tries:** Rance (39), Hill (50); **Goals:** Clavering 0/2.
THUNDER: 1 Lewis Young; 2 Joe Brown; 3 Ashley Gibson; 4 Kieran Gill; 5 Alex Clegg; 6 Quentin Laulu-Togaga'e; 7 Reece Dean; 8 Brenden Santi; 9 Bob Beswick; 10 Mikey Wood; 11 Adam Lawton; 12 Jed Charlton; 13 Evan Simons. Subs (all used): 14 Sam Blake; 15 Sam Luckley; 16 Harry Aldous; 17 Jake Lightowler.
Tries: Clegg (1), Gill (8), Young (25), Brown (30), Luckley (55), Blake (71); **Goals:** Dean 2/6.
Rugby Leaguer & League Express Men of the Match: *Bears:* Reece Rance; *Thunder:* Ashley Gibson.
Penalty count: 10-9; **Half-time:** 4-18;
Referee: Kevin Moore; **Attendance:** 384.

DONCASTER 22 BARROW RAIDERS 32

DONCASTER: 1 Jack Logan; 2 Josh Rickett; 3 Sam Smeaton; 4 Jason Tali; 5 Sam Doherty; 24 Watson Boas; 7 Matty Beharrell; 8 Russ Spiers; 14 Harry Carter; 10 Ryan Boyle; 12 Brad Foster; 19 Aaron Ollett; 22 Graeme Horne. Subs (all used): 9 Kieran Cross; 15 Brandon Douglas; 17 Ross Peltier; 27 Danny Bravo.
Tries: Boyle (23), Douglas (28), Rickett (46), Tali (76); **Goals:** Beharrell 3/4.
RAIDERS: 1 Luke Cresswell; 5 Theerapol Ritson; 3 Declan Hulme; 19 Perry Singleton; 2 Shane Toal; 6 Jamie Dallimore; 7 Ryan Johnston; 10 Carl Forster; 14 Wartovo Puara; 18 Lee Jewitt; 11 Jono Smith; 16 Danny Morrow; 13 Jordan Walne. Subs (all used): 23 Mark Tyson; 27 Tom Hopkins; 15 Dan Toal; 8 Ryan Duffy.
Tries: Duffy (36, 55), Puara (59), Dallimore (71), S Toal (80); **Goals:** Dallimore 6/6.
Sin bin: Morrow (33) - professional foul.
Rugby Leaguer & League Express Men of the Match: *Doncaster:* Graeme Horne; *Raiders:* Jamie Dallimore.
Penalty count: 9-9; **Half-time:** 12-8;
Referee: Billy Pearson; **Attendance:** 982.

LONDON SKOLARS 16 NORTH WALES CRUSADERS 40

SKOLARS: 1 Jacob Thomas; 5 Iliess Macani; 25 Kameron Pearce-Paul; 3 Max Clarke; 2 Jerome Yates; 21 Ben Steele; 7 Richard Wilkinson; 8 Matt Ross; 9 Neil Thorman; 10 Oscar Stone; 11 Lameck Juma; 19 Mike Greenhalgh; 13 Mike Bishay. Subs (all used): 14 Shay North; 17 Costa Charalambous; 12 Julius Hobbs; 18 Lamont Bryan.
Tries: Juma (2), Yates (24), Wilkinson (34);
Goals: Thorman 2/2, Bishay 0/1.
CRUSADERS: 1 Tommy Johnson; 2 Dave Eccleston; 3 Jordan Penny; 4 Earl Hurst; 5 Rob Massam; 6 Elliott Jenkins; 7 Jordy Gibson; 8 Brad Brennan; 9 Bob Billsborough; 10 Warren Thompson; 11 Matt Reid; 12 Gav Rodden; 13 Chris Barratt. Subs (all used): 14 Steve Roper; 15 Ryan Millington; 16 Jack Cottington; 17 James Tilley.
Tries: Thompson (11), Eccleston (14), Hurst (28), Rodden (47), Penny (62), Gibson (75); **Goals:** Johnson 8/8.
Rugby Leaguer & League Express Men of the Match: *Skolars:* Matt Ross; *Crusaders:* Matt Reid.
Penalty count: 10-10; **Half-time:** 16-18;
Referee: Michael Mannifield; **Attendance:** 223.

WEST WALES RAIDERS 10 HUNSLET 50

RAIDERS: 7 Phil Cowburn; 5 Dai Evans; 3 Emosi Nadaubale; 12 Rowland Kaye; 13 Robert Matamosi; 6 Bailey Liu; 1 Dan Price; 8 Sam Herron; 14 Dafydd Phillips; 15 Harry Boots; 21 Ryan Shallish; 11 Archie Snook; 9 Mitch Shaw. Subs (all used): 22 Jamie Laing; 20 Alan Pope; 10 Alex Hicken; 23 Charlie Bodman.
Tries: D Evans (3), Phillips (26); **Goals:** Price 1/2.
HUNSLET: 1 Jimmy Watson; 2 Ben Markland; 3 Ben Heaton; 4 Tom Ashton; 18 Kiedan Hartley; 6 Simon Brown; 7 Dom Brambani; 26 Alex Rowe; 9 Jack Lee; 10 Harry Kidd; 11 Josh Tonks; 12 Duane Straugheir; 13 Vila Halafihi. Subs (all used): 20 Nathan Conroy; 25 Jordan Andrade; 15 Harvey Hallas; 16 Jack Ray.
Tries: Watson (8), Hartley (16, 21, 43), Andrade (30), Conroy (40), Tonks (50), Halafihi (59), Markland (66), Ashton (76); **Goals:** Brown 0/2, Ashton 0/1, Brambani 5/7.
Rugby Leaguer & League Express Men of the Match: *Raiders:* Dafydd Phillips; *Hunslet:* Kiedan Hartley.
Penalty count: 4-8; **Half-time:** 10-24;
Referee: Neil Horton; **Attendance:** 304.

WORKINGTON TOWN 24 KEIGHLEY COUGARS 6

TOWN: 1 Gabriel Fell; 2 Elliot Hall; 3 Elliott Miller; 19 Tyler Lancaster; 5 Alex Young; 6 Jamie Doran; 7 Carl Forber; 8 Andrew Dawson; 14 Marcus O'Brien; 13 Conor Fitzsimmons; 12 Caine Barnes; 10 Stevie Scholey; 21 Hanley Dawson. Subs (all used): 15 Tom Curwen; 18 Blain Marwood; 25 Fuifui Moimoi; 33 Adam Ramsden.
Tries: Hall (19, 26, 37, 45), O'Brien (41); **Goals:** Forber 2/5.
COUGARS: 23 Alfie Seeley; 2 Mo Agoro; 4 Macauley Hallett; 3 Jake Webster; 5 Taylor Prell; 26 Billy Gaylor; 15 Jack Miller; 16 Dan Parker; 13 Kyle Kesik; 17 Dan Hawksworth; 11 Jason Muranka; 22 Lewis Wray; 12 Aaron Levy. Subs (all used): 1 Louis Sheriff; 8 Jack Coventry; 9 James Feather; 10 Dalton Desmond-Walker.
Try: Coventry (78); **Goals:** Miller 1/1.
Rugby Leaguer & League Express Men of the Match: *Town:* Marcus O'Brien; *Cougars:* Alfie Seeley.
Penalty count: 4-10; **Half-time:** 14-0;
Referee: Tom Crashley; **Attendance:** 887.

ROUND 3

Sunday 8th March 2020

BARROW RAIDERS 50 COVENTRY BEARS 6

RAIDERS: 1 Luke Cresswell; 5 Theerapol Ritson; 3 Declan Hulme; 23 Mark Tyson; 2 Shane Toal; 6 Jamie Dallimore; 7 Ryan Johnston; 10 Carl Forster; 14 Wartovo Puara; 15 Dan Toal; 11 Jono Smith; 27 Tom Hopkins; 20 Bradd Crellin. Subs (all used): 17 Jake Carter; 16 Danny Morrow; 15 Dan Toal; 8 Ryan Duffy.
Tries: S Toal (4, 42), Crellin (7), Ritson (12), Tyson (15), Cresswell (22), D Toal (39, 80), Dallimore (51); **Goals:** Dallimore 7/9.
Sin bin: D Toal (58) - trip.
BEARS: 1 Nathan Hill; 2 Hayden Freeman; 3 Liam Welham; 4 James Thornton; 5 Reece Rance; 6 Morgan Punchard; 7 Kieran Smith; 8 Kieran Moran; 23 Chris Cullimore; 25 Peter Ryan; 11 Brad Clavering; 12 Harry Kaufman; 13 Ben Gray. Subs (all used): 17 Ben Bradshaw; 21 Will Budd; 22 Leon Harber.
Try: Welham (66); **Goals:** Clavering 1/1.
Rugby Leaguer & League Express Men of the Match: *Raiders:* Jamie Dallimore; *Bears:* Nathan Hill.
Penalty count: 6-8; **Half-time:** 36-0;
Referee: Andrew Sweet; **Attendance:** 1,253.

DONCASTER 50 WEST WALES RAIDERS 10

DONCASTER: 1 Jack Logan; 2 Josh Rickett; 3 Sam Smeaton; 4 Jason Tali; 5 Sam Doherty; 6 Rangi Chase; 7 Matty Beharrell; 22 Graeme Horne; 14 Harry Carter; 15 Brandon Douglas; 27 Danny Bravo; 19 Aaron Ollett; 12 Brad Foster. Subs (all used): 9 Kieran Cross; 16 Brandan Wilkinson; 17 Ross Peltier; 21 Ryan Dixon.
Tries: Doherty (7, 15, 36, 54, 57), Foster (21), Peltier (31, 60), Cross (63); **Goals:** Beharrell 7/9.
Sin bin: Logan (66) - professional foul.
RAIDERS: 7 Phil Cowburn; 2 Robert Matamosi; 3 Emosi Nadaubale; 22 Jamie Laing; 5 Dai Evans; 6 Mitch Shaw; 1 Dan Price; 8 Sam Herron; 14 Dafydd Phillips; 15 Harry Boots; 6 Bailey Lui; 11 Archie Snook; 13 Morgan Evans. Subs (all used): 10 Alex Hicken; 20 Alan Pope; 21 Ryan Shallish; 23 Charlie Bodman.
Tries: M Evans (67), Matamosi (71); **Goals:** Price 1/2.
Rugby Leaguer & League Express Men of the Match: *Doncaster:* Sam Doherty; *Raiders:* Robert Matamosi.
Penalty count: 7-7; **Half-time:** 28-0;
Referee: Nick Bennett; **Attendance:** 540.

HUNSLET 29 NORTH WALES CRUSADERS 6

HUNSLET: 1 Jimmy Watson; 2 Ben Markland; 3 Ben Heaton; 4 Tom Ashton; 18 Kiedan Hartley; 6 Simon Brown; 7 Dom Brambani; 26 Alex Rowe; 9 Jack Lee; 10 Harry Kidd; 11 Josh Tonks; 12 Duane Straugheir; 13 Vila Halafihi. Subs (all used): 20 Nathan Conroy; 21 Jack Aldous; 25 Jordan Andrade; 15 Harvey Hallas.
Tries: Brambani (27, 69), Straugheir (31), Andrade (39), Hartley (62); **Goals:** Brambani 4/5.
Field goal: Brambani (60).
Sin bin: Hartley (9) - professional foul.
CRUSADERS: 1 Tommy Johnson; 2 Dave Eccleston; 3 Jordan Penny; 4 Dante Morley-Samuels; 5 Rob Massam; 6 Elliott Jenkins; 7 Jordy Gibson; 8 Brad Brennan; 9 Bob Billsborough; 10 Warren Thompson; 11 Matt Reid; 12 Gav Rodden; 13 Chris Barratt. Subs (all used): 14 Kieran Sherratt; 15 Ryan Millington; 16 Jack Cottington; 17 James Tilley.
Try: Massam (13); **Goals:** Johnson 1/1.
Rugby Leaguer & League Express Men of the Match: *Hunslet:* Dom Brambani; *Crusaders:* Matt Reid.
Penalty count: 4-6; **Half-time:** 18-6;
Referee: Jon Roberts; **Attendance:** 501.

NEWCASTLE THUNDER 30 WORKINGTON TOWN 22

THUNDER: 1 Lewis Young; 2 Ashley Gibson; 3 Matthew Wright; 4 Kieran Gill; 5 Alex Clegg; 6 Quentin Laulu-Togaga'e; 7 Reece Dean; 8 Brenden Santi; 9 Bob Beswick; 10 Mikey Wood; 11 Adam Lawton; 12 Harry Aldous; 13 Sam Luckley. Subs (all used): 15 Sam Blake; 14 Evan Simons; 16 Rhys Clarke; 17 Joe Brown.
Tries: Lawton (11), Gibson (15), Dean (19), Gill (48, 68); **Goals:** Dean 5/8.
TOWN: 1 Gabriel Fell; 2 Elliot Hall; 3 Elliott Miller; 4 Calvin Wellington; 5 Alex Young; 6 Jamie Doran; 7 Carl Forber; 8 Andrew Dawson; 14 Marcus O'Brien; 13 Conor Fitzsimmons; 12 Caine Barnes; 10 Stevie Scholey; 21 Hanley Dawson. Subs (all used): 18 Blain Marwood; 25 Fuifui Moimoi; 15 Tom Curwen; 24 Ryan Wilson.
Tries: H Dawson (24), Forber (32), Doran (38), Young (64); **Goals:** Forber 3/4.
Rugby Leaguer & League Express Men of the Match: *Thunder:* Kieran Gill; *Town:* Carl Forber.
Penalty count: 5-6; **Half-time:** 18-18;
Referee: Michael Mannifield; **Attendance:** 1,011.

ROCHDALE HORNETS 29 KEIGHLEY COUGARS 14

HORNETS: 1 Sam Freeman; 28 Brad Holroyd; 4 Ben Calland; 29 Jack Higginson; 2 Dale Bloomfield; 6 Lewis Sheridan; 27 Martyn Ridyard; 8 Callum Marriott; 9 Sean Penkywicz; 32 Sam Hopkins; 11 Jordan Syme; 12 Jamie Tracey; 13 Andy Lea. Subs (all used): 10 Adam Hesketh; 14 Declan Sheridan; 15 Luke Fowden; 18 Liam Whalley.
Tries: Lea (9), Tracey (21), Whalley (58), Hopkins (80); **Goals:** Freeman 6/6; **Field goal:** Ridyard (63).
COUGARS: 23 Alfie Seeley; 2 Mo Agoro; 4 Macauley Hallett; 3 Jake Webster; 30 Ritchie Hawkyard; 26 Billy Gaylor; 15 Jack Miller; 16 Dan Parker; 9 James Feather; 8 Jack Coventry; 11 Jason Muranka; 22 Lewis Wray; 12 Aaron Levy. Subs (all used): 1 Louis Sheriff; 14 Ryan Wright; 17 Dan Hawksworth; 19 Matthew Bailey.
Tries: Miller (32), Webster (36), Hawkyard (77); **Goals:** Miller 1/3.
Sin bin: Feather (26) - shoulder charge.
Rugby Leaguer & League Express Men of the Match: *Hornets:* Dale Bloomfield; *Cougars:* Dan Hawksworth.
Penalty count: 13-12; **Half-time:** 14-10;
Referee: Liam Staveley; **Attendance:** 541.

CHALLENGE CUP 2020
Round by Round

248

ROUND 3

Saturday 8th February 2020

ROCHDALE MAYFIELD 6 NORTH WALES CRUSADERS 64

MAYFIELD: 1 Ieuan Higgs; 2 Wayne Bannister; 3 Jack McConachie; 4 Lewis Butterworth; 5 Munya Samanyanga; 6 Chris Hough; 7 Cole Connolly; 8 Simon Moore; 9 Harry McDonald; 10 Shaun Hurley; 11 Rob Kershaw; 12 Sean Mulcahy; 13 Aidy Gleeson. Subs (all used): 14 Corey Newsham; 15 Nick Hargreaves; 16 Mark Biggins; 17 Andrew Taylor.
Try: Hough (52); **Goals:** Connolly 1/1.
CRUSADERS: 1 Tommy Johnson; 2 Dave Eccleston; 3 Jack Holmes; 4 Earl Hurst; 5 Rob Massam; 6 Steve Roper; 7 Jordy Gibson; 8 Brad Brennan; 9 Brad Billsborough; 10 Warren Thompson; 11 Kieran Sherratt; 12 Gav Rodden; 13 Chris Barratt. Subs (all used): 14 Elliott Jenkins; 15 Ryan Millington; 16 Jack Cottington; 17 James Tilley.
Tries: Rodden (21, 60, 64, 72), Jenkins (36), Sherratt (40), Massam (48, 74), Billsborough (58), Holmes (66, 69); **Goals:** Johnson 10/11.
Rugby Leaguer & League Express Men of the Match: *Mayfield:* Cole Connolly; *Crusaders:* Gav Rodden.
Penalty count: 8-12; **Half-time:** 0-16;
Referee: Steve Race; **Attendance:** 229.

SIDDAL 10 WEST HULL 6

SIDDAL: 1 Gareth Blackburn; 2 Sam Walsh; 3 Ben West; 4 Lewis Hosty; 5 Dom Booth; 6 Christian Ackroyd; 7 Will Scrimshaw; 8 Byron Smith; 9 Danny Rushworth; 10 Jack Georgiou; 11 Danny Williams; 12 Ben Hinsley; 13 Canaan Smithies. Subs (all used): 14 Jamie Greenwood; 15 Iain Davies; 16 Harry Georgiou; 17 Dom O'Keefe.
Tries: Hosty (46), Hinsley (70); **Goals:** Blackburn 1/2.
WEST HULL: 1 Luke Moss; 2 Jamie Leigh; 3 Tom Burke; 4 Josh Nicklin; 5 Ethan Shore; 6 Nathan Powley; 7 Danny Nicklas; 8 Will Gardiner; 9 Josh Wood; 10 Oscar Ellerington; 11 Jack Lazenby; 12 Louis Crowther; 13 Ryan Steen. Subs (all used): 14 Jack Watts; 15 George Tyson-Wilson; 19 Charlie Lumb; 20 Ryan Wilson.
Try: Lazenby (53); **Goals:** Wilson 1/1.
Rugby Leaguer & League Express Men of the Match: *Siddal:* Danny Williams; *West Hull:* Jack Lazenby.
Penalty count: 5-11; **Half-time:** 0-0;
Referee: Joe Stearne; **Attendance:** 450.

THORNHILL TROJANS 20 DONCASTER 24

TROJANS: 1 George Woodcock; 2 Declan Kaye; 3 William Gledhill; 4 Nick Mitchell; 5 Ross Roebuck; 6 Liam Morley; 7 Luke Haigh; 8 Tom Gledhill; 9 Matthew Tebb; 10 Jake Wilson; 11 Harry Woollard; 12 George Stott; 13 Casey Johnson. Subs (all used): 14 Jamie Searby; 15 Sam Ratcliffe; 17 Anthony Harris; 20 Joe Buggle.
Tries: Kaye (3), Stott (19), Mitchell (59);
Goals: Johnson 4/4.
DONCASTER: 1 Jack Logan; 5 Sam Doherty; 3 Sam Smeaton; 4 Jason Tali; 18 Tom Halliday; 9 Kieran Cross; 24 Watson Boas; 10 Ryan Boyle; 14 Harry Carter; 15 Brandon Douglas; 12 Brad Foster; 19 Aaron Ollett; 16 Brandan Wilkinson. Subs (all used): 17 Ross Peltier; 26 Alex Holdstock; 8 Russ Spiers; 20 Ben Howe.
Tries: Ollett (6), Cross (48), Doherty (58), Boas (78);
Goals: Logan 4/4.
Sin bin: Peltier (32) - dissent.
Rugby Leaguer & League Express Men of the Match: *Trojans:* Liam Morley; *Doncaster:* Alex Holdstock.
Penalty count: 7-10; **Half-time:** 14-6;
Referee: Andrew Sweet; **Attendance:** N/A
(at Tetley's Stadium, Dewsbury).

BRITISH ARMY 34 INCE ROSE BRIDGE 22

ARMY: 1 Kieron Roche; 2 Jefeti Vakalabure; 3 Jamie Laing; 4 Peter Holmes; 5 Uraia Naulusala; 6 Ben O'Connell; 7 Declan Baines; 8 Ryan Watkin; 9 Matthew Scott; 15 Micky Hoyle; 12 Sam Coleman; 11 Oli Toms; 13 Aaron McBride. Subs (all used): 16 Michael Harrison; 19 Sean Beevor; 20 Tom Zuger; 10 Alex Hicken.
Tries: Vakalabure (8, 57), Naulusala (42, 54), Laing (68), O'Connell (77); **Goals:** Roche 5/8.
ROSE BRIDGE: 1 Danny Cassidy; 2 Mitch Parr; 3 Jamie Malone; 4 Danny Dainty; 5 Callum Hughes; 6 Kieron Eccleston; 7 Connor Meaden; 8 Reece Cunningham; 9 Matthew Meaden; 10 Andrew Collier; 11 Pete Valentine; 12 Robbie Valentine; 13 Brad Smith. Subs (all used): 14 Alex Shaw; 15 Craig Sanby; 16 Scott Lomax; 17 Jack Morrison.
Tries: Dainty (17), Cassidy (32), Smith (73), Hughes (80);
Goals: Cassidy 3/4.
Rugby Leaguer & League Express Men of the Match: *Army:* Matthew Scott; *Rose Bridge:* Brad Smith.
Penalty count: 9-6; **Half-time:** 4-12;
Referee: Nick Bennett; **Attendance:** 100.

LEIGH MINERS RANGERS 20 BENTLEY 4

MINERS RANGERS: 1 Will Ashworth; 2 Rob Crompton; 3 Liam Kenyon; 4 Adam Thomason; 5 Lewis Grimes; 6 Ryan Horne; 7 Tom Worthington; 8 Harry Darby; 9 Owen Johnson; 10 Darryl Kay; 11 Jack Boulton; 12 Andy Badrock; 13 Matty McGeown. Subs (all used): 14 Danny Griffiths; 15 Mark Thomas; 16 Andy Philbin; 17 Jonny Carroll.
Tries: Thomason (15), Crompton (32), Grimes (50), Worthington (64); **Goals:** Worthington 2/4.
BENTLEY: 1 Alex Bates; 2 Grant Hill; 3 Jon Marshall; 4 Sean Richards; 5 Dean Colton; 6 Jonny Woodcock; 7 Jack Craswell; 8 David Royle; 9 Scott Smith; 10 Jordan Middleton; 11 Tom Flounders; 12 Ryan Craswell; 13 Jake Starbuck. Subs (all used): 14 Joe Barron; 15 Jordan Seaman; 16 Jamie I'Anson; 17 Lyndon Staley.
Try: Colton (6); **Goals:** Woodcock 0/1.
Rugby Leaguer & League Express Men of the Match: *Miners Rangers:* Ryan Horne; *Bentley:* Jack Craswell.
Penalty count: 5-3; **Half-time:** 8-4;
Referee: Michael Smaill; **Attendance:** 376.

Sunday 9th February 2020

WEST WALES RAIDERS 8 UNDERBANK RANGERS 30

RAIDERS: 1 Dan Price; 24 Lewys Thompson; 5 Dai Evans; 21 Ryan Shallish; 14 Dafydd Phillips; 7 Phil Cowburn; 6 Bailey Liu; 15 Harry Boots; 9 Mitch Shaw; 10 Chris Davies; 11 Archie Snook; 12 Rowland Kaye; 13 Morgan Evans. Subs (all used): 8 Sam Herron; 22 Sam Martin; 20 Alan Pope; 23 Charlie Bodman.
Tries: Cowburn (21), Phillips (55); **Goals:** Price 0/2.
Dismissal: C Davies (79) - fighting.
RANGERS: 1 Owen Restall; 2 Jamie Stringer; 3 Jakob Garside; 4 Alex Chatterton; 22 Courtney Allette; 6 Danny Hirst; 7 Richard Pogson; 8 Jordan Williams; 9 Ryan Maneely; 10 Tom Booth; 11 Nathan Chappell; 12 Tom Stringer; 13 Dom Newton. Subs (all used): 14 Steven Lockwood; 16 Nathan Richardson; 17 Mikey Holmes; 19 Mark Boothroyd.
Tries: Restall (5, 77), J Stringer (14), Pogson (60), Allette (74); **Goals:** Pogson 5/8.
Rugby Leaguer & League Express Men of the Match: *Raiders:* Dai Evans; *Rangers:* Richard Pogson.
Penalty count: 9-8; **Half-time:** 4-12;
Referee: James Jones; **Attendance:** 50.

HUNSLET 36 COVENTRY BEARS 4

HUNSLET: 18 Kiedan Hartley; 2 Ben Markland; 3 Ben Heaton; 4 Tom Ashton; 5 Matty Chrimes; 6 Simon Brown; 7 Dom Brambani; 8 Zach Braham; 9 Jack Lee; 10 Harry Kidd; 11 Josh Tonks; 12 Duane Straugheir; 13 Vila Halafihi. Subs (all used): 20 Nathan Conroy; 21 Jack Aldous; 25 Jordan Andrade; 17 Danny King.
Tries: Hartley (12, 29), Straugheir (45), Chrimes (53), Andrade (57), Tonks (63), Lee (72); **Goals:** Brambani 4/7.
Sin bin: Braham (17) - late challenge on Sheridan.
BEARS: 1 Nathan Hill; 2 Hayden Freeman; 3 Liam Welham; 4 Kadeem Williams; 5 Reece Rance; 6 Brad Sheridan; 7 Kieran Smith; 8 Peter Ryan; 23 Chris Cullimore; 10 Leon Harber; 11 Brad Clavering; 12 Harry Kaufman; 13 Ryan Langton. Subs (all used): 16 Will Budd; 19 Alex Williams; 21 Cameron Stewart; 22 Darius Hamilton.
Try: Freeman (19); **Goals:** Smith 0/1.
Rugby Leaguer & League Express Men of the Match: *Hunslet:* Simon Brown; *Bears:* Nathan Hill.
Penalty count: 14-6; **Half-time:** 8-4;
Referee: Cameron Worsley; **Attendance:** 225.

Saturday 15th February 2020

KEIGHLEY COUGARS 12 NEWCASTLE THUNDER 16

COUGARS: 23 Alfie Seeley; 2 Mo Agoro; 21 Matt Welham; 1 Louis Sheriff; 4 Macauley Hallett; 15 Jack Miller; 7 Benn Hardcastle; 16 Dan Parker; 13 Kyle Kesik; 10 Dalton Desmond-Walker; 28 Josh Lynam; 22 Lewis Wray; 12 Aaron Levy. Subs (all used): 8 Jack Coventry; 9 James Feather; 19 Matthew Bailey; 24 Spencer Darley.
Tries: Lynam (47), Levy (79); **Goals:** Hardcastle 2/2.
Sin bin: Desmond-Walker (8) - late challenge on Walker.
THUNDER: 1 Lewis Young; 2 Alex Donaghy; 3 Joe Brown; 4 Kieran Gill; 5 Alex Clegg; 6 Quentin Laulu-Togaga'e; 7 Reece Dean; 8 Brenden Santi; 9 Bob Beswick; 10 Mikey Wood; 11 Adam Lawton; 12 Colton Roche; 13 Brad Walker. Subs (all used): 14 Evan Simons; 15 Sam Blake; 16 Sam Luckley; 17 Harry Aldous.
Tries: Roche (6), Gill (32); **Goals:** Dean 4/5.
Dismissal: Roche (19) - late challenge on Parker.
On report: Wood (64) - alleged dangerous contact; Santi (71) - alleged dangerous contact.
Rugby Leaguer & League Express Men of the Match: *Cougars:* Alfie Seeley; *Thunder:* Bob Beswick.
Penalty count: 7-8; **Half-time:** 0-12;
Referee: Liam Staveley; **Attendance:** 402.

Sunday 16th February 2020

WORKINGTON TOWN 28 WEST BOWLING 22

TOWN: 1 Gabriel Fell; 2 Elliot Hall; 17 Russ Bolton; 19 Tyler Lancaster; 5 Alex Young; 6 Jamie Doran; 7 Carl Forber; 8 Andrew Dawson; 14 Marcus O'Brien; 13 Conor Fitzsimmons; 12 Caine Barnes; 10 Stevie Scholey; 21 Hanley Dawson. Subs (all used): 18 Blain Marwood; 25 Fuifui Moimoi; 15 Tom Curwen; 16 Gordon Maudling.
Tries: Young (5), Barnes (39), Hall (44), Fell (48), Bolton (65); **Goals:** Forber 4/5.
WEST BOWLING: 1 Ben Heald; 2 Jack Atkinson; 3 Louis Fraser; 19 Daniel Gregory; 5 Nicholas Fontaine; 6 Harry Williams; 7 Liam Darville; 8 Nathaniel Light; 9 Daniel Halmshaw; 10 Lewis Reed; 11 Richard Lumb; 18 Jack Milburn; 13 Oliver Bartle. Subs (all used): 14 Liam Coe; 15 Lewis Galtress; 16 Gavin Wilkinson; 17 Scott Smith.
Tries: Halmshaw (11), Lumb (52), Bartle (55), Gregory (75);
Goals: Heald 3/4.
Rugby Leaguer & League Express Men of the Match: *Town:* Carl Forber; *West Bowling:* Richard Lumb.
Penalty count: 7-2; **Half-time:** 12-4;
Referee: Kevin Moore; **Attendance:** 950.

BARROW RAIDERS 38 LONDON SKOLARS 18

RAIDERS: 1 Luke Cresswell; 5 Theerapol Ritson; 3 Declan Hulme; 19 Perry Singleton; 2 Shane Toal; 6 Jamie Dallimore; 7 Ryan Johnston; 8 Ryan Duffy; 14 Wartovo Puara; 10 Carl Forster; 11 Jono Smith; 16 Danny Morrow; 13 Jordan Walne. Subs (all used): 23 Mark Tyson; 15 Dan Toal; 18 Lee Jewitt; 27 Tom Hopkins.
Tries: Dallimore (14), Morrow (24, 80), Ritson (32, 47), Puara (67), Duffy (73); **Goals:** Dallimore 5/7.
SKOLARS: 1 Iliess Macani; 2 Jerome Yates; 3 Max Clarke; 16 Kameron Pearce-Paul; 12 Charles Hammond; 14 Richard Wilkinson; 7 Jacob Thomas; 8 Matt Ross; 9 Neil Thorman; 11 Costa Charalambous; 5 Dalton Grant; 19 Mike Greenhalgh; 13 Mike Bishay. Subs (all used): 20 Shay North; 17 Julius Hobbs; 4 Josh Spearing; 24 Ryan Cane.
Tries: Hammond (21), Thomas (35), Thorman (61);
Goals: Thorman 3/3.
Sin bin: Greenhalgh (19) - shoulder charge on Walne.
Rugby Leaguer & League Express Men of the Match: *Raiders:* Dan Toal; *Skolars:* Neil Thorman.
Penalty count: 7-7; **Half-time:** 14-12;
Referee: Brad Milligan; **Attendance:** 769.

ROCHDALE HORNETS 54 YORK ACORN 10

HORNETS: 1 Sam Freeman; 5 Shaun Ainscough; 4 Ben Calland; 29 Jack Higginson; 2 Dale Bloomfield; 6 Lewis Sheridan; 11 Jordan Syme; 10 Adam Hesketh; 20 Ben Moores; 32 Sam Hopkins; 12 Jamie Tracey; 18 Liam Whalley; 13 Andy Lea. Subs (all used): 15 Luke Fowden; 8 Callum Marriott; 16 Adam Carr; 14 Declan Sheridan.
Tries: Freeman (2, 38), Tracey (8), L Sheridan (16), Bloomfield (35), Ainscough (50), Calland (55), Hesketh (59), Higginson (78); **Goals:** Freeman 9/9.
Sin bin: Tracey (32) - high tackle on Sanderson.
ACORN: 1 Joe Budd; 2 Callum Worthington; 3 Ryan Gallacher; 4 Mark Sanderson; 20 Luke Swales; 6 Antony Chilton; 7 Lewis Brown; 8 Tim Stubbs; 9 Lewis Lord; 10 Adam Endersby; 11 Elliot Bulmer; 12 Jordan Hyde; 13 Thomas Holder. Subs (all used): 14 James Mountford; 15 Alex Hardcastle; 16 Jack Byrnes; 19 Adam Speck.
Tries: Gallacher (61), Hardcastle (71); **Goals:** Chilton 1/2.
Rugby Leaguer & League Express Men of the Match: *Hornets:* Sam Freeman; *Acorn:* Antony Chilton.
Penalty count: 9-8; **Half-time:** 30-0;
Referee: Andrew Sweet; **Attendance:** 200
(at AJ Bell Stadium, Salford).

ROUND 4

Friday 21st February 2020

LEIGH CENTURIONS 36 BATLEY BULLDOGS 10

CENTURIONS: 22 Craig Mullen; 28 Ryan Shaw; 3 Iain Thornley; 4 Junior Sa'u; 5 Adam Higson; 6 Ben Reynolds; 14 Matty Wildie; 27 Alex Gerrard; 9 Liam Hood; 10 Mark Ioane; 11 Ben Hellewell; 21 Nick Glohe; 13 Danny Addy. Subs (all used): 15 Jordan Thompson; 16 Sam Brooks; 18 Tom Spencer; 23 Callum Field.
Tries: Hood (3), Addy (10), Thornley (24, 39), Hellewell (59), Higson (63); **Goals:** Reynolds 6/6.
Sin bin: Brooks (68) - shoulder charge on Leak.
BULLDOGS: 1 Dave Scott; 2 Wayne Reittie; 18 George Senior; 4 Lewis Galbraith; 5 Johnny Campbell; 6 Ben White; 14 Luke Hooley; - Tyler Dupree; 9 Alistair Leak; 10 Toby Everett; 11 Dane Manning; 3 Keenen Tomlinson; 15 Jack Blagbrough. Subs (all used): - Tom Lillycrop; 16 Michael Ward; 21 Jo Taira; 24 Shaun Lunt.
Tries: Dupree (15), Senior (70); **Goals:** Hooley 1/2.

Rugby Leaguer & League Express Men of the Match: *Centurions:* Ben Reynolds; *Bulldogs:* Tyler Dupree.
Penalty count: 7-12; **Half-time:** 24-6;
Referee: Matt Rossleigh; **Attendance:** 1,586.

Saturday 22nd February 2020

SHEFFIELD EAGLES 20 HALIFAX 18

EAGLES: 1 Josh Guzdek; 2 Rob Worrincy; 19 Zack McComb; 18 Connor Bower; 5 Ryan Millar; 6 Corey Makelim; 7 Anthony Thackeray; 8 Scott Wheeldon; 14 Greg Burns; 11 Brad Knowles; 15 Olly Davies; 12 Joel Farrell; 13 Aaron Brown. Subs (all used): 9 James Davey; 17 Frankie Mariano; 21 Paddy Burns; 23 Lewis Taylor.
Tries: Davies (4, 76), J Farrell (22), Guzdek (63);
Goals: Guzdek 2/4.
HALIFAX: 1 Scott Grix; 2 Shaun Robinson; 3 Steve Tyrer; 18 James Saltonstall; 5 Jodie Broughton; 6 Scott Murrell; 4 James Woodburn-Hall; 10 Keegan Hirst; 9 Brandon Moore; 13 Jacob Fairbank; 11 Matt Garside; 15 Paul Brearley; 31 Kevin Larroyer. Subs (all used): 14 Keal Carlile; 12 Ed Barber; 29 Dan Fleming; 22 Will Calcott.
Tries: Garside (28), Brearley (35), Broughton (54), Fairbank (69); **Goals:** Tyrer 1/4.
Rugby Leaguer & League Express Men of the Match: *Eagles:* Joel Farrell; *Halifax:* Keegan Hirst.
Penalty count: 6-7; **Half-time:** 10-10;
Referee: James Vella; **Attendance:** 429
(at Mobile Rocket Stadium, Wakefield).

FEATHERSTONE ROVERS 18 BARROW RAIDERS 16

ROVERS: 1 Craig Hall; 28 Gareth Gale; 3 Josh Hardcastle; 5 Conor Carey; 2 Ben Blackmore; 6 Louis Jouffret; 20 Jake Sweeting; 17 Alec Susino; 9 Dean Parata; 15 Luke Cooper; 11 Brett Ferres; 16 Jack Bussey; 10 James Harrison. Subs: 13 James Lockwood; 22 Brandan French; 24 Sam Ottewell (not used); 29 Wellington Albert.
Tries: Hall (9), Parata (20), Gale (76); **Goals:** Hall 3/4.
Dismissal: Lockwood (38) - kicking D Toal.
RAIDERS: 1 Luke Cresswell; 5 Theerapol Ritson; 3 Declan Hulme; 19 Perry Singleton; 2 Shane Toal; 6 Jamie Dallimore; 7 Ryan Johnston; 10 Carl Forster; 14 Wartovo Puara; 30 Carl McBain; 27 Tom Hopkins; 16 Danny Morrow; 13 Jordan Walne. Subs (all used): 8 Ryan Duffy; 15 Dan Toal; 22 Connor Terrill; 23 Mark Tyson.
Tries: Cresswell (2), Terrill (32), Walne (72);
Goals: Dallimore 2/3.
Sin bin: Singleton (60) - repeated team offences; Hulme (64) - dangerous challenge on Cooper.
Rugby Leaguer & League Express Men of the Match: *Rovers:* Craig Hall; *Raiders:* Ryan Johnston.
Penalty count: 15-7; **Half-time:** 10-10;
Referee: Aaron Moore; **Attendance:** 1,120.

SIDDAL 10 NEWCASTLE THUNDER 30

SIDDAL: 1 Gareth Blackburn; 2 Sam Walsh; 3 Ben West; 4 Henry Turner; 5 Dom Booth; 6 Christian Ackroyd; 7 Will Scrimshaw; 8 Byron Smith; 9 Sean McCormack; 10 Jack Georgiou; 11 Danny Williams; 12 Ben Hinsley; 13 Canaan Smithies. Subs (all used): 14 Jamie Greenwood; 15 Harry Georgiou; 16 Dom O'Keefe; 17 Danny Rushworth.
Tries: Scrimshaw (20), Turner (31); **Goals:** Blackburn 1/2.
Sin bin: J Georgiou (65) - punching Aldous.
THUNDER: 1 Alex Donaghy; 2 Joe Brown; 3 Ashley Gibson; 4 Kieran Gill; 5 Alex Clegg; 6 Quentin Laulu-Togaga'e; 7 Reece Dean; 8 Brenden Santi; 9 Sam Blake; 10 Mikey Wood; 11 Adam Lawton; 12 Colton Roche; 13 Evan Simons. Subs (all used): 14 Jed Charlton; 15 Sam Luckley; 16 Kieran Hudson; 17 Harry Aldous.
Tries: Clegg (11), Blake (39, 40), Aldous (45), Wood (76), Brown (80); **Goals:** Dean 3/6.
Rugby Leaguer & League Express Men of the Match: *Siddal:* Byron Smith; *Thunder:* Sam Blake.
Penalty count: 7-12; **Half-time:** 10-18;
Referee: Neil Horton; **Attendance:** 450.

SWINTON LIONS 56 LEIGH MINERS RANGERS 0

LIONS: 1 Mike Butt; 2 Richard Lepori; 19 Sam Grant; 4 Mitch Cox; 5 Brandon Wood; 6 Jack Hansen; 20 Oscar Thomas; 8 Gavin Bennion; 9 Luke Waterworth; 10 Lewis Hatton; 11 Rhodri Lloyd; 12 Frankie Halton; 13 Will Hope. Subs (all used): 16 Paddy Jones; 21 Tayler Brown; 18 Louis Brogan; 23 Ben Heyes.
Tries: Butt (2, 13, 39, 69), Grant (23), Cox (36), Hope (50, 65), Lepori (56, 79), Halton (60);
Goals: Thomas 6/11.
MINERS RANGERS: 1 Tom Worthington; 18 Rob Crompton; 3 Liam Kenyon; 4 Adam Thomason; 5 Lewis Grimes; 6 Ryan Horne; 7 Callum Coleman; 8 Harry Darby; 9 Lee Hudson; 10 Darryl Kay; 11 Joe Connor; 12 Andy Badrock; 13 Matty McGeown. Subs (all used): 14 Owen Johnson; 17 Danny Griffiths; 20 Andy Philbin; 16 Jonny Carroll.
Rugby Leaguer & League Express Men of the Match: *Lions:* Mike Butt; *Miners Rangers:* Tom Worthington.
Penalty count: 5-2; **Half-time:** 26-0;
Referee: Kevin Moore; **Attendance:** 622.

Sunday 23rd February 2020

BRADFORD BULLS 22 UNDERBANK RANGERS 0

BULLS: 1 Brandon Pickersgill; 16 David Foggin-Johnston; 5 Joe Brown; 4 Ross Oakes; 19 Matty Dawson-Jones; 6 Rowan Milnes; 7 Jordan Lilley; 15 Liam Kirk; 9 Thomas Doyle; 10 Steve Crossley; 11 Adam Rooks; 28 Bradley Gallagher; 13 Sam Hallas. Subs (all used): 17 Levy Nzoungou; 29 Ebon Scurr; 20 Daniel Waite-Pullan; 14 George Flanagan.
Tries: Rooks (19), Flanagan (30), Nzoungou (37), Milnes (75); **Goals:** Milnes 3/4.
RANGERS: 1 Owen Restall; 2 Jamie Stringer; 3 Jakob Garside; 4 Alex Brown; 22 Courtney Allette; 6 Danny Hirst; 7 Richard Pogson; 8 Jordan Williams; 9 Ryan Maneely; 19 Mark Boothroyd; 11 Nathan Chappell; 12 Dom Newton; 13 Tom Stringer. Subs (all used): 10 Tom Booth; 14 Sam Rochford; 15 Olly Moorhouse; 17 Mikey Holmes.
Rugby Leaguer & League Express Men of the Match: *Bulls:* George Flanagan; *Rangers:* Ryan Maneely.
Penalty count: 12-8; **Half-time:** 18-0;
Referee: Cameron Worsley; **Attendance:** 1,458.

NORTH WALES CRUSADERS 18 HUNSLET 22

CRUSADERS: 1 Tommy Johnson; 2 Dave Eccleston; 17 Jordan Penny; 4 Earl Hurst; 5 Rob Massam; 7 Jordy Gibson; 6 Elliott Jenkins; 8 Brad Brennan; 9 Brad Billsborough; 10 Warren Thompson; 11 Kieran Sherratt; 12 Gav Rodden; 13 Chris Barratt. Subs: 14 Steve Roper; 15 Ryan Millington; 16 Jack Cottington; 3 Dante Morley-Samuels (not used).
Tries: Sherratt (25), Jenkins (30), Massam (39);
Goals: Johnson 3/4.
Sin bin: Hurst (64) - high tackle.
HUNSLET: 1 Jimmy Watson; 19 Liam Copland; 22 Anthony Boardman; 11 Josh Tonks; 4 Tom Ashton; 6 Simon Brown; 7 Dom Brambani; 15 Harvey Hallas; 9 Jack Lee; 10 Harry Kidd; 17 Danny King; 12 Duane Straugheir; 13 Vila Halafihi. Subs (all used): 20 Nathan Conroy; 21 Jack Aldous; 25 Jordan Andrade; 26 Alex Rowe.
Tries: Watson (16), Boardman (36, 76), Brambani (69);
Goals: Brambani 3/4.
Sin bin: Boardman (22) - dangerous challenge on Massam.
Rugby Leaguer & League Express Men of the Match: *Crusaders:* Tommy Johnson; *Hunslet:* Dom Brambani.
Penalty count: 5-13; **Half-time:** 16-10;
Referee: Billy Pearson; **Attendance:** 249.

LONDON BRONCOS 22 YORK CITY KNIGHTS 24

BRONCOS: 1 Olly Ashall-Bott; 27 Josh Hodson; 19 Jacob Ogden; 3 Guy Armitage; 2 Tuoyo Egodo; 6 Cory Aston; 17 James Meadows; 16 Olsi Krasniqi; 21 Sam Davis; 8 Eddie Battye; 20 Daniel Hindmarsh; 12 Rhys Curran; 14 Matty Fozard. Subs (all used): 9 Eloi Pelissier; 11 Josh Walters; 18 Dan Norman; 28 Will Blakemore.
Tries: Hindmarsh (1), Egodo (12), Curran (16), Pelissier (49), Armitage (53); **Goals:** Aston 1/5.
CITY KNIGHTS: 1 Matty Marsh; 24 Elliot Wallis; 3 Jimmy Keinhorst; 4 Liam Salter; 22 Brad Hey; 6 Ben Johnston; 7 Connor Robinson; 10 Jack Teanby; 9 Will Jubb; 16 Chris Clarkson; 11 Danny Washbrook; 12 Sam Scott; 13 Tim Spears. Subs (all used): 14 Kriss Brining; 15 James Green; 19 Jordan Baldwinson; 20 Marcus Stock.
Tries: Green (37), Baldwinson (44), Stock (46), Keinhorst (78); **Goals:** Robinson 4/4.
Rugby Leaguer & League Express Men of the Match: *Broncos:* Matty Fozard; *City Knights:* Matty Marsh.
Penalty count: 4-9; **Half-time:** 12-6;
Referee: Tom Grant; **Attendance:** 543.

ROCHDALE HORNETS 54 BRITISH ARMY 10

HORNETS: 1 Sam Freeman; 5 Shaun Ainscough; 4 Ben Calland; 29 Jack Higginson; 2 Dale Bloomfield; 6 Lewis Sheridan; 11 Jordan Syme; 10 Adam Hesketh; 20 Ben Moores; 32 Sam Hopkins; 12 Jamie Tracey; 8 Callum Marriott; 13 Andy Lea. Subs (all used): 15 Luke Fowden; 18 Liam Whalley; 16 Adam Carr; 14 Declan Sheridan.
Tries: Lea (5), Calland (10, 47, 68), Hopkins (22), Ainscough (31), Tracey (42, 77), Higginson (65), Hesketh (73); **Goals:** Freeman 7/10.
ARMY: 1 Kieron Roche; 14 Jefeti Vakalabure; 4 Peter Holmes; 3 Emosi Nadaubale; 5 Uraia Naulusala; 7 Declan Baines; 6 Ben O'Connell; 8 Ryan Watkin; 9 Matthew Scott; 10 Tom Zuger; 11 Sam Coleman; 13 Aaron McBride; 15 Micky Hoyle. Subs (all used): 17 Richard Cummings; 27 Michael Harrison; 29 Sean Beevor; 35 Oli Toms.
Tries: Holmes (2), Beevor (37); **Goals:** Roche 1/2.
Sin bin: Watkin (67) - fighting.
Rugby Leaguer & League Express Men of the Match: *Hornets:* Ben Calland; *Army:* Ben O'Connell.
Penalty count: 16-12; **Half-time:** 20-10;
Referee: John McMullen; **Attendance:** 400.

WIDNES VIKINGS 52 OLDHAM 12

VIKINGS: 1 Jack Owens; 2 Jack Johnson; 4 Lloyd Roby; 25 Joe Edge; 5 Deon Cross; 6 Danny Craven; 17 Matty Smith; 10 Ted Chapelhow; 9 Logan Tomkins; 14 Pat Moran; 12 Sam Wilde; 11 Shane Grady; 15 Kenny Baker. Subs (all used): 7 Joe Lyons; 13 MacGraff Leuluai; 16 Owen Farnworth; 19 Connor Dwyer.
Tries: Roby (2), Cross (4), Wilde (8, 41), Craven (15), Baker (21), Johnson (46, 73), Edge (49); **Goals:** Owens 8/9.
OLDHAM: 1 Dan Abram; 2 Dec Kay; 19 John Hutchings; 4 Cameron Leeming; 5 Kyran Johnson; 6 Lewis Charnock; 18 Adam Brook; 8 Phil Joy; 9 Gareth Owen; 10 Jack Spencer; 11 Danny Langtree; 12 Danny Bridge; 13 Liam Bent. Subs (all used): 7 Dave Hewitt; 14 Matty Wilkinson; 15 Ben Davies; 28 Matthew Fletcher.
Tries: Abram (35), Langtree (80); **Goals:** Abram 2/2.
Rugby Leaguer & League Express Men of the Match: *Vikings:* Jack Johnson; *Oldham:* Dan Abram.
Penalty count: 5-6; **Half-time:** 30-6;
Referee: Gareth Hewer; **Attendance:** 1,564.

WORKINGTON TOWN 22 DONCASTER 12

TOWN: 1 Gabriel Fell; 2 Elliot Hall; 3 Elliott Miller; 19 Tyler Lancaster; 5 Alex Young; 6 Jamie Doran; 7 Carl Forber; 8 Andrew Dawson; 14 Marcus O'Brien; 13 Conor Fitzsimmons; 12 Caine Barnes; 10 Stevie Scholey; 21 Hanley Dawson. Subs (all used): 15 Tom Curwen; 18 Blain Marwood; 25 Fuifui Moimoi; 33 Adam Ramsden.
Tries: H Dawson (31), Marwood (58), Doran (66), Hall (72);
Goals: Forber 3/4.
DONCASTER: 24 Watson Boas; 2 Josh Rickett; 3 Sam Smeaton; 4 Jason Tali; 5 Sam Doherty; 6 Rangi Chase; 7 Matty Beharrell; 8 Russ Spiers; 14 Harry Carter; 10 Ryan Boyle; 12 Brad Foster; 19 Aaron Ollett; 22 Graeme Horne. Subs (all used): 9 Kieran Cross; 15 Brandon Douglas; 17 Ross Peltier; 23 Jake McLoughlin.
Tries: Tali (5, 39); **Goals:** Beharrell 2/2.
Sin bin: Spiers (7) - high tackle on O'Brien.
Rugby Leaguer & League Express Men of the Match: *Town:* Elliott Miller; *Doncaster:* Jason Tali.
Penalty count: 6-5; **Half-time:** 6-12;
Referee: Tom Crashley; **Attendance:** 612.

Wednesday 11th March 2020

WHITEHAVEN 16 DEWSBURY RAMS 22

WHITEHAVEN: 1 Sam Forrester; 22 Brett Carter; 23 Jason Mossop; 4 Jessie Joe Parker; 5 Andrew Bulman; 13 Dion Aiye; 9 Callum Phillips; 24 Ethan Kelly; 18 James Newton; 10 Kris Coward; 12 Jake Moore; 15 Connor Holliday; 20 Jake Bradley. Subs (all used): 11 Brett Phillips; 14 Sam Dowsett; 17 Tom Walker; 25 Jamie Thackray.
Tries: Forrester (12), Bulman (37), Mossop (48);
Goals: Moore 1/1, Holliday 1/2.
RAMS: 4 Matty Fleming; 24 Tommy Brierley; 3 Adam Ryder; 5 Will Oakes; 18 Davey Dixon; 20 Morgan Punchard; 7 Liam Finn; 16 Connor Scott; 9 Dom Speakman; 23 Jon Magrin; 15 Liam Johnson; 25 James Thornton; 8 Frazer Morris. Subs (all used): 14 Sam Day; 29 Rhys Davies; 22 Luke Nelmes; 17 Martyn Reilly.
Tries: Speakman (19, 30), Scott (72); **Goals:** Finn 5/5.
Rugby Leaguer & League Express Men of the Match: *Whitehaven:* Tom Walker; *Rams:* Dom Speakman.
Penalty count: 7-8; **Half-time:** 12-12;
Referee: Jack Smith; **Attendance:** 427.

ROUND 5

Wednesday 11th March 2020

TORONTO WOLFPACK 18 HUDDERSFIELD GIANTS 0

WOLFPACK: 1 Gareth O'Brien; 5 Liam Kay; 3 Chase Stanley; 4 Ricky Leutele; 23 Hakim Miloudi; 6 Joe Mellor; 7 Josh McCrone (C); 8 Adam Sidlow; 9 Andy Ackers; 15 Gadwin Springer; 16 Tom Olbison; 12 Bodene Thompson; 11 Andrew Dixon. Subs: 10 Anthony Mullally; 14 Darcy Lussick (not used); 17 Blake Wallace (not used); 24 Tony Gigot (not used).
Tries: Leutele (3, 11); **Goals:** O'Brien 5/6.
GIANTS: 5 Darnell McIntosh; 2 Jermaine McGillvary; 3 Jake Wardle; 4 Jordan Turner; 27 Sam Wood; 23 Oliver Russell; 7 Aidan Sezer (C); 10 Suaia Matagi; 22 Tom Holmes; 8 James Gavet; 11 Kenny Edwards; 16 Aaron Murphy; 18 Paul Clough. Subs (all used): 9 Adam O'Brien; 13 Michael Lawrence; 26 Sam Hewitt; 15 Oliver Wilson.
Rugby Leaguer & League Express Men of the Match: *Wolfpack:* Joe Mellor; *Giants:* Adam O'Brien.
Penalty count: 10-8; **Half-time:** 16-0;
Referee: Scott Mikalauskas; **Attendance:** 1,488
(at John Smith's Stadium).

Friday 13th March 2020

FEATHERSTONE ROVERS 46 HUNSLET 6

ROVERS: 1 Craig Hall; 24 Sam Ottewell; 5 Conor Carey; 3 Josh Hardcastle; 2 Ben Blackmore; 6 Louis Jouffret; 7 Dane Chisholm; 13 James Lockwood; 20 Jake Sweeting; 15 Luke Cooper; 10 James Harrison; 11 Brett Ferres; 29 Wellington Albert. Subs (all used): 16 Jack Bussey; 17 Alec Susino; 18 Jimmy Beckett; 22 Brandan French.
Tries: Sweeting (2, 48), Ottewell (7), Chisholm (20, 63), Hardcastle (34), Blackmore (36, 57), Carey (78);
Goals: Chisholm 5/8, Jouffret 0/1.
HUNSLET: 18 Kiedan Hartley; 22 Anthony Boardman; 3 Ben Heaton; 4 Tom Ashton; 5 Matty Chrimes; 6 Simon Brown; 14 Danny Rowse; 8 Zach Braham; 20 Nathan Conroy; 26 Alex Rowe; 11 Josh Tonks; 12 Duane Straugheir; 13 Vila Halafihi. Subs (all used): 15 Harvey Hallas; 16 Jack Ray; 21 Jack Aldous; 25 Jordan Andrade.
Try: Heaton (66); **Goals:** Rowse 1/1.
Rugby Leaguer & League Express Men of the Match: *Rovers:* Dane Chisholm; *Hunslet:* Kiedan Hartley.
Penalty count: 8-4; **Half-time:** 26-0;
Referee: Aaron Moore; **Attendance:** 1,002.

WAKEFIELD TRINITY 17 BRADFORD BULLS 14

TRINITY: 1 Alex Walker; 3 Bill Tupou; 4 Reece Lyne; 28 Ryan Atkins; 2 Tom Johnstone; 6 Jacob Miller (C); 7 Danny Brough; 10 Tinirau Arona; 9 Kyle Wood; 36 Kelepi Tanginoa; 14 Jay Pitts; 11 Matty Ashurst; 13 Joe Westerman. Subs (all used): 8 David Fifita; 17 Chris Green; 22 George King; 23 Josh Wood.
Tries: Westerman (28), A Walker (59), Lyne (70);
Goals: Brough 2/3; **Field goal:** Miller (40).
BULLS: 1 Brandon Pickersgill; 16 David Foggin-Johnston; 19 Matty Dawson-Jones; 4 Ross Oakes; 5 Joe Brown; 6 Rowan Milnes; 7 Jordan Lilley; 8 Anthony England; 14 George Flanagan; 10 Steve Crossley; 11 Adam Rooks; 28 Bradley Gallagher; 13 Sam Hallas. Subs (all used): 9 Thomas Doyle; 29 Ebon Scurr; 18 Evan Hodgson; 17 Levy Nzoungou.
Tries: Lilley (20), Milnes (49); **Goals:** Milnes 3/3.
Rugby Leaguer & League Express Men of the Match: *Trinity:* Bill Tupou; *Bulls:* Rowan Milnes.
Penalty count: 5-5; **Half-time:** 7-6;
Referee: Marcus Griffiths; **Attendance:** 3,112.

Sunday 15th March 2020

SHEFFIELD EAGLES 34 WORKINGTON TOWN 18

EAGLES: 6 Corey Makelim; 2 Rob Worrincy; 19 Zack McComb; 18 Connor Bower; 5 Ryan Millar; 24 Izaac Farrell; 7 Anthony Thackeray; 8 Scott Wheeldon; 9 James Davey; 20 Blake Broadbent; 15 Olly Davies; 12 Joel Farrell; 13 Aaron Brown. Subs (all used): 11 Brad Knowles; 17 Frankie Mariano; 21 Paddy Burns; 23 Lewis Taylor.
Tries: J Farrell (3, 14), Millar (26), Davies (30), Makelim (34, 73), I Farrell (70); **Goals:** I Farrell 3/7.
TOWN: 1 Gabriel Fell; 2 Elliot Hall; 19 Tyler Lancaster; 4 Calvin Wellington; 5 Alex Young; 6 Jamie Doran; 7 Carl Forber; 15 Tom Curwen; 14 Marcus O'Brien; 10 Stevie Scholey; 12 Caine Barnes; 21 Hanley Dawson; 13 Conor Fitzsimmons. Subs (all used): 18 Blain Marwood; 25 Fuifui Moimoi; 8 Andrew Dawson; 24 Ryan Wilson.
Tries: Forber (23), Moimoi (52), Marwood (76);
Goals: Forber 3/3.
Rugby Leaguer & League Express Men of the Match: *Eagles:* Corey Makelim; *Town:* Carl Forber.
Penalty count: 10-8; **Half-time:** 26-6;
Referee: James Vella; **Attendance:** 323
(at Keepmoat Stadium, Doncaster).

HULL KINGSTON ROVERS 22 LEIGH CENTURIONS 19

ROVERS: 1 Adam Quinlan; 19 Will Dagger; 3 Shaun Kenny-Dowall (C); 22 Nick Rawsthorne (D); 23 Ethan Ryan; 7 Jordan Abdull; 20 Mikey Lewis; 15 George Lawler; 27 Elliot Minchella; 16 Daniel Murray; 11 Weller Hauraki; 4 Kane Linnett; 12 Harvey Livett. Subs (all used): 17 Kyle Trout; 18 Jez Litten; 21 Owen Harrison; 25 Matty Gee.
Tries: Linnett (23), Kenny-Dowall (26), Dagger (31), Rawsthorne (80); **Goals:** Lewis 3/4.
CENTURIONS: 1 Gregg McNally; 28 Ryan Shaw; 3 Iain Thornley; 4 Junior Sa'u; 5 Adam Higson; 6 Ben Reynolds; 17 Josh Woods; 27 Alex Gerrard; 9 Liam Hood; 10 Mark Ioane; 11 Ben Hellewell; 15 Jordan Thompson; 13 Danny Addy. Subs (all used): 14 Matty Wildie; 21 Nick Glohe; 18 Tom Spencer; 23 Callum Field.
Tries: Higson (7), Hellewell (18), Hood (65);
Goals: Reynolds 3/3; **Field goal:** Woods (70).
Sin bin: Higson (53) - professional foul, (73) - high tackle.
Rugby Leaguer & League Express Men of the Match: *Rovers:* Mikey Lewis; *Centurions:* Ben Reynolds.
Penalty count: 10-7; **Half-time:** 18-12;
Referee: Gareth Hewer; **Attendance:** 2,620.

NEWCASTLE THUNDER 38 DEWSBURY RAMS 30

THUNDER: 1 Lewis Young; 2 Ashley Gibson; 3 Tyler Craig; 4 Kieran Gill; 5 Alex Clegg; 6 Quentin Laulu-Togaga'e; 7 Reece Dean; 8 Brenden Santi; 9 Bob Beswick; 10 Mikey Wood; 11 Adam Lawton; 12 Rhys Clarke; 13 Sam Luckley. Subs: 14 Evan Simons; 15 Harry Aldous; 16 Colton Roche; 17 Sam Blake (not used).
Tries: Gill (4, 63), Laulu-Togaga'e (7), Gibson (18), Beswick (27), Lawton (57), Clegg (75); **Goals:** Dean 5/8.
RAMS: 1 Joe Martin; 2 Andy Gabriel; 5 Will Oakes; 15 Liam Johnson; 18 Davey Dixon; 6 Paul Sykes; 7 Liam Finn; 8 Frazer Morris; 9 Dom Speakman; 17 Martyn Reilly; 19 Sonny Esslemont; 12 Michael Knowles; 13 Chris Annakin. Subs (all used): 14 Sam Day; 16 Connor Scott; 23 Jon Magrin; 25 James Thornton.
Tries: Knowles (15), Sykes (24), Scott (34), Reilly (68), Oakes (72); **Goals:** Sykes 5/5.
Rugby Leaguer & League Express Men of the Match: *Thunder:* Lewis Young; *Rams:* Michael Knowles.
Penalty count: 5-5; **Half-time:** 20-18;
Referee: Billy Pearson; **Attendance:** 689.

WIDNES VIKINGS 32 SWINTON LIONS 16

VIKINGS: 7 Joe Lyons; 2 Jack Johnson; 25 Joe Edge; 3 Jake Spedding; 5 Deon Cross; 1 Jack Owens; 17 Matty Smith; 10 Ted Chapelhow; 34 Lewis Hulme; 14 Pat Moran; 12 Sam Wilde; 11 Shane Grady; 15 Kenny Baker. Subs (all used): 33 Callum Wood; 8 Jay Chapelhow; 13 MacGraff Leuluai; 4 Lloyd Roby.
Tries: Spedding (4), Johnson (34), Baker (56), Leuluai (62), Cross (75), Lyons (80); **Goals:** Owens 4/7.
LIONS: 1 Mike Butt; 2 Richard Lepori; 19 Sam Grant; 4 Mitch Cox; 5 Brandon Wood; 6 Jack Hansen; 7 Rob Fairclough; 8 Gavin Bennion; 9 Luke Waterworth; 10 Lewis Hatton; 11 Rhodri Lloyd; 12 Frankie Halton; 13 Will Hope. Subs (all used): 14 Billy Brickhill; 18 Louis Brogan; 20 Oscar Thomas; 3 Ben Morris.
Tries: Butt (9, 69), Hatton (16); **Goals:** Hansen 2/3.
Rugby Leaguer & League Express Men of the Match: *Vikings:* Lewis Hulme; *Lions:* Rob Fairclough.
Penalty count: 7-5; **Half-time:** 10-10;
Referee: Tom Grant; **Attendance:** 1,527.

YORK CITY KNIGHTS 70 ROCHDALE HORNETS 12

CITY KNIGHTS: 1 Matty Marsh; 5 Will Sharp; 3 Jimmy Keinhorst; 4 Liam Salter; 21 Jason Bass; 6 Ben Johnston; 7 Connor Robinson; 19 Jordan Baldwinson; 9 Will Jubb; 10 Jack Teanby; 16 Chris Clarkson; 12 Sam Scott; 13 Tim Spears. Subs (all used): 36 Reiss Butterworth; 15 James Green; 20 Marcus Stock; 11 Danny Washbrook.
Tries: Bass (6, 66, 72), Clarkson (16), Robinson (22, 77), Marsh (32, 48, 58, 80), Butterworth (34), Sharp (39), Johnston (69); **Goals:** Robinson 9/12, Spears 0/1.
HORNETS: 1 Sam Freeman; 28 Brad Holroyd; 4 Ben Calland; 26 Matt Whitehead; 2 Dale Bloomfield; 6 Lewis Sheridan; 11 Jordan Syme; 32 Sam Hopkins; 9 Sean Penkywicz; 10 Adam Hesketh; 18 Liam Whalley; 12 Jamie Tracey; 13 Andy Lea. Subs (all used): 14 Declan Sheridan; 15 Luke Fowden; 8 Callum Marriott; 30 Quinn Ngawati.
Tries: L Sheridan (44, 54); **Goals:** Freeman 2/2.
Sin bin: Whalley (38) - fighting.
Rugby Leaguer & League Express Men of the Match: *City Knights:* Matty Marsh; *Hornets:* Lewis Sheridan.
Penalty count: 7-4; **Half-time:** 34-0;
Referee: Jack Smith; **Attendance:** 400
(at LD Nutrition Stadium, Featherstone).

Featherstone Rovers, Newcastle Thunder, Sheffield Eagles, Toronto Wolfpack, Widnes Vikings and York City Knights withdrew from the Challenge Cup following Round 5.

New draws for Round 6 and the Quarter Finals were subsequently made.

ROUND 6

Saturday 22nd August 2020

CATALANS DRAGONS 36 WAKEFIELD TRINITY 24

DRAGONS: 25 Arthur Mourgue; 16 Tom Davies; 1 David Mead; 4 Israel Folau; 5 Fouad Yaha; 6 James Maloney; 7 Josh Drinkwater; 8 Remi Casty (C); 9 Michael McIlorum; 23 Antoni Maria; 11 Matt Whitley; 12 Joel Tomkins; 13 Benjamin Garcia. Subs (all used): 17 Benjamin Jullien; 19 Mickael Goudemand; 24 Jason Baitieri; 28 Sam Kasiano.
Tries: Mead (6, 37, 60), Yaha (24), Garcia (56), Whitley (64); **Goals:** Maloney 6/7.
Sin bin: McIlorum (55) - fighting.
TRINITY: 1 Alex Walker; 40 Innes Senior (D); 3 Bill Tupou; 24 Jack Croft; 21 Max Jowitt; 6 Jacob Miller (C); 29 Ryan Hampshire; 8 David Fifita; 9 Kyle Wood; 10 Tinirau Arona; 14 Jay Pitts; 11 Matty Ashurst; 13 Joe Westerman. Subs (all used): 19 Jordan Crowther; 36 Kelepi Tanginoa; 37 Romain Navarrete; 15 Craig Kopczak.
Tries: Pitts (31, 46), Arona (76), Miller (78);
Goals: Hampshire 4/4.
Sin bin: Pitts (55) - fighting.
Rugby Leaguer & League Express Men of the Match: *Dragons:* Josh Drinkwater; *Trinity:* Ryan Hampshire.
Penalty count: 5-6; **Half-time:** 20-6;
Referee: Chris Kendall.
(at John Smith's Stadium, Huddersfield).

Sunday 13th September 2020

CASTLEFORD TIGERS 16 HULL FC 29

TIGERS: 21 James Clare; 2 Derrell Olpherts; 18 Cheyse Blair; 4 Michael Shenton (C); 5 Sosaia Feki (D); 3 Peter Mata'utia; 7 Danny Richardson; 8 Liam Watts; 9 Paul McShane; 16 George Griffin; 11 Oliver Holmes; 12 Mike McMeeken; 22 Jacques O'Neill. Subs (all used): 10 Grant Millington; 13 Adam Milner; 24 Tyla Hepi; 26 Calum Turner.
Tries: Griffin (18), Holmes (45), Mata'utia (56);
Goals: Richardson 2/3.
HULL FC: 1 Jamie Shaul; 33 Ratu Naulago; 3 Carlos Tuimavave; 4 Josh Griffin; 2 Bureta Faraimo; 14 Albert Kelly; 6 Jake Connor; 29 Gareth Ellis; 16 Jordan Johnstone; 20 Brad Fash; 21 Jordan Lane; 12 Manu Ma'u; 15 Joe Cator. Subs (all used): 9 Danny Houghton (C); 10 Tevita Satae; 13 Ligi Sao; 24 Mahe Fonua.
Tries: Tuimavave (10, 40), Kelly (31), Naulago (43);
Goals: Connor 6/6; **Field goal:** Connor (78).
Rugby Leaguer & League Express Men of the Match: *Tigers:* Liam Watts; *Hull FC:* Carlos Tuimavave.
Penalty count: 4-3; **Half-time:** 6-18; **Referee:** Liam Moore.
(at Totally Wicked Stadium, St Helens).

QUARTER FINALS

Friday 18th September 2020

CATALANS DRAGONS 18 SALFORD RED DEVILS 22
(after golden point extra-time)

DRAGONS: 29 Sam Tomkins; 2 Lewis Tierney; 3 Samisoni Langi; 4 Israel Folau; 5 Fouad Yaha; 6 James Maloney; 7 Josh Drinkwater; 10 Sam Moa; 9 Michael McIlorum; 14 Julian Bousquet; 11 Matt Whitley; 13 Benjamin Garcia; 8 Remi Casty (C). Subs: 17 Benjamin Jullien (not used); 19 Mickael Goudemand; 24 Jason Baitieri; 28 Sam Kasiano.
Tries: Yaha (3), Maloney (22), Whitley (53);
Goals: Maloney 3/4.
Sin bin: Kasiano (77) - repeated team offences.
RED DEVILS: 4 Dan Sarginson; 5 Krisnan Inu; 3 Kris Welham; 32 Kallum Watkins (D); 22 Rhys Williams; 6 Tui Lolohea; 7 Kevin Brown; 10 Gil Dudson; 9 Joey Lussick; 17 Luke Yates; 21 James Greenwood; 13 Tyrone McCarthy; 19 Mark Flanagan (C). Subs: 12 Pauli Pauli; 14 Sebastine Ikahihifo; 16 Greg Burke; 24 Elliot Kear (not used).
Tries: Sarginson (28, 82), Inu (33), Greenwood (59);
Goals: Inu 3/4.
Sin bin: Pauli (45) - high tackle on Maloney.
Rugby Leaguer & League Express Men of the Match: *Dragons:* James Maloney; *Red Devils:* Dan Sarginson.
Penalty count: 12-3; **Half-time:** 12-10; **Referee:** Ben Thaler.
(at Totally Wicked Stadium, St Helens).

HULL KINGSTON ROVERS 18 LEEDS RHINOS 48

ROVERS: 19 Will Dagger; 23 Ethan Ryan; 3 Shaun Kenny-Dowall; 4 Kane Linnett; 5 Greg Minikin; 20 Mikey Lewis; 30 Jamie Ellis; 11 Weller Hauraki (C); 9 Matt Parcell; 15 George Lawler; 28 Matthew Storton; 13 Dean Hadley; 8 Robbie Mulhern. Subs (all used): 16 Daniel Murray; 18 Jez Litten; 25 Matty Gee; 32 Nathaniel Peteru.
Tries: Ellis (46, 72), Litten (63); **Goals:** Ellis 3/3.
On report: Ellis (34) - alleged bite on Donaldson.
RHINOS: 16 Richie Myler; 2 Tom Briscoe; 3 Harry Newman; 15 Liam Sutcliffe; 5 Ash Handley; 6 Robert Lui; 7 Luke Gale (C); 8 Ava Seumanufagai; 9 Kruise Leeming; 10 Matt Prior; 11 Alex Mellor; 12 Rhyse Martin; 19 Mikolaj Oledzki. Subs (all used): 23 Callum McLelland; 24 Luke Briscoe; 25 James Donaldson; 28 Tom Holroyd.
Tries: Seumanufagai (6), Handley (10), T Briscoe (16), Newman (20), Leeming (40, 54), L Briscoe (59), Martin (77); **Goals:** Martin 8/8.
Sin bin: Seumanufagai (45) - high tackle on Gee.
Rugby Leaguer & League Express Men of the Match: *Rovers:* Will Dagger; *Rhinos:* Rhyse Martin.
Penalty count: 4-6; **Half-time:** 0-30;
Referee: Liam Moore.
(at Totally Wicked Stadium, St Helens).

Saturday 19th September 2020

ST HELENS 18 WARRINGTON WOLVES 20

SAINTS: 1 Lachlan Coote; 22 Jack Welsby; 3 Kevin Naiqama; 4 Mark Percival; 5 Regan Grace; 6 Jonny Lomax;

Hull FC's Marc Sneyd gets to grips with Wigan's Bevan French

7 Theo Fages; 8 Alex Walmsley; 9 James Roby (C); 32 James Graham; 11 Zeb Taia; 20 James Bentley; 14 Morgan Knowles. Subs (all used): 13 Louie McCarthy-Scarsbrook; 15 Matty Lees; 16 Kyle Amor; 19 Aaron Smith.
Tries: Lomax (6), Grace (56), Naiqama (70);
Goals: Coote 3/4.
WOLVES: 26 Matty Ashton; 17 Jake Mamo; 3 Anthony Gelling; 4 Toby King; 5 Josh Charnley; 6 Blake Austin; 1 Stefan Ratchford; 8 Chris Hill (C); 9 Daryl Clark; 10 Mike Cooper; 11 Ben Currie; 12 Jack Hughes; 14 Jason Clark. Subs (all used): 13 Ben Murdoch-Masila; 15 Joe Philbin; 19 Matt Davis; 20 Danny Walker.
Tries: Gelling (29), Charnley (36, 64), Ashton (40);
Goals: Ratchford 2/4.
Rugby Leaguer & League Express Men of the Match:
Saints: Lachlan Coote; *Wolves:* Anthony Gelling.
Penalty count: 3-6; **Half-time:** 8-16;
Referee: Chris Kendall. *(at AJ Bell Stadium, Salford).*

HULL FC 4 WIGAN WARRIORS 36

HULL FC: 25 Connor Wynne; 24 Mahe Fonua; 3 Carlos Tuimavave; 4 Josh Griffin; 2 Bureta Faraimo; 6 Jake Connor; 7 Marc Sneyd; 19 Masi Matongo; 16 Jordan Johnstone; 20 Brad Fash; 12 Manu Ma'u; 21 Jordan Lane; 15 Joe Cator. Subs (all used): 9 Danny Houghton (C); 10 Tevita Satae; 13 Ligi Sao; 30 Jack Brown.
Try: Fonua (70); **Goals:** Sneyd 0/1.
WARRIORS: 6 Bevan French; 21 Dom Manfredi; 1 Zak Hardaker; 4 Oliver Gildart; 5 Joe Burgess; 7 Thomas Leuluai; 31 Jackson Hastings; 30 Ethan Havard; 9 Sam Powell; 17 Oliver Partington; 11 Willie Isa; 12 Liam Farrell; 13 Sean O'Loughlin (C). Subs (all used): 22 Mitch Clark; 15 Joe Greenwood; 28 Harry Smith; 33 Joe Shorrocks.
Tries: Powell (5), Farrell (10, 56), French (23, 38), J Burgess (40), Gildart (66); **Goals:** Hardaker 4/7.
Rugby Leaguer & League Express Men of the Match:
Hull FC: Tevita Satae; *Warriors:* Bevan French.
Penalty count: 7-3; **Half-time:** 0-26;
Referee: Robert Hicks. *(at AJ Bell Stadium, Salford).*

SEMI-FINALS

Saturday 3rd October 2020

LEEDS RHINOS 26 WIGAN WARRIORS 12

RHINOS: 16 Richie Myler; 5 Ash Handley; 4 Konrad Hurrell; 15 Liam Sutcliffe; 2 Tom Briscoe; 6 Robert Lui; 7 Luke Gale (C); 8 Ava Seumanufagai; 9 Kruise Leeming; 19 Mikolaj Oledzki; 11 Alex Mellor; 12 Rhyse Martin; 10 Matt Prior. Subs (all used): 14 Brad Dwyer; 22 Cameron Smith; 25 James Donaldson; 28 Tom Holroyd.
Tries: Martin (18), Handley (34, 69), T Briscoe (40);
Goals: Martin 5/7.
WARRIORS: 6 Bevan French; 21 Dom Manfredi; 1 Zak Hardaker; 23 Jake Bibby; 5 Joe Burgess; 31 Jackson Hastings; 7 Thomas Leuluai; 30 Ethan Havard; 9 Sam Powell; 17 Oliver Partington; 12 Liam Farrell; 11 Willie Isa; 13 Sean O'Loughlin (C). Subs (all used): 15 Joe Greenwood; 19 Joe Bullock; 28 Harry Smith; 33 Joe Shorrocks.
Tries: Smith (75), Hardaker (77); **Goals:** Hardaker 2/2.
Rugby Leaguer & League Express Men of the Match:
Rhinos: Luke Gale; *Warriors:* Zak Hardaker.
Penalty count: 5-5; **Half-time:** 20-0;
Referee: Chris Kendall.
(at Totally Wicked Stadium, St Helens).

SALFORD RED DEVILS 24 WARRINGTON WOLVES 22

RED DEVILS: 4 Dan Sarginson; 22 Rhys Williams; 32 Kallum Watkins; 3 Kris Welham; 5 Krisnan Inu; 6 Tui Lolohea; 7 Kevin Brown; 8 Lee Mossop (C); 9 Joey Lussick; 10 Gil Dudson; 13 Tyrone McCarthy; 21 James Greenwood; 19 Mark Flanagan. Subs: 16 Greg Burke; 14 Sebastine Ikahihifo; 24 Elliot Kear (not used); 12 Pauli Pauli.
Tries: Watkins (22), Inu (42), Greenwood (66), Lussick (74);
Goals: Inu 4/5.
Sin bin: McCarthy (11) - dangerous challenge on Ratchford.

WOLVES: 26 Matty Ashton; 17 Jake Mamo; 3 Anthony Gelling; 4 Toby King; 5 Josh Charnley; 1 Stefan Ratchford; 7 Gareth Widdop; 8 Chris Hill (C); 9 Daryl Clark; 10 Mike Cooper; 11 Ben Currie; 12 Jack Hughes; 6 Blake Austin. Subs (all used): 13 Ben Murdoch-Masila; 14 Jason Clark; 15 Joe Philbin; 20 Danny Walker.
Tries: King (13), Austin (36), Murdoch-Masila (62);
Goals: Ratchford 2/2, Widdop 3/3.
Rugby Leaguer & League Express Men of the Match:
Red Devils: Krisnan Inu; *Wolves:* Gareth Widdop.
Penalty count: 3-4; **Half-time:** 8-14; **Referee:** Liam Moore.
(at Totally Wicked Stadium, St Helens).

FINAL

Saturday 17th October 2020

LEEDS RHINOS 17 SALFORD RED DEVILS 16

RHINOS: 16 Richie Myler; 2 Tom Briscoe; 4 Konrad Hurrell; 15 Liam Sutcliffe; 5 Ash Handley; 6 Robert Lui; 7 Luke Gale (C); 8 Ava Seumanufagai; 9 Kruise Leeming; 19 Mikolaj Oledzki; 11 Alex Mellor; 12 Rhyse Martin; 10 Matt Prior. Subs (all used): 14 Brad Dwyer; 17 Adam Cuthbertson; 25 James Donaldson; 26 Alex Sutcliffe.
Tries: T Briscoe (12), Handley (31, 65); **Goals:** Martin 2/3;
Field goal: Gale (76).
RED DEVILS: 1 Niall Evalds; 22 Rhys Williams; 32 Kallum Watkins; 3 Kris Welham; 5 Krisnan Inu; 6 Tui Lolohea; 7 Kevin Brown; 8 Lee Mossop (C); 9 Joey Lussick; 10 Gil Dudson; 13 Tyrone McCarthy; 21 James Greenwood; 19 Mark Flanagan. Subs (all used): 12 Pauli Pauli; 14 Sebastine Ikahihifo; 16 Greg Burke; 17 Luke Yates.
Tries: Williams (19), Pauli (53), Greenwood (58);
Goals: Inu 2/3.
Rugby Leaguer & League Express Men of the Match:
Rhinos: Luke Gale; *Red Devils:* Kallum Watkins.
Penalty count: 6-5; **Half-time:** 12-6; **Referee:** Liam Moore.
(at Wembley Stadium).

Leeds' Konrad Hurrell halted by Salford's Kevin Brown and Pauli Pauli during the Challenge Cup Final

SUPER LEAGUE RECORDS
1996-2020

PLAYER RECORDS

COMPETITION
Includes play-off games & Super League Super 8s (2015-2018)

TRIES
Danny McGuire (Hull Kingston Rovers/Leeds Rhinos)
(2001-2019) 247

GOALS
Kevin Sinfield (Leeds Rhinos) (1997-2015) 1,566

FIELD GOALS
Lee Briers (Warrington Wolves/St Helens) (1997-2013) 70

POINTS
Kevin Sinfield (Leeds Rhinos) (1997-2015) 3,443

APPEARANCES
Kevin Sinfield (Leeds Rhinos) (1997-2015) 454

SEASON
Includes play-off games & Super League Super 8s (2015-2018)
(Play-offs in brackets)

TRIES
Denny Solomona (Castleford Tigers) (2016) 40 (-)

GOALS
Henry Paul (Bradford Bulls) (2001) 178 (13)

FIELD GOALS
Lee Briers (Warrington Wolves) (2002) 11 (-)

POINTS
Pat Richards (Wigan Warriors) (2010) 434 (46)

MATCH RECORDS

Includes play-off games & Super League Super 8s (2015-2018)

TRIES
Lesley Vainikolo (Bradford Bulls) 6
(v Hull FC (h), 2/9/05)

GOALS
Henry Paul (Bradford Bulls) 14
(v Salford City Reds (h), 25/6/00)

FIELD GOALS
Lee Briers (Warrington Wolves) 5
(v Halifax Blue Sox (a), 25/5/02)

POINTS
Iestyn Harris (Leeds Rhinos) 42
(v Huddersfield Giants (h), 16/7/99)

TEAM RECORDS

Includes play-off games & Super League Super 8s (2015-2018)

HIGHEST SCORE
Bradford Bulls 96 Salford City Reds 16 (25/6/00)

WIDEST MARGIN
Leeds Rhinos 86 Huddersfield Giants 6 (16/7/99)
Bradford Bulls 96 Salford City Reds 16 (25/6/00)
Warrington Wolves 80 Wakefield Trinity Wildcats 0 (11/4/15)

ATTENDANCE RECORDS

GRAND FINAL
73,512 Leeds Rhinos v Wigan Warriors (10/10/15)

PLAY-OFFS
21,790 Wigan Warriors v St Helens (3/10/03)

REGULAR SEASON *(includes Super League Super 8s (2015-2018)*
31,555 Catalans Dragons v Wigan Warriors (18/5/19)
(at Camp Nou, Barcelona)

2020 SEASON
Stats round-up

SUPER LEAGUE (*Regular season & play-offs; Toronto Wolfpack games excluded*)

FINAL TABLE

	P	W	D	L	F	A	D	Win %
Wigan Warriors	17	13	0	4	408	278	117	76.47
St Helens	17	12	0	5	469	195	274	70.59
Warrington Wolves	17	12	0	5	365	204	161	70.59
Catalans Dragons	13	8	0	5	376	259	117	61.54
Leeds Rhinos	17	10	0	7	369	390	-21	58.82
Hull FC	17	9	0	8	405	436	-31	52.94
Huddersfield Giants	18	7	0	11	318	367	-36	38.89
Castleford Tigers	16	6	0	10	328	379	-51	37.50
Salford Red Devils *	18	8	0	10	354	469	-123	27.78
Wakefield Trinity	19	5	0	14	324	503	-171	26.32
Hull Kingston Rovers	17	3	0	14	290	526	-236	17.65

* Salford Red Devils' win percentage reflects the removal of three wins for historic financial breaches

TRIES

1	Ash Handley	Leeds Rhinos	14
2	Tom Davies	Catalans Dragons	13
	Bevan French	Wigan Warriors	13
4	Ben Crooks	Hull Kingston Rovers	11
	Regan Grace	St Helens	11
	Sam Powell	Wigan Warriors	11
7	Krisnan Inu	Salford Red Devils	10
8	Lachlan Coote	St Helens	10
9	Fouad Yaha	Catalans Dragons	9
	Jermaine McGillvary	Huddersfield Giants	9
	Niall Evalds	Salford Red Devils	9
	Alex Walmsley	St Helens	9
	Jack Welsby	St Helens	9
	Tom Johnstone	Wakefield Trinity	9
	Jackson Hastings	Wigan Warriors	9

GOALS

1	Lachlan Coote	St Helens	70
2	Zak Hardaker	Wigan Warriors	62
3	James Maloney	Catalans Dragons	61
4	Marc Sneyd	Hull FC	56
5	Stefan Ratchford	Warrington Wolves	48
	Danny Richardson	Castleford Tigers	48
7	Aidan Sezer	Huddersfield Giants	38
8	Rhyse Martin	Leeds Rhinos	36
9	Ryan Hampshire	Wakefield Trinity	33
10	Krisnan Inu	Salford Red Devils	32

GOALS PERCENTAGE

			G	Att	%
1	Oliver Russell	Huddersfield Giants	11	12	91.66
2	Krisnan Inu	Salford Red Devils	32	35	91.42
3	Lachlan Coote	St Helens	70	80	87.50
4	Will Dagger	Hull Kingston Rovers	12	14	85.71
5	Stefan Ratchford	Warrington Wolves	48	59	81.35
	Danny Richardson	Castleford Tigers	48	59	81.35
7	James Maloney	Catalans Dragons	61	75	81.33
8	Marc Sneyd	Hull FC	56	70	80.00
9	Aidan Sezer	Huddersfield Giants	38	50	76.00
10	Ryan Hampshire	Wakefield Trinity	33	44	75.00
	Jake Connor	Hull FC	9	12	75.00

(10 minimum attempts to qualify)

POINTS

			T	G	FG	Pts
1	Lachlan Coote	St Helens	10	70	0	180
2	Zak Hardaker	Wigan Warriors	4	62	0	140
3	James Maloney	Catalans Dragons	2	61	0	130
4	Marc Sneyd	Hull FC	2	56	5	125
5	Danny Richardson	Castleford Tigers	2	48	1	105
	Aidan Sezer	Huddersfield Giants	7	38	1	105
7	Krisnan Inu	Salford Red Devils	10	32	0	104
	Stefan Ratchford	Warrington Wolves	2	48	0	104
9	Rhyse Martin	Leeds Rhinos	2	36	0	80
10	Ryan Hampshire	Wakefield Trinity	3	33	1	79

STEVE PRESCOTT MAN OF STEEL
Paul McShane (Castleford Tigers)

YOUNG PLAYER OF THE YEAR
Harry Newman (Leeds Rhinos)

COACH OF THE YEAR
Adrian Lam (Wigan Warriors)

SUPER LEAGUE DREAM TEAM

			Previous selections
1	Bevan French	Wigan Warriors	Debut
2	Ash Handley	Leeds Rhinos	2019
3	Toby King	Warrington Wolves	Debut
4	Konrad Hurrell	Leeds Rhinos	2019
5	Krisnan Inu	Salford Red Devils	Debut
6	Jonny Lomax	St Helens	2018
7	Aidan Sezer	Huddersfield Giants	Debut
8	Alex Walmsley	St Helens	2015
9	Paul McShane	Castleford Tigers	Debut
10	Mike Cooper	Warrington Wolves	Debut
11	Liam Farrell	Wigan Warriors	2015, 2019
12	Kelepi Tanginoa	Wakefield Trinity	Debut
13	Morgan Knowles	St Helens	2019

2020 Season - Stats round-up

TRIES

1	Ash Handley	Leeds Rhinos	20
2	Bevan French	Wigan Warriors	17
3	Tom Davies	Catalans Dragons	13
4	Krisnan Inu	Salford Red Devils	12
	Regan Grace	St Helens	12
	Sam Powell	Wigan Warriors	12
7	Fouad Yaha	Catalans Dragons	11
	Ben Crooks	Hull Kingston Rovers	11
9	Niall Evalds	Salford Red Devils	10
	Lachlan Coote	St Helens	10
	Alex Walmsley	St Helens	10
	Matty Ashton	Warrington Wolves	10
	Liam Farrell	Wigan Warriors	10

GOALS

1	Lachlan Coote	St Helens	73
2	Zak Hardaker	Wigan Warriors	72
3	James Maloney	Catalans Dragons	70
4	Rhyse Martin	Leeds Rhinos	62
5	Stefan Ratchford	Warrington Wolves	58
6	Marc Sneyd	Hull FC	56
7	Danny Richardson	Castleford Tigers	54
8	Krisnan Inu	Salford Red Devils	41
9	Aidan Sezer	Huddersfield Giants	38
10	Ryan Hampshire	Wakefield Trinity	37

POINTS

			T	G	FG	Pts
1	Lachlan Coote	St Helens	10	73	0	186
2	Zak Hardaker	Wigan Warriors	5	72	0	164
3	James Maloney	Catalans Dragons	3	70	0	152
4	Rhyse Martin	Leeds Rhinos	4	62	0	140
5	Krisnan Inu	Salford Red Devils	12	41	0	130
6	Marc Sneyd	Hull FC	2	56	5	125
7	Stefan Ratchford	Warrington Wolves	2	58	0	124
8	Danny Richardson	Castleford Tigers	2	54	1	117
9	Aidan Sezer	Huddersfield Giants	7	38	1	105
10	Ryan Hampshire	Wakefield Trinity	3	37	1	87

FIELD GOALS

1	Marc Sneyd	Hull FC	5
2	Blake Austin	Warrington Wolves	4
	Luke Gale	Leeds Rhinos	4
4	Izaac Farrell	Sheffield Eagles	2
	Jacob Miller	Wakefield Trinity	2
	Harry Smith	Wigan Warriors	2

Marc Sneyd

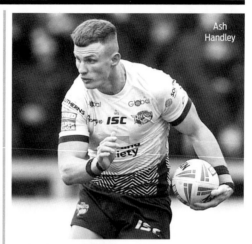

Ash Handley

Lachlan Coote

TRIES

1	Mike Butt	Swinton Lions	6
2	Ash Handley	Leeds Rhinos	5
3	Gav Rodden	North Wales Crusaders	4
	Ben Calland	Rochdale Hornets	4
	Matty Marsh	York City Knights	4

GOALS

1	Sam Freeman	Rochdale Hornets	18
2	Rhyse Martin	Leeds Rhinos	15
3	Tommy Johnson	North Wales Crusaders	13
	Connor Robinson	York City Knights	13
5	Reece Dean	Newcastle Thunder	12
	Jack Owens	Widnes Vikings	12

POINTS

			T	G	FG	Pts
1	Sam Freeman	Rochdale Hornets	2	18	0	44
2	Rhyse Martin	Leeds Rhinos	2	15	0	38
3	Connor Robinson	York City Knights	2	13	0	34
4	Krisnan Inu	Salford Red Devils	2	9	0	26
	Tommy Johnson	North Wales Crusaders	0	13	0	26